MW00596066

Computer Accounting
with
Sage 50 2016
[Formerly Peachtree]

Nineteenth Edition

Carol Yacht, M.A.

COMPUTER ACCOUNTING WITH SAGE 50 2016, NINETEENTH EDITION
Carol Yacht

Published by McGraw-Hill Education, 2 Penn Plaza, New York, NY 10121. Copyright © 2017 by McGraw-Hill Education. All rights reserved. Printed in the United States of America. Previous editions © 2015, 2013, and 2012. No part of this publication may be reproduced or distributed in any form or by any means, or stored in a database or retrieval system, without the prior written consent of McGraw-Hill Education, including, but not limited to, in any network or other electronic storage or transmission, or broadcast for distance learning.

Some ancillaries, including electronic and print components, may not be available to customers outside the United States.

This book is printed on acid-free paper.

1 2 3 4 5 6 7 8 9 0 QTN/QTN 1 0 9 8 7 6

ISBN 978-1-259-18392-8
MHID 1-259-18392-0

Senior Vice President, Products & Markets: *Kurt L. Strand*
Vice President, General Manager, Products & Markets: *Marty Lange*
Vice President, Content Design & Delivery: *Kimberly Meriwether David*
Managing Director:*Tim Vertovec*
Marketing Director: *Brad Parkins*
Brand Manager: *Steve Schuetz*
Director, Product Development: *Rose Koos*
Director of Digital Content: *Patricia Plumb*
Lead Product Developer: *Ann Torbert*
Marketing Manager: *Michelle Nolte*
Digital Product Developer: *Kevin Moran*
Digital Product Analyst: *Xin Lin*
Director, Content Design & Delivery: *Linda Avenarius*
Program Manager: *Daryl Horrocks*
Content Project Manager: *Dana M. Pauley*
Buyer: *Susan K. Culbertson*
Design: *Srdjan Savanovic*
Content Licensing Specialist: *Melissa Homer*
Cover Image: © *Ingram Publishing*
Compositor: *S4Carlisle Publishing Services*
Printer: *Quad/Graphics*

All credits appearing on page or at the end of the book are considered to be an extension of the copyright page.

The Internet addresses listed in the text were accurate at the time of publication. The inclusion of a website does not indicate an endorsement by the authors or McGraw-Hill Education, and McGraw-Hill Education does not guarantee the accuracy of the information presented at these sites.

www.mhhe.com

Software Installation

Install the software that millions of customers choose every year and accountants recommend. Sage provides small and medium-sized business software to **6 million customers worldwide**. Sage North America, a subsidiary of the Sage Group plc, has offices in the U.S. and Canada, employees more than 13,000 people, has $2 billion in revenue, and operates in 24 countries (http://na.sage.com/us/about-us).

Sage 50 accounting (formerly Peachtree) is an award-winning program (http://na.sage.com/us/our-news/press-releases/05/edison), is designed for sole proprietorships, partnerships, and corporations with up to 50 employees, and has more than 40 years of industry experience.

1. Sage 50 2016: Student Version and Educational Version, page iv
2. System Requirements, pages iv-vi
3. Sage 50 and Firewalls, page vi
4. Software Installation, page vi
5. Download Sage 50 2016, page vii
6. Install Sage 50 2016 with CD, pages viii-xviii
7. Expiration date, Student Version, Sage 50 2016, page xviii
8. Setting Global Options. Once global options are set, they are in effect for all Sage 50 companies, pages xix-xx
9. Computer Lab Installation, page xx
10. Student Version Software, pages xxi-xxii
11. Educational Version Software, pages xxii-xxiii
12. Deleting Sage 50, page xxiii

EDUCATIONAL VERSION FOR THE CLASSROOM

To obtain a serial number for classroom installation, email SageEducation@sage.com, *or* go online to www.mhhe.com/yacht2016, link to Install Sage 50.

Refer to the Note to Instructors/Schools on page ix, Step 6. If your school is already a Sage Education Partner, the 2016 software is sent automatically.

SAGE 50 2016: STUDENT VERSION AND EDUCATIONAL VERSION

Student Version

The Student Version is accessible for 14 months. The serial number for installing the student version is **41EC6-FBE6-86BE-3ØFF**. For Software Installation, refer to pages vi-xviii). After installation, activation is required (Step 14, pages xiv-xv).

Information about installation is on the Online Learning Center at www.mhhe.com/yacht2016, Install Sage 50 link. If your preference is downloading the software, the website is http://na.sage.com/us/about-us/education.

Educational Version

To install the software in the classroom, use the CD included with the textbook and the serial number emailed by SageEducation@sage.com. Sage Education emails a serial number to the school or instructor. Refer to Step 6, page ix, Note to Instructors/Schools.

The two versions, **Student Version** for individual installation and **Educational Version** for classroom installation, include the same features. The Educational Version does not have a time limit, *and* the serial number differs.

Sage 50 2016 was used to write the textbook. If you have an earlier version of the software installed, see Deleting Sage 50, page xxiii.)

 The serial number distinguishes the Educational Version from the Student Version. Sage 50 2016 can be downloaded (page vii), *or* installed with the CD included with the textbook (pages vii-xviii).

SYSTEM REQUIREMENTS: www.mhhe.com/yacht2016 > link to System Requirements

The *Sage Knowledgebase*[1] includes the system requirements. Go online to https://support.na.sage.com/selfservice/microsites/searchEntry.do >

---

[1]   Words that are in boldface and italics are defined in the glossary at www.mhhe.com/yacht2016 > link to Student Edition > Appendix D - Glossary.

type **Sage 50 2016 System Requirements** or ID **62337** in the Search field > link to System Requirements: Sage 50–U.S. Edition 2016.

Recommended Configuration:

- 2.4 GHz processor for single user and multiple users
- 1 GB of RAM for single user and 2GB for multiple users.

Minimum Requirements

- 1 GB of RAM for single user and multiple users
- Windows Vista SP2, Windows 7, or Windows 8 and 8.1, with the latest updates from Microsoft installed. **Note:** Sage 50 2016 was tested with Windows 10 and worked on an individual PC. No problems were encountered. Microsoft Windows XP and Server 2003 are <u>not</u> supported.
- 1 GB of disk space for installation.
- Internet Explorer 9.0, 10.0, and 11.0 supported
- Microsoft®.NET Framework 4.5.2; requires an additional 280 MB to 610 MB
- At least high color (16-bit) SVGA video; supports 1024x768 resolution with small fonts required
- DVD-ROM
- All online features/services require Internet access
- Excel®, Outlook®, and Word integration requires Microsoft Excel, Outlook, and Word 2007, 2010, or 2013 (32-bit)
- Printers supported by Microsoft Vista, Windows 7, or Windows 8
- In-product demos require Adobe® Flash™ Player 10 or greater
- Adobe® Reader® 9.0 required (https://get.adobe.com/reader/)
- Multiuser environments are supported in Sage 50 Premium Accounting and higher
- Multiuser mode is optimized for Windows Server 2003 or Windows Server 2008, or Windows Server 2012 client-server networks, and Windows Vista, Windows 7, or Windows 8 peer-to-peer networks
- A maximum of five licensed named users is allowed for Sage 50 Premium Accounting and 40 named users for Sage 50 Premium Accounting and 40 named users for Sage 50 Quantum Accounting; a named user account is granted a license when selected in the user maintenance screen.
- 1 GB of disk space for installation of components on server

- Windows Server 2008, Windows Server 2012 along with Remote Desktop Connection or Remote Desktop Web Connection client is required to run in a Windows Terminal Services environment; no more than 5 named users for Sage 50 Premium Accounting or 40 named users for Sage 50 Quantum Accounting.
- Terminal Server requires additional memory when more than one user is running under Terminal Services
- Product activation, registration and acceptance of License Agreement for Sage 50 Accounting software products. (For product activation, refer to Step 14, page xiv-xv)
- USB flash or thumb drive for backups

Read Me: Classroom software

To receive the serial number for the full Educational Version (no time limit) for classroom installation, email SageEducation@sage.com. Computer lab installation is on page xx.

Sage 50 and Firewalls

Sage 50 and its database, Pervasive, can be mistakenly identified as an intrusion threat by many firewall and anti-virus programs. If not addressed properly, this may cause installation to fail or Sage 50 may not start or run properly.

To read information about firewalls and antivirus software, search the Sage Knowledgebase at https://support.na.sage.com/selfservice/microsites/microsite.do > type **firewall** *or* ID **10903** in the Search field > link to Files to allow through firewall and antivirus.

SOFTWARE INSTALLATION

You can download the software *or* install from the CD included with the textbook. To download Sage 50 2016, refer to the steps on the next page. Software Installation with the CD is shown on pages vii-xviii, steps 1-21.

The author downloaded Sage 50 2016 on a Windows 8.1 computer and a Windows 7 computer. The installation steps differ slightly.

Download Sage 50 2016

Sage recommends using Internet Explorer for downloading the software. To download, follow these steps.

1. Go online to http://na.sage.com/us/about-us/education. Read the Software section. Complete Step 1, Register for your software.

2. Read Step 2, Download. Select  > click <Save>. The dialog box shows the download progress of the sage50_2016.0.exe file.

3. When the dialog box says "The sage50_2016.0.exe download has completed," click <View downloads>. The View Downloads – Internet Explorer window appears.

4. Click <Run>. When the Sage 50 Accounting 2016.0 window appears, the Destination folder shows c:\sage\SAGE50_2016_0. Click <Install>. The screen prompts "Extracting files." If the User Account Control window appears, click <Yes>.

5. The Sage 50 Accounting 2016 – InstallShield Wizard appears. Read the information. Click <Install>. Follow the screen prompts to install.

6. The Welcome to Sage 50 Accounting window appears. Read the information. Click <Next>. The License Agreement window appears. Go to Step 4 on the next page. Complete Steps 4-21 on pages viii-xviii. The serial number for the Student Version is **41EC6-FBE6-86BE-3ØFF** (Step 6, page ix).

   IMPORTANT: Sage 50 *must* be activated. For Product Activation, go to pages xiv-xv, step 14.

Install Sage 50 2016 with CD

Using the CD included with the textbook, install Sage 50 Accounting 2016 software. *After installation, you must activate the software* (step 14, pages xiv-xv). If you do <u>not</u> complete product activation, the software will stop working after a few startups.

Step 1:   Insert the Sage 50 Accounting 2016 CD. When the AutoPlay window appears, click Run autorun.exe. (*Or*, select Browse the CD. Select autorun.exe.) If the User Account Control window appears, click <Yes>.

Step 2:   At the Welcome to Sage 50 Accounting window, select Install Sage 50 Accounting. If a screen prompts Sage 50 Accounting 2016 requires the following items to be installed, click <Install>.

Step 3:   A Preparing to Install window appears. It may take a few minutes for the Welcome to Sage 50 Accounting window to appear. Click <Next>.

Step 4:   When the License Agreement window appears, click on the box next to I agree to the terms of the license agreement to place a checkmark.

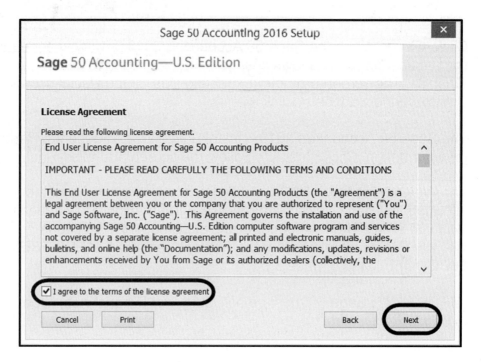

Step 5:   After clicking <Next>, the Windows Firewall window appears.
Accept the default for Yes (Recommended) by clicking <Next>.
If the Firewall Settings window appears, click <Next>.
NOTE: The Sage Knowledgebase includes information about firewalls
at https://support.na.sage.com/selfservice/microsites/microsite.do. In
the Search field, type **firewall** *or* ID **10903** > link to Files to allow
through firewall and antivirus.

Step 6:   The Serial Number window appears. Type **41EC6-FBE6-86BE-
3ØFF** in the Serial number field.

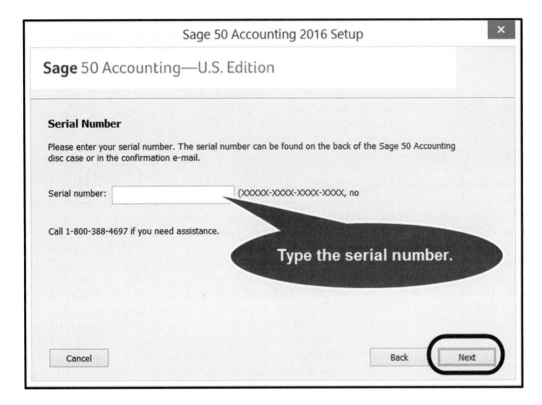

NOTE TO INSTRUCTORS/SCHOOLS: If your school is a member
of the Sage Education Partner Program, the Sage 50 2016 upgrade
is automatically sent to schools. When installing the software, use
the serial number emailed by SageEducation@sage.com, 800-256-
8807. The website for downloading free classroom software is
http://www.sage.com/us/about-us/education-instructor.

Step 7:   After clicking <Next>, the Single computer or Network window
appears. Accept the default for <Yes> by clicking <Next>.

Step 8:   The Choose Sage 50 Program Files Location window appears
          showing the directory for the Sage 50 program files:
          C:\Program Files (x86)\Sage\Peachtree.

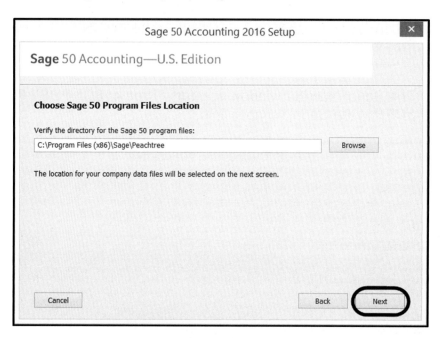

Step 9:   After clicking <Next>, the Company Data Files Location
          window appears, and is shown below.

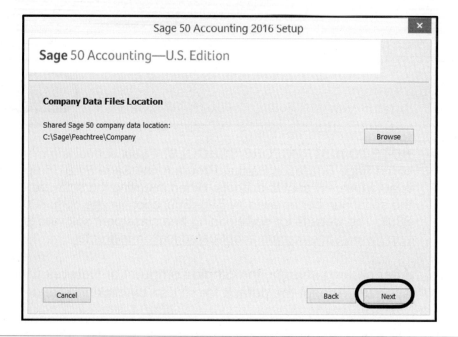

Step 10:   After clicking <Next>, the Summary window appears. Accept
the default locations for the Sage 50 program files and
company data files: C:\Program Files (x86)\Sage\Peachtree.
There are checkmarks for adding Sage 50 shortcuts to the
desktop and an icon on the quick launch toolbar. Review the
information on the Summary window.

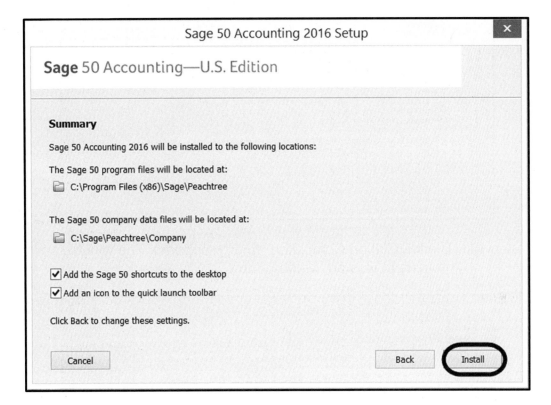

Step 11:   After clicking <Install>, The Installing Sage 50 Accounting—
U.S. Edition scale shows the progress of installation. Be
patient, installation takes a while.

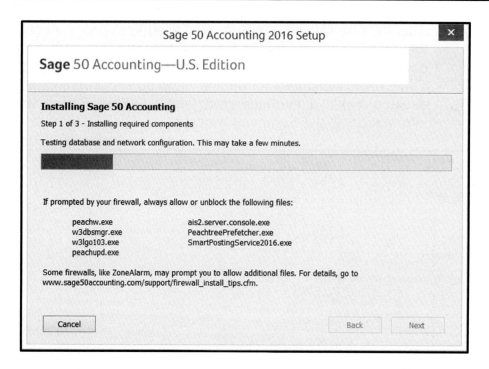

Step 12: The Installation Completed window appears. The window prompts to Restart Windows now.

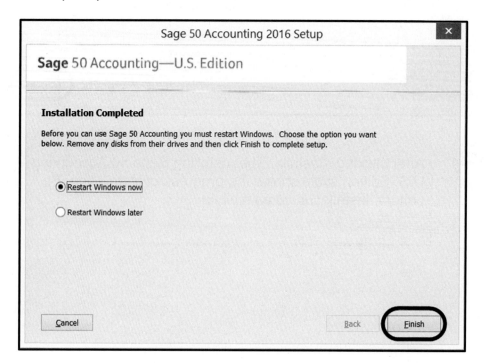

Step 13: After clicking <Finish>, wait for your computer to restart. To open Sage 50, select the Sage 50 Accounting 2016 icon. The Sage 50 Accounting startup window appears.

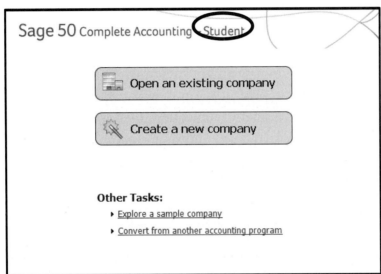

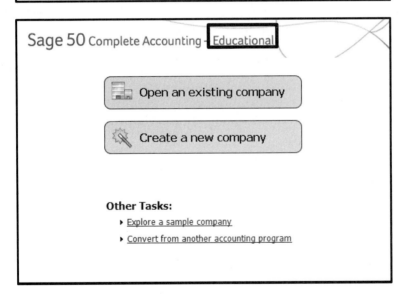

The version students install shows "Student," which is valid for 14 months. The version installed at school may show "Educational" which does not have a time limit. Instructors and schools can email SageEducation@sage.com to receive the serial number for the full, non-time limited "Educational" version.

Except for the time limit and serial number used during installation, the Student and Educational versions are the same.

 To restore backup files from lower versions of Sage 50, the "Educational" version must be used.

Step 14:   Complete *Product Activation*. From the startup window, select Help > Sage 50 Activation, Licensing, and Subscription Options.

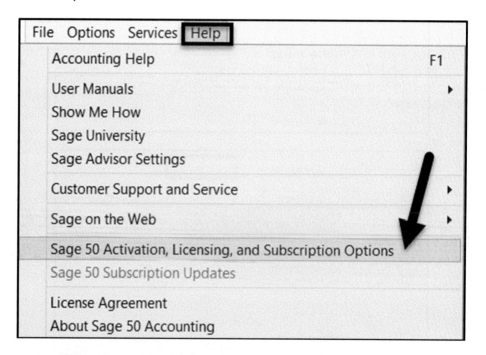

If the User Account window appears, click <Yes>.

Why do I need to activate?

If you do not complete product activation, Sage 50 will stop working after a few uses. If you start Sage 50 and a screen prompts to activate, follow these steps.

(*Hint:* If you started Sage 50 and a company opened, you can activate from the Help menu.)

a. The Product Activation window appears. Select Activate Online Now. *Or*, if you do not have an Internet connection, select <Activate Manually>. (If the User Account window appears, click <Yes>.)

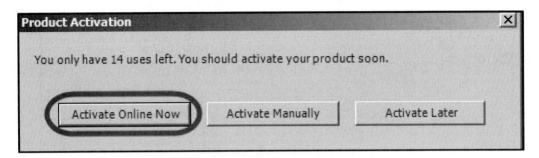

b. The Activation Complete window appears.

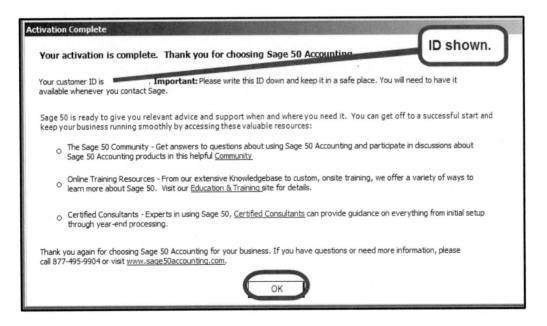

c. Click <OK> or press <Enter>.

Step 15: When Sage 50 starts, the **<u>Student version</u>** startup window shows "Sage 50 Accounting - Student." The Student version is accessible for 14 months.

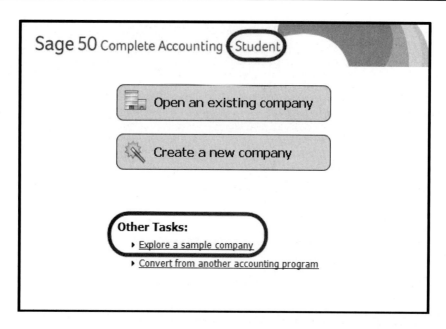

Or, in the classroom, the startup window may show **Educational** (serial number sent by Sage Education). The Educational version is the non-time limited multiuser software. Refer to page xx for Computer Lab Installation. If the school prefers that version, email SageEducation@sage.com.

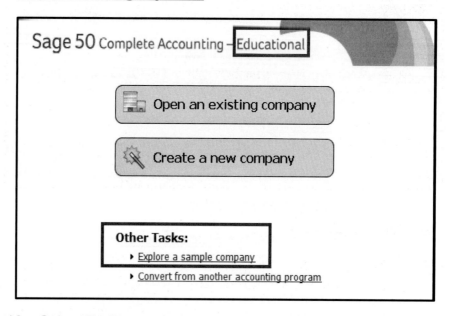

Step 16:   Select Explore a sample company. Bellwether Garden Supply is the default.

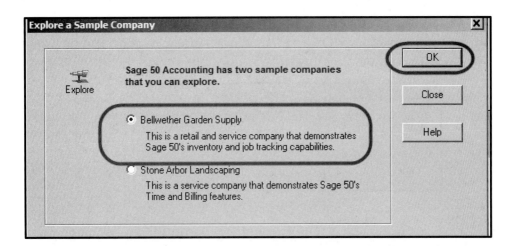

Step 17: Click 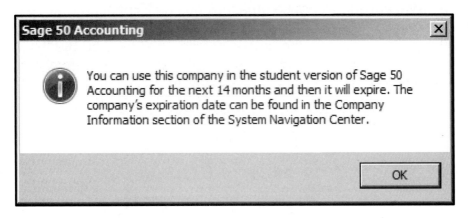 (or, press <Enter>). If you installed the Student Version, a Sage 50 Accounting window appears that says "You can use this company in the student version of Sage 50 for the next 14 months and then it will expire. The company's expiration date can be found in the Company Information section of the System Navigation Center. For more information about the expiration date, refer to page xviii.

Step 18: Click [OK].

Step 19: If the What's New? In Sage 50 window appears, read the information. To read more, select <Next>. Click on the box next to Do not display this screen again [☑ Do not display this screen again].

Step 20: To close the What's New?, click <Close>. When the window prompts Click <OK> to exit What's New, click on the box next to Do not display this message again.

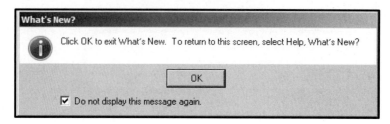

Step 21: Click [OK]. The Bellwether Garden Supply - Sage 50 Accounting window appears.

Expiration Date, Student Version, Sage 50 2016

To see when the Student Version of Sage 50 2016 expires, follow the steps below.

1. From the Navigation Bar > select [System].

2. The Company Maintenance area includes an Expiration Date field. The expiration date is 14 months after the day you installed the software. For example, the author installed the Sage 50 Student version on October 9, 2015. The expiration date is December 10, 2016.

Setting Global Options

Follow these steps to set Sage 50's Global Options. These options will be in effect for all Sage 50 companies.

1. From Sage 50's menu bar, select Options > Global. The Accounting tab is selected.

    •   In the **Decimal Entry** area, Manual and 2 decimal places should be selected in each field.

    •   In the **Hide General Ledger Accounts** area, the boxes *must* be unchecked.

    •   In the **Other Options** area, Warn if a record was changed but not saved and Recalculate cash balance automatically in Receipts, Payments, and Payroll Entry should be checked.

    Compare your Maintain Global Options/Accounting window to the one shown below.

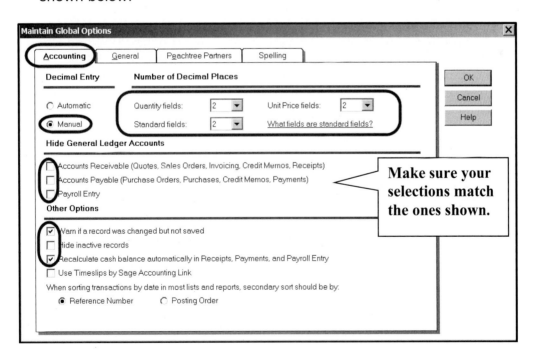

2. Click the General tab. Make sure your screen matches the one shown below.

3.   Click [OK]. The selections made in global options are now set for all companies.

4.   From Sage 50's menu bar, click File, Exit.

5.   If necessary, remove the CD. Observe that that icons have been set up on the desktop for Sage 50: Sage 50 Accounting 2016 and Sage 50 Accounting 2016 Automatic Backup Configuration.

COMPUTER LAB INSTALLATION

Before computer lab installation, make sure all versions of Peachtree or Sage 50 are deleted. Refer to Deleting Sage 50, page xxiii.

1.   Sage 50 Accounting 2016 - Educational Version should be installed locally. Do *not* put on server.

2.   Install software on local workstation then ghost (replicate) install. You can put the software on a standard lab image.

If you network Sage 50 2016-Educational Version, you will fall under the 5-seat license rule which will be an issue in a classroom where students may be working on the same data. For classroom installation, it is best to create a lab image.

STUDENT VERSION SOFTWARE

The software CD included with the textbook is Sage 50 Accounting 2016, Student Version. To see the default location where the currently displayed Sage 50 company resides, follow these steps.

1. Start Sage 50. Open the sample company, Bellwether Garden Supply.

2. From the menu bar, select Maintain > Company Information. The Directory field shows where the currently displayed Sage 50 company resides. The Student Version directory is shown below.

Student version directory:

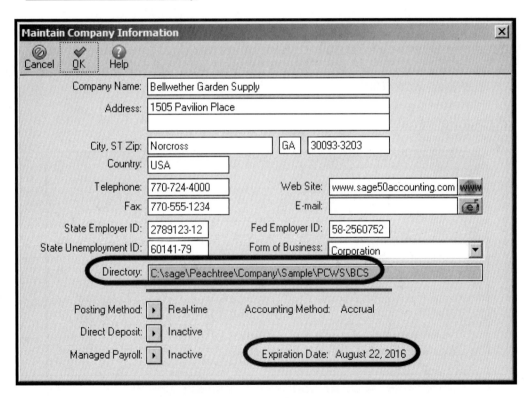

You can use company data in the Student Version of Sage 50 for 14 months. After 14 months, the Student Version software expires. Your expiration date will differ from the one shown.

Read me: Add student name to printouts

To add your name to reports, type your name or initials after the Company Name. The Company Name field is shown on Sage 50 printouts.

EDUCATIONAL VERSION SOFTWARE

If you are working in the computer lab, the default directory for Educational Version differs slightly when compared to the Student Version.

The Maintain Company Information window's Directory field differs slightly. Observe that the default folder for the Educational Version is \PCW**E** not \PCW**S**. *Before* adding your name to Bellwether Garden Supply in Chapter 1, the Directory field ends in \BCS. Once your name is added, the Directory field changes to **belgarsu** (first three letters from the first word (bel), three letters from the second word (gar), two letters from the third word (su)

Educational version Directory:

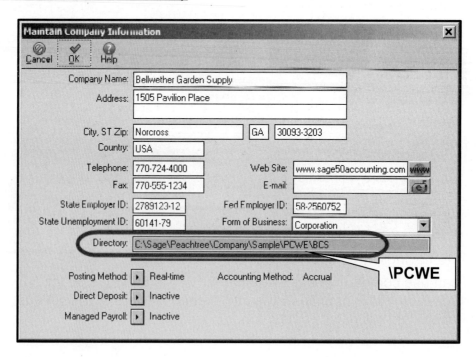

The features of the Student Version and Educational Version are the same, except for the Student Version's 14-month period of use. The serial numbers for installing the Student Version and Education Version also differ.

DELETING SAGE 50

Follow these steps to delete Sage 50 Accounting 2016. (Use similar steps to delete Sage 50 2015 or earlier version.)

1. Insert the Sage 50 CD. Select Run autorun.exe. *Or,* go to Control Panel > Programs and Features > Uninstall Sage 50 Accounting 2016 (*or* other year). The InstallWizard window appears briefly.

2. When the Maintenance Options window appears, select Remove > click <Next>.

3. The Confirm Uninstall prompts This will remove Sage 50 Accounting 2016 (all versions), click <OK>. Be patient. Removing Sage 50 Accounting will take a while.

4. When the Maintenance Complete window appears, click <Finish>. .

5. If necessary, remove the CD. Close Control Panel.

After removal, you may want to delete these two folders:

1. C:\Sage

2. C:\Program Files (x86)\Sage

Before removing the folders, backup data that you want to keep. Once the Sage folder is deleted, all company data files are removed. (In Windows Vista, the Sage folder is within C:\Program Files.)

After removing the folders, empty the recycle bin.

Preface

Computer Accounting with Sage 50 2016, 19th Edition, teaches you how to use Sage 50 2016 (formerly Peachtree) software. For more than 40 years[1], Sage Peachtree has produced award-winning accounting software. The Sage family of software products, which includes Sage 50, is the leading global supplier of business management solutions and services. Information about Sage Worldwide is shown on pages xxxv-xxxvi.

Sage operates in 24 countries and serves **6 million small and medium-sized businesses** (http://na.sage.com/us/about-us). Each year, tens of thousands of customers choose accountant-recommended Sage 50 for their business needs. Why? Because Sage 50 helps you do more to support the success of your business. Businesses that use Sage 50 include retail stores, healthcare, human resources/payroll, construction/real estate, transportation/distribution, payment processing, nonprofit, manufacturing, public utilities, legal, medical, accounting firms, home office businesses, and personal recordkeeping.

 Read Me: Multi-User Educational Version and Single User Student Version

For the Educational Version serial number, email SageEducation@sage.com. The full **Educational Version** is free to schools, does not have a time limit, and can be installed on multiple computers (http://www.sage.com/us/about-us/education-instructor). Refer to page xx for Computer Lab Installation.

The **Student Version** software can be installed on one computer and is valid for 14 months. The Student Version serial number is **41EC6-FBE6-86BE-3ØFF**.

In *Computer Accounting with Sage 50 2016, 19th Edition*, you learn about the relationship between Sage 50 software and fundamental accounting principles, procedures, and business processes.

---

[1] In 1976, Peachtree Accounting Software was available.

The diagram below illustrates the Sage 50 accounting system. Business processes are completed in this order:

- Software is installed,
- Companies are set up,
- Transactions are journalized in the special journals or general journal, then posted to the general ledger and subsidiary ledgers,
- After entering transactions, reports are printed.

Sage 50 is a real *double-entry accounting* system, not just an electronic checkbook. Double-entry accounting means that the equation Assets = Liabilities + Equity is always in balance. Since a debit in one account will be offset by a credit in another account, the sum of all debits is equal to the sum of all credits.

To assure double-entry accounting procedures, Sage 50 includes monthly accounting periods, the general journal and special journals, general ledger and subsidiary ledgers, account reconciliation, an audit trail, and numerous financial reports. The Sage 50 accounting system also includes closing the fiscal year.

SAGE 50 2016

The System Requirements for Sage 50 2016 are online at www.mhhe.com/yacht2016 > link to System Requirements. Each textbook includes a copy of the software, Sage 50 2016.

NEW The software, **Sage 50 2016**, is included with every textbook. For software installation instructions, see pages vi-xviii.

NEW Use this serial number **41EC6-FBE6-86BE-3ØFF** for installing the Student Version software. The student version is valid for **14 months** and then it expires. The expiration date can be found in the Company Information section of the System Navigation Center and on the Maintain > Company Information window.

NEW After installation, you must activate the software. Refer to Step 14, pages xiv-xv. The Help menu includes software activation.

Compatible with Windows 8, Windows 7, and Vista. System requirements at www.mhhe.com/yacht2016. Sage 50 2016 was tested with Windows 10.

NEW For installation on multiple classroom computers, email SageEducation@sage.com, 800-256-8807; instructor software, www.sage.com/us/about-us/education-instructor. Information for educators is included at www.mhhe.com/yacht2016, Install Sage 50 link. Refer to page xx, Computer Lab Installation.

GO GREEN & SAVE is included within the textbook chapters and on the Online Learning Center. There is no need for hard-copy printouts.

NEW Watch Sage Advisor video . Videos link to information about features and technical support.

Online Learning Center at www.mhhe.com/yacht2016 includes two appendixes: Appendix C, Review of Accounting Principles; Appendix D, Glossary.

NEW The Online Learning at www.mhhe.com/yacht2016 includes YouTube videos, narrated PowerPoints, Online quizzes include Multiple-Choice and True/False questions, QA Templates (end-of-chapter questions and analysis questions), Going to the Net exercises, and Assessment Rubrics.

How to fix?, **Troubleshooting**, **Comment**, and **Read Me** boxes within chapters identify and help resolve issues. To find How to fix?, Troubleshooting, Comment, and Read Me, use the chapter index.

NEW Bellwether Garden Supply project includes questions for analyzing the sample company data, identifying software features and functions, and reviewing sample company transactions and reports. The Bellwether Garden Supply project is online at www.mhhe.com/yacht2016.

Sage 50's emphasis on double-entry accounting and business processes is explained throughout the textbook. Accounting skills are applied to all facets of running a business. Students create 12 companies, complete the accounting cycle, and practice computer accounting skills.

NEW Financial Manager Analysis includes the Business Summary of financial ratios and Key Balances from the income statement and balance sheet.

NEW **Assessment online:** Rubrics, graded interactive quizzes, QA templates, and analysis questions.

NEW **Source document practice set**: The merchandising business practice set includes source documents, reviews special journals and subsidiary ledgers, and the accounting cycle. Online at www.mhhe.com/yacht2016.

Chapter 8, Stone Arbor Landscaping: Time and Billing. Use Sage 50's time and billing feature to record a time ticket, enter a sales invoice, and record payroll for jobs completed.

Chapters 1-18 include saving Sage 50 reports as Adobe Acrobat PDF files, and exporting reports to Excel.

Payroll tax tables for 50 states. Example payroll withholdings are included in Chapter 4, Employees; Chapter 15, Employees, Payroll, and Account Reconciliation; Exercise 15-1, Student Name Sales and Service; Project 2, Highland Sports; and Project 4, CW Manufacturing, Inc.

NEW End-of-chapter exercises include Check Your Figures.

Use Sage 50's import/export feature to copy lists into another company.

Sage 50's modular system design is explained and compared to other accounting information systems. Workflow diagrams illustrate Sage 50's system design.

An accounting software diagram illustrates where Sage 50 fits into the range of accounting software applications.

NEW   Illustrations show Sage 50's emphasize on the double-entry accounting system.

NEW   Sage 50 is compared to QuickBooks Online and Desktop versions and Microsoft Dynamics.

Computer Accounting with Sage 50 2016, 19th Edition, shows you how to set up service, merchandising, nonprofit, and manufacturing businesses. When the textbook is completed, you have a working familiarity with Sage 50 Complete Accounting 2016 software. You learn how computer accounting and the general ledger accounting cycle work together.

The Part 1, 2, 3, and 4 introductions include a chart showing the chapter number, Sage 50 backups, Excel and Adobe file names, size in kilobytes of each file backed up or saved, and page numbers where each backup, Excel, and Adobe PDF file is completed.

What's New in Sage 50 2016?

The Help menu includes the new Sage 50 2016 software features. To see that window, follow these steps:

1. Start Sage 50.

2. Open the sample company, Bellwether Garden Supply. (Detailed steps for installing the software and starting Bellwether are on pages vi-xviii.)

3. From Bellwether Garden Supply's menu bar, select Help > What's New. Getting started videos, show-me-how videos and quick reference guides are included.

4. On the What's New window, click [Next >] to see more. Read the information on these windows to review the new software features. Click [< Back] to review information. When through, click [Close].

PART 1: EXPLORING SAGE 50 2016

There are two sample companies included with the software: Bellwether Garden Supply and Stone Arbor Landscaping. Bellwether Garden Supply is a retail and service company that demonstrates Sage 50's inventory and job tracking capabilities. Stone Arbor Landscaping is a service company that demonstrates time and billing features.

> **Each part of the textbook includes a summary. Refer to pages 1 and 2 for a summary of Part 1**. Pages 2 and 3 include a chart showing chapter numbers, files backed up and saved (.ptb, .pdf, .xlsx), file sizes, and page numbers where work was completed.

Part 1, Chapters 1-8, shows how to backup (save) files, export Sage 50 reports to Excel and save reports as Adobe PDF files. Sage 50's system design is explained. This includes how Sage 50's user interface is organized into general ledger, accounts receivable, accounts payable, inventory, payroll, and job costing modules.

In Part 1 of the textbook, you complete eight chapters that demonstrate how Sage 50 is used. This introduces you to the procedures that will be used with all the chapters of the textbook. Beginning in Part 2, you set up companies from scratch.

NEW Chapter 1, Introduction to Bellwether Garden Supply, includes Sage 50's Navigation Centers and Restore Wizard for opening new or existing companies. The new Navigation Bar and menu bar selections are explained. Bellwether Garden Supply is updated to March 2016.

Chapter 2, Vendors, shows you how to view accounts payable lists and reports from the Vendors & Payables Navigation Center as well as custom date filtering and how to add columns to reports. New sections include Receive Inventory from a Purchase Order and Apply to Purchase Order. Sage 50's accounts payable system is explained.

Chapter 3, Customers, shows you how to view customer lists and reports from the Customers & Sales Navigation Center as well as custom date filtering and how to add columns to reports. Chapter 3 includes Sales Orders and Ship Items from a Sales Order. Sage 50's accounts receivable system is explained.

NEW Sage 50's Financial Manager includes financial ratios and key balances.

Chapter 4, Employees, shows you how to navigate Sage 50's Employees & Payroll system.

Chapter 5, General Ledger, Inventory, and Internal Control, shows you Sage 50's budget feature, how selected access for security is used, internal controls, and audit trail. Sage 50's inventory system is also included.

Chapter 6, Job Cost, shows you how to use Sage 50's job cost system.

Chapter 7, Financial Statements, shows the result of work completed in Chapters 1-6.

NEW After Chapter 7, the Bellwether Garden Supply Project can be completed. It is included online at www.mhhe.com/yacht2016.

In Chapter 8, Stone Arbor Landscaping: Time & Billing, you work with a service company that demonstrates Sage 50's time and billing features.

In Exercises 8-1 and 8-2, you record time and billing transactions, including a time ticket that is applied to a sales invoice and payroll entry.

PART 2: SAGE 50 2016 FOR SERVICE BUSINESSES

Chapters 9, 10, 11, Project 1, and Project 1A are included in this section of the textbook. The work completed in Chapter 9 is continued in Chapters 10 and 11. The accounting cycle is completed for the fourth quarter of the year and includes adjusting entries and closing the year.

> **For the Part 2 summary, refer to pages 251-256.** Pages 254-256 include a chart showing chapter numbers, files backed up and saved (.ptb, .pdf, .xlsx), file sizes, and page numbers where work was completed.

NEW In Chapter 9, New Company Setup and Beginning Balances, you set up two service companies—Donald Watson Designer and Crafts by Student Name with Sage 50's simplified chart of accounts. You use Sage 50's new Company Setup Wizard and enter beginning balances. The companies set up in Chapter 9 continue in Chapters 10 and 11.

In Chapter 10, Maintaining Accounting Records for Service Businesses, you record entries for October in the Write Checks and Receipts windows, use Sage 50's account reconciliation feature and print reports. You also backup, and save reports in Excel and Adobe PDF format.

Chapter 11, Completing Quarterly Activities and Closing the Fiscal Year, you complete transactions for November and December, record adjusting entries, print financial statements, and close the fiscal year.

NEW Exercises 9-1 through 11-2 include three months of transactions, account reconciliation, adjusting entries, financial statements, Sage 50's closing procedure, and Check Your Figures. Sage 50 reports are backed up, and saved in Adobe PDF format and exported to Excel.

NEW Project 1, Shelly Martin, Accounting, is a comprehensive project that reviews what you learned in Chapters 9, 10, and 11.

Project 1A, Student-Designed Service Business, shows you how to design a service business from scratch. You set up the business, choose a chart of accounts, create a Balance Sheet, write business transactions, complete the computer accounting cycle, and close the fiscal year.

PART 3: SAGE 50 2016 FOR MERCHANDISING BUSINESSES

Chapters 12, 13, 14, 15, Project 2, and Project 2A are included in this section of the textbook. Students set up two merchandising businesses in Chapter 12—Wendy's Service Merchandise *and* Student Name Sales and Service. The work started in Chapter 12 is continued in Chapters 13, 14 and 15.

> **For the Part 3 summary, refer to pages 399-402.** Pages 400-402 include a chart showing chapter numbers, files backed up and saved (.ptb, .pdf, .xlsx), file sizes, and page numbers where work was completed.

In Chapter 12, Vendors & Purchases, use Sage 50's accounts payable system, set up vendor defaults, record inventory purchases and payments from vendors, automatically track vendor discounts, and use vendor credit memos for purchase returns.

In Chapter 13, Customers & Sales, use Sage 50's accounts receivable system, set up customer defaults, record cash and credit sales and receive payments from customers, use credit memos for sales returns.

NEW Chapter 13 includes Financial Manager Analysis. Business summary financial ratios are shown and key balances for income statement and balance sheet accounts.

Chapter 14, Inventory & Services, shows you how to use Sage 50's inventory system.

Chapter 15, Employees, Payroll and Account Reconciliation, shows Sage 50's payroll system using two states, Arizona and Georgia, as an example for payroll withholdings. You set up payroll defaults, add employee information, learn about automatic payroll tax calculations, and complete payroll entry.

Account reconciliation shows you how Sage 50's Accounts Payable, Accounts Receivable, Inventory, and General Ledger systems work together. Chapter 15 includes account reconciliation for both the checking and payroll accounts. Check Your Figure amounts are included for Exercises 12-1 through 15-2.

NEW Project 2, Highland Sports, is a comprehensive project that incorporates what you have learned in Chapters 12 through 15. Project 2 includes payroll withholdings for Oregon.

Project 2A, Student-Designed Merchandising Business, asks you to create a merchandising business from scratch.

PART 4: ADVANCED SAGE 50 2016 APPLICATIONS

Chapters 16, 17, 18, Project 3, Project 4, and Project 4A are included in this part of the textbook. Chapter 16, Customizing Forms, shows you how to use Sage 50's design tools. Chapter 17, Import/Export, shows you how to export data from Sage 50 to a word processing program and how to import lists into a company. In Chapter 18, Microsoft Word and Templates, you copy a Sage 50 report to Word and look at vendor, customer, and employee templates included with the software.

> **For the Part 4 summary, refer to pages 617-618.** Page 618 includes a chart showing chapter numbers, files backed up and saved (.ptb, .pdf, .xlsx, .docx, .doc, .txt, .csv), file sizes, and page numbers where work was completed.

Chapter 16, Customizing Forms, includes design tools for report customization.

In Exercises 16-1 and 16-2, forms and financial statements are customized.

Chapter 17, Import/Export, includes how to import a chart of accounts into another company and export to a word processing program.

In Exercises 17-1 and 17-2 import lists from Bellwether Garden Supply into the new company set up in Chapter 17.

Chapter 18, Microsoft Word and Templates, includes copying reports to Word, using templates and the write letters feature.

NEW   Project 3, Springfield Computer Club, is a nonprofit business.

NEW   Project 4, CW Manufacturing, Inc., is the culminating project in your study of Sage 50 2016. Project 4 includes payroll withholdings for Pennsylvania.

Project 4A, Student-Designed Project, instructs you to write another month's transactions for one of the four projects completed.

Each chapter ends with an Index for that chapter. There is also an Index at the end of the book.

CONVENTIONS USED IN TEXTBOOK

As you work through *Computer Accounting with Sage 50 2016, 19e*, you should read and follow the step-by-step instructions. Numerous screen illustrations help you to check your work. The following conventions are used in this textbook:

1.   Information that you type appears in boldface; for example, Type **Supplies** in the Account ID field.

2.   Keys on the keyboard that should be pressed appear in angle brackets; for example, <Enter>.

3.   Sequences of software selections are indicated by a greater than symbol (>).

     Examples:  > New Bill
     From the menu bar, select File > Close Company

4.   When you see this icon ▶, there is a video, on the textbook website at www.mhhe.com/yacht2016 > Student Edition link > select the appropriate chapter > link to Videos or YouTube > then select the video.

5.   This icon—💾—reminds you to check the Sage 50 work completed.

6.   Buttons and picture icons are shown as they appear on the screen.

     Examples:  (Next button); (Display icon)

SAGE WORLDWIDE

Sage customers cover a wide range of small and medium-sized businesses. Sage software is used for personal recordkeeping and home-office customers, small businesses with just a few employees, and larger enterprises that distribute across North America.

- Established more than 40 years ago.
- Headquartered in the U.K. with offices across North America, Latin America, Europe, Africa, Middle East, Asia, and Oceania.
- Publicly traded on the London Stock Exchange (LSE: SGE).
- Generates more than $2 billion in revenue.
- Serves more than 6 million customers.
- Advises 1.9 million customers through support contracts.
- Manages 33,000 customer calls a day.
- Employs more than 13,000 people.
- Parent company of Sage North America.

About the Author, carol@carolyacht.com

Carol Yacht is an accounting educator and textbook author. Carol authors Sage Peachtree, and Intuit's QuickBooks Online and QuickBooks Desktop textbooks (www.mhhe.com/yacht2016).

Carol taught on the faculties of California State University-Los Angeles, West Los Angeles College, Yavapai College, and Beverly Hills High School. She started using accounting software in her classes in 1980. Carol's teaching career includes first and second year accounting courses, accounting information systems, and computer accounting.

Since 1989, Carol's textbooks have been published by McGraw-Hill. She contributes regularly to professional journals and is the Editor of the American Accounting Association's Teaching, Learning, and Curriculum section's *The Accounting Educator.*

Carol Yacht was an officer of AAA's Two-Year College section and recipient of its Lifetime Achievement Award. She is a board member of the Microsoft Dynamics Academic Alliance, worked for IBM Corporation as an education specialist, served on the AAA Commons Editorial Board, and works for Sage and Intuit as a consultant. Carol prepared AAA's Powerlytics Benchmark and Research Users' Guides. She is a frequent speaker at state, regional, and national conventions.

Carol earned her MA degree from California State University-Los Angeles, BS degree from the University of New Mexico, and AS degree from Temple University.

Acknowledgments

I would like to thank the following colleagues for their help in the preparation of this book: Steve Schuetz; Kevin Moran; Beth Woods, CPA; Donna Gillespie; and Matt Lowenkron. A special thank you to the following professors.

Kathy Blondell, St. Johns River Comm. Coll.
Linda Bolduc, Mt. Wachusett College
Anna Boulware, St. Charles Comm. College
Michael Bryan, Tidewater Community Coll.
Jim Burcicki, Penn Foster Career School
Lindy Bryd, Augusta Technical College
Vickie Campbell, Cape Fear CC
Sheree Corkern, Mississippi College
Leonard Cronin, Rochester Comm. College
Alan Davis, Comm. Coll. of Philadelphia
Dave Davis, Vincennes University
Vaun Day, Central Arizona College
Roger Dimick, Lamar Inst. of Technology
Brenda Douglas, Central Arizona College
Philip Empey, Purdue University-Calumet
Raul Enriquez, Laredo Community College
Bill Gaither, Dawson Community College
Vicki Garrison, Augusta Technical College
Harold Gellis, York College of CUNY
Christopher Gilbert, Glendale College
Marina Grau, Houston Community College
Nancy Greene, University of Cincinnati
Joyce Griffin, Kansas City Kansas CC
Bill Guidera, Texas State Technical College
Jim Hale, Vance-Granville Community Coll.
Mary Hauschen, Moraine Park Tech. Coll.
Paula E. Hegner, Folsom Lake College
Larry Heldreth, Danville Community College
Geoffrey Heriot, Greenville Tech. College
Tynia Kessler, Lake Land College
Jan Ivansek, Lakeland College
Jeff Jackson, San Jacinto College
Robert Jackson, Ivy Tech State College
Stacy Johnson, Iowa Central Comm. Coll.
Judy Kidder, Mohave Community College
Mary Kline, Black Hawk College
Linda Kropp, Modesto Junior College
Christine Kloezeman, Glendale Comm. Coll.
Sara Lagier, American Business College
Jan Lange, MN West Comm. & Tech. Coll.
Bruce Lindsey, Genesee Community Coll.
Susan Looney, Mohave Community Coll.
Susan Lynn, University of Baltimore
Josephine Mathias, Mercer County CC

J. Mike Metzcar, Indiana Wesleyan University
Julie Miller Millmann, Chippewa Valley Tech.
Rania Mousa, University of Evansville
LoAnn Nelson, Lake Region State College
Cory Ng, Comm. College of Philadelphia
Ahmed Omar, Peirce College
Vincent Osaghae, Chicago State University
Susan Pallas, Southeast Community College
Timothy Pearson, West Virginia University
Gerald Peterka, Mt. San Jacinto College
Simon Petravick, Bradley University
Tom Pinckney, Trident Technical College
Susan Pope, University of Akron
Robert Porter, Cape Fear Community College
Shirley Powell, Arkansas State University
Eric Primuth, Cuyahoga Community College
Jeffrey Pullen, Strayer University
Howard Randall, Mission College
Iris Lugo Renta, Interamerican University
Betty J. Reynolds, Arizona Western College
Monique Ring, So. New Hampshire University
Annalee Rothenberg, Tacoma Community Coll.
Helen Roybark, Radford University
Diane Sandefur, Elliott Bookkeeping School
Joann Segovia, Winona State University
Art Shroeder, Louisiana State University
Nancy Shoemake, Rochester Comm. Tech. Coll.
Lee Shook, Chipola College
Douglas L. Smith, Berry College
Mona Stephens, University of Phoenix
Charles Strang, Western New Mexico Univ.
Marilyn St. Clair, Weatherford College
Marie Stewart, Newport Business Institute
Maggie Stone, Pima Community College
Mel Sweet, University of Connecticut
Laurie Swinney, University of Nebraska
Eileen Taylor, North Carolina State University
Greg Thom, Parkland Community College
Tom Turner, Des Moines Area Community Coll.
Mazdolyn Winston, Calhoun Community Coll.
W. Brian Voss, Austin Community College
Bruce Whitaker, Diné College
Shandra Ware, Atlanta Technical College
Michele Wiltsie, Hudson Valley Comm. Coll.

Table of Contents

The Timetable for Completion on the next page is a guideline for in-class lecture/discussion/demonstration and hands-on work. Work not completed in class is homework. In most Accounting classes, students can expect to spend approximately two hours outside of class for every hour in class.

Two optional projects are on the textbook's Online Learning Center at www.mhhe.com/yacht2016. Select the Student Edition and then link to Practice Set or Bellwether Garden Supply Project.

The Bellwether Garden Supply project is in question/answer format. The Practice Set includes source documents for setting up and completing the accounting cycle for a merchandising business.

TIMETABLE FOR COMPLETION		Hours
Part 1: Exploring Sage 50 2016		
Chapter 1	Introduction to Bellwether Garden Supply	2.0
Chapter 2	Vendors	1.0
Chapter 3	Customers	1.0
Chapter 4	Employees	1.0
Chapter 5	General Ledger, Inventory, and Internal Control	1.0
Chapter 6	Job Cost	2.0
Chapter 7	Financial Statements	1.0
OLC	Bellwether Garden Supply Project, www.mhhe.com/yacht2016	varies
Chapter 8	Stone Arbor Landscaping: Time & Billing	1.0
	Subtotal Part 1	10.0
Part 2: Sage 50 2016 for Service Businesses		
Chapter 9	New Company Setup and Beginning Balances	2.0
Chapter 10	Maintaining Accounting Records for Service Businesses	2.0
Chapter 11	Completing Quarterly Activities and Closing the Fiscal Year	1.5
Project 1	Shelly Martin, Accounting	1.5
Project 1A	Student-Designed Service Business	2.0
	Subtotal Part 2	*9.0*
Part 3: Sage 50 2016 for Merchandising Businesses		
Chapter 12	Vendors & Purchases	3.0
Chapter 13	Customers & Sales	2.5
Chapter 14	Inventory & Services	2.0
Chapter 15	Employees, Payroll, and Account Reconciliation	2.0
Project 2	Highland Sports	3.5
Project 2A	Student-Designed Merchandising Business	3.0
OLC	Source Document Practice Set, www.mhhe.com/yacht2016	varies
	Subtotal Part 3	*16.0*
Part 4: Advanced Sage 50 2016 Applications		
Chapter 16	Customizing Forms	1.0
Chapter 17	Import/Export	1.0
Chapter 18	Microsoft Word and Templates	1.0
Project 3	Springfield Computer Club	1.0
Project 4	CW Manufacturing, Inc.	4.0
Project 4A	Student-Designed Project	2.0
	Subtotal Part 4	*10.0*
TOTAL HOURS: PARTS 1, 2, 3, 4		**45.0**

Part 1

Exploring Sage 50 2016

Part 1 introduces the basic features of Sage 50 2016. The purpose of Part 1 is to become familiar with the software rather than test accounting knowledge. Chapters 1 through 8 (Part 1) are an overview of Sage 50's user interface.

Beginning with Chapter 9, computer accounting skills are reviewed in depth. In Chapters 9-18 and Projects 1-4A, 12 businesses are set up from scratch. Part 1, Chapters 1-8, introduces two sample companies that are included with the software: Bellwether Garden Supply and Stone Arbor Landscaping.

Chapter 1:   Introduction to Bellwether Garden Supply
Chapter 2:   Vendors
Chapter 3:   Customers
Chapter 4:   Employees
Chapter 5:   General Ledger, Inventory, and Internal Control
Chapter 6:   Job Cost
Chapter 7:   Financial Statements
Chapter 8:   Stone Arbor Landscaping—Time & Billing
Online Learning Center–Bellwether Garden Supply Project, www.mhhe.com/yacht2016, Student Edition

In Chapters 1 through 7, the work completed with Bellwether Garden Supply is cumulative. That means all work within the chapter and end-of-chapter exercises need to be completed. Throughout Part 1, report illustrations and Check Your Figure amounts are shown. To insure that your work matches the textbook, complete *both* the work within the chapter and the end-of-chapter exercises. The Online Learning Center at www.mhhe.com/yacht2016, Student Edition link, includes a Bellwether Garden Supply Project. The project can be completed after Chapter 7.

The instructions in this book are written for Sage 50 2016. Sage 50 requires Windows 8, Windows 7, or Vista Service Pack 1 with the latest updates from Microsoft installed. To save reports in PDF format, the latest update of Adobe Acrobat Reader should be used (https://get.adobe.com/reader/).

Windows[1] uses pictures or ***icons*** to identify tasks. This is known as a ***user interface*** (***UI***), also known as the ***graphical user interface*** (***GUI***). For example, Sage uses common icons or symbols to represent tasks: a disk for saving, a question mark for help, a printer for printing, an envelope for email, etc. A ***mouse***, ***touchpad*** or other pointing device is used to perform various tasks. Software design can be described by the acronym ***WIMP*** -- Windows, Icons, Menus, and Pull-downs.

The chart below shows the size of the backup files, Excel files, and PDF files saved in Part 1–Chapters 1 through 8. (Excel 2007, 2010 and 2013 files end in an .xlsx extension.) The textbook shows how to back up to a USB drive. Backups can be made to the desktop, hard drive location, network location or external media.

Chapter	Sage 50 Backup (.ptb) Excel (.xlsx) and Adobe (.pdf)	Kilobytes[2]	Page Nos.
1	bgs.ptb[3]	3,305 KB	23-25
	Chapter 1.ptb	3,394 KB	41-42
	Chapter 1_Employee List.xlsx	15 KB	44-46
	Chapter 1_Employee List.pdf	27 KB	46-47
	Exercise 1-2.ptb	3,322 KB	51
	Exercise 1-2_Employee List.xlsx	15 KB	51
	Exercise 1-2_Employee List.pdf	28 KB	51
	Exercise 1-2_Chart of Accounts.xlsx	16 KB	51
	Exercise 1-2_Chart of Accounts.pdf	31 KB	52
2	Chapter 2.ptb	3,348 KB	84-85
	Chapter 2_Vendor List and Vendor Ledgers.xlsx	20 KB	85-87
	Chapter 2_Vendor List.pdf	15 KB	87-88
	Chapter 2_Vendor Ledgers.pdf	26 KB	88
	Exercise 2-2.ptb	3,369 KB	90
	Exercise 2-2_Vendor List_Vendor Ledgers_PO Register.xlsx	24 KB	90
	Exercise 2-2_Vendor List.pdf	16 KB	90
	Exercise 2-2_Vendor Ledgers.pdf	28 KB	90
	Exercise 2-2_Purchase Order Register.pdf	12 KB	90
3	Chapter 3.ptb	3,421 KB	127
	Exercise 3-2.ptb	3,436 KB	129
	Exercise 3-2_Customer Ledgers.xlsx	18 KB	129
	Exercise 3-2_Customer Ledgers.pdf	34 KB	129
4	Chapter 4.ptb	3,476 KB	149
	Exercise 4-2.ptb	3,564 KB	151

[1] Words that are boldfaced and italicized are defined in the Glossary online at www.mhhe.com/yacht2016 > Student Edition > Appendix D – Glossary.
[2] Your backup sizes may differ.
[3] This is the first backup and includes starting data for Bellwether Garden Supply.

Chapter	Sage 50 Backup (.ptb) Excel (.xlsx) and Adobe (.pdf)	Kilobytes[4]	Page Nos.
4	Exercise 4-2_Payroll Check Register.xlsx	13 KB	151
	Exercise 4-2_Payroll Check Register.pdf	19 KB	151
5	Chapter 5.ptb	3,554 KB	187
	Exercise 5-2.ptb	3,635 KB	188
	Exercise 5-2_General Ledger Trial Balance.xlsx	15 KB	188
	Exercise 5-2_General Ledger Trial Balance.pdf	23 KB	188
6	Chapter 6.ptb	3,611 KB	200
	Exercise 6-2.ptb[5]	3,631 KB	202
	Exercise 6-2_Job Profitability Report.xlsx	16 KB	202
	Exercise 6-2_Job Profitability Report.pdf	23 KB	202
7	No backups in Chapter 7	--	--
	Chapter 7_Financial Statements.xlsx	35 KB	223-225
	Chapter 7_Balance Sheet.pdf	7 KB	225
	Chapter 7_Income Statement.pdf	8 KB	225
	Chapter 7_Gross Profit by Departments.pdf	4 KB	225
	Chapter 7_Statement of Cash Flow.pdf	5 KB	225
	Chapter 7_Statement of Retained Earnings.pdf	4 KB	225
	Chapter 7_Statement of Changes in Financial Position.pdf	5 KB	225
OLC	Bellwether Garden Supply Project, www.mhhe.com/yacht2016		
8	Chapter 8.ptb	1,636 KB	243
	Chapter 8_Time Ticket Register.xlsx	14 KB	244-246
	Chapter 8_Time Ticket Register.pdf	21 KB	246
	Exercise 8-1.ptb	1,670 KB	248
	Exercise 8-2_Time and Billing Reports.xlsx	31 KB	249
	Exercise 8-2_Job Ledger.pdf	48 KB	249
	Exercise 8-2_Time Ticket Register.pdf	21 KB	249
	Exercise 8-2_Payroll Time Sheet.pdf	23 KB	249

Read Me: Problem Backing Up to USB Drive
If you encounter difficulties backing up to a USB drive, backup to the desktop first. Then, copy the backup file from the desktop to the USB drive. Refer to Appendix A, Troubleshooting, at www.mhhe.com/yacht2016.

---

[4]Your backup sizes may differ.
[5]The **Exercise 6-2.ptb** backup file is used in Part 4, Chapters 16, 17, and 18. If necessary, backup to external media. Do *not* delete the Exercise 6-2.ptb file.

Chapter 1 — Introduction to Bellwether Garden Supply

LEARNING OBJECTIVES

1. Start Sage 50 2016.
2. Explore the sample company, Bellwether Garden Supply.
3. Make sure global options are set ▶.[1]
4. Back up Bellwether Garden Supply data ▶.
5. Restore data with Sage 50's restore Wizard ▶.
6. Operate Sage 50's menus, drop-down lists, toolbar, and navigation bar.
7. Use File Explorer (also called Windows Explorer) to see file sizes.
8. Export Sage 50 reports to Excel, and save reports as Adobe PDF files.
9. Make three backups, save three Excel files, and three PDF files.[2]

In Chapters 1-7, the sample company Bellwether Garden Supply is used. Complete the work within the chapter and the end-of-chapter exercises because work continues in the next chapter. Use the sample company to become familiar with Sage 50's user interface and features. In Parts 2, 3 and 4 (Chapters 9-18, Projects 1-4A), you set up new service, merchandising, nonprofit, and manufacturing companies and computer accounting tasks are reviewed in depth.

MOUSE AND KEYBOARD BASICS

One of the first decisions is whether to use the mouse or keyboard. The instructions in this book assume that you are using a mouse. When the word click or select is used, it means to use the mouse, but you can also use the keyboard. The instructions that follow explain how to use the mouse or keyboard.

---

[1]This icon, ▶, means there is a video. Go online to www.mhhe.com/yacht2016 > link to Student Edition > select Chapter 1 > Videos.

[2]Refer to the chart on pages 2-3 for the size of files backed up and saved. Check with your instructor for his or her preference for receiving files—Adobe .pdf, Excel .xlsx, or Sage 50 .ptb backups.

Using the Mouse

➢ To single click: position the mouse cursor over the selection and click the left mouse button once.

➢ To double-click: position the mouse cursor over the selection and click the left mouse button twice, quickly.

➢ Use the right mouse button the same way as the left mouse button.

Using the Keyboard

➢ If there is an underlined letter on the menu bar, hold down the **<Alt>**[3] key and the underlined letter to make the selection. (*Hint:* Press the **<Alt>** key to underline menu bar letters.)

➢ If you have already held down the **<Alt>** key and the underlined letter and more selections appear with underlined letters, just type the underlined letter to select the item.

Using Shortcut Keys

Shortcut keys[4] enable you to perform common operations by using two or more keys together. The shortcut keys are shown below and on the next page.

<Ctrl> + <Letter> Shortcuts	
<Ctrl> + <X>	Cut
<Ctrl> + <C>	Copy
<Ctrl> + <V>	Paste
<Ctrl> + <E>	Delete Record
<Ctrl> + <F>	Find
<Ctrl> + <D>	Find Next
<Ctrl> + <N>	New Company
<Ctrl> + <O>	Open Company
<Ctrl> + <B>	Back Up Company
<Ctrl> + <R>	Restore Company
<Ctrl> + <P>	Print Displayed Report, Invoices, Quotes, etc.

---

[3]The angle brackets are used around words to indicate individual keys on your keyboard; for example, **<Alt>** is for the Alternate key, **<Enter>** for the Enter/Return key, **<Ctrl>** is for the Control key, **<Esc>** is for the Escape key.

[4] Words that are boldface and italics are defined in the Glossary, online at www.mhhe.com/yacht2016 > select Student Edition > Chapter 1 > link to Glossary.

Function Key Shortcuts	
<F1>	Displays the online Help topic for current window
<Shift> + <F1>	Changes mouse pointer to What's This Help selector
<F3>	Find transactions
<F5>	Saves records and posts (or saves) transactions in certain windows
<F7>	Check spelling
<F10>	Toggles between open window and menu bar
<CTRL>+<F4>	Close current document window
<ALT>+<F4>	Closes the application window
<CTRL>+<F6>	Moves to next window
<Shift>+<CTRL>+<F6>	Moves to the previous window

To learn more about Sage 50's shortcuts, use the Help menu. From the menu bar, select Help > Help >Index tab. Type **keyboard shortcuts** in the keyword field, then display the Sage 50 Keyboard Shortcuts. Additional links are listed in the Related topics and What do you want to do next? areas on the Sage 50 Help window.

SAGE 50'S STARTUP WINDOW

Sage 50's startup window displays a number of options.

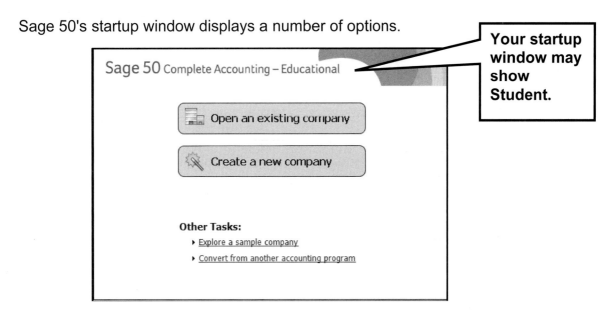

From the startup window, you can Open an existing company, Create a new company, Explore a sample company, and Convert from another accounting program.

Observe that the top-left of the Sage 50 Accounting window has four

menu bar options—   .

To exit from the startup window select File > Exit; *or,* click on the ☒ on
the upper right-hand side of the Sage 50 Accounting window.

THE WINDOWS INTERFACE

One of the benefits of Windows is that it standardizes terms and
operations used in software programs. Once you learn how to move
around Sage, you also know how to use other Windows applications.

To learn more about the Windows user interface, let's look at a Sage
window. On the next page, the Sage 50 Accounting window shows the
Business Status Navigation Center (the **dashboard**) and the menu
bar for Bellwether Garden Supply.

For now, let's study the parts of the Business Status Navigation Center.
Some features are common to all software programs that are written
for Windows. For example, in the upper right corner there is the Minimize

▬ button, Double Window 🗗 button, and the Exit or Close [☒]
button. The title bar, window border, and mouse pointer are also
common to Windows programs. Other features are specific to Sage:
menu bar, toolbar, and the Navigation Bar at the left side of Sage 50's
main window which offers access to the Navigation Centers.

Sage 50 includes a Navigation Bar on the left side of the window
with seven selections: Business Status, Customers & Sales, Vendors
& Purchases, Inventory & Services, Employees & Payroll, Banking, and
System. The Navigation Bar selections open Navigation Centers. For
example, the Business Status selection opens the Business Status
Navigation Center. The content of the Navigation Centers differ
depending on the selection from the Navigation Bar. The Business
Status Navigation Center is shown on the next page.

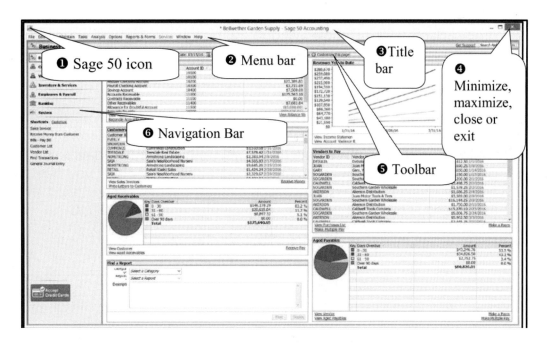

❶ Sage 50 icon: Click on the Sage 50 icon and a menu appears with options such as: Restore, Move, Size, Minimize, Maximize, Close. (Words that are gray are inactive selections.)

❷ Menu Bar: There are 10 (or 11) menu bar selections. If your menu bar selections have underlined letters that means you can make a selection by typing **<Alt>** and the underlined letter. For example, if you press the <Alt> key then press the <F> key, the menu bar shows underlined letters as well as the drop-down menu. You can also click with your left-mouse button on the menu bar headings to see a menu of options.

❸ *Title Bar*: The bar is at the top of the window. When a company is open, the name of the company is displayed on the Title Bar. If your window is minimized, you can put your mouse on the Title Bar, click and hold the left mouse button and drag the window around the *desktop*. The title bar shows Bellwether Garden Supply – Sage 50 Accounting.

❹ Minimize ▬, Double Window ⧉, or Maximize ⬜, and Close or Exit ✖ buttons: Clicking once on Double Window ⧉ returns the window to its previous size. This button appears when you maximize the window.

After clicking on the Double Window  button, the symbol changes to the Maximize button. Click once on the Maximize button to enlarge the window. Click once on the Exit or Close button to close the window, or exit the program.

❺ Toolbar: The gray bar[5] below the Business Status button shows the following selections: Hide, this allows you to hide the Navigation Centers; Refresh, you can update account balances; Print, you can print the Business Status Navigation Center; System Date; Period for accounting records (Bellwether defaults to Period 3 – 03/01/16-03/31/16); Make this the default page; Customize this page. (When Business Status is selected, this toolbar appears.)

  ⊗ Hide ⎅ Refresh 🖶 Print System Date: 03/15/16 Period 3 - 03/01/16-03/31/16 Make this the default page Customize this page

❻ Navigation Bar: The Navigation Bar includes seven selections. These selections open the Business Status, Customers & Sales, Vendors & Purchases, Inventory & Services, Employees & Payroll, Banking, and System Navigation Centers.

Business Status

Customers & Sales

Vendors & Purchases

Inventory & Services

Employees & Payroll

Banking

System

---

[5]Window colors may differ. Check with your instructor if you have a question.

TYPICAL SAGE 50 WINDOWS

When you make a Navigation Bar selection, access is provided to the Navigation Center for each area of the program. For example, when Customers & Sales is selected, a workflow diagram is shown for Customers & Sales tasks, and links to related areas. There is also a tab for Customer Management.

The Maintain Customers/Prospects window is shown below, one that is typical of Sage. Information about customers is entered into the Maintain Customers/Prospects window. There are five sections on this window: ❶ the icon bar, ❷ Previous or next record, ❸ drop-down list (down arrow), ❹ tabs, ❺ information about window.

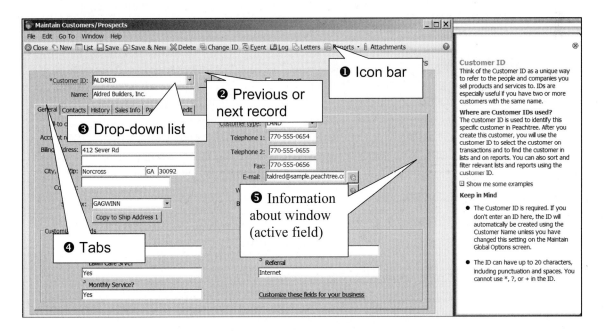

❶ *Icon bar*[6]: The icon bar shows pictures of commands or additional information that pertains to the window. Some icons are common to all windows while other icons are specific to a particular window.

The icons included in the Maintain Customers/Prospects window are shown on the next page.

---

[6]Notice that familiar business items are used for icons: disk for Save, an X for Delete, a paperclip for Attachments.

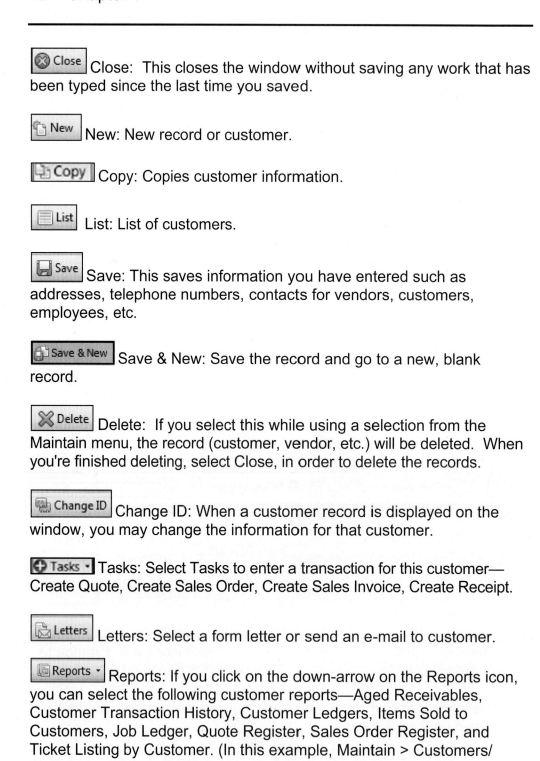

Close: This closes the window without saving any work that has been typed since the last time you saved.

New: New record or customer.

Copy: Copies customer information.

List: List of customers.

Save: This saves information you have entered such as addresses, telephone numbers, contacts for vendors, customers, employees, etc.

Save & New: Save the record and go to a new, blank record.

Delete: If you select this while using a selection from the Maintain menu, the record (customer, vendor, etc.) will be deleted. When you're finished deleting, select Close, in order to delete the records.

Change ID: When a customer record is displayed on the window, you may change the information for that customer.

Tasks: Select Tasks to enter a transaction for this customer—Create Quote, Create Sales Order, Create Sales Invoice, Create Receipt.

Letters: Select a form letter or send an e-mail to customer.

Reports: If you click on the down-arrow on the Reports icon, you can select the following customer reports—Aged Receivables, Customer Transaction History, Customer Ledgers, Items Sold to Customers, Job Ledger, Quote Register, Sales Order Register, and Ticket Listing by Customer. (In this example, Maintain > Customers/ Prospects > Aldred Builders, Inc. is selected as the customer.)

`⬚ Attachments` Attachments: Use this icon to add attachments for customer record.

`⬚ Event` Event: Select this button in various maintenance windows to create an event. The Create Event window allows you to schedule an event for a customer/prospect, vendor, or employee/sales representative. You can also use the Event log to record notes about telephone calls, meetings, letters, and create a listing of future activity.

`⬚ Log` Log: Shows you events recorded for an individual over a specified range of time. You can *filter* this list to see only certain types of activities and whether they're completed or not. You can mark activities as completed by placing a mark in the far left column. Double-clicking on any of the *line items* will take you to the Create an Event window. Line items appear on many of Sage 50's windows.

`⬚ ?` Help: Selecting this icon gives you information specific to the current window. The fields of the window are often listed at the bottom of the help message. When you have a question about how to use Sage 50, clicking on the Help icon often answers it.

❷ `◀ ▶` Previous or Next Record: Click on either the left arrow for the previous record; or the right arrow for the next record.

❸ *Drop-Down List*: The down arrow means that this field contains a list of information from which you can make a selection. Many of Sage's windows have drop-down lists that appear when you click on a down arrow next to a field. You can press **<Enter>** or click on an item to select it from the list.

❹ *Tabs*: The tabs that are shown in the Maintain Customers/Prospects window are General, Contacts, History, Sales Info, Payment & Credit. Once a customer is selected, you can select one of these folders to display information about a customer.

❺ On the right side of maintenance windows, information about the active field is shown. On the Maintain Customers/Prospects window on page 11, information about the CUSTOMER ID field is shown.

THE SAMPLE COMPANY: BELLWETHER GARDEN SUPPLY

Bellwether Garden Supply is one of the sample companies included with Sage 50. To help you become familiar with the software, the sample company is used.

GETTING STARTED

Follow these steps to start:

1. Start Sage 50 by clicking on the desktop icon. If Sage 50 2016 is not installed on your computer, refer to pages vi-xviii for software installation.

2. When Sage 50 was installed, a desktop icon is created. To start, place the mouse pointer on the Sage 50 icon and double-click with the left mouse button. (Or, click Start > go to Apps by name > Sage 50 Accounting 2016.)

3. From the startup window, you can Open an existing company, Create a new company, Explore a sample company, or Convert from another accounting program.

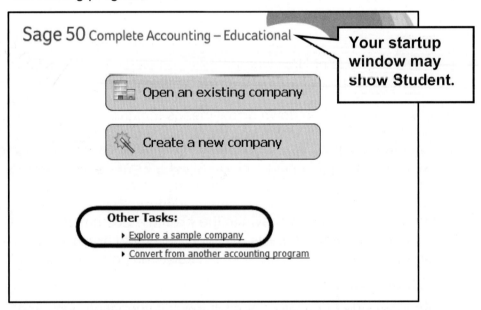

What is the difference between the Educational version and the Student version? The Student version is included with the textbook and can be used for 14 months. The Educational version does <u>not</u>

have a time limit, has a *different serial number,* can be installed on multiple computers in the classroom, and is available to instructors and schools. For more information, refer to Software Installation, page iv.

4. Select Explore a sample company.

5. The Explore a Sample Company window appears. Sage 2016 has two sample companies: Bellwether Garden Supply and Stone Arbor Landscaping. In Chapters 1 – 7, you use Bellwether Garden Supply to explore Sage 50. Then, in Chapter 8, you use Stone Arbor Landscaping to see how the time and billing feature works. Make sure that Bellwether Garden Supply is selected.

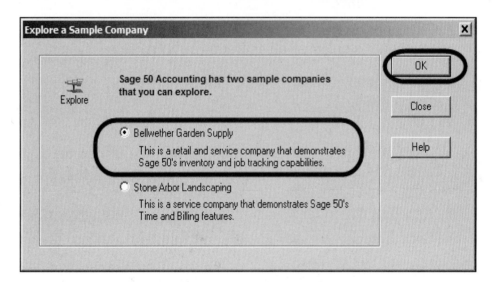

Troubleshooting: Why doesn't my Explore a Sample Company window show the <OK>, <Close>, and <Help> buttons? Screen resolution affects how Sage 50's windows look. The recommended screen resolution is 1024 X 768 with small fonts (refer to p. v). You can use a higher resolution but some of the windows will look different. If you do not have an <OK> button, press <Enter> to start Bellwether Garden Supply.

6. Click ⬚ OK ⬚ , *or* press <Enter>. On the Navigation Bar, select

    ⬚ **Business Status** ⬚. The Business Status Navigation Center appears. The Business Status Navigation Center, also known as the

Home page or dashboard, is separated into seven areas. The dashboard lets you see at a glance a variety of general business information. Scroll down the window to see all of it. Each area has underlined links shown in blue font.

a. Account Balances – observe the links from this area are <u>View Account List</u>; <u>Reconcile Accounts and Import Bank Statements</u>; <u>View Balance Sheet</u>. In Sage 50, you can link to reports from the Navigation Centers *or* from the menu bar.

b. Customers Who Owe Money – A customer list is shown with links to <u>View Sales Invoices List</u>, <u>Write Letters to Customers</u>, and <u>Receive Money.</u>

c. Aged Receivables – A graph is shown and links to <u>View Customer List</u>; <u>View Aged Receivables Report</u>; and <u>Receive Payment</u>.

d. Find a Report – Observe that fields are included for Category, Report, and Description. (If necessary, scroll down the Home page.)

e. Revenue: Year to Date – A graph shows the first quarter of 2016's revenue and links to <u>View Income Statement</u>; <u>Edit a Budget</u>; and <u>View Account Variance Report</u>.

f. Vendors to Pay – A vendor list is shown with links to <u>View Purchases List</u>, <u>Make Multiple Payments</u>, and <u>Make a Payment</u>.

g. Aged Payables – A graph is shown with links to <u>View Vendor List</u>, <u>View Aged Payables Report</u>, <u>Make a Payment</u>, and <u>Make Multiple Payments</u>.

DISPLAY PRODUCT INFORMATION

1. From the menu bar, click Help > About Sage 50 Accounting.

The About Sage 50 Accounting window shows the copyright information and the Release, Build, Serial Number, Installed Tax Service, and Registered Tax Service. The Release field shows Sage 50 Accounting 2016; the Build No. is 23.0.00.0090S (S for student) *or* Build No. 23.0.00.0090E (E for Educational); Serial Number,

Student Version or Educational Version, Customer ID: 0000000004; Installed Tax Service 20150101; Plan Level: None.

The About Sage 50 Accounting window is shown below for the Student Version.

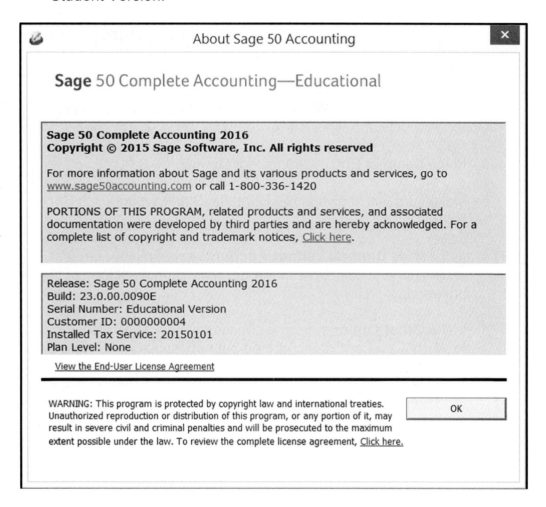

Troubleshooting: If you are using Sage 50 in the classroom or computer lab, the multi-user version may have been installed. When the multi-user version is installed, the Build field ends in E and the Serial Number field shows Educational Version.

When you install the student version software included with the textbook on your PC, the Build Number field ends in S and the Serial Number field shows Student Version. The Student Version software is valid for 14 months.

2. Click [OK] to close.

SETTING GLOBAL OPTIONS ▶[7]

Sage 50's *global options* are in effect for all companies. On pages xix-xx, steps are shown for setting global options. They are repeated here so you can make sure they are set. All companies in Chapters 1-18 and Projects 1-4 require these global options.

1. From the menu bar, select Options > Global. The Maintain Global Options window appears. The Accounting tab is selected.

   a. In the **Decimal Entry** area, select Manual.

   b. Make sure 2 is shown in the Quantity, Standard and Unit Price fields.

   c. In the **Hide General Ledger Accounts** area, make sure that there are no checkmarks in the boxes. (To uncheck one of the boxes, click on it.)

   d. In the **Other Options** area, a checkmark should be placed next to Warn if a record was changed but not saved; and Recalculate cash balance automatically in Receipts, Payments, and Payroll Entry. Compare your Maintain Global Options > Accounting tab window with the one shown on the next page.

---

[7]This icon, ▶, means there is a Global Options video. Go online to www.mhhe.com/yacht2016 > link to Student Edition > select Chapter 1 > Videos > Global Options.

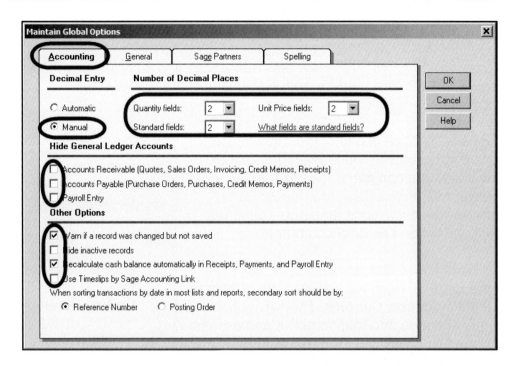

2. Click on the **General** tab. Make sure the Maintain Global Options > General window shows the following selections. The Color Scheme radio buttons are for choosing a different color. The color scheme options are not shown below.

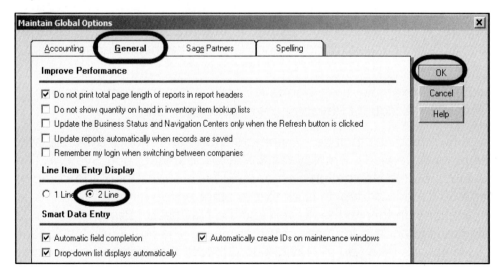

3. Click [OK] to save the global options, which will be in effect for all Sage 50 companies.

SAGE 50'S USER INTERFACE

A User Interface (UI) is the link between a user and a computer program. Sage 50's UI is designed for both Navigation Bar and menu-bar selections.

The user interface is one of the most important parts of any software because it determines how easily you can make the program do what you want. Graphical user interfaces (GUIs) that use windows, icons, and pop-up menus are standard on personal computers.

The **Navigation Bar** appears at the left side of the Sage 50 main window and offers access to the **Navigation Centers**. The Navigation Centers provide information about and access to Sage 50. The Navigation Bar includes seven selections: Business Status, Customers & Sales, Vendors & Purchases, Inventory & Services, Employees & Payroll, Banking, and System.

When you click one of the seven selections (for example, Customers & Sales), the panel to the right of the Navigation Bar displays a **workflow diagram** with additional links related to that **module**. Modules organize Sage 50's transaction windows and reports. The menu bar selections Tasks `Tasks` and Reports & Forms `Reports & Forms` – are also organized by module; for example, the Reports & Forms menu includes Accounts Receivable, Accounts Payable, General Ledger, etc.

Sage 50's modules include Customers & Sales, Vendors & Purchases, Inventory & Services, Employees & Payroll, Banking, and System. The Business Status Navigation Center includes a snapshot of the company. Sage 50's modular design is similar to other accounting software applications. In this textbook, you use the Navigation Bar and menu bar selections to access features of the program. The individual Navigation Bar selections take you to Navigation Centers. For example, if you select Customers & Sales, the tabs for Customers & Sales `Customers & Sales` and Customer Management `Customer Management` appear.

The [🧑 **Customers & Sales**] tab is the default with the Customer & Sales Tasks Navigation Center shown.

CHART OF ACCOUNTS

A **chart of accounts** is a list of all the account names and account numbers used in the General Ledger. Sage 50's **general ledger module** is the complete collection of accounts (chart of accounts) of a company, transactions associated with these accounts, and account balances for a specified period. In Chapter 5, General Ledger, Inventory, and Internal Control, you will learn more about Sage 50's general ledger module and the chart of accounts. For now, let's view Bellwether's chart of accounts so that you can familiarize yourself with the accounts that will be used in subsequent chapters.

Follow these steps to display Bellwether's chart of accounts.

1. From the Navigation Bar, select [📊 **Business Status**]. In the Account Balances area, link to View Account List. The Account List window appears. The Account List is also called the Chart of Accounts. A partial list is shown.

Account ID	Description	Type	Running Balance
10000	Petty Cash	Cash	$327.55
10100	Cash on Hand	Cash	$1,850.45
10200	Regular Checking Account	Cash	$23,389.83
10300	Payroll Checking Account	Cash	$3,711.09
10400	Savings Account	Cash	$7,500.00
11000	Accounts Receivable	Accounts Receivable	$175,563.10
11100	Contracts Receivable	Accounts Receivable	$0.00
11400	Other Receivables	Accounts Receivable	$7,681.84
11500	Allowance for Doubtful Account	Accounts Receivable	($5,000.00)
12000	Inventory	Inventory	$12,786.56
14000	Prepaid Expenses	Other Current Assets	$14,221.30
14100	Employee Advances	Other Current Assets	$3,000.65
14200	Notes Receivable-Current	Other Current Assets	$11,000.00
14700	Other Current Assets	Other Current Assets	$120.00
15000	Furniture and Fixtures	Fixed Assets	$62,769.25
15100	Equipment	Fixed Assets	$38,738.33
15200	Vehicles	Fixed Assets	$86,273.40
15300	Other Depreciable Property	Fixed Assets	$6,200.96
15400	Leasehold Improvements	Fixed Assets	$0.00
15500	Buildings	Fixed Assets	$185,500.00
15600	Building Improvements	Fixed Assets	$26,500.00
16900	Land	Fixed Assets	$0.00
17000	Accum. Depreciation-Furniture	Accumulated Depreciation	($54,680.57)
17100	Accum. Depreciation-Equipment	Accumulated Depreciation	($33,138.11)
17200	Accum. Depreciation-Vehicles	Accumulated Depreciation	($51,585.26)
17300	Accum. Depreciation-Other	Accumulated Depreciation	($3,788.84)
17400	Accum. Depreciation-Leasehold	Accumulated Depreciation	$0.00
17500	Accum. Depreciation-Buildings	Accumulated Depreciation	($34,483.97)
17600	Accum. Depreciation-Bldg Imp	Accumulated Depreciation	($4,926.28)
19000	Deposits	Other Assets	$15,000.00
19100	Organization Costs	Other Assets	$4,995.10
19150	Accum Amortiz - Organiz Costs	Other Assets	($2,000.00)
19200	Notes Receivable- Noncurrent	Other Assets	$5,004.90
19900	Other Noncurrent Assets	Other Assets	$3,333.00
20000	Accounts Payable	Accounts Payable	($80,626.01)
23000	Accrued Expenses	Other Current Liabilities	($3,022.55)
23100	Sales Tax Payable	Other Current Liabilities	($18,028.08)
23200	Wages Payable	Other Current Liabilities	($2,320.30)

Note: The numbers in parentheses are credit balances. The Account List's icon bar includes a Send To selection. When you make that selection, you can send the Account List to Excel, E-mail, or PDF (Adobe Acrobat). Exporting Sage 50 reports to Microsoft Excel is shown on pages 44-46. Saving PDF files is shown on pages 46-47.

2. Close the Account List by clicking ☒ on its title bar.

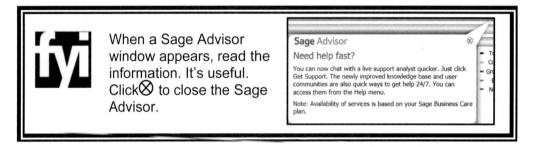

When a Sage Advisor window appears, read the information. It's useful. Click⊗ to close the Sage Advisor.

BACKING UP BELLWETHER GARDEN SUPPLY ▶[8]

Before making changes to Bellwether Garden Supply, you should back up the sample company data. When using Sage 50, information is automatically saved to the hard drive of the computer. In a classroom, a number of students may be using the same computer. This means that when you return to the computer lab or classroom, your data will be gone. **Backing up** means saving a copy of the data to a hard drive, network drive, or external media. Backing up insures that you can start where you left off the last time Sage 50 was used.

When backing up, you have choices–accept the hard-drive default location or back up to a USB flash drive (or other external media). In the steps that follow, backups are made to a USB drive also called flash drives, thumb drives, or pen/stick drives. In this book, the term **USB drive** is used to identify USB storage media. USB is an abbreviation of Universal Serial Bus.

Backups should be made each time you complete work. In the textbook, the following backup file names are suggested.

---

[8]The arrow indicates there is a video. Go online to www.mhhe.com/yacht2016 > link to Student Edition > select Chapter 1 > Videos > Backup.

- For the first backup, *before* any data has been added, the suggested file name is bgs.ptb. [The extension .ptb is added to backups.]
- Chapter number.ptb for work completed within the chapter.
- Exercise number.ptb for work completed in the exercises.

When work is completed, back up. This could be before it is shown in the textbook.

Comment: Backing up data to the hard-drive default location

The author suggests backing up the sample company *before* any changes are made. In the textbook, backups are made to **external media** or a USB drive. Backups can also be made to the desktop or other locations.

You may also backup to the default location at C:\Sage\Peachtree\Company\Sample\PCWS\BCS. (*Hint:* To see the default directory where Bellwether is located, from the menu bar select Maintain > Company Information. The Directory field shows the location of the BCS folder. BCS is the folder where Bellwether Garden Supply data is stored.)

Education Version directory:

Directory:	C:\Sage\Peachtree\Company\Sample\PCWE\BCS

Student Version directory: | C:\Sage\Peachtree\Company\Sample\PCWS\BCS |

When you add your name to Bellwether's reports on page 43, the folder where Bellwether data is stored is changed to \belgarsu.

When a backup is made, data is saved to the current point. To distinguish between backups, a different backup name (file name) should be used. Use Sage 50's **restore** feature to retrieve information that was backed up.

In the business world, backups are unique to each business: daily, weekly, monthly. Think of your backups this way and you will see why individual backups at different points in the data are necessary. *You should never leave the computer lab or classroom without backing up your data.*

Follow these steps to back up Bellwether Garden Supply.

The text directions assume that you are backing up to a USB drive. *You can also backup to the desktop, hard drive, or network location. One USB flash, thumb or pen drive, CD-R or DVD-R can be used for all (Chapters 1-18 and the projects).* The chart on pages 2 and 3 (Part 1 introduction) shows the size of each backup made in Chapters 1-8.

1. Insert a USB flash or thumb drive into the USB drive.

2. From the Navigation Bar, click [**System**]. In the Back Up and Restore Data area, click [Back Up Now]. The Back Up Company window appears. If necessary, uncheck the box next to Include company name in the backup file name. Compare your Back Up Company window to the one shown below.

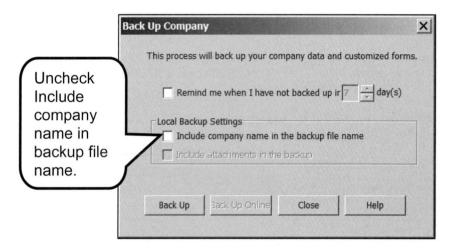

3. Click [Back Up]. The Save Backup for Bellwether Garden Supply as window appears.

4. In the Save in field, select your USB drive. The illustration below shows drive D, which is the location of the author's USB drive. Your USB drive letter may differ. Type **bgs** in the File name field.

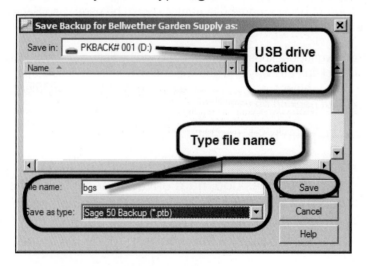

Observe that the Save as type field shows that you are making a Sage 50 Backup (*.ptb), which is abbreviated ptb. This is the extension for Sage 50 backups.

Comment

If your Save as type field does *not* show Sage 50 Backup (*.ptb), follow these steps:

1. Go to File Explorer.
2. From the menu bar, select View. Make sure there is a checkmark next to File name extensions.
3. Close File Explorer.

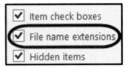

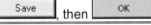 **Read Me: "Student Version" or "Educational Version"**

If you are backing up to the default hard-drive location, the Student Version hard-drive location for backups is C:\Sage\Company\Sample\PCW**S**\ BCS. If your folder shows …\Sample\PCW**E**, you are using the Educational Version's sample company data. Your hard-drive location may differ.

Accept the hard-drive default for backing up. Click [Save], then [OK].

5. Click [Save].

6. A window appears that says This company backup will require approximately 1 diskette. If you are backing up to USB flash drive, this window appears. If backing up to a hard-drive location, a window appears showing the file size.

7. Click [OK]. When the window prompts Please insert the first disk, click [OK]. When Back Up Company scale is 100% complete, you have successfully backed up the sample company.

Follow these steps to see the size of the backup file.

1. Go to File Explorer. The folder icon 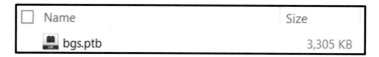 also opens File Explorer.

2. Select your USB drive (or the location where you backed up Bellwether Garden Supply).

   The Name of the file is bgs.ptb; the size of the file is 3,305 KB;[9] and File Type is PTB File. Compare this information to the bcs folder on your hard drive, network drive, USB drive, or DVD. Your backup size may differ.

Name	Size
bgs.ptb	3,305 KB

   Refer to the chart on pages 2 and 3 for estimated back up sizes. Sage 50 backs up to the current point in the data. The author suggests backing up to a USB flash drive, CD-R, DVD-R, or hard drive location.

Follow these steps to exit Sage 50:

1. Close File Explorer.

2. From the menu bar, click File > Exit. You are returned to the desktop.

COPYING THE BCS FOLDER TO A CD-RW OR DVD-RW DRIVE

The instructions on pages 22-25 show how to use Sage 50's Back Up feature. Sage 50's Back Up feature works with Restore, which is shown on pages 29-33. *What if your instructor prefers that all the company data files be copied or saved?*

1. Go to your Windows desktop.

---

[9]The size of your backup file may differ.

2. Put your CD-R or DVD-R into the drive. In this example, Roxio Easy Media Creator is being used to copy files to a DVD-R. An AutoPlay window appears.

3. Select Add Files, then Data Disc.

4. Open File Explorer.

5. Select the location of the BCS folder: C:\Sage\Peachtree\Company\Sample\PCWE (or \PCWS).

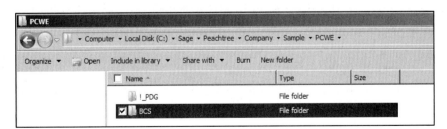

6. Copy/Paste or Drag Drop the BCS folder to the Easy Media Creator window. (Your window may differ. The Author is using Roxio Easy Media Creator software.)

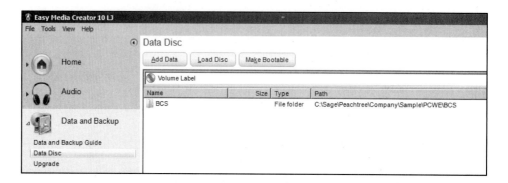

7. Click  to continue. The Project Running window appears while the folder is being copied to the CD-R or DVD-R. When the drive opens, the file is copied.

Click [Done], close the Easy Media Creator window. Do not save the current Data Disc project.

8. Close the File Explorer window.

USING FILE EXPLORER

To see the size of the folder you copied, follow these steps.

1. Close your CD or DVD drive. When the AutoPlay window appears, select Open folder to view files using File Explorer.

2. On the CD or DVD drive window, there is a Files Currently on the Disc (1) area. Right-click on the BCS folder. Left-click Properties. The BCS Properties window appears. The Location and Size of the BCS folder is shown. (Your file size may differ.)

3. Click [OK   ] to close the BCS Properties window. Close File Explorer.

USING SAGE 50'S RESTORE WIZARD ▶[10]

In order to start where you left off the last time you backed up, use the Restore Wizard. Your instructor may prefer that you use File Explorer to copy/paste instead of the Restore feature. You may need to check with your instructor on the preferred method. This textbook shows Sage 50's Restore Wizard.

Follow these steps to use the Restore Wizard.

1. Start Sage 50. (*Hint:* If another company opens, from the menu bar select File > Close Company to go to the startup window.) Open the sample company, Bellwether Garden Supply.

 Read Me: What if Bellwether Garden Supply is *not* shown as an existing company *or* when you select Explore a sample company?

Some schools delete company folders from the hard drive. For example, you have a backup file but the company, Bellwether Garden Supply, is *not* listed as a Sage 50 company. Follow these steps to restore *and* create Bellwether from a backup file.

1. If necessary, click File > Close Company to go to the Startup window. To double-check that Bellwether is *not* listed, select Open an existing company. Make sure Bellwether Garden Supply is *not* listed in the Company Name list. Click

    [Close]. **NOTE:** Complete steps 2, 3, and 4 within this Read Me box if the sample company, Bellwether Garden Supply, *cannot* be opened from the Startup window *or* from the Open an existing company selection.

2. The startup window shows four menu bar options—[File Options Services Help]. Select File > Restore.

3. Browse to the location of your backup file. Click on the backup file to highlight it. Click <Open>, then <Next>.

4. On the Select Company/Choose how to restore your backup window, select Create
    [⦿ Create a new company using the restored data]
    a new company using the restored data [   ].
    The Company Name field shows Bellwether Garden Supply, click <Next>. Continue with step 10, page 32.

---

[10]The arrow indicates a video at www.mhhe.com/yacht2016. Select Student Edition > Chapter 1 > Videos > Restore.

2. Insert your USB flash drive. The steps that follow assume you are restoring from a USB drive.

3. From the Navigation Bar > click  > Restore Now . The Select Backup File window appears > click Browse .

4. The Open Backup File window appears. In the Look in field, select the location of your USB drive. Select the bgs.ptb file.

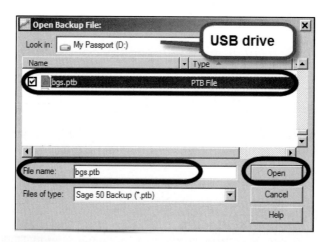

5. Click Open . The Restore Wizard – Select Backup File window appears showing the location of your backup file, X:\bgs.ptb. (Substitute X for your drive letter.)

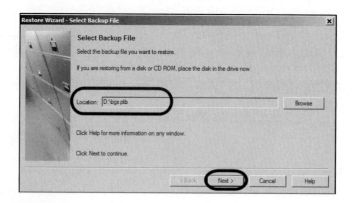

6. Click Next > .

7. The Select Company, Choose how to restore your backup window appears. Observe that Overwrite existing company data is the default. Since Bellwether is open and you are <u>not</u> creating a new company, accept the Overwrite existing company data default. The Company Name field shows Bellwether Garden Supply and the Location shows Bellwether's location. Your Location field may differ.

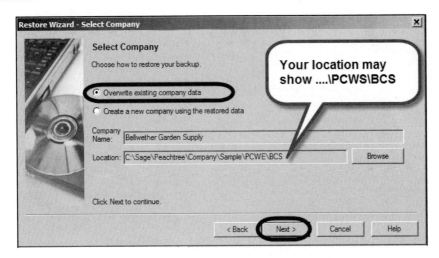

8. Read the information on the Select Company > Choose how to restore your backup window > click [Next >].

9. The Restore Options window appears. Make sure that the check mark is next to Company Data.

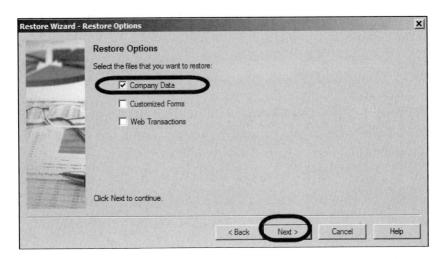

10. On the Restore Options window, click | Next > |.

11. The Confirmation window appears. Read the information. Check the Backup file and Location fields.

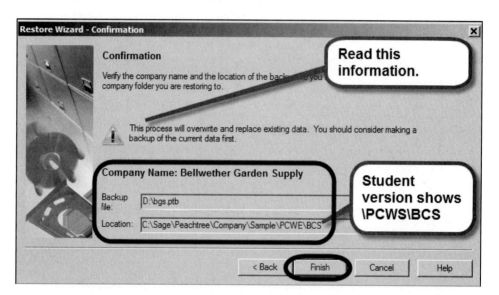

12. Click | Finish |. The window prompts "This process will overwrite and replace existing data permanently. Do you want to continue?"

   Click | Yes |. When the scale is 100% complete, the Bellwether Garden Supply data is restored.

   A window prompts that you can use this company in the student version of Sage 50 for the next 14 months and then it will expire.

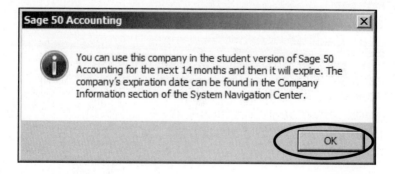

13. Click ⬚ OK ⬚. The Bellwether Garden Supply - Sage 50
     Accounting window appears. (*Hint:* If you are using the Educational
     Version of Sage 50, the student version 14 month window does <u>not</u>
     appear.)

Once Bellwether's files are restored, you are ready to continue using the
sample company. *Remember before you exit, make a backup of your
work.* The following information demonstrates the horizontal menu bar
selections. In this book, you are going to use *both* the menu bar
selections and the Navigation Bar.

MENU BAR

The menu bar has 10 active selections: File, Edit, Lists, Maintain, Tasks,
Analysis, Options, Reports & Forms, (Services is inactive), Window, and
Help. (Once a file is restored, the Services menu appears.) Follow these
steps to look at each menu bar selection.

1. From the menu bar, click File to see its
    menu, *or*, press <Alt> + F to display the
    File menu. If you use <Alt> + F instead
    of your mouse, notice that the individual
    letters on the menu bar are underlined.
    In this example, the mouse is used. The
    File menu selections are shown.

    The File menu allows you to open a
    company, open previous company,
    create a new company, close the
    company, go to the setup guide, print
    preview, print, create a PDF (Adobe
    Acrobat) file, go to user login manager
    (inactive), Back Up, Restore, Automatic
    Backup, Online Backup/Restore
    (inactive), select import/export, convert
    a company, data verification, update
    encryption, enter payroll formulas, and
    exit. (The grayed out selections are
    inactive.)

    Menu choices that are followed by an
    ellipsis (…) are associated with ***dialog***

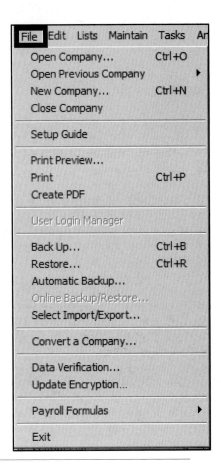

boxes or windows that supply information about a window. An arrow (▶) next to a menu item (Open Previous Company and Payroll Formulas) indicates that there is another menu with additional selections. To cancel the drop-down menu, click File or **<Esc>**.

2. The Edit selection shows Find Transactions.

3. Click Lists to see its menu. The Lists selection shows Customers & Sales, Vendors & Purchases, Employees & Payroll, Chart of Accounts, General Journal Entries, Inventory & Services, Jobs, and Time/Expense. The Lists menu is an alternative to using the Navigation Bar.

4. Click Maintain to see its menu.

From the Maintain menu, you can enter, view, or edit required information for your company's customers or prospects, vendors, employees or sales reps, payroll, chart of accounts, budgets, inventory items, item prices, job costs, make records inactive, and fixed assets. (Fixed Assets requires that FAS for Sage 50 has been purchased.) You can also edit company information; enter memorized transactions; or go to ***default*** information, sales tax codes, and users

(passwords and security). Defaults are commands that Sage automatically selects. Default information automatically displays in windows. You can change the default by choosing another command.

5.   Click Tasks to see its menu.

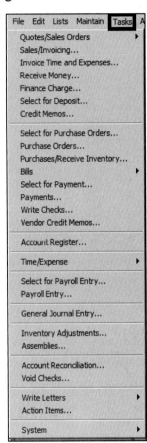

From the Tasks menu, you can enter quotes and sales orders, sales invoices, invoice time and expenses, receive money, finance charges, select for deposit, issue credit memos, select for purchase orders, purchase orders, purchases/ receive inventory, bills, select for payment, payments, write checks, vendor credit memos, account register, record time and expenses, select for payroll entry, payroll entry, make general journal entries, inventory adjustments, assemblies, account reconciliation, void checks, write letters, action items, and system.

6.   Click Analysis to see its menu.

The Analysis menu includes the cash flow manager, collection manager, payment manager, and financial manager.

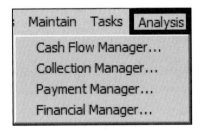

7. Click Options to see its menu.

The Options menu includes setting global options, change the system date, start with the Last Opened Company, and enter default information. The checkmark next to Start with Last Opened Company means that each time you start Sage 50, the last company worked with opens.

8. Click Reports & Forms to see its menu.

The Reports & Forms menu allows you to *queue* reports for printing or displaying. You can also create and edit the format for forms, reports, and financial statements.

9. Click Window to see its menu. The Window menu allows you to close all windows.

10. Click Help to see its menu.

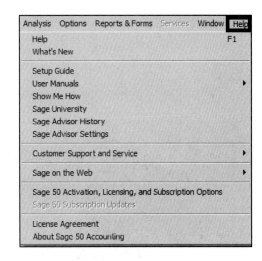

The Help menu allows you to open a window of context-sensitive help, see what's new in this version, go to the setup guide, open Sage 50's user manuals, go to Show Me How videos, Sage University, Sage Advisor History and Settings, Customer Support and Service, Sage on the Web, Sage 50 Activation, Licensing, and Subscription Options, and the About Sage 50 Accounting window. Select About Sage 50 Accounting to display product information. Detailed steps for displaying product information are shown on pages 16-17.

BECOMING AN EMPLOYEE OF BELLWETHER GARDEN SUPPLY

Before adding yourself as an employee of Bellwether Garden Supply, let's use the Navigation Bar to open the Maintain Employees & Sales Reps window. The Navigation Bar selections include: Business Status, Customers & Sales, Vendors & Purchases, Inventory & Services, Employees & Payroll, Banking, and System.

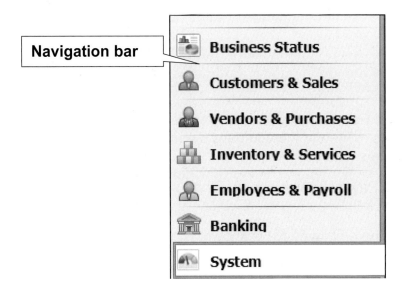

Follow these steps to add yourself as an employee.

1. On the Navigation Bar, select **Employees & Payroll** . The
   Employees & Payroll Navigation Center appears.

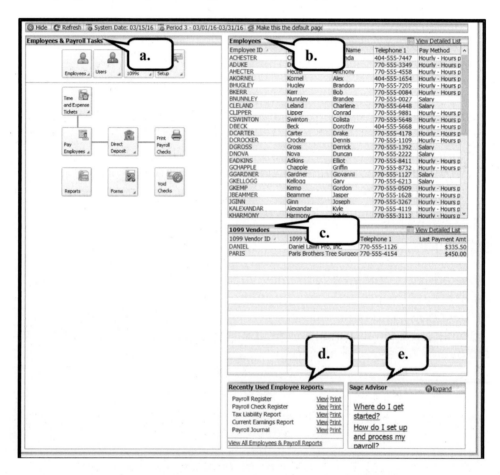

The Employees & Payroll Navigation Center displays information
and access points related to the company's employees. It is
organized into five sections.

a. Employees & Payroll Tasks: The flowchart shows how Sage 50
   processes payroll.

b. Employees: The employee list is shown.

c. 1099 Vendors: These are vendors who receive 1099's from
   Bellwether Garden Supply.

d. Recently Used Employee Reports: This section includes links to payroll reports.

e. Sage Advisor: Link to <u>Expand</u>. The Sage Advisor Getting Started window includes videos ▶ that you can watch about Sage's features.

2. Click [Employees ◢] > New Employee. The Maintain Employees & Sales Reps window appears.

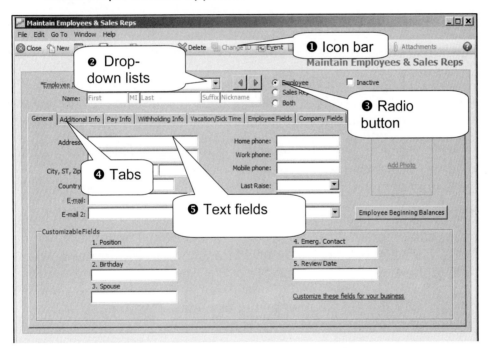

❶ The icon bar at the top of most windows shows graphical representations of commands or functions that are accessible from the window.

❷ Drop-down lists: Click on the down-arrow to see lists. On the Maintain Employees & Sales Reps window, employee IDs are shown.   When you are in the text portion of the field, the cursor changes to an I-bar and a question mark <I?>. Type a question mark **<?>** in the field, or click the right mouse button, to display lists.

❸ *Radio Button or Option Button:* These buttons allow you to select one by clicking with the mouse. The default is Employee shown by the radio button next to Employee.

❹ Tabs are common to most windows. They provide a subtitle to the various windows that store and organize information. Here, for example, the information you can choose to track is subdivided into categories: General, Additional Info, Pay Info, Withholding Info, Vacation/Sick Time, Employee Fields, and Company Fields.

❺ Text fields are rectangular fields where information is typed.

Adding Yourself as an Employee

Follow these steps to add yourself as an employee.

1. Type an Employee ID code for yourself in the Employee ID field. For example, in all caps type **CYACHT** (type *the first initial of your first name and your full last name in all capital letters)* > press **<Enter>**.[11]

2. Using upper and lowercase letters, in the Name field, type your first name, press **<Enter>** > type your middle initial, if any > press **<Enter>** > then type your last name. Press **<Enter>** five times.[12]

3. In the Address field, type your street address. There are two lines so you can enter an ATTENTION line or PO Box, if necessary. If you are using just one line for your address, press **<Enter>** two times to go to the City, ST, Zip fields.

4. In the City, ST Zip field, type your city, state (two-digits), and zip code, pressing **<Enter>** after each.

5. None of the other information is required. You work with the other fields in Chapter 15, Employees, Payroll, and Account Reconciliation. Click [Save]. To check that your Employee ID has been added, click on the down-arrow in the Employee ID field.

---

[11]Set up Employee IDs that are consistent with how Bellwether identifies employees. For example, use uppercase for the first initial and last name.

[12]You can use **<Enter>** or **<Tab>** to move between fields. Use **<Shift>+<Enter>** or **<Shift>+<Tab>** to move back a field. You can also hold the **<Alt>** key and press the underlined letter of a text box to move between fields.

6. Click 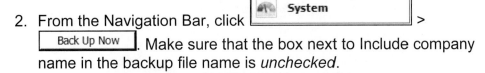 Close to return to the Employees & Payroll Navigation Center. To see your name on the Employees list, click ↻ Refresh.

BACKING UP CHAPTER 1 DATA

Follow these steps to back up Chapter 1 data:

1. Insert your USB flash drive.

2. From the Navigation Bar, click ⛰ **System** > Back Up Now . Make sure that the box next to Include company name in the backup file name is *unchecked*.

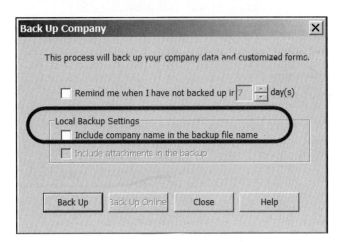

3. Click Back Up .

4. In the Save in field, select the appropriate drive letter for your USB drive.[13] (*Or,* save to the hard-drive default location or other location.) Type **Chapter 1** in the File name field. Compare your Save Backup for Bellwether Garden Supply as window with the one shown below. (Your Save in field may differ.)

---

[13]If you are having difficulty backing up to USB flash drive, backup to the desktop, then copy the file to a USB flash drive. Refer to www.mhhe.com/yacht2016 > Troubleshooting Tips > Problem Backing Up to USB Drive or Other External Media.

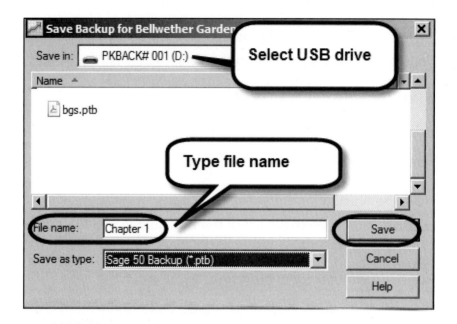

5. Click [Save].

6. When the window prompts This company backup will require approximately 1 diskette, click [OK]. When the window prompts Please insert the first disk, click [OK]. When the Back Up Company scale is 100% complete, you have successfully backed up to the current point in Chapter 1. (Step 6 will differ slightly if you are backing up to the default or other hard-drive location.)

> **Read Me: Problem Backing Up to USB Drive**
>
> If you encounter difficulties backing up to a USB drive, backup to your desktop first. Then copy the backup file from your desktop to a USB drive. Refer to www.mhhe.com/yacht2016 > Troubleshooting > Problem Backing Up to USB Drive or Other External Media.

7. Continue with the next section, Add Your Name to Reports.

ADD YOUR NAME TO REPORTS

Your instructor may want to have your name or initials on all report printouts. To do that, follow these steps.

1. From the Navigation Bar > select [🔘 **System**]. If necessary, scroll down the page to Company Maintenance.

2. Click [Edit Company Information Now]. The Maintain Company Information Window appears. In the Company Name field, add your name or initials after Bellwether Garden Supply.

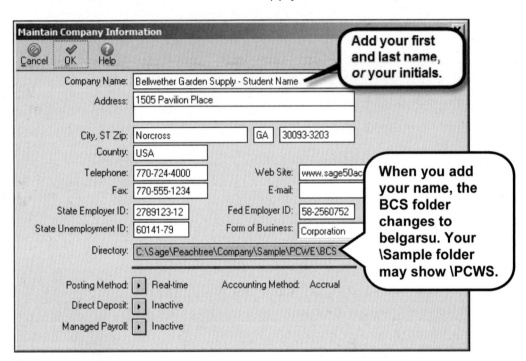

3. Click [✓ OK]. Your name is added to reports. To see the change from \BCS to \belgarsu, exit Sage 50. Then start Sage and open Bellwether Garden Supply. Go to Maintain > Company Information. The Directory field ends in belgarsu.

Directory: C:\Sage\Peachtree\Company\Sample\PCWE\belgarsu

EXPORTING SAGE 50 REPORTS TO MICROSOFT EXCEL

On page 40, you added yourself as an employee of Bellwether Garden Supply. To see an Employee List and export the list to Excel, follow these steps. In order to export reports to Excel, you need Excel 2003 or higher.

1. From the Navigation Bar > select Employees & Payroll. In the Recently Used Employee Reports section, link to View All Employees & Payroll Reports. The Select a Report or Form window appears > select Employee List.

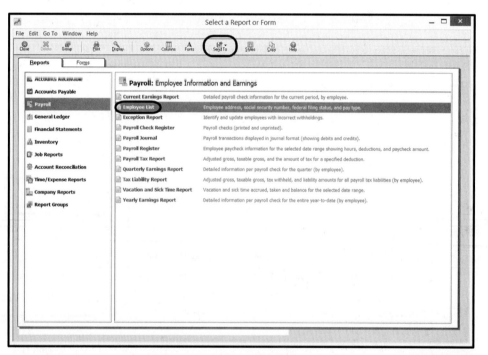

2. On the icon bar, select Send To > then Excel.

3. The Modify Report – Employee List window appears. Accept the defaults by clicking [OK].

4. The Copy Report to Excel window appears. Accept the File option, Create a New Microsoft Excel workbook. In the Report header option area, select Show header in Excel worksheet.

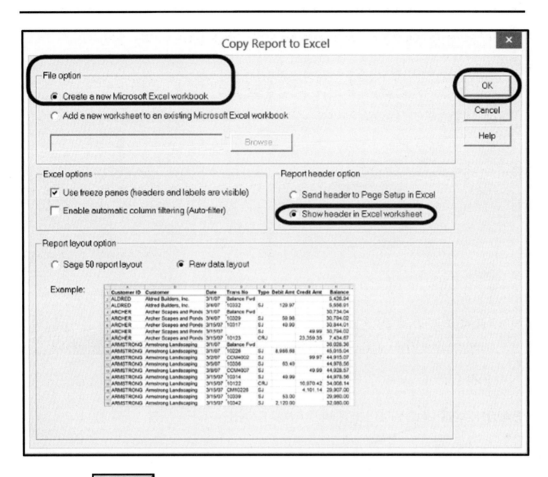

5. Click [OK]. The Copying Employee List to Excel window appears. When the Bellwether Garden Supply Employee List displays, check that your name has been added to the list of employees.

6. Save the Excel worksheet to your USB flash drive. Use **Chapter 1_Employee List.xlsx** as the file name. (If you are using Excel 2003 or earlier, the file extension is .xls.) The Employee List shows Student Name on the title bar. Your name should be shown.

	A	B	C	D	E	F	G	H
1	Your name is shown.				Bellwether Garden Supply - Student Name			
2					Employee List			
3								
4	Filter Criteria includes: Report order is by ID.							
5	Employee ID	Employee	Address line 1	Address line 2	City ST ZIP	Masked SS No	Fed Filing Status	Pay Type
6	ACHESTER	Amanda W. Chester	4599 West Paces Ferry Road		Atlanta, GA 30328	XXX-XX-1337	Single	Hourly
7	ADUKE	Al L. Duke	3905 Alpharetta Hwy		Alpharetta, GA 30039	XXX-XX-1134	Single	Hourly
8	AHECTER	Anthony H. Hecter	67 Lenox Rd		Atlanta, GA 30319	XXX-XX-5656	Single	Hourly
9	AKORNEL	Alex C. Kornel	847 Clairmont Road		Atlanta, GA 30329	XXX-XX-8778	Married	Hourly
10	BHUGLEY	Brandon A. Hugley	920 Gainesville Hwy		Buford, GA 30518	XXX-XX-8991	Married	Hourly
11	BKERR	Bob G. Kerr	1066 Gwinnett Drive		Lawrenceville, GA 30045	XXX-XX-8992	Single	Hourly
12	BNUNNLEY	Brandee M. Nunnley	2777 Sweetwater Trail		Norcross, GA 30093	XXX-XX-6894	Married	Salaried
13	CLELAND	Charlene M. Leland	834 Chamblee Tucker Rd		Atlanta, GA 30341	XXX-XX-6555	Married	Salaried
14	CLIPPER	Conrad C. Lipper	588 Hammond Dr		Chamblee, GA 30341	XXX-XX-2331	Married	Hourly
15	CSWINTON	Colista A. Swinton	36 Piper Lane		Duluth, GA 30155	XXX-XX-8997	Married	Hourly
16	CYACHT	Carol Yacht					Single	Hourly
17	DBECK	Dorothy L. Beck	3743 North Druid Hills Road		Atlanta, GA 30325	XXX-XX-7745	Married	Hourly
18	DCARTER	Drake V. Carter	1679 Chattahoochee Lane		Flowery Branch, GA 30542	XXX-XX-8990	Single	Hourly
19	DCROCKER	Dennis V. Crocker	3222 Sidney Marcus Blvd		Atlanta, GA 30319	XXX-XX-8526	Single	Hourly
20	DGROSS	Derrick P. Gross	1264 Oak Lane		Lawrenceville, GA 30245-1209	XXX-XX-7746	Married	Salaried
21	DNOVA	Duncan S. Nova	212 Landing Lane		Norcross, GA 30093	XXX-XX-9113	Single	Salaried
22	EADKINS	Elliot U. Adkins	11475 Lakefield Drive		Duluth, GA 30155-1511	XXX-XX-8554	Single	Hourly
23	GCHAPPLE	Griffin E. Chapple	8265 Champlain Ave		Cumming, GA 30028	XXX-XX-5761	Single	Hourly
24	GGARDNER	Giovanni V. Gardner	4328 Old Peachtree Rd		Norcross, GA 30093	XXX-XX-2594	Married	Salaried
25	GKELLOGG	Gary A. Kellogg	522 Neese Road		Woodstock, GA 30188	XXX-XX-6931	Married	Salaried
26	GKEMP	Gordon B. Kemp	634 Winter Chapel Rd		Doraville, GA 30342	XXX-XX-5379	Married	Hourly
27	JBEAMMER	Jasper L. Beammer	21 Pembroke Lane		Hiram, GA 30025	XXX-XX-5162	Single	Hourly
28	JGINN	Joseph W. Ginn	22 Piedmont Rd		Atlanta, GA 30319	XXX-XX-7002	Married	Hourly
29	KALEXANDAR	Kyle B. Alexandar	627 Brookwood Road		Snellville, GA 30039	XXX-XX-8998	Single	Hourly
30	KHARMONY	Kelvin R. Harmony	544 Dunhill Dr		Norcross, GA 30092	XXX-XX-4446	Married	Hourly
31	KIRELAND	Kari M. Ireland	5243 Lupus Lane		Lawrenceville, GA 30044	XXX-XX-3425	Married	Salaried
32	LAKERSON	Lyle E. Akerson	988 Sentinel Lane		Lawrenceville, GA 30365	XXX-XX-8563	Married	Salaried
33	LSWEET	Leonard Sweet	6983 Crabapple Court		Alpharetta, GA 30049	XXX-XX-6399	Married	Hourly
34	MCHAMBERLIN	Mark T. Chamberlin	1015 Velvet Court		Alpharetta, GA 30066-4557	XXX-XX-3325	Single	Salaried
35	MFROST	Melvin H. Frost	275 13th Street	Apt. E 406	Atlanta, GA 30309-0406	XXX-XX-8878	Single	Salaried
36	MMULHERN	Marianna S. Mulhern	256 Mt. Paran Court		Atlanta, GA 30085-1305	XXX-XX-4477	Married	Hourly
37	MRHODES	Matt Q. Rhodes	1220 Neptune Circle		Grayson, GA 30098	XXX-XX-0024	Single	Salaried

Employee List   (+)

7. Exit Excel.

SAVING EMPLOYEE LIST AS AN ADOBE PDF FILE

Check with your instructor to see if he or she would like you to save the Employee list as a PDF file. If so, follow these steps.

1. From the Select a Report or Form window > select Send To > PDF. To save reports as PDF files, Adobe Reader must be installed. If necessary, go online to https://get.adobe.com/reader/ and download the free Adobe Acrobat Reader. (*Hint:* If you cannot save the Employee List as a PDF file, make sure you have the latest Adobe Reader update.)

2. The Modify Report - Employee List window appears. Click **OK**.

3. The Save As window appears. If necessary, insert your USB drive. Select the USB drive. Type **Chapter 1_Employee List** in the File name field. Observe that the Save as Type field shows Adobe PDF Files (*.pdf).

4. Click [Save]. Close the Select a Report & Form window. Continue or exit Sage 50.

How to Fix? My PDF button is not active. What should I do?

1. Display the report. Select the Print icon instead of the PDF icon.
2. The Print window appears. In the Name field, click on the down-arrow.
3. Select Adobe PDF. Click <OK>. Save the file to your USB drive.

MANUAL VS. COMPUTERIZED ACCOUNTING

Because there are differences between manual and computerized accounting, notice there are several instances where the procedures used in Sage are different than those outlined in the steps of the manual accounting cycle. The steps of the manual accounting cycle shown in most accounting textbooks differ slightly from Sage's computer accounting cycle.

The differences between the Manual and Computer Accounting Cycle are shown on the next two pages. The first step of the Computer Accounting Cycle is setting up a new company, which includes the option for selecting a Chart of Accounts. Starting with Chapter 9 you will set up 11 companies from scratch. In Chapters 1-8 you work with the two sample companies that are included with the installation of Sage 50.

The Manual Accounting Cycle does not include creating a new company. In manual accounting, the chart of accounts is the same as the accounts in the general ledger.

Step five of the manual cycle shows a worksheet. There is no worksheet in the computerized cycle. In Sage you can complete account reconciliation. Account reconciliation automates bank reconciliation. Another important difference is that in the Computer Accounting Cycle, the adjusting entries are journalized and posted before printing the financial statements.

In the computerized cycle, Step 10, change accounting periods, is similar to closing the month manually except that the temporary accounts maintain balances so a post-closing trial balance is not available. Sage tracks income and expense data for an entire year. At the end of the year, all revenue and expense accounts are closed to equity. In all Sage 50 companies (including sole proprietorships), a retained earnings account is needed so that posting to the general ledger can be done.

MANUAL ACCOUNTING CYCLE	SAGE'S COMPUTER ACCOUNTING CYCLE
1. Analyze transactions.	1. Create a new company *or* restore A New Company.
2. Journalize entries.	2. Analyze transactions.
3. Post to the ledger.	3. Journalize entries.
4. Prepare unadjusted trial balance.	4. Post to the ledger.
5. Prepare worksheet.	5. Print general ledger trial balance (unadjusted).
6. Prepare financial statements: income statement, statement of changes in owner's equity, and balance sheet.	6. Account reconciliation: reconciling the bank statement.
7. Adjust the ledger accounts: journalize and post adjusting entries.	7. Journalize and post adjusting entries.
8. Close the temporary accounts: journalize and post the closing entries.	8. Print the general ledger trial balance (adjusted).
Continued	

9. Prepare post-closing trial balance.	9. Print financial statements: balance sheet, income statement, statement of cash flow, and statement of changes in financial position.
10. Reverse entries (optional).	10. Change accounting periods.
11. Interpret accounting information	

ONLINE LEARNING CENTER (OLC): www.mhhe.com/yacht2016

Complete end-of-chapter activities at www.mhhe.com/yacht2016 > select Student Edition > then Chapter 1. Link to the appropriate *atom*, for example, Multiple Choice Quiz. Website atoms are underlined. The following chapter resources are available.

1. Quizzes: Multiple Choice Quiz and True or False. Interactive online tests that are graded and can be emailed to your instructor.

2. More Resources:

   a. QA Templates: 10 true/make true questions. Analysis Questions are also included. The Microsoft Word file, with answers, can be emailed to your instructor.

   b. Videos: In Chapter 1, the videos include Global Options, Backup, and Restore. Watch the videos using an Internet browser, iPod, iPad, or iPhone.

   c. Narrated PowerPoints: Listen to narrated PowerPoints.

   d. Going to the Net Exercises: Complete Internet research about accounting careers.

   e. Assessment Rubric: Complete the rubric to review Sage 50's journals, navigation centers, modules, task windows, and reports.

The OLC also includes links to the Appendixes:

- Appendix A: Troubleshooting
- Appendix B: Accounting Information Systems
- Appendix C: Review of Accounting Principles

- Appendix D: Glossary (words that are boldfaced and italicized in chapter)

Exercise 1-1: Follow the instructions below to complete Exercise 1-1:

1. Start Sage. Open the sample company, Bellwether Garden Supply - Student Name.

2. Restore the Chapter 1.ptb file. This backup was made on pages 41-42. For detailed restore steps, refer to pages 29-33. If needed, add your name to Bellwether Garden Supply (refer to page 43, Add Your Name to Reports).

Read Me: Do I need to restore?

If you are working in the computer lab or classroom, open Bellwether Garden Supply - Student Name (your name or another name). Restore the Chapter 1.ptb file from your USB flash drive. Restoring replaces [overwrites] an existing file.

If you are working on your own computer or laptop, you can skip restore. In Chapter 1 on pages 40-41, you added yourself as an employee. Display the employee list. Make sure your name is shown. If *not*, restore.

---

3. Display Company Information. (*Hint:* Maintain > Company Information; *or* select [System], Company Maintenance.). Observe that the Directory field ends in \belgarsu. Why is it different than the Directory field shown on page 43

   Directory: C:\Sage\Peachtree\Company\Sample\PCWS\belgarsu ? (*Hint:* After restarting Bellwether Garden Supply – Student name on page 43, the \belgarsu Directory was shown. Your \Sample folder may show \PCWS; "S" for Student version.)

   When you added your name to Bellwether Garden Supply, Sage changed the shortened company name. Shortened company names are comprised of 8 characters: the first three letters from the first and second word (belgar), and two letters from the third word (su). The shortened company name is belgarsu.

4. Continue with Exercise 1-2.

Exercise 1-2: Follow the instructions below to complete Exercise 1-2:

1. Add Sam Wittner as a new employee.

Employee I<u>D</u>:	SWITTNER [use all caps]
N<u>a</u>me:	Sam Wittner [use upper and lowercase]
Address:	1400 East Canal Street
City, ST <u>Z</u>ip:	Atlanta, GA 30307
Home phone:	770-555-9645

2. Print the Employee List. Select . In the Employees area, link to <u>View Detailed List</u>. (*Hint:* Click 🔄 Refresh to see Sam Wittner.)

Employees				⊞ View Detailed List
Employee ID ↗	Last Name	First Name	Telephone 1	Pay Method
ACHESTER	Chester	Amanda	404-555-7447	Hourly - Hours
ADUKE	Duke	Al	770-555-3349	Hourly - Hours
AHECTER	Hecter	Anthony	770-555-4558	Hourly - Hours

3. Click 🖨 Print, then make the selections to print. If necessary, click on Employee ID to display the list in alphabetical order. (*Hint:* The Employee List should show your name after Bellwether Garden Supply. Adding your name, or initials, to reports was shown on page 43.)   After printing the Employee List, close the Employee List window.

4. Back up. The suggested file name is **Exercise 1-2**. For detailed backing up steps, refer to pages 23-25, steps 1-7.

5. Export the Employee List to Excel. Save. Use **Exercise 1-2_Employee List.xlsx** as the file name. Refer to pages 44-46 for exporting reports to Excel. Click Send To Excel to Create a new Microsoft Excel workbook. (If you are using Excel 2003 or lower, the file extension is .xls.)

6. Save the Employee List as a PDF file. Use **Exercise 1-2_Employee List.pdf** as the file name. Refer to pages 46-47 for saving files as PDFs.

7. Export the Chart of Accounts to Excel. Use **Exercise 1-2_Chart of Accounts.xlsx** as the file name. (Refer to pages 21-22 for displaying the account list or chart of accounts.)

8. Save the Chart of Accounts as a PDF file. Use **Exercise 1-2_Chart of Accounts.pdf** as the file name.

   Check your figures: Account No. 10200, Regular Checking Account: $23,389.83.

9. Exit Excel and Sage 50.

Comment: If your instructor would like Sage 50 reports attached for grading purposes, see pages 44-47, Exporting Sage 50 Report Data to Microsoft Excel or Saving as a PDF File. To export two Sage 50 reports to one Excel file, see pages 85-87. For grading purposes, your instructor may prefer receiving an Adobe file (.pdf) or an Excel file (.xlsx).

CHAPTER 1 INDEX

Chapter

2 Vendors

LEARNING OBJECTIVES

1. Restore data from Exercise 1-2. This backup was made on page 51. (Refer to the Read me box on page 50, Do I need to restore?)
2. Enter a purchase order.
3. Apply receipt of inventory to existing purchase order.
4. Enter and post a vendor invoice in the Purchases/Receive Inventory window.
5. Go to the Payments window to pay a vendor.
6. Print a check in payment of the vendor invoice.
7. Add a Terms column to the Vendor Ledgers report.
8. Analyze payments and vendor credit memos.
9. Export the Vendor List and Vendor Ledgers to Excel.
10. Save the Vendor List and Vendor Ledgers as PDF files.
11. Make two backups, save two Excel files, and save four PDF files.[1]

Chapter 2 explains how Sage 50 works with vendors. The first thing you do is select **Vendors & Purchases** from the Navigation Bar to go to the Vendors & Purchases Navigation Center.

When Bellwether Garden Supply orders and receives inventory from vendors, Account No. 12000, Inventory, is debited. Accounts Payable and the vendor account are credited.

Vendors offer Bellwether a *purchase discount* for purchase invoices paid within a discount period. Purchase discounts are cash discounts from vendors in return for early payment of an invoice; for example, 2% 10, net 30 days. If Bellwether pays an invoice within 10 days, they can deduct two percent from the invoice amount. In Sage 50, the purchase discount is entered when the vendor is paid. If the payment is not made within 10 days, the full invoice amount is paid within 30 days.

---

[1]Refer to the chart on page 2 for the size of backups and saved Excel and PDF files.

In this chapter, you learn how Sage handles accounts payable transactions with vendors.

GETTING STARTED

Follow these steps to start:

1. Start Sage 50. If an activate window appears, follow the screen prompts. (For more information, refer to Step 14, pages xiv-xv.)

2. Since Bellwether Garden Supply - Student Name was the last company opened, it should start automatically. (*Hint:* If Bellwether does <u>not</u> open, select File > Close Company to go to the startup window. Then, Open an Existing Company. Select Bellwether Garden Supply - Student Name > click <OK>.) On the Options menu, check that Start with Last Opened Company is checked.

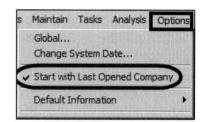

> ➤ **Troubleshooting: Bellwether Garden Supply - Student Name is not listed on Sage 50's Company Name list.**
>
> Refer to the Read Me box on page 29 to review the steps for restoring a company that is not listed. The steps on page 29 show how to Create a new company using the restored data.

RESTORING DATA FROM EXERCISE 1-2

On page 51, Exercise 1-2 is backed up (saved). In order to begin where you left off, restore the Exercise 1-2.ptb file. After completing Exercise 1-2, restore allows you to start where you left off. For detailed restore steps, refer to pages 29-33

 Read Me: Do I need to restore?
You may be able to skip restore. In Chapter 1 (pages 40-41) and Exercise 1-2 (page 51), you added two employees. Refer to the disk icon 💾 on the next page to make sure you are starting with the work completed in Chapter 1 and Exercise 1-2. If your employee list and Regular Checking Account's balance agrees with Exercise 1-2, you can skip Restore. Go to the next section, Accounts Payable Tasks. *If you are working in the computer lab or classroom, open Bellwether Garden Supply - Student Name. Restore the Exercise 1-2.ptb file from your USB drive.* Detailed steps are shown on pages 29-33, Using Sage 50's Restore Wizard. Restoring replaces [overwrites] an existing file.

To make sure you are starting in the appropriate place in the data (Exercise 1-2 backup), display the Employee list. (*Hint:* From the

Navigation Bar > select 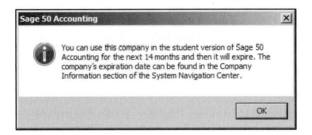). In the Employees area, link to <u>View Detailed List</u>. Your name and SWITTNER should appear. You added yourself as an employee on pages 40-41, and added SWITTNER in Exercise 1-2, page 51. Confirm that Account No. 10200, Regular Checking Account, is $23,389.83 (*Hint:* On the Business Status Navigation Center, link to View Account List.)

If you are restoring from the Student Version, a window appears that says You can use this company in the student version of Sage 50 for the next 14 months then it will expire.

Sage 50 Accounting

> You can use this company in the student version of Sage 50
> Accounting for the next 14 months and then it will expire. The
> company's expiration date can be found in the Company
> Information section of the System Navigation Center.

OK

ACCOUNTS PAYABLE SYSTEM

Sage 50's **Accounts Payable System** provides the summary information needed for the entry that credits Accounts Payable and debits the various asset and expense accounts that the vendor invoices represent. Since Bellwether Garden Supply buys on credit from a number of vendors, the company keeps close track of the amount owed and the due dates of the bills.

Vendor transactions are a five-step process:

1. Maintain Vendors: Set up a new vendor.

2. Purchase Orders: Order items from one of Bellwether's vendors.

3. Purchase Invoices: Receive inventory or services from one of Bellwether's vendors. Apply a purchase order to a purchase invoice.

4. Payments: Pay a vendor or record a cash purchase. (Sage also includes vendor credit memos.)

5. Print Checks: Print a check for payment to a vendor or for expenses.

Before you begin adding accounts payable transactions, examine the Vendors & Purchases Navigation Center. Follow these steps to do that.

1. From the Navigation Bar > select [Vendors & Purchases]. The Vendors & Purchases Navigation Center appears. Vendors & Purchases illustrate Sage 50's **accounts payable module** or accounts payable system. The Vendors & Purchases Navigation Center includes Vendors & Purchases Tasks and its workflow diagram, Vendors, Recently Used Vendor Reports, Aged Payables, and Sage 50 Advisor. (*Hint:* The Sage Advisor includes video links.)

    Modules organize Sage 50's transaction windows and reports. When the Navigation Bar's Vendors & Purchases selection is made, Sage 50's accounts payable system is shown. The menu bar selections, Tasks and Reports & Forms, are also organized by module; for example, the Reports & Forms menu includes Accounts Receivable, Accounts Payable, General Ledger, etc. Compare your Vendors & Purchases Navigation Center with the one shown.

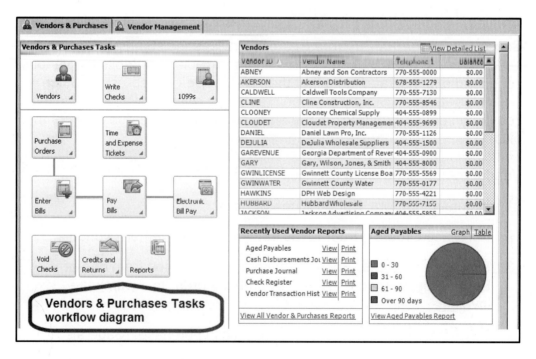

The Vendors & Purchases Navigation Center displays information and access points related to the company's vendors. It includes a summary of vendor information, access to recently used vendor reports, and an overview of the company's aged payables. In addition, the Navigation Center shows the flow of vendor-related tasks. You can also link or drill down to various areas.

The Vendors & Purchases Navigation Center includes two tabs: Vendors & Purchases and Vendor Management. Vendors & Purchases is the default and shows the workflow diagram for Vendors & Purchases Tasks. The Vendor Management tab lists information regarding transactions and history for an individual vendor, including purchase orders, purchases, and payments.

2. If necessary, click on the Vendors & Purchases tab. In the Vendors area (on the right side of the screen), click ABNEY. The Maintain Vendors window appears with information about Abney and Son Contractors.

3. Click [⊗ Close] to return to the Vendors & Purchases Navigation Center.

4. Click on the Vendor Management tab. In the Vendor ID field > select Abney > in the Date Range field > select All Transactions.

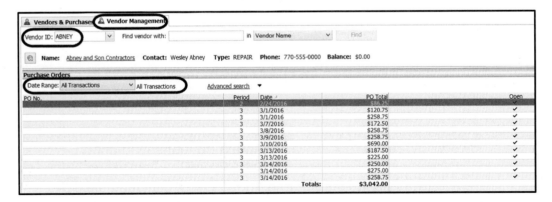

Vendor Management shows historical information about Abney and Son Contractors – Purchase Orders, Payments, and Item Purchase History. If necessary, scroll down.

5. To return to the workflow diagram, select the Vendors & Purchases tab.

The Purchase Order Window

Purchase orders are used to place an order from a vendor. When you post a purchase order, you do not update accounting information. A purchase order is used to request items from a vendor. When the Apply to Purchase Order tab is selected on the Purchases/Receive Inventory window and the transaction is posted, accounting information (inventory, accounts payable subsidiary ledger, general ledger) is updated.

Changing Global Settings for Accounting Behind the Screens

Sage 50 is a double-entry accounting system. There is a selection in Options/Global that allows you to hide general ledger accounts. This is called Accounting Behind the Screens. The windows in this book show the general ledger accounts. To check the Accounting Behind the Screens settings, follow the steps shown below.

1. From the menu bar > click Options > Global. The <u>A</u>ccounting tab is selected. The boxes in the Hide General Ledger Accounts section *must* be unchecked. (If necessary, click on the boxes to uncheck them.)

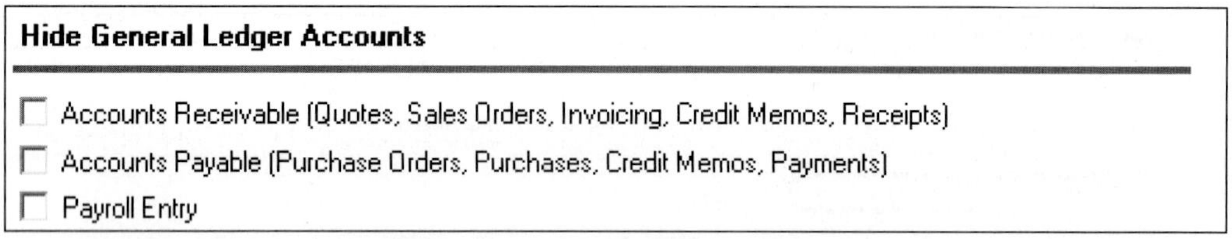

Hide General Ledger Accounts

  ☐ Accounts Receivable (Quotes, Sales Orders, Invoicing, Credit Memos, Receipts)

  ☐ Accounts Payable (Purchase Orders, Purchases, Credit Memos, Payments)

  ☐ Payroll Entry

---

2. Observe that two boxes need to be checked in the Other Options section: Warn if a record was changed but not saved and Recalculate cash balance automatically in Receipts, Payments, and Payroll Entry. Make sure *both* of these Other Options boxes are checked.

Other Options

☑ Warn if a record was changed but not saved

☐ Hide inactive records

☑ Recalculate cash balance automatically in Receipts, Payments, and Payroll Entry

☐ Use Timeslips by Sage Accounting Link

3. Click on the <u>G</u>eneral tab. Make sure your Line Item Entry Display has 2 Line selected; and that the Smart Data Entry area has all three boxes checked.

Line Item Entry Display

○ 1 Line   ⦿ 2 Line

Smart Data Entry

☑ Automatic field completion   ☑ Automatically create IDs on maintenance windows

☑ Drop-down list displays automatically

4. Click [OK]. Once Global Settings are saved by clicking the <OK> button, they are in effect for all companies.

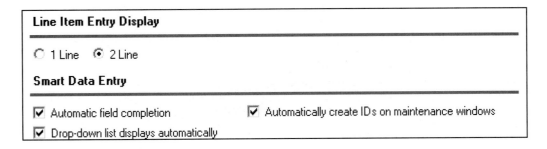

5. From the Vendors & Purchases Navigation Center, select [Purchase Orders]

> New Purchase Order. If necessary, click . The Purchase Orders window displays.

If your Purchase Orders window does *not* show an A/P Account

A/P Account
20000 🔍

GL Account

lookup field or a GL Account field, the option to hide general ledger accounts is selected. Uncheck the Hide General Ledger Accounts boxes in Options > Global. (*Hint: See the instructions on pages 60-61 steps 1-4, for changing the global settings.*)

6. Your cursor is in the Vendor ID lookup field. Type **A** (use capital A). ABNEY displays in the lookup field.

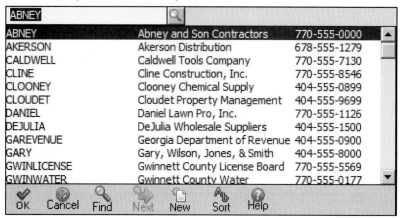

Comment: If the Vendor ID field is not completed, the Automatic Field Completion option is *not* selected. Click Options, then Global. Click on the General tab. In the Smart Data Entry section, make sure that a check mark is placed next to Automatic field completion. Click [OK] when you are finished.

7. After clicking <OK>, click on the Date field. Highlight the date, then type **28** and press **<Enter>**. Your cursor moves to the Good thru field. Press **<Enter>** to accept the default. Your cursor moves to the PO No. field.

8. Click on the Quantity field. Type **20** as the Quantity. If necessary, refer to the Comment below.

Comment: If 20.00 does *not* display in the Quantity field, click Options > Global. Make sure that the Decimal Entry shows Manual, and that the Number of decimal places is 2.

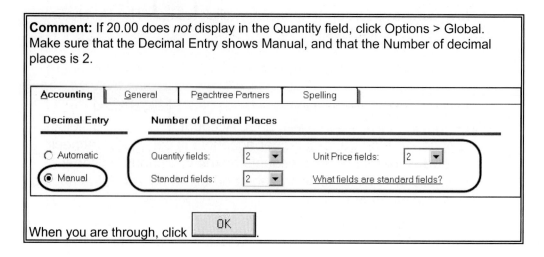

9. Press **<Enter>**. Your cursor is in the Item field.

10. Click once on the magnifying-glass icon in the Item field. Click AVRY-10150 Bird Bath - Stone Gothic 2pc. The Description field is automatically completed with detailed information.

11. Press the **<Enter>** key and your cursor moves to the GL Account field. Notice that Account No. 12000 is automatically selected. Account No. 12000 is the Inventory account. The word Inventory is also displayed on the line below the Description. (*Hint:* If Inventory is *not* shown, refer to step 1, page 60.)

12. Press the **<Enter>** key to go to the Unit Price field. The Unit Price of 51.95 automatically displays.

13. Press the **<Enter>** key to go to the Amount field. Sage 50 calculates the quantity times the unit price and enters the result in the Amount field (20 X $51.95 = $1,039.00).

14. Press the **<Enter>** key to go to the Job field. The Job field is also a lookup field. It contains a list of the jobs and their descriptions. Since Bellwether does not apply this purchase to a job, press the **<Enter>** key to skip this field. Complete the following information:

Quantity: **50**
Item: **AVRY-10100** - Bird House Kit

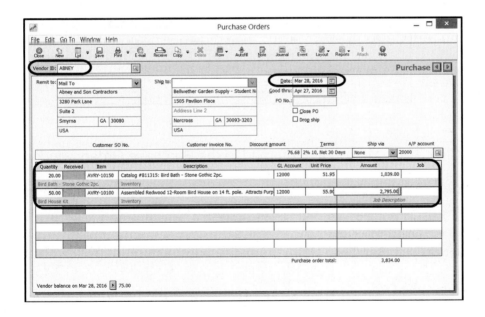

When you selected Abney and Son Contractors, the Vendor Account Balance as of March 28, 2016 also appears on the lower left side of the Purchase Orders window. You can drill down to Abney and Son Contractors vendor ledger by clicking on the right arrow (▶) in the Vendor Balance area. Observe that the icon bar also includes a Reports [Reports] button. Click on the down-arrow next to the Reports button.

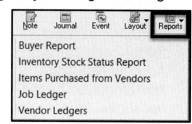

15. Click [Journal]. The Accounting Behind the Screens, Purchase Order Journal window displays. Compare your Accounting Behind the Screens window to the one below. This window shows that Account No. 12000, Inventory, was debited for two items and that Accounts Payable was credited. (The vendor account, Abney and Sons, is also credited.)

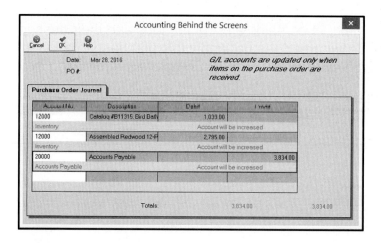

16. Click [OK] You are returned to the Purchase Orders window.

Printing Purchase Orders

When you select [Print], Sage prints the purchase order and posts it to the Purchase Order Journal. [Save] also posts the Purchase Order.

1. Click [🖨 Print ▼]. (*Or,* if you are <u>not</u> going to print, click on the down-arrow next to Print and select Print Preview to display the purchase order.)

2. The Print Forms: Purchase Orders window appears. Accept the default for First PO Number 101 by clicking [Print]. (If you selected Print Preview, there is a Print Preview button — [Print Preview].) Compare your Purchase Order to the one below. If you are <u>not</u> printing, refer to the How to Fix? on page 66.

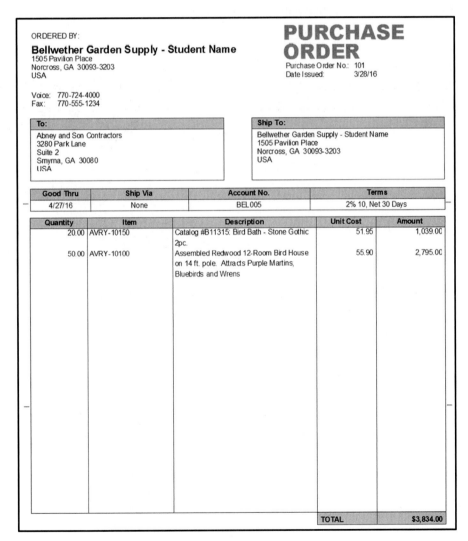

ORDERED BY:

Bellwether Garden Supply - Student Name
1505 Pavilion Place
Norcross, GA 30093-3203
USA

Voice: 770-724-4000
Fax: 770-555-1234

PURCHASE ORDER

Purchase Order No.: 101
Date Issued: 3/28/16

To:	Ship To:
Abney and Son Contractors 3280 Park Lane Suite 2 Smyrna, GA 30080 USA	Bellwether Garden Supply - Student Name 1505 Pavilion Place Norcross, GA 30093-3203 USA

Good Thru	Ship Via	Account No.	Terms
4/27/16	None	BEL005	2% 10, Net 30 Days

Quantity	Item	Description	Unit Cost	Amount
20.00	AVRY-10150	Catalog #B11315: Bird Bath - Stone Gothic 2pc.	51.95	1,039.00
50.00	AVRY-10100	Assembled Redwood 12-Room Bird House on 14 ft. pole. Attracts Purple Martins, Bluebirds and Wrens	55.90	2,795.00
			TOTAL	$3,834.00

Comment

The purchase order form that printed is called Purchase Order. To print a different form, click | Select Form |. Then, select Purchase Order Preprinted as the form to print. When you select a different form, the information is the same but the look of the form changes.

3. If you displayed the report and are printing, click | Print |. The Purchase Orders window is ready for the next entry. If you are <u>not</u> printing, refer to the How to fix? Information below.

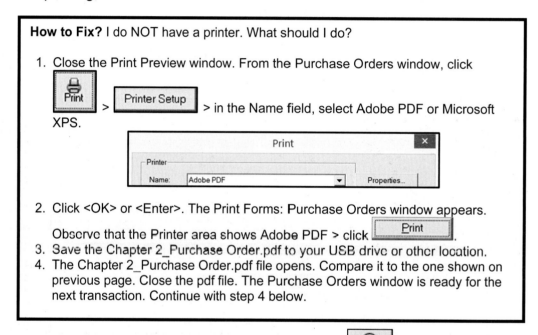

How to Fix? I do NOT have a printer. What should I do?

1. Close the Print Preview window. From the Purchase Orders window, click | Print | > | Printer Setup | > in the Name field, select Adobe PDF or Microsoft XPS.

2. Click <OK> or <Enter>. The Print Forms: Purchase Orders window appears. Observe that the Printer area shows Adobe PDF > click | Print |.
3. Save the Chapter 2_Purchase Order.pdf to your USB drive or other location.
4. The Chapter 2_Purchase Order.pdf file opens. Compare it to the one shown on previous page. Close the pdf file. The Purchase Orders window is ready for the next transaction. Continue with step 4 below.

4. To close the Purchase Orders window, click | Close |.

Troubleshooting: Selecting | Save | posts and saves Purchase Orders. Selecting | Print | also saves and posts Purchase Orders.

Receive Inventory from a Purchase Order

After you have entered a purchase order, the next step is to receive the inventory. Sage 50 allows you to receive a different quantity for an item

---

than you originally ordered. In other words, you can receive less than or more than the originally ordered quantity.

Let's see how Bellwether's purchase orders match up to the inventory received.

1. From the Vendors & Purchases Navigation Center > select Purchase Orders > View and Edit Purchase Orders.

2. Double-click DEJULIA, PO No. 10300. Observe that some of the items are received and some are not. For example, six BGS Gardening Handbooks (BOOK-11010) have not been received. Twelve Clay Flower Pots – 6 in. (POTS-30210) were received.

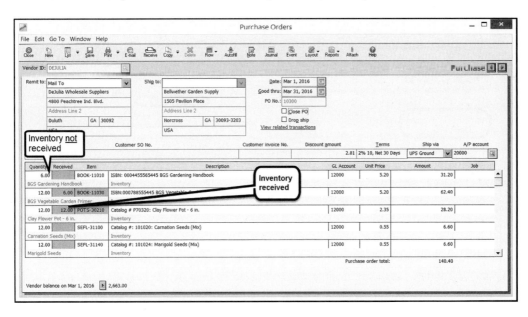

The Received field shows items added to inventory.

3. Select [Reports] > Inventory Stock Status Report. The Inventory Stock Status Report shows the Inventory items purchased from DeJulia Wholesale Suppliers, item class, stocking units/measures, quantity on hand, minimum stock order, reorder quantity, and the inventory location. Close the Inventory Stock Status Report.

Apply to Purchase Order

To see if inventory items from PO No. 10300 have been applied, follow these steps.

1. On the Purchase Orders window, link to <u>View related transactions</u>.

2. Double-click Purchase 22113. The Purchases/Receive Inventory window appears. (*Hint:* If necessary, enlarge the window.) This is Sage 50's Purchase Journal. Observe that some of the items from PO No. 10300 are shown. (The Apply to Purchase Order No. field shows 10300, the PO number.)

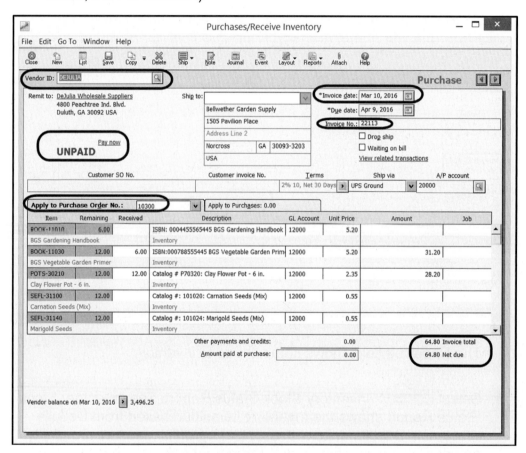

When purchase orders are applied, the transaction appears in Sage 50's Purchase Journal. Click [Journal] to see how the Purchase Journal was debited and credited. When the Purchases/Receive Inventory window (Purchase Journal) is posted, the vendor, DeJulia

Wholesale Suppliers, is updated in the vendor ledger, and the controlling account, Accounts Payable, is updated in the general ledger. Inventory is also updated. Observe that the Purchases/Receive Inventory window shows Unpaid. Also, the Invoice total and Net due fields show $64.80 (the items received so far). The entire purchase order was for $140.40. As of March 10, Bellwether has not received all the items requested on PO 10300. Payment will be made at a later date.

From the Purchases/Receive Inventory window, link to <u>View related transactions</u> to go to Purchase Order 10300. This is the same Purchases/Receive Inventory window shown on page 68.

3. Close all windows. (*Hint:* From the menu bar, select Window > Close All.)

The Purchases/Receive Inventory Window

In Sage 50, the Purchases/Receive Inventory window is the Purchase Journal. The Apply to Purchases tab is the default. The lower half of the window shows fields for Quantity, Item (inventory items), Description, GL Account, Unit Price, Amount, and Job. Observe that the default for the A/P Account is 20000, Accounts Payable. The Purchases/Receive Inventory window looks like a purchase order. Similar to other windows, the icon bar appears at the top of the window.

Follow these steps to record vendor transactions.

1. From the Vendors & Purchases Navigation Center > select > New Bill. The Purchases/Receive Inventory window appears. Observe that the Apply to Purchases tab is the default. The cursor is in the Vendor ID field. To see more lines in the Quantity/Item/Description table, make the Purchases/Receive Inventory window larger. You can do this by putting your mouse on the bottom border of the window and pulling down. The mouse changes to a double-arrow [ ]. With the cursor on the bottom border of the window, pull the window down to make it larger. If necessary, repeat this step on the left and right borders.

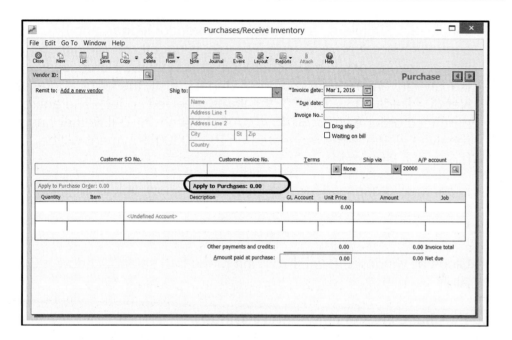

2. With the cursor in the Vendor ID field, press the plus key **<+>** and the Maintain Vendors window appears.

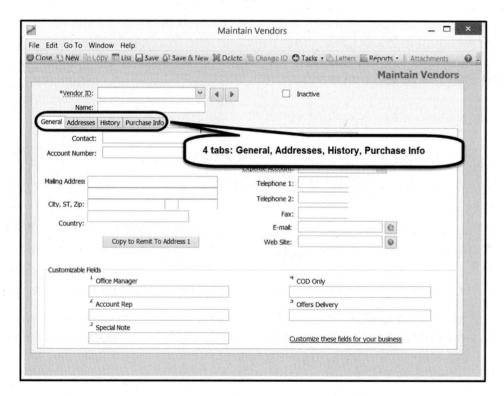

Adding a New Vendor

You are going to enter a new vendor, Adler's Landscaping. Since a *coding system* has already been established for Bellwether's vendors, you should continue to use the same one. The coding system used has uppercase letters. To be consistent, Adler's Landscaping will use ADLER. Notice that the name of the company is typed in all capital letters. What if two companies have the same name, such as, Adler's Landscaping and Adler's Suppliers? They could be coded as ADLER and ADLSUPPL.

You have choices for coding. Here are some other suggestions for coding Adler's Landscaping:

ADLE :   the first four letters of the company's name.
ADLL: the first three letters of a company's name, the first letter of the second word.
ADLER: An alphabetic code for a company name, using the first word. This is the Vendor ID used for Adler's Landscaping and is consistent with Bellwether's other vendors.

Follow these steps to continue in the Maintain Vendors window:

1. Make sure the Maintain Vendors window is displayed. Type **ADLER** in the Vendor ID field and press **<Enter>**. Your cursor is in the Name field.

2. Type **Adler's Landscaping** in the Name field.

3. Press **<Enter>** two times. Your cursor is in the Contact field. The person who handles sales for Adler's Landscaping is Raymond Adler. Type **Raymond Adler** and press **<Enter>**.

4. Your cursor is in the Account Number field. Click on the Vendor type
    field. (Skip the Account Number and Address fields.) The Vendor
    Type field is used for classifying vendors. In the Vendor Type field,
    click on the down arrow. Scroll down, then select SUPPLY.

5. Click on the down-arrow in the Expense Account field. Scroll down
    the list. Select Account No. 57200, Materials Cost. Press **<Enter>**.
    When Adler's Landscaping is selected as the vendor, Account No.
    57200, Materials Cost, will be automatically debited.

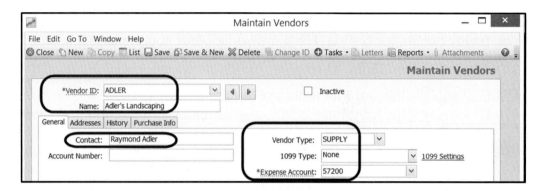

If you need to move between fields to make corrections, use the
<Tab> key to move forward and the **<Shift> + <Tab>** to move
backwards.

6. Click on the Purchase Info tab. Notice that the Vendor ID and Name
    fields stay the same: ADLER and Adler's Landscaping. Also,
    observe the Terms and Credit are 2% net 10, 30 days. Purchase
    discounts are described on page 55.

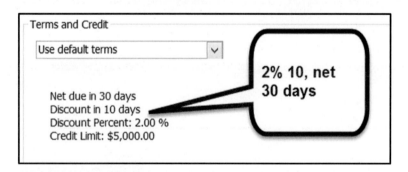

7. Click to return to the Purchases/Receive
    Inventory window.

Entering a Vendor Invoice

Make sure that the Purchases\Receive Inventory window is displayed and that the cursor is in the Vendor ID field. Follow the steps below to enter the transaction.

Date	*Transaction Description*
03/15/2016	Invoice No. AD107 was received from Adler's Landscaping for the purchase of Plant Food, $45. (*Hint:* Debit Account No. 57200, Materials Cost; Credit Account No. 20000, Accounts Payable/Adler's Landscaping.)

1. In the Vendor ID field, click 🔍. Select ADLER, Adler's Landscaping.

2. Select or type 15 as the date.

3. In the Invoice No. field, type **AD107**.

4. Click on the Quantity field and type **1** and press **<Enter>**.

5. Since you are not purchasing an inventory item, press the **<Enter>** key again.

6. The cursor moves to the Description field. In the Description field, type **Plant Food** and press **<Enter>**.

7. In the GL Account field press **<Enter>** to accept Account No. 57200, the Materials Cost account.

8. In the Unit Price field, type **45** and press **<Enter>**. Compare your Purchases/Receive Inventory window to the one shown on the next page.

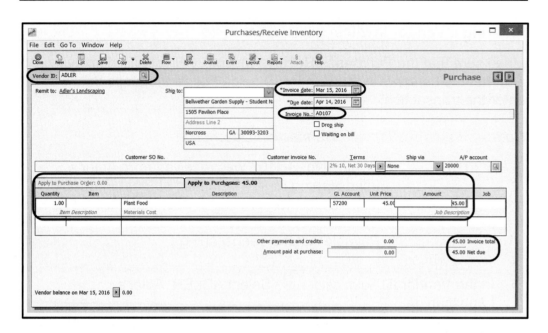

Comment: What if your Purchases/Receive Inventory window does *not* show an A/P Account field or GL Account field?

You should check your settings in the Options/Global selection. Make sure that the boxes in the Hide General Ledger Accounts section are unchecked. These steps were shown on pages 60-61, steps 1-4.

Editing a Journal Entry. Observe that the Purchases/Receive Inventory window includes a ⊞ List icon. Selecting List displays the Purchase List window. From the Purchase List, you can drill down to an entry that you want to edit or change. The Purchases/Receive Inventory window is Sage 50's Purchase Journal. The List icon is included on journal-entry windows.

Posting a Purchase Transaction

When you made this entry in the Purchases/Receive Inventory window, you debited Account No. 57200, Material Cost, which is a General Ledger Cost of Sales account; and credited Accounts Payable/Adler's Landscaping. ADLER is the vendor account. (To see this account distribution, click ⊞ Journal .)

Acct. #	Account Description	Debit	Credit
57200	Materials Cost (Plant Food)	45.00	
20000/ ADLER	Accounts Payable/ Adler's Landscaping		45.00

Follow these steps to post this transaction.

1. Click <OK> to close the Accounting Behind the Screens Purchases Journal window. The Purchases/Receive Inventory window is displayed. Compare it to page 74.

2. Click [Save] to post the vendor invoice.

3. Click [Close] to return to the Vendors & Purchases Navigation Center.

Read Me

The Vendors area on the Vendors & Purchases Navigation Center does *not* show the vendor that I added. How do I update the list?

The toolbar (above Vendors & Purchases Tasks) includes a [Refresh] button. Click it. Observe that the Vendors list now includes ADLER, Adler's Landscaping.

VENDOR PAYMENTS

When you make a payment to a vendor, use the Payments window. The Payments window is the Cash Disbursements Journal. On pages 71-72, you added a new vendor; then entered and posted an invoice to that vendor on pages 73-75. *Both* the new vendor and invoice *must* be completed *before* a vendor payment can be made.

Date   *Transaction Description*

03/18/2016   Issued Check No. 10215 to Adler's Landscaping in payment of Invoice No. AD107.

Follow these steps to pay the Adler's Landscaping invoice:

1. From the Vendors & Purchases Navigation Center > 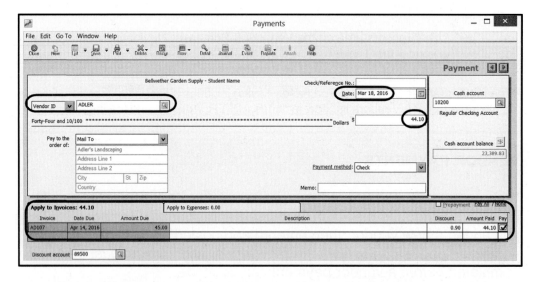 >
   Pay Bill. There are two parts to the Payments window: the check
   section at the top; and the invoice section at the bottom.

   In the Vendor ID field, click on the magnifying-glass icon, then select
   ADLER, Adler's Landscaping. Look at the invoice section. The
   invoice number AD107 is shown with the amount that Bellwether
   owes to Adler's Landscaping.

2. Click on the Date field. Type or select **18** > press <Enter>.

3. Click on the Pay box for Invoice AD107. Notice that the check
   portion of the window is completed. The amount paid is 44.10. This
   is the amount of the invoice less the 2% discount ($45 -.90 =
   $44.10).

> **Troubleshooting:** Observe that the Check/Reference No. field is
   blank. The check number is assigned when you print. Enter check
   number 10215 if checks are *not* going to be printed. Checks are
   printed on pages 78-80.

4. To see the Cash Disbursements Journal entry, click [Journal]. Observe the debits and credits. Account distribution is shown below. Click [OK] to close Accounting Behind the Screens.

5. Click [Save] to post the Payments window (Cash Disbursements Journal).

6. Click [Close] to return to the Vendors & Purchases Navigation Center.

When you post this payment, the Accounts Payable account is debited for the full invoice amount ($45), which offsets the credit created when you entered the invoice. The cash account is decreased (credited) by the amount of the check ($44.10) and the Discounts Taken account is increased (credited) for the purchase discount ($.90). Purchase discounts (Account No. 89500 Purchase Disc-Expense Items) was already set up for Bellwether Garden Supply.

Acct. #	Account Description	Debit	Credit
20000/ ADLER	Accounts Payable/Adler's Landscaping; Invoice AD107	45.00	
10200	Regular Checking Account		44.10
89500	Purchase Disc-Expense Items		.90

PRINTING CHECKS

You can print a batch of checks or print one check at a time. Since there is only one check to print, you are going to print an individual check. Sage also includes special check forms to use for printing checks. These may be purchased from Sage. Since you do not have check forms, print the check on a blank piece of paper.

GO GREEN & SAVE: Instead of printing, select Display or Print Preview, and save as an Adobe PDF file or Microsoft XPS file. In other words, you do not need to print hard copy. Check with your instructor for his or her preference. Instead of printing, email PDFs or Microsoft XPS files.

Follow these steps to print a check:

1. From the menu bar, select Reports & Forms > Forms > Checks. The Select a Report or Form window appears.

2. Observe that the Forms tab is selected. If necessary, in the Form Types list, select Checks. In the Forms list, OCR AP Laser Preprinted is automatically selected. (If not, select OCR AP Laser Preprinted.)

> **Comment**
>
> Step 2 instructs you to select OCR AP Laser Preprinted as the form to print. If this form does *not* print, select another one. The form you select is tied to the kind of printer you are using. Depending on your printer, you may need to make a different selection.

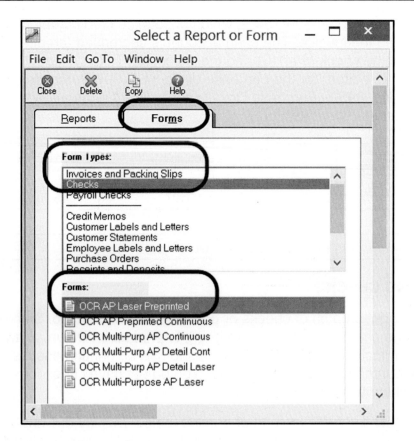

3. Double-click OCR AP Laser Preprinted.

4. The Preview and Print Checks window appears. In the Include checks through field, type **3/18/2016**.

5. Type **10215** in the Number the first check field.

6. In the Filter vendors by area, select ADLER to ADLER in the ID fields.

7. Click [↻ Refresh List].

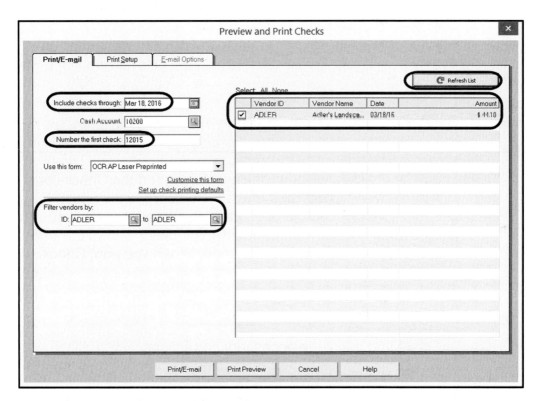

8. Click [Print/E-mail] or [Print Preview]. The check prints or displays. Compare Check No. 10215 to the one shown below. The top half of the check is shown. **If you are NOT connected to a printer, refer to page 66, How to fix.**

AD107			3/15/16	45.00	0.90	44.10

3/18/16	12015	Adler's Landscaping		0.90		$44.10

Check Number: 12015   Mar 18, 2016

Memo:

44.10

Forty-Four and 10/100 Dollars

Adler's Landscaping

If you print the check, a window displays asking Did the Checks print properly, and is it OK to assign the check numbers to the checks? Make sure the check printed properly and the amount is correct. (See the Payments window on page 76.) The check shows the check stub (top portion) and check portion. When you print Check No. 10215, there is also a bottom portion.

9. If the check printed property, click [Yes]. If needed, click [Cancel] and make the necessary corrections.

10. Close the Select a Report or Form window.

DISPLAYING THE VENDOR LEDGERS

To display the Vendor Ledgers, follow these steps.

1. On the Vendors & Purchases Navigation Center, Recently Used Vendor Reports area > link <u>View All Vendor & Purchases Reports</u> > select Vendor Ledgers > [Display] (*Or,* in the Recently Used Vendor Reports area, link to View next to Vendor Ledgers.)

2. The Vendor Ledgers displays. To see the terms for the vendor, click

   Columns. The Vendor Ledgers/Columns window displays. Scroll down
   the Show list. Select Terms. (Click on the box to place a checkmark.)

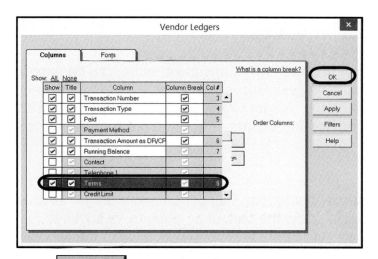

3. After clicking OK, a Terms column is added to the Vendor
   Ledgers report. A partial Vendor Ledgers report is shown below.

Bellwether Garden Supply - Student Name
Vendor Ledgers
For the Period From Mar 1, 2016 to Mar 31, 2016

Filter Criteria includes: Report order is by ID.

Vendor ID Vendor	Date	Trans No	Typ	Pai	Debit Amt	Credit Amt	Balance	Terms
ABNEY	3/1/16	B1000	PJ			75.00	75.00	2% 10, Net 30
Abney and Son Contractor	3/9/16	B1015	PJ	*		195.65	270.65	
	3/12/16	VCM30001	PJ	*	195.65		75.00	
	3/15/16		CD		50.00	50.00	75.00	
ADLER	3/15/16	AD107	PJ	*		45.00	45.00	2% 10, Net 30
Adler's Landscaping	3/18/16	10215	CD		0.90	0.90	45.00	
	3/18/16	10215	CD		45.00		0.00	
AKERSON	3/1/16	Balance Fw					9,398.75	2% 10, Net 30
Akerson Distribution	3/7/16	VCM30002	PJ	*	27.20		9,371.55	
	3/8/16	4	PJ			5,179.20	14,550.75	
	3/13/16		CD		1,000.00	1,000.00	14,550.75	
	3/14/16	B1016	PJ	*		27.20	14,577.95	
CALDWELL	3/1/16	Balance Fw					21,214.10	2% 10, Net 30
Caldwell Tools Company	3/4/16	B1004	PJ			90.00	21,304.10	
	3/6/16	B1017	PJ	*		45.90	21,350.00	
	3/9/16	VCM30003	PJ	*	45.90		21,304.10	

The Vendor Ledger is the Accounts Payable subsidiary ledger. When
you entered and posted the vendor invoice (pages 73-75) in the

Purchases/Receive Inventory window, the Accounts Payable subsidiary ledger for Adler's Landscaping was credited for $45. Once the invoice was entered, there is a balance of $45. When you posted the payment (step 5, page 77), Sage debited the vendor for the same amount. The balance after posting the payment is zero ($0.00).

VENDOR CREDIT MEMOS

Vendor credit memos are returns to vendors. You can apply vendor credit memos to any existing vendor invoice that has *not* been paid. All entries made on the Vendor Credit Memos window are posted to the general ledger, vendor records, and when applicable, inventory and job records.

You are going to use Sage 50's *drill down* feature to go to the original entry from the vendor ledger. Using the vendor ledger as an example, use drill down to follow the path of an entry to its origin. In Sage 50 reports, you can click transactions to drill down to the window that includes the original transaction information.

1. The vendor ledger should be displayed. Using the vendor, Abney and Son Contractors, put your cursor over the 3/9/16 vendor ledger entry. Your cursor changes to a magnifying-glass with a Z (for zoom) in it.

ABNEY	3/1/16	B1000	PJ			75.00	75.00	2% 10, Net 30
Abney and Son Cont	3/9/16	B1015 ②	PJ	*		195.65	270.65	
	3/12/1	VCM30001	PJ	*	195.65		75.00	
	3/15/1		CD		50.00	50.00	75.00	

2. To drill down to the 3/9/16 transaction, double-click on it with your left mouse button. The Purchases/Receive Inventory window appears showing the original purchase of inventory items.

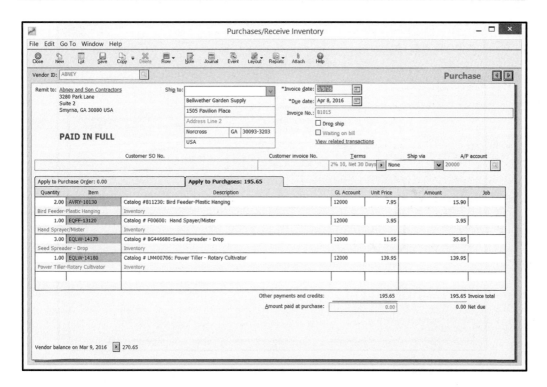

> **Troubleshooting:** On my Purchases/Receive Inventory window, the Quantity, Item, Description, GL Account, Unit Price, and Amount table does *not* show multiple lines. If that is the case, you can use the arrows next to the Job field to scroll through the multiple lines. Try enlarging your screen with the cursor. If that doesn't work, read the next paragraph about screen resolution.

The number of lines on the Quantity, Item, Description, GL Account, Unit Price, and Amount table is determined by your screen resolution. On page v, the minimum system requirements suggest 1024x768 resolution with small fonts.

3. Click ⊗ Close. You are returned to the Vendor Ledgers. Drill down on the 3/12/16 vendor credit memo (VCM30001). The Vendor Credit Memos window appears. Observe that the Apply to Invoice No. tab shows B1015. This is the same merchandise that was purchased on 3/9/16. (See the Purchases/ Receive inventory window.) The returned field shows the items returned.

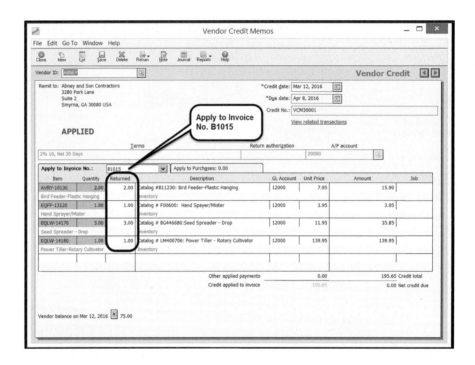

4. Click [Close]. You are returned to the Vendor Ledgers. Click [Close] again to return to the Vendors & Purchases Navigation Center. (*Hint:* You can also select Window > Close All.)

BACKING UP CHAPTER 2 DATA

After completing the work within Chapter 2, back up. The suggested file name is **Chapter 2.ptb**. Detailed steps for backing up data are shown on pages 22-25.

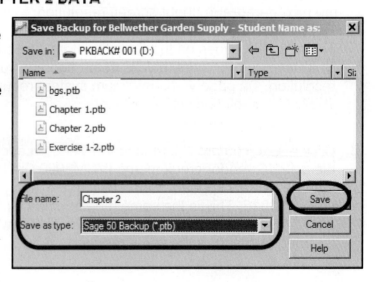

Backing up saves your data to that point in your work. Each time you back up, use a different file name; for example, the suggested file name at this point is Chapter 2.ptb. (Sage 50 automatically adds the file extension .ptb to backups.) Using a unique name allows you to restore at different points in the data.

EXPORT TWO SAGE 50 REPORTS TO EXCEL

The steps that follow demonstrate how to add a new worksheet to an existing Excel file. These steps show how two Sage 50 reports, the Vendor List and the Vendor Ledgers, are saved to one Excel file.

1. From the Navigation Bar, click [Vendors & Purchases]. In the Recently Used Vendor Reports area, link to <u>View All Vendor & Purchases Reports</u>. The Select a Report or Form window appears.

2. Select Vendor List > Se<u>n</u>d To > Excel. When the Modify Report – Vendor List window appears, click [OK]. (*Hint:* You may want to display the Vendor list, reformat the columns, then from the displayed report click [Excel])

3. The Copy Report to Excel window appears. In the File option area make sure Create a new Microsoft Excel workbook is selected. In the Report header option, Show header in Excel worksheet should also be selected.

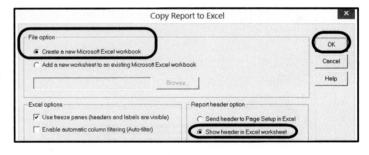

option, Show header in Excel worksheet should also be selected.

4. After clicking [OK], the report is exported to Microsoft Excel. Bellwether Garden Supply's Vendor List is shown.

5. Save the Vendor List. Use **Chapter 2_Vendor List and Vendor Ledgers.xlsx** as the file name. (Excel 2003 ends in the file extension .xls.)

6. Go to Bellwether. (*Hint:* Select a Report or Form.)

7. From the Select a Report or Form window, double-click Vendor Ledgers. The Vendor Ledgers displays.

   There are two ways to export to Excel.

   a. From the Select a Report or Form window, highlight the report and then select Se_n_d To Excel.

   b. Display the report and select Excel [Excel]. (This is shown below.)

8. Click. [Excel] On the Copy Report to Excel window, select Add a new worksheet to an existing Microsoft Excel workbook. Select [Browse...] Go to the location of the saved file, Chapter 2_Vendor List and Vendors Ledgers.xlsx. Select [Open]

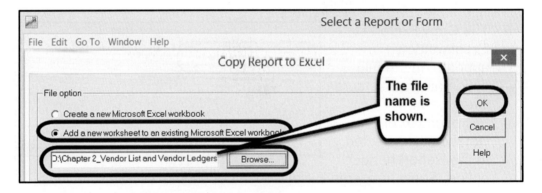

9. After clicking [OK], Bellwether Garden Supply's Vendor Ledgers appear. Observe that the two sheets are shown: Vendor List and Vendor Ledgers (tabs at the bottom of the window.)

10. Save. The Excel file, Chapter 2_Vendor List and Vendor Ledgers, includes two sheets: the Vendor List and the Vendor Ledgers. Click ☒ on the title bar to exit Excel and return to Sage 50.

11. Close all windows.

SAVE VENDOR LIST AND VENDOR LEDGERS AS PDF FILES

Follow these steps to save the Vendor List as a PDF file.

1. Go to the Vendor List. From the Reports & Forms menu > Accounts Payable > double-click Vendor List.

2. The Vendor List appears. On the icon bar, click ⬚PDF⬚. The Save As window appears. Select the location of your USB drive.

➢ **Troubleshooting**: If you are having difficulty saving a PDF file, go online to www.adobe.com. Update or download the Free Adobe Reader.

3. Type **Chapter 2_Vendor List** in the File name field.

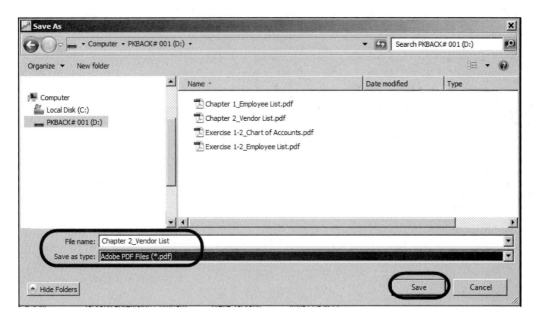

4. Click ⬚Save⬚.

5. Complete similar steps to save the Vendor Ledgers as a PDF file. Use the file name **Chapter 2_Vendor Ledgers.pdf**.

6. Close all windows.

ONLINE LEARNING CENTER

Complete the following end-of-chapter activities online at www.mhhe.com/yacht2016 > select the Student Edition > Chapter 2.

1. Interactive Multiple-Choice and True/False questions.
2. Going to the Net exercise: Internet Corporation for Assigned Names and Numbers.
3. QA Templates: 10 multiple-choice questions and one analysis question.
4. Assessment Rubric: review journals, navigation centers, modules, and task windows.
5. Listen to narrated PowerPoint slides.

The OLC also includes links to the Appendixes:

- Appendix A: Troubleshooting
- Appendix B: Accounting Information Systems
- Appendix C: Review of Accounting Principles
- Appendix D: Glossary of Terms (words that are boldfaced and italicized in chapter)

Exercise 2-1: Follow the instructions below to complete Exercise 2-1.

1. Start Sage 50. Open Bellwether Garden Supply - Student Name [your first and last name].[2]

2. If necessary, restore the Chapter 2.ptb backup file. This file was backed up on pages 84-85.

3. Add the following vendor:

Vendor ID: OFCSUPPL
Name: Office Supplies & More

---

[2]If Bellwether Garden Supply is *not* shown in the Company Name field, refer to the Read Me box on page 29. If an Activation window appears, follow the screen prompts to activate (see Step 14, pages xiv-xv).

Contact: Ron Barber
Vendor Type: OFFICE
Expense Account: Account No. 71000, Office Expense

4. Enter the following transaction.

   Date   *Transaction Description*

   03/15/2016   Invoice No. H788 was received from Office Supplies
                & More for the purchase of five boxes of letter-size
                file folders, $10.95 each. (*Hint:* Account No. 71000,
                Office Expense, should be debited.)

5. Post this purchase.

6. Continue with Exercise 2-2.

Exercise 2-2: Follow the instructions below to complete Exercise 2-2.

1. Enter the following transaction.

   Date   *Transaction Description*

   03/18/16   Pay Office Supplies & More for Invoice H788, $53.65.
                (*Hint:* The payment is less a 2% discount: $54.75 -1.10
                = $53.65.)

2. Post the Cash Disbursements Journal. (*Hint:* The Payments window
   is the Cash Disbursements Journal.)

3. Print Check No. 10216. (*Hint: On the OCR AP Laser Preprinted
   Filter window, select the payment date and vendor.*)

   If you do NOT have a printer, refer to page 66, How to Fix.

4. Print the Vendor Ledgers. Add a Terms column. Adjust the Vendor
   Ledgers report so that it prints on one page. (*Hint:* Place the mouse
   over the column. The cursor changes to a double-arrow. Adjust the
   column.)

5. Print the March 1, 2016 to March 31, 2016 Purchase Order Register.
   (*Hint:* The Purchase Order Register is an Accounts Payable report. If
   necessary, select <Options>, from Mar 1, 2016 to Mar 31, 2016.)

Check Your Figures: PO No. 10300, $140.40
PO No. 101, $3,834.00

6. Backup. The suggested file name is **Exercise 2-2.ptb**.

7. Save three Sage 50 reports: the Vendor List, Vendors Ledgers, and Purchase Order Register to one Excel file. (*Hint:* Refer to pages 85-87, Export Two Sage 50 Reports to One Excel File.) Add the terms column to the Vendor Ledgers. Use **Exercise 2-2_Vendor List_Vendor Ledgers_PO Register.xlsx** as the file name.

8. Save the Vendor List, Vendor Ledgers, and Purchase Order Register as PDF files. Use **Exercise 2-2_Vendor List**, **Exercise 2-2_Vendor Ledgers.pdf**, **Exercise 2-2_Purchase Order Register.pdf** as the file names.

   Check Your figures: Vendor Ledgers balance: $80,826.01.

9. Close all windows. Exit Sage 50.

CHAPTER 2 INDEX

Chapter

3 Customers

LEARNING OBJECTIVES

1. Restore data from Exercise 2-2. This backup was made on page 90. (Refer to the Read me box on page 56, Do I need to restore?)
2. Go to the Customers & Sales Navigation Center to enter quotes and sales orders.
3. Enter a sales order.
4. Ship items from a sales order.
5. Enter customer terms.
6. Record a sales invoice on the Sales/Invoicing window.
7. Print a sales invoice.
8. Analyze customer payments and credit memos.
9. Post a customer payment for previously invoiced amounts.
10. Add a Customer Terms column to the Customer Ledgers report.
11. Export Customer Ledgers to Excel.
12. Save the Customer Ledgers as a PDF file.
13. Make two backups, save one Excel file, and one PDF file.[1]

Chapter 3 introduces the basics of how Sage 50 works with customer transactions. First you learn about quotes and *sales orders*. A sales order is a document containing a list of items or services that a customer wants to buy. When a sales order is posted, no accounting information is updated. Once sales orders are completed, you learn how the information entered in customer maintenance is used when posting entries. For example, in the Maintain Customers/Prospects window, you set a range of days within which a customer can receive a discount and set the discount percentage. This information will print on the sales invoices you record. The discount is automatically applied when you enter a customer payment within the allotted time. The Collection Manager, included on the Analysis Menu, shows an overview of all outstanding invoices.

---

[1]Refer to the chart on page 2 for the size of backups, and saved Excel and PDF files.

GETTING STARTED

1. Start Sage 50. Open Bellwether Garden Supply - Student Name.

   > **Troubleshooting: Bellwether Garden Supply is not listed on Sage 50's Company Name list.**

   Refer to the Read Me box on page 29 to review steps to "Create a new company using the restored data." The steps within the Read Me box show how to restore a backup file and set up a company at the same time.

2. If necessary, restore the Exercise 2-2 file. This file was backed up on page 90.

   To make sure you are starting in the appropriate place in the data (Exercise 2-2 backup) check that these vendors, Adler's Landscaping and Office Supplies & More, are shown in the Vendors area of the Vendors & Purchases Navigation Center. (*Hint:* You may need to click ⟳ Refresh to update your Vendors list.) The Vendor Ledgers report

shows a zero balance for both Adler's Landscaping and

ADLER	3/15/16	AD107	PJ	*		45.00	45.00
Adler's Landscaping	3/18/16	10215	CD		0.90	0.90	45.00
	3/18/16	10215	CD		45.00		0.00
OFCSUPPL	3/15/16	H788	PJ	*		54.75	54.75
Office Supplies & More	3/18/16	10216	CD		1.10	1.10	54.75
	3/18/16	10216	CD		54.75		0.00

Office Supplies & More. The Vendor Ledgers Report Total is $80,826.01.

Bellwether Garden Supply - Student Name
Vendor Ledgers
For the Period From Mar 1, 2016 to Mar 31, 2016

Filter Criteria includes: Report order is by ID.

Vendor ID Vendor	Date	Trans No	Typ	Paid	Debit Amt	Credit Amt	Balance
PAYNE	3/9/16	10212V	CD		50.00	50.00	0.00
Payne Enterprises	3/15/16	10212	CD		50.00	50.00	0.00
SAFESTATE	3/15/16	10210	CD		530.64	530.64	0.00
Safe State Insurance Compa							
SOGARDEN	3/1/16	Balance Fw					31,079.25
Southern Garden Wholesale	3/4/16	11544	PJ	*		255.65	31,334.90
	3/14/16	SG-11657	PJ			50.90	31,385.80
	3/14/16	SG-11658	PJ			239.85	31,625.65
	3/14/16	10208	CD		5.11	5.11	31,625.65
	3/14/16	10208	CD		255.65		31,370.00
SOPOWER	3/11/16	B1011	PJ			226.88	226.88
Southern Power Co.							
STANLEY	3/1/16	VCM30009	PJ		103.60		-103.60
Stanley Shipping Express	3/12/16	B1012	PJ			19.99	-83.61
SULLEY	3/5/16	14223	PJ			675.00	675.00
Sulley Printing	3/9/16	B1024	PJ			17.10	692.10
WATKINS	3/2/16	B1013	PJ			60.00	60.00
Watkins Financial Planning	3/5/16	VCM30010	PJ		35.35		24.65
Report Total					8,131.74	18,603.12	80,826.01

ACCOUNTS RECEIVABLE SYSTEM

Accounts Receivable represents amounts owed by customers for items or services sold to them when cash is not received at the time of sale. Typically, accounts receivable balances are recorded on sales invoices that include terms of payment. Accounts receivable is used if you are setting up accrued income that customers owe.

The four basic tasks in Accounts Receivable are:

1. Quotes: Allows you to enter a quote for a customer.

2. Sales Orders: Sales orders provide you with a means of tracking backorders for your customers.

3. Sales/Invoicing: When items are ready for shipment, the sales/invoicing window is used.

4. Receive Money from Customers: Used for recording payments from customers. (Sage 50 also includes credits and returns.)

Before adding accounts receivable transactions, examine the Customers & Sales Navigation Center. Follow these steps to do that.

1. From the Navigation Bar > select . The Customers & Sales Navigation Center displays information and access points related to the company's customers. In Sage 50, this represents the *accounts receivable module* or *accounts receivable system*.

   Modules organize Sage 50's transaction windows and reports. When the Navigation Bar's Customers & Sales selection is made, Sage 50's accounts receivable system is shown. The menu bar selections, Tasks and Reports & Forms, are also organized by module; for example, the Reports & Forms menu includes Accounts Receivable, Accounts Payable, General Ledger, etc.

   Sage 50's Customers & Sales Navigation Center has two tabs that display information and access points related to Bellwether's customers.

- 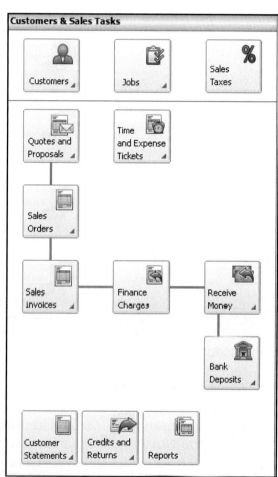 **Customers & Sales** The Customers & Sales tab is a summary of customer information, includes access to recently used customer reports and an overview of the company's aged receivables. Scroll down the Customers & Sales window to see the Customers, Recently Used Customer Reports, Aged Receivables, and Sage Advisor.

- **Customer Management**

  On the Customer Management tab, you can see lists of information regarding transactions and customer history, including invoices, receipts, and finance charges.

  The Customers & Sales Tasks workflow diagram is shown. Scroll down the window to see the rest of the Customers & Sales Navigation Center.

  Link to a couple of areas to explore the Customers & Sales Navigation Center. Close any open windows, then continue with the next section. (*Hint:* If multiple windows are open, from the menu bar select Window, Close All.)

2. Click on the **Customer Management** tab. In the Customer ID field, select ARCHER. On the Customer Management window, there are 3 sections:

   - Sales Invoices
   - Receipts

- Credit Memos

  In the Receipts, Date Range field select All Transactions
  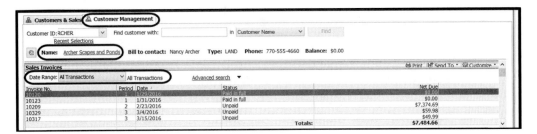. The sections list sales invoices, receipts, and credit memos. A partial Customer Management window is shown.

3. To see detail for Invoice No. 10123 > drill down on Invoice No. 10123. The Sales/Invoicing window appears > link to <u>View related transactions</u> > drill down on Receipt Reference No. 10123. The Receive Money window appears showing a partial payment of $23,359.35. Unpaid amounts are unchecked.

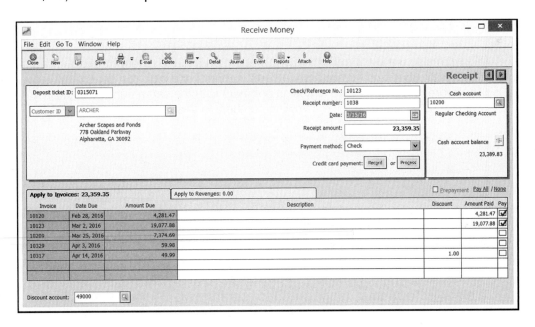

4. After reviewing the Receive Money window, close all windows.

Entering a Quote

When you enter a quote for a customer, you are *not* updating any accounting information or inventory amounts. Sage calculates what the total cost of the sale will be for a customer, including sales tax and freight. You can then print the quote for the customer. Follow these steps to enter a sales quote.

1. Select the  Customers & Sales tab. From the Customers & Sales Tasks diagram > click Quotes and Proposals > New Quote.

2. The Quotes window displays. Your cursor is in the <u>C</u>ustomer ID field. Type **D** (use capital D). Press the **<Enter>** key. Dash Business Systems displays.

3. Click on the <u>D</u>ate field. Type **15** (or select 15). Press the **<Enter>**. The Quote No. field is blank. This is okay. Sage 50 assigns a quote number automatically.

Comment

You can also enter a number that you want to print in the Quote No. field. If you assign your own number, Sage sorts numbers one digit at a time. Therefore, it is a good idea to assign numbers with the same number of digits. For example, Sage sorts the following numbers in this order:
    1
    104
    12
    2
    23

---

4. Your cursor should be in the Customer <u>P</u>O field. Observe that this field is blank. Since this customer does not have a purchase order number, you are going to leave this field blank. Click on Quantity field. Type **1** and press **<Enter>**. (If the Quantity field shows .01, refer to the steps 1a. and b. on page 18 for setting two decimal places.)

5. In the Item field, select EQFF-13110 Fertilizer Compression Sprayer. (*Hint: Scroll down the Item list to make this selection, or you can type the item ID.*) The Description, GL Account, Unit Price, Tax, and Amount fields are automatically completed.

> **Comment**
>
> If the GL Account field is not displayed on the Quotes window, you need to check your global settings. Refer to step 1c. on page 18 (Chapter 1) to make sure that the boxes in the Hide General Ledger Accounts section are unchecked (see Options > Global).

6. Click on the Quantity field. Type **4** then select EQWT-15120 Garden Hose - 75 ft. for the item.

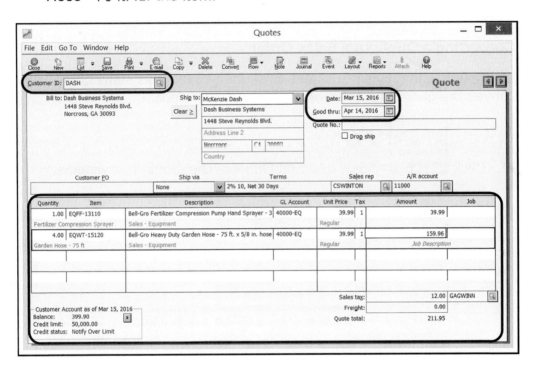

When you selected Dash Business Systems, the Customer Account balance as of March 15, 2016 also appears on the lower left side of the Quotes window, along with the Credit Limit and Credit Status. You can drill down to Dash Business Systems' customer ledger by clicking on the right arrow ( ) in the Customer Account area.

7. To see the journal entry, click Journal . The Quotes Journal lists the sales taxes that are paid for the transaction, the price for each item, and the amount that Bellwether will receive from the customer on this quote. Close the Accounting Behind the Screens window by clicking OK .

---

8. Click [Save] , then click [Close] to return to the Customers & Sales Navigation Center.

Comment

When a sales quote is saved, you are *not* posting or updating general ledger accounts. That is handled through the Sales/Invoicing window, which you work with after converting the quote and printing the sales order.

Converting a Quote to a Sales Order

Let's assume that Dash Business Systems accepts this sales quote. To convert the quote to a sales order, follow these steps.

1. Click [Quotes and Proposals] > View and Edit Quotes. The Quote List window appears.

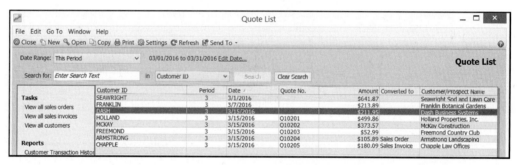

2. Double-click DASH. The Quotes window appears showing the March 15, 2016 quote. Compare this to the Quotes window shown on page 99.

3. Click [Convert]. There are three options: Sale/Invoice, Sale/Invoice and Print Now, Sales Order. Click on the radio button next to Sales Order. The SO # field is completed automatically.

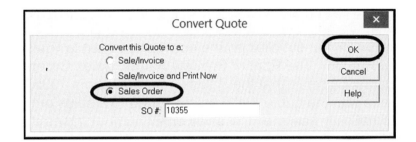

4. Click [OK]. A blank Quotes window appears. Click [Close].
   You just converted the sales quote to a sales order. Now you can
   invoice the customer for shipment.

5. Close all windows. (*Hint:* Select Window > Close All.)

Printing (or Displaying) a Sales Order

Printing a sales order gives you the ability to confirm customer orders
and fill these orders more efficiently. Follow these steps to print.

1. From the Customers & Sales Navigation Center > select [Sales Orders] >
   View and Edit Sales Orders. On the Sales Order List window, double-
   click DASH. The Quote converted to Sales Order No. 10355 displays.

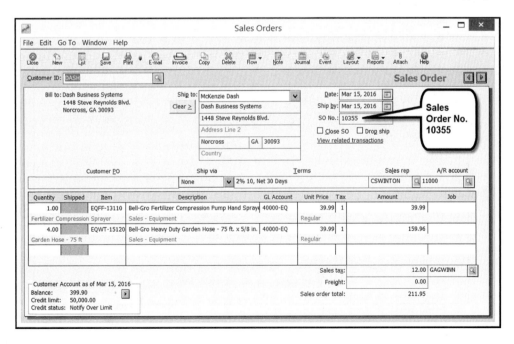

2. Click [Print]. *Or,* click on the down arrow next to Print and select Print Preview. The Print or Preview Forms: Sales Orders window appears. Observe that the Sales Order number is 10355. This agrees with the quote that was converted to a sales order. Sage 50 automatically assigned the sales order number. (*Hint:* If you do <u>not</u> have a printer, see How to Fix on the next page.)

3. Accept the Use this form – Sales Order w/Totals. Click [Print] (*or* [Print Preview]). The sales order starts to print or displays.

Bellwether Garden Supply - Student Name
1505 Pavilion Place
Norcross, GA 30093-3203
USA

Voice: 770-724-4000
Fax: 770-555-1234

SALES ORDER

Sales Order Number: 10355
Sales Order Date: Mar 15, 2016
Ship By: Mar 15, 2016
Page: 1

To:
Dash Business Systems
1448 Steve Reynolds Blvd.
Norcross, GA 30093

Ship To:
Dash Business Systems
1448 Steve Reynolds Blvd.
Norcross, GA 30093

Customer ID	PO Number	Sales Rep Name
DASH		Colista A. Swinton

Customer Contact	Shipping Method	Payment Terms
McKenzie Dash	None	2% 10, Net 30 Days

Quantity	Item	Description	Unit Price	Amount
1.00	EQFF-13110	Bell-Gro Fertilizer Compression Pump Hand Sprayer - 3 Gallon	39.99	39.99
4.00	EQWT-15120	Bell-Gro Heavy Duty Garden Hose - 75 ft. x 5/8 in. hose	39.99	159.96

Subtotal		199.95
Sales Tax		12.00
Freight		0.00
TOTAL ORDER AMOUNT		**211.95**

4. If you previewed the Sales Order, click . (Printing saves and posts.)

How to Fix? I don't have a printer? From the Sales Orders window, select <Print Preview>. In the Printer area, select <Printer Setup>. Select Adobe PDF or Microsoft XPS Document Writer. Save to USB drive. For detailed steps, refer to page 66.

---

5. Close all windows. (*Hint:* From the menu bar, click Window, Close All.)

Ship Items from a Sales Order

To ship items from a sales order, open the Sales/Invoicing window, select the customer, then choose the open sales order you want to invoice. Once the shipped field is completed, an invoice is created with the appropriate sales tax and the amount of the sale. When the Sales/Invoicing window is saved (posted), accounting information is updated. That includes the accounts receivable controlling account in the general ledger, the customer's subsidiary account in the customer ledger, and inventory amounts.

Follow these steps to ship items from Sales Order No. 10355.

1. Click  > New Sales Invoice. The Sales/Invoicing window appears.

2. In the Customer ID field, select DASH, Dash Business Systems.

3. In the Date field type **15** (or select the date).

4. The Apply to Sales Order No. tab is selected. Click on the down-arrow and select number 10355.

5. Since we are receiving both items on this Sales Order, type **1** and **4** in the Shipped fields. Once you complete the Shipped fields, the Invoice totals are computed (sales tax and amount paid at sale.)

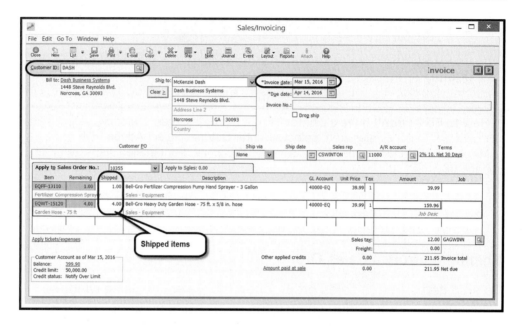

6. To see how this transaction is journalized in the Sales Journal, click
   ▣ Journal . After the entry is saved (posted), Cost of Sales is computed.
   Close the Sales Journal window.

7. Click 💾 Save to post. Close the Sales/Invoicing window.

THE MAINTAIN CUSTOMERS/PROSPECTS WINDOW

The first step is to select the customer you are going to invoice and to change one item of information: the discount percentage offered for timely payment.

1. From the Customers & Sales Navigation Center > 👤 Customers > New Customer. The Maintain Customers/Prospects window displays. The cursor is in the Customer ID field.

2. Click on the down-arrow in the Customer ID field to open the customers/prospects list.[2]

---

[2]There are three ways to open the list in a lookup field. Your cursor should be in the Customer ID field: 1) Press the right mouse button; 2) type a question mark **<?>**; 3) left-click the down-arrow.

3. The customer file you are going to use is Teesdale Real Estate. Click on the down-arrow, then select **TEESDALE**.

The Maintain Customers/ Prospects window shows a completed record for Teesdale Real Estate.

Entering a Discount for a Customer

Because Teesdale Real Estate is such a good customer, Bellwether Garden Supply is going to increase their discount from 2% to 5%. In accounting, this is called a ***sales discount***. The standard sales discount for Bellwether is 2% if paid within 10 days. Teesdale's new sales discount is 5% if paid within 15 days. Sales discounts are applied when payment is received from the customer within the discount period. In this case, 5% discount if payment is received within 15 days.

Follow these steps to enter a discount for a customer:

1. The Maintain Customers/Prospects window for Teesdale Real Estate should be displayed. Click on the Payment & Credit tab

   Payment & Credit .

2. In the Terms and Credit Area (right side of window), click on the down-arrow. Select Customize terms for this customer.

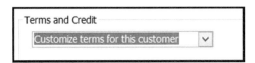

3. If necessary, click on the radio button next to Due in number of days.

4. Click on the Discount in field. Type **15** and press **<Enter>**. The cursor moves to the Discount percent field.

5. In the Discount percent field, type **5** and press **<Enter>**.[3]

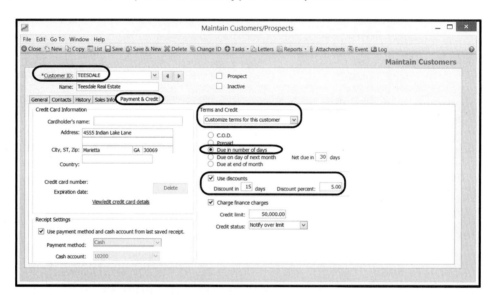

6. Click . If the Sage Advisor window appears, read it. You may want to follow the links. Close the window when through.

7. Close all windows.

Entering a Sale to a Customer

To print or record an invoice, enter a sales invoice for a customer on the Sales/Invoicing window. Similar to a Sales Journal, the Sales/Invoicing window is reserved for sales from credit customers.

---

[3]You should have set two decimal places in Chapter 1 (see page 18, 1 a. and b.).

Date	Transaction Description

03/01/16   Bellwether Garden Supply sold 5 hand sprayer/misters, $49.95, to Teesdale Real Estate, Customer ID, TEESDALE, and cleaned the parking lot, $100, for a total of $149.95 plus $9.00 sales tax; $158.95.

Follow these steps to learn how to use the Sales/Invoicing window:

1. From the Customers & Sales Navigation Center > 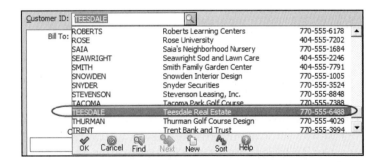 > New Sales Invoice. The Sales/Invoicing window appears.

   Use the Sales/Invoicing window for credit sales from customers. The Sales/Invoicing window is for credit customers only. If the transaction involves an accounts receivable credit sale, enter it in the Sales/Invoicing window. The Sales/Invoicing window posts to the Sales Journal.

   The Sales/Invoicing window should be displayed. The cursor is in the Customer ID field. Don't worry if you have forgotten Teesdale's customer ID number because Sage knows it. The Customer ID field has a lookup field.

2. With the cursor in the Customer ID field, click the right mouse button (or type a question mark, **<?>**). You may also click ⌕.

3. Highlight TEESDALE, Teesdale Real Estate.

4. Click .

   The Sales/ Invoicing window appears. Observe that the Bill to and Ship to fields are completed automatically. Sage provides an invoice number when the sales invoice is printed so there is no need to enter an invoice number now.

5. Click on the Invoice date field. Type **1** for the date.

   Sage offers flexibility when entering dates. For example, you can enter March 1, 2016 as 030116 and the program will format the date correctly. Or, you can enter just the day portion of the date and the date is formatted in the current period. For example, if you're working in March of 2016, you can type 4 in the Invoice date field and the program formats the date as March 4, 2016. You can also use the calendar to select the date.

6. Make sure the Invoice date field shows Mar 1, 2016. Press **<Enter>** two times to go to the Invoice No field. The cursor moves to the Invoice No. field, which you are going to leave blank. Sage 50 will assign an invoice number when you print the sales invoice.

7. Click on the Apply to Sales tab **Apply to Sales: 0.00** .

8. Click on the Quantity field, type **5** and press **<Enter>**. Your cursor goes to the Item lookup field.

9. Click ⊞ to open the list of inventory items.

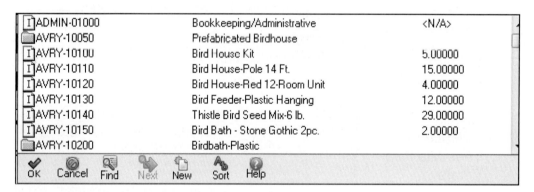

ADMIN-01000	Bookkeeping/Administrative	<N/A>
AVRY-10050	Prefabricated Birdhouse	
AVRY-10100	Bird House Kit	5.00000
AVRY-10110	Bird House-Pole 14 Ft.	15.00000
AVRY-10120	Bird House-Red 12-Room Unit	4.00000
AVRY-10130	Bird Feeder-Plastic Hanging	12.00000
AVRY-10140	Thistle Bird Seed Mix-6 lb.	29.00000
AVRY-10150	Bird Bath - Stone Gothic 2pc.	2.00000
AVRY-10200	Birdbath-Plastic	

OK   Cancel   Find   Next   New   Sort   Help

There are two ways to enter transaction lines for an invoice:

➤ By Inventory Item: Because the price of each inventory item is stored in the Maintain Inventory Items file, you only have to enter the quantity supplied. The program will compute the credit amount.

> ➢ By Account Number: If there is no line item set up for a particular commodity you sell, or if you don't use the Inventory module, you can distribute directly against the proper General Ledger account.

10. The Inventory Item list should be open. Let's see what happens if the Sort icon is selected. Click [Sort] which is located at the bottom of the lookup list on the right side.

    By selecting Sort, you change the order of the list. The list was sorted by ID number; now the list is sorted alphabetically by name. This feature is available in all lookup lists.

11. Select Hand Sprayer/Mister as the item for this sale. EQFF-13120 displays in the Item field (*Hint:* You can also type the item ID.)

12. Your cursor should be in the Description field with the following description highlighted: Bell-Gro Plant All-Purpose Plastic Sprayer/Mister. Since you are not going to add a comment or explanation about this inventory item, press **<Enter>** to move to the GL Account field. The default account is Account No. 40000-EQ, Sales – Equipment. The account name, Sales – Equipment, is shown below the transaction line. This account will be credited unless you change the account number in this GL Account field. The debit is automatically made to Accounts Receivable–Teesdale Real Estate.

13. Press **<Enter>** to accept Account No. 40000-EQ. The cursor moves to the Unit Price field and 9.99 is automatically completed. Since the price has been set up in the Maintain Inventory Items file, the unit price is automatically completed for you.

14. Press **<Enter>** to go to the tax field. Type a **<?>** to display the lookup list. Inventory Item tax types are set up in the Maintain Inventory Item file. This lookup list lets you specify certain items as exempt or having special tax situations. There is no need to specify any special tax situation.

15. Press **<Enter>** to go to the Amount field. Sage calculates the total, $49.95, and enters it in the field.

16. Press **<Enter>** to go to the Job field. The job field also has a lookup list. In Chapter 6, you learn about assigning Jobs.

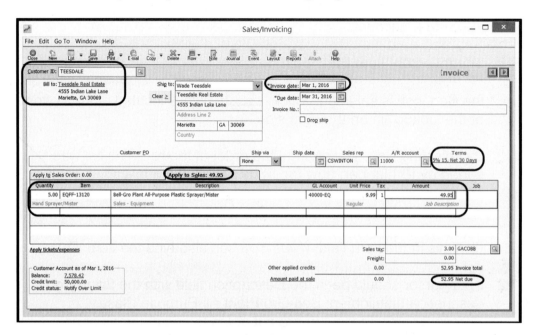

> ➤ **Troubleshooting:** Observe that the Invoice No. field is blank and that the Terms field shows 5% 15, Net 30 Days. The invoice number, similar to the check number, is assigned when you print. If you are <u>not</u> going to print, enter 101 in the Invoice No. field.

Notice that the Invoice Total and Net Due in the lower right of the window shows $52.95. The Invoice Total displays a running total of the customer's account. Accounts Receivable subsidiary ledger is increased (debited). When you add the next transaction line, this figure will increase. In accounting, two things happen when the Accounts Receivable subsidiary ledger is used.

a. The Accounts Receivable controlling account in the General Ledger is increased by the amount of the credit sale.

b. The credit to the applicable revenue account is offset by a debit to the Customer's account in the Accounts Receivable ledger.

17. To go to a new transaction line, press **<Enter>**.

Distributing Against a Specific Account

In this part of the transaction, Bellwether Garden Supply contracted with Teesdale Real Estate to clean up their parking lot for $100. Because no inventory item is stored in the maintenance records, this transaction is different than the one you just completed (entering a sale to a customer for an inventory item). In this part of the transaction, you need to distribute the amount ($100.00) directly against the Other Income account.

1. Your cursor is in the Quantity field. Since you don't have a quantity number to enter with this transaction, press **<Enter>**. Your cursor should be in the Item field.

2. Press **<Enter>** to leave the Item field blank. Your cursor moves to the Description field.

3. Type **Cleaned parking lot** in the Description field and press **<Enter>**. Your cursor moves to the GL Account field. The default account displays, but it needs to be changed.

4. Type **41000** (for Other Income) and press **<Enter>**. Now the account description below the current transaction line reads Other Income and your cursor moves to the Unit Price field.

    The account number that automatically displayed, 40000, Sales, was the default account. Since we want to distribute this revenue to a specific account, 41000, Other Income, you must type this account number (41000); otherwise, the program will accept the default account number.

5. Press **<Enter>** to skip the Unit Price field. Your cursor moves to the Tax field.

6. Press **<Enter>** to accept the default tax code. Your cursor moves to the Amount field.

7. Type **100** and press **<Enter>** two times. Notice the Sales/Invoicing window shows the two amounts entered for this invoice. The Invoice Total, including sales tax, is $158.95.

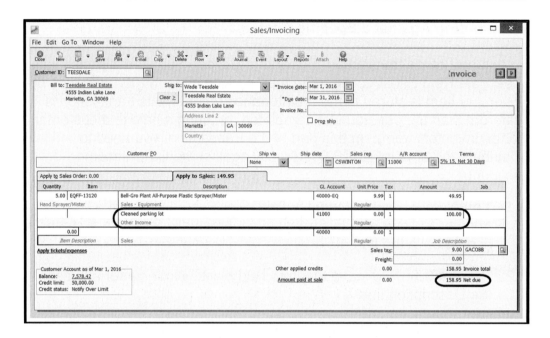

For purposes of this example, the cleaning service is taxed. In some states, services such as cleaning a parking lot would not be subject to sales tax.

Discount Information

In this chapter you changed the sales discount for Teesdale Real Estate. Let's check to make sure that the discount information is current for the invoice you just entered.

1. Link to Terms, <u>5% 15, Net 30 Days</u>. The Terms Information window appears. Since the Discount Amount was computed automatically on the items sold plus sales tax, the Discount Amount of 7.95 needs to be changed. In Sage 50, you can enter a different sales discount amount.

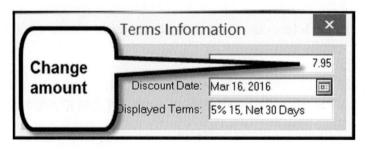

In this example, the sales discount is calculated on the amount of the items sold which is $149.95. (Refer to the Sales/Invoicing window on page 112.)

> Items sold: $49.95 + $100 = $149.95
> Times sales discount   .05
> **Discount Amount**   **$7.50**

2. Type **7.50** in the Discount Amount field, then press **<Enter>**.

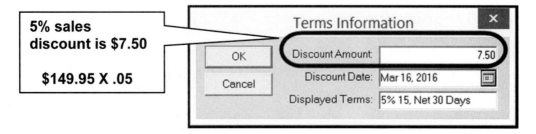

The Discount Date, March 16, 2016, is the date when the customer must pay to receive the discount. The Displayed Terms are the percentage of discount (5%), the time period in days for receiving the discount (15), and the number of days before the invoice is due (Net 30).

3. Click OK to close the Terms Information window.

POSTING THE INVOICE

The sample company, Bellwether Garden Supply, uses **_real-time posting_**. When real-time posting is used, the transactions that you enter are posted when you select the Save icon.

There is another type of posting. It is called **_batch posting_**. When using batch posting, the transactions you enter are saved to a temporary holding area where you can review them before posting to the general ledger. Follow these steps to save and post the invoice.

1. Click Save. The Sales/Invoicing window is ready for another transaction.
2. Close all windows.

PRINTING (OR DISPLAYING) INVOICES

Follow these steps to print the invoice for Teesdale Real Estate:

1. From the menu bar, select Reports & Forms > Forms > Invoices and Packing Slips.

2. Observe that the Form Types field shows Invoices and Packing Slips highlighted. In the Forms list, select Invoice.

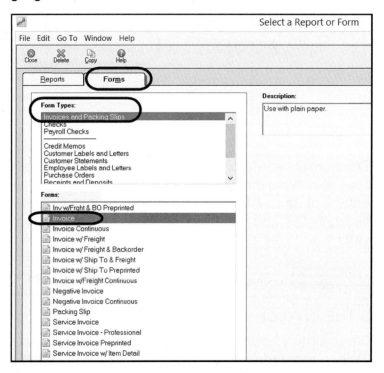

3. Double-click Invoice. The Preview and Print Invoices and Packing Slips window appears.

4. In the through field, type or select 3/1/16.

5. In the Filter customers by field select Teesdale in the ID and to fields.

6. Click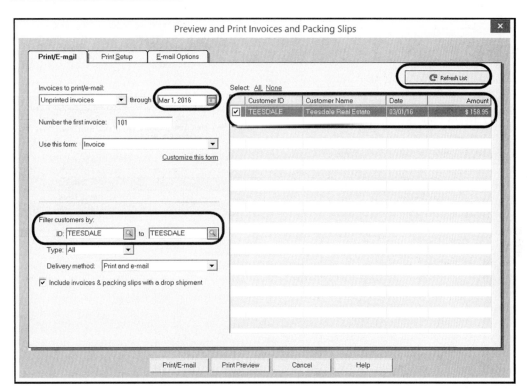

7. Select the E-mail Options tab. Select Print only a paper copy.

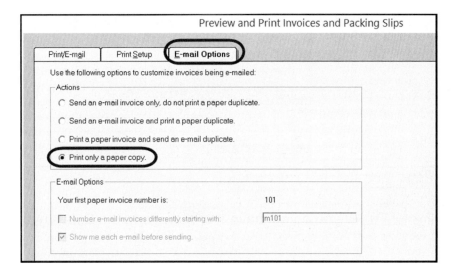

8. Click **Print Preview**. Compare Invoice 101 to the one shown.

Bellwether Garden Supply - Student Name
1505 Pavilion Place
Norcross, GA 30093-3203
USA

INVOICE

Invoice Number: 101
Invoice Date: Mar 1, 2016
Page: 1

Voice: 770-724-4000
Fax: 770-555-1234

Bill To:	Ship to:
Teesdale Real Estate 4555 Indian Lake Lane Marietta, GA 30069	Teesdale Real Estate 4555 Indian Lake Lane Marietta, GA 30069

Customer ID	Customer PO	Payment Terms	
TEESDALE		5% 15, Net 30 Days	
Sales Rep ID	**Shipping Method**	**Ship Date**	**Due Date**
CSWINTON	None		3/31/16

Quantity	Item	Description	Unit Price	Amount
5.00	EQFF-13120	Bell-Gro Plant All-Purpose Plastic Sprayer/Mister	9.99	49.95
		Cleaned parking lot		100.00

Subtotal		149.95
Sales Tax		9.00
Total Invoice Amount		158.95
Payment/Credit Applied		
TOTAL		**158.95**

Check/Credit Memo No:

9. Click [Print]. If you do <u>not</u> have a printer, go to the Sales/Invoicing window – close all windows > [Sales Invoices] > View and Edit Sales Invoices > double-click Invoice No. 101 > type **101** in the Invoice No. field > <u>S</u>ave.

> **Read Me:**
>
> When I try to print Invoice 101, a Sage 50 Accounting window appears that says There are no forms to preview. What should I do?
>
> 1. Click <OK>.
> 2. Close the Select a Report and Forms window.
> 3. On the Customers & Sales Navigation Center > select Sales Invoices > View and Edit Sales Invoices.
> 4. Double-click Teesdale, Invoice 101, to go to the Sales/Invoicing window.
> 5. Make the selections to Print from the Sales/Invoicing window. Compare Invoice 101 to the one shown above.
> 6. Close all windows.

Notice the Payment Terms are 5% 15, Net 30 Days. This is the information you entered for Customer Terms on pages 105-106.

10. A message displays asking if the invoice printed and emailed properly. When you answer Yes, Sage updates the invoice number and flags the invoice as printed so that it will not print again. Click .

11. Close all windows.

RECEIVE MONEY FROM CUSTOMER

Teesdale Real Estate has sent a check in payment of their invoice. Follow these steps to enter the following transaction.

Date   *Transaction Description*

03/15/16   Received Check No. 8818 from Teesdale Real Estate in payment of Invoice No. 101, $151.45. (*Hint:* The sales discount is applied to the items sold in the amount of $149.95. Refer to Discount Information, step 2, page 113.)

The customer payment is calculated like this:

Items sold:	$149.95
5% sales discount:	(7.50)
Sales tax:	9.00
Customer payment:	$151.45

1. From the Customers & Sales Navigation Center, click [Receive Money] >
    Receive Money from Customer. The Receive Money window
    appears.

    The Receive Money window is also the Cash Receipts Journal.
    There is a table in the lower half of the window that lists distribution
    lines for the current transaction. There is an icon bar at the top of
    the window. The item descriptions and account descriptions appear
    beneath each transaction line. The title bar identifies the window
    being used. In this case, the title bar says, Receive Money.

2. Your cursor is in the Deposit ticket ID field. Type **03/15/16** (the
    customer payment date). This Deposit ticket ID field defaults to the
    current date (today's date) and is used to combine receipts for bank
    reconciliation. Press **<Enter>**.

3. In the Customer ID field, type the Customer ID for Teesdale:
    TEESDALE and press **<Enter>**.

    When you enter a Customer ID, the window shows a list of invoices.
    When the customer is paying for invoiced amounts, you can select
    an invoice from the list. The invoice amounts, including discounts,
    complete the Apply to Invoices table.

4. Click on the Check/Reference No. field. Type **8818** for the
    customer's check number (a Reference number must be entered).
    Press **<Enter>** key two times and the cursor moves to the Date field.
    Type **15** (or select 15).

    This date is important because it is used to determine if a discount
    applies. For example, if the transaction date for the invoice was
    March 1, 2016, and the discount terms were 5% for 10 days, the
    customer payment entered for March 15, 2016 would miss qualifying
    for a discount. The discount amount is computed automatically and
    displays the discount when there is one.

5. The terms for Teesdale are 5% 15 days, Net 30. Since March 15, 2016 is within the discount period, accept the March 15, 2016 date. Press **<Enter>**. In the Payment method field, select Check. Press **<Enter>**.

6. If the Cash Account field does *not* show Account No. 10200, Regular Checking Account, select it. Press **<Enter>**.

7. If necessary, select the Apply to Invoices tab.

8. Click on the Pay box for Invoice 101.

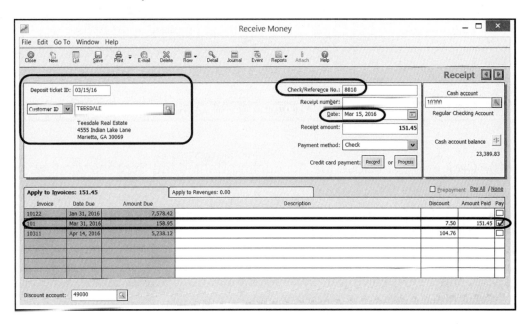

Notice that the Discount field displays the amount of the discount, $7.50. The discount displays because payment was received within the discount period (5%, 15 days). Therefore, the customer gets the 5% discount and the amount is automatically entered in the Discount field. Then, the check amount for the invoice is automatically computed: $151.45 (149.95 – 7.50 + 9.00 = $151.45). The Receipt amount in the check portion of the Receive Money window shows 151.45, Teesdale's invoice minus the 5% discount, plus sales tax.

9. Click [Journal] to see the account distribution in the Cash Receipts Journal.

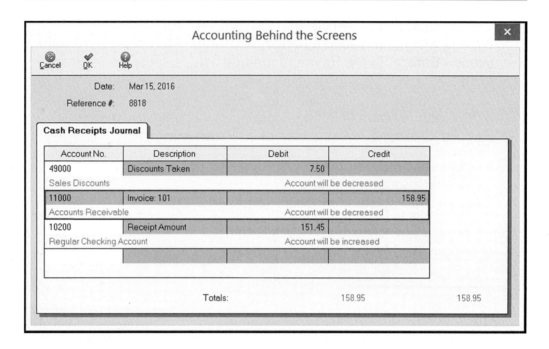

10. Click [OK] to close the Accounting Behind the Screens window.

11. Click [Save] and the customer payment is posted to the Cash Receipts Journal.

12. Close the Receive Money to return to Customers & Sales Navigation Center.

ANALYZING CUSTOMER PAYMENTS

How well does Bellwether Garden Supply manage its collections of payments from customers? To look at customers and aging amounts, use the Collection Manager. Follow these steps to learn how to use the Collection Manager:

1. From the menu bar, click Analysis > Collection Manager. The Collection Aging bar graph appears.

2. In the As of Date field, type or select 3/15/16.

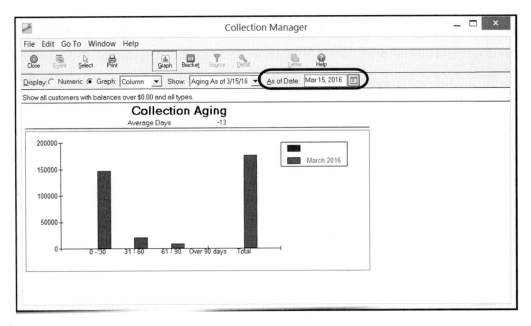

There are four aging brackets along the horizontal or X axis: 0 - 30 days, 31 - 60 days, 61 - 90 days, and over 90 days. The vertical or Y axis shows dollar amounts due.

3. Click 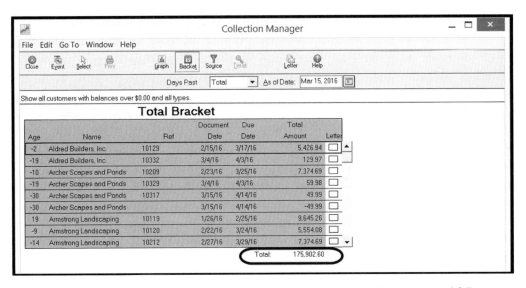 . The Total Bracket table is shown below.

The Total agrees with the Customer Ledgers total on page 125. The Collection Manager's Total Bracket window shows the age of the invoice in days, the customer name, the reference (Ref) number, the document date or transaction date, the due date, the total amount due, and whether a letter was sent.

4. Scroll down the window to highlight the invoice for Teesdale Real Estate (Age, -30; Ref, 10311; Amt Due, 5,238.12). Then, click

   [Source]. The Customer Detail window is shown below.

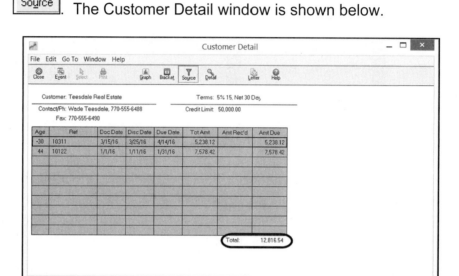

The Total agrees with Teesdale Real Estate's Customer Ledgers balance shown on page 125. At this level you can see all of Teesdale Real Estate's invoices. If you want to send a collection

letter you can do that from this window. By clicking [Letter] on the icon bar you can send a collection letter. (If you print a letter, Sage 50 defaults to a letter addressed to Thurman Golf Course Design.)

5. Click [Close] to exit the Collection Manager.

FINANCIAL MANAGER

The Financial Manager provides a brief, overall financial picture of how the business is performing. The business summary data includes *financial ratios*. These financial ratios are included.

- Cost of sales as a percentage of sales
- Gross profits as a percentage of sales

- Net income as a percentage of sales
- Return on total assets as a percentage
- Return on net worth as a percentage
- Current assets
- Current liabilities
- Current ratio
- Inventory turnover
- Days accounts receivable outstanding

Follow these steps to see the Financial Manager and the ratios that Sage 50 calculates.

1. From the Analysis menu > select Financial Manager. The defaults are March 31, 2016 and Business Summary. (If needed, type 033116 as the date.) The Financial Manager includes these sections: Operational Analysis, Resource Management, Profitability, and Working Capital. Financial ratios are included within each section.

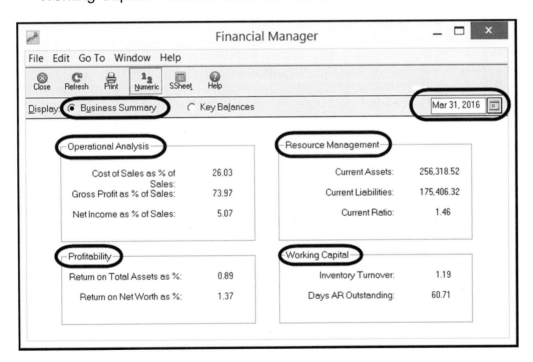

2. Review the ratios shown on the Financial Manager, then close all windows.

DISPLAYING THE CUSTOMER LEDGERS

Sage 50's accounts receivable system includes the customer ledgers. *Customer Ledgers* lists customers with detail transaction information including outstanding balances for each customer.

To display the Customer Ledgers, follow these steps.

1. From the Customers & Sales Navigation Center, link to <u>View All Customer & Sales Reports</u> in the Recently Used Customer Reports area. The Select a Report or Form window appears.

2. Double-click Customer Ledgers.

3. The Customer Ledgers report appears. Click Columns. The Customer Ledgers/Columns window appears. Select Customer Terms.

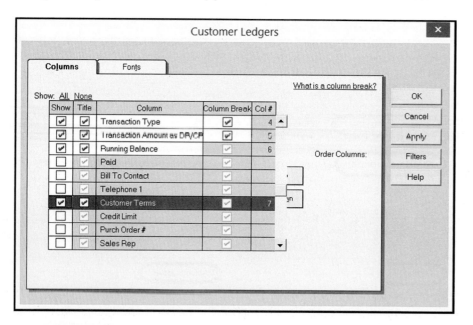

4. Click OK. A Terms column is added to the Customer Ledgers report. Scroll down the report to TEESDALE. Observe the terms are 5% 15, Net 30 Days and the account balance is $12,816.54. The Customer Detail window on page 122 shows the same balance.

```
                                                Bellwether Garden Supply - Student Name
                                                          Customer Ledgers
                                             For the Period From Mar 1, 2016 to Mar 31, 2016
Filter Criteria includes: Report order is by Name. Report is printed in Detail Format.
```

Customer ID Customer	Date	Trans No	Type	Debit Amt	Credit Amt	Balance	Terms
SNYDER Snyder Securities	3/1/16 3/4/16 3/13/16	Balance Fw 10334 CC0006	 SJ CRJ	 59.98 99.98	 99.98	2,981.04 3,041.02 3,041.02	2% 10, Net 30
STEVENSON Stevenson Leasing, Inc.	3/8/16 3/12/16	10318 10118	SJ SJ	49.99 7,790.42		49.99 7,840.41	2% 10, Net 30
TACOMA Tacoma Park Golf Course	3/1/16 3/14/16 3/15/16	Balance Fw 10322 10327	 SJ SJ	 49.99 1,049.01		4,675.57 4,725.56 5,774.57	2% 10, Net 30
TEESDALE Teesdale Real Estate	3/1/16 3/1/16 3/15/16 3/15/16 3/15/16	Balance Fw 101 10311 8818 8818	 SJ SJ CRJ CRJ	 158.95 5,238.12 7.50 	 7.50 158.95	7,578.42 7,737.37 12,975.49 12,975.49 12,816.54	5% 15, Net 30
THURMAN Thurman Golf Course Desig	3/1/16 3/15/16	Balance Fw 10343	 SJ	 9,998.00		3,610.39 13,608.39	2% 10, Net 30
TRENT Trent Bank and Trust		No Activity				0.00	2% 10, Net 30
WILLIAMS Williams Industries	3/3/16 3/3/16 3/15/16	4452 10312V 10312	CRJ SJ SJ	220.31 939.72	220.31 939.72 	0.00 -939.72 0.00	2% 10, Net 30
Report Total				**91,904.25**	**80,942.32**	**175,902.60**	

The Report Total, 175,902.60, agrees with the Total Bracket table's total on page 121, and Teesdale's Customer Detail total page 122.

CREDIT MEMOS

Credit Memos are issued to customers for returned merchandise or service refunds. Use the Credit Memos window to enter credit memos for customer returns and credits. You can apply credit memos to any existing sales invoice. All entries made on this window are posted to the General Ledger, customer records, if appropriate, and to inventory and job records.

The customer ledgers should be displayed on your screen. Scroll up the customer ledger to Saia's Neighborhood Nursery. Observe that Saia's Neighborhood Nursery has a customer credit memo (CCM4003) on 3/14/16.

Follow these steps to see how the credit was applied.

1. The customer ledgers should be displayed. Scroll up the Customer Ledgers window to Saia's Neighborhood Nursery.

2. Double-click on the 3/14/16 CCM4003 transaction to drill down to Credit memos window.

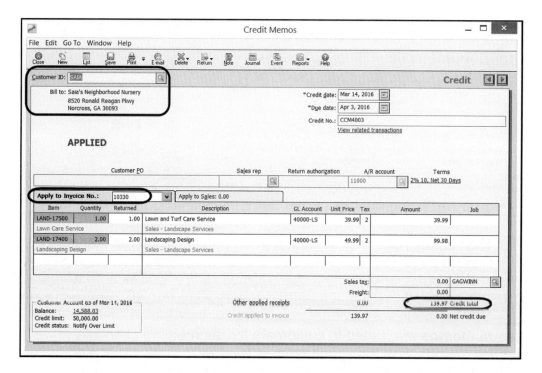

3. Observe that there is a $139.97 Credit total which was applied to Invoice No. 10330. Close the Credit Memos window. You are returned to the Customer Ledgers. The amount of the credit memo is subtracted from the Customer Ledger's balance forward amount: $14,728.00 − 139.97 = $14,588.03.

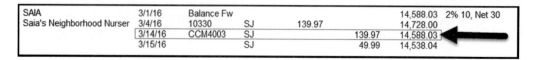

4. Close all windows.

BACKING UP CHAPTER 3 DATA

After completing the work within Chapter 3, back up. The suggested file name is **Chapter 3.ptb**. Detailed steps for backing up data are shown on pages 22-25.

Backing up saves your data to that point in your work. Each time you back up, use a different file name; for example, the suggested file name at this point is Chapter 3.ptb. (Sage 50 automatically adds the file extension .ptb to backups.) Using a unique file name allows you to restore at different points in the data.

ONLINE LEARNING CENTER

Complete the following end-of-chapter activities online at www.mhhe.com/yacht2016 > Student Edition > Chapter 3.

1. Interactive Multiple-Choice and True/False questions.
2. Going to the Net exercise: Access the Financial Accounting Standards Board (FASB) website.
3. Feature Quiz: Review of user interface and accounting principles that provide immediate feedback.
4. QA Templates: 10 short-answer questions and one analysis question.
5. Assessment Rubric: review journals, navigation centers, modules, and task windows.
6. Listen to narrated PowerPoint slides.

The OLC also includes links to the Appendixes:

- Appendix A: Troubleshooting
- Appendix B: Accounting Information Systems
- Appendix C: Review of Accounting Principles
- Appendix D: Glossary of Terms (words that are boldfaced and italicized in chapter)

Exercise 3-1: Follow the instructions below to complete Exercise 3-1.

1. Start Sage 50. Open Bellwether Garden Supply - Student Name [your first and last name].

2. If necessary, restore data from the end of Chapter 3. This backup was made on this page.

3. Record the following transaction.

Date	Transaction Description
03/03/16	Bellwether Garden Supply sold one Rotary Mower – Riding 4HP to Teesdale Real Estate, Invoice 102, $299.99; plus $18 sales tax; total, $317.99. (*Hint*: If you do <u>not</u> have a printer, type 102 in the Invoice No. field. Select the Apply to Sales tab. Type **1** in the Quantity field > select EQLW-14140 > Bell-Gro Riding Lawn Mower - 4HP as the Item.)

4. Print or post. (*Hint*: When you print from the Sales/Invoicing window, the sales invoice saves and posts. If you do <u>not</u> print, click <Save> to post to the Sales Journal.)

5. Continue with Exercise 3-2.

Exercise 3-2: Follow the instructions below to complete Exercise 3-2.

1. Record the following transaction:

Date	Transaction Description
03/15/16	Received Check No. 9915 in the amount of $302.99 from Teesdale Real Estate in payment of Invoice 102. (*Hint: Type **3/15/16** in the Deposit ticket ID field. Remember to use the check number in the Check/Reference field.* **IMPORTANT: Calculate the discount on the item sold. On the Receive Money window, type the appropriate amount in the Discount field.** *Do* not *include sales tax in the sales discount computation.*)

2. Post the customer payment.

   The 5% discount for Teesdale's 3/15/16 transactions is shown on the Cash Receipts Journal. From the menu bar, select Reports & Forms > Accounts Receivable > Cash Receipts Journal > Columns > GL Account Description > then <OK>. The Cash Receipts Journal displays with an Account Description column.

3. Print the Customer Ledgers. Add a Customer Terms column to the Customer Ledgers report. Adjust the columns so that the Terms for each customer prints on the same page.

If needed, on the Print window, select Adobe PDF or Microsoft XPS Document Writer as the printer. Refer to page 66, How to Fix. If you save as PDF file, use file name shown in step 6.

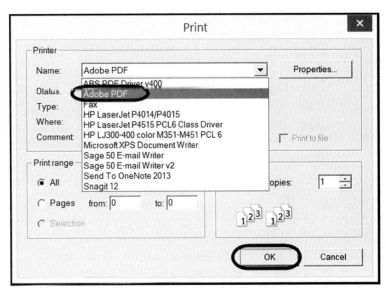

4. Back up Exercise 3-2. Use **Exercise 3-2.ptb** as the file name.

5. Export the Customer Ledgers to Excel. Use **Exercise 3-2_Customer Ledgers.xlsx** as the file name. (*Hint:* Refer to pages 44-46, Exporting Sage 50 Reports to Microsoft Excel. A Terms column should be included on the Customer Ledgers.)

6. Save the Customer Ledgers as PDF file. Use **Exercise 3-2_Customer Ledgers.pdf** as the file name.

   Check your figures: Customer Ledgers balance, $175,902.60.

7. Exit.

CHAPTER 3 INDEX

Chapter 4

Employees

LEARNING OBJECTIVES

1. Restore data from Exercise 3-2. (This backup was made on page 128.)
2. Enter and store information using the Maintain Employees/Sales Reps window.
3. Set up default information for payroll.
4. Store information about payroll payment methods.
5. Transfer funds from the regular checking account to the payroll checking account.
6. Enter paychecks in the Payroll Entry window.
7. Print employee paychecks.
8. Make two backups, save one Excel file, and save one PDF file.[1]

In Chapter 4 you learn how Sage 50 processes payroll. Once default and employee maintenance information is set up, payroll is a simple process.

The first step in setting up payroll is to go to the Employees & Payroll Navigation Center. Sage 50's Employees & Payroll Navigation Center displays information and access points related to the company's employees. It includes a summary of employee information including 1099 vendors and access to recently used employee reports.

On the left side of the Employees & Payroll Navigation Center, there is a workflow diagram showing employee and payroll tasks, represented by icons. The Employees & Payroll workflow diagram is shown on the next page.

---

[1]Refer to the chart on pages 2-3 for the size of backup files and saved Excel and PDF files.

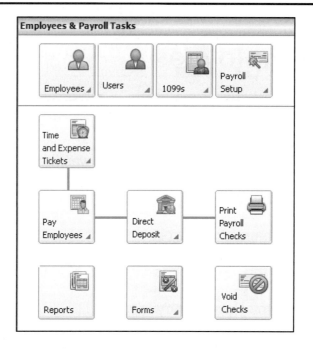

Click the icons to see menus that take you to various payroll-related tasks.

Sage 50's **employees and payroll system** is another example of the software's modular design. Sage 50's modules organize lists, transaction windows, and reports related to a specific Navigation Bar selection. In Chapter 2, Vendors, you used Sage 50's accounts payable system. In Chapter 3, Customers, you used Sage 50's accounts receivable system. In this chapter, you see how the payroll system is organized.

Another way to use Sage 50's modules is to select Tasks or Reports & Forms from the menu bar. For example, if you select Tasks from the menu bar, observe that selections for Payroll—Select for Payroll Entry and Payroll Entry—are listed together. If you select Reports & Forms from the menu bar, there is a selection for Payroll. Selections from the Tasks and Reports & Forms menus are also organized by module.

Some of the information that appears in the Employees & Payroll Navigation Center can be accessed with the drill down feature. Drill down is the act of following a path to its origin for further analysis. In certain Sage 50 reports, click on a transaction to drill down to the window that includes the original transaction information. From financial statements, you can drill down to the General Ledger report, and then use drill down again to see original transaction detail. You can also drill down to transaction detail from other Navigation Bar selections.

The diagram below describes the payroll process. These steps show how payroll accounting is set up.

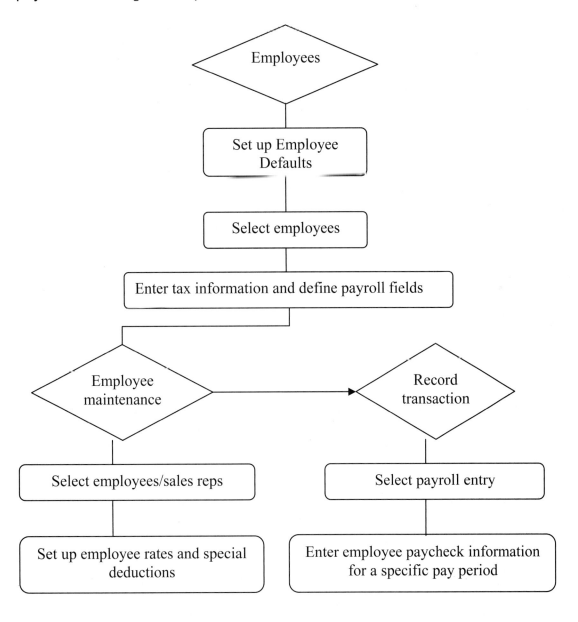

GETTING STARTED

Follow these steps to start:

1. Start Sage 50. Open Bellwether Garden Supply - Student Name [your first and last name].

   Troubleshooting: If Bellwether Garden Supply - Student Name does not open, or is not shown on the Company Name list, refer to the Read Me box on page 29 to review the steps to "Create a new company using the restored data." To see the window below, go to the startup window. Select Open an existing company. To make sure Bellwether is not listed, click [Browse]. Some schools delete company folders so you may need to restore. Go to step 2 below.

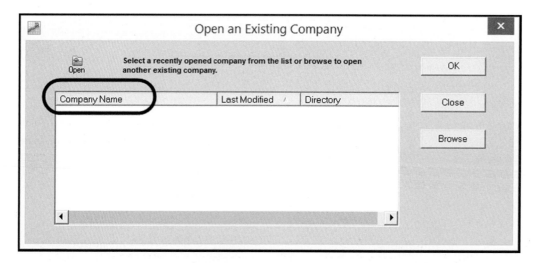

2. If necessary, restore data from the Exercise 3-2 back up. The Exercise 3-2.ptb backup was made on page 129. (*Hint:* To verify data, restore data periodically from your USB drive.)

   To make sure you are starting in the appropriate place in the data (Exercise 3-2.ptb backup) check the account balance for Teesdale Real Estate.

3. Go to the Customers & Sales Navigation Center. In the Recently Used Customer Reports area, link to View All Customer & Sales Reports. Double-click Customer Ledgers.

4. Scroll down to TEESDALE. The balance for Teesdale Real Estate is $12,816.54.

Bellwether Garden Supply - Student Name							
Customer Ledgers							
For the Period From Mar 1, 2016 to Mar 31, 2016							

Filter Criteria includes: Report order is by ID. Report is printed in Detail Format.

Customer ID Customer	Date	Trans No	Type	Debit Amt	Credit Amt	Balance
TEESDALE	3/1/16	Balance Fwd				7,578.42
Teesdale Real Estate	3/1/16	101	SJ	158.95		7,737.37
	3/3/16	102	SJ	317.99		8,055.36
	3/15/16	10311	SJ	5,238.12		13,293.48
	3/15/16	8818	CRJ	7.50	7.50	13,293.48
	3/15/16	8818	CRJ		158.95	13,134.53
	3/15/16	9915	CRJ	15.00	15.00	13,134.53
	3/15/16	9915	CRJ		317.99	12,816.54

5. Close all windows.

DEFAULT INFORMATION

In Sage, you can set up default information for your business. This information is important for payroll, customer receivables, and vendor payables. Bellwether Garden Supply already has the receivable and payable default information set up. Processing payroll is automatic once defaults are set up.

Follow these steps to set up payroll Default Information:

1. From the Navigation Bar > select  >

![Employees] > Set Up Employee Defaults. Compare your Employee Defaults window with the one on the next page.

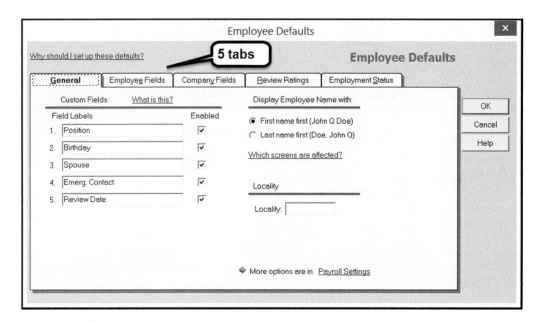

There are five tabs on the Employee Defaults window: General, Employee Fields, Company Fields, Review Ratings, Employment Status. You can set up a lot of information within these tabs. This will make your payroll processing almost automatic.

2. Click on the Employee Fields tab.

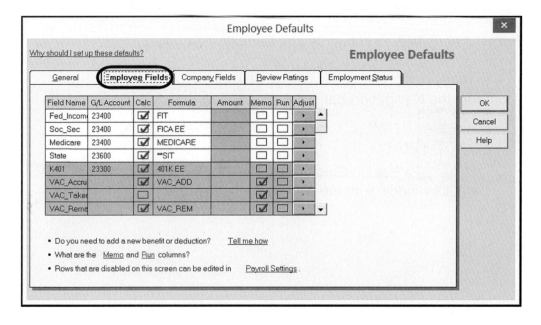

Notice that there are numerous items checked in the Calc column: Fed_Income (FIT), Soc_Sec (FICA EE), Medicare (MEDICARE), State (**SIT), K401 (401K EE), etc. (Scroll down to see the Field Name's complete list.) These fields work together with the payroll tax tables to calculate common employee deductions.

The check marks in the Calc and Memo columns indicate common deductions. Bellwether Garden Supply computes Federal Income Tax, Social Security, Medicare, State Income Taxes, 401K, and vacation deductions. These deductions are calculated according to the appropriate tax tables and formulas entered for payroll deductions, 401K's and vacation calculations.

The accounts affected by paychecks are liability accounts set up specifically to handle these kinds of deductions. Notice that the GL Account field shows the account numbers. All the accounts that are checked off are liability accounts. You can also set up voluntary deductions (called allowances). Voluntary allowances that are individually entered on the employee paycheck could include gas allowances, union dues, and savings bonds.

There is a Memo column with a place to put check marks for amounts that should not be posted to the company's books. The Memo check box is used when you want the employee record to show amounts not on the company's books. An example would be a restaurant business that needed to show employees' tips.

3. Click on the Company Fields tab. The Company Fields tab is for the employer's portion of Soc_Sec_ER (Social Security), Medicare_ER (Medicare), FUTA_ER (Federal Unemployment Tax Act) SUI_ER (State Unemployment Insurance), and K401_ER (401K contribution). The Employee Defaults/Company Fields window is shown on the next page.

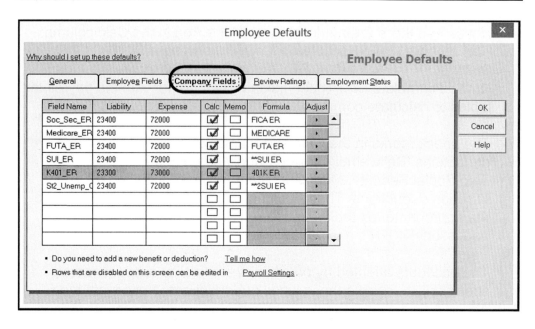

4. Click on the Review Ratings tab. You can add up to 10 performance ratings.

5. Click on the Employment Status tab. This shows different statuses for Bellwether's employees: Current Employee, Terminated, Leave of Absence, etc.

6. Select [OK] to return to the Employees & Payroll Navigation Center.

EMPLOYEE MAINTENANCE

When default information is completed, Sage sets guidelines for processing the company's payroll. On the Maintain Employees/Sales Reps window, information is entered for each employee.

1. From the Employees & Payroll Navigation Center > click > View and Edit Employees. The Employee List appears.

2. Double-click BNUNNLEY, Nunnley, Brandee. The Maintain
    Employees & Sales Reps window appears. Let's look at this
    employees' record. (*Hint:* In Chapter 15, you learn about Sage 50's
    payroll features in more detail.)

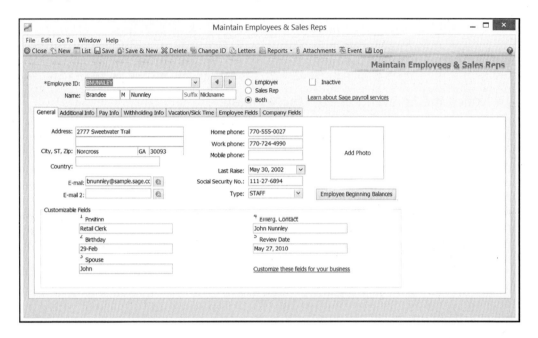

3. Click on the Pay Info tab.

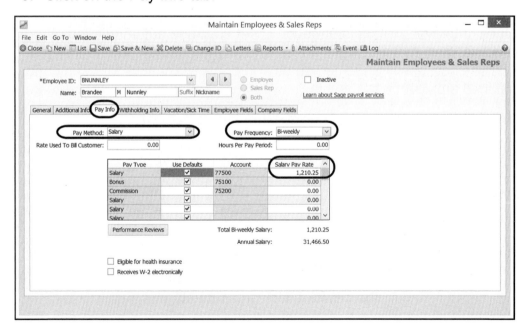

Observe that there is a Performance Reviews button. Select Performance Reviews to see if any information has been added for this employee. On page 136, the Employee Defaults window included a Review Ratings tab. When the Review Ratings tab is selected up to ten performance ratings can be set up. Click Close. You are returned to the Maintain Employees & Sales Reps window and the Pay Info tab is selected.

Notice the following about Ms. Nunnley:

a. She is paid a salary of $1,210.25.
b. She is paid bi-weekly (once every two weeks).

4. Click on the down-arrow in the Employee ID field.

5. Select employee **DCARTER** > **Drake V. Carter**. If necessary, select the Pay Info tab. Notice that Mr. Carter is paid an hourly wage of $9.00; overtime pay of $13.50; and special rate of $18.00. Observe that Mr. Carter is paid bi-weekly.

6. Close all windows.

PAYROLL SYSTEM

Once employee default information is set up, Sage automates the payroll process. Now that you have looked at Bellwether's payroll defaults, you can see how easily Sage computes and prints paychecks for hourly and salaried employees.

Transferring Cash to the Payroll Checking Account

Before making a payroll entry, you need to transfer $8,000 from Account No. 10200, Regular Checking Account; to Account No. 10300, the Payroll Checking Account. The following transaction is recorded in the general journal.

Date	Transaction Description
3/29/16	Transfer $8,000 from the regular checking account to the payroll checking account.

Follow these steps to record this transaction in the general journal.

1. From the Navigation Bar > select  >

   General Journal Entry > New General Journal Entry. (*Hint:* You can also link to General Journal Entry in the Shortcuts list.) The General Journal Entry window appears.

2. Select **29** as the date. Click on the Reference field. Type **Transfer** in the Reference field. Press the **<Enter>** key two times.

3. Your cursor is in the GL Account field. Select Account No. 10300, Payroll Checking Account (or you can type **10300**). Press **<Enter>**.

4. Your cursor should be in the Description field. Type **Payroll Checking Account** (or you can type a description) in the Description field. Press **<Enter>**.

5. Type **8000** in the Debit field. Press the **<Enter>** key three times to go to the Account No. field.

6. Your cursor should be in the GL Account field. Select Account No. 10200, Regular Checking Account. Press **<Enter>**.

7. Type **Regular Checking Account** in the Description field. Press the **<Enter>** key two times to go to the Credit field.

8. Your cursor is in the Credit field. Type **8000** in the Credit field. Press **<Enter>**. Observe that at the bottom of the General Journal Entry window, the Out of Balance field shows 0.00. This shows that debits equal credits, therefore, out of balance equals zero.

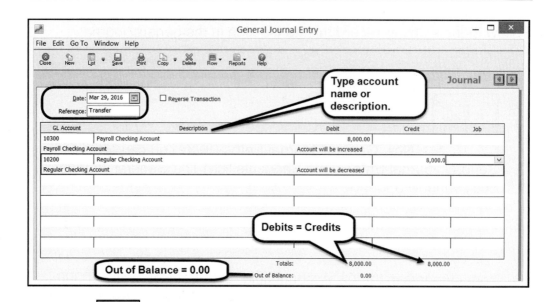

9. Click Save to post the entry to the general ledger.

10. Close the General Journal Entry window.

Payroll Entry for a Salaried Employee

In the next section you enter paychecks for these two employees: Brandee M. Nunnley and Drake V. Carter. When processing payroll checks, the information stored in Default Information and in the Maintain Employees file is important. Processing payroll is simple once you have set the defaults correctly.

Follow these steps to see how a paycheck for a salaried employee is done.

1. From the Navigation Bar > select **Employees & Payroll** >
    Pay Employees > Enter Payroll For One Employee. The Payroll Entry window appears.

2. In the Employee ID field, type **BN** for Brandee M. Nunnley and press **<Enter>**.

3. To print a check, leave the Check Num̱ber field blank by pressing **<Enter>**. If you type a check number and then print, Duplicate is printed on the check. (*Hint:* If you do <u>not</u> have a printer, type 1294 in the Check Number field.)

4. Type **29** in the Ḏate field, then press **<Enter>**. (*Remember you can also click on the Calendar icon* 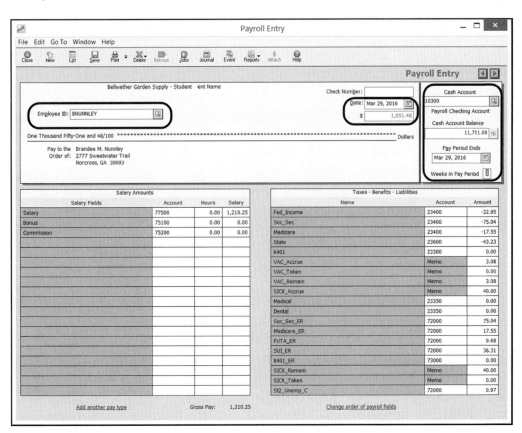 *and select 29. If necessary, enlarge the Payroll Entry window.*) Your cursor goes to the Cash Account field. This check will be charged against the Payroll Checking Account (Account No. 10300) which is displayed in the Cash Account field.

5. Press **<Enter>**. Your cursor is in the Pa̱y Period Ends field. Type **29** then press **<Enter>**. Your cursor goes to the Weeks in Pay Period box. The number 2 is displayed. Ms. Nunnley is on a bi-weekly pay period which means that Ms. Nunnley has two weeks in her pay period.

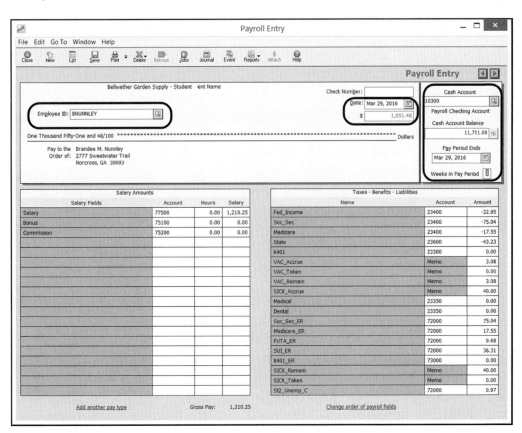

Notice that Brandee M. Nunnley has a Salary Amounts table that includes Salary, Bonus, and Commission. If necessary, these amounts can be adjusted. All of the Taxes - Benefits - Liabilities fields that were completed, which include Fed_ Income, Soc_Sec, Medicare and State tax, etc., have been calculated and display as negative amounts. They display as negative amounts because they decrease the check amount. The amounts shown as positive numbers are *not* deducted from the employee's check. Once payroll defaults and employees are set up, payroll processing is easy. Compare your Payroll Entry window for Brandee M. Nunnley to the one shown on the previous page.

Observe that the Cash Account Balance field on the upper right side of the Payroll Entry window shows 11,711.09. This is because the default is to recalculate the cash balance automatically for receipts, payments, and payroll entries. From the menu bar, select Options, Global, and notice that a check mark <✓> is placed next to the Recalculate cash balance automatically in the Receipts, Payments, and Payroll Entry field. If your balance field does *not* show an amount, then place a check mark in the recalculate cash balance automatically field. Also, notice that Ms. Nunnley's paycheck amount is $1,051.48.

6. Click [Save] to post this payroll entry.

Payroll Entry for an Hourly Employee

1. In the Employee ID field, click 🔍. Select Drake V. Carter. ((*Hint:* If you do not have a printer, type 1295 in the Check Number field.

2. If necessary, type **29** in the Date field and press **<Enter>** two times.

3. If necessary, type **29** in the Pay Period Ends field.

   Since Drake V. Carter is an hourly employee, the Hours Worked table lists his regular and overtime hours. If necessary, these categories can be adjusted.

4. To see how to adjust the hours that he worked, do the following: in the Hours Worked table, click on Overtime. The Overtime row is

highlighted. Make sure your cursor is in the Hours field. Type **3** and press **<Enter>**. Notice that the amounts in the Taxes - Benefits - Liabilities fields are automatically adjusted. The check amount also changed.

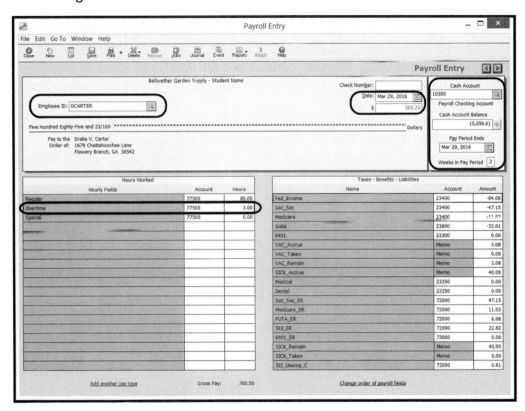

Observe that the Cash Account Balance field on the upper right side of the Payroll Entry window changed to 10,659.61. This is because the default for Sage 50 is to recalculate the cash balance automatically for receipts, payments, and payroll entries. (If your Cash Account Balance did *not* automatically recalculate, refer to Chapter 1, page 18 step 1d; Other Options area, Recalculate cash balance automatically in Receipts, Payments, and Payroll Entry should be *checked*.)

5. Select [Save] to post this paycheck. Close the Payroll Entry window.

Printing Payroll Checks

Similar to vendor disbursements, there is a choice: you may print each check as you enter it in the Payroll Entry window or you can print all the checks at once. Batch posting involves printing checks before posting. Real time posting allows you to print checks later. Since real-time posting is used with Bellwether, you print checks later. (You may also use the Preview icon to display checks instead of printing them.) Follow these steps to print the checks previously entered in the Payroll Entry window.

1. From the Recently Used Employee Reports area of the Employees & Payroll Navigation Center, link to <u>View All Employees & Payroll Reports</u>. The Select a Report or Form window appears. Observe that in the <u>R</u>eports list, Payroll is selected.

2. On the Select a Report or Form window, click on the For<u>m</u>s tab.

3. In the Form Types list, select Payroll Checks.

4. In the Forms list, double-click OCR Multi-Purpose PR Laser. The Preview and Print Payroll Checks window appears.

5. In the Include checks through field, select March 29, 2016.

6. Type **1294** in the Number the first check field.

7. In the Filter employees by field > select ID, Brandee M. Nunnley to Drake V. Carter.

8. Click [C Refresh List]. The two employee names, both check marked, appear in the table on the right side of the Preview and Print Payroll Checks window.

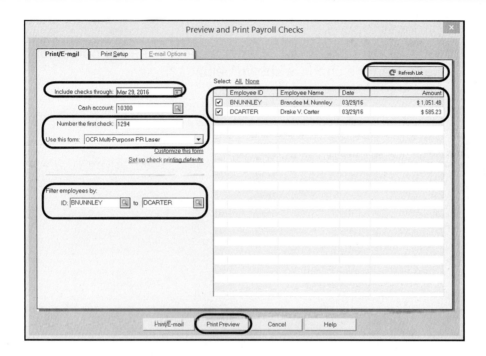

9. After clicking [Print Preview], the Print Preview window appears. The top portion of Brandee M. Nunnley's check is shown below.

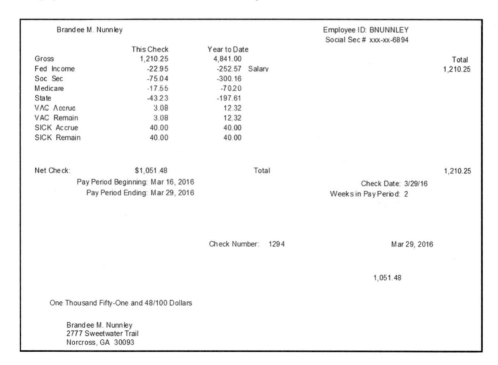

10. Click [Next] to see Drake V. Carter's check. The top portion of Drake V. Carter's check is shown below.

Drake V. Carter			Employee ID: DCARTER		
			Social Sec # xxx-xx-8990		
	This Check	Year to Date			
Gross	760.50	2,920.50	Hours	Rate	Total
Fed Income	-84.08	-362.21 Regular	80.00	9.00	720.00
Soc Sec	-47.15	-181.07 Overtime	3.00	13.50	40.50
Medicare	-11.03	-42.35			
State	-33.01	-124.75			
VAC Accrue	3.08	12.32			
VAC Remain	3.08	12.32			
SICK Accrue	40.00	40.00			
SICK Remain	40.00	40.00			
Net Check:	$585.23	Total	83.00		760.50

Pay Period Beginning: Mar 16, 2016   Check Date: 3/29/16
Pay Period Ending: Mar 29, 2016   Weeks in Pay Period: 2

Check Number: 1295   Mar 29, 2016

585.23

Five Hundred Eighty-Five and 23/100 Dollars

Drake V. Carter
1679 Chattahoochee Lane
Flowery Branch, GA 30542

11. Click [Print] to print Check Nos. 1294 and 1295. Observe that the employee statement information (also known as the pay stub) is printed first, then the check is printed.

If needed, on the Preview and Print Payroll Checks window, select the Printer Setup tab. In the Default Printer area, select Adobe PDF or Microsoft XPS Document Writer.

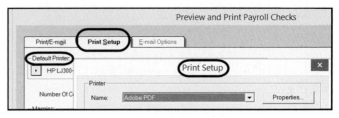

12. A window appears that says Did the Checks print properly and is it is OK to assign the check numbers to the checks? If your checks are correct, click [Yes].

13. Close the Select a Report or Form window to return to the Employees & Payroll Navigation Center.

> **Comment**
>
> In Chapter 15, Employees, Payroll, and Account Reconciliation, you learn how to set the defaults for the payroll accounts. Each employee and employer deduction will be set for individual liability accounts and expense accounts. The sample company is used as an example of automatic payroll processing but does *not* reflect correct payroll accounting procedures.

JOURNAL ENTRY FOR PAYROLL

What happens when you post payroll? In the most common case, the Cash Account that you entered in the Payroll Default window is automatically credited for the net paycheck amount when the payroll check is posted. The employee salary expense account is debited for the gross amount of the check and any deductions used are credited. The following table shows the payroll journal entry for the hourly employee, Drake V. Carter.

Account Description	Debit	Credit
Wages Expense (Regular Hours)	720.00	
Wages Expense (Overtime Hours)	40.50	
Federal Payroll Taxes Payable (Fed_Income)		84.08
Social Security (Soc_Sec for the Employee)		47.15
Medicare (Medicare for the Employee)		11.03
State Payroll Taxes Payable		33.01
Payroll Checking Account		585.23

BACKING UP CHAPTER 4 DATA

After completing the work within Chapter 4, back up. The suggested file name is **Chapter 4.ptb**. Detailed steps for backing up data are shown on pages 22-25.

Backing up saves data to that point in your work. Each time you back up, use a different file name; for example, the suggested file name at this point is Chapter 4.ptb. (Sage 50 automatically adds the file extension .ptb to backups.) Using a unique file name allows you to restore at different points in the data.

ONLINE LEARNING CENTER

Complete the following end-of-chapter activities online at
www.mhhe.com/yacht2016 > select the Student Edition > Chapter 4.

1. Interactive Multiple-Choice and True/False questions.
2. Going to the Net exercise: Access the All Accounting Careers website.
3. QA Templates: 10 short-answer questions and two analysis questions.
4. Assessment Rubric: Review journals, navigation centers, modules, and task windows.
5. Listen to narrated PowerPoint slides.

The OLC also includes links to the Appendixes:

- Appendix A: Troubleshooting
- Appendix B: Accounting Information Systems
- Appendix C: Review of Accounting Principles
- Appendix D: Glossary of Terms

Exercise 4-1: Follow the instructions below to complete Exercise 4-1:

1. Start Sage 50. Open Bellwether Garden Supply - Student Name [your first and last name].

2. If necessary, restore data from the end of Chapter 4. This back up was made on page 149.

3. Record the following transaction.

Date	Transaction Description
03/29/16	Record paycheck information for Brandon A. Hugley. Mr. Hugley worked 80 regular hours during this pay period. (If you do not have a printer, type 1296 in the Check No. field.)

4. Post the payroll entry.

5. Continue with Exercise 4-2.

Exercise 4-2: Follow the instructions below to complete Exercise 4-2:

1. Record the following transaction:

   Date   *Transaction Description*

   03/29/16   Record paycheck information for Derrick P. Gross.
                   Mr. Gross is a salaried employee. (If you do <u>not</u> have
                   a printer, type 1297 in the Check No. field.)

2. Post the payroll entry.

3. Print Check Nos. 1296 and 1297. (*Hint: Select OCR Multiple-Purpose PR Laser as the form. Type **3/29/16** in the Include checks through field. The Number the first check field should display 1296. If not, type 1296. Filter employees by Brandon A. Hugley to Derrick P. Gross.* Click [🔄 Refresh List] .)

   Not printing? Select Adobe PDF or Microsoft XPS Document Writer as the printer. Refer to page 66, How to Fix.

4. Print the Payroll Check Register. (*Hint*: In the Recently Used Employee Reports area of the Employees & Payroll Navigation Center, link to <u>Print</u> the Payroll Check Register. Accept the default for This Period.)

5. Close all windows. Back up Exercise 4-2. Use **Exercise 4-2** as the file name.

6. Export the Payroll Check Register to Excel. Use **Exercise 4-2_Payroll Check Register.xlsx** as the file name.

7. Save the Payroll Check Register as a PDF file. Use **Exercise 4-2_Payroll Check Register.pdf** as the file name.

   Check your figures: Payroll Check Register, 3/1/16 thru 3/31/16, $37,631.02

CHAPTER 4 INDEX

Chapter 5

General Ledger, Inventory, and Internal Control

LEARNING OBJECTIVES

1. Restore data from Exercise 4-2. (This backup was made on page 151.)
2. Use Sage 50's help feature.
3. Enter a new account in the Chart of Accounts.
4. Look at Sage 50's budget feature.
5. Record and post a General Journal entry to transfer funds.
6. Display the General Ledger Trial Balance.
7. Set up an Inventory Item.
8. Record an inventory adjustment.
9. Look at Sage 50's internal controls, user security and access, and audit trail.
10. Make two backups, save one Excel file, and save one PDF file.

In Chapter 5, the Bellwether's General Ledger Chart of Accounts is used. In Parts 2, 3, and 4 (Chapters 9-18 and Projects 1 through 4A), you create 12 new companies from scratch. The accounting cycle is completed in depth with service, merchandising, nonprofit, and manufacturing businesses.

When a new company is set up, the following initial steps are performed: set up a chart of accounts and enter beginning balances or budget amounts. After completing work with the sample companies (Chapters 1-8), you learn how to set up new companies (Chapters 9-18 and projects).

Chapter 5 also shows how to use the Inventory system. Sage 50 lets you track inventory items both at the purchasing and the sales level. When an inventory item is set up, the General Ledger accounts that are updated by purchases and sales are established. Sage 50 keeps track of cost of goods sold, stock levels, sales prices, and vendors. Sage 50 uses a *perpetual inventory* system. In a perpetual inventory system, an up-to-date record of inventory is maintained, recording each purchase and each sale as they occur.

Another Sage 50 feature is user security. On pages 178-186, Security and Internal Control, you look at how Sage 50 keeps company data secure.

GETTING STARTED

1. Start Sage 50. Open Bellwether Garden Supply - Student Name [your first and last name]. (If Bellwether Garden Supply is not shown, Restore data to Create a new company using the restored data. Refer to the Read Me box on page 29.)

2. Restore data from the Exercise 4-2 backup. This back was completed on page 151, step 5. The steps that follow review the steps for restoring the backup file.

    a. Insert your USB flash drive. From the Navigation Bar > select

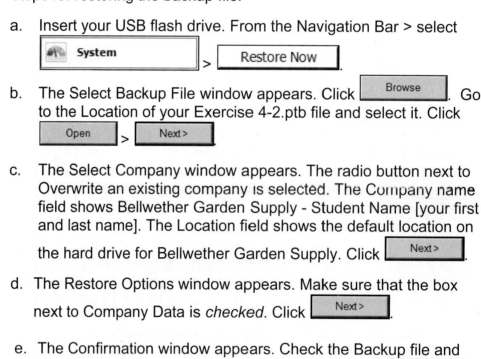

    b. The Select Backup File window appears. Click [Browse]. Go to the Location of your Exercise 4-2.ptb file and select it. Click [Open] > [Next >]

    c. The Select Company window appears. The radio button next to Overwrite an existing company is selected. The Company name field shows Bellwether Garden Supply - Student Name [your first and last name]. The Location field shows the default location on the hard drive for Bellwether Garden Supply. Click [Next >].

    d. The Restore Options window appears. Make sure that the box next to Company Data is *checked*. Click [Next >].

    e. The Confirmation window appears. Check the Backup file and Location fields to make sure they are correct. Click [Finish]. When the window prompts "This process will overwrite....", click [Yes]. When the Restore Company scale is 100% complete, your data is restored. (*Hint:* The Student Version of Sage 50 prompts that company data can be used for 14 months.

After that time the data expires. Click [OK]. Bellwether Garden Supply opens.)

💾 To make sure you are starting in the appropriate place in the data (Exercise 4-2.ptb backup) check the Payroll Check Register. View the Payroll Check Register from the Employee's & Payroll Navigation Center. Make sure Check Nos. 1294-1297 are listed. A partial Payroll Check Register is shown below.

Bellwether Garden Supply - Student Name
Payroll Check Register
For the Period From Mar 1, 2016 to Mar 31, 2016
Filter Criteria includes: Report order is by Check Date. Report is printed in Detail Format.

Reference	Date	Employee	Amount
1281	3/15/16	Mitchell K. Trotter	681.40
1282	3/15/16	Michelle Y. Wagner	612.75
1283	3/15/16	Nola I. Bigalow	787.54
1284	3/15/16	Ray J. Mosley	740.47
1285	3/15/16	Raffaello M. Saulny	770.44
1286	3/15/16	Steve N. Barkley	694.03
1287	3/15/16	Susan T. Prichard	559.22
1288	3/15/16	Samuel R. Prather	1,148.62
1289	3/15/16	Thatcher G. Leverne	759.00
1290	3/15/16	Tim O. Maske	1,380.01
1291	3/15/16	Tyler F. Riddell	756.11
1292	3/15/16	Virginia L. Ansell	965.72
1293	3/15/16	Vincent O. Kilborune	759.00
1294	3/29/16	Brandee M. Nunnley	1,051.48
1295	3/29/16	Drake V. Carter	585.23
1296	3/29/16	Brandon A. Hugley	650.25
1297	3/29/16	Derrick P. Gross	1,058.87
	3/1/16 thru 3/31/16		37,631.02
	3/1/16 thru 3/31/16		37,631.02

➤ **Troubleshooting:** My Payroll Check Register does *not* agree. Make sure you completed paychecks 1294 through 1297 in Chapter 4, pages 142-151. You should also check the 3/29/16 transfer, pages 141-142. To display the General Journal, select Reports & Forms > General Ledger > General Journal.

Bellwether Garden Supply - Student Name
General Journal
For the Period From Mar 1, 2016 to Mar 31, 2016

Filter Criteria includes: Report order is by Date. Report is printed with Accounts having Zero Amounts and with shortened descriptions and in Detail Format.

Date	Account I	Reference	Trans Description	Debit Amt	Credit Amt
3/29/16	10300	Transfer	Payroll Checking Account	8,000.00	
	10200		Regular Checking Account		8,000.00

3. Close all windows.

SAGE 50 HELP: CHART OF ACCOUNTS

The chart of accounts is a list of all the accounts used by a company showing the identifying number assigned to each account. Sage 50 includes over 75 sample Charts of Accounts. A Chart of Accounts can be set up from scratch or you can select an industry-specific simplified or extensive Chart of Accounts.

To see the sample Charts of Accounts, follow these steps:

1. From the menu bar, click Help > then Help. The Sage 50 Help window appears. Sage 50 Help topics are displayed in the *HTML* (Hypertext Markup Language).

2. Click on the Contents tab > then the plus signs (+) next to Getting Started > Initial Decisions > Your chart of accounts > link to View the chart of accounts for over 75 sample companies.

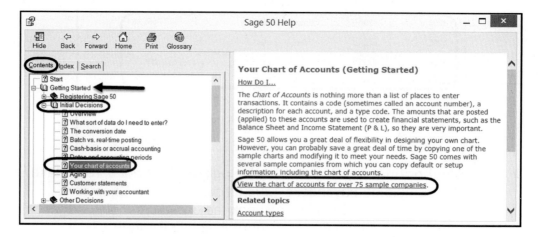

3. The right pane shows sample charts of accounts by industry.

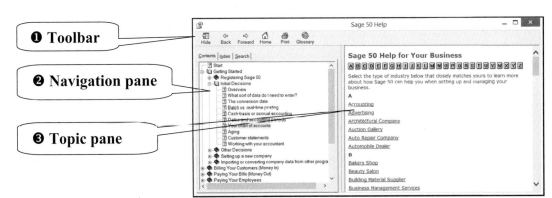

Observe that there are three panes on the Sage 50 Help window:

❶ Toolbar is located below the Sage 50 Help title bar. The toolbar appears on individual windows and contains buttons that let you perform certain functions within that window.

❷ On the left side of the window is the Navigation pane. It contains three tabs: Contents, Index, and Search. Use the Navigation pane to browse or search for topics.

❸ On the right side of the window is the Topic pane. The topic pane displays each Help topic or Web page selected in the Navigation pane. In this example, the topic pane shows charts of accounts by industry.

4. In the list of sample charts of accounts, click Accounting. The Accounting Agency window appears. Scroll down the window. In the What do you want to do next? area, click Display a sample chart of accounts for this type of business. A sample chart of accounts for an Accounting Company appears.

5. Click ![X] on the Sage 50 Help title bar to close the Help window.

ADD AN ACCOUNT TO THE CHART OF ACCOUNTS

1. From the Navigation Bar, select ▥ **Banking** > Chart of Accounts
   > New Account. The Maintain Chart of Accounts window appears.

2. To add a new Money Market account, do this:

   a. In the Account ID field, type **10500** and press **<Enter>**
   b. Your cursor is in the Description field. Type the name of the
      account **Money Market Fund**, and press **<Enter>**.

   c. Your cursor is in the Account Type field. There is a drop-down list
      indicated by a down arrow. The default Account Type is Cash.

      *Account Type: Cash ▼. In the Account Type field
      specify the kind of account you are creating; for example, Cash,
      Cost of Sales, Equity-doesn't close, Equity-gets closed, etc. Select
      the drop-down list by clicking on the down arrow in the Account
      Type field to display the list of available account types.

      Make sure **Cash** is highlighted and press **<Enter>**. *The Account
      Type is important; it sorts each account for the financial statements.*
      Compare your Maintain Chart of Accounts window to the one
      shown below. (The top portion of the Maintain Chart of Accounts
      window is shown.)

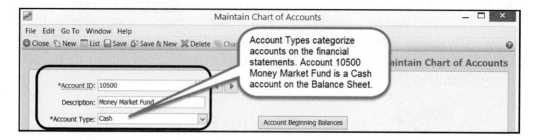

      Remember to check the Account Type field. The selection made
      in the Account Type field classifies accounts on the financial
      statements.

3. Click ![Save] then close the Maintain Chart of Accounts window.

BUDGETS

Bellwether Garden Supply already has a budget set up. To see Bellwether's budget, do the following.

1. From the Navigation Bar, select ![Banking] > ![Analysis Tools] > View and Edit Budgets.

2. The Maintain Budgets window appears. Observe that the Maintain Budgets window shows an icon bar with an Excel icon—![Excel]. Most Sage 50 reports can be exported to Excel.

The Maintain Budgets window defaults to Income Statement Accounts. This is shown in the Account Filters/Type field –

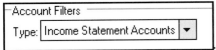

The Maintain Budgets window lets you build a forecast of dollar amounts for selected accounts for each fiscal period. You can filter the accounts you budget by account type (income statement accounts, expenses, etc.). For example, the amount budgeted to Account No. 40000-AV, Sales - Aviary for 3/31/16 is $7,000.00. Let's look at the Income Statement to see how close that amount was to the actual sales for Account No. 40000-AV, Sales - Aviary. (*Hint:* The Total column shows the accumulated total for 1/31/16 through 12/31/16.) A partial Maintain Budgets window is shown on the next page.

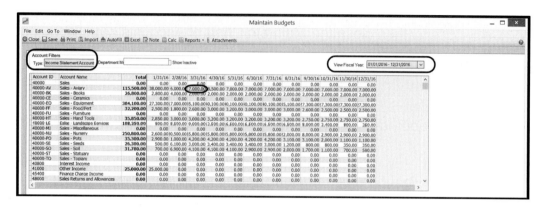

To compare the March 31, 2016 budgeted amount for Account No. 40000, Sales-Aviary to the actual amount, display the <Standard> Income/Budget report.

1. Minimize the Maintain Budgets window.

2. From the menu bar, select Reports & Forms > Financial Statements > then <Standard> Income/Budget.

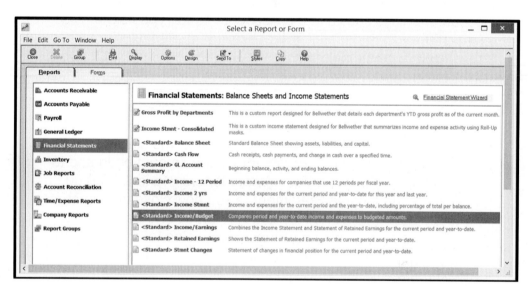

3. Click [Display]. The <Standard> Income/Budget window appears. Observe that the title of the report shows Income Statement, Compared with Budget. Observe that Sales - Aviary for the Current Month Actual is 7,127.71. The Current Month Budget shows 7,000.00.

The Total Revenues section is shown. Current Month Actual, Budget and Variance; and Year to Date Actual, Budget, and Variance are also shown.

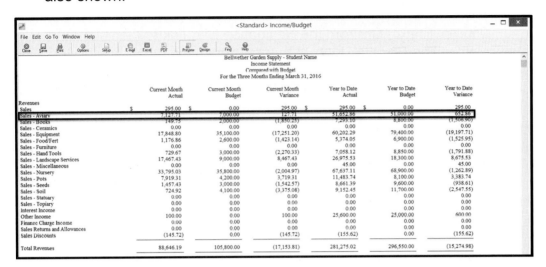

What does the Income/Budget report show? For the Current Month, March 31, 2016, the budgeted amount of $7,000 was exceeded by the actual sales amount of $7,127.71 for Sales-Aviary. The current month variance is 127.71—sales exceeded the budget by that amount. Amounts shown in parentheses indicate that sales were lower than budgeted amounts.

4. Close all windows.

GENERAL JOURNAL

To open the Money Market Fund, transfer $4,500 from Bellwether's regular checking account to Account No. 10500, Money Market Fund. Also, transfer $1,000 from Bellwether's regular checking account to the payroll checking account (10300, Payroll Checking Account). The transfer of funds is recorded in the General Journal, and then posted to the General Ledger.

Date	Transaction Description
03/15/16	Transfer $4,500 to the Money Market Fund and $1,000 to the Payroll Checking Account from the Regular Checking Account.

The transfer is shown on the next two pages.

1. From the Banking Navigation Center, select [General Journal Entry] > New General Journal Entry. (*Or,* from the Navigation Bar, link to General Journal Entry.) The General Journal Entry window appears.

2. In the <u>D</u>ate field, type **3/15/16** or select the day. Press **<Enter>**.

3. Your cursor is in the Refere<u>n</u>ce field. Type **Transfer** and press **<Enter>** two times.

4. Your cursor is in the GL Account field. Type the account number for the Money Market Fund account, **10500**, and press the **<Enter>** or **<Tab>**. Observe that Money Market Fund appears below the account number.

5. Type **Money Market Fund** in the Description field. In this textbook, the account name is used as the description. You may prefer to type a description instead; for example, Established money market account. When a description is typed, it will repeat automatically on each Description line. Press **<Enter>** or **<Tab>** to go to the Debit field.

6. You are going to increase this account by $4,500. Type a debit amount of **4500** and press **<Enter>** three times. (It doesn't matter whether you type the debit or credit part of the entry first.) Notice that the Totals field displays 4,500.00 below the Debit column. The Out of Balance amount beneath it totals 4,500.00.

7. Your cursor is in the Account No. field. Type **10300** and press **<Enter>**. Payroll Checking Account displays on the line below the account number. Type **Payroll Checking Account** in the Description field. Press **<Enter>** to go to the Debit field.

8. Type **1000** in the Debit field. Press **<Enter>** three times.

9. Your cursor is in the Account No. field. Type **10200** > press **<Enter>**. Type **Regular Checking Account** in the Description field. Press **<Enter>** two times to go to the Credit field.

10. Type **5500** in the Credit field > press **<Enter>**. Notice that the Totals field beneath the Credit column displays 5,500.00. The Out of Balance amount equals zero (0.00). This means that the General Journal is in balance and can be posted.

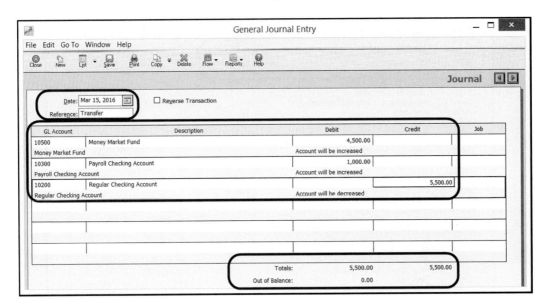

11. Click ![Save] to post to the General Ledger. Close the General Journal Entry window.

To check that the account   transfers have been made, follow these steps:

1. From the menu bar, select Reports & Forms > General Ledger. The Select a Report or Form window displays.

2. In the General Ledger: Account Information List > double-click General Ledger Trial Balance. The General Ledger Trial Balance is shown on the next two pages.

Bellwether Garden Supply - Student Name
General Ledger Trial Balance
As of Mar 31, 2016

Filter Criteria includes: Report order is by ID. Report is printed in Detail Format.

Account I	Account Description	Debit Amt	Credit Amt
10000	Petty Cash	327.55	
10100	Cash on Hand	1,850.45	
10200	Regular Checking Account	10,246.52	
10300	Payroll Checking Account	9,365.26	
10400	Savings Account	7,500.00	
10500	Money Market Fund	4,500.00	
11000	Accounts Receivable	175,775.05	
11400	Other Receivables	7,681.84	
11500	Allowance for Doubtful Account		5,000.00
12000	Inventory	12,547.11	
14000	Prepaid Expenses	14,221.30	
14100	Employee Advances	3,000.65	
14200	Notes Receivable-Current	11,000.00	
14700	Other Current Assets	120.00	
15000	Furniture and Fixtures	62,769.25	
15100	Equipment	38,738.33	
15200	Vehicles	86,273.40	
15300	Other Depreciable Property	6,200.96	
15500	Buildings	185,500.00	
15600	Building Improvements	26,500.00	
17000	Accum. Depreciation-Furniture		54,680.57
17100	Accum. Depreciation-Equipment		33,138.11
17200	Accum. Depreciation-Vehicles		51,585.26
17300	Accum. Depreciation-Other		3,788.84
17500	Accum. Depreciation-Buildings		34,483.97
17600	Accum. Depreciation-Bldg Imp		4,926.28
19000	Deposits	15,000.00	
19100	Organization Costs	4,995.10	
19150	Accum Amortiz - Organiz Costs		2,000.00
19200	Notes Receivable- Noncurrent	5,004.90	
19900	Other Noncurrent Assets	3,333.00	
20000	Accounts Payable		80,626.01
23000	Accrued Expenses		3,022.55
23100	Sales Tax Payable		18,067.08
23200	Wages Payable		2,320.30
23300	401 K Deductions Payable		2,490.32
23350	Health Insurance Payable	530.64	
23400	Federal Payroll Taxes Payable		41,791.17
23500	FUTA Tax Payable		258.20
23600	State Payroll Taxes Payable		6,857.05
23700	SUTA Tax Payable		658.67
23800	Local Payroll Taxes Payable		113.25
23900	Income Taxes Payable		11,045.75
24000	Other Taxes Payable		2,640.15
24100	Current Portion Long-Term Debt		5,167.00
24300	Contracts Payable- Current		2,000.00
24700	Other Current Liabilities		54.00
27000	Notes Payable-Noncurrent		4,000.00
39003	Common Stock		5,000.00
39004	Paid-in Capital		100,000.00
39005	Retained Earnings		189,037.60
40000	Sales		295.00
40000-AV	Sales - Aviary		51,652.86
40000-BK	Sales - Books		7,293.10
40000-EQ	Sales - Equipment		60,202.29
40000-FF	Sales - Food/Fert		5,374.05
40000-HT	Sales - Hand Tools		7,058.12
40000-LS	Sales - Landscape Services		26,975.53
40000-MI	Sales - Miscellaneous		45.00
40000-NU	Sales - Nursery		67,637.11
40000-PO	Sales - Pots		11,483.74
40000-SE	Sales - Seeds		8,661.39
40000-SO	Sales - Soil		9,152.45
41000	Other Income		25,600.00
49000	Sales Discounts	155.62	
50000	Product Cost		68.50

Bellwether Garden Supply - Student Name
General Ledger Trial Balance
As of Mar 31, 2016

Filter Criteria includes: Report order is by ID. Report is printed in Detail Format.

Account I	Account Description	Debit Amt	Credit Amt
50000-AV	Product Cost - Aviary	20,821.45	
50000-BK	Product Cost - Books	2,361.37	
50000-EQ	Product Cost - Equipment	24,154.95	
50000-FF	Product Cost - Food/Fert	2,127.54	
50000-HT	Product Cost - Hand Tools	2,813.85	
50000-PO	Product Cost - Pots	3,423.60	
50000-SE	Product Cost - Seeds	3,450.65	
50000-SO	Product Cost - Soil	4,075.97	
57000-NU	Direct Labor - Nursery	3,062.50	
57200	Materials Cost	1,397.45	
57200-NU	Materials Cost - Nursery	9,668.50	
57300-LS	Subcontractors - Landscaping	335.50	
57500	Freight	50.00	
60000	Advertising Expense	1,325.00	
61000	Auto Expenses	274.56	
61500	Bad Debt Expense	1,341.09	
62000	Bank Charges	18.00	
64000	Depreciation Expense	8,394.00	
68500	Legal and Professional Expense	510.00	
69000	Licenses Expense	150.00	
70000	Maintenance Expense	75.00	
71000	Office Expense	534.64	
72000	Payroll Tax Exp	15,857.60	
74000	Rent or Lease Expense	1,100.00	
74500	Repairs Expense	3,694.00	
75500	Supplies Expense	2,873.42	
77000	Utilities Expense	303.45	
77500	Wages Expense	138,465.46	
89000	Other Expense	464.90	
89500	Purchase Disc- Expense Items		10.11
	Total:	**946,261.38**	**946,261.38**

On page 164, Account No. 10200, Regular Checking Account, has a debit balance of $10,246.52; Account No. 10300, Payroll Checking Account, has a debit balance of $9,365.26; and Account No. 10500, Money Market Fund, has a debit balance of $4,500.00. This shows that the General Journal entry that you completed is posted correctly. To see the rest of the General Ledger Trial Balance, scroll down the General Ledger Trial Balance window.

3. Close all windows.

> **How to fix?** What if an account balance does <u>not</u> agree with the General Ledger Trial Balance shown on pages 164-165? Suggestions follow.
>
> - Determine the difference in the amounts. Is the difference the amount of an entry? Refer to Audit Trail report on page 185. For example, display the Audit Trail for the month(s)/year you have been completing work.
> - Did you record an entry twice? For example, display the general journal. If you recorded an entry twice, drill down to the original entry, then select
>
>   to remove the entry. (*Hint:* To check if you duplicated an entry, you could also display the Customer and Vendor Ledgers.)
> - Did you forget to record an entry? Both work within the chapter and the exercises should be completed.
> - If needed, restore an earlier backup file and then continue from that point. Refer to the chart on pages 2-3 for the backups made in Chapters 1-5.

SETTING UP AN INVENTORY ITEM

This part of Chapter 5 explains the Inventory system. The sample company, Bellwether Garden Supply, has decided to track cleaning supplies as stock inventory items and to bill clients for supplies used. First, you need to enter the cleaning supplies they stock as Inventory Items.

Sage 50's Inventory & Services Navigation Center shows Sage 50's **Inventory System**, another module within the software. The Navigation Bar's selection displays information and access points related to the company's inventory items. It includes a summary of item information, access to recently used inventory reports, and a graphic analysis of how the cost of sales is trending. In addition, the Inventory & Services Navigation Center shows the flow of inventory-related tasks and takes you where you need to go to perform those tasks. Observe that drill down links are also available. If necessary, scroll down and across the Inventory & Services Navigation Center window to see all the areas.

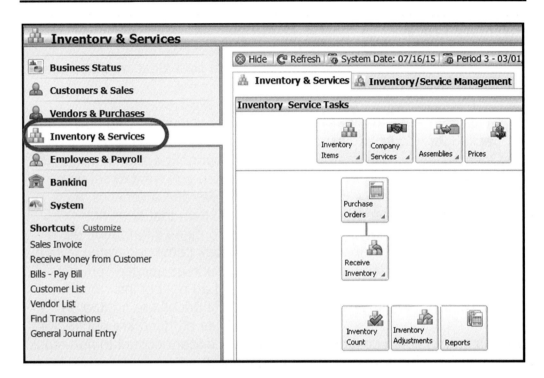

The Inventory & Services Navigation Center also includes an Inventory/ Service Management tab. The Inventory and Service Management selection is a dashboard that allows you to quickly find and view information about inventory and service items. This helps you do research, make comparisons, and make decisions regarding the items sold and the services offered by the business.

Follow these steps to set up an Inventory Item:

1. From the Inventory & Services Navigation Center, select 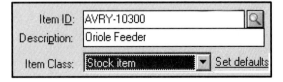 > New Inventory Item. The Maintain Inventory Items window displays.

2. In the Item I**D** field, type **AVRY-10300** — the first four characters should be in uppercase and press **<Enter>**.

3. In the Descri**p**tion field, type **Oriole Feeder** and press **<Enter>**.

Item I**D**:	AVRY-10300	🔍
Description:	Oriole Feeder	
Item Class:	Stock item ▼	Set defaults

4. In the Item Class field, select Stock item.

Inventory Types

If you click on the down-arrow next to the Item field, observe that there are several types of Inventory Items:

➤ Stock item: Use this item class for traditional inventory items that are tracked for quantities, average costs, vendors, low stock points, etc. Once an item is assigned to this class, it cannot be changed.

➤ Master Stock Item: Use this item class when you want to set up a group of related stock items that have similar characteristics or attributes. A master stock item is a special item that does not represent inventory you stock but rather contains information (item attributes) shared with a number of substock items generated from it.

➤ Non-stock item: Use this class for items, such as service contracts and office supplies that you buy or sell but do not put into your inventory. Quantities, descriptions, and unit prices are printed on invoices and purchase orders, but quantities on hand are not tracked. You can assign a cost of goods General Ledger account to non-stock items, but it is not affected by a costing method.

➤ Description only: Use this item class when nothing is tracked except the description. For example, "comments" that can be added to sales or purchase transactions are description-only items.

➤ Service: Use this item class for services you perform and sell, such as monthly maintenance work. You can enter a cost for the service, which would include your employee's wage, overhead, materials, and such used in the course of performing the service.

➤ Labor: Use this item class for labor that is part of an assembly item or for outside labor that you use for projects; you can enter a cost for the service. In the case of assembly items, this labor will become part of the cost of goods for the assembled item.

➤ Assembly: Use this class for items that consist of components that can be built or dismantled. For each assembly item, select the Bill of Materials tab, and define the components of the assembly before you click the Save button on the Maintain Inventory Items window. Once a transaction uses an assembly, it cannot be changed.

➤ Activity item: Use this item class for different types of work that are performed for a customer or job. These are very useful for professional businesses, such as law firms, that want to track employee time for a customer and job and then bill the customer. Activity items are used in Time & Billing and are recorded on employee or vendor time tickets.

> Charge item: Use this item class to identify items that are expenses recorded by an employee or vendor when various services are performed for a customer or job. Charge items are used in Time & Billing and are recorded on employee or vendor expense tickets. Use charge items when you plan on billing customers for reimbursable expenses, such as parking fees, mileage, and so on.

Follow these steps to continue setting up an Inventory Item:

1. If necessary, press the **<Enter>** key to go to the Description field. Type **Oriole Feeder** and press **<Enter>**.

2. Your cursor is in the Price Level 1 field. Click on the right arrow button [Price Level 1: 0.00 ▸] in this field. The Multiple Price Levels window appears. In the Price Level 1 row > click on the Price field > type **15** on the Price Level 1 row > press **<Enter>**. You can set up ten different sales prices per item.

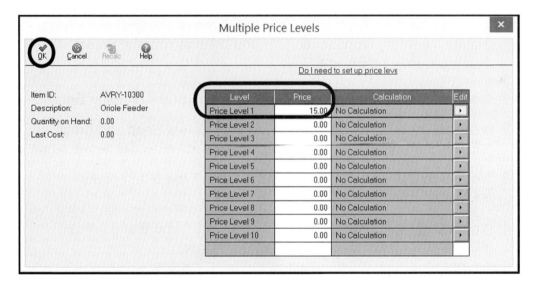

3. After clicking [✔ OK], close the Multiple Price Levels window. The Price Level 1 field shows 15.00.

4. Click on the Last Unit Cost field. Type **7** and press **<Enter>**. (*Hint:* Delete 0.00 in the Last Unit Cost field, then type 7.)

5. Observe that the Cost Method is FIFO. Sage 50 includes three inventory cost methods: FIFO, LIFO and Average. Press **<Enter>**.

6. Your cursor is in the GL Sales Account field. Click 🔍, then select Account No. 40000-AV, Sales – Aviary, as the sales account. Press **<Enter>**.

7. Accept the default for the GL Inventory Acct, Account No. 12000, Inventory, by pressing **<Enter>**.

8. Your cursor is in the GL Cost of Sales Acct field. Select Account No. 50000-AV, Product Cost – Aviary, as the product cost account. Press **<Enter>**.

9. Click 🔍 in the Item Tax Type field. Observe that the default, 1, means that this is a regular, taxable item. Press **<Enter>**. UPC/SKU information pops up. Read the information.

10. Click on the Item Type field. The Item Type is a way of classifying similar inventory items for sorting and printing reports. Select SUPPLY. Press **<Enter>**.

11. Your cursor is in the Location field. Select AISLE 1. Press **<Enter>**.

12. Your cursor is in the Stocking U/M field. Select Each and press **<Enter>** two times.

13. Your cursor is in the Minimum Stock field. Type **6** and press **<Enter>**.

14. Your cursor is in the Reorder Quantity field. Type **6** and press **<Enter>**

15. Select DEJULIA, DeJulia Wholesale Suppliers as the Preferred Vendor ID. Leave the Buyer ID field blank. Your Maintain Inventory Items window should agree with the one shown on the next page.

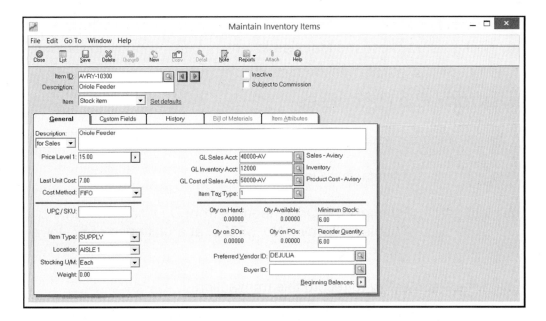

When you purchase inventory stock items from a vendor, this is the Purchase Journal entry: debit the Inventory account and credit Accounts Payable/Vendor account. When you sell Inventory stock items on account, a compound Sales Journal entry is recorded.

➢ Debit Accounts Receivable and Cost of Sales accounts.

➢ Credit Sales, Sales Tax Payable, and Inventory accounts.

The Maintain Inventory Items window should be displayed.

Observe that you set the following account defaults for this stock item:

GL Sales Acct	40000-AV	Sales - Aviary
GL Inventory Acct	12000	Inventory
GL Cost of Sales Acct	50000-AV	Product Cost - Aviary

You also selected a preferred vendor. The Preferred Vendor ID field should display DEJULIA, which is the Vendor ID for DeJulia Wholesale Suppliers. Bellwether purchases oriole feeders from this vendor.

16. Click 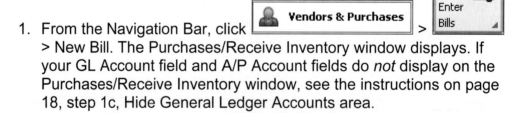. Close the Maintian Inventory Items window to return to the Inventory & Services Navigation Center.

INVENTORY AND PURCHASES

In the following transaction, journalize and post a purchase of inventory.

Date   *Transaction Description*

03/17/16   Purchased 6 Oriole feeders from DeJulia Wholesale Suppliers, Invoice No. 55522, at a unit price of $7, for a total of $42.

Follow the steps below to record this transaction.

1. From the Navigation Bar, click **Vendors & Purchases** > **Enter Bills** > New Bill. The Purchases/Receive Inventory window displays. If your GL Account field and A/P Account fields do *not* display on the Purchases/Receive Inventory window, see the instructions on page 18, step 1c, Hide General Ledger Accounts area.

2. In the Vendor ID field, type **DEJULIA** and press **<Enter>** (or use the lookup icon to find DeJulia Wholesale Suppliers).

3. Click on the Invoice date field. Type or select **17** as the date.

4. In the Invoice No. field, type **55522** and press **<Enter>**. This is a required field.

5. Click on the Apply to Purchases tab.

6. Click on the Quantity field. Type **6** and press **<Enter>**.

7. Your cursor is in the Item field. Type or select the code you just created, **AVRY-10300** and press **<Enter>** three times. The description and the GL Account automatically default to the information you assigned in the Maintain Inventory Items window.

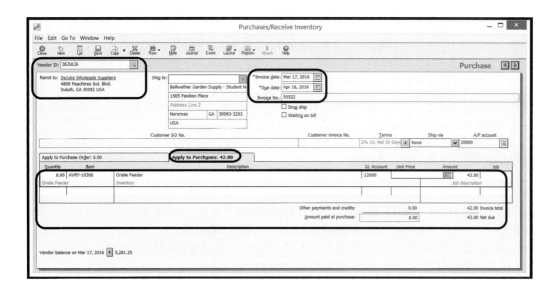

8. To see how this inventory purchase is journalized, click . The Accounting Behind the Screens, Purchases Journal appears: Account No. 12000, Inventory, is debited for 42.00; Account No. 20000, Accounts Payable is credited for 42.00. The vendor, DeJulia Wholesale Suppliers is also credited. The entry to the vendor is shown in the Vendor Ledgers.

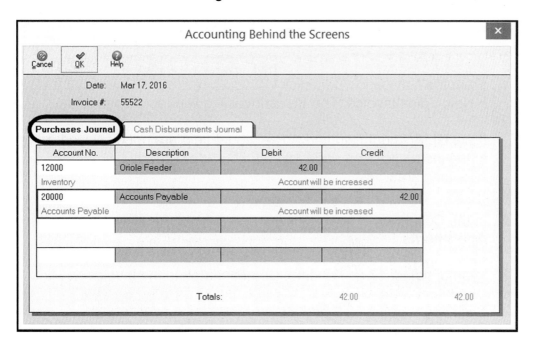

9. Click  to return to the Purchases/Receive Inventory window.

10. Click 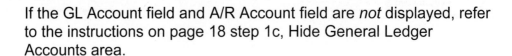 to post this purchase. Close the Purchases/Receive Inventory window.

INVENTORY AND SALES

When a stock item is sold, Sage updates Accounts Receivable and computes the Cost of Goods Sold (product cost), using one of three costing methods. In the General Ledger, a single entry encompassing all sales in the current period is made to the Product Cost account. This entry is dated the last day of the accounting period.

Henton Park Apartments wants three Oriole feeders. The following steps show you how to invoice Henton Park Apartments for three Oriole feeders.

Date	*Transaction Description*
03/17/16	Sold three Oriole feeders on account to Henton Park Apartments for $15 each plus sales tax.

1. From the Navigation Bar, click ⬛ **Customers & Sales** > ⬛ Sales Invoices > New Sales Invoice. The Sales/Invoicing window displays.

    If the GL Account field and A/R Account field are *not* displayed, refer to the instructions on page 18 step 1c, Hide General Ledger Accounts area.

2. In the Customer ID field, click 🔍 and select **HENTON, Henton Park Apartments**.

3. Type or select **17** as the date. Do not complete the Invoice No. field.

4. Click on the Apply to Sales tab.

5. Click on the Quantity field. Type **3** and press **<Enter>**.

6. The cursor is in the Item field. Type **AVRY-10300** and press **<Enter>** five times. (*Hint:* This is the inventory item added on page 167. Observe that the default GL Account is Account No. 40000-AV, Sales - Aviary. If the GL Account is <u>not</u> 40000- AV, you did <u>not</u> complete step 6, page 170. In the GL Account field, select 40000-AV *or* redo step 6, page 170.)

   Sage computes the amount based on the quantity times the sales price that was established when setting up the inventory item. All the other lines for this invoice are automatically completed based on the inventory item information.

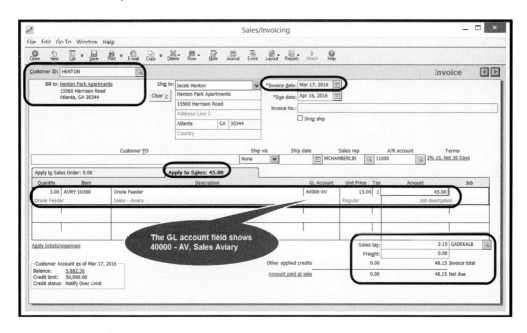

7. Click [Journal] to see how Sage 50 journalizes this entry in the Sales Journal. Scroll down the Accounting Behind the Screens, Sales Journal window, to see the whole entry. Observe that in a perpetual inventory system (Sage 50's default) the cost of sales accounts (50000-AV, Product Cost-Aviary; and 12000, Inventory) are "To be calculated." Once the sales invoice is posted, the cost of sales amounts will be calculated. Click [OK] to close the Accounting Behind the Screens window to return to the Sales/Invoicing window.

8. Click [Save] to post this sales invoice. Close the Sales/Invoicing window to return to the Customers & Sales Navigation Center.

Let's review the last two sections: Inventory and Purchases and Inventory and Sales. When Bellwether purchased six Oriole Feeders (an inventory stock item) on pages 172-174, the entry is recorded in the Purchase Journal with these accounts debited and credited.

Account #	Account Description	Debit	Credit
12000/ AVRY-10300	Inventory	42.00	
20000/ DEJULIA	Accounts Payable/DeJulia Wholesale Suppliers		42.00

When three Oriole Feeders were sold on pages 174-176, the entry in the Sales Journal was:

Account #	Account Description	Debit	Credit
11000/ HENTON	Accts. Rec./Henton Park Apartments	48.15	
40000-AV	Sales-Aviary		45.00
23100	Sales Tax Payable		3.15
50000-AV	Product Cost-Aviary	21.00	
12000	Inventory		21.00

When three Oriole feeders were sold, they were sold for $15 each, plus sales tax. The total sale to Henton Park Apartments is $45 plus sales tax of $3.15, for a total of $48.15. When Bellwether Garden Supply bought the Oriole Feeders from the vendor (DeJulia Wholesale Suppliers), they paid $7 each. The last two lines of the journal entry (Account nos. 50000-AV and 12000) reflect the product cost of the stock items, $7 X 3 = $21.

The journal entries shown above are examples of how purchases and sales are recorded in Sage 50's perpetual inventory system.

INVENTORY ADJUSTMENTS

It may become necessary to adjust the amount of Inventory Items due to faulty records, pilferage, spoilage, or inventory changes. You use the Inventory Adjustment Journal to make inventory adjustment entries.

In the example that follows, one of Bellwether's employees dropped two bird house kits which damaged them beyond repair. To adjust inventory for this loss, follow these steps.

1. From the Navigation Bar, click **Inventory & Services** > Inventory Adjustments. The Inventory Adjustments window appears.

2. Type **AVRY-10100** (for Bird House Kit) in the Item ID field and the press **<Enter>**.

3. In the Date field, type **15** or select the day.

4. Type **-2** in the Adjust quantity by field to decrease the current inventory by two. Press the **<Enter>** key. The New Quantity field shows that you have 28.00 bird house kits.

5. Type **Damaged** as the Reason to Adjust.

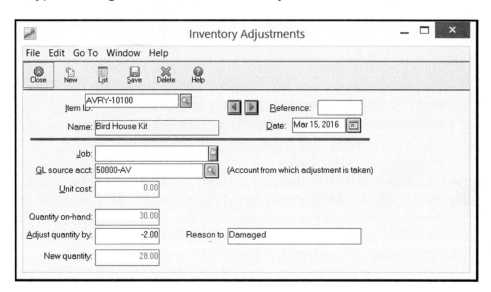

6. Click [Save] to post this adjustment, then close the Inventory Adjustments window.

   Adjustments to inventory, like the one just made, only affect the average cost of the item. For example, let's say you purchased two bird house kits at $30 each and then damaged one. For accounting purposes you now have one bird house kit that costs $30.

SECURITY AND INTERNAL CONTROL

Internal control is an integrated system of people, processes, and procedures that minimize or eliminate business risks, protect assets, facilitate reliable accounting, and promote efficient operations. If changes are made to company records, Sage 50's *audit trail* provides documentation. An audit trail records all entries and changes related to the company's data, including actions by specific users.

Sage 50 has several methods to track information. For example, a combination of the general ledger, journals, reports, and financial statements can be used to trace transactions and balances. If you want to track when an action is performed, Sage 50's audit trail provides this information. The audit trail provides accountability of users, deters users from fraudulent activity or mistakes, and tracks transaction history. Four internal control methods are built into the software:

- Setting up user names, passwords, and access rights.
- The ability to associate the user currently logged into the Sage 50 company with the data that is being entered.
- Limit access to information in Sage 50's Navigation Centers.
- Audit Trail reports that show what each user entered.

In order to get the most use out of the audit trail feature, user records need to be set up. If User Security is set up, Sage 50 can associate the user currently logged into the company with the data being entered. For example, USER1 adds a customer record. USER2 then logs on and modifies the customer record. The Audit Trail report will show that USER2 was the last person who worked with the customer record, and it will display what was changed.

By limiting access to accounting data, Sage 50's user security feature addresses an important purpose of internal control. For example, assigning users to one Navigation Center increases the accuracy of records and reports. Also, since one user assumes responsibility for repetitive tasks, the efficiency of operations increases. User security reduces the business's risk of users changing or deleting data inappropriately which also safeguards accounting data. User security establishes accountability and allows the company to track who has performed various maintenance and recording tasks.

User Security and Access to the Sage 50 Navigation Centers

If you are an administrator responsible for setting up and maintaining user access to Sage 50, you can choose settings that will limit access to information in Sage 50's Navigation Centers. For example, if you want a user to have limited access to company revenue information, you could make sure the user has no access to the general ledger master list and transaction list reports or financial statements. However, you might want that same user to be able to view company budgets but not change them in any way.

When you set up Sage 50 security, you can fine-tune settings to give users exactly the kind of access you want them to have. The Selected AccessRole Setup window has embedded Help for each security setting— just select a setting to see Help about it. This will aid you in deciding which areas users have access to and which areas are not accessible.

Selected Access

The Selected Access window allows the administrator to grant rights to work in certain areas of the Sage 50 program within the current company. Sage 50 program areas include the following roles:

- Customers & Sales
- Vendors & Purchases
- Inventory & Services
- Employees & Payroll
- Banking & General Ledger
- System

In addition to full or no access, the administrator can set different levels of access within subareas such as maintenance, tasks, and reports. For example, in the Customers & Sales area, the administrator could choose to give a user limited access to Customer Information or Customer Beginning Balances. Drop-down lists let the administrator set different access levels for different subareas of the program; for example, Payments; Write Checks.

User Security

Sage 50 allows custom access for different individuals. If you want to take advantage of this security feature, you set up user rights for each person who will be using Sage 50. When set up, each user is issued a user name and password that will be required before opening and working with company data.

Once user names and passwords are set up, Sage 50 prompts each user for a user name and password whenever he or she opens a company. As long as users properly enter their passwords, they can access the areas of the program to which they have rights.

Setting Up Company Users, Passwords, and Access Rights

In order to have data security and password protection, you need to set up user records. When user names and passwords are set up, Sage 50 prompts you for a user name and password when you open a company. This is a two-step process:

- Set up the company administrator.
- Set up individual users.

The steps below are for example purposes only. Check with your instructor to see if he or she would like you to set up user access. *Remember, if you set up a user name and password you have to use it each time you start Sage 50.* To learn about setting up company users, passwords, and access rights, go to the following Help windows.

1. From Sage 50's menu bar select, Help < Help > Index tab.

2. Type **Password** in the Type in the keyword to find. Select setting up, click Display .

3. The Set Up Company Users, Passwords, and Access Rights window appears. Enlarge the window. In the right pane, link to Setting up the first user (administrator). Read the information.

4. Link to Setting up additional company users. Read the information.

5. Link to Setting up users with selected access. Read the information. This Help window explains how to set up users, passwords and access rights.

   Check with your instructor to see if he or she would like you do this.

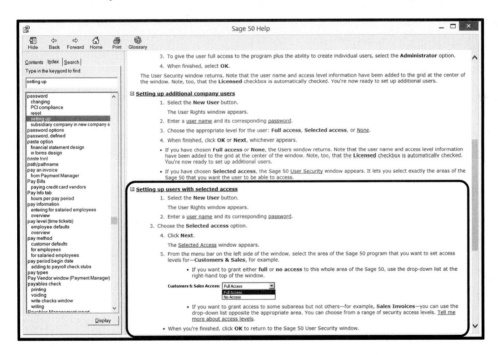

Note: Passwords must be at least seven characters. They must contain both numbers and letters. It's a good idea to include both upper and lowercase letters, although that is not required. An example of a strong password is MLsmith707. Passwords are **case sensitive**. You need to remember if letters are capitalized or not.

6. Click [×] on the Sage 50 Help title bar to close.

Audit Trail Report

The Audit trail is an historical record of financial data that is used to examine the data's correctness. Sage 50's audit trail feature records all entries and changes related to company data, including actions by specific users. The Audit Trail report can trace fraudulent activity and other accounting adjustments you may not know were completed.

The System Navigation Center shows a link to Run Audit Trail report. Once date options are selected, the Audit Trail report can be viewed from this link, or from the Reports & Forms, Company selection. On page 185, the Audit Trial Report is displayed from the Reports & Forms menu.

The audit trail feature records the following items with each activity performed while operating in the Sage 50 company:

- Date: System (computer) date of action.
- Time: System (computer) time of action.
- User Name: User Name (if available); otherwise, Sage 50 displays "Not Available."
- Action: Add, Change, or Delete.
- Window/Description: Window where action occurred or name of system function implemented (for example, Backup Company Data Files, Maintain Employees & Sales Reps).

- Transaction ID: For maintenance records, the ID associated with the record; for tasks, the ID associated with the transaction after change. (*Hint:* To see entire column, widen it.)
- Transaction Reference: Reference number associated with the transaction after change.
- Amount: Amount of transaction after change.

Sage 50's audit trail tracks the following:

1. Records and Transactions

   Records include customers, vendors, employees, inventory items, etc. Transactions include quotes, sales orders, invoices, payments, general journal entries, inventory adjustments, etc.

   These include:

   - adding records or transactions (when Save is selected).
   - editing records or transactions (when Save is selected).
   - deleting records or transactions (when Delete is selected).
   - entering or maintaining record beginning balances (when OK or Save is selected).
   - voiding checks and paychecks.
   - making payments in Cash Manager and Payment Manager.

2. Miscellaneous Actions

   - reconciling accounts.
   - maintaining company information and options.
   - maintaining and loading user-maintained and Sage 50-maintained payroll tax tables.
   - importing data into the company.
   - adding transactions using Dynamic Data Exchange (DDE).

3. System Functions

   - posting and unposting journals (Batch mode only).
   - closing the fiscal year.
   - closing the payroll tax year.
   - backing up company data.

Displaying the Audit Trail Report & Find Transactions Report

Follow these steps to print an Audit Trail Report.

1. From the menu bar, select Reports & Forms > Company. The Select a Report or Form window appears. The Audit Trail Report is the default.

2. Click [Options].

3. In the Date field, select Range.

4. Type **1/1/2006** in the From field. Press **<Tab>**.

5. Type **12/31/2016** in the To field. Press **<Tab>**.

   ➢ **Troubleshooting:** If the current date is *after* 12/31/2016, type today's date in the To field. The Audit Trail Report shows the dates that you recorded entries.

6. Click [OK]. The Audit Trail Report for the period from Jan 1, 2006 to Dec. 31, 2016 (*or, today's date*) appears. Observe that each transaction shows the Date; Time; User Name, Action, Window/ Description, Transaction ID, Transaction Reference, and Amount. If users had been set up, the User Name column would show that. Scroll down to see the whole report. A partial report is shown on the next page.

   Observe that the work completed in Chapters 1-5 is shown on the Audit Trail Report; for example, the employees added in Chapter 1 (CYACHT, or your name, and SWITTNER) the vendors added (Maintain Vendors), purchases (Purchases/Receive Inventory), and payments to ADLER and OFCSUPPL in Chapter 2. From Chapter 4, the DASH and TEESDALE transactions are also shown. Scroll down the Audit Trail Report to see your work. (Your date column will differ. It shows the date you recorded the entries.)

The Audit Trial Report provides a listing of the changes made to the maintenance items and transactions. Depending on when you made additions and changes, your time and date column will differ. The Audit Trail Report shows when the author made changes.

A partial Audit Trail Report is shown below. If you are working *after* December 31, 2016, your Audit Trail Report may show a different ending date. Observe that the work you completed up to this point is shown. For example, adding your name as an employee (CYACHT is shown below), backing up, adding SWITTNER as an employee, adding the vendor OFCSUPPLY, and the transactions completed.

Bellwether Garden Supply - Student Name

Audit Trail Report

For the Period From Jan 1, 2006 to Dec 31, 2016

Filter Criteria includes: 1) All Actions.

Date	Time	User Name	Action	Window/Description	Transaction ID	Transaction Reference	Amount
6/24/15	1:59 PM	Not Available	Change	Backup Company Data Files			
6/24/15	2:53 PM	Not Available	Add	Maintain Employees & Sales Reps	CYACHT		
6/24/15	2:57 PM	Not Available	Change	Backup Company Data Files			
6/24/15	2:58 PM	Not Available	Change	Backup Company Data Files			
6/24/15	3:05 PM	Not Available	Change	Maintain Company	BCS	Bellwether Garden Supply - Student	
6/24/15	3:11 PM	Not Available	Change	Maintain Company	BELGARSU	Bellwether Garden Supply - Student	
6/27/15	1:20 PM	Not Available	Add	Maintain Employees & Sales Reps	SWITTNER		
6/27/15	1:21 PM	Not Available	Change	Maintain Employees & Sales Reps	SWITTNER		
6/27/15	1:37 PM	Not Available	Change	Backup Company Data Files			
6/27/15	1:37 PM	Not Available	Change	Backup Company Data Files			
6/30/15	2:19 PM	Not Available	Add	Purchase Orders	ABNEY	101	3,834.00
7/1/15	2:26 PM	Not Available	Add	Maintain Vendors	ADLER		
7/1/15	2:33 PM	Not Available	Add	Purchases/Receive Inventory	ADLER	AD107	45.00
7/1/15	2:40 PM	Not Available	Add	Payments	ADLER		44.10
7/6/15	10:21 AM	Not Available	Change	Backup Company Data Files			
7/6/15	10:56 AM	Not Available	Add	Maintain Vendors	OFCSUPPL		
7/6/15	10:59 AM	Not Available	Add	Purchases/Receive Inventory	OFCSUPPL	H788	54.75
7/6/15	11:02 AM	Not Available	Add	Payments	OFCSUPPL	10216	53.65
7/6/15	11:17 AM	Not Available	Change	Backup Company Data Files			
7/7/15	12:56 PM	Not Available	Add	Quotes	DASH		211.95
7/7/15	1:00 PM	Not Available	Add	Quotes	DASH	10355	211.95
7/7/15	1:00 PM	Not Available	Add	Auto Purchase Orders	SOGARDEN		191.40
7/7/15	1:00 PM	Not Available	Change	Quotes	DASH		211.95
7/7/15	1:00 PM	Not Available	Change	Convert to Sales Order	DASH		
7/7/15	1:20 PM	Not Available	Add	Sales/Invoicing	DASH		211.95
7/8/15	10:22 AM	Not Available	Change	Maintain Customers/Prospects	TEESDALE		
7/8/15	10:45 AM	Not Available	Add	Sales/Invoicing	TEESDALE		158.95
7/8/15	11:17 AM	Not Available	Add	Receive Money	TEESDALE	8818	151.45
7/8/15	11:44 AM	Not Available	Change	Backup Company Data Files			
7/8/15	1:10 PM	Not Available	Add	Sales/Invoicing	TEESDALE	102	317.99
7/8/15	1:14 PM	Not Available	Add	Receive Money	TEESDALE	9915	302.99
7/8/15	1:14 PM	Not Available	Change	Backup Company Data Files			
7/9/15	11:37 AM	Not Available	Add	General Journal Entry		Transfer	8,000.00
7/9/15	11:41 AM	Not Available	Add	Payroll Entry	BNUNNLEY		1,051.48
7/9/15	11:44 AM	Not Available	Add	Payroll Entry	DCARTER		585.23
7/9/15	12:47 PM	Not Available	Change	Backup Company Data Files			
7/11/15	11:22 AM	Not Available	Add	Payroll Entry	BHUGLEY		650.25
7/11/15	11:23 AM	Not Available	Add	Payroll Entry	DGROSS		1,058.87
7/11/15	11:34 AM	Not Available	Change	Backup Company Data Files			
7/16/15	10:05 AM	Not Available	Add	Maintain Chart of Accounts	10500		
7/16/15	10:48 AM	Not Available	Add	General Journal Entry		Transfer	5,500.00
7/16/15	11:16 AM	Not Available	Add	Maintain Inventory Items	AVRY-10300		
7/16/15	12:47 PM	Not Available	Add	Purchases/Receive Inventory	DEJULIA	55522	42.00
7/16/15	1:12 PM	Not Available	Add	Sales/Invoicing	HENTON		48.15
7/16/15	1:12 PM	Not Available	Add	Auto Purchase Orders	DEJULIA		42.00
7/16/15	1:15 PM	Not Available	Add	Inventory Adjustments	AVRY-10100		-2.00

7. Close the Audit Trail Report.

8. Display the Find Transactions Report from 3/15/16 to 3/15/16. The Find Transactions Report provides a way to easily search for Sage 50 Transactions. You can drill down to the original entry from each transaction.

   A partial Find Transactions Report is shown below.

Bellwether Garden Supply - Student Name
Find Transactions Report
For the Period From Mar 15, 2016 to Mar 15, 2016
Filter Criteria includes: 1) All Transaction Types. Report order is by Date.

Date	Type	Reference	ID	Name	Amount
3/15/16	Credit Memo		ARCHER	Archer Scapes and Ponds	-49.99
3/15/16	Credit Memo		SAIA	Saia's Neighborhood Nursery	-49.99
3/15/16	General Journal Entry	ADJ0303103			0.11
3/15/16	General Journal Entry	Transfer			5,500.00
3/15/16	Inventory Adjustment		AVRY-10100	Bird House Kit	-2.00
3/15/16	Inventory Adjustment		AVRY-10050-SM-HTL	Prefabricated Birdhouse	8.00
3/15/16	Inventory Adjustment		AVRY-10050-LG-EFL	Prefabricated Birdhouse	4.00
3/15/16	Inventory Adjustment		AVRY-10050-SM-EFL	Prefabricated Birdhouse	8.00
3/15/16	Inventory Adjustment		AVRY-10050-SM-PYR	Prefabricated Birdhouse	4.00
3/15/16	Inventory Adjustment		AVRY-10050-SM-HTL	Prefabricated Birdhouse	6.00
3/15/16	Payment		ABNEY	Abney and Son Contractors	50.00
3/15/16	Payment	10210	SAFESTATE	Safe State Insurance Company	530.64
3/15/16	Payment	10212	PAYNE	Payne Enterprises	50.00
3/15/16	Payment	10213	CLINE	Cline Construction, Inc.	100.00
3/15/16	Payment	10214	HAWKINS	DPH Web Design	100.00
3/15/16	Payroll Entry	1250	ACHESTER	Amanda W. Chester	809.22
3/15/16	Payroll Entry	1251	ADUKE	Al L. Duke	379.50
3/15/16	Payroll Entry	1252	AHECTER	Anthony H. Hecter	787.54
3/15/16	Payroll Entry	1253	AKORNEL	Alex C. Kornel	845.06
3/15/16	Payroll Entry	1254	BHUGLEY	Brandon A. Hugley	612.75
3/15/16	Payroll Entry	1255	BKERR	Bob G. Kerr	559.22
3/15/16	Payroll Entry	1256	BNUNNLEY	Brandee M. Nunnley	989.66

9. Close all windows.

BACKING UP CHAPTER 5 DATA

After completing the work within Chapter 5, back up. The suggested file name is **Chapter 5.ptb**. Detailed steps for backing up data are shown on pages 22-25.

Backing up saves data to that point in your work. Each time you back up, use a different file name; for example, the suggested file name at this point is Chapter 5.ptb. (Sage 50 automatically adds the file extension .ptb to backups.) Using a unique file name allows you to restore at different points in the data.

ONLINE LEARNING CENTER

Complete the following end-of-chapter activities online at www.mhhe.com/yacht2016 > Student Edition > Chapter 5.

1. Interactive Multiple-Choice and True/False questions.
2. Going to the Net exercise: Go online to the Bookkeeping and Accounting Basics website.
3. QA Templates: 10 multiple-choice questions and three analysis questions.
4. Assessment Rubric: Review journals, navigation centers, modules, and task windows.
5. Listen to narrated PowerPoint slides.

The OLC also includes links to the Appendixes:

*   Appendix A: Troubleshooting
*   Appendix B: Accounting Information Systems
*   Appendix C: Review of Accounting Principles
*   Appendix D: Glossary of Terms

Exercise 5-1: Follow the instructions below to complete Exercise 5-1.

1. Start Sage 50. Open Bellwether Garden Supply - Student Name [your first and last name].

2. Restore data from the end of Chapter 5. This back up was made on page 187.

3. Journalize and post the following transactions:

   Date   *Transaction Description*

   03/18/16   Transfer $1,200 from the Regular Checking Account
                     to the Payroll Checking Account.

   03/19/16   Purchased two (2) Oriole Feeders from DeJulia
                     Wholesale Suppliers, Invoice No. 94977, $14.

4. Continue with Exercise 5-2.

Exercise 5-2: Follow the instructions below to complete Exercise 5-2.

1. Print the General Ledger Trial Balance.

How to Fix? I am NOT connected to a printer. What should I do?

1. Display the General Ledger Trial Balance. Select [🖨 Print]. In the
   Name field, click on the down-arrow.
2. Select Adobe PDF *or* Microsoft XPS Document Writer.

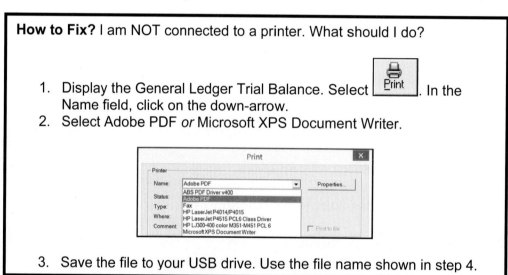

3. Save the file to your USB drive. Use the file name shown in step 4.

---

2. Back up Exercise 5-2. Use **Exercise 5-2** as the file name.

3. Export the General Ledger Trial Balance to Excel. Use **Exercise
   5-2_General Ledger Trial Balance.xlsx** as the file name.

4. Save the General Ledger Trial Balance as a PDF file. Use **Exercise
   5-2_General Ledger Trial Balance.pdf** as the file name.

Check your figures:

Account No. 10200, Regular Checking Account $9,046.52
Account No. 10300, Payroll Checking Account   10,565.26
Account No. 11000, Accounts Receivable   175,823.20
Account No. 20000, Accounts Payable   80,682.01

5. Exit Sage 50.

CHAPTER 5 INDEX

Chapter

6 Job Cost

LEARNING OBJECTIVES

1. Restore data from Exercise 5-2. (This backup was made on page 188.)
2. Learn about Sage 50's Job Cost system.
3. Set up a job.
4. Coordinate job costs with purchases, sales, and payroll.
5. Display the Job Profitability Report.
6. Make two backups, save one Excel file, and save one PDF file.

This chapter shows how to use the Job Cost system. In Sage 50, you can assign Job ID codes to purchases, sales, and employee hours. In this way, Sage 50 tracks how each of these factors impacts job costs. The diagram below illustrates how job costing works with purchases, sales, and payroll.

Sage 50's *job costing* feature allows you to track the costs incurred while performing a job. To use job costing, identify the project for which you want to track expenses and income and then determine how much detail is needed.

There are several advantages to using job costing:

- It allows you to track income and expenses for each project the company undertakes. You can create estimates for each job. As you enter invoices for materials or services used in the job through accounts payable, they can be assigned to a job so actual costs can be compared with job estimates.

- You can exercise greater control over costs and revenues by tracking customer invoices and payments received for each job. You can print reports during a job's progress to find out the total amount spent and net revenues due for each job.

- You can also maintain statistics on various jobs including starting date, completion date, and the progress of each job and view these by printing various job-costing reports.

- If phases or cost codes are used, you can generate reports to display this information, showing whether a job is over or under budget for any phase or task involved. This helps control costs by adjusting one phase or task prior to the job's completion.

Job costing gives you greater insight into all the company's jobs or projects so that you know what you are spending, how long it is taking, and how much profit was made on each job.

The diagram below shows how Sage 50 organizes job costing.

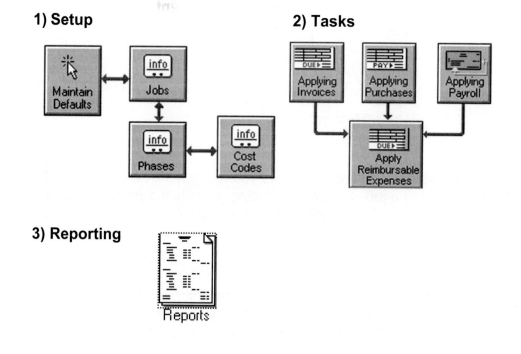

GETTING STARTED

Bellwether Garden Supply has a customer named Franklin Botanical Gardens. Once a Job ID is set up for Franklin Botanical Gardens, you can track supplies and employee hours charged to this customer.

1. Start Sage 50. Open Bellwether Garden Supply - Student Name. (If Bellwether Garden Supply - Student Name is not shown, Create a new company using the restored data. Refer to the Read me box on page 29.)

2. If necessary, restore data from the Exercise 5-2 backup. (The Exercise 5-2.ptb backup was made on page 188.) Restoring overwrites or replaces an existing file.

💾 To make sure you are starting in the appropriate place in the data (Exercise 5-2.ptb backup) check the General Ledger Trial Balance. A partial trial balance is shown below. The General Ledger Trial Balance was completed in Exercise 5-2, step 1, page 188.

Bellwether Garden Supply - Student Name
General Ledger Trial Balance
As of Mar 31, 2016

Filter Criteria includes: Report order is by ID. Report is printed in Detail Format.

Account ID	Account Description	Debit Amt	Credit Amt
10000	Petty Cash	327.55	
10100	Cash on Hand	1,850.45	
10200	Regular Checking Account	9,046.52	
10300	Payroll Checking Account	10,565.26	
10400	Savings Account	7,500.00	
10500	Money Market Fund	4,500.00	
11000	Accounts Receivable	175,823.20	
11400	Other Receivables	7,681.84	
11500	Allowance for Doubtful Account		5,000.00
12000	Inventory	12,470.31	
14000	Prepaid Expenses	14,221.30	
14100	Employee Advances	3,000.65	
14200	Notes Receivable-Current	11,000.00	
14700	Other Current Assets	120.00	

3. From the Navigation Bar, select  >

 > New Job. The Maintain Jobs window appears.

4. In the Job ID field > type **FRANKLIN** > press **<Enter>**. (*Hint:* To match other Job IDs, use uppercase.)

5. In the Description field > type **Franklin Botanical Gardens** > press **<Enter>** two times.

6. Type **3/4/16** in the Start Date field > press **<Enter>** to go to the For Customer field. (*Hint:* Or, click on the For Customer field).

7. In the For Customer field, select FRANKLIN.

8. Click on the Job Type field, select LAND. Compare your Maintain Jobs window to the one shown below.

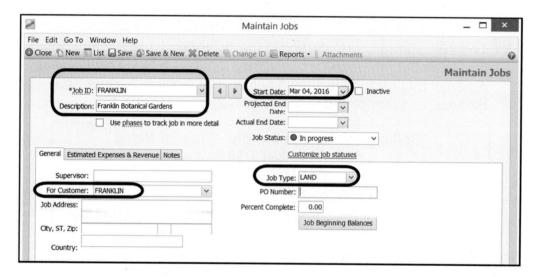

9. Save this job. Close the Maintain Jobs window to return to the Customers & Sales Navigation Center.

JOB COSTING AND PURCHASING: Purchasing Inventory Items for Jobs

This new job has some special circumstances; namely, Franklin Botanical Gardens has a new building overlooking a park. In the park, there are several picnic tables. According to the terms of the contract with Franklin Botanical Gardens, Bellwether Garden Supply purchases and provides a special wood treatment to the picnic benches.

When inventory items are purchased for jobs, you need to do the following:

➢ Record the purchase directly as a job expense. You could indicate a Non-stock or a Description only Inventory Item but not a Stock Item.

➢ Record the purchase into Inventory. When you bill the customer, enter the Item and the Job. The system posts the price as Job revenue and the Cost of Goods Sold as Job Expense.

Let's see how this works.

Date	Transaction Description
3/20/16	Invoice No. AD501 was received from Adler's Landscaping for the purchase of special wood treatment, $85; terms 2% 10, Net 30 Days. Apply this purchase to the Franklin Botanical Gardens job.

1. From the Navigation Bar, select  > New Bill. The Purchases/Receive Inventory window displays.

2. Type or select **AD** (Adler's Landscaping) for the Vendor ID.

3. Select or type **20** in the Invoice date field > press **<Enter>**.

4. Type **AD501** for the Invoice No. (This is a *required* field.) Press **<Enter>**.

5. The Apply to Purchases tab is selected. Type **1** in the Quantity field > press **<Enter>** two times.

6. In the Description field, type **Special wood treatment** > press **<Enter>** two times.

7. Account No. 57200, Materials Cost, is the default account displayed in the GL Account field. Your cursor is in the Unit Price field. Type **85** > press **<Enter>** two times.

8. Type or select **FRANKLIN**, the new Job, in the Job field.

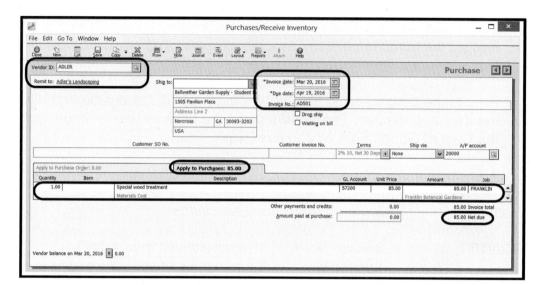

If your GL Account field and A/P Account field are *not* displayed on the Purchases/Receive Inventory window, see the instructions on page 18, step 1c, Hide General Ledger Accounts area.

9. Click Save to post this purchase. Close the Purchases/Receive Inventory window to return to the Vendors & Purchases Navigation Center.

JOB COSTING AND SALES

Follow these steps to invoice Franklin Botanical Gardens for a drip irrigation system and apply this sale to Franklin Botanical Gardens, Job ID, FRANKLIN.

Date	Transaction Description
3/21/16	Bellwether Garden Supply sold one Bell-Gro Home Irrigation System, Item No. EQWT-15100, to Franklin Botanical Gardens on account, $129.99, plus $9.10 sales tax, total $139.09; terms 2% 10, Net 30 Days.

1. Select [Customers & Sales] > [Sales Invoices] > New Sales Invoice. The Sales/Invoicing window displays.

2. In the Customer ID field, click 🔍 > select Franklin Botanical Gardens as the Customer > press **<Enter>**.

3. Select or type **21** in the Invoice date field.

4. If necessary, click on the Apply to Sales tab.

5. Click on the Quantity field, type **1** > press **<Enter>**.

6. In the Item field, type **EQWT-15100** (Drip Irrigation System).

7. Press **<Enter>** until you are in the Job field. (You are accepting all of the displayed information when you do this.)

8. Type or select **FRANKLIN**, the Job ID for Franklin Botanical Gardens.

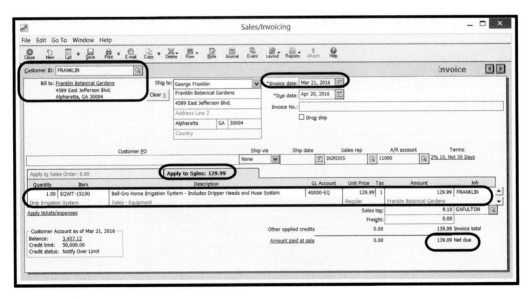

If your GL Account field and A/R Account field are *not* displayed on the Sales/Invoicing window, see the instructions on page 18, 1c, Hide General Ledger Accounts area.

9. Click ![Save] to post this invoice. Close the Sales/Invoicing window to return to the Customers & Sales Navigation Center.

JOB COST AND PAYROLL

In the example that follows, one employee applied the special wood treatment to the picnic tables at Franklin Botanical Gardens. The employee spent one hour applying the wood treatment.

1. From the Navigation Bar, select ![Employees & Payroll] >
   ![Pay Employees] > Enter Payroll for One Employee. The Payroll Entry window appears.

2. Click ![magnifier] in the Employee ID field, select **Alex C. Kornel** > press **<Enter>**.

3. Type **29** as the Date > press **<Enter>** two times.

4. Type **29** in the Pay Period Ends field.

5. On the icon bar, select the Jobs icon ![Jobs]. The Labor Distribution to Jobs window appears.

6. In the Job field, click on the down arrow >select FRANKLIN.

7. Press the <**Enter**> key. Type **1** in the Hours field > press <**Enter**>. In the Amount field, 14.00 is shown.

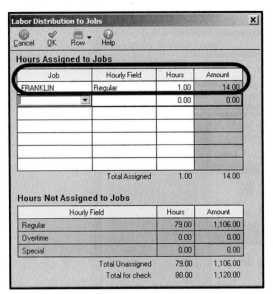

8. Click [OK]. You are returned to the Payroll Entry window.

9. Click [Save] to post the paycheck. Close the Payroll Entry window to return to the Employees & Payroll window.

JOB COST REPORTS

Job cost reports tell you how jobs are progressing. Follow these steps to look at Job Cost Reports.

1. From the menu bar, select Reports & Forms > Jobs. The Select a Report or Form window displays.

2. In the Job Reports: Project Information list, double-click Job Profitability Report. The Job Profitability Report appears.

3. Scroll down to FRANKLIN.

Job ID	Phase ID	Cost Code ID	GL Acct ID	Actual Rev.	Actual Exp.	Profit $	Profit %
FRANKLIN			40000-EQ	129.99			
			50000-EQ		59.95		
			57200		85.00		
			77500		14.00		
				129.99	158.95		
FRANKLIN	Total			129.99	158.95	-28.96	-22.28

The report breaks down each job according to what was spent or earned for each affected general ledger account. It also shows the profit or loss for each job.

4. Close all windows.

BACKING UP CHAPTER 6 DATA

After completing the work within Chapter 6, back up. The suggested file name is **Chapter 6.ptb**. Detailed steps for backing up data are shown on pages 22-25.

Backing up saves your data to that point in your work. Each time you back up, use a different file name; for example, the suggested file name at this point is Chapter 6.ptb. (Sage 50 automatically adds the file extension .ptb to backups.) Using a unique file name allows you to restore at different points in the data.

ONLINE LEARNING CENTER

Complete the following end-of-chapter activities online at www.mhhe.com/yacht2016 > Student Edition > Chapter 6.

1. Interactive Multiple-Choice and True/False questions.
2. Going to the Net exercise: Access the Sage website.
3. QA Templates: 10 short-answer questions and one analysis question.
4. Assessment Rubric: Review journals, navigation centers, modules, and task windows.
5. Listen to narrated PowerPoint slides.

The OLC also includes links to the Appendixes:

- Appendix A: Troubleshooting
- Appendix B: Accounting Information Systems
- Appendix C: Review of Accounting Principles
- Appendix D: Glossary of Terms

Exercise 6-1: Follow the instructions below to complete Exercise 6-1.

1. Start Sage 50. Open Bellwether Garden Supply - Student Name.

2. If necessary, restore data from the end of Chapter 6. This backup was made on page 200.

3. Journalize and post the following transactions:

Date	Transaction Description
03/26/16	Sold two Bell-Gro Impulse Sprinklers (EQWT-15160) to Franklin Botanical Gardens, $64.18 (includes sales tax); terms 2% 10, Net 30 Days; Job ID Franklin Botanical Gardens.
03/26/16	Invoice No. AD967 was received from Adler's Landscaping for the purchase of one container of special wood treatment for $85; terms 2% 10, Net 30 Days; Job ID Franklin Botanical Gardens. (Debit Materials Cost.)
03/29/16	Amanda W. Chester worked one hour on the Franklin Botanical Gardens job. Apply her paycheck to this job. (*Hint:* Remember to select the appropriate job and hour worked. Refer to pages 198-199, steps 6 and 7. The Job Profitability Report completed in Exercise 6-2 depends on selecting the appropriate job and entering the hour worked.)

4. Continue with Exercise 6-2.

Exercise 6-2: Follow the instructions below to complete Exercise 6-2.

1. Print a Job Profitability Report. (*Hint*: If needed, select Adobe PDF or Microsoft XPS Document Writer as the printer. If you save as a PDF file, use the file name shown in step 4. Refer to page 66, How to Fix - I do not have a printer.)

2. Back up Exercise 6-2. Use **Exercise 6-2** as the file name.

Read Me
This backup is important. If you are using external media; for example, a USB drive, do *not* delete the Exercise 6-2.ptb file. You restore the Exercise 6-2.ptb backup file to complete work in Part 4, Chapters 16, 17, and 18.

---

3. Export the Job Profitability Report to Excel. Use **Exercise 6-2_Job Profitability Report.xlsx** as the file name.

4. Save the Job Profitability Repot as a PDF file. Use **Exercise 6-2_Job Profitability Report.pdf** as the file name.

Check Your Figures: Job Profitability Report, FRANKLIN

Actual Revenue, $189.97
Actual Expenses, $281.85
Profit dollars, -$91.88
Profit percentage, -48.37

CHAPTER 6 INDEX

Chapter

7

Financial Statements

LEARNING OBJECTIVES

1. Restore data from Exercise 6-2. This backup was made on page 202.
2. Explore Sage 50's Help feature.
3. Print the financial statements.
4. Use drill down to go from the income statement to the general ledger, then to the original entry window.
5. Complete Bellwether Garden Supply project online at www.mhhe.com/yacht2016 > Student Edition link.
6. Make an optional backup of Chapter 7, save one Excel file, and save six PDF files. (The Exercise 6-2.ptb backup, page 202, includes the data needed for Chapter 7.)

FINANCIAL STATEMENTS

In Chapters 1 through 6, you explored the sample company, Bellwether Garden Supply. You learned how Sage's user interface works and how to navigate the software. In Chapters 1 through 6, you also journalized and posted various types of transactions. Beginning with Chapter 9, you learn how to use these features to set up service businesses from scratch.

In Chapter 7, you look at the financial statements. Once journal entries have been recorded and posted, Sage 50 automatically calculates financial statements. Since business managers and owners have the primary responsibility for the organization, they depend on accounting information in the form of financial statements to understand what is happening.

All the financial statements reflect the current month and year-to-date amounts.

In this chapter, six financial statements are printed.

1. Balance Sheet.

2. Gross Profit by Departments.

3. Income Statement.

4. Statement of Cash Flow.

5. Statement of Retained Earnings.

6. Statement of Changes in Financial Position (SCFP). Even though current accounting standards do not require a SCFP, Sage 50 includes it. (Refer to Read Me on page 221.)

Balance Sheet

A balance sheet is a list of assets, liabilities, and capital of a business entity as of a specific date, such as the last day of an accounting period or the last day of the year.

Each financial statement may be modified to fit your needs. Sage 50 includes a Design icon for that purpose. Later in this chapter, you learn about how to use the Help feature to design financial statements. In Chapter 16, Customizing Forms, you learn more about modifying Sage 50's standard forms.

Gross Profit by Departments

A departmentalized accounting system provides information that management can use to evaluate the profitability or cost effectiveness of a department's activities. The Gross Profit by Departments financial statement is a custom report designed for Bellwether that details each department's year-to-date gross profit as of the current month.

Some of Bellwether's chart of account numbers have a dash, then an AV or a BK. For example, Account No. 40000-AV, Sales - Aviary; and Account No. 40000-BK, Sales - Books show the departmental designation.

Sage 50 includes a feature called masking which allows organization of the business by department. Then, custom forms can be designed to accommodate a departmentalized accounting system. The wrench [] to the left of some of Bellwether's financial statements indicates custom-designed forms.

Income Statement

The income statement is a summary of the revenues and expenses a company accrues over a period of time, such as an accounting period or a year. Only revenue and expense accounts are displayed on the income statement. *Net income* is computed by subtracting total expenses from total revenues. Net income results when revenues exceed expenses. An excess of expenses over revenues results in a *net loss*. Bellwether's net loss for the current month, March 1 through March 31, 2016, is $2,523.21. A net loss is indicated on the income statement with parenthesis ($2,523.21). Bellwether's year-to-date net income is $25,579.22. On page 218, the Income Statement is shown.

In addition to dollar figures, the income statement also includes percentage-of-revenue columns for the current month and year to date. The percentages shown for each expense, total expenses, and net income (or net loss) indicate the relationship of each item to total revenues.

Statement of Cash Flow

The cash flow from operations is roughly the same as income from operations plus depreciation, depletion, and adjusted for any other operating transactions that had no effect on cash during the period. The statement of cash flow also reports cash transactions associated with the purchase or sale of fixed assets (Investing Activities) and cash paid to or received from creditors and owners (Financing Activities).

The statement of cash flow provides the answers to three questions:

1. Where did cash receipts come from?

2. What were cash payments used for?

3. What was the overall change in cash?

Statement of Retained Earnings

The Statement of Retained Earnings shows beginning and ending retained earnings amounts, adjustments made to retained earnings within the report period, and the detail for all Equity-gets closed accounts. The retained earnings balance is the cumulative, lifetime earnings of the company less its cumulative losses and dividends.

Statement of Changes in Financial Position

The statement of changes in financial position describes changes in a company's financial position that may not be obvious from other financial statements. The statement of changes shows the change in working capital, assets, and liabilities for a given period of time. (Sage 50 includes this report. For more information, refer to Read me, page 221.)

Interrelationship of Financial Statements

The financial statements work together. The net income (or net loss) from the income statement is reported on the balance sheet's capital section. The net income or net loss is used to update the balance sheet's capital amount: Capital Beginning of the Year – Net Loss (or + Net Income) = Total Capital.

On the statement of retained earnings, the Ending Retained Earnings balance is $214,616.82. On the balance sheet, if you add the net income $25,579.22 to the balance sheet's retained earnings amount, $189,037.60, the result is $214,616.82. This amount, $214,616.82, is the same as the Ending Retained Earnings balance on the Statement of Retained Earnings.

The total of all the cash accounts on the Balance Sheet (Petty Cash, Cash on Hand, Regular Checking Account, Payroll Checking Account, Savings Account, and Money-Market Fund) is shown as the Cash Balance at End of Period on the statement of cash flow, $32,060.92. The statement of cash flow uses information from both the balance sheet and income statement.

The statement of changes in financial position uses information from the income statement and balance sheet. The net income is shown on the income statement. Current assets and current liabilities are derived from the balance sheet.

No single financial statement tells the entire story. The income statement indicates how much revenue a business has earned during a specific period of time, but it says nothing about how much of that amount has or has not been received in cash. For information about cash and accounts receivable, we have to look at the balance sheet, statement of cash flow, and statement of changes in financial position.

GETTING STARTED

1. Start Sage 50. Open the sample company, Bellwether Garden Supply - Student Name.

2. If necessary, restore data from the Exercise 6-2 backup. (This backup was made on page 202.) Restoring overwrites or replaces an existing file.

To make sure you are starting in the appropriate place in the data (Exercise 6-2.ptb backup) check the Job Profitability Report. The results for Franklin Botanical Gardens are shown below.

FRANKLIN		40000-EQ	129.99			
			59.98			
		50000-EQ		59.95		
				23.90		
		57200		85.00		
				85.00		
		77500		14.00		
				14.00		
			189.97	281.85		
FRANKLIN	Total		189.97	281.85	-91.88	-48.37

USING SAGE 50'S HELP FEATURE

In Chapter 5 on pages 156-157 you used the Help feature to access sample charts of accounts. Later in Chapter 5, on pages 180-181, you used Sage 50's Help feature to learn about security and internal controls. In this chapter, you learn how to access Sage 50's Help feature to learn more about financial statements.

Follow these steps to use Help:

1. From the menu bar, click Help > Help. The Sage 50 Help window displays. If necessary, click on the Index tab.

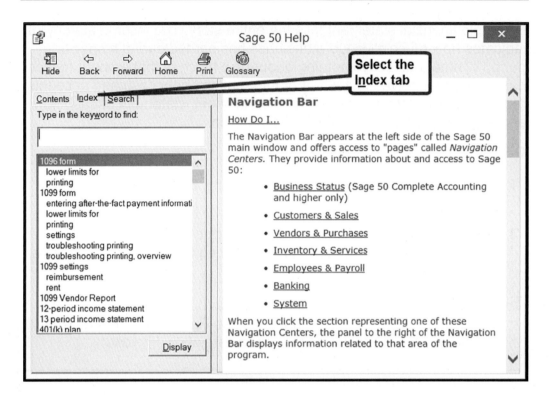

2. Type **balance sheet** in the Type in keyword to find field. Observe that Balance Sheet is highlighted.

3. Click [Display]. Read the information in the right pane.

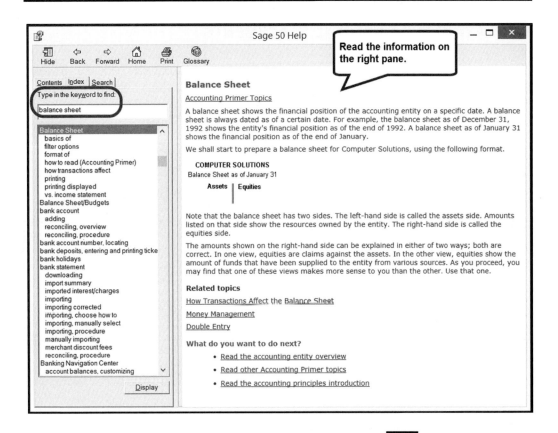

4. If necessary, on the Sage 50 Help title bar click 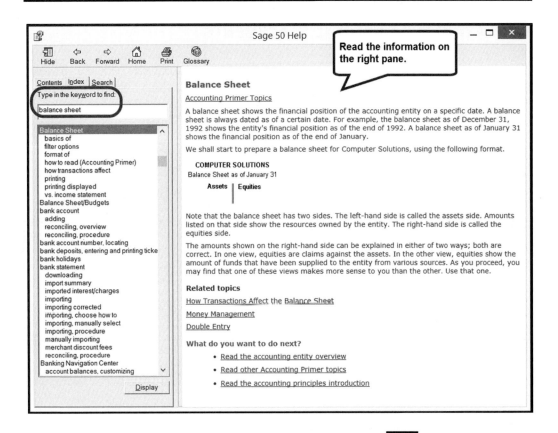 to enlarge the Sage 50 Help window, *or* scroll down. Link to <u>How Transactions Affect the Balance Sheet</u>. Read the information. From that page you can link to <u>Accounting Primer Topics</u>, or you can scroll down and link to other areas.

5. Click on the Sage 50 Help title bar to close the window.

DISPLAYING THE FINANCIAL STATEMENTS

You have already used the Reports & Forms menu to print reports. In the steps that follow you use the Business Status Navigation Center to print financial statements.

1. From the Navigation Bar, click [▣ **Business Status**]. In the Find a Report area's Category field > select Financial Statements.

2. In the Report field > select <Standard> Balance Sheet.

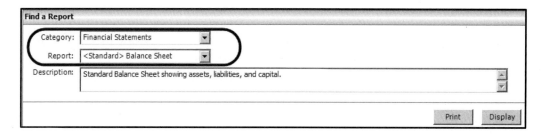

3. Click [Display]. The <Standard> Balance Sheet appears.

Standard refers to statements that Sage 50 has already set up. As noted in the Help window, Sage 50 has a feature that allows you to design financial statements to fit your company's needs. For example, if you select Financial Statements from the Reports & Forms menu,

reports with a wrench [🔧] next to them are customized forms. Compare your balance sheet with the one shown on the next two pages. If you printed the report, observe that a line at the bottom of the reports says "Unaudited – For Management Purposes Only."

Bellwether Garden Supply - Student Name
Balance Sheet
March 31, 2016

ASSETS

Current Assets		
Petty Cash	$ 327.55	
Cash on Hand	1,850.45	
Regular Checking Account	9,046.52	
Payroll Checking Account	8,836.40	
Savings Account	7,500.00	
Money Market Fund	4,500.00	
Accounts Receivable	176,026.47	
Other Receivables	7,681.84	
Allowance for Doubtful Account	(5,000.00)	
Inventory	12,386.46	
Prepaid Expenses	14,221.30	
Employee Advances	3,000.65	
Notes Receivable-Current	11,000.00	
Other Current Assets	120.00	
Total Current Assets		251,497.64
Property and Equipment		
Furniture and Fixtures	62,769.25	
Equipment	38,738.33	
Vehicles	86,273.40	
Other Depreciable Property	6,200.96	
Buildings	185,500.00	
Building Improvements	26,500.00	
Accum. Depreciation-Furniture	(54,680.57)	
Accum. Depreciation-Equipment	(33,138.11)	
Accum. Depreciation-Vehicles	(51,585.26)	
Accum. Depreciation-Other	(3,788.84)	
Accum. Depreciation-Buildings	(34,483.97)	
Accum. Depreciation-Bldg Imp	(4,926.28)	
Total Property and Equipment		223,378.91
Other Assets		
Deposits	15,000.00	
Organization Costs	4,995.10	
Accum Amortiz - Organiz Costs	(2,000.00)	
Notes Receivable- Noncurrent	5,004.90	
Other Noncurrent Assets	3,333.00	
Total Other Assets		26,333.00
Total Assets	$	501,209.55

LIABILITIES AND CAPITAL

Current Liabilities

Accounts Payable	$	80,852.01
Accrued Expenses		3,022.55
Sales Tax Payable		18,083.53
Wages Payable		2,320.30
401 K Deductions Payable		2,579.92
Health Insurance Payable		(530.64)
Federal Payroll Taxes Payable		42,381.73
FUTA Tax Payable		258.20
State Payroll Taxes Payable		6,946.31
SUTA Tax Payable		658.67
Local Payroll Taxes Payable		113.25
Income Taxes Payable		11,045.75
Other Taxes Payable		2,640.15
Current Portion Long-Term Debt		5,167.00
Contracts Payable- Current		2,000.00
Other Current Liabilities		54.00

Total Current Liabilities	177,592.73

Long-Term Liabilities

Notes Payable-Noncurrent	4,000.00

Total Long-Term Liabilities	4,000.00

Total Liabilities	181,592.73

Capital

Common Stock	5,000.00
Paid-in Capital	100,000.00
Retained Earnings	189,037.60
Net Income	25,579.22

Total Capital	319,616.82

Total Liabilities & Capital	$	501,209.55

Unaudited - For Management Purposes Only

Follow these steps to display the Gross Profit by Departments financial statement for the current period.

1. Close the Balance Sheet. In the Find a Report area of the Business Status Navigation Center, the Category field shows Financial Statements. In the Report field, select Gross Profit by Departments.

2. Click **Display** The Departmental Gross Profit Totals report appears. Compare yours with the one shown on the next page.

Bellwether Garden Supply - Student Name
Departmental Gross Profit Totals
Year To Date Totals For the Month Ending March 31, 2016

	Aviary		Books		Equipment	
Revenues						
Sales	$ 51,697.86	100.00	$ 7,293.10	100.00	60,392.26	100.00
Total Revenues	51,697.86	100.00	7,293.10	100.00	60,392.26	100.00
Cost of Sales						
Product Cost - Aviary	20,954.25	40.53	0.00	0.00	0.00	0.00
Product Cost - Books	0.00	0.00	2,361.37	32.38	0.00	0.00
Product Cost - Equipment	0.00	0.00	0.00	0.00	24,238.80	40.14
Total Cost of Sales	20,954.25	40.53	2,361.37	32.38	24,238.80	40.14
Gross Profit	30,743.61	59.47	4,931.73	67.62	36,153.46	59.86

For Management Purposes Only

The Departmental Gross Profit Totals report lists the departmental gross profit totals for the following departments: Aviary, Books, and Equipment.

3. Close the Departmental Gross Profit Totals window.

Departmental Masking

The Departmental Gross Profit report shown above is separated into three departments: Aviary, Books, and Equipment. A feature included in Sage 50 called *masking* allows you to departmentalize financial statements. Masking is the ability to limit information on the report to a single division, department, location, or type code.

For masking, account numbers could be set up like this.

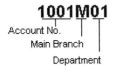

When you print or display a report, you can filter the report using *wildcard* characters. In this example, you would type *****01 to include all departments ending in 01. You would type ****M** to show only main branch numbers on the report. You could type 10***** to find all asset-type accounts for all branches and departments (assuming your asset accounts all begin with 10).

Wildcards make it easy to select a range of account numbers. In Sage 50, the only valid wildcard character is an asterisk. An asterisk represents any number of characters.

You can filter or mask the information that appears on certain general ledger reports. This is done by the use of 15 characters that are allowed in the Account ID field of your general ledger accounts. To see the account masking option, do this.

1. Select Reports & Forms.

2. Select General Ledger.

3. Highlight the Chart of Accounts.

4. On the toolbar, click [Options]

5. In the Select a filter area, highlight Department Mask.

6. In the Select an option area, select Use wildcards. Type **10*****.**
   (*Hint*: After 10, type 5 asterisks.)

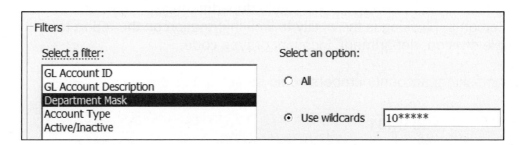

7. Click [OK]. The Chart of Accounts appears with account numbers starting with 10.

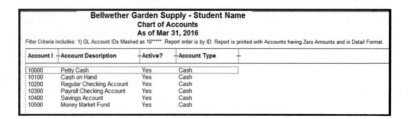

8. Close the Chart of Accounts and the Select a Report or Form window.

Bellwether Garden Supply masks departments by adding a suffix for the department name—AV for Aviary, BK for Books, etc.

Follow these steps to display the income statement:

1. In the Find a Report area of the Business Status Navigation Center, the Category field shows Financial Statements. In the Report field > select <Standard> Income Stmnt.

2. Click [Display]. When the Income Statement displays > click [Options], then uncheck Show Zero Amounts > [OK].

How to fix? What if your financial statements do <u>not</u> agree? Suggestions follow.

- Determine the difference in the amounts. Is the difference the amount of an entry?
- Display the Audit Trail report for the month(s)/year you have been completing work. A partial Audit Trail Report is shown in Chapter 5, page 185. Verify amounts. Is an entry missing or has an entry been recorded twice? If needed, drill down to the original entry.
- You may also find it useful to display the General Ledger Trial Balance and drill down to specific accounts.
- If needed, restore an earlier backup file and then continue from that point. Refer to the chart on pages 2-3 for the backups made in Chapters 1-7.
- Display the financial statement again and compare to textbook illustration.

The income statement is shown on the next page.

Bellwether Garden Supply - Student Name
Income Statement
For the Three Months Ending March 31, 2016

	Current Month			Year to Date	
Revenues					
Sales	$ 295.00	0.33	$	295.00	0.10
Sales - Aviary	7,172.71	8.07		51,697.86	18.36
Sales - Books	149.75	0.17		7,293.10	2.59
Sales - Equipment	18,038.77	20.30		60,392.26	21.45
Sales - Food/Fert	1,176.86	1.32		5,374.05	1.91
Sales - Hand Tools	729.67	0.82		7,058.12	2.51
Sales - Landscape Services	17,467.43	19.65		26,975.53	9.58
Sales - Miscellaneous	0.00	0.00		45.00	0.02
Sales - Nursery	33,795.03	38.02		67,637.11	24.03
Sales - Pots	7,919.31	8.91		11,483.74	4.08
Sales - Seeds	1,457.43	1.64		8,661.39	3.08
Sales - Soil	724.92	0.82		9,152.45	3.25
Other Income	100.00	0.11		25,600.00	9.09
Sales Discounts	(145.72)	(0.16)		(155.62)	(0.06)
Total Revenues	88,881.16	100.00		281,509.99	100.00
Cost of Sales					
Product Cost	(68.50)	(0.08)		(68.50)	(0.02)
Product Cost - Aviary	2,210.60	2.49		20,954.25	7.44
Product Cost - Books	14.27	0.02		2,361.37	0.84
Product Cost - Equipment	7,482.30	8.42		24,238.80	8.61
Product Cost - Food/Fert	466.30	0.52		2,127.54	0.76
Product Cost - Hand Tools	287.15	0.32		2,813.85	1.00
Product Cost - Pots	3,148.60	3.54		3,423.60	1.22
Product Cost - Seeds	584.45	0.66		3,450.65	1.23
Product Cost - Soil	310.72	0.35		4,075.97	1.45
Direct Labor - Nursery	1,750.00	1.97		3,062.50	1.09
Materials Cost	1,567.45	1.76		1,567.45	0.56
Materials Cost - Nursery	5,438.40	6.12		9,668.50	3.43
Subcontractors - Landscaping	335.50	0.38		335.50	0.12
Total Cost of Sales	23,527.24	26.47		78,011.48	27.71
Gross Profit	65,353.92	73.53		203,498.51	72.29
Expenses					
Freight	0.00	0.00		50.00	0.02
Advertising Expense	1,325.00	1.49		1,325.00	0.47
Auto Expenses	274.56	0.31		274.56	0.10
Bad Debt Expense	1,341.09	1.51		1,341.09	0.48
Bank Charges	18.00	0.02		18.00	0.01
Depreciation Expense	2,761.30	3.11		8,394.00	2.98
Legal and Professional Expense	150.00	0.17		510.00	0.18
Licenses Expense	150.00	0.17		150.00	0.05
Maintenance Expense	75.00	0.08		75.00	0.03
Office Expense	534.64	0.60		534.64	0.19
Payroll Tax Exp	5,854.46	6.59		16,115.88	5.72
Rent or Lease Expense	550.00	0.62		1,100.00	0.39
Repairs Expense	125.00	0.14		3,694.00	1.31
Supplies Expense	2,873.42	3.23		2,873.42	1.02
Utilities Expense	303.45	0.34		303.45	0.11
Wages Expense	51,086.42	57.48		140,705.46	49.98
Other Expense	464.90	0.52		464.90	0.17
Purchase Disc- Expense Items	(10.11)	(0.01)		(10.11)	0.00
Total Expenses	67,877.13	76.37		177,919.29	63.20
Net Income	$ (2,523.21)	(2.84)	$	25,579.22	9.09

For Management Purposes Only

Drill Down from the Income Statement to Original Entry

Follow these steps to follow an account balance from the income statement, to the general ledger, then to the original entry window. This is called drill down.

1. The income statement should be displayed. Place your cursor over 7,172.71, Sales – Aviary

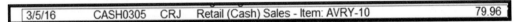

| Sales - Aviary | ⓩ 7,172.71 |

Observe that the cursor becomes a magnifying glass icon with a Z in the middle. (Z is an abbreviation for zoom). Double-click with your left mouse button.

2. The General Ledger Account 40000-AV, Sales - Aviary, appears. From the general ledger you can drill down to the Receive Money window. For example, double click on the 3/5/2016 Cash Receipts Journal (CRJ) entry for $79.96.

| 3/5/16 | CASH0305 | CRJ | Retail (Cash) Sales - Item: AVRY-10 | 79.96 |

3. This takes you to the Receive Money window. The original entry for 4 Thistle Bird Seed Mix-6 lb. (AVRY-10140) is shown (19.99 x 4 = 79.96). Close the Receive Money window to go back to the General Ledger Account No. 40000-AV.

4. Drill down from one of the Sales Journal (SJ) entries. The Sales/Invoicing window appears.

5. When you are through using drill down, close the Sales/Invoicing window, General Ledger, and Income Statement windows.

Follow these steps to display the Statement of Cash Flow.

1. In the Find a Report area of the Business Status Navigation Center, the Category field shows Financial Statements. In the Report field, select <Standard> Cash Flow > Display

2. From the Statement of Cash Flow window, click Options > uncheck Show Zero Amounts > OK. If printed, observe that the bottom of the report says "Unaudited - For Internal Use Only."

Bellwether Garden Supply - Student Name
Statement of Cash Flow
For the three Months Ended March 31, 2016

	Current Month	Year to Date
Cash Flows from operating activities		
Net Income	$ (2,523.21) $	25,579.22
Adjustments to reconcile net income to net cash provided by operating activities		
Accum. Depreciation-Furniture	420.80	1,262.40
Accum. Depreciation-Equipment	385.05	1,265.25
Accum. Depreciation-Vehicles	1,437.89	4,313.67
Accum. Depreciation-Other	64.57	193.71
Accum. Depreciation-Buildings	396.37	1,189.11
Accum. Depreciation-Bldg Imp	56.63	169.87
Accounts Receivable	(11,085.80)	(172,928.03)
Other Receivables	0.00	(3,672.24)
Inventory	13,650.37	6,211.73
Accounts Payable	10,497.38	76,949.26
Sales Tax Payable	4,386.16	15,622.98
401 K Deductions Payable	825.32	2,135.22
Health Insurance Payable	(530.64)	(530.64)
Federal Payroll Taxes Payable	14,617.04	40,794.88
State Payroll Taxes Payable	2,138.64	5,960.98
Other Taxes Payable	50.00	50.00
Other Current Liabilities	150.00	150.00
Total Adjustments	37,459.78	(20,861.85)
Net Cash provided by Operations	34,936.57	4,717.37
Cash Flows from investing activities Used For		
Net cash used in investing	0.00	0.00
Cash Flows from financing activities Proceeds From Used For		
Net cash used in financing	0.00	0.00
Net increase <decrease> in cash	$ 34,936.57 $	4,717.37
Summary		
Cash Balance at End of Period	$ 32,060.92 $	32,060.92
Cash Balance at Beg of Period	2,875.54	(27,343.66)
Net Increase <Decrease> in Cash	$ 34,936.46 $	4,717.26

Unaudited - For Management Purposes Only

3. Close the Statement of Cash Flow.

Follow these steps to display the Statement of Retained Earnings:

1. In the Report field, select <Standard> Retained Earnings.

2. Click [Display]. When the Statement of Retained Earnings displays >
   click [Options] > uncheck Show Zero Amounts > [OK]. The
   Statement of Retained Earnings appears.

Bellwether Garden Supply - Student Name
Statement of Retained Earnings
For the Three Months Ending March 31, 2016

Beginning Retained Earnings	$	189,037.60
Adjustments To Date		0.00
Net Income		25,579.22
Subtotal		214,616.82
Dividends Paid		0.00
Ending Retained Earnings	$	214,616.82

For Management Purposes Only

---

3. Close the Statement of Retained Earnings.

Follow the steps on the next page to print the Statement of Changes in
Financial Position.

 Read Me: Statement of Changes in Financial Position

Sage 50 includes the Statement of Changes in Financial Position even though current
accounting standards require that a statement of cash flow is needed as part of a full set of
financial statements in place of a statement of changes in financial position.

---

1. In the Report field, select <Standard> Stmnt Changes > [Display].
   Select the option to uncheck Show Zero amounts.

Bellwether Garden Supply - Student Name
Statement of Changes in Financial Position
For the three months ended March 31, 2016

	Current Month	Year To Date
Sources of Working Capital		
Net Income	$ (2,523.21)	$ 25,579.22
Add back items not requiring working capital		
Accum. Depreciation-Furniture	420.76	1,262.36
Accum. Depreciation-Equipment	384.99	1,265.19
Accum. Depreciation-Vehicles	1,437.89	4,313.67
Accum. Depreciation-Other	64.57	193.71
Accum. Depreciation-Buildings	396.36	1,189.10
Accum. Depreciation-Bldg Imp	56.63	169.87
Working capital from operations	237.99	33,973.12
Other sources		
Total sources	237.99	33,973.12
Uses of working capital		
Total uses	0.00	0.00
Net change	$ 237.99	$ 33,973.12
Analysis of componants of changes		
Increase <Decrease> in Current Assets		
Petty Cash	$ 227.55	$ 227.55
Regular Checking Account	(631.21)	(2,280.03)
Payroll Checking Account	30,840.12	2,269.74
Money Market Fund	4,500.00	4,500.00
Accounts Receivable	11,085.80	172,928.03
Other Receivables	0.00	3,672.24
Inventory	(13,650.37)	(6,211.73)
<Increase> Decrease in Current Liabilities		
Accounts Payable	(10,497.38)	(76,949.26)
Sales Tax Payable	(4,386.16)	(15,622.98)
401 K Deductions Payable	(825.32)	(2,135.22)
Health Insurance Payable	530.64	530.64
Federal Payroll Taxes Payable	(14,617.04)	(40,794.88)
State Payroll Taxes Payable	(2,138.64)	(5,960.98)
Other Taxes Payable	(50.00)	(50.00)
Other Current Liabilities	(150.00)	(150.00)
Net change	$ 237.99	$ 33,973.12

For Management Purposes Only

How to Fix? I do NOT have a printer. What should I do?

1. Display the financial statement > select 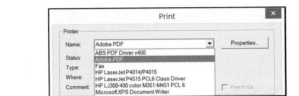. In the Name field, click on the down-arrow.
2. Select Adobe PDF *or* Microsoft XPS Document Writer.

3. Save the file to your USB drive.
4. Verify your displayed reports with those shown on pages 213-222.

If needed, the PDF or XPS file can be emailed to your instructor. When selecting an Adobe PDF or XPS file, no printer is required.

---

2. If instructed, print or save. Close all windows.

BACKING UP CHAPTER 7 DATA (Optional Backup)

You have not added any new data in Chapter 7.

If you would prefer to make a backup, the suggested file name is **Chapter 7.ptb**. Detailed steps for backing up data are shown on pages 22-25.

Backing up saves your data to that point in your work. Each time you back up, use a different file name; for example, the suggested file name at this point is Chapter 7.ptb. (Sage 50 automatically adds the file extension .ptb to backups.) Using a unique file name allows you to restore at different points in the data.

EXPORT FINANCIAL STATEMENTS TO EXCEL

Follow these steps to have separate sheets for each financial statement on one Excel workbook.

1. Display the <Standard> Balance Sheet > click .

---

2. The Copy Report to Excel window appears. The default File Option is Create a new Microsoft Excel workbook. The Default Report header option is Show header in Excel worksheet. If necessary, make these selections.

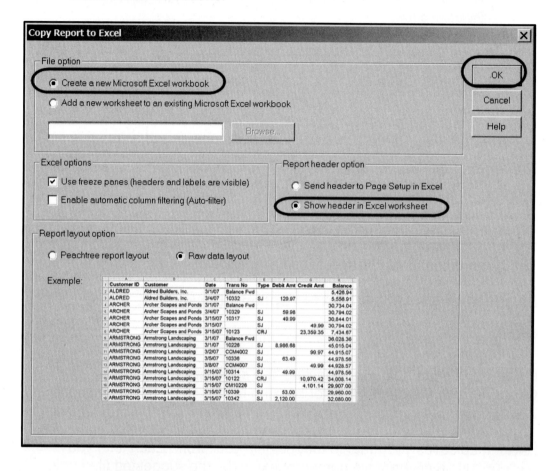

3. Click [OK]. The Balance Sheet appears as an Excel workbook.

4. Save. Use the file name **Chapter 7_Financial Statements.xlsx**. Minimize Excel.

5. Close Sage 50's Balance Sheet.

6. Display the \<Standard\> Income Statement. From the displayed Income Statement, click [Excel].

7. On the Copy Report to Excel window, select Add a new worksheet to an Existing Microsoft Excel workbook. Then, Browse to the location of the saved file (Chapter 7_Financial Statements.xlsx). Double-click on the Chapter 7_Financial Statements file (or highlight it and click <Open>).

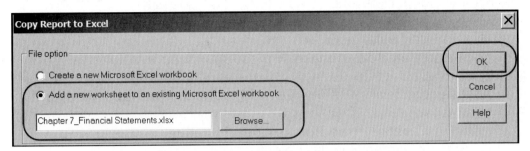

8. Click [OK]. Maximize Excel. (From the taskbar, click on the Microsoft Excel button.) Observe that the Excel file shows two sheets—Balance Sheet and Income Stmnt –
    [Balance Sheet   **Income Stmnt**].

9. Save. Add the following financial statements to the Excel file: Gross Profit by Departments, Statement of Cash Flow, Retained Earnings Statement, and Statement of Changes in Financial Position. When you are finished, the Excel file should have 6 sheets: Balance Sheet, Income Stmnt, Gross Profit by Departments, Cash Flow, Retained Earnings, Stmnt Changes.

    Check your figures:

Total Liabilities & Capital	$501,209.55
Year to Date Gross Profit	203,498.51
Year-to-date Net Income	$25,579.22
Year-to-date Net Increase in Cash	$4,717.26
Ending Retained Earnings	$214,616.82

10. Save. Exit Excel.

11. Save the financial statements as PDF files. Use the financial statement's name, then save. For example, use the file name Chapter 7_Balance Sheet.pdf, Chapter 7_Income Statement, etc.

ONLINE LEARNING CENTER

Complete the following end-of-chapter activities online at
www.mhhe.com/yacht2016 > Student Edition > Chapter 7.

1. Interactive Multiple-Choice and True/False questions.
2. Going to the Net exercise: Access the article How to Value Stocks: How to Read Balance Sheet.
3. QA Templates: 10 true/make true questions and three analysis questions.
4. Assessment Rubric: Review journals, navigation centers, modules, and task windows.
5. Listen to narrated PowerPoint slides.
6. Bellwether Garden Supply Project.

The OLC also includes links to the Appendixes:

- Appendix A: Troubleshooting
- Appendix B: Accounting Information Systems
- Appendix C: Review of Accounting Principles
- Appendix D: Glossary of Terms

Exercise 7-1: Answer the following questions about the balance sheet and income statement:

1. The total assets are: _____

2. The total capital is: _____

3. Indicate the amount of the net income or
   (net loss) for the month of March: _____

4. The current month's gross profit is: _____

5. The current month's total expenses are: _____

Exercise 7-2: Answer the following questions about the statement of cash flow and the statement of retained earnings:

1. The current month's cash balance at the
   beginning of the period is: _____

2. The year-to-date's cash balance at the
   beginning of the period is: _____

3. The cash balance at end of period for the
   current month is: _____

4. The beginning Retained Earnings balance is: _____

5. The ending Retained Earnings balance is: _____

BELLWETHER GARDEN SUPPLY PROJECT

To answer questions about Bellwether Garden Supply, go online to www.mhhe.com/yacht2016 > Student Edition > link to Bellwether Garden Supply Project. In this project, you examine Bellwether's transactions, reports, and internal controls. The project includes comparing controlling account balances to the subsidiary ledgers and describing why some balances may differ.

CHAPTER 7 INDEX

Chapter 8

Stone Arbor Landscaping: Time & Billing

LEARNING OBJECTIVES

1. Start the sample company, Stone Arbor Landscaping.
2. Explore Sage 50's time and billing feature.
3. Use the time and billing feature to complete a time ticket, sales invoice, and payroll entry.
4. Make two backups, save two Excel files, and save four PDF files.

STONE ARBOR LANDSCAPING

When you installed Sage 50 2016, two sample companies were included with the software: Bellwether Garden Supply and Stone Arbor Landscaping. In Chapters 1–7 you worked with Bellwether Garden Supply. Chapter 8 focuses on how the second sample company, Stone Arbor Landscaping, uses the time and billing feature.

TIME & BILLING

Time & Billing can track time spent on various activities and record internal use of company resources associated with customers or jobs. Recorded time and expenses can be billed later to customers on sales invoices. If you use payroll, timed activities can be applied to an employee's paycheck. Time & Billing can also be used to effectively manage administrative activities and overhead expenses for your business.

The purpose of Sage 50's time and billing feature is to provide the tools to record customer-related work or expenses. Time & Billing gives you a way to track expenses and time when working with customers. Time and expenses are recorded for customers, jobs, or administrative tasks.

Customers: Time and expenses can be associated with customers that you intend to bill later in Sales/Invoicing. Record time and expenses for customers only if you are not using job costing.

Jobs: If you are tracking jobs in Job Costs, you can record time and expense for jobs, phases, or cost codes. Then, you can apply billable time and expense items to the customer's invoice. The advantage of recording time and expense for jobs is that you can track details related to the completion of the project, including overhead and labor costs. Also, you can manage job profitability more effectively in reports.

Administrative: You can track internal activities to manage process control and overhead costs for the business. You may want to track the number of hours an employee spends preparing proposals or bookkeeping. Or, you may want to track an employee's mileage or travel expenses.

To track time and expenses, Sage uses two forms or tickets: the time ticket and the expense ticket. Each ticket type can be specific to a customer, job, or non-billable administrative tasks (miscellaneous items). Each ticket has its own special type of inventory item: the activity item for time tickets and the charge item for expense tickets.

Time Tickets

Time tickets are used to record time-based activities such as research or consultations. They record the activities of either an employee or a vendor. The two methods of entering time ticket information are weekly or daily.

The billing rate used for a recorded activity can be based on the employee who records the ticket or one of the five billing rates assigned to the activity item. Or, you can record the billing at the time you enter the time ticket.

Expense Tickets

Expense tickets are used to track and aid in the recovery of customer-related expenses. These expenses are *not* based on time. Expenses can be based on the various charges related to the service being offered. For example, if you were an accountant, you might charge your client for copying fees or faxing fees.

Both time and expense tickets can be used in the Sales/Invoicing window to bill your customers. The Sales/Invoicing window includes a feature called Apply Tickets/Reimbursable Expenses which takes you to the time and billing feature. The rate for expense tickets is determined by the unit price of the charge item multiplied by the quantity.

The chart below shows how time and billing works:

Time & Billing Ticket Types			
Ticket Type	**Inventory Item Class**	**Examples**	**Billing Amount Equals**
Time Ticket	Activity Item	Research Consultants Writing Reports	Billing Rate Times Activity Divisions
Expense Ticket	Charge Item	Copying Faxing Court Fees	Unit Price of the Charge Item Times Quantity

GETTING STARTED

1. Start Sage 50. From the startup window, select Explore a sample company. (*Hint:* If another company opens, select File > Close Company. Stone Arbor Landscaping will be listed in the Company Name list after the first time it is opened.)

2. The Explore a Sample Company window appears. Select Stone Arbor Landscaping.

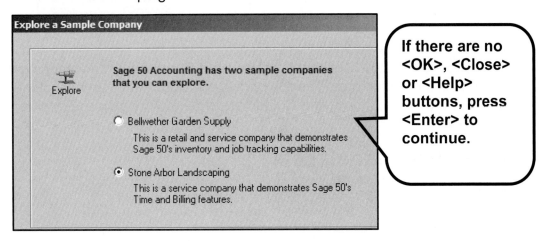

> **Troubleshooting:** Why doesn't my Explore a Sample Company window show the <OK>, <Close>, and <Help> buttons?

Screen resolution affects how windows look. The recommended screen resolution is 1024X768 with small fonts (refer to page v, Software Installation). You can use a higher resolution but some of the windows will look different. If you do not have an OK button, press <Enter> to start Stone Arbor Landscaping.

Software Expiration. If you are using the Student Version of Sage 50 2016 included with the textbook, a Sage 50 Accounting window appears that says "You can use this company in the student version of Sage 50 for the next 14 months and then it will expire. The company's expiration date can be found in the Company Information section of the System Navigation Center." For more information about the expiration date, refer to page xviii, Expiration Date, Student Version, Sage 50 2016.

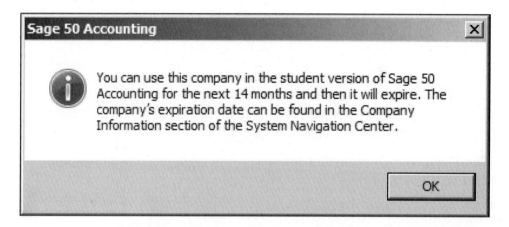

3. Click [OK]. The first time you start Stone Arbor Landscaping it takes a few moments. The title bar shows Stone Arbor Landscaping – Sage 50 Accounting. The Customers & Sales Navigation Center is shown.

ADD YOUR NAME TO REPORTS

To add your name to reports, follow these steps.

1. From the Navigation Bar, select [System]. If necessary, scroll down the page to Company Maintenance.

2. Click ⎢Edit Company Information Now⎥. The Maintain Company Information
   Window appears. In the Company Name field, add your name or
   initials after Stone Arbor Landscaping.

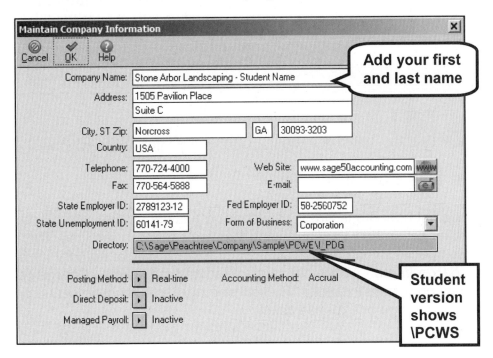

3. Click ⎢OK⎥. Click File > Exit Sage 50. (Exit so you can see how the
   Maintain Company Information window changes.)

4. Start Sage 50 > ⎢Open an existing company⎥ Open Stone Arbor
   Landscaping - Student Name (your first and last name.) In the Last
   field, the current date is shown. Your date will differ.

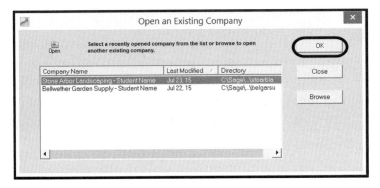

5. Display the Maintain Company Information window (Maintain > Company Information). Observe that the Directory field has changed. After adding your name to the Stone Arbor Landscaping, the Directory field ends in **\stoarbla** – three letters from the first word (**sto**ne), three letters from the second word (**arb**or), and two letters from the third word (**la**ndscaping).

Directory: C:\Sage\Peachtree\Company\Sample\PCWE\stoarbla ◄───────

6. Click [OK] to close the Maintain Company Information window.

USING TIME & BILLING

Let's look at how Stone Arbor Landscaping has set up time and billing. First, they set up how they are going to invoice for their services. There are two special inventory item classes for Time & Billing: *activity items* and *charge items*. Activity items are used on time tickets. Charge items are used on expense tickets. These inventory items must be set up prior to entering a time or expense ticket.

There are four steps to complete Time & Billing.

Step 1:   Set up the inventory item.
Step 2:   Enter the time ticket.
Step 3:   Record the sales invoice.
Step 4:   Payroll.

Inventory Item Maintenance

You use maintenance windows to set up defaults. Follow these steps to look at the inventory maintenance information for Stone Arbor Landscaping.

1. From the Navigation Bar, click [Inventory & Services] > [Inventory Items] > View and Edit Inventory Items. The Inventory List appears. Click once on INSTL HARD – COMM to highlight it.

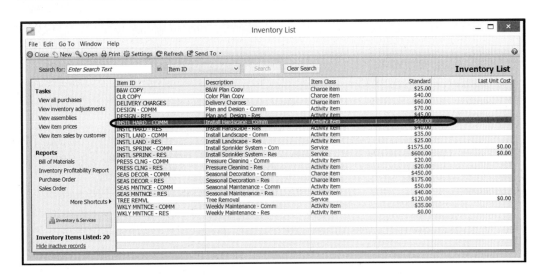

2. Double-click INSTL HARD – COMM. The Maintain Inventory
   Items window appears for INSTL HARD – COMM, Install Hardscape
   – Comm. If the Sage Advisor appears, read it. To close it, click ⊗.

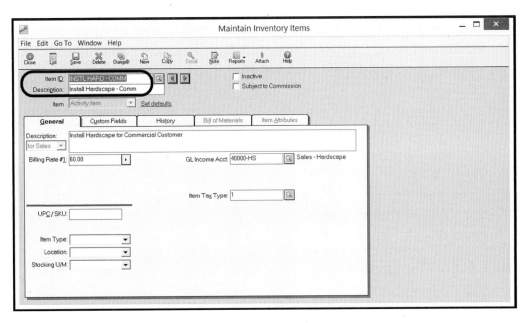

Review the information on the Maintain Inventory Items window.
Observe that $60.00 is shown in the Billing Rate #1 field. Click on
the right-arrow to see other billing rates, then close the Multiple Price
Levels window. The GL Income Acct is Account No. 40000-HS,
Sales – Hardscape. The Item Tax Type is 1 (for Taxable). This
maintenance window is similar to ones that you have set up before.

Remember, defaults are set up in maintenance windows.

3. Close all windows to return to the Inventory & Services Navigation Center.

Time Ticket

The Time Ticket shows how much was billed to the customer. To see how time is billed, look at a job that Alan Hardman has already completed.

Follow these steps to see time tickets.

1. From the Navigation Bar, click 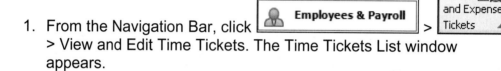 > 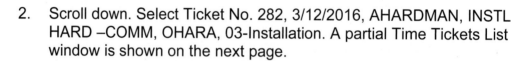 > View and Edit Time Tickets. The Time Tickets List window appears.

2. Scroll down. Select Ticket No. 282, 3/12/2016, AHARDMAN, INSTL HARD –COMM, OHARA, 03-Installation. A partial Time Tickets List window is shown on the next page.

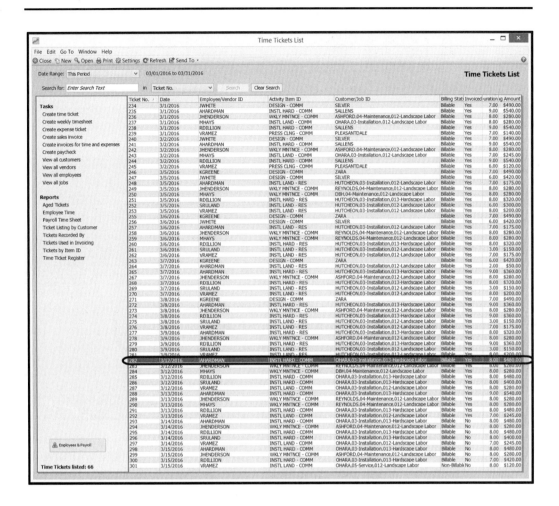

3. Click 🔍 Open. The Time Tickets window appears. Notice that the Activity Item is for INSTL HARD – COMM, Install Hardscape - Comm, and that the Job name is O'Hara Homes Contract. The Invoice description is Installation of Decking/Patio. Mr. Hardman worked for eight hours on March 12, 2016; and the Bill amount is 480.00. The Time Tickets window shows one instance, March 12, 2016 (refer to the Ticket date field.)

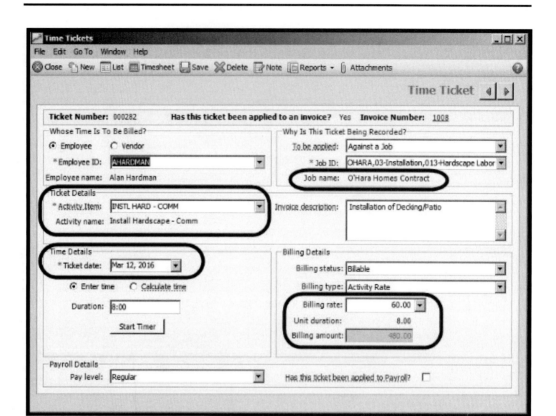

4. Click 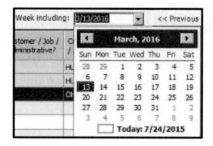. The Time Ticket Weekly Timesheet Entry window appears. In the Week including field, click on the down arrow. The calendar appears. Select March 13, 2016. (*Hint:* The Week including field may default to the current date. To select the date, use the calendar.)

The Time Ticket Weekly Timesheet Entry window is shown on the next page. The OHara job completed on 3/12 is shown.

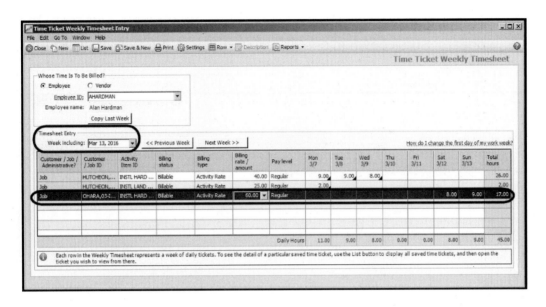

5. Close all windows.

Sales Invoice

In order to see how Mr. Hardman's charges were billed to the customer, O'Hara Homes, follow these steps.

1. From the Navigation Bar, click [Customers & Sales] > [Sales Invoices] > View and Edit Sales Invoices. The Sales Invoice List appears. Click on OHARA, Invoice No. 1008, 3/13/2016 to highlight it.

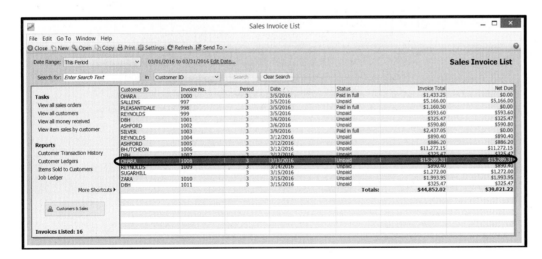

2. Double-click OHARA, Invoice 1008. A partial Sales/Invoicing window appears. Scroll down to see all of it, *or* enlarge the Sales/Invoicing window.

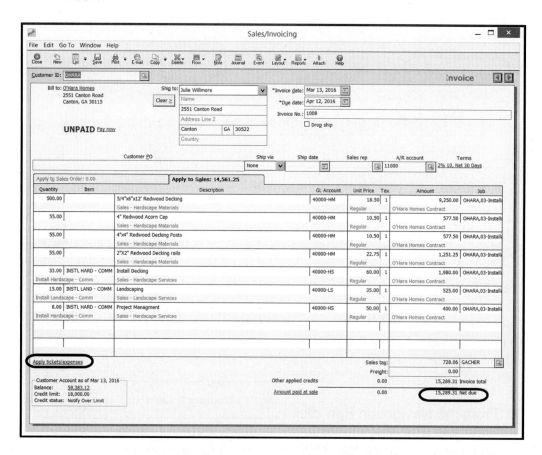

3. Link to Apply tickets/expenses. (*Hint: This is located in the lower left of the window.*)

4. The Apply Tickets/Reimbursable Expenses window appears. Observe that Alan Hardman's work is billed, along with other employees that worked on this customer's job.

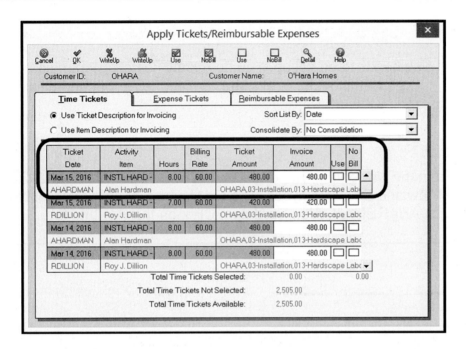

The time ticket shows Alan Hardman's Ticket Amount of 480.00 for 8 hours at a billing rate of $60.00 ($60 x 8 = $480).

5. Click [✔ OK] to close the Apply Tickets/Reimbursable Expenses window. You are returned to the O'Hara Homes Sales/Invoicing window.

6. Close all windows to return to the Customers & Sales Navigation Center.

Payroll

Payroll also needs to be set up. You do this by selecting Hourly-Time Ticket Hours for employees. Let's see how Stone Arbor Landscaping sets this up.

1. From the Navigation Bar, click **Employees & Payroll** > **Employees**, > View and Edit Employees. The Employee List appears. Double-click AHARDMAN, Alan Hardman. Click on the Pay Info tab.

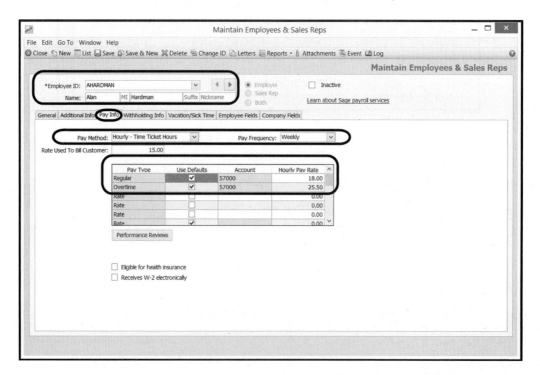

Observe that Mr. Hardman's Pay Method is Hourly – Time Ticket Hours. He is paid weekly. Also notice that Mr. Hardman's regular pay account number is 57000.

2. Close all windows. If prompted, do not save this record.

BACKING UP CHAPTER 8 DATA

Follow these steps to back up Chapter 8 data:

1. If necessary, insert your USB flash drive. From the System Navigation Center, link to [Back Up Now]. Make sure that the box next to Include company name in the backup file name is *unchecked*.

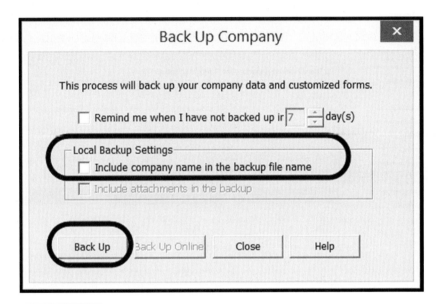

2. Click [Back Up].

3. In the Save in field, select the appropriate drive letter for your USB drive. (*Or,* save to the hard-drive default location or other location.) Type **Chapter 8** in the File name field.

4. Click [Save].

5. When the window prompts This company backup will require approximately 1 diskette, click [OK]. When the window prompts Please insert the first disk, click [OK]. When the Back Up Company scale is 100% complete, you have successfully backed up to the current point in Chapter 8. (Step 5 will differ slightly if you are backing up to the default or other hard-drive location.)

EXPORT TIME TICKET REGISTER TO EXCEL

Follow these steps to export the Time Ticket Register to Excel.

1. From the Reports & Forms menu, select Time/Expense > highlight Time Ticket Register

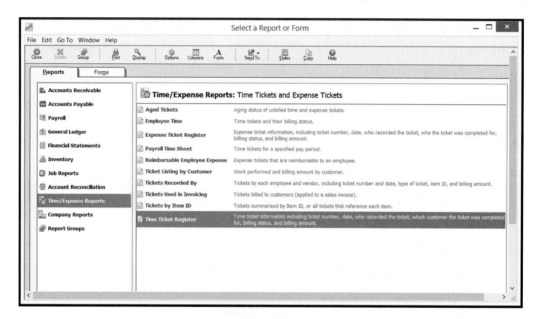

2. Click Send To, Excel.

3. The Modify Report – Time Ticket Register window appears, click OK

4. The Copy Report to Excel window appears. In the File option area, make sure Create a new Microsoft Excel workbook is selected.

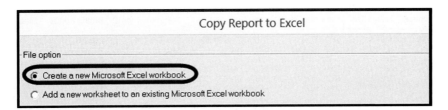

5. In the Report header option area, Show header in Excel worksheet should be selected.

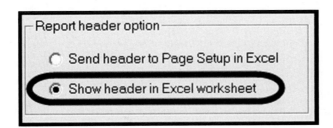

6. Click [OK]. Stone Arbor Landscaping's Time Ticket Register is exported to Excel. Scroll down the Register. Ticket No. 282 for AHardman is shown. The Time Tickets List window on page 237 also shows this job. A partial Time Ticket Register is shown on the next page.

Stone Arbor Landscaping - Student Name
Time Ticket Register
For the Period From Mar 1, 2016 to Mar 31, 2016

Filter Criteria includes: Report order is by Ticket Number.

Ticket Number	Ticket Dat	Recorded by ID	Item ID	Completed for ID	Billing Status	Billing Amount
234	3/1/16	JWHITE	DESIGN - COMM	SILVER	Billable	490.00
235	3/1/16	AHARDMAN	INSTL HARD - COM	SALLENS	Billable	540.00
236	3/1/16	JHENDERSON	WKLY MNTNCE - C	ASHFORD,04-Ma	Billable	280.00
237	3/1/16	MHAYS	INSTL LAND - COM	OHARA,03-Install	Billable	280.00
238	3/1/16	RDILLION	INSTL HARD - COM	SALLENS	Billable	540.00
239	3/1/16	VRAMEZ	PRESS CLNG - CO	PLEASANTDALE	Billable	140.00
240	3/2/16	JWHITE	DESIGN - COMM	SILVER	Billable	490.00
241	3/2/16	AHARDMAN	INSTL HARD - COM	SALLENS	Billable	540.00
242	3/2/16	JHENDERSON	WKLY MNTNCE - C	ASHFORD,04-Ma	Billable	280.00
243	3/2/16	MHAYS	INSTL LAND - COM	OHARA,03-Install	Billable	245.00
244	3/2/16	RDILLION	INSTL HARD - COM	SALLENS	Billable	540.00
245	3/2/16	VRAMEZ	PRESS CLNG - CO	PLEASANTDALE	Billable	120.00
246	3/5/16	KGREENE	DESIGN - COMM	ZARA	Billable	490.00
247	3/5/16	JWHITE	DESIGN - COMM	SILVER	Billable	420.00
248	3/5/16	AHARDMAN	INSTL LAND - RES	HUTCHEON,03-I	Billable	175.00
249	3/5/16	JHENDERSON	WKLY MNTNCE - C	REYNOLDS,04-M	Billable	280.00
250	3/5/16	MHAYS	WKLY MNTNCE - C	DBH,04-Maintena	Billable	280.00
251	3/5/16	RDILLION	INSTL HARD - RES	HUTCHEON,03-I	Billable	320.00
252	3/5/16	SRULAND	INSTL LAND - RES	HUTCHEON,03-I	Billable	300.00
253	3/5/16	VRAMEZ	INSTL LAND - RES	HUTCHEON,03-I	Billable	200.00
255	3/6/16	KGREENE	DESIGN - COMM	ZARA	Billable	490.00
256	3/6/16	JWHITE	DESIGN - COMM	SILVER	Billable	420.00
257	3/6/16	AHARDMAN	INSTL LAND - RES	HUTCHEON,03-I	Billable	175.00
258	3/6/16	JHENDERSON	WKLY MNTNCE - C	REYNOLDS,04-M	Billable	280.00
259	3/6/16	MHAYS	WKLY MNTNCE - C	REYNOLDS,04-M	Billable	280.00
260	3/6/16	RDILLION	INSTL HARD - RES	HUTCHEON,03-I	Billable	320.00
261	3/6/16	SRULAND	INSTL LAND - RES	HUTCHEON,03-I	Billable	150.00
262	3/6/16	VRAMEZ	INSTL LAND - RES	HUTCHEON,03-I	Billable	175.00
263	3/7/16	KGREENE	DESIGN - COMM	ZARA	Billable	420.00
264	3/7/16	AHARDMAN	INSTL LAND - RES	HUTCHEON,03-I	Billable	50.00
265	3/7/16	AHARDMAN	INSTL HARD - RES	HUTCHEON,03-I	Billable	360.00
267	3/7/16	JHENDERSON	WKLY MNTNCE - C	ASHFORD,04-Ma	Billable	280.00
268	3/7/16	RDILLION	INSTL HARD - RES	HUTCHEON,03-I	Billable	320.00
269	3/7/16	SRULAND	INSTL LAND - RES	HUTCHEON,03-I	Billable	150.00
270	3/7/16	VRAMEZ	INSTL LAND - RES	HUTCHEON,03-I	Billable	200.00
271	3/8/16	KGREENE	DESIGN - COMM	ZARA	Billable	490.00
272	3/8/16	AHARDMAN	INSTL HARD - RES	HUTCHEON,03-I	Billable	360.00
273	3/8/16	JHENDERSON	WKLY MNTNCE - C	ASHFORD,04-Ma	Billable	280.00
274	3/8/16	RDILLION	INSTL HARD - RES	HUTCHEON,03-I	Billable	360.00
275	3/8/16	SRULAND	INSTL LAND - RES	HUTCHEON,03-I	Billable	150.00
276	3/8/16	VRAMEZ	INSTL LAND - RES	HUTCHEON,03-I	Billable	175.00
277	3/9/16	AHARDMAN	INSTL HARD - RES	HUTCHEON,03-I	Billable	320.00
278	3/9/16	JHENDERSON	WKLY MNTNCE - C	ASHFORD,04-Ma	Billable	280.00
279	3/9/16	RDILLION	INSTL HARD - RES	HUTCHEON,03-I	Billable	360.00
280	3/9/16	SRULAND	INSTL LAND - RES	HUTCHEON,03-I	Billable	150.00
281	3/9/16	VRAMEZ	INSTL LAND - RES	HUTCHEON,03-I	Billable	200.00
282	3/12/16	AHARDMAN	INSTL HARD - COM	OHARA,03-Install	Billable	480.00
283	3/12/16	JHENDERSON	WKLY MNTNCE - C	REYNOLDS,04-M	Billable	280.00
284	3/12/16	MHAYS	WKLY MNTNCE - C	DBH,04-Maintena	Billable	280.00
285	3/12/16	RDILLION	INSTL HARD - COM	OHARA,03-Install	Billable	480.00

7. Save. Use the file name **Chapter 8_Time Ticket Register.xlsx**. Close all windows.

8. Save the Time Ticket Register as a PDF file. Use **Chapter 8_Time Ticket Register.pdf** as the file name.

ONLINE LEARNING CENTER

Complete the following end-of-chapter activities online at
www.mhhe.com/yacht2016 > Student Edition > Chapter 8.

1. Interactive Multiple-Choice and True/False questions.
2. Going to the Net exercise: Access the Sage Advice website.
3. QA Templates: 10 multiple choice questions and one analysis
   question.
4. Assessment Rubric: Review journals, navigation centers, modules,
   and task windows.
5. Listen to narrated PowerPoint slides.

The OLC also includes links to the Appendixes:

- Appendix A: Troubleshooting
- Appendix B: Accounting Information Systems
- Appendix C: Review of Accounting Principles
- Appendix D: Glossary of Terms

Exercise 8-1: Complete the following time ticket, sales invoice, and
payroll entry.

1. If necessary, restore the Chapter 8.ptb file. This backup was made on
   page 243.

2. Enter a new time ticket for the employee, Mike E. Hays. Complete the
   following Time Ticket fields.

Employee ID: Mike E. Hays
To be applied: Against a Job
Job ID: DBH
          04-Maintenance
          012 Landscape Labor

Hint: Click on the plus sign next
to DBH to expand the list.
Expand 04-Maintenance, then select 012 Landscape Labor.

Activity item: Weekly Maintenance - Comm
Invoice description: Weekly Maintenance
Ticket Date: Mar 15, 2016

Duration: 8:00
Billing status: Billable
Billing type: Activity Rate

3. Save the Time Ticket.

4. Record the following sales invoice.

Date   *Description*

03/22/16   Apply the completed time ticket to Invoice 1019.
            (*Hint:* Enter a new sales invoice.) On the Sales/Invoicing
            window, complete these fields:

            Customer ID: DBH Enterprises
            Date: March 22, 2016
            Invoice No.:   1019

Select [▸ Apply tickets/expenses]. The Apply Tickets/Reimbursable
Expenses window appears showing the Time Ticket information.
Select the Use box to place a checkmark in it. Click <OK>. The Apply
to Sales portion of the Sales/Invoicing window is completed. Observe
that the Net due shows $295.40. Post the sales invoice.

5. Display the Time Ticket for Mike E. Hays. Observe that Invoice No.
   1019 is applied.

6. Record the following payroll entry.

03/23/16   Pay employee, Mike E. Hays for 24 regular hours.
            Select the Jobs icon to see the two jobs Mr. Hays
            completed during this pay period. Post the payroll entry.

7. Backup. The suggested file name is **Exercise 8-1**.

Exercise 8-2: To complete Exercise 8-2, do the following.

1. If necessary, restore the Exercise 8-1.ptb backup file.

2. Print the Job Ledger Report. (*Hint:* Reports & Forms > Jobs > Job
   Ledger.

How to Fix? I don't have a printer?

Select <Print>, then in the Name field, Adobe PDF or Microsoft XPS Document Writer. Save to USB drive. For detailed steps, refer to page 66. Use for steps 2 through 4. If you save as PDF files, use the file names shown in step 6 on the next page.

4. Print the Payroll Time Sheet. (*Hint:* Reports & Forms > Time/Expense Reports > Payroll Time Sheet. Select [Options]. The Pay End Date is 3/15/16.

5. Save the three Time & Billing Reports as an Excel file: Job Ledger, Time Ticket Register, and Payroll Time Sheet. The suggested file name is **Exercise 8-2_Time and Billing Reports.xlsx**.

6. Save three PDF files: **Exercise 8-2_Job Ledger.pdf**, **Exercise 8-2_Time Ticket Register.pdf**, and **Exercise 8-2_Payroll Time Sheet.pdf**.

CHAPTER 8 INDEX

Part 2

Sage 50 2016 for Service Businesses

In Part 2 of *Computer Accounting with Sage 50 2016, 19th Edition,* you are the owner of an accounting practice. Your accounting business does monthly record keeping for local service businesses.

In Chapters 9, 10, 11, Projects 1 and 1A (Part 2), you use Sage 50 to set up four service businesses, complete the accounting cycle, and close the fiscal year. In Part 2, entries are recorded in the Receive Money window (Cash Receipts Journal) and the Write Checks window (Cash Disbursements Journal). Also, adjusting entries are recorded in the General Journal. At the end of each month, you reconcile the bank statement and print the general ledger trial balance and financial statements. At the end of the fourth quarter, you use Sage 50 to complete end-of-quarter adjusting entries, print the adjusted trial balance, print financial statements, close the fiscal year, and print a postclosing trial balance.

After entering deposits and payments, the next step is to post them to the general ledger. One of the best features of a computerized accounting system is how quickly **posting** is done. Once entries are recorded and checked for accuracy, posting is a click of the mouse. All entries are posted to the correct accounts in the general ledger and account balances are calculated–fast, easy, and accurate. Think of it as a process where journalizing and posting is the first step, then ledgers and financial statements are next. The diagram below illustrates this process.

Journalize and Post → General Ledger → Financial Statements

This illustration shows the *Sage 50 accounting system*.

- Software is installed.
- Companies are set up.
- Transactions are journalized in the general journal or special journals, and then posted to the general ledger and subsidiary ledgers.
- After entering transactions, reports are printed.

Sage 50 is a *double-entry accounting* system which means that the equation Assets = Liabilities + Equity is always in balance. Since a debit in one account will be offset by a credit in another account, the sum of all debits is equal to the sum of all credits.

To assure double-entry accounting procedures, Sage 50 includes accounting periods, the general journal and special journals, general ledger and subsidiary ledgers, account reconciliation, an audit trail, and financial reports. The Sage 50 accounting system also includes closing the fiscal year.

In Part 2, you set up companies, journalize transactions in the Cash Receipts and Cash Disbursements Journals, post to the General Ledger, complete account reconciliation, print the Financial Statements, and close the fiscal year. The accounting cycle is completed for the fourth quarter.

The accuracy of your general ledger and financial statement reports depends on the accuracy of the entries recorded on the Write Checks (Cash Disbursements Journal) and Receive Money (Cash Receipts Journal) windows. Once entries are posted, account reconciliation is completed.

Chapters 9, 10 and 11 work together. The service businesses set up in Chapter 9 are continued in Chapters 10 and 11. Part 2 ends with two comprehensive projects.

Chapter 9:   New Company Setup and Beginning Balances
Chapter 10: Maintaining Accounting Records for Service Businesses
Chapter 11: Completing Quarterly Activities and Closing the Fiscal Year
Project 1:   Shelly Martin, Accounting
Project 1A: Student-Designed Service Business

Part 2 includes three chapters and two projects: Chapters 9, 10, and 11 and Projects 1 and 1A. In Chapters 9, 10, and 11, you set up two service businesses from scratch—Donald Watson Designer and Crafts by Student Name (after Crafts by, students add their first and last name).

You complete accounting tasks for the fourth quarter–October, November and December 2016. You also complete end-of-quarter adjusting entries. At the end of Chapter 9, a new service business is set up in Exercise 9-1. The service business set up in Exercise 9-1 is continued in Exercises 9-2, 10-1, 10-2, 11-1 and 11-2.

In Project 1, you complete the accounting cycle for Shelly Martin, Accounting. This project gives you an opportunity to apply what you have learned in Chapters 9, 10, and 11. At the end of Project 1, there is a Check Your Progress assessment.

Project 1A is an opportunity to design a service business of your own. You select a chart of accounts, write and journalize transactions, reconcile the bank statement, and complete the accounting cycle for the business.

The chart below and on pages 255-256 shows the size of the backups, Excel files, and PDF files saved in Part 2–Chapters 9, 10, 11, and Project

1. The textbook shows how to back up to a USB drive. Backups can be made to the desktop, hard drive location, network location or external media.

Chapter	Sage 50 Backup (.ptb) Excel (.xlsx) and Adobe (.pdf)	Kilobytes	Page Nos.
9	Chapter 9 Chart of Accounts.ptb	941 KB	275-278
	Chapter 9 Beginning Balances.ptb	961 KB	291-292
	Chapter 9_Chart of Accounts and Beginning Balances.xlsx	17 KB	292-294
	Chapter 9_Balance Sheet.pdf	10 KB	295
	Chapter 9_Chart of Accounts.pdf	15 KB	295
	Exercise 9-1.ptb	911 KB	299
	Exercise 9-2.ptb	914 KB	302
	Exercise 9-2_Chart of Accounts and Beginning Balances.xlsx	17 KB	302
	Exercise 9-2_Chart of Accounts.pdf	15 KB	302
	Exercise 9-2_Balance Sheet.pdf	12 KB	302
10	Chapter 10 Transaction Register October.ptb	987 KB	315-316
	Chapter 10 October.ptb	1,002 KB	329
	Chapter 10_October Trial Balance and Financial Statements.xlsx	20 KB	329-331
	Chapter 10_October Trial Balance.pdf	13 KB	331
	Chapter 10_October Balance Sheet.pdf	12 KB	331
	Chapter 10_October Income Statement.pdf	11 KB	331
	Exercise 10-1.ptb	941 KB	333
	Exercise 10-2.ptb	947 KB	335
	Exercise 10-2_October Trial Balance and Financial Statements.xlsx.	20 KB	335
	Exercise 10-2_October Trial Balance.pdf	12 KB	335
	Exercise 10-2_October Balance Sheet.pdf	10 KB	335
	Exercise 10-2_October Income Statement.pdf	11 KB	335

Chapter/ Project	Sage 50 Backup (.ptb) Excel (.xlsx) and Adobe (.pdf)	Kilobytes	Page Nos.
11	Chapter 11 November.ptb	1,019 KB	350
	Chapter 11 December UTB.ptb	1,026 KB	357
	Chapter 11 December.ptb	1,038 KB	367
	Chapter 11_Adjusted Trial Balance and Financial Statements.xlsx	28 KB	368-369
	Chapter 11_Adjusted Trial Balance.pdf	14 KB	369
	Chapter 11_December Balance Sheet.pdf	11 KB	369
	Chapter 11_December Income Statement.pdf	12 KB	369
	Chapter 11_December Statement of Cash Flow.pdf	13 KB	369
	Chapter 11_December Statement of Retained Earnings.pdf	8 KB	369
	Chapter 11 EOY.ptb	1,039 KB	376
	Chapter 11_Postclosing Trial Balance.xlsx	12 KB	376
	Chapter 11_Postclosing Trial Balance.pdf	12 KB	376
	Asset depreciation.xlsx (Going to the Net)	15 KB	OLC
	Exercise 11-1.ptb	968 KB	380
	Exercise 11-2 Unadjusted Trial Balance.ptb	1,007 KB	383
	Exercise 11-2 Financial Statements.ptb	1,014 KB	383
	Exercise 11-2_Adjusted Trial Balance and Financial Statements.xlsx	27 KB	383
	Exercise 11-2_Adjusted Trial Balance.pdf	13 KB	383
	Exercise 11-2_Balance Sheet.pdf	10 KB	383
	Exercise 11-2_Income Statement.pdf	12 KB	383
	Exercise 11-2_Statement of Cash Flow.pdf	11 KB	383
	Exercise 11-2_Statement of Retained Earnings.pdf	8 KB	383
	Exercise 11-2 End of Year.ptb	1,022 KB	384
	Exercise 11-2_Postclosing Trial Balance.xlsx	12 KB	384
	Exercise 11-2_Postclosing Trial Balance.pdf	11 KB	384
Project 1	Shelly Martin Chart of Accounts.ptb	907 KB	390
	Shelly Martin Beginning Balances.ptb	912 KB	391
	Shelly Martin UTB.ptb	954 KB	393
	Shelly Martin December.ptb	986 KB	394
	Shelly Martin_Adjusted Trial Balance and Financial Statements.xlsx	27 KB	394

Chapter/ Project	Sage 50 Backup (.ptb) Excel (.xlsx) and Adobe (.pdf)	Kilobytes	Page Nos.
Project 1	Project 1_Adjusted Trial Balance.pdf	9 KB	394
	Project 1_Balance Sheet.pdf	5 KB	394
	Project 1_Income Statement.pdf	11 KB	394
	Project 1_Statement of Cash Flow.pdf	12 KB	394
	Project 1_Statement of Retained Earnings.pdf	8 KB	394
	Shelly Martin EOY.ptb	997 KB	394
	Shelly Martin_Postclosing Trial Balance.xlsx	12 KB	394
	Project 1_Postclosing Trial Balance.pdf	12 KB	394

Chapter

9 New Company Setup and Beginning Balances

LEARNING OBJECTIVES

1. Set up company information for Donald Watson Designer.
2. Select a Service Company from the simplified chart of accounts list.
3. Edit the chart of accounts.
4. Enter beginning balances.
5. Use Windows or File Explorer to see the company's file size.
6. Export the chart of accounts and beginning balances to Excel, and save PDF files.
7. Make four backups, save two Excel files, and save four PDF files.[1]

Chapter 9 begins Part 2 of the book–Sage 50 2016 for Service Businesses. In this part of the book you are the owner of an accounting practice that does the monthly record keeping for several service businesses.

The chapters in Part 2 work together--the service businesses set up in Chapter 9 are continued in Chapters 10 and 11. The two businesses set up in Chapter 9 are Donald Watson [your first and last name] Designer, and another service business in Exercise 9-1, Crafts by your first and last name. In Chapter 9, you set up a service business using one of Sage 50's sample companies. Then, edit a chart of accounts and enter beginning balances. When setting up companies, use your first and last name — Your Name Designer and Crafts by Your Name.

GETTING STARTED: NEW COMPANY SETUP

Donald Watson is a designer and educator. His sources of income are: design work, book royalties, and part-time teaching at Milwaukee Community College. He is single and has no dependents.

---

[1]Refer to the chart on pages 254-256 for the file names and size of backups, Excel files, and PDF files.

▶ Follow these steps to set up the company, Donald Watson Designer. (*Hint:* The arrow indicates a video at www.mhhe.com/yacht2016. Link to Student Edition > select Chapter 9 > Videos > Set up a new company.)

1. Start Sage 50. (If a company opens, click File > Close Company.)

2. At the startup window, click **✦ Create a new company** .
    The Create a New Company window appears. Read the information.

3. After clicking Next > , type the company information shown on the next page. Press the **<Tab>** or **<Enter>** key between each field.

Company Information

Company Name:	**Donald Watson Designer (use your name)**[2]
Address Line 1:	**3024 University Drive**
City, State, Zip:	**Milwaukee, WI 53202**
Country:	**USA**
Telephone:	**414-555-8211**
Fax:	**414-555-8213**
Business Type:	Select Sole Proprietorship
Web Site:	**www.donaldwatson.com**
E-Mail:	**info@donaldwatson.com**

Compare your Create a New Company - Company Information window to the one below. *The company name field should show your first and last name Designer. Do not complete the ID fields. (Hint: Observe that there is a red asterisk next to Company Name. The asterisk indicates a required field.)*

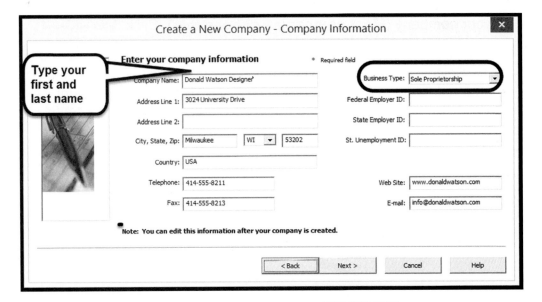

4. Check the company information > click [Next >]. The Select a method to create your company window appears.

---

[2]Boldface indicates information that you type. Substitute your name for Donald Watson. If you use your first and last name Designer as the company name, Sage 50 printouts show your name.

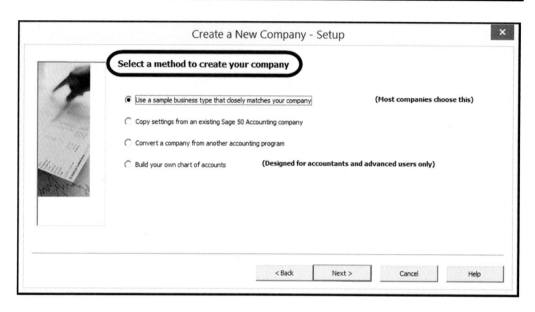

5. Accept the default to Use a sample business that closely matches your company **(Most companies choose this)**. Click Next >.

6. Read the information about selecting a business type. Observe that the Select a business type list shows Service Company selected, and that the Chart of Accounts shows four digits for the account numbers. Four-digit account numbers are used with Sage's simplified chart of accounts.

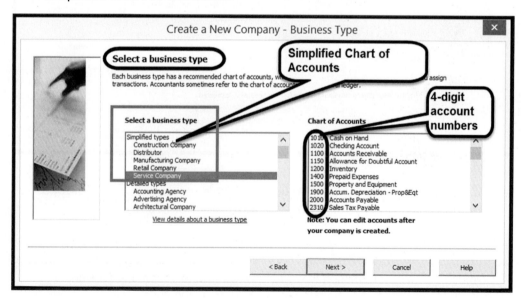

7. Make sure that Simplified types, Service Company is highlighted, and the Chart of Accounts numbers show 4 digits > click Next >

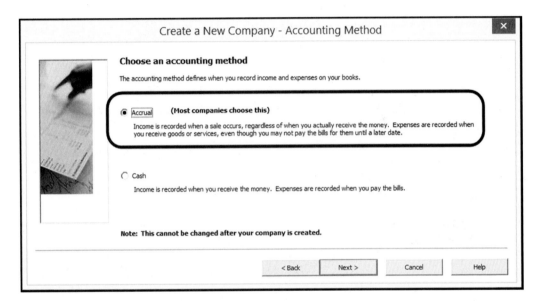

8. Accept the default for Accrual, by clicking Next > . The Choose a posting method window appears. Real Time posting is the default.

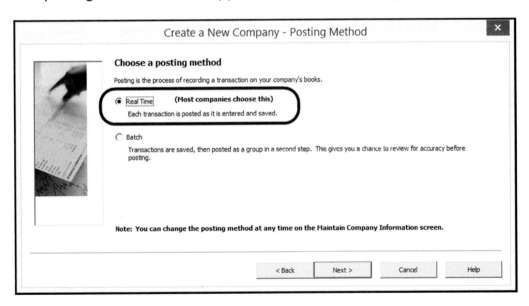

9. Accept the default for Real Time posting, by clicking Next > .
   The Choose an accounting period structure window appears.

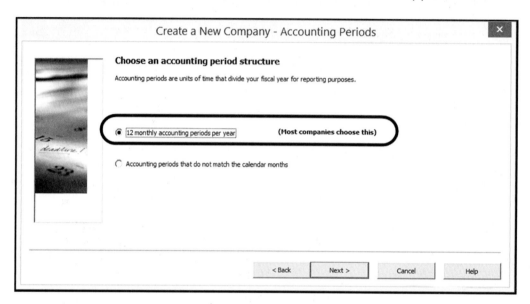

10. Accept the default for 12 monthly accounting periods per year by
    clicking Next > . The Choose the first period of your fiscal year
    window appears. **Select 2016**.

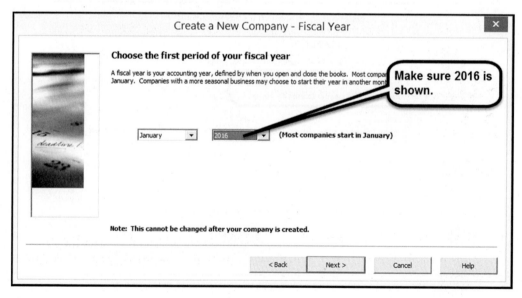

11. Make sure the Choose the first period of your fiscal year window shows **January 2016. This window is important. The year cannot be changed after your company is created.** Click

    Next > . You are ready to create your company window appears.

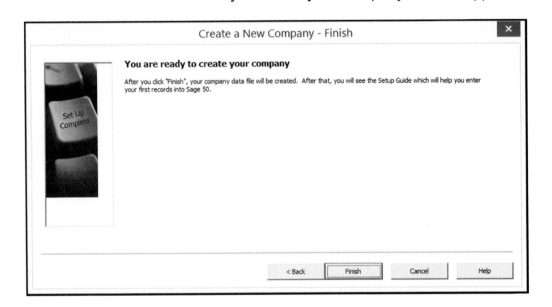

12. Read the information on the Finish window. Click Finish . If the screen prompts You can use this company in the student version of Sage 50 for the next 14 months and then it will expire, click

    OK . After a few moments (be patient), the Donald Watson Designer - Sage 50 Accounting window appears. (Substitute your first and last name for Donald Watson.)

13. When the Setup Guide window appears, read the information. Click on the box next to ☑ Don't show this screen at startup. > click

    Close . When the Sage 50 Setup Guide appears, click on the box next to Do not display this message again

    ☑ Do not display this message again. , then OK to close it. If the Sage Advisor Getting Started window appears in the right pane, click on ⊗ to close it (*or*, you may want to watch the videos).

14. On the Navigation Bar, click [Business Status]. To set the Business Status Navigation Center as your default page, from the toolbar select [Make this the default page]. When you open Donald Watson Designer, the Business Status Navigation Center will appear.

15. On the toolbar (below the menu bar and Business Status), click on the Period button [Period]. The Change Accounting Period window appears. Click 10 – Oct 01, 2016 to Oct 31, 2016 to highlight it.

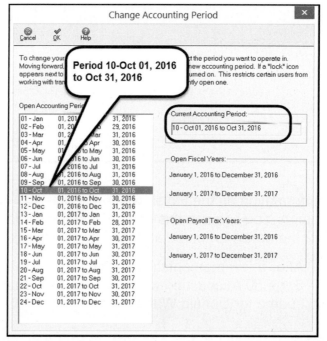

Selecting the accounting period sets up the month for recording transactions.

16. Make sure Period 10 is selected. October 2016 is the first month for recording transactions >click [OK]. If a window prompts that transactions may need to be reviewed, click on the box next to Do not display this message again. Then, click [No].

17. Check that Period 10 – 10/01/16-10/31/16 appears on the toolbar
 . The Period appears next to the System Date,
which is the current (today's) date. A partial window is shown. Scroll
down to see all the information. (*Hint:* Depending on your screen
resolution, your Business Status Navigation Center may look
different.)

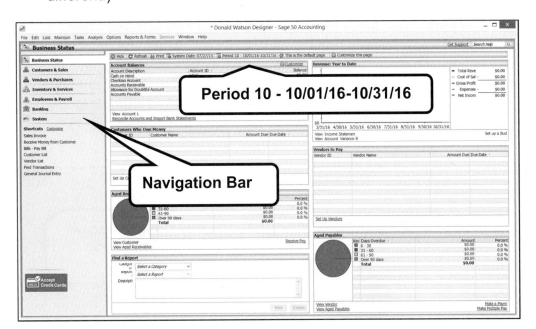

Read Me: *What is Sage 50's shortened name?*

1. From the menu bar, select Help > Customer Support and Service, File Statistics. The
    company's shortened name is shown on the title bar. The Data File Statistics for
    XXXXXXDE window appears. (Substitute the Xs with your shortened name.) This
    represents the shortened name of the open company. Observe that there is also a
    Directory field at the bottom of the Data File Statistics window. The directory where
    Donald Watson Designer resides on the computer is C:\Sage\Peachtree\Company\
    donwatde. (Since you used your first and last name, the first six letters of the shortened
    name will differ.)

2. Click OK to close the Data File Statistics window.

Company Maintenance Information

Follow these steps to see information.

1. From the menu bar, select Maintain > Company Information. You can also display Company Information from the System Navigation Center.

2. Compare these fields to the company information below. They should agree. Notice that the Directory field shows the default location where your company is stored: C:\Sage\Peachtree\ Company\donwatde. Since you used your first and last name, the Directory field ends with the shortened company name assigned by Sage 50. For example, if your company name is Janet Williams Designer, the Directory field ends in \janwilde.

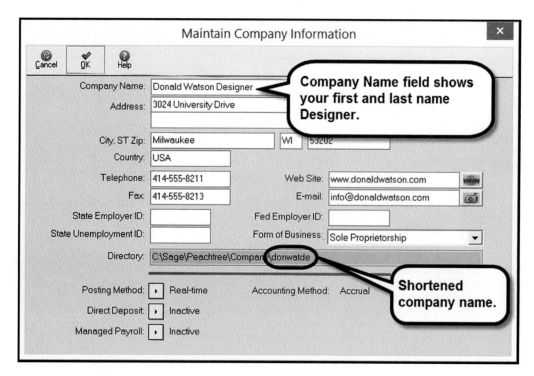

3. Click [OK] to return to the Business Status Navigation Center.

CHART OF ACCOUNTS

The chart of accounts is a list of all the accounts in the general ledger. When you selected Service Company from the list of business types, a chart of accounts was included. Follow these steps to edit the sample chart of accounts.

Delete Accounts

1. From the Business Status Navigation Center, link to <u>View Account List</u>. The Account List appears. (*Or,* you can use the menu bar. Select Maintain > Chart of Accounts > in the Account ID field, click the down-arrow, continue with step 2.)

2. Double click Account ID, 1150, Allowance for Doubtful Account. The Maintain Chart of Accounts window appears.

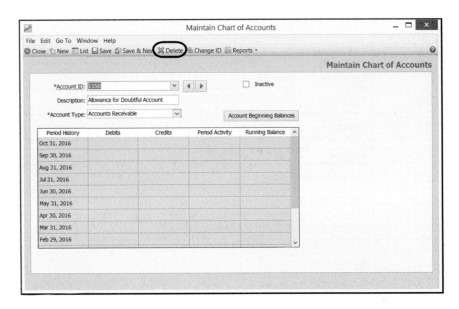

3. Click .

4. The Sage 50 Accounting - Are you sure you want to delete this record? window appears.

5. Click  .

6. Delete the accounts shown on the chart below. (*Hint:* On the Maintain Chart of Accounts window, type the account number in the Account ID field to expedite editing the chart of accounts.)

Acct. ID	Account Description
2310	Sales Tax Payable
2320	Deductions Payable
2330	Federal Payroll Taxes Payable
2340	FUTA Payable
2350	State Payroll Taxes Payable
2360	SUTA Payable
2370	Local Taxes Payable
2500	Current Portion Long-Term Debt
2700	Long-Term Debt-Noncurrent
4300	Other Income
5900	Inventory Adjustments
6050	Employee Benefit Programs Exp
6250	Other Taxes Expense
6650	Commissions and Fees Expense
7100	Gain/Loss - Sale of Assets Exp

Change Accounts

To change the name of an account, follow these steps:

1. On the Maintain Chart of Accounts window, type **3920** > Press <Tab> or <Enter>. Owner's Contribution appears in the Description field.

2. Type **Donald Watson, Capital** (use your first and last name, Capital). Press <Tab> or <Enter>.

3. In the Account Type field, click on the down arrow. Select Equity-doesn't close.

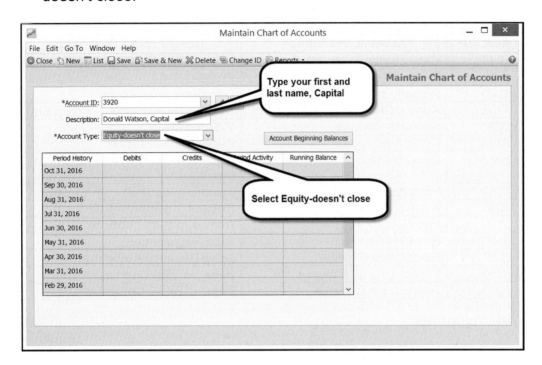

Read Me: Account Type

The Account Type is important. Make sure the Capital account shows Equity-doesn't close. The Account Type determines how the account is used and where it appears on financial reports. The Account Type classifies the account for financial reports *and* the automatic closing process.

Once you set up an account and post transactions, you should be very careful about changing the account type. Changing the account type could cause your financial reporting to be incorrect or inconsistent. If you need to change the account type, you should make the account inactive and create a new account with the correct account type.

4. Click ⊟ Save .

5. Change the names of the accounts shown below. (*Hint:* When you change the Account Description, the Account Type does not need to be changed.

Acct. ID	Account Description	New Account Description
1010	Cash on Hand	**Money Market Account**
1400	Prepaid Expenses	**Prepaid Rent**
1500	Property and Equipment	**Computer Equipment**
1900	Accum. Depreciation – Prop&Eqt	**Accum. Depreciation – Comp Eqt**
2000	Accounts Payable	**VISA Payable**
2400	Customer Deposits	**Publisher Advances**
3930	Owner's Draw	**Donald Watson, Draw** (your name, Draw)
4000	Professional Fees	**Teaching Income**
4050	Sales of Materials	**Royalty Income**
6100	Payroll Tax Expense	**Dues and Subscriptions**
6150	Bad Debt Expense	**Auto Registration**
6550	Other Office Expense	**Long Distance Company**
6850	Service Charge Expense	**Bank Service Charge**
7050	Depreciation Expense	**Deprec. Exp. - Comp Eqt**

Add Accounts

To add an account to the Chart of Accounts, follow these steps:

1. On the Maintain Chart of Accounts window, click [New].

2. In the Account ID field, type **1040** and press **<Enter>**.

3. In the Description field, type **IRA Savings Account** and press **<Enter>**.

4. In the Account Type field, Cash is the default. Click on the down arrow. A list of account types drops down. Make sure that Cash is highlighted. If not, click once on Cash to select it.

On the right side of the Maintain Chart of Accounts window is an explanation of Account Type (if necessary, go to the Account Type field). Read the information. (*Hint*: If necessary, click on Advisor – vertical bar on the right side of Maintain Chart of Accounts.)

ⓧ

Account Type

This determines where the account should be used in Sage 50 and how it is used for financial reporting.

For example, on the Maintain Vendors screen, you must select an expense account. In this case, you should select an account with the account type of Expenses. In financial reporting, the Income Statement reports information from income and expense accounts.

The account type appears in lists and reports and is also used to filter lists and reports.

▶ What are the available account types?

Keep in Mind

- Once you set up an account and start using it, you should be very careful about changing the account type. Changing the account type could cause your financial reporting to be incorrect or inconsistent. If you feel like you need to change the account type, you might want to make the account inactive and create a new account with the correct account type.

    Read Me: *Why is the Account Type field important?*

Observe that the Account Type field shows Cash for the IRA Savings Account. This is an important field – the Account Type field classifies each account for the financial statements. For example, Account No. 1040, IRA Savings Account, is classified as Cash, which means this account will appear on the Balance Sheet and Statement of Cash Flow, but *not* on the Income Statement or Statement of Retained Earnings.

The companies you set up in Chapter 9 continue in Chapters 10 and 11. If you select the *wrong* Account Type, transactions will post incorrectly and the financial statements will be inaccurate. The automatic closing process is also affected because Account Type selections affect the postclosing trial balance.

When using accounting software, each process relates to the next step.

---

5. Click ⬚ Save & New . (*Hint:* What is the difference between Save & New and Save? If you click Save, the Account Type does not change. If you have a couple of accounts with the same Account Type, click Save, then change the Account ID and Description. The Account Type stays the same.)

Important – Account Type field. The Account Type field determines where the accounts appear on financial statements. For example, the Income Statement lists information from the Income and Expense accounts. Make sure you select the account types shown below.

Add the following accounts:

Acct. ID	Account Description	Account Type
1045	WI State Retirement	Cash
1300	Prepaid Insurance	Other Current Assets
1450	Supplies	Other Current Assets
1510	Furniture	Fixed Assets
1520	Automobile	Fixed Assets
1910	Accum. Depreciation – Furnitur	Accumulated Depreciation
1920	Accum. Depreciation – Automobi	Accumulated Depreciation
6560	Internet Service Provider	Expenses
7060	Deprec. Exp. - Furniture	Expenses
7070	Deprec. Exp. - Automobile	Expenses

6. Click ⬚ Close after completing the Chart of Accounts. If necessary, close all windows. You are returned to the Business Status Navigation Center.

Display the Chart of Accounts

1. From the menu bar, click Reports & Forms > General Ledger. Click on the Chart of Accounts to highlight it > select ⬚ Display .

Donald Watson Designer
Chart of Accounts
As of Oct 31, 2016

Filter Criteria includes: Report order is by ID. Report is printed with Accounts having Zero Amounts and in Detail Format.

Account I	Account Description	Active?	Account Type
1010	Money Market Account	Yes	Cash
1020	Checking Account	Yes	Cash
1040	IRA Savings Account	Yes	Cash
1045	WI State Retirement	Yes	Cash
1100	Accounts Receivable	Yes	Accounts Receivable
1200	Inventory	Yes	Inventory
1300	Prepaid Insurance	Yes	Other Current Assets
1400	Prepaid Rent	Yes	Other Current Assets
1450	Supplies	Yes	Other Current Assets
1500	Computer Equipment	Yes	Fixed Assets
1510	Furniture	Yes	Fixed Assets
1520	Automobile	Yes	Fixed Assets
1900	Accum. Depreciation - Comp Eqt	Yes	Accumulated Depreciation
1910	Accum. Depreciation - Furnitur	Yes	Accumulated Depreciation
1920	Accum. Depreciation - Automobi	Yes	Accumulated Depreciation
2000	VISA Payable	Yes	Accounts Payable
2380	Income Taxes Payable	Yes	Other Current Liabilities
2400	Publisher Advances	Yes	Other Current Liabilities
3910	Retained Earnings	Yes	Equity-Retained Earnings
3920	Donald Watson, Capital	Yes	Equity-doesn't close
3930	Donald Watson, Draw	Yes	Equity-gets closed
4000	Teaching Income	Yes	Income
4050	Royalty Income	Yes	Income
4100	Interest Income	Yes	Income
4200	Finance Charge Income	Yes	Income
4900	Sales/Fees Discounts	Yes	Income
5000	Cost of Sales	Yes	Cost of Sales
5400	Cost of Sales-Salary & Wage	Yes	Cost of Sales
6000	Wages Expense	Yes	Expenses
6100	Dues and Subscriptions	Yes	Expenses
6150	Auto Registration	Yes	Expenses
6200	Income Tax Expense	Yes	Expenses
6300	Rent or Lease Expense	Yes	Expenses
6350	Maintenance & Repairs Expense	Yes	Expenses
6400	Utilities Expense	Yes	Expenses
6450	Office Supplies Expense	Yes	Expenses
6500	Telephone Expense	Yes	Expenses
6550	Long Distance Company	Yes	Expenses
6560	Internet Service Provider	Yes	Expenses
6600	Advertising Expense	Yes	Expenses
6800	Freight Expense	Yes	Expenses
6850	Bank Service Charge	Yes	Expenses
6900	Purchase Disc-Expense Items	Yes	Expenses
6950	Insurance Expense	Yes	Expenses
7050	Deprec. Exp. - Comp Eqt	Yes	Expenses
7060	Deprec. Exp. - Furniture	Yes	Expenses
7070	Deprec. Exp. - Automobile	Yes	Expenses

How to Fix? Width of columns

Move the mouse to the blue arrows ⬌ between columns. The cursor becomes a crossbar.
Left click on the crossbar and drag the mouse to the right. After you have adjusted the Account
Description column, click on the Print icon to print the chart of accounts.

Carefully check the Account Type column. Account types classify each account for the financial statements.

Observe that the chart of accounts is dated As of Oct 31, 2016. Since Sage 50 posts on the last day of the month, your reports will show October 31, 2016 as the date.

Notice that Donald Watson's chart of accounts includes Account No. 3910, Retained Earnings. At the end of every fiscal year, the temporary owner's equity accounts (revenues, expenses, and drawing) are closed to a permanent owner's equity account. In Sage 50, there are two permanent owner's equity accounts: the owner's capital account and the Retained Earnings account. Sage 50 closes the temporary accounts to the Retained Earnings account. This will be discussed in more detail in Chapter 11 when you close the fiscal year. In order to post to the general ledger, a Retained Earnings account is required.

2. To print the Chart of Accounts, click [Print]. When the Print window appears, make the selections to print. (*Hint:* If you do not have a printer, you can save the Chart of Accounts as an Adobe PDF or Microsoft XPS Document Writer file instead of printing.)

   GO GREEN & SAVE: Instead of printing, select Display, and save as an Adobe PDF file or Microsoft XPS file. In other words, you do <u>not</u> need to print hard copy. Check with your instructor for his or her preference. Instead of printing, email PDFs or Microsoft XPS files.

3. Click [Close] two times to return to the Business Status Navigation Center. If you need to edit the Chart of Accounts, select Maintain, then Chart of Accounts, *or* from the Business Status Navigation Center, link to <u>View Account List</u>.

When using accounting software, each step in the process affects the next step – setting up the company affects the chart of accounts, the chart of accounts affects beginning balances, those balances influence transaction processing, and posting affects financial reporting and the closing process. The steps in the computer accounting cycle work together to produce a company's financial records.

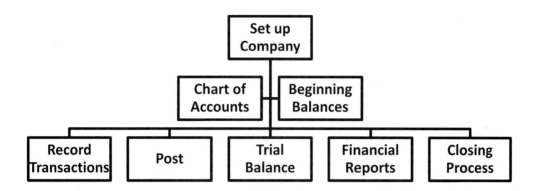

The work completed in Chapter 9 continues in Chapters 10 and 11. In this chapter, the Chart of Accounts (page 273) and Beginning Balance Sheet (page 283) are important to accurate processing in the next two chapters. Similar to the accounting software's steps working together, the work in Chapters 9, 10, and 11 are also related to each other.

BACKING UP THE CHART OF ACCOUNTS

When using Sage, information is automatically saved to the hard drive of the computer. In a classroom setting, a number of students may be using the same computer. This means that when you return to the computer lab, your data will be gone. Backing up data simply means saving it to a hard drive location or external media. Saving data (backing up) means that it will be available when you want to work again.

In this textbook, detailed steps are shown for backing up to a USB drive. The chart on pages 254-256 shows the size of Part 2 backup files (Chapters 9, 10, 11 and Project 1).

When this backup is done, you are saving the new company set up information (pages 258-265) and the revised chart of accounts (pages 267-274).

In the next section, detailed steps are shown for backing up your data to this point.

> **Comment: Backup & Restore**
>
> When a backup is made, you are saving to the current point. Each backup should have a different backup name (file name) to distinguish one backup from another. In this way, if you need to restore to an earlier backup, you have the data for that purpose.
>
> Remember, you can Restore if you need to go back to an earlier point in the company's data. Without a backup file, you cannot go back to an earlier point. Since Chapters 9, 10, and 11 work together, your backup files are important.
>
> In the business world, backups are unique to each business: daily, weekly, monthly. *Remember, back up before you leave the computer lab!*

Follow these steps to back up Donald Watson's company and the chart of accounts.

1. Insert your USB flash drive. From the Navigation Bar, click
    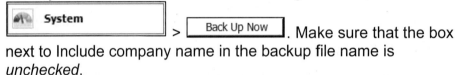 . Make sure that the box next to Include company name in the backup file name is *unchecked*.

    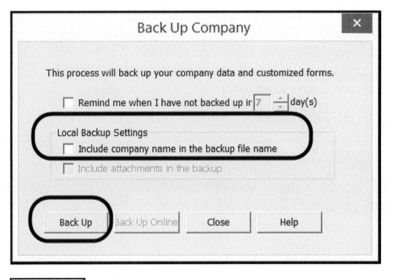

2. Click Back Up .

3. Go to the location of your USB drive. (*Or,* backup to the hard-drive or other location.) Type **Chapter 9 Chart of Accounts** in the File name field.

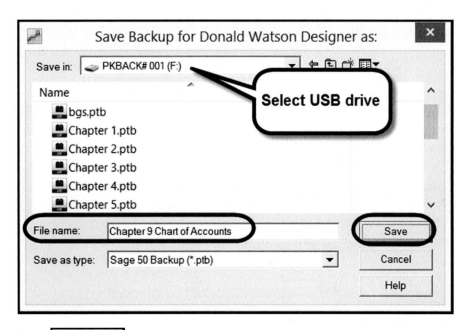

4. Click [Save].

5. When the window prompts This company backup will require approximately 1 diskette, click [OK]. When the window prompts Please insert the first disk, click [OK]. When the Back Up Company scale is 100% complete, you have successfully backed up to the current point in Chapter 9. (This step will differ slightly if you are backing up to the default or other hard-drive location.)

Read Me: Problem Backing Up to USB Drive

If you encounter difficulties backing up to an external USB drive, backup to your desktop first. Then, copy the backup file from the desktop to the USB drive. Refer to Appendix A, Troubleshooting, Problem Backing Up to USB Drive, and on page 712.

Some USB drives work better than others for backing up directly from Sage 50 to the flash drive.

Follow these steps to see the size of the backup file.

1. Open Windows or File Explorer.

2. Go to the location of your backup file; for example, the USB drive.

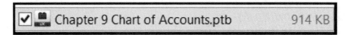

The Name of the file is Chapter 9 Chart of Accounts.ptb, the Size of the file is 914 KB. (Your file size may differ.) Backups can also be made to a hard drive, network location, or external media. Close Explorer.

How to Fix? .PTB extension

If you do *not* have a .PTB extension, follow these steps:

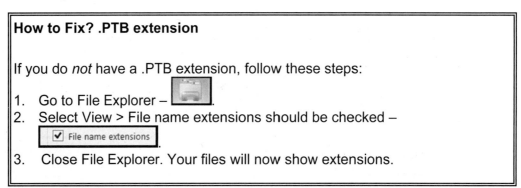

1. Go to File Explorer –   .
2. Select View > File name extensions should be checked –   .
3. Close File Explorer. Your files will now show extensions.

RESTORING COMPANY DATA

After completing new company setup and editing the chart of accounts, you backed up (saved) Donald Watson Designer company information. In order to start where you left off the last time you backed up, use the Restore Wizard.

In the steps that follow you are shown how to restore a backup file (.ptb extension). This backup was made on pages 276-277. Sage 50 backups are compressed files which means that the file is made smaller.

1. If necessary, insert your USB flash drive. Start Sage 50.

2. These instructions assume that the Donald Watson [your name] Designer - Sage 50 Accounting window appears. If *not*, click File > Close Company. If a screen prompts to keep two companies open, select   No . Open Donald Watson [your name] Designer.

> ➤ **Troubleshooting: What if Donald Watson Designer (or another name Designer) is not shown on the title bar?**

a. Click File > Close Company.

b. From the startup window, select

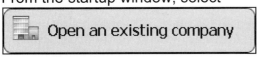

.

c. Click Browse . The Open Company window appears.

d. If Donald Watson Designer (or, other name Designer) is shown select it, and then click OK . Go to page 280, step 3, and follow the steps to restore your data.

e. If *no Designer company is shown*, click Cancel then Close .

f. There are four menu bar options--

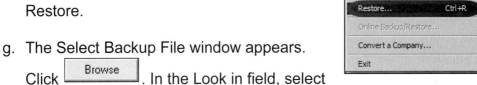

File Options Services Help . Select File > Restore.

g. The Select Backup File window appears. Click Browse . In the Look in field, select the appropriate location of your backup file; for example, your USB drive.

h. Select the Chapter 9 Chart of Accounts.ptb backup file > click Open .

i. Make sure the Location field shows the Chapter 9 Chart of Accounts.ptb backup file. Click Next > .

j. The Select Company window appears. Click on the radio button next to Create a new company using the restored data.

 Read Me

Observe that there are two options on the Select Company window: Overwrite existing company data *or* Create a new company using restored data. If you select Create a new company using restored data, the company will be named exactly the same as the backup file selected.

Let's say you want to restore a backup file for a company that was *not* set up in Sage 50. Some computer labs delete directories from the hard drive. For example, you have a back up file but the company, Donald Watson [or your name *or* other student name] Designer, is *not* listed as a Sage 50 company. If you start Sage 50 and you *cannot* select the appropriate company, use the Restore Wizard's Create a new company using the restored data selection to restore and set up the company.

---

   k. The Company Name field shows Donald Watson Designer. The Location field shows the location of your backup file. The last two letters of the location field shows "de." Click ⬚Next >⬚. Continue with step 7 on page 281.

3. From the Navigation Bar, select ⬚ System ⬚ > click ⬚Restore Now⬚. The Select Backup File window appears.

4. Click ⬚Browse⬚. The Open Backup File window appears. Go to the Location of your Chapter 9 Chart of Accounts.ptb file and select it.

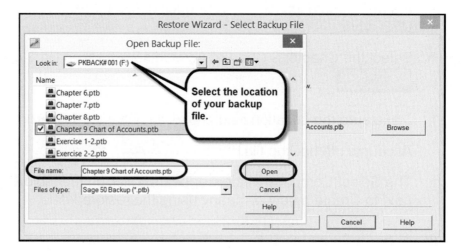

---

5. Click ⬚Open⬚ The Select Backup File window shows the location of your backup file, X:\Chapter 9 Chart of Accounts.ptb. (Substitute X for your drive letter.) Click ⬚Next >⬚.

6. The Select Company window appears. The radio button next to Overwrite existing company data is selected. The Company Name field shows Donald Watson Designer (*or,* your first and last name, Designer). The Location field shows the default location on the hard drive for Donald Watson Designer – C:\Sage\Peachtree\Company\ donwatde.

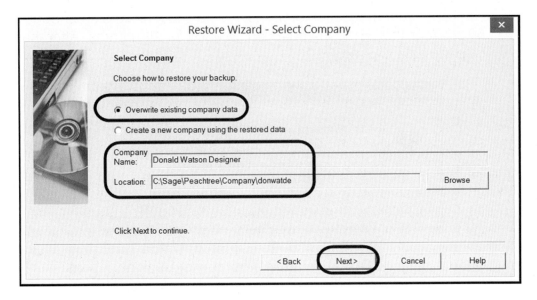

7. Click ⬚Next >⬚. The Restore Options window appears. Make sure that the box next to Company Data is checked. Click ⬚Next >⬚.

8. The Confirmation window appears. Check the Backup file and Location fields to make sure they are correct. Click ⬚Finish⬚.

9.   A window prompts "This process will overwrite and replace existing data permanently."

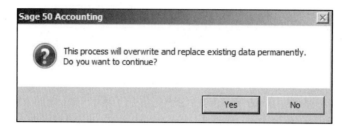

10.   Click 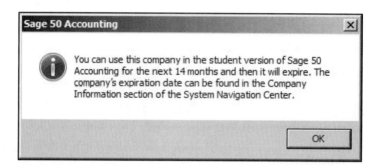 . When the Restore Company scale is 100% complete, your data is restored. (*Hint:* The Student Version of Sage 50 prompts that company data can be used for 14 months. After that time the data expires.)

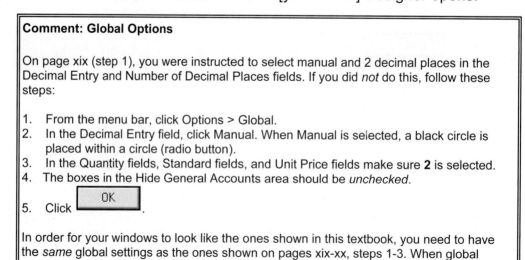

11.   Click [OK] . Donald Watson [your name] Designer opens.

Comment: Global Options

On page xix (step 1), you were instructed to select manual and 2 decimal places in the Decimal Entry and Number of Decimal Places fields. If you did *not* do this, follow these steps:

1.   From the menu bar, click Options > Global.
2.   In the Decimal Entry field, click Manual. When Manual is selected, a black circle is placed within a circle (radio button).
3.   In the Quantity fields, Standard fields, and Unit Price fields make sure **2** is selected.
4.   The boxes in the Hide General Accounts area should be *unchecked*.
5.   Click [OK] .

In order for your windows to look like the ones shown in this textbook, you need to have the *same* global settings as the ones shown on pages xix-xx, steps 1-3. When global options are selected, this feature is in effect for all companies.

ENTERING CHART OF ACCOUNTS BEGINNING BALANCES

Mr. Watson hired you to do his monthly record keeping. In order to begin accounting tasks for Mr. Watson, you asked him for a **Balance Sheet**. A Balance Sheet lists the types and amounts of assets, liabilities, and equity as of a specific date. A balance sheet is also called a **statement of financial position**.

Donald Watson Designer Balance Sheet **October 1, 2016**		
ASSETS		
Current Assets		
1010 - Money Market Account	$ 10,700.00	
1020 - Checking Account	11,750.75	
1040 - IRA Savings Account	27,730.35	
1045 - WI State Retirement	35,612.00	
1300 - Prepaid Insurance	2,100.00	
1400 - Prepaid Rent	600.00	
1450 - Supplies	1,771.83	
Total Current Assets		$ 90,264.93
Property and Equipment		
1500 - Computer Equipment	$ 6,800.00	
1510 - Furniture	5,000.00	
1520 - Automobile	19,000.00	
Total Property and Equipment		30,800.00
Total Assets		$ 121,064.93
LIABILITIES AND CAPITAL		
Current Liabilities		
2000 - VISA Payable	$ 5,250.65	
Total Current Liabilities		$ 5,250.65
Capital		
3920 - Donald Watson, Capital		115,814.28
Total Liabilities and Capital		$ 121,064.93

The information in this Balance Sheet is the basis for recording Mr. Watson's beginning balances.

Follow these steps to record Donald Watson's beginning balances.

1. From the menu bar, select Maintain > Chart of Accounts.

2. Click **Account Beginning Balances** .

> Observe that the balance sheet on page 283 is dated October 1, 2016. **Beginning balances must be set for the previous month– September 1 through 30, 2016**. You select 9/1/16 through 9/30/16 because Sage 50 posts on the last day of the month. When 9/1/16 through 9/30/16 is selected as the chart of accounts beginning balance period, transaction windows start on October 1, 2016, and reports are dated October 31, 2016. **The September 30 ending balance is the October 1 beginning balance.**
>
> In Chapter 11, you print end-of-year financial statements. In order for your end-of-year financial statements to show the correct current month and year-to-date amounts, you *must* enter beginning balances for the previous month. **Select From 9/1/16 through 9/30/16 as the period for setting beginning balances**. *The beginning balance period cannot be changed later.*

3. Scroll down the Select Period list. Click From 9/1/16 through 9/30/16 to highlight it.

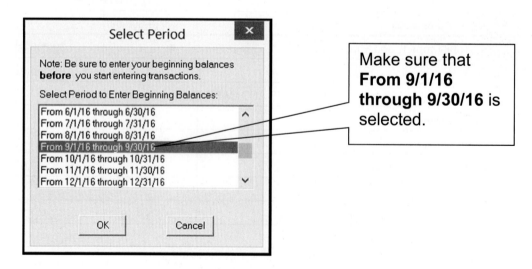

IMPORTANT: Check the Select Period window. The period you select should be From 9/1/16 through 9/30/16. The period selected affects financial statement current month and year-to-date account balances. Make sure that **From 9/1/16 through 9/30/16** is selected. *The beginning balance period <u>cannot</u> be changed later.*

4. On the Select Period window, make sure that you have selected **From 9/1/16 through 9/30/16**. You *cannot* change the period later. Click OK .

5. The Chart of Accounts Beginning Balances window appears. Observe that **Beginning Balances as of September 30, 2016** is shown. For Account ID 1010, Money Market Account, type **10700** in the Assets, Expenses field. Press **<Enter>**.

6. Account No. 1020, Checking Account is selected. Type **11750.75** and press **<Enter>**.

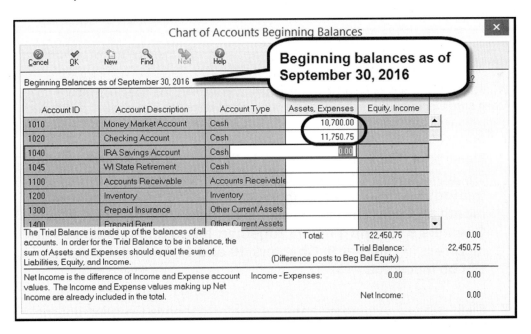

Continue entering the beginning balances using the Balance Sheet on page 283. If necessary, for credit balances, click on the Liabilities, Equity, Income field. When you are finished, the Assets, Expenses column equals the Liabilities, Equity, and Income column. This indicates that there are equal debits and credits.

Compare your completed Chart of Accounts Beginning Balances window with the one shown below.

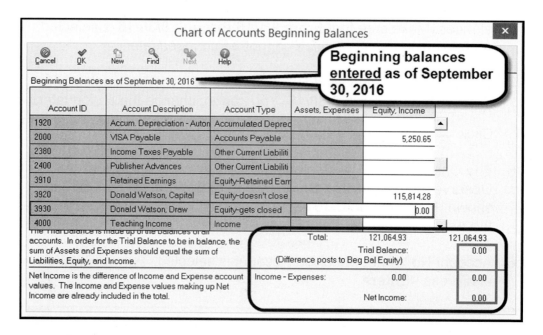

How to Fix?
What if your Trial Balance, Income-Expenses, and Net Income does *not* show 0.00? Make sure that debit balances for assets and credit balances for liabilities and capital accounts are entered correctly.

Make sure that your beginning balances are as of September 30, 2016. If you enter your balances for the wrong month (period), your financial statements will not show the current month and year-to-date amounts correctly. Remember, Chapters 9, 10 and 11 work together. If beginning balances are incorrect in Chapter 9, Chapters 10 and 11 financial statements will be incorrect.

7. Click [OK]. A window appears briefly that says Creating Journal Entries.

8. At the Maintain Chart of Accounts window, click [Close] to return to the Business Status Navigation Center.

To check your chart of accounts beginning balances, select Maintain > Chart of Accounts > [Account Beginning Balances] > then select the From 9/1/16 through 9/30/16 > [OK]. Make any needed corrections. Refer to pages 283-287 for entering the chart of accounts beginning balances. When through, click [✔ OK]. Close the Maintain Chart of Accounts window.

Display the September 30, 2016 Balance Sheet

On page 283, the beginning balances for Donald Watson Designer were shown on the October 1, 2016 Balance Sheet. It's important to record account beginning balances for the month *before* the business's start date. That means you should make sure that you entered the appropriate period for beginning balances–From 9/1/16 through 9/30/16 (refer to steps 2 and 3, page 284).

To check that you entered account beginning balances as of September 30, 2016, follow these steps. September 30 ending balances are October 1 beginning balances.

1. From the menu bar, select Reports & Forms > Financial Statements > double-click <Standard> Balance Sheet.

2. The <Standard> Balance Sheet Options window appears. In the Time Frame field, select Range.

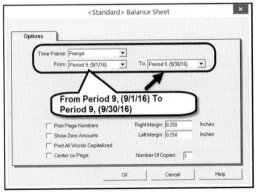

3. In the From field, select Period 9, (9/1/16). In the To Field, select Period 9, (9/30/16). Click [OK].

Compare the balance sheet with the one shown on the next page. The September 30, 2016 account balances match the ones shown on the October 1, 2016 balance sheet on page 283. If your account balances do not agree, or if they show zeroes, you should redo the account beginning balances. (*Hint:* Restore the Chapter 9 Chart of Accounts.ptb file. Redo steps 1-8, pages 284-287.)

Donald Watson Designer
Balance Sheet
September 30, 2016

ASSETS

Current Assets		
Money Market Account	$ 10,700.00	
Checking Account	11,750.75	
IRA Savings Account	27,730.35	
WI State Retirement	35,612.00	
Prepaid Insurance	2,100.00	
Prepaid Rent	600.00	
Supplies	1,771.83	
Total Current Assets		90,264.93
Property and Equipment		
Computer Equipment	6,800.00	
Furniture	5,000.00	
Automobile	19,000.00	
Total Property and Equipment		30,800.00
Other Assets		
Total Other Assets		0.00
Total Assets		$ 121,064.93

LIABILITIES AND CAPITAL

Current Liabilities		
VISA Payable	$ 5,250.65	
Total Current Liabilities		5,250.65
Long-Term Liabilities		
Total Long-Term Liabilities		0.00
Total Liabilities		5,250.65
Capital		
Donald Watson, Capital	115,814.28	
Net Income	0.00	
Total Capital		115,814.28
Total Liabilities & Capital		$ 121,064.93

Unaudited - For Management Purposes Only

Observe when you print the report, "Unaudited - For Management Purposes Only" is shown at the bottom.

> **Troubleshooting: The companies set up in Chapter 9 continue in Chapters 10 and 11. If account beginning balances are <u>not</u> set up for September 30, 2016, your financial statements year-to-date column in Chapter 11 will not show the correct account balances.**

4. Close the Balance Sheet and the Select a Report or Form windows.

5. On the Business Status Navigation Center's toolbar, click ⟳ Refresh. Notice that the account balances are updated. Balances shown in red are credit balances.

Account Balances		Customize
Account Description	Account ID	Balance
Money Market Account	1010	$10,700.00
Checking Account	1020	$11,750.75
IRA Savings Account	1040	$27,730.35
WI State Retirement	1045	$35,612.00
Accounts Receivable	1100	$0.00
VISA Payable	2000	($5,250.65)

6. Link to <u>View Account List</u> to see all the accounts and their Running Balance. A partial Account List is shown below. (*Hint:* Accounts shown in red with a parenthesis are credit balances.) These account balances agree with the Balance Sheet shown on page 288.

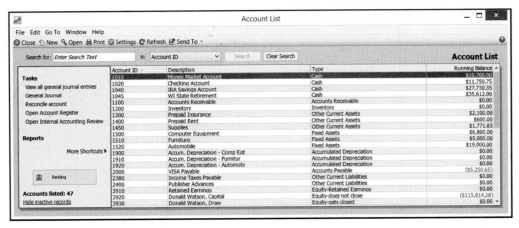

7. Close the Account List.

USING WINDOWS OR FILE EXPLORER TO SEE THE FILE SIZE

To see the size of the Donald Watson Designer file, following these steps.

1. Open Windows or File Explorer –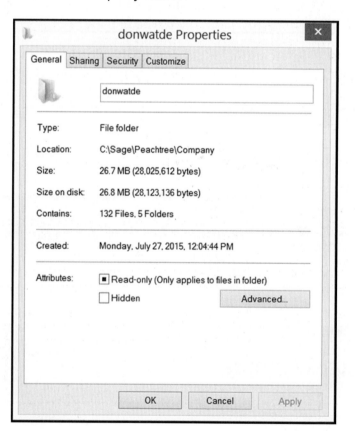

2. Go to the location of the company data. The default location is C:\Sage\Peachtree\Company. Click on the Company folder.

3. Right-click on the donwatde folder, *or* the folder with your shortened name. (*Hint:* Sage 50 shortens the company name using the first three letters of the first word, first three letters from the second word, and two letters from the third word. There are eight characters in the shortened company name.)

4. Left-click Properties. The default location is drive C. The title bar shows the shortened company name.

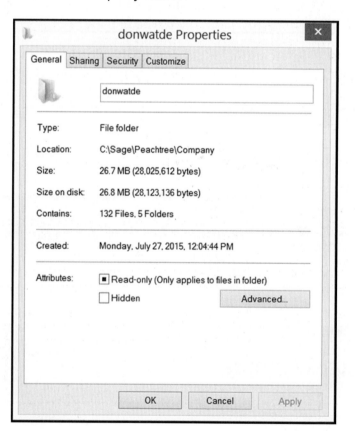

Observe that the size of the file is 26.7 MB (28,025,612 bytes). To save all the data contained in the Donald Watson [or your name] folder, use Windows or File Explorer to copy, then paste the donwatde folder from drive C to a USB drive, CD, or DVD. (Your file size may differ from the donwatde Properties window. This is okay.)

5. When you are finished comparing your properties window, click OK , then ✕ on the Explorer title bar.

BACKING UP BEGINNING BALANCES

Follow these steps to back up the work completed so far. This backup saves the Donald Watson Designer company set up on pages 258-265, the chart of accounts (pages 267-274), and the beginning balances (pages 283-287).

The idea is to make periodic backups so that you can go back to an earlier point in the data. Use a different file name for each backup so that you can distinguish one file from another one.

1. If necessary, close all windows and insert your USB flash drive. From the System Navigation Center, select Back Up Now . (*Or, from the* menu bar, select File > Back Up.)

2. If necessary, uncheck the box next to Include company name in the backup file name. Click Back Up .

3. In the Save in field, go to the location of your USB drive.

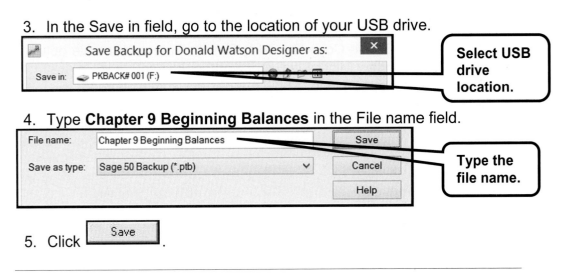

4. Type **Chapter 9 Beginning Balances** in the File name field.

5. Click Save .

6. When the window prompts that This company backup will require approximately 1 diskette, click [OK]. Click [OK] again when the window prompts Please insert the first disk. When the Back Up Company scale is 100% complete, you have successfully backed up to this point in Chapter 9. (This step will differ slightly if you are backing up to the default or other hard drive location.)

In Chapter 9, you learned how to set up a new Sage 50 company, edit the chart of accounts, and how to use information from a balance sheet to enter beginning balances. Because two files were backed up in Chapter 9—the Chapter 9 Chart of Accounts.ptb file and the Chapter 9 Beginning Balances.ptb file—you could restore either file to start at that point in the data. For example, what if you notice a mistake and need to start at an earlier place in the data? By saving two files, you have two different backup files to restore. *Remember, in the business world backups are made frequently.*

EXPORT THE CHART OF ACCOUNTS AND BEGINNING BALANCES TO EXCEL

Follow these steps to export the October 1, 2016 Balance Sheet to Excel.

1. From the menu bar, select Reports & Forms > General Ledger > double-click Chart of Accounts. The Chart of Accounts appears. If needed, expand the Accounts Description and Account Type columns. (Click [ ] to widen the column.)

2. Click [Excel]. On the Copy Report to Excel window, in the file option area, Create a new Microsoft Excel workbook is selected. In the Report header option field, Show header in Excel worksheet is selected.

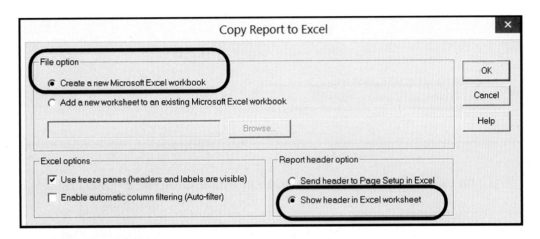

3. Click [OK]. The chart of accounts exports to Excel.

4. Save. Use the file name **Chapter 9_Chart of Accounts and Beginning Balances.xlsx**. (*Hint:* If you are using Excel 2003, your file extension is .xls.)

5. Go back to the Select a Report or Form window. In the Reports list, select Financial Statements > double-click <Standard> Balance Sheet. Change the date range to Period 9, 9/1/2016 to 9/30/2016.

   (Refer to page 287, steps 1-3.) Click [OK].

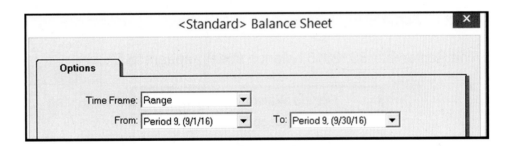

6. Click [OK] > select [Excel]. On the Copy Report to Excel window, select Add a new worksheet to an existing Microsoft Excel workbook.

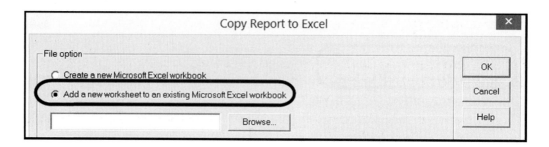

7. Click [Browse...] to go to the location of the Chapter 9_Chart of Accounts and Beginning Balances.xlsx file. Click [Open]. You are returned to the Copy Report to Excel window. Observe that the Browse field shows the location of the Chapter 9_Chart of Accounts and Beginning Balances file.

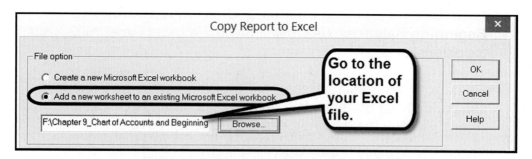

8. Click [OK].

9. The September 30, 2016 balance sheet appears in Excel.

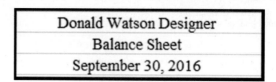

Donald Watson Designer
Balance Sheet
September 30, 2016

10. Observe that two sheets are shown at the bottom of the Excel file: Chart of Accounts and Balance Sheet.

Chart of Accounts / Balance Sheet

11. Save the file. Exit Excel. Close all windows.

SAVE PDF FILES

Follow these steps to save the September 30, 2016 Balance Sheet and Chart of Accounts as Adobe PDF file.

1. Display the <Standard> Balance Sheet. Change the Time Frame to Range. Select From Period 9, (9/1/16) To Period 9, (9/30/16).

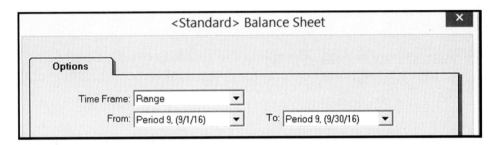

2. Click <OK>. The September 30, 2016 Balance Sheet appears. Click
   . (*Hint:* If the PDF icon is not active, select Print > in the Name field, select Adobe PDF > click <OK>.) Select your USB drive. Save the file. The suggested file name is **Chapter 9_Balance Sheet.pdf**. (*Hint:* The September 30 ending balances are the October 1, 2016 beginning balances.) Compare the balance sheet to the one shown on page 288.

3. Display the Chart of Accounts. Save as a PDF file. The suggested file name is **Chapter 9_Chart of Accounts.pdf.** (*Hint:* Sage automatically dates reports the last day of the month. By default, the Chart of Accounts is dated October 31, 2016.)

4. Exit Sage 50.

ONLINE LEARNING CENTER

Complete end-of-chapter activities at www.mhhe.com/yacht2016 > Student Edition > Chapter 9.

1. Quizzes: Multiple Choice Quiz and True or False. Interactive online tests that are graded and can be emailed to your instructor.

2. More Resources:

   a. <u>Quizzes</u>: <u>Multiple-Choice</u> and <u>True/False</u> questions. Interactive online tests that are graded and can be emailed to your instructor.

   b. <u>Going to the Net Exercises</u>: Access Wikipedia's Chart of Accounts website.

   c. <u>QA Templates</u>: 10 multiple-choice questions and two Analysis Questions.

   d. <u>Assessment Rubric</u>: Complete the rubric to review Sage 50's journals, navigation centers, modules, task windows, and reports.

   e. <u>Narrated PowerPoints</u>: Listen to narrated PowerPoints.

   f. <u>Videos</u>: In Chapter 9, the video is New Company Set Up. Watch the videos using an Internet browser, iPod, iPad, or iPhone.

The OLC also includes links to the Appendixes:

- Appendix A: Troubleshooting
- Appendix B: Accounting Information Systems
- Appendix C: Review of Accounting Principles
- Appendix D: Glossary (words that are boldfaced and italicized in chapter)

Exercise 9-1: Follow the instructions below to complete Exercise 9-1:

1. Start Sage 50. If Donald Watson [your name] Designer or other company opens, select File > New Company. When the window prompts, Do you want to keep Donald Watson (your name) Designer open?, click [No]. The Create a New Company – Introduction window appears. Click [Next >]. (*Or,* from the startup window, select [Create a new company].)

2. Type the following company information:

Company Name:	Crafts by Your Name (*Use your first and last name*)
Address Line 1:	Your address
City, State, Zip	Your city, Your State, Your Zip code
Country:	USA
Telephone:	Your telephone number
Fax:	Your fax number (if any)
Business Type:	Sole Proprietorship
E-mail:	Type your email address

Leave the Tax ID Numbers fields blank.

The Company Name field should show Crafts by *your first and last name*. The Business Type field shows Sole Proprietorship.

3. Click [Next >]. At the Select a method to create your company window, select Copy settings from an existing Sage 50 Accounting company.

4. Click [Next >].

5. Highlight Donald Watson [or your name] Designer, then click [Next >].

6. At the Copy Company Information window, accept the default selections by clicking [Next >].

7. Accept the default for accrual accounting by clicking [Next >].

8. Accept the default for Real Time posting by clicking [Next >].

9. At the You are ready to create your company window, click [Finish]. If the screen prompts You can use this company in the student version of Sage 50 for the next 14 months and then it will expire, click [OK].

10. If the Setup Guide window appears, click on the box next to Don't show this screen at startup. Click [Close]. Close the Getting Started window.

11. The Crafts by your first and last name - Sage 50 Accounting window appears. Make sure the period is Period 10 - 10/01/16-10/31/16 – [Period 10 - 10/01/16-10/31/16].

12. Make the following changes to the Chart of Accounts:

   a. Change the name of the following accounts:

   • Account No. 1020, Checking Account to Midway Bank
   • Account No. 2000, VISA Payable to Accounts Payable
   • Account No. 3920, Donald Watson, Capital to Your Name, Capital (Make sure the Account Type is Equity-doesn't close)
   • Account No. 3930, Donald Watson, Draw to Your Name, Draw
   • Account No. 4050, Royalty Income to Crafts Income
   • Account No. 6800, Freight Expense to Conference Expense

b. Delete the following accounts:

- Account No. 1010, Money Market Account
- Account No. 1040, IRA Savings Account
- Account No. 1045, WI State Retirement
- Account No. 2400, Publisher Advances

c. Add the following accounts:

- Account No. 6180, Automobile Expense
- Account No. 6420, Water and Power Expense
- Account No. 7400, Postage Expense

13. Print the chart of accounts.

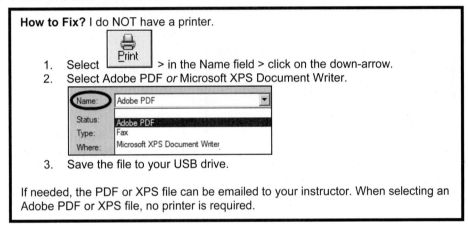

How to Fix? I do NOT have a printer.

1. Select [🖶 Print] > in the Name field > click on the down-arrow.
2. Select Adobe PDF *or* Microsoft XPS Document Writer.

Name:	Adobe PDF ▼
Status:	Adobe PDF
Type:	Fax
Where:	Microsoft XPS Document Writer

3. Save the file to your USB drive.

If needed, the PDF or XPS file can be emailed to your instructor. When selecting an Adobe PDF or XPS file, no printer is required.

14. Backup. The suggested file name is **Exercise 9-1**.

15. Click File > Exit or continue.

Exercise 9-2: Follow the instructions below to complete Exercise 9-2. Exercise 9-1 *must* be completed before starting Exercise 9-2.

1. Start Sage. If necessary, open the company that you set up in Exercise 9-1, Crafts by Your Name. (*Hint:* If a different company opens, select File > Open Previous Company. When the screen prompts do you want to open two companies, select <No>.)

2. If necessary, restore the Exercise 9-1.ptb file.[3] If you are continuing from Exercise 9-1, you do <u>not</u> need to restore.

3. Use the Balance Sheet on the next page to record chart of accounts beginning balances. (*Hint:* Select **9/1/16 through 9/30/16** as the period for entering chart of accounts beginning balances. Enter beginning balances as of September 30, 2016.)

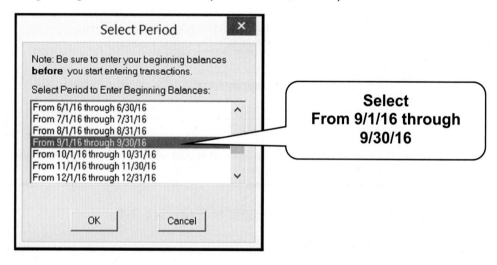

_____

[3]You can restore from your back up file even if *no* Sage 50 company exists. Refer to Troubleshooting, pages 279-280.

Crafts by Your Name Balance Sheet October 1, 2016		
ASSETS		
Current Assets		
Midway Bank	$17,500.00	
Prepaid Insurance	1,000.00	
Prepaid Rent	700.00	
Supplies	850.00	
Total Current Assets		$20,050.00
Property and Equipment		
Computer Equipment	6,500.00	
Furniture	3,500.00	
Automobile	19,000.00	
Total Property and Equipment		29,000.00
Total Assets		$ 49,050.00
LIABILITIES AND CAPITAL		
Current Liabilities		
Accounts Payable	$1,050.00	
Total Current Liabilities		$1,050.00
Capital		
Your Name, Capital		48,000.00
Total Liabilities and Capital		$ 49,050.00

4. Print the September 30, 2016 balance sheet.

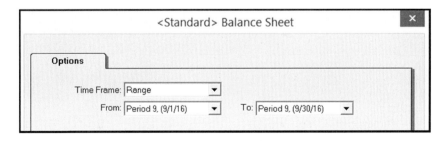

CHECK YOUR FIGURES: Chart of Accounts & Balance Sheet

Account No. 3930, Student Name, Draw
Account No. 4050, Crafts Income
Account No. 7400, Postage Expense
Account No. 1020, Midway Bank, $17,500
Account No. 3920, Student Name, Capital, $48,000

5. Backup. The suggested filename is **Exercise 9-2**.

6. Export the chart of accounts and balance sheet to Excel. Use the file name **Exercise 9-2_Chart of Accounts and Beginning Balances.xlsx**. Change the date on the balance sheet to September 30, 2016.

7. Save the Chart of Accounts and September 30, 2016 Balance Sheet as PDF files. Use the file names **Exercise 9-2_Chart of Accounts.pdf** and **Exercise 9-2_Balance Sheet.pdf** as the file names.

CHAPTER 9 INDEX

Chapter 10 — Maintaining Accounting Records for Service Businesses

LEARNING OBJECTIVES

1. Restore data from Chapter 9. (This backup was made on pages 291-292.)[1]
2. Record and post deposits, checks and ATMs.
3. Complete account reconciliation.
4. Display the Account Register.
5. Display the Cash Receipts Journal, Cash Disbursements Journal, and General Journal.
6. Display the general ledger trial balance.
7. Print financial statements.
8. Export the October General Ledger Trial Balance, Balance Sheet and Income Statement to Excel and save as PDF files.
9. Make four backups, save two Excel files, and save four PDF files.[2]

In Chapter 10, you continue the work started in Chapter 9. You complete the computer accounting cycle for the month of October using your client's transaction register and bank statement as **source documents**. Source documents are used to show written evidence of a business transaction. For Donald Watson Designer, the source documents used are his transaction register and bank statement. The **transaction register** shows Mr. Watson's checking account activity.

Remember, Chapter 9 must be completed before starting Chapter 10.

GETTING STARTED

Follow the steps on the next page to continue using Donald Watson [your first and last name] Designer company data.

---

[1]All activities in Chapter 9 must be completed before starting Chapter 10.

[2]Refer to the chart on pages 254-256 for the file names and size of backup files, Excel files, and Adobe PDF files.

1. Start Sage 50. Open Donald Watson Designer [or another name Designer]. (*Hint:* If a different company opens, select File > Open a Previous Company > select Donald Watson Designer. When the window prompts, Do you want to keep [company name] open?, click No . If you prefer to keep two companies open, click Yes .)

2. If necessary, restore the Chapter 9 Beginning Balances.ptb backup file. This backup was made on pages 291-292.[3]

Read Me: Do I need to restore?

If you are working on your own PC or laptop, you may be able to skip restore. Refer to the disk icon below to make sure you are starting with the work completed in Chapter 9.

If you are working in the computer lab or classroom, start Donald Watson Designer [or other name Designer]. Restore the Chapter 9 Beginning Balances.ptb file from your USB drive.

To make sure you are starting in the appropriate place in the data (Chapter 9 Beginning Balances.ptb backup) check the balance sheet. A partial balance sheet is shown on the next page. The complete balance sheet is shown on page 288.

Unless you change the date range, the balance sheet shows October 31, 2016. Sage 50 dates reports the last day of the period (month). For the balance sheet shown on page 288, you changed the date range to check that you entered beginning balances as of September 30.

---

[3]You can restore from your back up file even if *no* designer company exists. Refer to Troubleshooting, pages 279-280.

Donald Watson Designer
Balance Sheet
October 31, 2016

ASSETS

Current Assets		
Money Market Account	$ 10,700.00	
Checking Account	11,750.75	
IRA Savings Account	27,730.35	
WI State Retirement	35,612.00	
Prepaid Insurance	2,100.00	
Prepaid Rent	600.00	
Supplies	1,771.83	
Total Current Assets		90,264.93
Property and Equipment		
Computer Equipment	6,800.00	
Furniture	5,000.00	
Automobile	19,000.00	
Total Property and Equipment		30,800.00
Other Assets		
Total Other Assets		0.00
Total Assets	$	121,064.93

RECORDING DEPOSITS, CHECKS AND ATMs

In Sage, the Receive Money window is used to record deposits. When you save a receipt, Sage automatically journalizes the entry in the Cash Receipts Journal. When Mr. Watson writes a check, the disbursement is recorded in the Write Checks window. When you save the check or ATM, the entry is automatically journalized in the Cash Disbursements Journal and posted to the appropriate general ledger accounts.

Sage 50's Write Checks window is a simplified version of the Payments window. In this chapter, use the Write Checks window to issue a check for expenses, assets, owner's draw, or ATM withdrawals.

Mr. Watson's transaction register has the information necessary to record entries for the month of October. Since Mr. Watson is a new client, information from his Balance Sheet was used for an opening entry. His transaction register lists the information for the rest of the month.

Follow these steps to show the cash balance on the Receive Money window and Payments window.

1. From the menu bar, click Options > Global.

2. Make sure the box next to Recalculate cash balance automatically in Receipts, Payments, and Payroll Entry has a checkmark next to it.

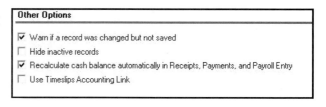

3. Click [OK]. When you use the Receive Money window or Write Checks window, the transaction register balance agrees with the Cash Account balance shown on these windows.

Mr. Watson's transaction register shows an October 1 deposit of $11,000. A section of Mr. Watson's transaction register is shown.

Check Number	Date	Description of Transaction	Payment	Deposit	Balance
	9/30				11,750.75
	10/1	Deposit (publisher's advance)		11,000.00	22,750.75

▶ Follow these steps to record the October 1 deposit from Mr. Watson's transaction register. (The arrow indicates a video at www.mhhe.com/yacht2016 > Student Edition > select Chapter 10 > Videos > Deposits.)

1. From the menu bar, select Tasks > Receive Money. The Select a Cash Account window displays. If necessary click on the down arrow to select Checking Account.

2. Click [OK]. The Receive Money window displays. (*Hint:* If a Sage Advisor window appears, read it. Then close.)

3. Your cursor is in the Deposit ticket ID field. Type **10/1/16**. (*Hint: Use the date of the deposit for the Deposit ticket ID field.*)

4. Click on the Name field. Type **Deposit** in the Name field.

5. Click on the Check/Reference No. field. Type **Advance** in the Check/Reference No. field. Press **<Enter>** two times.

6. Accept the default for Oct 1, 2016 in the Date field by pressing **<Enter>**.

   Verify that the Payment Method is Check and that Account 1020, Checking Account, is displayed in the Cash account field. The Cash Account Balance field displays 11,750.75. This agrees with the partial transaction register balance shown on page 308 and the Checking Account balance shown on the Balance Sheet, page 307.

7. Make sure that the Apply to Revenues tab is selected. Click once on the Quantity field. Type **1** in the Quantity field. Press the **<Enter>** key two times.

8. Type **Publisher's advance** in the Description field. Press **<Enter>**.

9. Click 🔍 in the GL Account field. Select Account No. 2400, Publisher Advances. (*Hint:* In the GL Account field, you can also type 2400.)

10. Type **11000** in the Unit Price field.

How to Fix? 11,000.00 does <u>not</u> appear in the Unit Price field.

1. From the menu bar, click Options > Global.
2. In the Decimal Entry field > click Manual. When Manual is selected, a black circle is placed within a circle (radio button).
3. The Quantity fields, Standard fields, and Unit Price fields, should have **2** selected.
4. Make sure the boxes in the Hide General Ledger Accounts section are *unchecked*.
5. Click [OK].

When global options are selected, this feature is in effect for all companies.

---

11. Press the **<Enter>** key two times. Compare your Receive Money window to the one shown below. (*Hint:* If the GL Account field is <u>not</u> shown, refer to the How to Fix box on the previous page. In order to show account numbers (1020 is debited; 2400 is credited), the boxes in the Hide General Ledger Accounts area must be *unchecked.*)

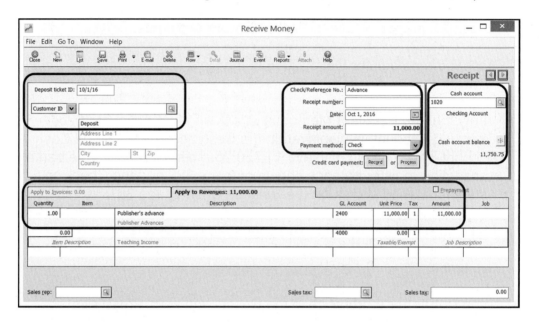

12. Click 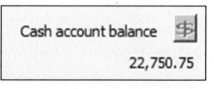 to post this entry. After you post, the Cash account balance field shows the same balance, $22,750.75, as the partial transaction register shown on the next page. The Receive Money window is ready for another entry. When the entry is saved, it is posted to the general ledger. The Cash Receipts Journal shows the debits and credits for this deposit.

13. Click 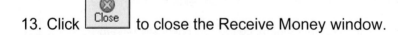 to close the Receive Money window.

▶ Use Write Checks for Check No. 4001. A section of the transaction register is shown on the next page. (The arrow indicates a video at www.mhhe.com/yacht2016 > Student Edition > Chapter 10 > Videos > Checks.)

Italics, and a broken line, indicate entries that have already been entered and saved.

Ck. No.	Date	Description of Transaction	Payment	Deposit	Balance
	9/30				*11,750.75*
	10/1			*11,000.00*	*22,750.75*
4001	**10/2**	**Transfer to Money Market Account**	**6,000.00**		**16,750.75**

From the Navigation Bar, click 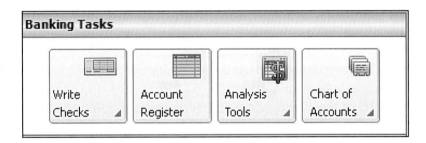. Observe that the Banking Tasks diagram appears. In this chapter you focus on banking; in Part 3 (Chapters 12-15), you work with customers and vendors and record customer receipts and vendor payments.

Banking Tasks

Write Checks   Account Register   Analysis Tools   Chart of Accounts

---

Read Me: Navigation Bar or Menu Bar

In this textbook, you are going to use *both* menu bar selections and the Navigation Bar. Sage 50 2016 includes various ways to access features. You can make selections from the menu bar *or* the Navigation Bar. Throughout the textbook, these two methods are shown.

Use these steps to enter Check No. 4001 and post to the Cash Disbursements Journal.

1. From the Banking Navigation Center, click  > New Check. The Select a Cash Account window appears. If necessary, click on the down-arrow to select the Checking Account.

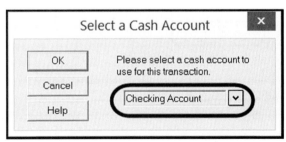

2. Click [OK].

3. The Write Checks window displays. Click on the Pay to the order of, Name field. Type **Money Market Account**.

4. Click 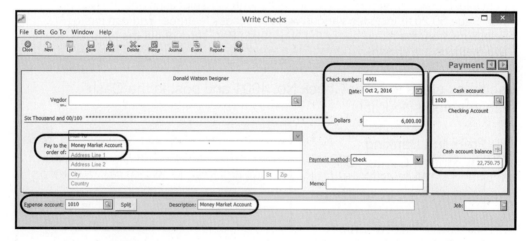 in the Expense account field. The Chart of Accounts list is displayed. Even though you are *not* charging Check No. 4001 against an expense account, you use the Expense Account field to select the appropriate account to debit. Select Account No.1010, Money Market Account. The Description field is automatically completed with Money Market Account.

5. Click on the Check number field. Type **4001** in the Check number field and press **<Enter>**.

6. Type **2** in the Date field and press **<Enter>**.

   Verify that the Cash Account Balance field shows $22,750.75. This agrees with the partial transaction register on page 311 (beginning balance plus publisher's advance, $11,750.75 + 11,000 = $22,750.75. If the Cash Account Balance field does not agree with your transaction register, see the instructions on page 308, steps 1-3, for setting the global options for recalculating the cash balance for receipts, payments, and payroll.

7. Type **6000** in the $ field. Press **<Enter>**. The check is completed.

8. Click ![Save] to post to the general ledger. The debits and credits for this entry are in the Cash Disbursements Journal. Verify that the Cash Account Balance field displays the October 2 balance (this is the same balance, $16,750.75, as the partial transaction register on page 311).You are ready for the next entry. (*Hint: you may need to change the date to 10/2/16 to see the correct cash balance.*)

9. Click ![Close] to return to the Banking Navigation Center.

Comment

Sage automatically completes the Check number field once the first number is typed. After typing another reference in the Check number field (for example, ATM), you need to type the appropriate check number. ATM is an acronym for Automated Teller Machine. When an ATM card is used, cash is withdrawn from the checking account.

Source documents are used to show written evidence of a business transaction or event. Examples of source documents are sales invoices, purchase invoices, and in this case, Mr. Watson's transaction registers which show checking account activity. Starting with the ATM withdrawal on October 3 for $200, record the entries shown on the transaction register on pages 314 and 315 in the Write Checks window (Banking Navigation Center) or the Receive Money window (Tasks > Receive Money). Assign each entry on the transaction register an appropriate account number from Mr. Watson's Chart of Accounts. Record individual entries for each check number, deposit, or ATM transaction.

Each deposit (cash or check received) is a debit to Account No. 1020, Checking Account, and is recorded on the Receive Money window (Cash Receipts Journal). On the Receive Money window, you select the appropriate general ledger account for the credit part of the entry. The offsetting debit is automatically entered in Account No. 1020, Checking Account.

Each payment (check issued and ATM withdrawal) listed on the transaction register is a credit to Account No. 1020, Checking Account, and is recorded on the Write Checks window (Cash Disbursements Journal). On the Write Checks window, you select the appropriate general ledger account for the debit part of the entry. The offsetting credit is automatically entered in Account No. 1020, Checking Account.

After recording each check, deposit, or ATM, you should verify that the Balance field on the Write Checks window and Receive Money window agrees with the transaction register balances below and on page 315. You have already recorded the first two entries for October 1 and October 2. Continue recording entries with the October 3 ATM transaction.

Remember, click *to post each entry (ATMs, Deposits, Checks). The transaction register entries are listed individually on the table below and on page 315.*

> **Read Me:** *Why should I use Write Checks instead of the Payments window?*
>
> The Write Checks window is a simplified version of the Payments window. Both Write Checks and Payments post to the Cash Disbursements Journal. In Chapter 10, you use the Write Checks window for checks and ATM withdrawals. You could use the Payments window for checks and ATMs but it is quicker to use Write Checks.

Italics and a broken line, indicate entries that have already been made. Start with the 10/3 ATM.

		Transaction Register Donald Watson Designer			
Ck. No.	**Date**	**Description of Transaction**	**Payment**	**Deposit**	**Balance**
	9/30				*11,750.75*
	10/1			*11,000.00*	*22,750.75*
	10/2		*6,000.00*		*16,750.75*
	10/3	**ATM**[4]	**200.00**		**16,550.75**
	10/4	Deposit (book royalty)		3,965.05	20,515.80
4002	10/4	Office Time (computer equipment)	1,105.68		19,410.12
4003	10/9	U.S. Post Office[5]	49.00		19,361.12

---

[4]For each ATM use Account No. 3930, Donald Watson, Draw [or, your name, Draw]. Type **ATM** in the Check number and Pay to the order of fields. For the next check, you need to type the check number in the Check number field.

[5]Add account No. 7400, Postage Expense. (*Hint:* In the Expense Account field, click

 > . In the Account Type field, select Expenses.)

4004	10/9	Bayside News (newspaper subscription); debit 6100 Dues and Subscriptions	45.00		19,316.12
4005	10/9	MIL Gas (utilities)	39.64		19,276.48
4006	10/10	Water and Power Company, add account 6420 Water and Power Expense	98.59		19,177.89
4007	10/10	Lake Telephone (telephone expense)	35.00		19,142.89
4008	10/10	Long Distance Company	46.20		19,096.69
	10/13	Deposit (Milwaukee Community College)		2,716.19	21,812.88
	10/14	ATM (Read warning, click <OK>.	400.00		21,412.88
4009	10/15	Auto Parts - car headlight; add account 6180 Automobile Expense	201.00		21,211.88
4010	10/16	Matt Lozano (install headlight; automobile expense)	110.00		21,101.88
4011	10/29	WI Dept. of Transportation (auto registration)	210.00		20,891.88
4012	10/29	Supplies & More (letterhead and envelopes); debit 1450, Supplies	215.98		20,675.90
4013	10/30	Internet Service Provider	29.99		20,645.91

BACKING UP THE OCTOBER TRANSACTION REGISTER

Follow these steps to back up the October transaction register.

1. If necessary, close all windows and insert your USB flash drive. From the System Navigation Center, select `Back Up Now`. (*Or*, from the menu bar, select File > Back Up. If necessary, uncheck the box next to Include company name in the backup file name. Click `Back Up`).

2. In the Save in field, go to the location of your USB drive or back up to another location. Type **Chapter 10 Transaction Register October** in the File name field.

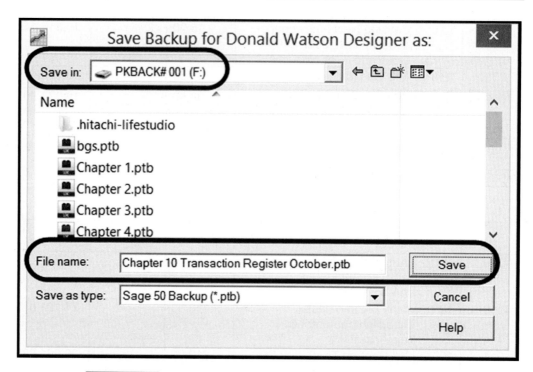

3. Click [Save].

4. When the window prompts that This company backup will require approximately 1 diskette, click [OK]. Click [OK] again when the window prompts Please insert the first disk. When the Back Up Company scale is 100% complete, you have successfully backed up to this point in Chapter 10. (This step will differ slightly if you are backing up to the default or other hard drive location.)

ACCOUNT RECONCILIATION

Donald Watson receives a bank statement every month for his checking account (Account No. 1020). The bank statement shows which checks, ATMs, and deposits cleared the bank. The Account Reconciliation feature allows you to reconcile his bank statement.

Statement of Account			Donald Watson Designer
Checking Account			3024 University Dr.
October 1 to October 31, 2016	Account No. 248531-90		Milwaukee, WI 54202
REGULAR CHECKING			
Previous Balance		$ 11,750.75	
3 Deposits (+)		17,681.24	
9 checks (-)		7,690.47	
2 Other Deductions (-)		600.00	
Service Charges (-)	10/31/16	10.00	
Ending Balance	10/31/16	**$21,131.52**	
DEPOSITS			
	10/4/16	11,000.00	
	10/7/16	3,965.05	
	10/17/16	2,716.19	
CHECKS (Asterisk * indicates break in check number sequence)			
	10/2/16	4001	6,000.00	
	10/6/16	4002	1,105.68	
	10/15/16	4003	49.00	
	10/16/16	4004	45.00	
	10/16/16	4006*	98.59	
	10/17/16	4007	35.00	
	10/20/16	4008	46.20	
	10/23/16	4009	201.00	
	10/30/16	4010	110.00	
OTHER DEDUCTIONS (ATM's)			
	10/3/16	ATM	200.00	
	10/14/16	ATM	400.00	

Follow these steps to reconcile Mr. Watson's bank statement balance to Account No. 1020, Checking Account.

1. From the Navigation Bar, select [Banking] > [Reconcile Accounts].
   (*Hint:* You may also use the menu bar selections Tasks > Account Reconciliation.) The Account Reconciliation window appears.

2. In the Account to Reconcile field, select Account No. 1020, Checking Account. If necessary, enlarge the window.

3. On the Account Reconciliation window, click on the up-arrow 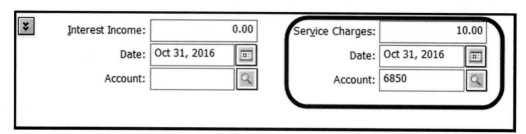 next to Statement Ending Balance to expand the area. Type **10** in the Service Charges field. The Date defaults to October 31, 2016. In the Account field, select Account No. 6850, Bank Service Charge.

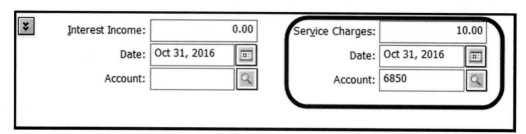

4. In the Statement Ending Balance field (at the bottom of the window), type **21131.52**. (This is the ending balance on Mr. Watson's bank statement.)

5. In the Deposit/Bank Credit; Check/Bank Debit table, place a checkmark <✓> in the Status column for each deposit, check, and ATM that is listed on the bank statement. For each deposit, check, and ATM cleared, the Status column shows a checkmark. Do not check off the outstanding checks: 4005, 4011, 4012, 4013.

> **Comment:** Observe that the Unreconciled Difference is zero (0.00). This zero balance is proof that Account No. 1020, Checking Account, is reconciled.
>
> The GL (System) Balance is $20,635.91. The transaction register on page 315 shows an October 30 balance of $20,645.91. When you subtract the service charge of $10, the transaction register balance (20,645.91 – 10 = 20,635.91) agrees with the GL (System) Balance shown on the Account Reconciliation window.

The Account Reconciliation window is shown on the next page.

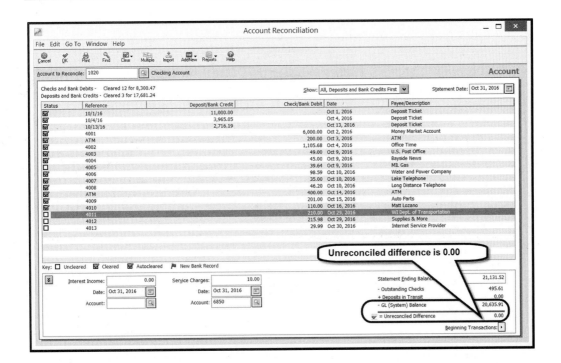

6. When you are finished, click 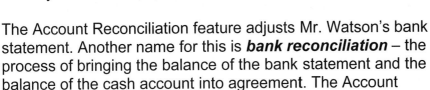.

The Account Reconciliation feature adjusts Mr. Watson's bank statement. Another name for this is **bank reconciliation** – the process of bringing the balance of the bank statement and the balance of the cash account into agreement. The Account Reconciliation can be used with other accounts, too.

DISPLAYING THE ACCOUNT REGISTER

Entries for deposits and withdrawals are shown on the Account Register.

1. From the Banking Navigation Center's Recently Used Banking Reports area, select <u>View</u> Account Register. Compare your Account Register to the one shown on the next page.

Donald Watson Designer
Account Register
For the Period From Oct 1, 2016 to Oct 31, 2016
1020 - Checking Account

Filter Criteria includes: Report order is by Date.

Date	Trans No	Type	Trans Desc	Deposit Amt	Withdrawal Amt	Balance
			Beginning Balance			11,750.75
10/1/16	10/1/16	Deposit	Deposit	11,000.00		22,750.75
10/2/16	4001	Withdrawal	Money Market Account		6,000.00	16,750.75
10/3/16	ATM	Withdrawal	ATM		200.00	16,550.75
10/4/16	10/4/16	Deposit	Deposit	3,965.05		20,515.80
10/4/16	4002	Withdrawal	Office Time		1,105.68	19,410.12
10/9/16	4003	Withdrawal	U.S. Post Office		49.00	19,361.12
10/9/16	4004	Withdrawal	Bayside News		45.00	19,316.12
10/9/16	4005	Withdrawal	MIL Gas		39.64	19,276.48
10/10/16	4006	Withdrawal	Water and Power Compa		98.59	19,177.89
10/10/16	4007	Withdrawal	Lake Telephone		35.00	19,142.89
10/10/16	4008	Withdrawal	Long Distance Telephone		46.20	19,096.69
10/13/16	10/13/16	Deposit	Deposit	2,716.19		21,812.88
10/14/16	ATM	Withdrawal	ATM		400.00	21,412.88
10/15/16	4009	Withdrawal	Auto Parts		201.00	21,211.88
10/16/16	4010	Withdrawal	Matt Lozano		110.00	21,101.88
10/29/16	4011	Withdrawal	WI Dept. of Transportatio		210.00	20,891.88
10/29/16	4012	Withdrawal	Supplies & More		215.98	20,675.90
10/30/16	4013	Withdrawal	Internet Service Provider		29.99	20,645.91
10/31/16	10/31/16	Other	Service Charge		10.00	20,635.91
			Total	**17,681.24**	**8,796.08**	

2. The Account Register and Mr. Watson's transaction register on pages 314-315 show the same results, *except* for the 10/31/16 service charge of 10.00. Similar to the transaction register, the Account Register lists deposits (receive money or receipts) and withdrawals (checks and ATMs). If you notice a discrepancy use drill down to follow the path of the entry's origin. Follow these steps to use drill down.

   a. Double-click on the 10/4/16 Deposit of $3,965.05. Notice that your cursor turns into a magnifying glass with a Z in the center.

   | 10/4/16 | 10/4/16 | Deposit | Deposit | 3,965.05 | Ⓩ | 20,515.80 |

   b. The Receive Money window appears with the October 4, 2016 deposit shown.

   c. If there is no need to make a correction, close the Receive Money window. You are returned to the Account Register window.

   Observe that the Account Register shows the Beginning Balance, Deposits, and Withdrawals (Checks, ATMs, bank service charge). It is okay if the Trans Desc (transaction descriptions) differs.

You can also drill down from the Account Register to the Write Checks, Receive Money, or General Journal windows. Drill down shows the original entry. For example, if you double-click on the check number, you go to the Write Checks window; if you double-click on the 10/31/16 entry for the service charge (10.00) you go to the General Journal Entry window.

3. Close the Account Register and any other open windows.

4. Follow these steps to display the General Journal.

   a. From the menu bar, click Reports & Forms > General Ledger.

   b. Click General Journal > Display .

Donald Watson Designer
General Journal
For the Period From Oct 1, 2016 to Oct 31, 2016

Filter Criteria includes: Report order is by Date. Report is printed with Accounts having Zero Amounts and with shortened descriptions and in Detail Format.

Date	Account ID	Reference	Trans Description	Debit Amt	Credit Amt
10/31/16	1020	10/31/16	Service Charge		10.00
	6850		Service Charge	10.00	
		Total		10.00	10.00

   c. Close the General Journal report.

PRINTING THE CASH RECEIPTS JOURNAL

Follow these steps to print the Cash Receipts Journal.

1. From the Select a Report or Form window, select Accounts Receivable in the Reports area. (*Hint:* From the menu bar, select Reports & Forms > Accounts Receivable.)

2. Double-click Cash Receipts Journal. The Cash Receipts Journal appears.

   Troubleshooting: Why does my Cash Receipts Journal show blue lines between columns? Most of the screen images are done with the PDF file image.

Donald Watson Designer
Cash Receipts Journal
For the Period From Oct 1, 2016 to Oct 31, 2016

Filter Criteria includes: Report order is by Check Date. Report is printed in Detail Format.

Date	Account ID	Transaction Re	Line Description	Debit Amnt	Credit Amnt
10/1/16	2400	Advance	Publisher's advance		11,000.00
	1020		Deposit	11,000.00	
10/4/16	4050	Book royalty	Book royalty		3,965.05
	1020		Deposit	3,965.05	
10/13/16	4000	Milwaukee CC	Teaching income		2,716.19
	1020		Deposit	2,716.19	
				17,681.24	17,681.24

Comment

The information in the Transaction Ref column may differ. The Transaction Ref column shows the same information as what you typed in the Check/Reference No. field of the Receive Money window.

3. Close the Cash Receipts Journal.

PRINTING THE CASH DISBURSEMENTS JOURNAL

1. The Select a Report or Form window should be displayed. In the Reports area, highlight Accounts Payable.

2. Double-click the Cash Disbursements Journal.

Donald Watson Designer
Cash Disbursements Journal
For the Period From Oct 1, 2016 to Oct 31, 2016
Filter Criteria includes: Report order is by Date. Report is printed in Detail Format.

Date	Check #	Account ID	Line Description	Debit Amount	Credit Amount
10/2/16	4001	1010	Money Market Account	6,000.00	
		1020	Money Market Account		6,000.00
10/3/16	ATM	3930	Donald Watson, Draw	200.00	
		1020	ATM		200.00
10/4/16	4002	1500	Computer Equipment	1,105.68	
		1020	Office Time		1,105.68
10/9/16	4003	7400	Postage Expense	49.00	
		1020	U.S. Post Office		49.00
10/9/16	4004	6100	Dues and Subscriptions	45.00	
		1020	Bayside News		45.00
10/9/16	4005	6400	Utilities Expense	39.64	
		1020	MIL Gas		39.64
10/10/16	4006	6420	Water and Power Expense	98.59	
		1020	Water and Power Company		98.59
10/10/16	4007	6500	Telephone Expense	35.00	
		1020	Lake Telephone		35.00
10/10/16	4008	6550	Long Distance Company	46.20	
		1020	Long Distance Telephone		46.20
10/14/16	ATM	3930	Donald Watson, Draw	400.00	
		1020	ATM		400.00
10/15/16	4009	6180	Automobile Expense	201.00	
		1020	Auto Parts		201.00
10/16/16	4010	6180	Automobile Expense	110.00	
		1020	Matt Lozano		110.00
10/29/16	4011	6150	Auto Registration	210.00	
		1020	WI Dept. of Transportation		210.00
10/29/16	4012	1450	Supplies	215.98	
		1020	Supplies & More		215.98
10/30/16	4013	6560	Internet Service Provider	29.99	
		1020	Internet Service Provider		29.99
	Total			8,786.08	8,786.08

3. Close the Cash Disbursements Journal; close the Select a Report or Form window.

EDITING JOURNAL ENTRIES

Compare your journal entries to the ones shown on pages 322–323. Some of the Line Descriptions may differ. This is okay. If your dates, check numbers, or account numbers are different, you should edit the journal entry. Follow these steps to edit the Cash Receipts Journal:

1. From the menu bar, click Tasks > Receive Money. The Receive Money window displays.

2. Click [List]. The Receipt List window appears showing the three deposits and the total.

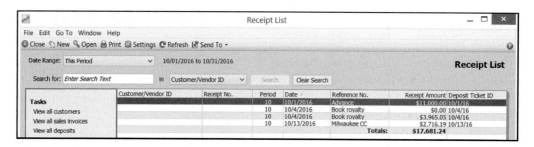

3. If you need to edit a deposit, double-click on it to drill down to the original entry on the Receive Money window.

4. Make any necessary corrections, then click [Save] to post.

5. Close all windows. (*Hint:* From the menu bar, select Window > Close All.)

6. Editing the Cash Disbursements Journal is similar. Go to [Write Checks] > View and Edit Checks. The Write Checks List appears. Drill down to the check or ATM that needs to be edited.

7. Close all windows.

DISPLAYING THE GENERAL LEDGER TRIAL BALANCE

Follow these steps to display the General Ledger Trial Balance.

1. From the menu bar, click Reports & Forms > General Ledger > General Ledger Trial Balance.

2. Click . Compare your General Ledger Trial Balance with the one shown below.

Donald Watson Designer
General Ledger Trial Balance
As of Oct 31, 2016

Filter Criteria includes: Report order is by ID. Report is printed in Detail Format.

Account I	Account Description	Debit Amt	Credit Amt
1010	Money Market Account	16,700.00	
1020	Checking Account	20,635.91	
1040	IRA Savings Account	27,730.35	
1045	WI State Retirement	35,612.00	
1300	Prepaid Insurance	2,100.00	
1400	Prepaid Rent	600.00	
1450	Supplies	1,987.81	
1500	Computer Equipment	7,905.68	
1510	Furniture	5,000.00	
1520	Automobile	19,000.00	
2000	VISA Payable		5,250.65
2400	Publisher Advances		11,000.00
3920	Donald Watson, Capital		115,814.28
3930	Donald Watson, Draw	600.00	
4000	Teaching Income		2,716.19
4050	Royalty Income		3,965.05
6100	Dues and Subscriptions	45.00	
6150	Auto Registration	210.00	
6180	Automobile Expense	311.00	
6400	Utilities Expense	39.64	
6420	Water and Power Expense	98.59	
6500	Telephone Expense	35.00	
6550	Long Distance Company	46.20	
6560	Internet Service Provider	29.99	
6850	Bank Service Charge	10.00	
7400	Postage Expense	49.00	
	Total:	**138,746.17**	**138,746.17**

3. To print the general ledger trial balance, select ⊟ Print, then make

the selections to print (or save as a PDF or Microsoft XPS file.) Observe that the Checking Account (Account No. 1020) balance on the General Ledger Trial Balance and the GL (System) Balance on the Account Reconciliation window on page 319 are the same: 20,635.91.

PRINTING FINANCIAL STATEMENTS

The Computer Accounting Cycle shows that adjusting entries are needed at this point. (See the Computer Accounting Cycle on pages 48-49.) There is no need to complete adjusting entries at the end of October since quarterly adjusting entries are done on December 31, 2016. Instead, print Mr. Watson's financial statements.

Print the following financial statements:

1. <Standard> Balance Sheet. (*Hint:* Reports & Forms > Financial Statements. *Or,* from the Business Status Navigation Center's Find a Report area, in the *Select a Category* field, select Financial Statements. In the *Select a Report* field, select <Standard> Balance Sheet. Click Display . The October 31, 2016 balance sheet is shown on the next page.

Donald Watson Designer
Balance Sheet
October 31, 2016

ASSETS

Current Assets			
Money Market Account	$	16,700.00	
Checking Account		20,635.91	
IRA Savings Account		27,730.35	
WI State Retirement		35,612.00	
Prepaid Insurance		2,100.00	
Prepaid Rent		600.00	
Supplies		1,987.81	
Total Current Assets			105,366.07
Property and Equipment			
Computer Equipment		7,905.68	
Furniture		5,000.00	
Automobile		19,000.00	
Total Property and Equipment			31,905.68
Other Assets			
Total Other Assets			0.00
Total Assets		$	137,271.75

LIABILITIES AND CAPITAL

Current Liabilities			
VISA Payable	$	5,250.65	
Publisher Advances		11,000.00	
Total Current Liabilities			16,250.65
Long-Term Liabilities			
Total Long-Term Liabilities			0.00
Total Liabilities			16,250.65
Capital			
Donald Watson, Capital		115,814.28	
Donald Watson, Draw		(600.00)	
Net Income		5,806.82	
Total Capital			121,021.10
Total Liabilities & Capital		$	137,271.75

Unaudited - For Management Purposes Only

2. Display or print the <Standard> Income Stmnt.

Comment

To print an Income Statement without zero balances, select , uncheck Show Zero Amounts.

Donald Watson Designer
Income Statement
For the Ten Months Ending October 31, 2016

	Current Month			Year to Date	
Revenues					
Teaching Income	$	2,716.19	40.65	$ 2,716.19	40.65
Royalty Income		3,965.05	59.35	3,965.05	59.35
Total Revenues		6,681.24	100.00	6,681.24	100.00
Cost of Sales					
Total Cost of Sales		0.00	0.00	0.00	0.00
Gross Profit		6,681.24	100.00	6,681.24	100.00
Expenses					
Dues and Subscriptions		45.00	0.67	45.00	0.67
Auto Registration		210.00	3.14	210.00	3.14
Automobile Expense		311.00	4.65	311.00	4.65
Utilities Expense		39.64	0.59	39.64	0.59
Water and Power Expense		98.59	1.48	98.59	1.48
Telephone Expense		35.00	0.52	35.00	0.52
Long Distance Company		46.20	0.69	46.20	0.69
Internet Service Provider		29.99	0.45	29.99	0.45
Bank Service Charge		10.00	0.15	10.00	0.15
Postage Expense		49.00	0.73	49.00	0.73
Total Expenses		874.42	13.09	874.42	13.09
Net Income	$	5,806.82	86.91	$ 5,806.82	86.91

For Management Purposes Only

Observe that both the balance sheet and income statement include a line at the bottom of the report that says "For Management Purposes Only."

In addition to dollar amounts, observe that the income statement also includes percentage of revenue columns for both the current month and the year to date. The percentages shown for each expense, total expenses, and net income indicate the percentage of each expense or revenue account divided by total revenues.

For example, here is how 13.09% was calculated for Total Expenses:

$$874.42 \div 6,681.24 = 13.09\%$$

At the end of the quarter (in Chapter 11), more financial statements are printed.

BACKING UP CHAPTER 10 DATA

Backup your data to this point. The suggested file name is **Chapter 10 October**. This backup saves the following data: new company set up (pages 258-265), chart of accounts (pages 267-274), beginning balances (pages 283-287), the entries recorded in the Receive Money and Write Checks windows (refer to the transaction register, pages 314-315); Account Reconciliation (pages 316-319); the Account Register, General Journal, Cash Receipts Journal, Cash Disbursements Journal, the General Ledger Trial Balance, and Financial Statements (pages 319-329).

Each backup allows you to restore data to different points. Observe that each time you backup, the instructions show a different file name. This allows you to distinguish one backup file from another one.

EXPORT THE GENERAL LEDGER TRIAL BALANCE, INCOME STATEMENT AND BALANCE SHEET TO EXCEL

Follow the steps on the next page to export the October general ledger trial balance and financial statements to Excel.

1. Display the General Ledger Trial Balance.

2. Click [Excel]. On the Copy Report to Excel window, in the file option area, Create a new Microsoft Excel workbook should be selected. In the Report header option field, Show header in Excel worksheet is selected.

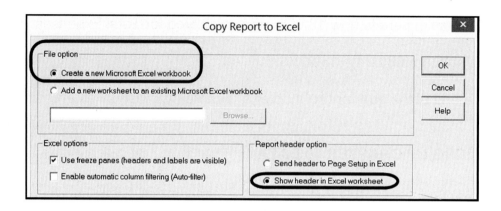

3. Click [OK]. The general ledger trial balance appears in Excel. Save. Use the file name **Chapter 10_October Trial Balance and Financial Statements.xlsx**.

4. Maximize Sage 50. Go to the Select a Report or Form window. Select Financial Statements. Double-click <Standard> Income Statement. Uncheck Show Zero Amounts. Click [OK]. On the Income Statement window, click [Excel].

5. On the Copy Report to Excel window, select Add a new worksheet to an existing Microsoft Excel workbook. Click [Browse...] to go to the location of the saved file. Click [Open].

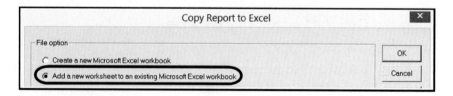

6. Click [OK]. Go to Sage 50 and add the <Standard> Balance Sheet to the Excel file.

7. Click [OK]. The Excel file opens. Observe that three sheets are shown at the bottom: General Ledger Trial Balance, Income Stmnt, Balance Sheet.

| ⏮ ◀ ▶ ⏭ | General Ledger Trial Balance | Income Stmnt | **Balance Sheet** |

8. Save the Excel file. Exit Excel. Close all Sage 50 windows.

SAVE GENERAL LEDGER TRIAL BALANCE AND FINANCIAL STATEMENTS AS PDF FILES

1. Display the General Ledger Trial Balance. Click [PDF]. Save the **Chapter 10_October Trial Balance.pdf**.

2. Display the <Standard> Income Statement. Click [PDF]. Save the **Chapter 10_October Income Statement.pdf**.

3. Display the <Standard> Balance Sheet. Click [PDF]. Save the **Chapter 10_October Balance Sheet.pdf**.

ONLINE LEARNING CENTER

Complete the following end-of-chapter activities online at www.mhhe.com/yacht2016 > Student Edition > Chapter 10.

1. Interactive Multiple-Choice and True/False questions.

2. Going to the Net exercise: Describe Sage 50 Quantum Accounting features.

3. QA Templates: 10 short-answer questions and one analysis question.

4. Assessment Rubric: review journals, navigation centers, modules, and task windows.

5. Listen to narrated PowerPoint slides.

6. Videos: In Chapter 10, the videos demonstrate recording checks and deposits.

The OLC also includes links to the Appendixes:

- Appendix A: Troubleshooting
- Appendix B: Accounting Information Systems
- Appendix C: Review of Accounting Principles
- Appendix D: Glossary of Terms (words that are boldfaced and italicized in chapter)

Exercise 10-1: Follow the instructions below to complete Exercise 10-1. Exercises 9-1 and 9-2 *must* be completed before starting Exercise 10-1.

1. Start Sage. Open the company that you set up in Exercise 9-1, Crafts by Your Name. The suggested company name for Exercise 9-1, pages 296-297, is Crafts by your first and last name. (*Hint*: If a different company opens, select File > Open Previous Company. Select No to opening two companies.)

2. If necessary, restore the Exercise 9-2.ptb file.[6] This backup was made on page 302. *Or,* if you are using your own individual PC or laptop, select File, Open Previous Company to resume work with Crafts by Student Name (your first and last name).

3. To make sure you are starting in the correct place, display the Balance Sheet. Compare it to October 1, 2016 balance sheet on page 301.

How to Fix? Check that beginning balances are entered for September 30, 2016

1. To display the September 30, 2016 Balance Sheet, change the Range of dates to From Period 9, (9/1/16) To Period 9, (9/30/16).

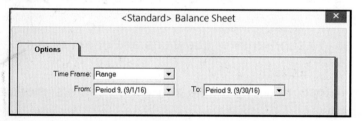

2. The September 30, 2016 balance sheet displays.

In order for the current month and year-to-date balances to post correctly from the general ledger to the financial statements, beginning balances must be entered for September 30, 2016. If you do <u>not</u> have a September 30, 2016 balance sheet, restore the Exercise 9-1.ptb file and redo the chart of accounts beginning balances, pages 300-301, Exercise 9-2.

---

[6]You can restore from your back up file even if *no* Sage 50 company exists. Refer to Troubleshooting, pages 279-280.

4. Use the transaction register below to record and post checks, ATMs, and deposits. (*Hint:* From the Banking Navigation Center, use Write Checks for checks and ATMs. From the menu bar, use Tasks > Receive Money for deposits.)

   Start recording transactions on **10/1/16**. The balance brought forward is Account 1020, Midway Bank's balance of $17,500. Refer to the October 1, 2016 balance sheet on page 301.

		Transaction Register			
Ck. No.	**Date**	**Description of Transaction**	**Payment**	**Deposit**	**Balance**
	9/30/16	*Balance brought forward*			*17,500.00*
	10/1/16	Deposit (Crafts Income)		2,300.00	19,800.00
	10/2/16	ATM	100.00		19,700.00
1001	10/3/16	Accounts Payable	1,050.00		18,650.00
	10/8/16	Deposit (Teaching Income)		2,105.00	20,755.00
1002	10/9/16	Utilities Company; debit 6400 Utilities Expense	45.80		20,709.20
1003	10/10/16	Western Advertising	115.00		20,594.20
1004	10/13/16	U.S. Post Office	49.00		20,545.20
1005	10/13/16	Crafts Workshop; debit 6800 Conference Expense	195.00		20,350.20
1006	10/15/16	ARL Telephone	55.15		20,295.05
1007	10/16/16	DSL Service; debit 6560 Internet Service Provider	29.95		20,265.10
	10/20/16	ATM	100.00		20,165.10
1008	10/28/16	Prospect Avenue Office Supplies; debit 1450 Supplies	137.80		20,027.30
	10/30/16	ATM	200.00		19,827.30

5. Backup. The suggested file name is **Exercise 10-1**.

6. Exit Sage 50 or continue with Exercise 10-2.

Exercise 10-2: Follow the instructions below to complete Exercise 10-2. Exercises 9-1, 9-2, and 10-1 must be completed before starting Exercise 10-2.

1. If necessary, start Sage. Open the company that you set up in Exercise 9-1, Crafts by Your Name.

2. If necessary, restore the Exercise 10-1.ptb backup file.

3. Use the Bank Statement below to complete Account Reconciliation. *Record the bank service charge on the Account Reconciliation window.* (*Hint:* Click [image] to expand the Account Reconciliation window.)

Statement of Account Midway Bank October 1 to October 31, 2016		Account No. 732600-51	Crafts by Your Name Your Address Your City, State, Zip	
REGULAR CHECKING				
Previous Balance	9/30/16	17,500.00		
2 Deposits(+)		4,405.00		
6 Checks (-)		1,484.75		
3 Other Deductions (-)		400.00		
Service Charges (-)	10/31/16	12.00		
Ending Balance	10/31/16	**20,008.25**		
DEPOSITS				
	10/6/16	2,300.00		
	10/8/16	2,105.00		
CHECKS (Asterisk * indicates break in check number sequence)				
	10/10/16	1001	1,050.00	
	10/10/16	1002	45.80	
	10/24/16	1003	115.00	
	10/24/16	1004	49.00	
	10/27/16	1005	195.00	
	10/30/16	1007*	29.95	
OTHER DEDUCTIONS (ATM's)				
	10/2/16	100.00		
	10/20/16	100.00		
	10/30/16	200.00		

4. Print an Account Reconciliation report. (*Hint:* Reports & Forms > Account Reconciliation.) If you are not connected to a printer, refer to the How to Fix box on page 299.

5. Print the Account Register.

6. Print the General Journal.

7. Print the Cash Receipts Journal.

8. Print the Cash Disbursements Journal.

9. Print the General Ledger Trial Balance.

10. Print the Balance Sheet and Income Statement.

    Check Your Figures:

Account No 1020, Midway Bank	$19,815.30
Total Liabilities & Capital	$51,503.10
Net Income	$3,903.10

11. Backup. The suggested file name is **Exercise 10-2**.

12. Export the General Ledger Trial Balance, Income Statement and Balance Sheet to Excel. Use the file name **Exercise 10-2_October Trial Balance and Financial Statements.xlsx**.

13. Save the General Ledger Trial Balance, Balance Sheet and Income Statement as PDF files. Use the files names **Exercise 10-2_October Trial Balance.pdf, Exercise 10-2_October Balance Sheet.pdf** and **Exercise 10-2_October Income Statement.pdf** as the file names.

    Your instructor may also require additional PDFs: Account Reconciliation report, Account Register, General Journal, Cash Disbursements Journal, and Cash Receipts Journal.

14. Exit Sage 50.

CHAPTER 10 INDEX

Chapter 11

Completing Quarterly Activities and Closing the Fiscal Year

LEARNING OBJECTIVES

1. Restore data from Chapter 10.[1] (This backup was made on page 329.)
2. Define Sage 50's General Ledger System.
3. Change accounting periods.
4. Record and post deposits, checks, and ATM transactions for November and December.
5. Complete account reconciliation.
6. Display Sage 50's data file statistics window.
7. Print a General Ledger Trial Balance (unadjusted).
8. Journalize and post end-of-quarter adjusting entries in the General Journal.
9. Print the Adjusted Trial Balance and financial statements.
10. Close the fiscal year.
11. Print a Postclosing Trial Balance.
12. Make eight backups, save four Excel files, and save 12 PDF files.[2]

Chapters 9, 10 and 11 work together. In Chapter 11 you continue recording financial information for Donald Watson Designer. You complete the computer accounting cycle for November and December. Mr. Watson's transaction registers and bank statements are used as source documents. At the end of December, which is also the end of the fourth quarter, you complete adjusting entries, print financial statements, and close the fiscal year.

GENERAL LEDGER SYSTEM (GL)

Sage 50's *General Ledger System* is the complete collection of accounts (chart of accounts) of a company, transactions associated with these accounts, and account balances for a specified period of time. In Sage 50, the GL is the combination of all journal entries that have been

---

[1]All activities in Chapters 9 and 10 must be completed before starting Chapter 11.

[2]For the size of backup files, Excel files, and PDFs, refer to the chart on pages 254-256.

recorded and posted. The account balances are shown on the company's financial statements.

Similar to other modules, the General Ledger System is organized within Sage 50's interface. On the Reports & Forms menu, the General Ledger selection shows the GL system in one place: Chart of Accounts, General Journal, General Ledger, etc. The Navigation Bar's Banking selection shows the Account Register, Chart of Accounts, General Journal Entry (three icons associated with the GL system). The journal associated with the General Ledger System is the general journal. Observe that the Tasks menu includes General Journal entry in one section--

General Journal Entry...
.

The steps of the computer accounting cycle that are completed in Chapter 11 are shown below.

Sage 50's Computer Accounting Cycle
1. Change accounting periods.
2. Journalize entries.
3. Post entries to the General Ledger.
4. Account Reconciliation.
5. Print the General Ledger Trial Balance (unadjusted).
6. Journalize and post adjusting entries.
7. Print the General Ledger Trial Balance (adjusted).
8. Print the financial statements: Balance Sheet, Income Statement, Statement of Cash Flow, and Statement of Retained Earnings .
9. Close the fiscal year.
10. Interpret accounting information.

GETTING STARTED

Follow these steps to continue using Donald Watson's company data.

1. Start Sage 50. Open an existing company, Donald Watson Designer (or your name Designer).[3] (*Hint:* If a different company opens, select File > Open a Previous Company. Select Donald Watson [your name] Designer. If the screen prompts Do you want to keep Crafts by Your Name open?, click [No].)

2. If necessary, restore the Chapter 10 October.ptb backup file. This backup was made on page 329.

   To make sure you are starting in the appropriate place in the data (Chapter 10 October.ptb backup), display the General Ledger Trial Balance. This is also shown on page 325.

Donald Watson Designer
General Ledger Trial Balance
As of Oct 31, 2016

Filter Criteria includes: Report order is by ID. Report is printed in Detail Format.

Account I	Account Description	Debit Amt	Credit Amt
1010	Money Market Account	16,700.00	
1020	Checking Account	20,635.91	
1040	IRA Savings Account	27,730.35	
1045	WI State Retirement	35,612.00	
1300	Prepaid Insurance	2,100.00	
1400	Prepaid Rent	600.00	
1450	Supplies	1,987.81	
1500	Computer Equipment	7,905.68	
1510	Furniture	5,000.00	
1520	Automobile	19,000.00	
2000	VISA Payable		5,250.65
2400	Publisher Advances		11,000.00
3920	Donald Watson, Capital		115,814.28
3930	Donald Watson, Draw	600.00	
4000	Teaching Income		2,716.19
4050	Royalty Income		3,965.05
6100	Dues and Subscriptions	45.00	
6150	Auto Registration	210.00	
6180	Automobile Expense	311.00	
6400	Utilities Expense	39.64	
6420	Water and Power Expense	98.59	
6500	Telephone Expense	35.00	
6550	Long Distance Company	46.20	
6560	Internet Service Provider	29.99	
6850	Bank Service Charge	10.00	
7400	Postage Expense	49.00	
	Total:	138,746.17	138,746.17

3. Follow these steps to change accounting periods:

   a. From the menu bar, select Tasks > System.

---

[3]You can restore from your back up file even if *no* designer company exists. Refer to Troubleshooting, pages 279-280.

b. From the System menu, select Change Accounting Period.

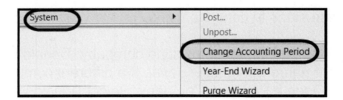

Comment: Can I Unpost journal entries?

If your company is operating in the Batch Posting Method, you can Unpost journal entries to edit a batch of transactions. Because you are using Real Time posting with the design company, you <u>cannot Unpost</u>. (Refer to steps 8 and 9, pages 261-262.) Observe that both *Post* and *Unpost* are inactive because they are grayed out.

---

c. From the Open Accounting Periods list, select 11-Nov 01, 2016 to Nov 30, 2016.

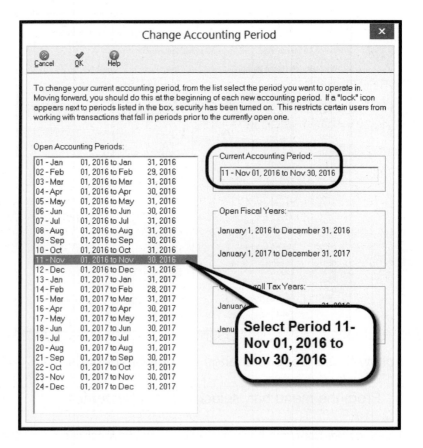

d. Make sure you selected period 11 - Nov 01, 2016 to Nov 30, 2016. Click 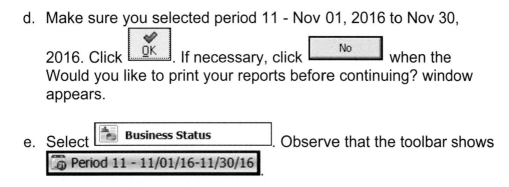. If necessary, click when the Would you like to print your reports before continuing? window appears.

e. Select . Observe that the toolbar shows .

When accounting periods are changed, you prepare Sage 50 to record November's entries. Windows and reports are updated to November 2016.

TRANSACTION REGISTER AND BANK STATEMENT: NOVEMBER 2016

Use Mr. Watson's transaction register to journalize and post transactions for the month of November. (*Hint: Use Write Checks from the Banking Navigation Center for recording checks and ATMs; use Receive Money from the Tasks menu for recording deposits. Remember to Save after each transaction.* Saving posts the entry to the appropriate journal and the general ledger.) Italics and a broken line, indicate entries that have already been made. Start with the 11/3 Deposit.

Comment
Before journalizing November's entries, make sure that you are starting with correct data. To do that, display the General Ledger Trial Balance and compare it to the one shown on page 325 in Chapter 10. Since you changed accounting periods on pages 340-341, your trial balance will be dated November 30, 2016. Verify that Account No. 1020, Checking Account, shows a balance of $20,635.91 which is the same as the starting balance on the transaction register below.

Transaction Register Donald Watson Designer					
Check Number	Date	Description of Transaction	Payment	Deposit	Balance
	10/31	*Starting balance*			*20,635.91*
	11/3	Deposit (book royalty)		2,455.85	23,091.76
	11/5	ATM	200.00		22,891.76
	11/6	Deposit (Milwaukee CC)		2,716.19	25,607.95

4014	11/11	Water and Power Company	90.50		25,517.45
4015	11/11	MIL Gas	53.90		25,463.55
4016	11/12	Lake Telephone	45.08		25,418.47
4017	11/14	Long Distance Company	81.50		25,336.97
	11/16	ATM	200.00		25,136.97
4018	11/27	VISA card payment	5,250.65		19,886.32
4019	11/28	Internet Service Provider	29.99		19,856.33
	11/28	ATM	200.00		19,656.33

Follow these steps to complete the computer accounting cycle.

1. Journalize and post the checks and deposits using the transaction register. (*Hint: Start entries with the November 3 deposit. Remember to record each transaction--checks, deposits, ATM withdrawals--as a separate entry. Save to post after each transaction*).

2. Use Mr. Watson's bank statement to complete the account reconciliation for Account No. 1020, Checking Account.

   Remember to record the bank service charge (Account No. 6850) on the Account Reconciliation window.

Statement of Account Checking Account November 1 to November 30, 2016 Account No. 248531-90			Donald Watson Designer 3024 University Avenue Milwaukee, WI 53202	
REGULAR CHECKING				
Previous Balance	10/31/16	21,131.52		
2 Deposits(+)		5,172.04		
8 checks (-)		766.59		
3 Other deduction (-)		600.00		
Service Charges (-)	11/30/16	10.00		
Ending Balance	11/30/16	**24,926.97**		
DEPOSITS				
	11/3/16	2,455.85		
	11/8/16	2,716.19		

Continued

CHECKS (Asterisk * indicates break in check number sequence)			
	11/3/16	4005*	39.64	
	11/3/16	4011	210.00	
	11/3/16	4012	215.98	
	11/5/16	4013	29.99	
	11/17/16	4014	90.50	
	11/27/16	4015	53.90	
	11/28/16	4016	45.08	
	11/28/16	4017	81.50	
OTHER DEDUCTIONS (ATM's)			
	11/5/16	200.00		
	11/16/16	200.00		
	11/28/16	200.00		

3. Follow these steps to display the Account Register.

   a. From Banking Navigation Center's Recently Used Banking Reports area, select <u>View</u> Account Register. (*Hint:* You can also go to the menu bar selection Reports & Forms > Account Reconciliation > Account Register.*)

   b. Compare the Account Register to the transaction register on pages 341-342. If necessary, drill down to make corrections.

Donald Watson Designer
Account Register
For the Period From Nov 1, 2016 to Nov 30, 2016
1020 - Checking Account

Filter Criteria includes: Report order is by Date.

Date	Trans No	Type	Trans Desc	Deposit Amt	Withdrawal Am	Balance
			Beginning Balance			20,635.91
11/3/16	11/3/16	Deposit	Deposit	2,455.85		23,091.76
11/5/16	ATM	Withdrawal	ATM		200.00	22,891.76
11/6/16	11/6/16	Deposit	Deposit	2,716.19		25,607.95
11/11/16	4014	Withdrawal	Water and Power Compan		90.50	25,517.45
11/11/16	4015	Withdrawal	MIL Gas		53.90	25,463.55
11/12/16	4016	Withdrawal	Lake Telephone		45.08	25,418.47
11/14/16	4017	Withdrawal	Long Distance Company		81.50	25,336.97
11/16/16	ATM	Withdrawal	ATM		200.00	25,136.97
11/27/16	4018	Withdrawal	VISA card payment		5,250.65	19,886.32
11/28/16	4019	Withdrawal	Internet Service Provider		29.99	19,856.33
11/28/16	ATM	Withdrawal	ATM		200.00	19,656.33
11/30/16	11/30/16	Other	Service Charge		10.00	19,646.33
			Total	5,172.04	6,161.62	

4. Close the Account Register report.

5. Follow these steps to print an Account Reconciliation report:

a. From the menu bar, click Reports & Forms > Account Reconciliation.

b. At the Select a Report window, highlight Account Reconciliation.

c. Click Print or Display. If you are printing, the Modify Report – Account Reconciliation window appears. Observe that the As of field shows Current Period, and the GL Account ID field shows 1020. Click OK.

d. At the Print window, click OK.

Donald Watson Designer				
Account Reconciliation				
As of Nov 30, 2016				
1020 - Checking Account				
Bank Statement Date: November 30, 2016				

Filter Criteria includes: Report is printed in Detail Format.

Beginning GL Balance				20,635.91
Add: Cash Receipts				5,172.04
Less: Cash Disbursements				(6,151.62)
Add (Less) Other				(10.00)
Ending GL Balance				19,646.33
Ending Bank Balance				24,926.97
Add back deposits in transit				
Total deposits in transit				
(Less) outstanding checks	Nov 27, 2016	4018	(5,250.65)	
	Nov 28, 2016	4019	(29.99)	
Total outstanding checks				(5,280.64)
Add (Less) Other				
Total other				
Unreconciled difference				0.00
Ending GL Balance				19,646.33

6. Close the account reconciliation report.

7. Print or display the Cash Receipts Journal.

Donald Watson Designer
Cash Receipts Journal
For the Period From Nov 1, 2016 to Nov 30, 2016

Filter Criteria includes: Report order is by Check Date. Report is printed in Detail Format.

Date	Account ID	Transaction Ref	Line Description	Debit Amnt	Credit Amnt
11/3/16	4050	Book royalty	Royalty income		2,455.85
	1020		Deposit	2,455.85	
11/6/16	4000	Milwaukee CC	Teaching income		2,716.19
	1020		Deposit	2,716.19	
				5,172.04	5,172.04

8. Print or display your Cash Disbursements Journal and compare it to the one shown.

Donald Watson Designer
Cash Disbursements Journal
For the Period From Nov 1, 2016 to Nov 30, 2016

Filter Criteria includes: Report order is by Date. Report is printed in Detail Format.

Date	Check #	Account ID	Line Description	Debit Amount	Credit Amount
11/5/16	ATM	3930	Donald Watson, Draw	200.00	
		1020	ATM		200.00
11/11/16	4014	6420	Water and Power Expense	90.50	
		1020	Water and Power Company		90.50
11/11/16	4015	6400	Utilities Expense	53.90	
		1020	MIL Gas		53.90
11/12/16	4016	6500	Telephone Expense	45.08	
		1020	Lake Telephone		45.08
11/14/16	4017	6550	Long Distance Company	81.50	
		1020	Long Distance Company		81.50
11/16/16	ATM	3930	Donald Watson, Draw	200.00	
		1020	ATM		200.00
11/27/16	4018	2000	VISA Payable	5,250.65	
		1020	VISA card payment		5,250.65
11/28/16	4019	6560	Internet Service Provider	29.99	
		1020	Internet Service Provider		29.99
11/28/16	ATM	3930	Donald Watson, Draw	200.00	
		1020	ATM		200.00
	Total			6,151.62	6,151.62

9. Print or display the general journal to see the bank service charge.

Donald Watson Designer
General Journal
For the Period From Nov 1, 2016 to Nov 30, 2016
Filter Criteria includes: Report order is by Date. Report is printed with Accounts having Zero Amounts and with shortened descriptions and in Detail Format.

Date	Account ID	Reference	Trans Description	Debit Amt	Credit Amt
11/30/16	1020	11/30/16	Service Charge		10.00
	6850		Service Charge	10.00	
		Total		10.00	10.00

If your journals do not agree with the ones shown, edit the journals and post again. (Refer to page 324 Editing Journal Entries.)

10. Print or display the General Ledger Trial Balance.

Donald Watson Designer
General Ledger Trial Balance
As of Nov 30, 2016
Filter Criteria includes: Report order is by ID. Report is printed in Detail Format.

Account I	Account Description	Debit Amt	Credit Amt
1010	Money Market Account	16,700.00	
1020	Checking Account	19,646.33	
1040	IRA Savings Account	27,730.35	
1045	WI State Retirement	35,612.00	
1300	Prepaid Insurance	2,100.00	
1400	Prepaid Rent	600.00	
1450	Supplies	1,987.81	
1500	Computer Equipment	7,905.68	
1510	Furniture	5,000.00	
1520	Automobile	19,000.00	
2400	Publisher Advances		11,000.00
3920	Donald Watson, Capital		115,814.28
3930	Donald Watson, Draw	1,200.00	
4000	Teaching Income		5,432.38
4050	Royalty Income		6,420.90
6100	Dues and Subscriptions	45.00	
6150	Auto Registration	210.00	
6180	Automobile Expense	311.00	
6400	Utilities Expense	93.54	
6420	Water and Power Expens	189.09	
6500	Telephone Expense	80.08	
6550	Long Distance Company	127.70	
6560	Internet Service Provider	59.98	
6850	Bank Service Charge	20.00	
7400	Postage Expense	49.00	
	Total:	138,667.56	138,667.56

11. Print or display the Balance Sheet.

Donald Watson Designer
Balance Sheet
November 30, 2016

ASSETS

Current Assets		
Money Market Account	$ 16,700.00	
Checking Account	19,646.33	
IRA Savings Account	27,730.35	
WI State Retirement	35,612.00	
Prepaid Insurance	2,100.00	
Prepaid Rent	600.00	
Supplies	1,987.81	
Total Current Assets		104,376.49
Property and Equipment		
Computer Equipment	7,905.68	
Furniture	5,000.00	
Automobile	19,000.00	
Total Property and Equipment		31,905.68
Other Assets		
Total Other Assets		0.00
Total Assets		$ 136,282.17

LIABILITIES AND CAPITAL

Current Liabilities		
Publisher Advances	$ 11,000.00	
Total Current Liabilities		11,000.00
Long-Term Liabilities		
Total Long-Term Liabilities		0.00
Total Liabilities		11,000.00
Capital		
Donald Watson, Capital	115,814.28	
Donald Watson, Draw	(1,200.00)	
Net Income	10,667.89	
Total Capital		125,282.17
Total Liabilities & Capital		$ 136,282.17

Unaudited - For Management Purposes Only

12. Print or display the Income Statement.

Donald Watson Designer
Income Statement
For the Eleven Months Ending November 30, 2016

		Current Month			Year to Date	
Revenues						
Teaching Income	$	2,716.19	52.52	$	5,432.38	45.83
Royalty Income		2,455.85	47.48		6,420.90	54.17
Total Revenues		5,172.04	100.00		11,853.28	100.00
Cost of Sales						
Total Cost of Sales		0.00	0.00		0.00	0.00
Gross Profit		5,172.04	100.00		11,853.28	100.00
Expenses						
Dues and Subscriptions		0.00	0.00		45.00	0.38
Auto Registration		0.00	0.00		210.00	1.77
Automobile Expense		0.00	0.00		311.00	2.62
Utilities Expense		53.90	1.04		93.54	0.79
Water and Power Expense		90.50	1.75		189.09	1.60
Telephone Expense		45.08	0.87		80.08	0.68
Long Distance Company		81.50	1.58		127.70	1.08
Internet Service Provider		29.99	0.58		59.98	0.51
Bank Service Charge		10.00	0.19		20.00	0.17
Postage Expense		0.00	0.00		49.00	0.41
Total Expenses		310.97	6.01		1,185.39	10.00
Net Income	$	4,861.07	93.99	$	10,667.89	90.00

For Management Purposes Only

➢ **Troubleshooting:** Why are my Current Month and Year to Date balances different than the Income Statement shown?

On the Income Statement, the Year to Date column accumulates balances for October *and* November; the Current Month column reflects November only.

In Chapter 9, on page 284, step 2, the instructions said "Beginning balances must be set for the previous month, September 1-30, 2016." If you did <u>not</u> set your chart of accounts beginning balances From 9/1/16 through 9/30/2016, the Current Month and Year to Date columns will differ from those shown above. To see when your beginning balances were set, display the General Ledger from Period 9 (9/1/2016) to Period 11 (11/30/2016).

To display the General Ledger from Sep 1, 2016 to Nov 30, 2016 do this:

a. From the Reports & Forms menu, select General Ledger, select General Ledger. Click [Options].

b. In the From field, select Period 9, (9/1/16). The To field shows Period 11, (11/30/16).

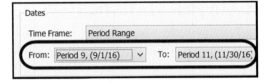

c. Click [OK].

Donald Watson Designer
General Ledger
For the Period From Sep 1, 2016 to Nov 30, 2016

Filter Criteria includes: Report order is by ID. Report is printed with shortened descriptions and in Detail Format.

Account ID Account Description	Date	Reference	Jrnl	Trans Description	Debit Amt	Credit Amt	Balance
1010 Money Market Account	9/1/16			Beginning Balance			
	9/1/16	BEGBAL	GENJ		10,700.00		
				Current Period Cha	10,700.00		10,700.00
	10/1/16			Beginning Balance			10,700.00
	10/2/16	4001	CDJ	Money Market Acco	6,000.00		
				Current Period Cha	6,000.00		6,000.00
	11/1/16			Beginning Balance			16,700.00
	11/30/16			**Ending Balance**			**16,700.00**

How to Fix? Beginning balances were <u>not</u> set up correctly.

Ask your instructor if points will be deducted if you use one of the backup files available to the instructor. If that is okay, restore the Chapter 10 October.ptb file. Continue on page 339.

OR,

Restore your Chapter 9 Beginning Balances.ptb file. Go to Maintain > Chart of Accounts > Beginning Balances. Delete the beginning balances entered for October [or another incorrect month]. Enter the beginning balances for 9/1/16 through 9/30/16 (refer to page 284). Make sure you have NOT entered the beginning balances twice by displaying the October 31, 2016 balance sheet. (Sage 50 dates reports on the last day of the period or month.) Compare your September 30, 2016 balance sheet to the one shown on page 288. Back up the Chapter 9 Beginning Balances.ptb file. Continue on page 307, Recording Deposits, Checks and ATMs.

BACKING UP NOVEMBER DATA

Backup. The suggested file name is **Chapter 11 November**. This backup saves the work completed for Donald Watson [your name] Designer in Chapters 9, 10, and up to this point in Chapter 11.

DATA FILE STATISTICS

To display information about your company data files, follow these steps.

1. From the menu bar, click Help > Customer Support and Service > File Statistics.

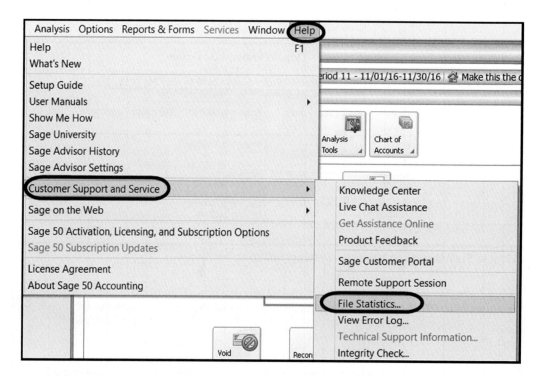

2. The Data File Statistics window lists the number of records and sizes in kilobytes for each data file for the company that is open. It also provides a grand total (scroll down).

   Sage 50 displays the company's shortened name (DONWATDE) on the title bar.[4] This represents the name of the folder where the

---

[4]Since you used your first and last name, the company's shortened name will differ.

opened company resides. Observe that the Directory field shows where the company resides on your hard drive: C:\Sage\Peachtree\Company\donwatde [*or, your shortened name*].

Note: In Chapter 9, pages 290-291, the donwatde Properties window shows the shortened company name that Sage 50 assigned.

Compare your Data File Statistics window to the one shown below.

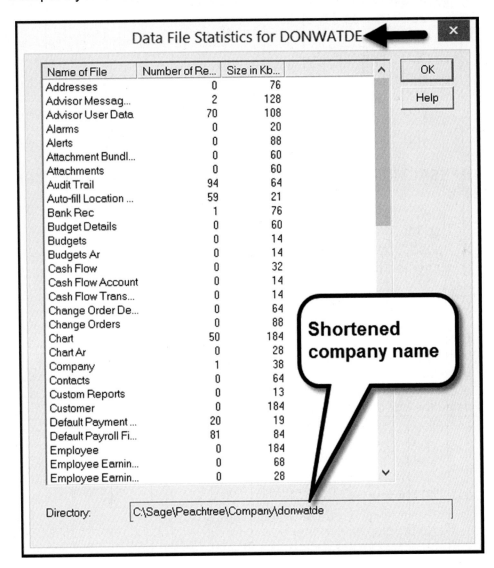

3. To close the Data File Statistics window, click OK .

CHANGING ACCOUNTING PERIODS

Follow these steps to change accounting periods:

1. From the menu bar, select Tasks > System.

2. From the System menu, select Change Accounting Period.

   a. In the Open Accounting Periods list, select period 12 - Dec 01, 2016 to Dec 31, 2016.

   b. Click **OK**. When the window prompts Would you like to print your reports before continuing?, click **No**. Observe that your toolbar shows **Period 12 - 12/01/16-12/31/16**.

TRANSACTION REGISTER AND BANK STATEMENT: DECEMBER 2016

1. Use Mr. Watson's transaction register to journalize and post transactions for the month of December. His transaction register is shown on the next page.

> **Comment**
>
> Before you start journalizing December entries, make sure that you are starting with correct data. To do that, display the General Ledger Trial Balance and compare it to the one shown on page 346. Since you changed accounting periods to December, your General Ledger Trial Balance is dated the last day of the month, December 31, 2016.

Transaction Register Donald Watson Designer					
Check Number	Date	Description of Transaction	Payment	Deposit	Balance
	11/30	*Starting balance*			*19,646.33*
	12/3[5]	ATM	400.00		19,246.33
	12/8	Deposit (Milwaukee CC)		2,716.19	21,962.52
4020	12/11	Water and Power Company	75.45		21,887.07
4021	12/11	MIL Gas (utilities)	102.92		21,784.15
4022	12/12	Lake Telephone	45.95		21,738.20
4023	12/15	The Gallery (business cards; debit 1450 Supplies)	115.25		21,622.95
4024	12/18	Long Distance Company	75.49		21,547.46
4025	12/18	Internet Service Provider	29.99		21,517.47
	12/19	ATM	400.00		21,117.47
	12/29	ATM	400.00		20,717.47

2. Use Mr. Watson's bank statement to complete account reconciliation. (*Remember to record the bank service charge on the Account Reconciliation window.*)

Statement of Account Checking Account December 1 to December 31, 2016 Account No. 248531-90			Donald Watson Designer 3024 University Drive Milwaukee, WI 53202	
REGULAR CHECKING				
Previous Balance	11/30/16	24,926.97		
1 Deposit(+)		2,716.19		
7 Checks (-)		5,695.70		
3 Other Deduction (-)		1,200.00		
Service Charges (-)	12/31/16	10.00		
Ending Balance	12/31/16	**20,737.46**		
DEPOSITS				
	12/8/16	2,716.19		

---

[5]Start your journal transactions with the December 3 ATM transaction.

	CHECKS (Asterisk * indicates break in check number sequence)			
	12/8/16	4018	5,250.65	
	12/8/16	4019	29.99	
	12/22/16	4020	75.45	
	12/29/16	4021	102.92	
	12/29/16	4022	45.95	
	12/31/16	4023	115.25	
	12/31/16	4024	75.49	
	OTHER DEDUCTIONS (ATM's)			
	12/3/16	400.00		
	12/19/16	400.00		
	12/29/16	400.00		

3. Display the Account Register (Reports & Forms > Account Reconciliation, Account Register > Display). Compare the Account Register below to the transaction register on the previous page.

Donald Watson Designer
Account Register
For the Period From Dec 1, 2016 to Dec 31, 2016
1020 - Checking Account

Filter Criteria includes: Report order is by Date.

Date	Trans No	Type	Trans Desc	Deposit Amt	Withdrawal A	Balance
			Beginning Balance			19,646.33
12/3/16	ATM	Withdrawal	ATM		400.00	19,246.33
12/8/16	12/8/16	Deposit	Deposit	2,716.19		21,962.52
12/11/16	4020	Withdrawal	Water and Power Compan		75.45	21,887.07
12/11/16	4021	Withdrawal	MIL Gas		102.92	21,784.15
12/12/16	4022	Withdrawal	Lake Telephone		45.95	21,738.20
12/15/16	4023	Withdrawal	The Gallery		115.25	21,622.95
12/18/16	4024	Withdrawal	Long Distance Company		75.49	21,547.46
12/18/16	4025	Withdrawal	Internet Service Provider		29.99	21,517.47
12/19/16	ATM	Withdrawal	ATM		400.00	21,117.47
12/29/16	ATM	Withdrawal	ATM		400.00	20,717.47
12/31/16	12/31/16	Other	Service Charge		10.00	20,707.47
			Total	**2,716.19**	**1,655.05**	

4. Print or display the Account Reconciliation report.

Donald Watson Designer
Account Reconciliation
As of Dec 31, 2016
1020 - Checking Account
Bank Statement Date: December 31, 2016

Filter Criteria includes: Report is printed in Detail Format.

Beginning GL Balance				19,646.33
Add: Cash Receipts				2,716.19
Less: Cash Disbursements				(1,645.05)
Add (Less) Other				(10.00)
Ending GL Balance				20,707.47
Ending Bank Balance				20,737.46
Add back deposits in transit				
Total deposits in transit				
(Less) outstanding checks	Dec 18, 2016	4025	(29.99)	
Total outstanding checks				(29.99)
Add (Less) Other				
Total other				
Unreconciled difference				0.00
Ending GL Balance				20,707.47

5. Print or display the General Journal.

Donald Watson Designer
General Journal
For the Period From Dec 1, 2016 to Dec 31, 2016
Filter Criteria includes: Report order is by Date. Report is printed with Accounts having Zero Amounts and with shortened descriptions and in Detail Format.

Date	Account I	Reference	Trans Description	Debit Amt	Credit Amt
12/31/16	1020	12/31/16	Service Charge		10.00
	6850		Service Charge	10.00	
		Total		**10.00**	**10.00**

6. Print or display the Cash Receipts Journal.

Donald Watson Designer
Cash Receipts Journal
For the Period From Dec 1, 2016 to Dec 31, 2016

Filter Criteria includes: Report order is by Check Date. Report is printed in Detail Format.

Date	Account ID	Transaction Ref	Line Description	Debit Amnt	Credit Amnt
12/8/16	4000	Milwaukee CC	Teaching income		2,716.19
	1020		Deposit	2,716.19	
				2,716.19	2,716.19

7. Print or display the Cash Disbursements Journal. Compare your cash disbursements journal to the one shown below.

Donald Watson Designer
Cash Disbursements Journal
For the Period From Dec 1, 2016 to Dec 31, 2016

Filter Criteria includes: Report order is by Date. Report is printed in Detail Format.

Date	Check #	Account ID	Line Description	Debit Amount	Credit Amount
12/3/16	ATM	3930	Donald Watson, Draw	400.00	
		1020	ATM		400.00
12/11/16	4020	6420	Water and Power Expense	75.45	
		1020	Water and Power Company		75.45
12/11/16	4021	6400	Utilities Expense	102.92	
		1020	MIL Gas		102.92
12/12/16	4022	6500	Telephone Expense	45.95	
		1020	Lake Telephone		45.95
12/15/16	4023	1450	Supplies	115.25	
		1020	The Gallery		115.25
12/18/16	4024	6550	Long Distance Company	75.49	
		1020	Long Distance Company		75.49
12/18/16	4025	6560	Internet Service Provider	29.99	
		1020	Internet Service Provider		29.99
12/19/16	ATM	3930	Donald Watson, Draw	400.00	
		1020	ATM		400.00
12/29/16	ATM	3930	Donald Watson, Draw	400.00	
		1020	ATM		400.00
	Total			1,645.05	1,645.05

If your journals do not agree with the ones shown, edit and post again.

8. Display or print a General Ledger Trial Balance (unadjusted). Compare your trial balance to the one shown below.

Donald Watson Designer
General Ledger Trial Balance
As of Dec 31, 2016

Filter Criteria includes: Report order is by ID. Report is printed in Detail Format.

Account ID	Account Description	Debit Amt	Credit Amt
1010	Money Market Account	16,700.00	
1020	Checking Account	20,707.47	
1040	IRA Savings Account	27,730.35	
1045	WI State Retirement	35,612.00	
1300	Prepaid Insurance	2,100.00	
1400	Prepaid Rent	600.00	
1450	Supplies	2,103.06	
1500	Computer Equipment	7,905.68	
1510	Furniture	5,000.00	
1520	Automobile	19,000.00	
2400	Publisher Advances		11,000.00
3920	Donald Watson, Capital		115,814.28
3930	Donald Watson, Draw	2,400.00	
4000	Teaching Income		8,148.57
4050	Royalty Income		6,420.90
6100	Dues and Subscriptions	45.00	
6150	Auto Registration	210.00	
6180	Automobile Expense	311.00	
6400	Utilities Expense	196.46	
6420	Water and Power Expense	264.54	
6500	Telephone Expense	126.03	
6550	Long Distance Company	203.19	
6560	Internet Service Provider	89.97	
6850	Bank Service Charge	30.00	
7400	Postage Expense	49.00	
	Total:	**141,383.75**	**141,383.75**

BACKING UP THE UNADJUSTED TRIAL BALANCE

Backup. The suggested file name is **Chapter 11 December UTB**. (UTB is an abbreviation for Unadjusted Trial Balance.) This backup saves the work completed for Donald Watson [your name] Designer in Chapters 9, 10, and up to this point in Chapter 11. After you journalize and post the end-of-quarter adjusting entries, you print the financial statements.

END-OF-QUARTER ADJUSTING ENTRIES

It is the policy of your accounting firm to record adjusting entries at the end of the quarter. Mr. Watson's accounting records are complete through December 31, 2016. The adjusting entries are recorded in the General Journal. Use these steps for entering the seven adjusting entries that follow. The first adjusting entry is shown below; adjusting entries 2 through 7 are on pages 359-360.

1. From the Banking Navigation Center, select > New General Journal Entry. The General Journal Entry window appears. (*Or,* from the Navigation Bar, link to General Journal Entry. *Or,* from the menu bar, click Tasks > General Journal Entry.

2. Type **31** in the Date field. Press **<Enter>** three times.

3. In the GL Account field, select the appropriate account to debit. Type the account name in the Description field (or type a description). Press the **<Enter>** key once to go to the Debit field. Type the debit amount, then press the **<Enter>** key three times.

4. In the GL Account field, select the appropriate account to credit. Type the account name in the Description field. (If you typed a description with the debit part of the entry, it appears automatically.) Press the **<Enter>** key two times to go to the Credit field. Type the credit amount. Press the **<Enter>** key.

5. Click to post each adjusting entry.

Journalize and post the following December 31, 2016 adjusting entries:

1. Office supplies on hand are $1,700.00. (It is the policy of Mr. Watson's company to do an adjustment for supplies at the end of the quarter.)

Acct. #	Account Name	Debit	Credit
6450	Office Supplies Expense	403.06	
1450	Supplies		403.06

Computation: Supplies $2,103.06
              Office supplies on hand   - 1,700.00
              Adjustment $ 403.06

Hint: To post your transaction to the general ledger, click *after each general journal entry.*

2. Adjust three months of prepaid insurance ($2,100 X 3/12 = $525).
    Mr. Watson paid a one year insurance premium on 10/1/16.

Acct. #	Account Name	Debit	Credit
6950	Insurance Expense	525.00	
1300	Prepaid Insurance		525.00

3. Adjust three months of prepaid rent ($200 X 3 = $600.)

Acct. #	Account Name	Debit	Credit
6300	Rent or Lease Expense	600.00	
1400	Prepaid Rent		600.00

4. Use straight-line depreciation for Mr. Watson's computer equipment.
    His computer equipment has a three-year service life and a $1,000
    salvage value. To depreciate computer equipment for the fourth
    quarter, use this calculation:

    $7,905.68 – $1,000 ÷ 3 years × 3/12 = $575.47

    Computer Equipment, 10/1/16 $6,800.00
    Hardware Upgrade, 10/4/16   1,105.68
    Total computer equipment, 12/31/16 $7,905.68

Acct. #	Account Name	Debit	Credit
7050	Deprec. Exp.- Comp Eqt	575.47	
1900	Accum. Depreciation - Comp Eqt		575.47

5. Use straight-line depreciation to depreciate Mr. Watson's furniture. His furniture has a 5-year service life and a $500 salvage value. To depreciate furniture for the fourth quarter, use this calculation:

$5,000 − $500 ÷ 5 × 3/12 = $225.00

Acct. #	Account Name	Debit	Credit
7060	Deprec. Exp.- Furniture	225.00	
1910	Accum. Depreciation - Furniture		225.00

6. Mr. Watson purchased his automobile on October 1, 2016. Use the following adjusting entry. The computation is:

$19,000 × 20% × 3/12 = $950.00

Acct. #	Account Name	Debit	Credit
7070	Deprec. Exp. - Automobile	950.00	
1920	Accum. Depreciation - Automobile		950.00

7. Mr. Watson received an $11,000 advance from his publisher. This was recorded as ***unearned revenue*** on October 2, 2016. Unearned revenue is a liability account used to report advance collections from customers or clients. The amount of this adjusting entry is based on Mr. Watson's royalty statement.

Acct. #	Account Name	Debit	Credit
2400	Publisher Advances	3,500.00	
4050	Royalty Income		3,500.00

8. After journalizing and posting the end-of-quarter adjusting entries, print the General Journal for December 31, 2016. Follow these steps to print your December 31, 2016 General Journal:

   a. From the menu bar, click Reports & Forms > General Ledger. Highlight General Journal.

b. Click 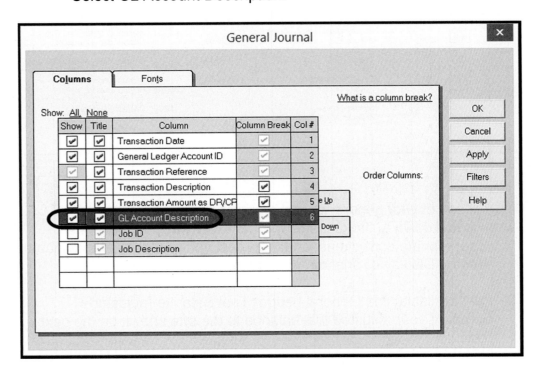. The General Journal report appears.

c. To see the account ID for each account debited and credited,
    click ⊞ Columns. The General Journal Columns window appears.
    Select GL Account Description.

General Journal

| Columns | Fonts |

What is a column break?

Show: All, None

Show	Title	Column	Column Break	Col #
✔	✔	Transaction Date	✔	1
✔	✔	General Ledger Account ID	✔	2
✔	✔	Transaction Reference	✔	3
✔	✔	Transaction Description	✔	4
✔	✔	Transaction Amount as DR/CR	✔	5
✔	✔	GL Account Description	✔	6
☐	✔	Job ID	✔	
☐	✔	Job Description	✔	

Order Columns:

Up   Down

OK
Cancel
Apply
Filters
Help

d. Click **OK**. Adjust the report so it appears on one page.
    Observe that an Account Description column is added. If you
    used a description on the general journal entry window, you may
    want to show the account ID on the general journal report. The
    December 31 adjustments and bank charges, which post on
    12/31/16, are shown on the next page.

Donald Watson Designer
General Journal
For the Period From Dec 1, 2016 to Dec 31, 2016

Filter Criteria includes: Report order is by Date. Report is printed with Accounts having Zero Amounts and with shortened descriptions and in Detail Format.

Date	Account	Reference	Trans Description	Debit Amt	Credit Amt	Account Description
12/31/16	6450		Office Supplies Expense	403.06		Office Supplies Expense
	1450		Supplies		403.06	Supplies
	6950		Insurance Expense	525.00		Insurance Expense
	1300		Prepaid Insurance		525.00	Prepaid Insurance
	6300		Rent or Lease Expense	600.00		Rent or Lease Expense
	1400		Prepaid Rent		600.00	Prepaid Rent
	7050		Deprec. Exp. - Comp Eqt	575.47		Deprec. Exp. - Comp Eqt
	1900		Accum. Depreciation - Comp Eq		575.47	Accum. Depreciation - Comp E
	7060		Deprec. Exp. - Furniture	225.00		Deprec. Exp. - Furniture
	1910		Accum. Depreciation - Furniture		225.00	Accum. Depreciation - Furnitur
	7070		Deprec. Exp. - Automobile	950.00		Deprec. Exp. - Automobile
	1920		Accum. Depreciation - Automobi		950.00	Accum. Depreciation - Automo
	2400		Publisher Advances	3,500.00		Publisher Advances
	4050		Royalty Income		3,500.00	Royalty Income
12/31/16	1020	12/31/16	Service Charge		10.00	Checking Account
	6850		Service Charge	10.00		Bank Service Charge
		Total		**6,788.53**	**6,788.53**	

If any of your general journal entries are incorrect, click to drill down to the General Journal Entry window. Make the appropriate corrections, and then post your revised general journal entry. Display or print the general journal report.

9. Print or display the General Ledger Trial Balance (adjusted). Compare your adjusted trial balance to the one shown on the next page.

Donald Watson Designer
General Ledger Trial Balance
As of Dec 31, 2016

Filter Criteria includes: Report order is by ID. Report is printed in Detail Format.

Account ID	Account Description	Debit Amt	Credit Amt
1010	Money Market Account	16,700.00	
1020	Checking Account	20,707.47	
1040	IRA Savings Account	27,730.35	
1045	WI State Retirement	35,612.00	
1300	Prepaid Insurance	1,575.00	
1450	Supplies	1,700.00	
1500	Computer Equipment	7,905.68	
1510	Furniture	5,000.00	
1520	Automobile	19,000.00	
1900	Accum. Depreciation - Comp Eq		575.47
1910	Accum. Depreciation - Furnitur		225.00
1920	Accum. Depreciation - Automob		950.00
2400	Publisher Advances		7,500.00
3920	Donald Watson, Capital		115,814.28
3930	Donald Watson, Draw	2,400.00	
4000	Teaching Income		8,148.57
4050	Royalty Income		9,920.90
6100	Dues and Subscriptions	45.00	
6150	Auto Registration	210.00	
6180	Automobile Expense	311.00	
6300	Rent or Lease Expense	600.00	
6400	Utilities Expense	196.46	
6420	Water and Power Expense	264.54	
6450	Office Supplies Expense	403.06	
6500	Telephone Expense	126.03	
6550	Long Distance Company	203.19	
6560	Internet Service Provider	89.97	
6850	Bank Service Charge	30.00	
6950	Insurance Expense	525.00	
7050	Deprec. Exp. - Comp Eqt	575.47	
7060	Deprec. Exp. - Furniture	225.00	
7070	Deprec. Exp. - Automobile	950.00	
7400	Postage Expense	49.00	
	Total:	**143,134.22**	**143,134.22**

10. Print or display the Balance Sheet.

Donald Watson Designer
Balance Sheet
December 31, 2016

ASSETS

Current Assets		
Money Market Account	$ 16,700.00	
Checking Account	20,707.47	
IRA Savings Account	27,730.35	
WI State Retirement	35,612.00	
Prepaid Insurance	1,575.00	
Supplies	1,700.00	
Total Current Assets		104,024.82
Property and Equipment		
Computer Equipment	7,905.68	
Furniture	5,000.00	
Automobile	19,000.00	
Accum. Depreciation - Comp Eqt	(575.47)	
Accum. Depreciation - Furnitur	(225.00)	
Accum. Depreciation - Automobi	(950.00)	
Total Property and Equipment		30,155.21
Other Assets		
Total Other Assets		0.00
Total Assets		$ 134,180.03

LIABILITIES AND CAPITAL

Current Liabilities		
Publisher Advances	$ 7,500.00	
Total Current Liabilities		7,500.00
Long-Term Liabilities		
Total Long-Term Liabilities		0.00
Total Liabilities		7,500.00
Capital		
Donald Watson, Capital	115,814.28	
Donald Watson, Draw	(2,400.00)	
Net Income	13,265.75	
Total Capital		126,680.03
Total Liabilities & Capital		$ 134,180.03

Unaudited - For Management Purposes Only

11. Print or display the Income Statement.

Donald Watson Designer
Income Statement
For the Twelve Months Ending December 31, 2016

	Current Month			Year to Date	
Revenues					
Teaching Income	$ 2,716.19	43.70	$	8,148.57	45.10
Royalty Income	3,500.00	56.30		9,920.90	54.90
Total Revenues	6,216.19	100.00		18,069.47	100.00
Cost of Sales					
Total Cost of Sales	0.00	0.00		0.00	0.00
Gross Profit	6,216.19	100.00		18,069.47	100.00
Expenses					
Dues and Subscriptions	0.00	0.00		45.00	0.25
Auto Registration	0.00	0.00		210.00	1.16
Automobile Expense	0.00	0.00		311.00	1.72
Rent or Lease Expense	600.00	9.65		600.00	3.32
Utilities Expense	102.92	1.66		196.46	1.09
Water and Power Expense	75.45	1.21		264.54	1.46
Office Supplies Expense	403.06	6.48		403.06	2.23
Telephone Expense	45.95	0.74		126.03	0.70
Long Distance Company	75.49	1.21		203.19	1.12
Internet Service Provider	29.99	0.48		89.97	0.50
Bank Service Charge	10.00	0.16		30.00	0.17
Insurance Expense	525.00	8.45		525.00	2.91
Deprec. Exp. - Comp Eqt	575.47	9.26		575.47	3.18
Deprec. Exp. - Furniture	225.00	3.62		225.00	1.25
Deprec. Exp. - Automobile	950.00	15.28		950.00	5.26
Postage Expense	0.00	0.00		49.00	0.27
Total Expenses	3,618.33	58.21		4,803.72	26.58
Net Income	$ 2,597.86	41.79	$	13,265.75	73.42

For Management Purposes Only

How to Fix? My Income Statement's Year to Date column does not agree

Check the beginning balances on the general ledger. (Refer to Troubleshooting, pages 348-349.) If you did <u>not</u> enter chart of accounts beginning balances for 9/1/16 through 9/30/16, the Year to Date column does not agree with December's Income Statement or the Statement of Cash Flow on page 367. You can also check your beginning balances by displaying a September 30, 2016 Balance Sheet and comparing it to page 288.

After posting transactions for October, November, and December, the chart of accounts beginning balances cannot be changed. What can you do?

Ask your instructor if you can restore the Chapter 11 December.ptb file (or another backup file) that the instructor can provide. Refer to the chart on page 255 for the files backed up in Chapter 11. Print or display the financial statements and compare with the textbook.

12. Follow these steps to print or display the Statement of Retained Earnings.

    a. In the Financial Statement list, click <Standard> Retained Earnings to highlight it.

    b. Click [Print] (or to display, click [Options]).

    c. Uncheck Show Zero Amounts. Make the selections to print. Compare your Statement of Retained Earnings to the one shown below.

Donald Watson Designer
Statement of Retained Earnings
For the Twelve Months Ending December 31, 2016

Beginning Retained Earnings	$	0.00
Adjustments To Date		0.00
Net Income		13,265.75
Subtotal		13,265.75
Donald Watson, Draw		(2,400.00)
Ending Retained Earnings	$	10,865.75

For Management Purposes Only

The Statement of Retained Earnings shows the net income at the end of the quarter, $13,265.75, minus Mr. Watson's drawing, $2,400. When you close the fiscal year, the Ending Retained Earnings amount, $10,865.75, will be shown on the postclosing trial balance, page 375.

13. Print or display the Statement of Cash Flow. Compare it to the one shown on the next page.

Donald Watson Designer
Statement of Cash Flow
For the twelve Months Ended December 31, 2016

	Current Month	Year to Date
Cash Flows from operating activities		
Net Income	$ 2,597.86 $	13,265.75
Adjustments to reconcile net income to net cash provided by operating activities		
Accum. Depreciation - Comp Eqt	575.47	575.47
Accum. Depreciation - Furnitur	225.00	225.00
Accum. Depreciation - Automobi	950.00	950.00
Prepaid Insurance	525.00	(1,575.00)
Prepaid Rent	600.00	0.00
Supplies	287.81	(1,700.00)
Publisher Advances	(3,500.00)	7,500.00
Total Adjustments	(336.72)	5,975.47
Net Cash provided by Operations	2,261.14	19,241.22
Cash Flows from investing activities		
Used For		
Computer Equipment	0.00	(7,905.68)
Furniture	0.00	(5,000.00)
Automobile	0.00	(19,000.00)
Net cash used in investing	0.00	(31,905.68)
Cash Flows from financing activities		
Proceeds From		
Donald Watson, Capital	0.00	115,814.28
Used For		
Donald Watson, Draw	(1,200.00)	(2,400.00)
Net cash used in financing	(1,200.00)	113,414.28
Net increase <decrease> in cash	$ 1,061.14 $	100,749.82
Summary		
Cash Balance at End of Period	$ 100,749.82 $	100,749.82
Cash Balance at Beg of Period	(99,688.68)	0.00
Net Increase <Decrease> in Cash	$ 1,061.14 $	100,749.82

Unaudited - For Internal Use Only.

BACKING UP DECEMBER DATA

Backup. The suggested file name is **Chapter 11 December**. (This backup saves the work completed for Donald Watson [your name] Designer in Chapters 9, 10, and up to this point in Chapter 11.

EXPORT FINANCIAL STATEMENTS TO EXCEL AND SAVE PDF FILES

Follow these steps to export the General Ledger Trial Balance (Adjusted), Balance Sheet, Income Statement, Statement of Cash Flow, and Statement of Retained Earnings to Excel and save as Adobe PDF files. For detailed steps exporting multiple reports to Excel, refer to pages 329-331.

1. Display the General Ledger Trial Balance.

2. Export the General Ledger Trial Balance to Excel. Create a new Microsoft Excel workbook.

3. Save. Use **Chapter 11_Adjusted Trial Balance and Financial Statements.xlsx** as the file name.

4. Display the Balance Sheet. Export to Excel. Add a new worksheet to an existing Microsoft Excel workbook. (*Hint:* Add the sheet to the file saved in step 3–Chapter 11_Adjusted Trial Balance and Financial Statements.xlsx.)

5. Display the Income Statement. (*Hint:* Select Options to uncheck Show Zero Amounts.) Export to Excel. Add a new worksheet to an existing Microsoft Excel workbook. *(Hint:* Add the sheet to the file saved in step 3—Chapter 11_Financial Statements.xlsx).

6. Display the Statement of Cash Flow. Export to Excel. Add this sheet to the saved file.

7. Display the Statement of Retained Earnings. Export to Excel. Add this sheet to the saved file.

8. Your Excel file should have five sheets: General Ledger Trial Balance, Balance Sheet, Income Stmnt, Cash Flow, and Retained Earnings.

9. Save the file. Exit Excel.

10. Save the General Ledger Trial Balance, Balance Sheet, Income Statement, Statement of Cash Flow, and Statement of Retained Earnings as PDF files. Use Chapter 11_Adjusted Trial Balance, Chapter 11_December Balance Sheet.pdf, Chapter 11_December Income Statement.pdf, etc. as the file names. (Your instructor may require additional reports saved as PDF files.)

11. Close all Sage 50 windows.

CLOSING THE FISCAL YEAR

The Retained Earnings account is updated at the close of the fiscal year with the ending balance of income and expenses (net income or net loss). The balance in the retained earnings account continues to accrue at the end of each fiscal year.

At the end of the year, Sage automatically completes the closing procedure. Follow these steps to close Donald Watson's fiscal year:

1. If necessary, start Sage 50, then open Donald Watson Designer. (*Hint:* If necessary, restore the Chapter 11 December.ptb file.) From the menu bar, select Tasks > System > Year-End Wizard. (*Hint:* You can also select [🗠 **System**] > [Run Year End Wizard].)

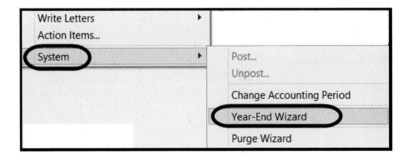

2. The Year-End Wizard - Welcome window appears. Read the information on the Welcome to the Sage 50 Year-End Wizard window.

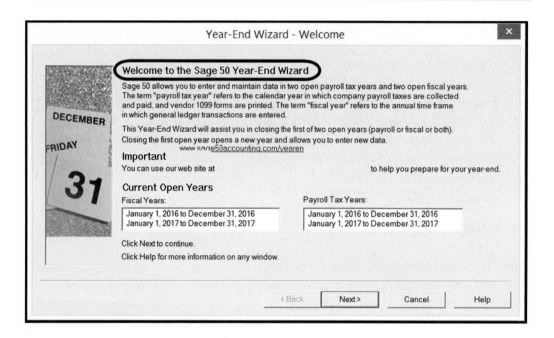

3. Click . The Close Options window appears. In the Years to Close list, Fiscal and Payroll Tax Years is the default. Read the information on this window.

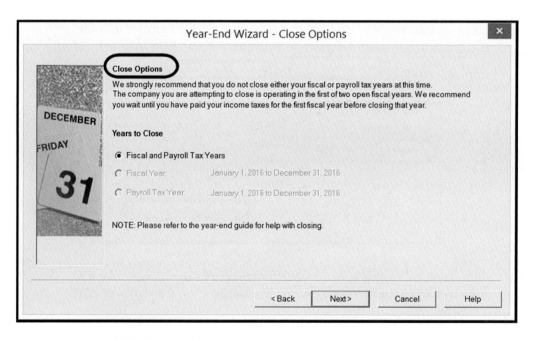

4. Click .

5. The Print Fiscal Year-End Reports window appears. Read the information on this window. Since you have already printed reports, click [Check None] to uncheck all.

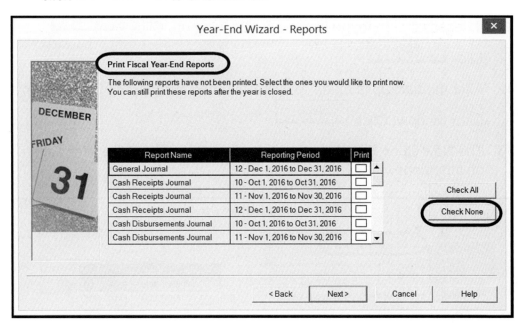

Hint: If you do not uncheck the boxes, the general ledger prints.

6. Click [Next >] .

7. The Internal Accounting Review window appears. Read the information on this window. Click [Next >] .

8. The Back Up Company Data window appears. You already made a back up on page 367 but you should make another one. Read the information on this window. Click [Back Up] . The Back Up Company window appears.

9. Observe that the box next to Include company name in the backup file name is checked. Click [Back Up] .

10. The Save Backup for Donald Watson Designer as window appears. Observe that the File name field includes the name of the company and today's date.

11. If necessary, go to the location for backing up. Click [Save]. Click [OK].

12. After the backup is made, you are returned to the Back Up Company Data window. Click [Next >].

13. The New Open Fiscal Years window appears. Read the information on this window.

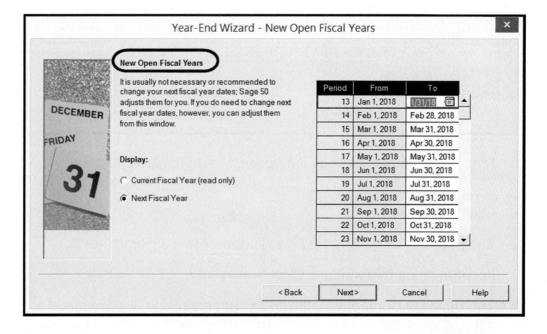

14. Accept the default for Next Fiscal Year by clicking on [Next >].

15. The Important - Confirm Year-End Close window appears. Read the information on this window.

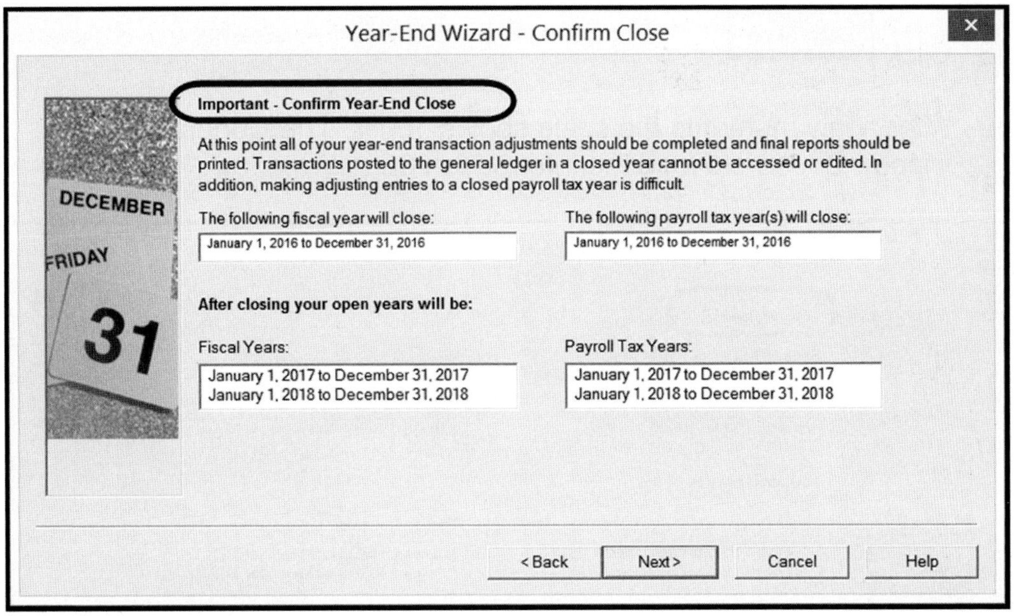

16. Click 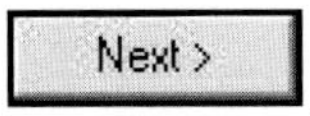

.

17. The Begin Close-Year Process window appears. Read the information on this window.

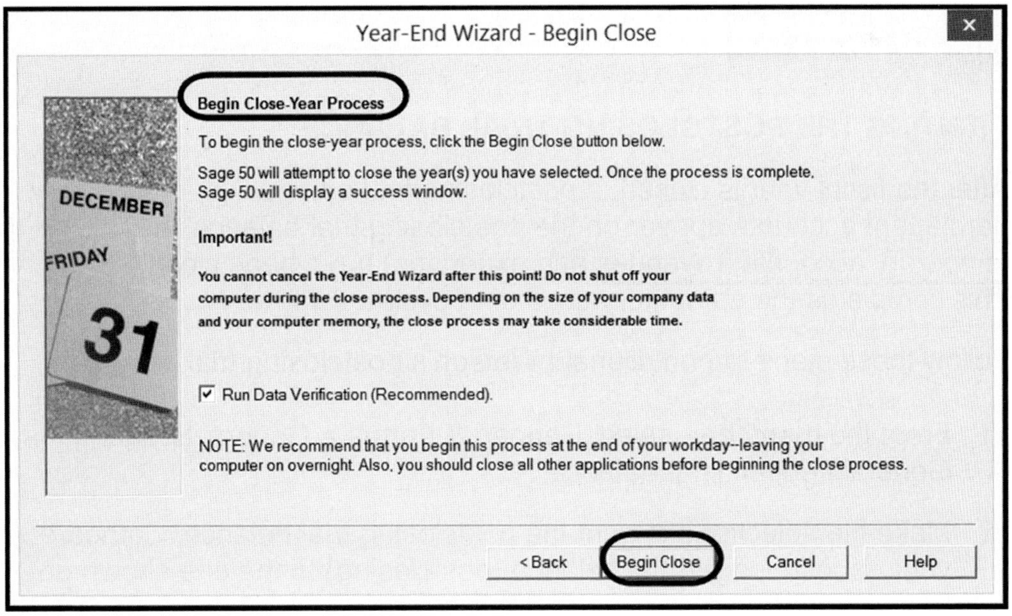

18. Click [Begin Close].

19. After a few moments the scale shows 100%. The Congratulations! window appears. Read the information on this window.

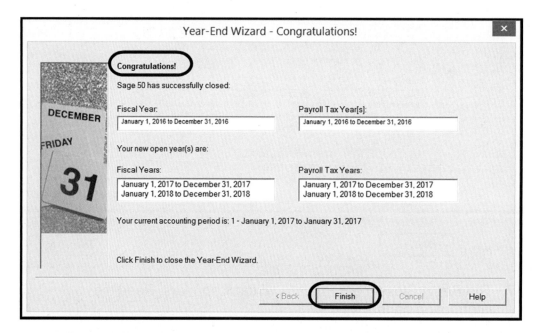

20. Click [Finish].

PRINTING THE POSTCLOSING TRIAL BALANCE

After the fiscal year is closed, a postclosing trial balance is printed. Only permanent accounts appear on the postclosing trial balance. All temporary accounts (revenues and expenses) have been closed. This completes the computer accounting cycle.

Follow these steps to print Donald Watson's postclosing trial balance:

1. From the menu bar, select Reports & Forms > General Ledger > General Ledger Trial Balance.

2. Make the selections to print the postclosing trial balance. Compare your general ledger trial balance (postclosing) to the one shown on the next page.

Donald Watson Designer
General Ledger Trial Balance
As of Jan 31, 2017

Filter Criteria includes: Report order is by ID. Report is printed in Detail Format.

Account ID	Account Description	Debit Amt	Credit Amt
1010	Money Market Account	16,700.00	
1020	Checking Account	20,707.47	
1040	IRA Savings Account	27,730.35	
1045	WI State Retirement	35,612.00	
1300	Prepaid Insurance	1,575.00	
1450	Supplies	1,700.00	
1500	Computer Equipment	7,905.68	
1510	Furniture	5,000.00	
1520	Automobile	19,000.00	
1900	Accum. Depreciation - Comp Eqt		575.47
1910	Accum. Depreciation - Furnitur		225.00
1920	Accum. Depreciation - Automobi		950.00
2400	Publisher Advances		7,500.00
3910	Retained Earnings		10,865.75
3920	Donald Watson, Capital		115,814.28
	Total:	**135,930.50**	**135,930.50**

Observe that the postclosing trial balance is dated January 31, 2017. The balance in Account 3910, Retained Earnings, is Mr. Watson's year-to-date net income minus the total of his drawing account (13,265.75 – 2,400 = 10,865.75). The Retained Earnings balance was also shown on page 366, Statement of Retained Earnings.

How to Fix? Postclosing trial balance is not the same

On the chart of accounts, the Account Type field is important. Display the chart of accounts and compare your Account Types to the ones shown on page 273.

If you need to change the account type, you should make the account inactive and create a new account with the correct Account Type and balance. Then, try to complete the closing process again.

If changing the account type does not work, you may need to ask your instructor for an earlier backup. Restore that file and continue work from that point. Refer to the Part 2 introduction, pages 254-256 for the appropriate file to restore. Consult with your instructor about using one of the backup files available to instructors.

BACKING UP YEAR-END DATA

Backup. The suggested file name is **Chapter 11 EOY**. (*Hint:* EOY is an abbreviation of End of Year. If necessary, uncheck Include company name in the backup file name.) When this backup is made, you have saved the work completed for Donald Watson [your name] Designer in Chapters 9, 10, and 11.

EXPORT POSTCLOSING TRIAL BALANCE TO EXCEL AND SAVE PDF FILE

Follow these steps to export the postclosing trial balance to Excel.

1. Display the General Ledger Trial Balance.

2. Export to Excel. Create a new Microsoft Excel workbook. Change General Ledger Trial Balance to Postclosing Trial Balance. Change the date to December 31, 2016.

3. Save. Use **Chapter 11_Postclosing Trial Balance.xlsx** as the file name. On the Excel file, change title to Postclosing Trial Balance and date to December 31, 2016.

4. Save the General Ledger Trial Balance (postclosing) as a PDF file. The suggested file name is **Chapter 11_Postclosing Trial Balance.pdf**.

5. Close all windows.

ONLINE LEARNING CENTER

Complete end-of-chapter activities at www.mhhe.com/yacht2016 > Student Edition > Chapter 11.

1. Quizzes: Multiple Choice and True False questions. Interactive online tests that are graded and can be emailed to your instructor.

2. More Resources:

    a. QA Templates: 10 true/make true questions and three Analysis Questions.

b. Narrated PowerPoints: Listen to narrated PowerPoints.

c. Going to the Net Exercises: Complete depreciation exercise using the Chapter 11_Asset depreciation schedule1.xlsx file at www.mhhe.com/yacht2016 > Student Edition > Chapter 11 > Going to the Net.

d. Assessment Rubric: Complete the rubric to review Sage 50's journals, navigation centers, modules, task windows, and reports.

The OLC also includes links to the Appendixes:

- Appendix A: Troubleshooting
- Appendix B: Accounting Information Systems
- Appendix C: Review of Accounting Principles
- Appendix D: Glossary (words that are boldfaced and italicized in chapter)

Exercise 11-1: Follow the instructions below to complete Exercise 11-1. You must complete Exercises 9-1, 9-2, 10-1, and 10-2 *before* you can do Exercise 11-1.

1. Start Sage 50. Open the company that you started in Exercise 9-1, Crafts by your first and last name. (*Hint:* From the menu bar, select File > Open Previous Company > Crafts by your first and last name. When the screen prompts Do you want to keep Donald Watson [or your name] Designer open, click <No>.)

2. If necessary, restore the Exercise 10-2.ptb file.[6] This back up was made on page 335. (Hint: To make sure you are starting in the right place, display the general ledger trial balance and compare it to the one printed for Exercise 10-2, step 9, page 335. Compare the Midway Bank account balance on the general ledger trial balance with the 10/31/16 balance on the transaction register below.)

3. Change accounting period to November 1 through November 30, 2016.

---

[6]You can restore from your back up file even if *no* Sage 50 company exists. Refer to Troubleshooting, pages 279-280.

4. To record and post checks, ATMs, and deposits, use the transaction register. (*Hint:* Use Write Checks for checks and ATMs; use Receive Money for deposits.)

Transaction Register					
Check Number	**Date**	**Description of Transaction**	**Payment**	**Deposit**	**Balance**
	10/31/16	*Starting balance*			*19,815.30*
	11/2/16	ATM	100.00		19,715.30
	11/3/16	Deposit (Crafts Income)		2,200.00	21,915.30
1009	11/3/16	Hudson Maintenance and Repairs	75.00		21,840.30
	11/8/16	Deposit (Teaching income)		2,105.00	23,945.30
1010	11/9/16	Utilities Company	55.75		23,889.55
1011	11/10/16	Western Advertising	175.00		23,714.55
1012	11/13/16	U.S. Post Office	49.00		23,665.55
1013	11/15/16	ARL Telephone	41.97		23,623.58
1014	11/16/16	DSL Service	29.95		23,593.63
	11/20/16	ATM	100.00		23,493.63
1015	11/28/16	Prospect Avenue Office Supplies; debit 1450 Supplies	47.80		23,445.83
	11/29/16	ATM	200.00		23,245.83

5. To complete Account Reconciliation, use the Bank Statement on the next page. (*Hint: Remember to record the bank service charge on the Account Reconciliation window.*)

Statement of Account Midway Bank November 1 to November 30, 2016		Account No. 732600-51	Crafts by Your Name Your Address Your city, state, Zip	
REGULAR CHECKING				
Previous Balance	10/31/16	20,008.25		
2 Deposits(+)		4,305.00		
6 Checks (-)		547.70		
3 Other Deductions (-)		400.00		
Service Charges (-)	11/30/16	12.00		
Ending Balance	11/30/16	**23,353.55**		
DEPOSITS				
	11/6/16	2,200.00		
	11/8/16	2,105.00		
CHECKS (Asterisk * indicates break in check number sequence)				
	11/10/16	1006*	55.15	
	11/10/16	1008	137.80	
	11/24/16	1009	75.00	
	11/24/16	1010	55.75	
	11/27/16	1011	175.00	
	11/30/16	1012	49.00	
OTHER DEDUCTIONS (ATM's)				
	11/2/16	100.00		
	11/20/16	100.00		
	11/29/16	200.00		

6. Print an Account Reconciliation report.

7. Print the Account Register.

8. Print the General Journal.

9. Print the Cash Receipts Journal.

10. Print the Cash Disbursements Journal.

11. Print the General Ledger Trial Balance.

12. Print a Balance Sheet and Income Statement.

Check Your Figures:

Account No. 1020, Midway Bank, $23,233.83
Account No. 3920, Student Name, Capital, $48,000.00
Account No. 3930, Student Name, Draw, $800.00

13. Backup. The suggested file name is **Exercise 11-1**.

14. Ask your instructor if you should save these reports as Adobe PDF or Excel files. The suggested file name is Exercise 11-1_November Account Reconcilation.pdf, etc. For the saved Excel files use Exercise 11-1.xlsx. Save multiple sheets within one Excel file.

Exercise 11-2: Follow the instructions below to complete Exercise 11-2. Exercises 9-1, 9-2, 10-1, 10-2 and 11-1 *must* be completed before starting Exercise 11-2.

1. Start Sage. Open the company that you set up in Exercise 9-1 (Crafts by your first and last name).

2. If necessary, restore Exercise 11-1.[7] To make sure you are starting in the correct place, display the General Ledger Trial Balance (refer to step 11, above).

3. Change accounting period to December 1 through December 31, 2016.

4. Use the transaction register on the next page to record and post checks, ATMs, and deposits. (*Hint:* On the Business Status Navigation Center, the balance, $23,233.83, should match Account No. 1020 for Midway Bank. In the Account Balances area, the balance shows $23,233.83. This is the same balance as the Transaction Register on the next page. You may need to click Refresh.)

---

[7]You can restore from your backup file even if *no* Sage 50 company exists. Refer to Troubleshooting, pages 279-280.

		Transaction Register			
Check Number	Date	Description of Transaction	Payment	Deposit	Balance
	11/30/16	*Starting balance*	*12.00*		*23,233,83*
	12/2/16	ATM	100.00		23,133.83
	12/3/16	Deposit (Crafts Income)		2,850.00	25,983.83
1016	12/3/16	Western Advertising	100.00		25,883.83
	12/7/16	Deposit (Teaching income)		2,105.00	27,988.83
1017	12/8/16	Hudson Maintenance and Repairs	75.00		27,913.83
1018	12/9/16	Utilities Company	95.75		27,818.08
1019	12/13/16	U.S. Post Office	49.00		27,769.08
1020	12/15/16	ARL Telephone	45.05		27,724.03
1021	12/16/16	DSL Service	29.95		27,694.08
	12/20/16	ATM	100.00		27,594.08
1022	12/28/16	Prospect Avenue Office Supplies; debit 1450 Supplies	137.80		27,456,28
	12/30/16	ATM	200.00		27,256.28

5. To complete Account Reconciliation, use the Bank Statement on the next page. *Record the bank service charge on the Account Reconciliation window.*

Statement of Account Midway Bank December 1 to December 31, 2016		Account No. 732600-51	Crafts by Your Name Your Address Your City, State, Zip	
REGULAR CHECKING				
Previous Balance	11/30/16	23,353.55		
2 Deposits(+)		4,955.00		
6 Checks (-)		390.47		
3 Other Deductions (-)		400.00		
Service Charges (-)	12/31/16	12.00		
Ending Balance	12/31/16	**27,506.08**		
DEPOSITS				
	12/6/16	2,850.00		
	12/8/16	2,105.00		
CHECKS (Asterisk * indicates break in check number sequence)				
	12/10/16	1013	41.97	
	12/10/16	1014	29.95	
	12/24/16	1015	47.80	
	12/24/16	1016	100.00	
	12/27/16	1017	75.00	
	12/30/16	1018	95.75	
OTHER DEDUCTIONS (ATM's)				
	12/2/16	100.00		
	12/20/16	100.00		
	12/31/16	200.00		

6. Print an Account Reconciliation report.

7. Print the Account Register.

8. Print the General Journal.

9. Print the Cash Receipts Journal.

10. Print the Cash Disbursements Journal.

11. Print the General Ledger Trial Balance (unadjusted).

12. Backup. The suggested file name is **Exercise 11-2 Unadjusted Trial Balance**.

13. Complete the following end-of-quarter adjusting entries.

    a. Supplies on hand: $850.00.
    b. Depreciation for Computer Equipment: $458.33.
    c. Depreciation for Furniture: $150.00.
    d. Depreciation for the Automobile: $950.00.
    e. Adjust three months prepaid rent: $700.00.
    f. Adjust three months prepaid insurance: $250.00.

14. Print the December 31, 2016 general journal.

15. Print the General Ledger Trial Balance (adjusted).

16. Print the financial statements: Balance Sheet, Income Statement, Statement of Cash Flow, and Statement of Retained Earnings.

    Check Your Figures:

    Account No. 1020, Midway Bank, $27,244.28
    Account No. 3920, Student Name, Capital, $48,000.00
    Total Liabilities & Capital, $56,285.95
    Net Income, Current Month, $1,716.52; Year to Date, $9,485.95

17. Backup. The suggested filename is **Exercise 11-2 Financial Statements**.

18. Export the General Ledger Trial Balance (Adjusted), Balance Sheet, Income Statement, Statement of Cash Flow, and Statement of Retained Earnings to Excel. Use **Exercise 11-2_Adjusted Trial Balance and Financial Statements.xlsx** as the file name.

19. Save the General Ledger Trial Balance (Adjusted), Balance Sheet, Income Statement, Statement of Cash Flow and Statement of Retained Earnings as PDF files. Use Exercise 11-2 and the reports' title for each file name.

20. Close the fiscal year.

21. Print the General Ledger Trial Balance (Postclosing).

Check Your Figures:

Account No. 3910, Retained Earnings, $8,285.95

22. Backup. The suggested filename is **Exercise 11-2 End of Year**.

23. Export the Postclosing Trial Balance to Excel. Create a new Microsoft Excel workbook. Change General Ledger Trial Balance to Postclosing Trial Balance. Change the date to December 31, 2016

24. Save. Use **Exercise 11-2_Postclosing Trial Balance.xlsx** as the file name. On the Excel file, change title and date (refer to step 23).

25. Save the Postclosing Trial Balance as a PDF file. Use **Exercise 11-2_Postclosing Trial Balance.pdf** as the file name.

CHAPTER 11 INDEX

In Project 1, you complete the computer accounting cycle for Shelly Martin, Accounting. Ms. Martin started her accounting practice on December 1, 2016 in Phoenix, Arizona. Ms. Martin employs two accounting technicians and one administrative assistant. Ms. Martin's employees are independent contractors. Further study of payroll accounting will be done in Chapter 15.

In this project, you complete the accounting cycle for the month of December 2016. Shelly Martin's balance sheet, transaction register, and bank statement are provided as source documents.

At the end of Project 1, a checklist is shown listing the printed reports recommended. The step-by-step instructions remind you to print reports at certain intervals. Your instructor may require reports for grading purposes. Remember to make backups at periodic intervals. Project 1 ends with a Check Your Progress assessment.

Follow these steps to complete Project 1:

Step 1: Start Sage 50. If a company opens, select File > New Company. One company should be opened. The Create a New Company – Introduction window appears. Click Next > .

Step 2: Type the following company information:

Company Name:	**Shelly Martin, Accounting** (substitute your first and last name for Shelly Martin)
Address Line 1:	**3342 West Missouri Avenue**
City, State, Zip	**Phoenix, AZ 85040**
Country:	**USA**
Telephone:	**602-555-4403**
Fax:	**602-555-4415**
Business Type:	Select Sole Proprietorship

Leave the Tax ID Numbers fields blank.
Web Site: www.shellymartin.com
E-mail: info@shellymartin.com

Step   3:   Accept the default to Use a sample business type that closely matches your company.

Step   4:   Select Service Company. (*Hint:* Simplified types have four-digit account numbers.)

Step   5:   Accept the default for Accrual accounting.

Step   6:   Accept the default for Real Time posting.

Step   7:   Accept the default for Choose an accounting period structure, 12 monthly accounting periods per year.

Step   8:   The Choose the first period of your fiscal year window appears. Select January 2016.

Step   9:   At the You are ready to create your company window, click Finish . If the screen prompts You can use this company in the student version of Sage 50 for the next 14 months and then it will expire, click OK . At the Sage 50 Setup Guide window, click on the box next to Don't show this screen at startup. Click Close . Close the Sage Advisor Getting Started window.

Step 10:   Change the accounting period to Period 12 – Dec 01, 2016 to Dec. 31, 2016. (*Hint:* On the toolbar, click Period > select Period 12. The toolbar shows Period 12 - 12/01/16-12/31/16 .)

Step 11:   Make the following changes to the Chart of Accounts:

Delete these accounts:

    1010   Cash on Hand
    1150   Allowance for Doubtful Account
    2310   Sales Tax Payable
    2320   Deductions Payable

2330	Federal Payroll Taxes Payable	
2340	FUTA Payable	
2350	State Payroll Taxes Payable	
2360	SUTA Payable	
2370	Local Taxes Payable	
2400	Customer Deposits	
2700	Long Term Debt–Noncurrent	
4300	Other Income	
5900	Inventory Adjustments	
6250	Other Taxes Expense	
6650	Commissions and Fees Expense	
7100	Gain/Loss – Sale of Assets Exp	

Change these accounts:[1]

1020	Checking Account	**Second Street Bank**
1400	Prepaid Expenses	**Prepaid Rent**
1500	Property and Equipment	**Computer Equipment**
1900	Accum. Depreciation-Prop&Eqt	**Accum. Depreciation - Comp Eqt**
2500	Current Portion Long-Term Debt	**Notes Payable**
3920	Owner's Contribution	**Shelly Martin, Capital** (Use your name; *Account Type: Equity-doesn't close*)
3930	Owner's Draw	**Shelly Martin, Draw** (Use your name)
4000	Professional Fees	**Accounting Fees**
6000	Wages Expense	**Wages Expense – Adm Asst**
6050	Employee Benefit Programs Exp.	**Wages Expense - Acctg Tech**
6150	Bad Debt Expense	**Subscriptions Expense**
6450	Office Supplies Expense	**Supplies Expense**
6550	Other Office Expense	**Internet Service**
7050	Depreciation Expense	**Deprec Exp – Comp Eqt**

---

[1]New account names are shown in boldface. Click between accounts.

Add these accounts:

1450	**Supplies**	Other Current Assets
1510	**Furniture and Fixtures**	Fixed Assets
1520	**Automobile**	Fixed Assets
1910	**Accum. Depreciation – Furn&Fix**	Accum. Depreciation
1920	**Accum. Depreciation – Automobi**	Accum. Depreciation
7060	**Deprec Exp - Furn&Fix**	Expenses
7070	**Deprec Exp - Automobile**	Expenses
7400	**Postage Expense**	Expenses

Step 12: Print or display the Chart of Accounts. Check Account IDs (numbers) and Account Types.

Step 13: Back up the chart of accounts. The suggested file name is **Shelly Martin Chart of Accounts**.

Step 14: Use Shelly Martin's Balance Sheet to enter the beginning balances. **Important:** When selecting the beginning balance period, select From 11/1/16 through 11/30/16—Beginning Balances as of November 30, 2016.

Shelly Martin, Accounting Balance Sheet December 1, 2016		
ASSETS		
Current Assets		
Second Street Bank	$34,500.00	
Accounts Receivable	17,400.00	
Prepaid Rent	4,000.00	
Supplies	3,300.00	
Total Current Assets		$59,200.00
Property and Equipment		
Computer Equipment	12,600.00	
Furniture and Fixtures	15,000.00	
Automobile	21,500.00	
Total Property and Equipment		49,100.00
Total Assets		$108,300.00
Continued		

LIABILITIES AND CAPITAL		
Current Liabilities		
Accounts Payable	$11,200.00	
Notes Payable	8,400.00	
Total Current Liabilities		19,600.00
Capital		
Shelly Martin, Capital		88,700.00
Total Liabilities and Capital		$ 108,300.00

Step 15: To check your beginning balances, display or print the November 30, 2016 balance sheet.

Step 16: Back up beginning data. The suggested file name is **Shelly Martin Beginning Balances**.

Step 17: The transaction register below and on the next page provides the information necessary for December's journal entries. Remember to post (save) between each transaction.

		Transaction Register **Shelly Martin, Accounting**			
Ck. No.	**Date**	**Description of Transaction**	**Payment**	**Deposit**	**Balance**
	11/30	*Starting balance*			*34,500.00*
	12/1	Deposit (accounting fees)		3,500.00	38,000.00
9001	12/1	Second Street Bank (Notes Payable)	2,700.00		35,300.00
9002	12/1	AAA Office Equipment - laser printer (computer equipment)	625.87		34,674.13
9003	12/9	Administrative Asst.	1,250.00		33,424.13
9004	12/9	Acctg. Technician	690.00		32,734.13
9005	12/12	Worth's Office Supplies (letterhead - supplies)	105.65		32,628.48
9006	12/16	Administrative Asst.	1,250.00		31,378.48
9007	12/16	Acctg. Technician	690.00		30,688.48
	12/16	Deposit (accounting fees)		3,500.00	34,188.48
9008	12/17	Adobe Telephone (telephone bill)	70.47		34,118.01
9009	12/17	U.S. Post Office	49.00		34,069.01
9010	12/17	Journal of Accounting (subscription)	545.00		33,524.01
Continued					

9011	12/23	Administrative Asst.	1,250.00		32,274.01
9012	12/23	Acctg. Technician	620.00		31,654.01
	12/23	Deposit (accounting fees)		4,000.00	35,654.01
9013	12/24	S3R Electric (utilities bill)	105.20		35,548.81
	12/24	Deposit (accounting fees)		4,000.00	39,548.81
9014	12/30	Administrative Asst.	1,250.00		38,298.81
9015	12/30	Acctg. Technician	750.00		37,548.81
	12/30	Deposit (payment received from client on account)		1,500.00	39,048.81
9016	12/30	Internet Service	29.99		39,018.82

Step 18:   Shelly Martin's bank statement is shown below. (*Hint:* Remember to record the bank service charge.)

Statement of Account Second Street Bank December 1 to December 31, 2016 Account No. 3133-861123			Shelly Martin, Accounting 3342 West Missouri Avenue Phoenix, AZ 85040		
REGULAR CHECKING					
Previous Balance	11/30/16	34,500.00			
4 Deposits(+)		15,000.00			
12 Checks (-)		10,607.19			
Service Charges (-)	12/31/16	25.00			
Ending Balance	12/31/16	**38,867.81**			
DEPOSITS					
	12/3/16	3,500.00	12/27/16	4,000.00	
	12/17/16	3,500.00	12/30/16	4,000.00	
CHECKS (Asterisk * indicates break in check number sequence)					
	12/10/16	9001	2,700.00		
	12/11/16	9002	625.87		
	12/13/16	9003	1,250.00		
	12/13/16	9004	690.00		
	12/17/16	9005	105.65		
	12/17/16	9006	1,250.00		
	12/17/16	9007	690.00		
	12/24/16	9008	70.47		
	12/24/16	9011*	1,250.00		
Continued					

	12/24/16	9012	620.00	
	12/27/16	9013	105.20	
	12/31/16	9014	1,250.00	

Step 19:   Print an Account Reconciliation report.

Step 20:   Print the Account Register.

Step 21:   Print a General Ledger Trial Balance (unadjusted).

Step 22:   Back up the unadjusted trial balance. The suggested file name
is **Shelly Martin UTB**. (UTB is an abbreviation for unadjusted
trial balance.)

Step 23:   Complete these adjusting entries:

   a. Supplies on hand: $3,250.00.
   b. Depreciation for Computer Equipment: $353.50.
   c. Depreciation for Furniture and Fixtures: $166.67.
   d. Depreciation for the Automobile: $358.33.
   e. Rent was paid for two months on November 30, 2016.
        Adjust one month's rent.[2]

Step 24:   Print the General Journal, Cash Receipts Journal, and Cash
Disbursements Journal.

Step 25:   Print the General Ledger Trial Balance (adjusted).

Step 26:   Print the General Ledger. (*Hint: Select Reports & Forms >
General Ledger > highlight General Ledger, make the
selections to print.*)

Step 27:   Print the financial statements: balance sheet, income
statement, statement of retained earnings, and statement of
cash flow.

---

[2]Refer to the December 1, 2016, Balance Sheet for the account balance in the
Prepaid Rent account.

Step 28: Back up December data. The suggested file name is **Shelly Martin December**.

Note: For grading purposes, your instructor may require that you turn in reports. Ask your instructor what type of files they prefer: Adobe (.pdf), Excel (.xlsx), or Sage 50 backup (.ptb).

Step 29: Export the adjusted trial balance, balance sheet, income statement, statement of cash flow, and statement of retained earnings to Excel. Use **Shelly Martin_Adjusted Trial Balance and Financial Statements.xlsx** as the file name. (Change the name of the General Ledger Trial Balance to Adjusted Trial Balance.)

Step 30: Save the adjusted trial balance and financial statements as PDF files. Use Project 1, then the report's title for the file name; for example, **Project 1_Adjusted Trial Balance**, **Project 1_Balance Sheet.pdf**.

Step 31: Close the fiscal year. (If a window appears saying that The current Sage 50 system date falls within the first of two open fiscal years. Do you still want to open the Year-End Wizard?

Click [Yes]. Continue closing the fiscal year.)

Step 32: Print the Postclosing Trial Balance.

Step 33: Back up year-end data. The suggested file name is **Shelly Martin EOY**.

Step 34: Export the postclosing trial balance to Excel. Use **Shelly Martin_Postclosing Trial Balance.xlsx** as the file name; December 31, 2016 as the data. Change the name of the trial balance.

Step 35: Save the postclosing trial balance as a PDF file. **Use Project 1_Postclosing Trial Balance.pdf** as the file name.

Your instructor may want to collect this project. A Checklist of Printouts is shown below.

Checklist of Printouts, Project 1: Shelly Martin, Accounting
	Chart of Accounts
	November 30, 2016 Balance Sheet
	Account Reconciliation
	Account Register
	General Ledger Trial Balance (unadjusted)
	December 31, 2016 General Journal
	Cash Receipts Journal
	Cash Disbursements Journal
	General Ledger Trial Balance (adjusted)
	General Ledger
	Balance Sheet
	Income Statement
	Statement of Retained Earnings
	Statement of Cash Flow
	Postclosing Trial Balance

Student Name_____ **Date**_____

CHECK YOUR PROGRESS: PROJECT 1, Shelly Martin, Accounting

1. What are the total debit and credit balances on your
   unadjusted trial balance?   _____

2. What are the total debit and credit balances on your
   adjusted trial balance?   _____

3. According to your account reconciliation report,
   what is the Ending GL Balance?   _____

4. What is the depreciation expense for furniture
   and fixtures on December 31?   _____

5. What is the depreciation expense for computer
   equipment on December 31?   _____

6. What is the amount of total revenues as of
   December 31?   _____

7. How much net income (or net loss) is reported
   on December 31?   _____

8. What is the account balance in the Supplies
   account on December 31?   _____

9. What is the account balance in the Accounts Payable
   account on December 31?   _____

10. What is the total liabilities and capital balance on
    December 31?   _____

11. Is there an Increase or Decrease in cash for the
    the month of December?   _____

12. Were any Accounts Payable incurred during the
    month of December? (Circle your answer).   YES   NO

Project 1A — Student-Designed Service Business

In Chapters 9, 10, 11, and Project 1, you learned how to complete the Computer Accounting Cycle for a service business. Project 1A gives you a chance to design a service business of your own.

You create a service business, edit your business's Chart of Accounts, create source documents, and complete the Computer Accounting Cycle. Project 1A also gives you an opportunity to review the software features learned so far.

You should think about the kind of business to create. Since you have been working on sole proprietorship service businesses in Part 2, you might want to design a business similar to these. Service businesses include: accountants, beauty salons, architects, hotels, airlines, cleaning stores, doctors, artists, etc. If you have a checking account and receive a monthly bank statement, you could use your own records for this project.

Before you begin you should design your business. You will need the following:

1. Company information that includes business name, address, and telephone number. (*Hint: Set your company up for Period 12, December 1 - 31, so that you can close the fiscal year.*)

2. One of Sage 50's sample companies.

3. A Chart of Accounts: 25 accounts minimum; 30 maximum.

4. One month's transactions for your business. You will need a Balance Sheet, check register, and bank statement. Your check register should include a minimum of 15 transactions and a maximum of 25. You should have at least four adjusting entries.

If you don't want to use a check register and bank statement, you could write 15 to 25 narrative transactions.

After you have designed your business, you should follow the steps of Sage 50's Computer Accounting Cycle to complete Project 1A.

For grading purposes, Project 1A should include the following printouts:

Checklist of Printouts **Project 1A** **Student-Designed Project**	
	Chart of Accounts
	Account Reconciliation
	Account Register
	General Ledger Trial Balance (unadjusted)
	Cash Receipts Journal
	Cash Disbursements Journal
	December 31, 20XX General Journal
	General Ledger Trial Balance (adjusted)
	General Ledger
	Balance Sheet
	Income Statement
	Statement of Retained Earnings
	Statement of Cash Flow
	Postclosing Trial Balance

<table>
<tr><td>**Part**

3</td><td>**Sage 50 2016 for Merchandising Businesses**</td></tr>
</table>

In Part 3 of *Computer Accounting with Sage 50 2016*, 19th Edition, your accounting business is hired to do the monthly record keeping for three merchandising businesses: Wendy's Service Merchandise; the end-of-chapter exercise, Your Name Sales and Service; and Highland Sports.

Part 3 includes four chapters and two projects.

Chapter 12: Vendors & Purchases

Chapter 13: Customers & Sales

Chapter 14: Inventory & Services

Chapter 15: Employees, Payroll and Account Reconciliation

Project 2: Highland Sports

Project 2A: Student-Designed Merchandising Business

Merchandising businesses purchase products ready-made from a vendor and then resell these products to their customers. (Merchandising businesses are also called retail businesses.) Items purchased by a retail business for resale are referred to as merchandise. A merchandising business earns revenue from buying and selling goods. Items purchased for use by the business are *not* merchandise; for example, supplies or computer equipment are *not* sold to customers.

In Part 1 you were shown how the sample company, Bellwether Garden Supply, used Sage 50's customer, vendor, payroll, and inventory features. The chapters that follow illustrate these features in detail.

Chapters 12 through 15 are cumulative. This means that the businesses you set up in Chapter 12, Wendy's Service Merchandise; and Exercise 12-1, Student Name Sales and Service, are continued in Chapters 13, 14, and 15.

At the end of Part 3, you complete Project 2, Highland Sports, which reviews Sage 50's merchandising business features. At the end of Project 2, there is a Check Your Progress assessment that your instructor may want you to turn in. Project 2A, Student-Designed Merchandising Business, gives you an opportunity to create a merchandising business from scratch.

The chart below shows the size of the backups, Excel files, and Adobe PDF files in Part 3–Chapters 12, 13, 14, 15, and Project 2. The textbook shows how to back up to a USB drive. Backups can be made to the desktop, hard drive location, network location, or external media.

Chapter	Backup (.ptb extension) Excel (.xlsx)	Kilobytes	Page Nos.
12	Chapter 12 Chart of Accounts.ptb	924 KB	414
	Chapter 12 Starting Balance Sheet.ptb	927 KB	417
	Chapter 12 Begin.ptb	992 KB	431
	Chapter 12.ptb	1,068 KB	455
	Chapter 12_CofA_PJ_CDJ_VL_GLTB.xlsx	28 KB	455-457
	Exercise 12-1 Chart of Accounts.ptb	912 KB	460
	Exercise 12-1 Starting Balance Sheet.ptb	913 KB	462
	Exercise 12-1_Dec 31 2015 Balance Sheet.pdf	10 KB	465
	Exercise 12-1.ptb	922 KB	465
	Exercise 12-2.ptb	939 KB	467
	Exercise 12-2_ CofA_PJ_CDJ_VL_GLTB. xlsx	27 KB	467
	Exercise 12-2_Purchase Journal.pdf	11 KB	467
	Exercise 12-2_Cash Disbursements Journal.pdf	12 KB	467
	Exercise 12-2_Vendor Ledgers.pdf	6 KB	467
	Exercise 12-2_General Ledger Trial Balance.pdf	12 KB	467
13	Chapter 13 Begin.ptb	1,070 KB	482
	Chapter 13.ptb	1,085 KB	511
	Chapter 13_SJ_CRJ_CL_GLTB.xlsx	24 KB	511
	Exercise 13-1.ptb	970 KB	514
	Exercise 13-2.ptb	981 KB	515

Chapter	Backup (.ptb extension) Excel (.xlsx) and Adobe (.pdf)	Kilobytes	Page Nos.
13	Exercise 13-2_SJ_CRJ_CL_GLTB.xlsx	22 KB	515
	Exercise 13-2_Sales Journal.pdf	12 KB	515
	Exercise 13-2_Cash Receipts Journal.pdf	12 KB	515
	Exercise 13-2_Customer Ledgers.pdf	12 KB	515
	Exercise 13-2_General Ledger Trial Balance.pdf	13 KB	515
14	Chapter 14 Begin.ptb	1,112 KB	526
	Chapter 14.ptb	1,130 KB	539
	Chapter 14_ CL_VL_CGSJ_IAJ_IPR_GLTB.xlsx	30 KB	540
	Exercise 14-1.ptb	990 KB	542
	Exercise 14-2_CRJ_PJ_CGSJ_IAJ_IPR_GLTB.xlsx	29 KB	542
	Exercise 14-2_Cash Receipts Journal.pdf	6 KB	543
	Exercise 14-2_Purchase Journal.pdf	6 KB	543
	Exercise 14-2_Cost of Goods Sold Journal.pdf	6 KB	543
	Exercise 14-2_Inventory Adjustment Journal.pdf	6 KB	543
	Exercise 14-2_Inventory Profitability Report.pdf	6 KB	543
	Exercise 14-2_General Ledger Trial Balance.pdf	6 KB	543
15	Chapter 15 Begin.ptb	1,127 KB	562
	Chapter 15.ptb	1,171 KB	586
	Chapter 15_PayJ_GLTB_BS_IS_SCF.xlsx	31 KB	586
	Exercise 15-1_General Journal.pdf	47 KB	591
	Exercise 15-1.ptb	1,010 KB	591
	Exercise 15-2.ptb	1,046 KB	594
	Exercise 15-2_EL_CL_VL_IVR_ PayJ_GLTB_ BS_IS_SCF.xlsx	47 KB	594
	Exercise 15-2_Employee List.pdf	7 KB	594
	Exercise 15-2_Vendor Ledgers.pdf	6 KB	594
	Exercise 15-2_Customer Ledgers.pdf	6 KB	594
	Exercise 15-2_Inventory Valuation Report.pdf	5 KB	594
	Exercise 15-2_Payroll Journal.pdf	11 KB	594
	Exercise 15-2_General Ledger Trial Balance.pdf	7 KB	594

Chapter	Backup (.ptb extension) Excel (.xlsx) and Adobe (.pdf)	Kilobytes	Page Nos.
15	Exercise 15-2_Balance Sheet.pdf	6 KB	594
	Exercise 15-2_Income Statement.pdf	5 KB	594
	Exercise 15-2_Statement of Cash Flow.pdf	5 KB	594
Project 2	Highland Sports Chart of Accounts.ptb	920 KB	600
	Highland Sports_Dec 31 2015 Balance Sheet.pdf	4 KB	600
	Highland Sports Starting Balance Sheet.ptb	920 KB	601
	Highland Sports Begin.ptb	981 KB	608
	Highland Sports January.ptb	1,031 KB	611
	Highland Sports Financial Statements.ptb	1,048 KB	612
	Highland Sports_CofA_CL_VL_ GLTB_AcctRec_ BS_ IS_SCF.xlsx	40 KB	612
	Project 2_Chart of Accounts.pdf	23 KB	612
	Project 2_Customer Ledgers.pdf	11 KB	612
	Project 2_Vendor Ledgers.pdf	12 KB	612
	Project 2_General Ledger Trial Balance.pdf	14 KB	612
	Project 2_Account Reconciliation.pdf	28 KB	612
	Project 2_Balance Sheet.pdf	11 KB	612
	Project 2_Income Statement.pdf	12 KB	612
	Project 2_Statement of Cash Flow.pdf	12 KB	612

The size of your files may differ from those shown.

The extension for Excel 2007, 2010, and 2013 files is .xlsx.

Chapter

12 Vendors & Purchases

LEARNING OBJECTIVES

1. Set up company information for Wendy's Service Merchandise, a merchandising business.
2. Enter general ledger information – chart of accounts and beginning balances.
3. Enter accounts payable information – vendor defaults and vendor records.
4. Enter inventory information – inventory defaults, inventory items, and inventory beginning balances.
5. Record and post Vendors & Purchases transactions.
6. Make eight backups, save two Excel files, and save five PDF files.[1]

Chapter 12 begins Part 3 of the book, Sage 50 2016 for Merchandising Businesses. Merchandising businesses are retail stores that resell goods and services. In this chapter, you set up a merchandising business called Wendy's Service Merchandise. Wendy's Service Merchandise is a partnership owned by Alex Ziegler and Wendy Lincoln. Mr. Ziegler and Ms. Lincoln divide their income equally.

Merchandising businesses purchase the merchandise they sell from suppliers known as **vendors**. Vendors are the businesses that offer Wendy's Service Merchandise credit to buy merchandise and/or assets, or credit for expenses incurred. When Wendy's Service Merchandise makes purchases on account from vendors, the transactions are known as **accounts payable transactions**.

Sage 50 organizes and monitors Wendy's Service Merchandise's **accounts payable**. Accounts Payable is the amount of money the business owes to suppliers or vendors.

When entering a purchase, you enter a vendor code first. The vendor's name and address information, the standard payment terms, and the

---

[1]Refer to the chart on page 400 for the size of files backed up and saved.

general ledger purchase account are automatically entered in the appropriate places. This information can be edited if any changes are needed. This works similarly for accounts receivable.

Once you have entered purchase information, printing a check to pay for a purchase is simple. When you enter the vendor's code, a list of purchases displays. You simply select the ones you want to pay and click on the Pay box. You can print the check or wait to print a batch of checks later. You can also pay a whole batch of vendors at one time, using the Select for Payment option. The diagram below illustrates how vendors are paid.

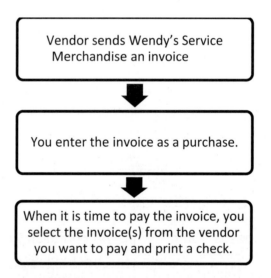

In Chapter 12, the merchandising businesses that you set up are continued in Chapters 13, 14, and 15.

GETTING STARTED

Wendy's Service Merchandise started operations on January 1, 2016. It is a partnership owned by Alex Ziegler and Wendy Lincoln and is located in Tucson, AZ. Follow these steps to set up the company.

1. Start Sage 50. If a company opens, select File > New Company, click ⬚ OK ⬚. If a screen prompts do you want to keep another company open, click ⬚ No ⬚. (*Hint:* If the startup window appears, select Create a new company.)

2. The Create a New Company – Introduction window appears. Click
    Next > .

3. The Enter your company information window appears. (Observe that
    a red asterisk (*) indicates a required field.) Complete the following
    fields. Press the **<Tab>** key between each field.

Company Information

Company Name: **Wendy's Service Merchandise** *(use your first name then Service Merchandise)*
Address Line 1:   **1341 Farrington Road**
City, State, Zip: **Tucson, AZ 85750**
Country: **USA**
Telephone: **520-555-3900**
Fax: **520-555-3902**
Business Type: Select Partnership

Tax ID Information

Federal Employer ID: **41-2259912**
State Employer ID: **15-7904378**
State Unemployment ID: **1553229-3**
Web Site: **www.wendyservmdse.biz**
E-mail: **info@wendyservmdse.biz**

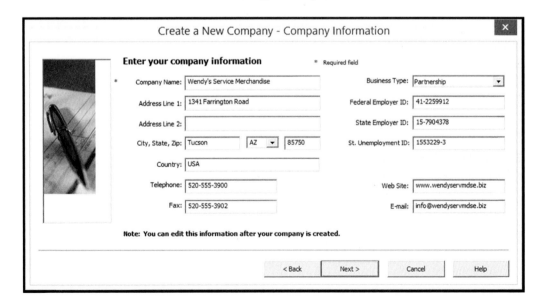

> **Comment**
>
> Use your first name in the Company Name field so that your first name will appear on all printouts.

4. Check the information you just typed, then click [Next >]. The Select a method to create your Company window appears.

   Accept the default for Use a sample business type that closely matches your company.

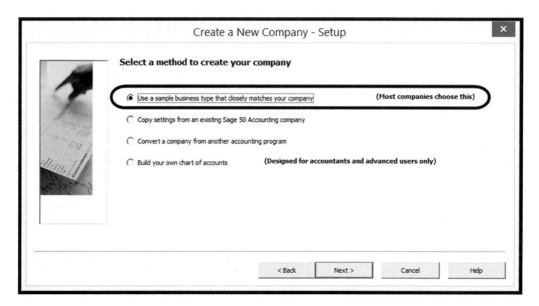

5. Click [Next >].

6. Read the information about selecting a business type. Numerous business types are available. Scroll down. In the Detailed types list, select Retail Company. Compare your selection to the one shown on the next page. The detailed types list includes five-digit chart of accounts numbers.

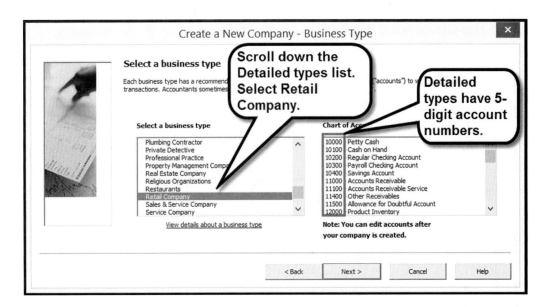

IMPORTANT: Make sure that Retail Company is selected from the **Detailed types** list <u>not</u> the Simplified types list. Check the Chart of Accounts on the right pane. The Detailed types list has a more extensive chart of accounts than the Simplified types list. Observe that the chart of accounts has account numbers with five digits; for example, 10000 – Petty Cash. (The Simplified types list has four-digit account numbers.)

7. Make sure that Retail Company is selected from the Detailed types list. Click Next > .

8. Read the information about the Accounting Method. Accept the default for Accrual by clicking Next > .

9. Read the information about Posting Method. Sage 50 Software recommends real-time posting for networked computers. Accept the default for real-time posting by clicking Next > .

10. At the Choose an accounting period structure window, accept the default for 12 monthly accounting periods per year by clicking Next > .

11. The Choose the first period of your fiscal year window appears. Select **2016** as the year.

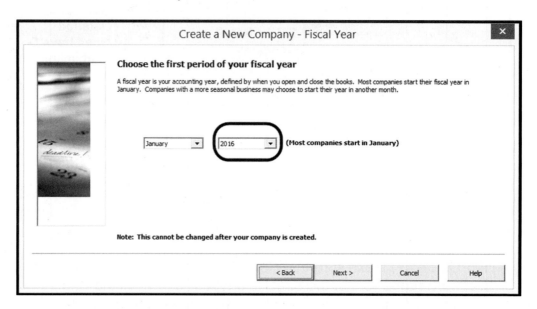

Check this window carefully. You cannot change it later.

12. Click Next > .

13. The You are ready to create your company window appears. Click Finish . If the screen prompts You can use this company in the student version of Sage 50 for the next 14 months and then it will expire, click OK .

14. The Sage 50 Setup Guide window appears. Click on the box next to Don't show this screen at startup to place a checkmark in it-- ☑ Don't show this screen at startup. Click Close . Close the Sage Advisor Getting Started window. Wendy's (your first name) Service Merchandise - Sage 50 Accounting appears on the title bar (above the menu bar).

15. The Period shown on the toolbar defaults to the current period (month). (*Hint:* Click on the Period shown on the toolbar to change accounting periods.)

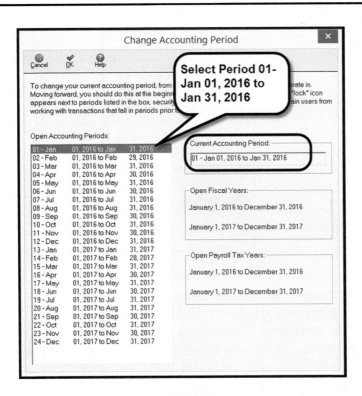

16. After selecting Period 1, click ☑ OK. The Period shows
    🗓 **Period 1 - 01/01/16-01/31/16** (next to the System Date or current
    date).

17. Click 📊 **Business Status**. The Business Status Navigation
    Center shows the following sections:

    - Account Balances
    - Customers Who Owe Money
    - Aged Receivables
    - Find a Report
    - Revenue: Year to Date
    - Vendors to Pay
    - Aged Payables

In Chapters 12 through 15, you use links from the Business Status
Navigation Center and the Navigation Bar to record transactions.
Observe that the Navigation Bar's selections include:

These selections provide ways to navigate the software for Wendy's Service Merchandise, a retail business. The Navigation Bar's selections also indicate Sage 50's modules: Business Status represents an overview of the company; Customers & Sales is the accounts receivable system; Vendors & Purchases is the accounts payable system, etc. A Navigation Bar is used with other Windows software, for example, Microsoft Outlook and Microsoft Dynamics use a Navigation Bar. QuickBooks Online and Desktop versions has a Home page that includes Vendors, Customers, Company and Banking modules. Similar to Sage 50's Business Status center, Account Balances are also included on QuickBooks' home page.

To make the Business Status Navigation Center the default, on the toolbar, click [Make this the default page]. This icon changes to This is the default page [This is the default page].

GENERAL LEDGER

Sage 50's general ledger system includes the collection of accounts of a company (chart of accounts), then summarizes the transactions associated with these accounts and their related account balances for a specified period of time. After setting up a new company, the next step is editing the chart of accounts, and then entering the beginning balances. Sage 50's general ledger system is used for that purpose. Think of the general ledger as the core of an accounting system.

Observe how the general ledger system is organized within Sage 50's user interface; for example, the Navigation Bar's Banking selection shows general ledger system choices such as the chart of accounts general journal entries, and banking reports. Also, the Reports & Forms menu shows the general ledger system's contents.

Most accounting software organizes the user interface into system modules: Accounts Payable (Vendors & Purchases); Accounts Receivable (Customers & Sales), Banking, etc. For this reason, Sage 50, QuickBooks, and Microsoft Dynamics work similarly.

The major differences between accounting software applications include the depth of processing, enhanced features and functions, and the size of the *database* (an organized body of related information). As the database gets larger, the depth of processing increases and more features and functions are available. As companies grow in size, their accounting software needs change.

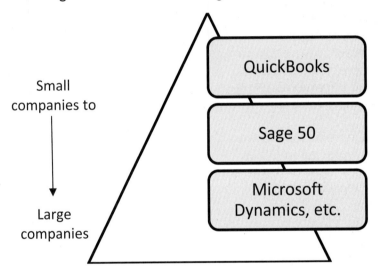

Sage 50 and QuickBooks Online and Desktop versions are used by small companies. As the company grows to mid-size, Sage 50, Microsoft Dynamics, and NetSuite can be used. Large companies use Microsoft Dynamics, Oracle and SAP.

Company size	No. of Employees
Small business	1-50 employees
Mid-sized business	50-500 employees
Large business	500+ employees

Chart of Accounts

From the Navigation Bar, click  >
View and Edit Accounts.

1. Delete the following accounts.

Comment

Double-click on the account you want to delete. Then, click 🗶 Delete From the
Maintain Chart of Accounts window, you can also type the account number into the
Account ID field, then delete.

10000	Petty Cash
10100	Cash on Hand
11400	Other Receivables
14100	Employee Advances
14200	Notes Receivable-Current
14700	Other Current Assets
15200	Automobiles
15300	Other Depreciable Property
15400	Leasehold Improvements
15600	Building Improvements
16900	Land
17200	Accum. Depreciation-Automobi
17300	Accum. Depreciation-Other
17400	Accum. Depreciation-Leasehol
17600	Accum. Depreciation-Bldg Imp
19000	Deposits
19100	Organization Costs
19150	Accum. Amortiz -Org. Costs
19200	Notes Receivable-Noncurrent
19900	Other Noncurrent Assets
23300	Deductions Payable
23800	Local Payroll Taxes Payable
24800	Other Current Liabilities
24900	Suspense-Clearing Account
58000	Cost of Sales-Other
60500	Amortization Expense
61000	Auto Expenses
62500	Cash Over and Short
63000	Charitable Contributions Exp
63500	Commissions and Fees Exp

65000 Employee Benefit Programs Exp
68000 Laundry and Cleaning Exp
73000 Other Taxes
74000 Rent or Lease Expense
76500 Travel Expense
77000 Salaries Expense

2. Change the following accounts.

10200	Regular Checking Account	**Southern Bank**
10400	Savings Account	**Tucson Savings & Loan**
12000	Product Inventory	**Merchandise Inventory**
14000	Prepaid Expenses	**Prepaid Insurance**
15100	Equipment	**Computers & Equipment**
17000	Accum. Depreciation-Furnitur	**Accum. Depreciation - Furn&Fix**
17100	Accum. Depreciation-Equipmen	**Accum. Depreciation - Comp&Eqt**
24000	Other Taxes Payable	**Soc. Sec. Employee Taxes Payab**
24100	Employee Benefits Payable	**Soc. Sec. Employer Taxes Payab**
24200	Current Portion Long-Term Debt	**Medicare Employee Taxes Payabl**
24400	Customer Deposits	**Medicare Employer Taxes Payabl**
27000	Notes Payable-Noncurrent	**Long-Term Notes Payable**
27400	Other Long Term-Liabilities	**Mortgage Payable**
39006	Partner's Contribution	**Alex Ziegler, Capital** *(Note: Account Type, Equity-doesn't close)*
39007	Partner's Draw	**Alex Ziegler, Drawing**
40000	Sales-Merchandise	**Sales-Hardware**
40200	Sales-Services	**Sales-Wall**
40400	Sales-Clearance	**Sales-Floor**
40600	Interest Income	**Service Fees**
50000	Cost of Goods Sold	**Cost of Sales-Hardware**
50500	Cost of Sales-Service	**Cost of Sales-Wall**
57000	Cost of Sales-Salaries and Wag	**Cost of Sales-Floor**
64000	Depreciation Expense	**Deprec Exp-Furn & Fixtures**
64500	Dues and Subscription Exp	**Deprec Exp-Computers & Equip**

3. Add the following accounts.

                                                    Account Type:

      13000 Supplies   Other Current Assets
      39008 Wendy Lincoln, Capital   Equity-doesn't close
      39009 Wendy Lincoln, Drawing   Equity- gets closed
      64600 Deprec Exp-Building   Expenses
      72510 Soc. Sec. Expense   Expenses
      72520 Medicare Expense   Expenses
      72530 FUTA Expense   Expenses
      72540 SUTA Expense   Expenses
      77600 Overtime Expense   Expenses

Backing up the Chart of Accounts

Follow these steps to back up the work completed so far. This backup saves the new company set up on pages 404-409 and the general ledger chart of accounts, pages 412-414.

1. Insert your USB flash drive. From the Navigation Bar, select

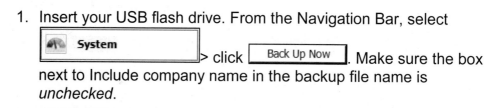

    > click [Back Up Now]. Make sure the box next to Include company name in the backup file name is *unchecked*.

2. Click [Back Up].

3. Go to the location of your USB drive. (Or, backup to another location.) Type **Chapter 12 Chart of Accounts** in the File name field.

4. Click [Save].

5. When the window prompts This company backup will require approximately 1 diskette, click [OK]. When the window prompts Please insert the first disk, click [OK]. When the Back Up Company scale is 100% complete, you have successfully backed up to the current point in Chapter 12. (If you are backing up to the default or another location, this step will differ slightly.)

Beginning Balances

1. From the Maintain Chart of Accounts window, click

    Account Beginning Balances

2. The Select Period window appears. Highlight From 12/1/15 through
    12/31/15. Beginning balances *must* be set for the previous month.
    The starting balance sheet on pages 416-417 is dated January 1,
    2016. This means that the period for entering beginning balances
    must be the *previous month* From 12/1/15 through 12/31/15. See the
    screen illustration below number 3.

Comment

Select December 1 - 31, 2015 as your Chart of Accounts Beginning Balance period
so that your journals will start on January 1, 2016. Your reports will be dated January
31, 2016. Remember, Sage 50 posts on the last day of the month. The December
31, 2015 account balances are the January 1, 2016 starting balances.

---

3. Compare your Select Period window to the one shown. Make sure
    From 12/1/15 through 12/31/15 is selected.

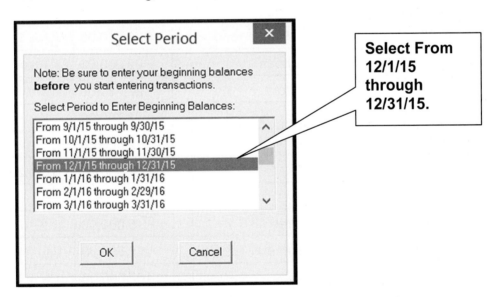

**Select From
12/1/15
through
12/31/15.**

**Check the Select Period window carefully. Once the beginning
balance period is selected, you cannot change it later.**

4. Click [OK]. The Chart of Accounts Beginning Balances window appears. Observe that this window shows that you are going to enter Beginning Balances as of December 31, 2015.

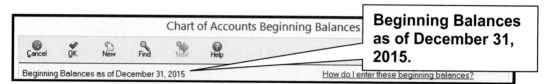

Beginning Balances as of December 31, 2015.

5. Alex Ziegler and Wendy Lincoln purchased Wendy's Service Merchandise in December 2015. Use the Balance Sheet below and on the next page to record the Chart of Accounts Beginning Balances. If you need to review how to record beginning balances, see Chapter 9 pages 283-287, steps 1-8.

Wendy's Service Merchandise		
Balance Sheet		
January 1, 2016		
ASSETS		
Current Assets:		
10200 - Southern Bank	$76,500.00	
10400 - Tucson Savings & Loan	22,000.00	
12000 - Merchandise Inventory	27,740.00	
13000 - Supplies	1,750.00	
14000 - Prepaid Insurance	2,400.00	
Total Current Assets		$130,390.00
Property and Equipment:		
15000 - Furniture and Fixtures	5,000.00	
15100 - Computers & Equipment	7,500.00	
15500 - Building	100,000.00	
Total Property and Equipment		112,500.00
Total Assets		$242,890.00

Continued

LIABILITIES AND CAPITAL		
Long-Term Liabilities:		
27000 - Long-Term Notes Payable	20,500.00	
27400 - Mortgage Payable	75,000.00	
Total Long-Term Liabilities		$95,500.00
Capital:		
39006 - Alex Ziegler, Capital	73,695.00	
39008 - Wendy Lincoln, Capital	73,695.00	
Total Capital		147,390.00
Total Liabilities and Capital		$242,890.00

6. When you are finished entering the beginning balances, click

.

Troubleshooting: To make sure your beginning balances were entered correctly, display the December 31, 2015 balance sheet. (*Hint:* Reports & Forms > Financial Statements > double-click <Standard> Balance Sheet. In the Time Frame field, select Range, From Per start (12/1/15) To Per end (12/31/15).

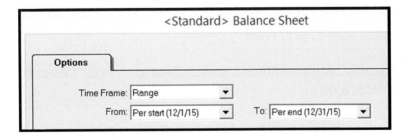

7. Close the Maintain Chart of Accounts window.

Backing up Beginning Balances

Back up. This backup saves the new company set on pages 404-409; the general ledger chart of accounts, pages 412-414; and the beginning balances, pages 415-417. The suggested file name is **Chapter 12 Starting Balance Sheet**.

ACOUNTS PAYABLE: VENDORS

The next section shows how to set up Accounts Payable defaults. This is where you set up information about the vendors who offer credit to Wendy's Service Merchandise. Vendors offer Wendy's Service Merchandise a 2 percent discount for invoices paid within 10 days (2% 10, Net 30 Days).

In Chapter 2, Vendors, you used Bellwether Garden Supply to explore Sage 50's accounts payable system. The accounts payable system provides the information needed for the entry that credits the Accounts Payable account and debits asset or expense accounts that vendor invoices represent.

Since Wendy's Service Merchandise buys on credit from various vendors, the business wants to keep track of the amount owed and the due dates of bills. The accounts payable system does that.

Follow these steps to enter vendor default information.

1. From the Navigation Bar, select [Vendors & Purchases] > [Vendors]. If the Sage Advisor Getting Started window appears, watch the videos ⊙ — Pay your bills, Record the expense, Use the Vendor Management Center, View reports. There are also PDFs [📄] that you can link to and read.

2. After watching the videos, select Set Up Vendor Defaults (within the Vendors icon).

3. Due in number of days is selected in the Standard Terms list. In the Discount in field, type **10** for the number of days. Press **<Tab>**.

4. In the Discount % field, type **2** then press **<Tab>**.

5. In the Credit Limit field, type **10000** then press **<Tab>**.

6. In the Expense Account field, click [🔍]. Select Account No. 12000, Merchandise Inventory.

7. In the Discount GL Account field, click 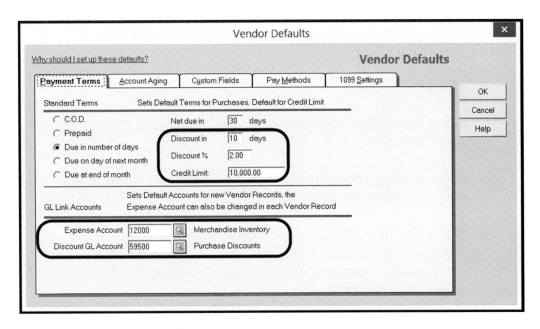. Select Account No. 59500, Purchase Discounts.

Make sure that the Expense Account field shows Account No. 12000, Merchandise Inventory; and that the Discount GL Account field shows Account No. 59500, Purchase Discounts. This sets up the default accounts for merchandise purchases and vendor discounts.

In Sage 50, the Merchandise Inventory account contains summary information about the total cost of the merchandise on hand and available for sale. In addition, Sage tracks vendor discounts in Account No. 59500, Purchase Discounts. Sage also keeps a detailed inventory record for each item of merchandise in stock. Sage automatically updates subsidiary records every time there is a change in the Merchandise Inventory account caused by a purchase, sale, or return of merchandise.

8. Click OK. You are returned to the Vendors & Payables Navigation Center.

9. Click **Vendors** ▲ > New Vendor. The Maintain Vendors window displays. To enter vendor information, follow these steps.

    a. In the Vendor ID field, type **JJH06** (use a zero) then press the **<Enter>** key.

    b. In the Name field, type **James Jarvis Hardware** then press the **<Enter>** key four times.

    c. In the Mailing Address field, type **7713 Sunset Avenue** then press the **<Enter>** key two times.

    d. In the City, ST, Zip field, type **Los Angeles** then press the **<Enter>** key. Click on the down arrow ▼ then select CA from the list of states. Press the **<Enter>** key. Type **90046** as the Zip code, press **<Enter>**.

    e. In the Country field, type **USA** then press **<Enter>**.

    f. In the Vendor Type field, type **hardware** then press **<Enter>**.

    g. In the 1099 Type field, click on the down arrow ▼ and select Independent Contractor. Press the **<Enter>** key. Observe that the Expense Account automatically displays 12000. This is the default Expense Account entered on page 418, step 6.

    h. In the Telephone 1 field, type **323-555-1400** then press **<Enter>** two times.

    i. In the Fax field, type **323-555-1402** then press **<Enter>**.

    j. In the E-mail field, type **james@jarvishardware.com** and then press **<Enter>**.

    k. Type **www.jarvishardware.com** in the Web Site field. Compare your Maintain Vendor window to the one shown on the next page.

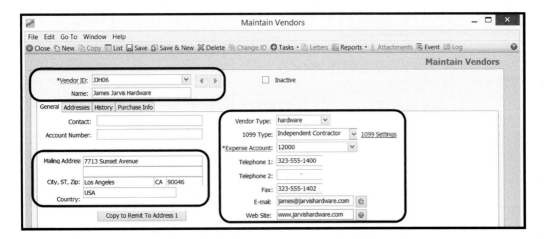

10. Click on the Purchase Info tab. Follow these steps to complete the fields:

   a. Type **81-3329477** in the Tax ID Number field. Observe that the credit terms entered on pages 418-419 are shown. Compare your Maintain Vendors/Purchase Info window to the one shown below.

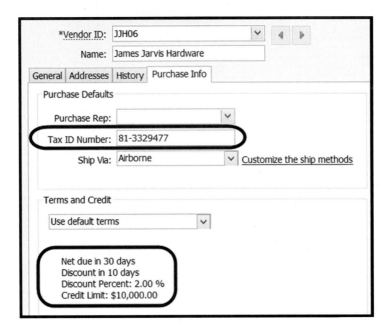

Comment

The Ship Via field on this window shows Airborne. You complete shipping information when you set the defaults for inventory.

---

b. Click [Save & New].

c. Click on the General tab. Add the next vendor.

1) Vendor ID: **LLP07**
    Name: **Len Lacey Products**
    Mailing Address: **1802 West Third Street**
    City, ST, Zip   **San Diego, CA 97022**
    Country: **USA**
    Vendor Type: **floor**
    1099 Type: **Independent Contractor**
    Expense Account: Defaults to 12000
    Telephone 1:   **619-555-8311**
    Fax: **619-555-8313**
    E-mail: **len@laceyproducts.com**
    Web Site: **www.laceyproducts.com**

Purchase Info:

    Tax ID Number: **31-8899123**
    Terms and Credit: Defaults to 2% 10 Net 30

2) Vendor ID: **RBF08**
    Name: **Ronnie Becker Fabrics**
    Mailing Address: **2064 East 31 Avenue**
    City, ST, Zip   **Tucson, AZ 85750**
    Country: **USA**
    Vendor Type: **wall**
    1099 Type: **Independent Contractor**
    Expense Account: Defaults to 12000
    Telephone 1:   **520-555-3200**
    Fax: **520-555-3300**
    E-mail: **ronnie@beckerfabrics.net**
    Web Site: **www.beckerfabrics.net**

Purchase Info:

    Tax ID Number: **82-2344899**
    Terms and Credit: Defaults to 2% 10 Net 30

11. Check your vendor information carefully. When you are finished entering vendor information, close the Maintain Vendors window.

How does vendor information work? The diagram below shows how vendor maintenance information, vendor default information and purchases and payments work together.

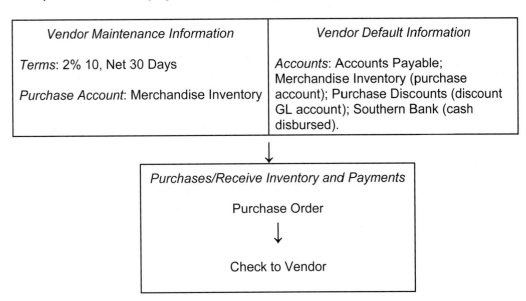

Vendor Maintenance Information	Vendor Default Information
Terms: 2% 10, Net 30 Days *Purchase Account*: Merchandise Inventory	*Accounts*: Accounts Payable; Merchandise Inventory (purchase account); Purchase Discounts (discount GL account); Southern Bank (cash disbursed).

Purchases/Receive Inventory and Payments

Purchase Order

↓

Check to Vendor

On the Vendors & Purchases Navigation Center, Sage 50 illustrates its accounts payable system. In Chapter 12, you work with vendors, entering bills, credits and returns, paying vendor bill, and issuing checks for expenses and owners' withdrawals, (*Hint*: To see Vendors, click 🔄 Refresh .)

Compare your Vendors to the one shown below

Vendors				View Detailed List
Vendor ID ⁄	Vendor Name	Telephone 1		Balance
JJH06	James Jarvis Hardware	323-555-1400		$0.00
LLP07	Len Lacey Products	619-555-8311		$0.00
RBF08	Ronnie Becker Fabrics	520-555-3200		$0.00

INVENTORY & SERVICES

The Inventory & Services Navigation Center displays information and access points related to the company's inventory items. It includes a summary of item information, access to recently used inventory reports, and a graphic analysis of how the cost of sales is trending. In addition, the Inventory & Services Navigation Center shows the flow of inventory-related tasks and takes you where you need to go to perform those tasks. Sage 50's inventory system is an example of another module within its user interface.

In the next section, default information for inventory items is completed. Because the Merchandise Inventory account is increased or decreased for every purchase, sale or return, its balance in the general ledger is current.

Inventory Defaults

Follow these steps to set up inventory items.

1. From the Navigation Bar, select [Inventory & Services]. (*Hint:* When the Sage Advisor Getting Started window appears, watch the videos ⊙ and read the PDF files.) Observe how the Inventory & Services Tasks are organized. The workflow diagram illustrates a sequence of connected steps within Sage 50's inventory system.

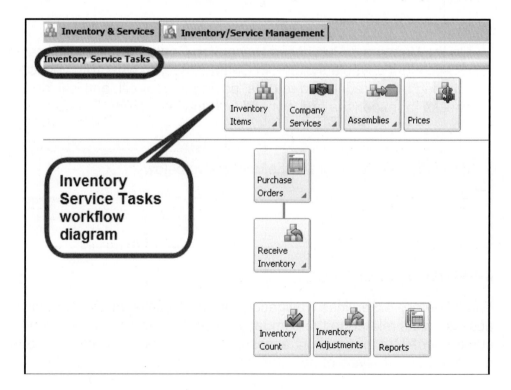

2. Click 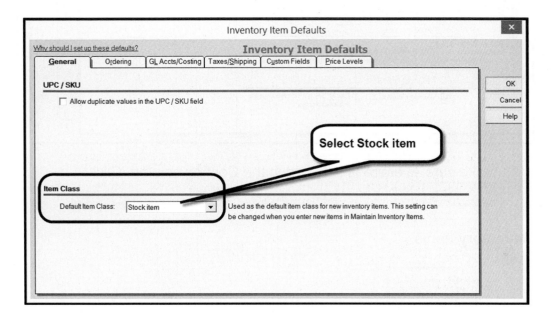 > Set Up Inventory Defaults. The Inventory Item Defaults window appears.

3. Click on the <u>G</u>eneral tab. In the Default Item Class field, select Stock item.

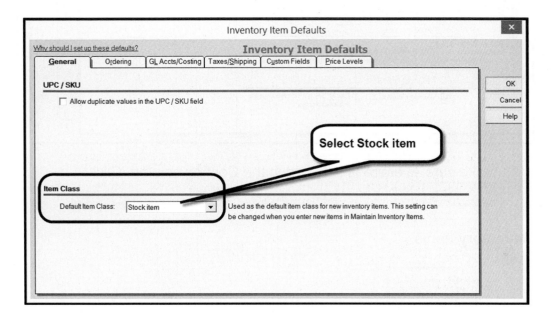

4. Click on the G<u>L</u> Accts/Costing tab. In the Stock item row, click on the down arrow ▾ next to FIFO in the Costing column. Select Average.

Comment
Further study of inventory costing methods will be done in Chapter 14, Inventory & Services.

5. On the Master Stock item row, change FIFO to Average.

6. On the Assembly row, change FIFO to Average.

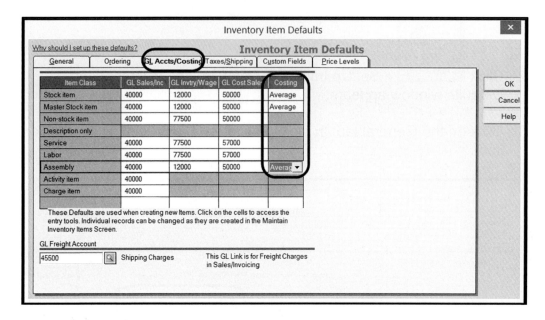

7. Make sure Average is selected in the Costing column. Click
   OK .

Inventory Items

1. Click Inventory Items > New Inventory item. Follow these steps to add inventory items.

   a. In the Item ID field, type **001hardware**, then press the **<Enter>** key.

   b. In the Description field, type **hardware** then press **<Enter>**. In the Item field, Stock item appears automatically. (Refer to step 3, page 425.) Press **<Enter>** two times.

   c. In the Description: for Sales field, type **restoration hardware** then press **<Enter>**.

   d. Click on the right arrow ► in the Price Level 1 field. The Multiple Price Levels window appears. Type **150** in the Price field of Price Level 1, then press **<Enter>**.

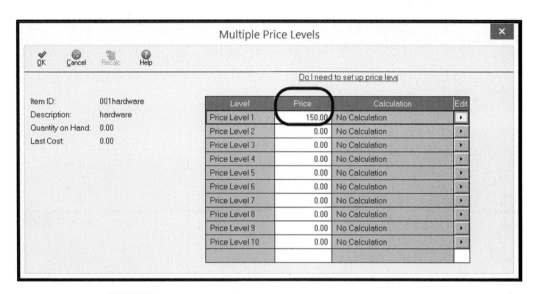

e. Click  .

How to Fix?: What if your Price Level 1 field does not display 150.00 but 1.50? Follow these steps to set the decimal point:

1. From the menu bar, click Options > Global. If necessary, select the Accounting tab.
2. In the Decimal Entry field, click Manual. Make sure that the number 2 is shown in the Number of decimal places field.
3. Click [OK] . This sets your decimal place globally. That means from now on all numbers with decimal places will be set automatically; for example, 150 will display as 150.00.

---

f. Type **50** in the Last Unit Cost field. Press **<Enter>**.

g. Accept the default for Account No. 40000, Sales-Hardware as the GL Sales Acct.

h. Accept the default for Account No. 12000, Merchandise Inventory, as the GL Inventory Acct by pressing **<Enter>**

i. Accept the default for Account No. 50000, Cost of Sales-Hardware as the GL Cost of Sales Acct by pressing **<Enter>** three times.

j. In the Item Type field, type **hardware** then press **<Enter>** two times.

---

k. In the Stocking U/M field (U/M is an abbreviation for Unit of Measure), type **each** then press **<Enter>** two times.

l. In the Minimum Stock field, type **10** then press **<Enter>**.

m. In the Reorder Quantity field, type **4** then press **<Enter>**.

n. In the Preferred Vendor ID field, click 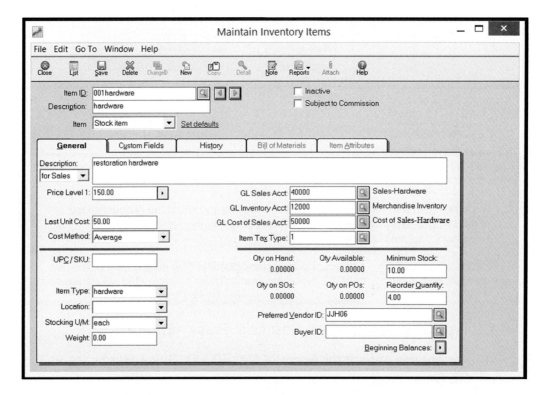. Select James Jarvis Hardware, JJH06, as the vendor. Compare your Maintain Inventory Items window with the one below.

o. Click .

p. Click .

Enter the following stock items:

1) Item ID: **002wall**

    Description: **wall**

    Item Class: Stock item

    Description for Sales: **wall coverings**

    Price Level 1:   **100**

    Last Unit Cost: **30**

    Cost Method: Average

    GL Sales Acct: **40200 Sales-Wall**

    GL Inventory Acct: **12000 Merchandise Inventory**

    GL Cost of Sales Acct: **50500 Cost of Sales-Wall**

    Item Type: **wall**

    Stocking U/M: **each**

    Minimum Stock: **10**

    Reorder Quantity: **4**

    Preferred Vendor ID: **RBF08**, Ronnie Becker Fabrics

2) Item ID: **003floor**

    Description: **floor**

    Item Class: Stock item

    Description for Sales: **flooring**

    Price Level 1:   **160**

    Last Unit Cost: **54**

    Cost Method: Average

    GL Sales Acct: **40400 Sales-Floor**

    GL Inventory Acct: **12000 Merchandise Inventory**

    GL Cost of Sales Acct: **57000 Cost of Sales-Floor**

    Item Type: **floor**

    Stocking U/M: **each**

    Minimum Stock: **25**

    Reorder Quantity: **10**

    Preferred Vendor ID: **LLP07**, Len Lacey Products

2. Save. Then, click on the arrow next to Beginning Balances. The Inventory Beginning Balances window displays. Follow these steps to record beginning balances.

    a. In the Item ID table, click on 001hardware. Press the **<Tab>** key.

    b. In the Quantity field, type **90** then press **<Enter>**.

c. In the Unit Cost field, type **50** then press **<Enter>**.

d. The Total Cost field displays 4,500.00. Press the **<Enter>** key.

e. Enter the beginning balances for walls and floors:

Item ID	Description	Quantity	Unit Cost	Total Cost
002wall	wall	148	30	4,440.00
003floor	floor	200	54	10,800.00

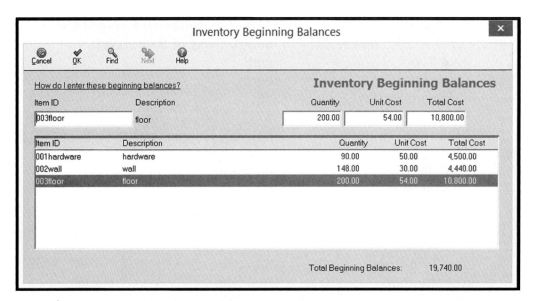

f. Observe that the Total Beginning Balance is 19,740. You add additional inventory in Chapter 14, Inventory & Services.[2] Click OK.

g. Close the Maintain Inventory Items window.

When you have completed entering Inventory items, the Inventory & Services Navigation Center shows these Inventory items. (*Hint:* If necessary, click Refresh, and if needed close the Sage Advisor.)

---

[2] If you compare the total beginning balance in inventory, $19,740, to the balance sheet on pages 416-417, observe that the Merchandise Inventory account has a $27,740 balance. Additional inventory valued at $8,000 is added in Chapter 14.

Inventory			View Detailed List
Item ID	Description	No. Units Sold	Qty on Hand
001hardware	hardware	0.00	90.00
002wall	wall	0.00	148.00
003floor	floor	0.00	200.00

Inventory/Service Management

On the Inventory & Services Navigation Center, there is a tab for Inventory/Service Management. When you select Inventory/Service Management, you can access windows where you enter/maintain inventory items and services. This page shows Item/Service Information, Purchase Orders, Sales Orders, and Sales Backorders.

BACKING UP YOUR DATA

Back up. This backup saves the new company set on pages 404-409; the general ledger chart of accounts, pages 412-414; the beginning balances, pages 415-417, and accounts payable defaults, vendors, inventory defaults, and inventory items, pages 418-431 The suggested file name is **Chapter 12 Begin**.

VENDORS & PURCHASES: PURCHASES/RECEIVE INVENTORY

The Vendors & Purchases Tasks workflow diagram includes a selection for Enter Bills; New Bill. This selection takes you to the Purchases/ Receive Inventory window. In Sage, all information about a purchase is recorded in the Purchases/Receive Inventory window. Then, Sage takes the necessary information from the window and journalizes the transaction in the Purchase Journal.

In Sage 50, the Purchases/Receive Inventory window is the *Purchase Journal*. On the Purchases/Receive Inventory window, you can enter vendor purchase invoices or receive inventory for purchase orders. The Purchases/Receive Inventory window includes two tabs.

- **Apply to Purchase Order**: When you select a vendor who has open purchase orders, Sage 50 displays this tab, allowing you to select which purchase order to receive items against.
- **Apply to Purchases**: If you select a vendor with no open purchase orders, by default Sage 50 displays this tab, where you can enter a purchase that did not originate on a purchase order. In addition, if

items were included on the purchase invoice that are not included on the purchase order, you can add them here.

After recording vendor purchases in the Purchases/Receive Inventory window, you can display or print the Purchase Journal by selecting Reports, then Accounts Payable and highlighting the Purchase Journal. These steps are included in this chapter. Remember, each time you use the Purchases/Receive Inventory window you are also journalizing in the Purchase Journal.

Purchases are posted both to the General Ledger and to the **Vendor Ledger** or **Accounts Payable Ledger**. You can also apply purchases to Inventory Items or Jobs.

Purchases work hand in hand with paying bills. On the Vendors & Purchases Tasks flowchart, Pay Bills is one of the selections. Once you have entered and posted a purchase (vendor invoice), that invoice is available when you enter the Vendor's ID code in Payments. You can select the invoice, then save (post) the payment; Sage distributes the appropriate amounts.

▶ Recording Purchases: Purchases/Receive Inventory Window

(*Hint:* This icon, ▶, means there is a video at www.mhhe.com/yacht2016.)

1. If you exited, start Sage 50. Open Wendy's Service Merchandise and, if necessary, restore the Chapter 12 Begin.ptb backup file.

2. From the Navigation Bar, select [Vendors & Purchases] > [Enter Bills]
   > New Bill. The Purchases/Receive Inventory window displays. Observe that the window looks like a typical purchase order or invoice form.

   Check that *both* the A/P Account lookup field and GL Account field are shown on your Purchases/Receive Inventory window. If *not*, read the paragraph below the Purchases/Receive Inventory window. (*Hint:* To see multiple lines in the Apply to Purchases table, use your cursor to enlarge the Purchases/Receive Inventory window.)

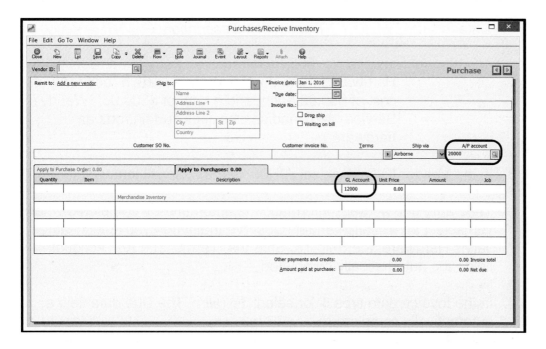

If the A/P Account lookup field and GL Account field are *not* shown, check your global settings. To do that, click Options, Global. If necessary, select the Accounting tab. The boxes in the Hide General Ledger Accounts section *must* be unchecked. (See steps 1-3 pages xix-xx, Setting Global Options.)

On the Purchases/Receive Inventory window, your cursor is in the Vendor ID field. There are three ways to select a vendor or add a new vendor.

➢ In the Vendor ID field, type a question mark **<?>** and the vendor list displays.

➢ With the mouse pointer in the Vendor ID field, click on the right mouse button. The vendor list displays.

➢ In the Vendor ID field, click ⌕ and the vendor list displays. The transaction is shown on the next page.

Date	Transaction Description
1/3/16	Invoice No. 56JJ was received from James Jarvis Hardware for the purchase of six curtain rods for a unit cost of $50.00 each, and a total of $300.00. (Wendy's Service Merchandise classifies curtain rods as hardware.)

3. In the Vendor ID field, select JJH06, James Jarvis Hardware.

The name and address information is automatically completed when you select an existing vendor. Observe that when you select James Jarvis Hardware, the Ship To, Ship Via, Terms, and A/P Account[3] fields are automatically completed.

4. In the Invoice date type **3** (or select 3). (*Hint:* The Due date field s automatically completed.)

5. In the Invoice # field, type **56JJ** and press the **<Enter>** key.

6. Click on the Quantity field and type **6** then press the **<Enter>** key.

7. In the Item field, click 🔍 and select 001hardware. Accept the description. Press the **<Tab>** key. Observe that the following purchase information is automatically completed:

   a. Description field, restoration hardware.
   b. GL Account 12000, Merchandise Inventory. (If the account name, Merchandise Inventory does *not* show, go to Options > Global > General tab. In the Line Item Entry Display area, make sure 2 Line is selected > click <OK>. Click on the Purchases/Receive Inventory button on the taskbar to enlarge the window.)
   c. Unit Price 50.00.
   d. Amount 300.00.
   e. Invoice Total and Net Due, 300.00
   f. Vendor Balance on Jan 3, 2016 is 0.00.

---

[3]If the A/P Account lookup field does not display, click Options, Global. The boxes in the Hide General Ledger Accounts section *must* be unchecked.

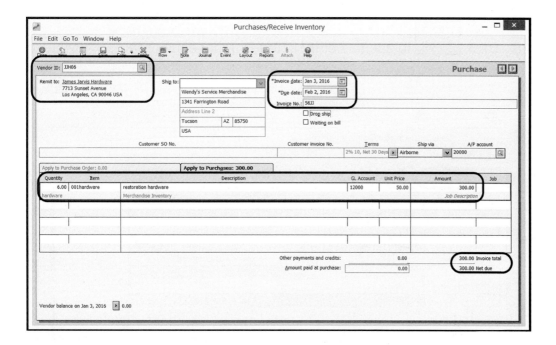

Read Me

On the Purchases/Receive Inventory window, if the Quantity, Item, Description, GL Account, Unit Price, and Amount table does *not* show multiple lines you can use the arrows next to the Job field to scroll through the multiple lines. *Or,* try using the cursor to enlarge the window.

The number of lines on the Quantity, Item/Description table is determined by how the screen resolution is set. If your Purchases/Receive Inventory window shows one line on the Quantity, Item table, then your computer is probably set up for 800 X 600 pixels. If your screen resolution is set at 1024 X 768 pixels, your Purchases/Receive Inventory window shows multiple lines in the Quantity/Item area. To check your screen resolution, go to the desktop and right click > left click Properties > select the Settings tab. The screen resolution area shows the number of the monitor's pixels.

Invoice Total: The Invoice Total keeps a running total of the entry lines you have added to the Purchase Journal. Before you post a Purchase Journal entry, you should check to see that the amount field is the same as the total invoice amount (Net Due) on the vendor invoice.

The total that shows in the Amount field is automatically credited to the accounts payable account (Account No. 20000, Accounts Payable and the vendor account, James Jarvis Hardware). The information entered on the Purchases/Receive Inventory window is recorded in the Purchase Journal.

8. Click 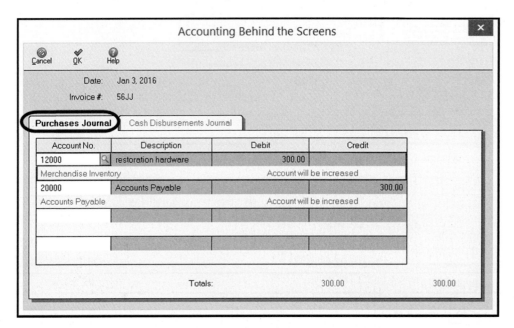 to see this entry in the Purchases Journal.

Inventory Items and Purchases: Since you entered an Inventory Item (hardware), the debit amount is shown in the merchandise inventory account (Account No. 12000). (On page 418, step 6, you set up the Expense Account default for Account No. 12000, Merchandise Inventory.)

9. Click ☑ OK to return to the Purchases/Receive Inventory window.

10. Click 💾 Save to post this entry. The Purchases/Receive Inventory window is ready for the next transaction. When you enter and post purchases of inventory items, three things happen:

    a. The amount or stock level of the item is updated.

    b. The ***Average Cost*** is updated based on the Unit Price entered. Average cost is computed using the ***weighted-average method*** for inventory. The Average Cost is used by Sage to compute Cost of Goods Sold when these Inventory Items are entered as Sales.

For Stock-Type items, the Inventory account is debited and Accounts Payable is credited (debit, Account No. 12000, Merchandise Inventory; credit, Account No. 20000, Accounts Payable/Vendor.)

Additional Purchases

The following transactions need to be entered in the Purchases Journal. Remember to click [Save] after each transaction to post.

Date	Transaction Description
1/21/16	Invoice 90 was received from Len Lacey Products for the purchase of eight rolls of vinyl flooring at $54 each, for a total of $432. (*Hint: Select 003floor as the inventory item.*)
1/21/16	Invoice 210 was received from Ronnie Becker Fabrics for four pairs of curtains at $30 each, for a total vendor invoice of $120. (*Hint: Select 002wall as the inventory item.*)
1/21/16	Invoice 78JJ was received from James Jarvis Hardware for the purchase of 10 curtain rods at $50 each, for a total of $500. (*Hint: Select 001hardware as the inventory item.*)

CASH PURCHASES: Write Checks

Wendy's Service Merchandise pays cash for some purchases. Usually these cash disbursements are for expenses. All payments of cash are recorded in the ***cash disbursements journal***. Follow these steps to see how cash purchases are entered.

> **Read Me:**
>
> The Write Checks window is a simplified version of the Payments window. Both the Write Checks window and the Payments window post to the Cash Disbursements Journal.

1. From the Vendors & Purchases Navigation Center, click [Write Checks], New Check. When the Select a Cash Account window appears, make sure Southern Bank is selected. Then, click [OK]. The Write Checks window displays.

    Date   *Transaction Description*

    1/24/16   Wendy's Service Merchandise issued check 3030 in the amount of $160 to Morgan Knapp for cleaning (debit Account No. 70000, Maintenance Expense). Print Check No. 3030.

> **Comment**
>
> Your Write Checks window will show a cash account balance in the Balance field. Your Cash Account Balance field shows the same amount as the January 1, 2016 balance sheet, page 416, Southern Bank, $76,500.00.

2. Click on the Pay to the order of Name field and type **Morgan Knapp.**

3. Type **24** in the Date field and press **<Enter>**.

4. Type **160** in the $ field.

5. In the Expense Account field, select Account No. 70000, Maintenance Expense.

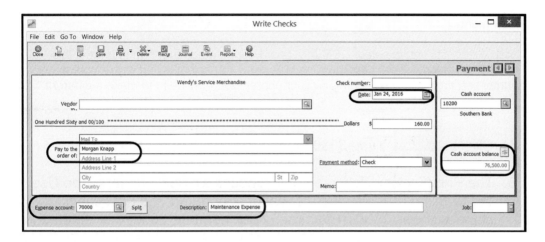

The next section shows you how to print or display Check 3030. If you are <u>not</u> connected to a printer, refer to the How to Fix box on page 441. (*Hint:* Type **3030** in the Check num<u>b</u>er field, then <Save>.)

Printing (or Displaying) the Check

Follow these steps to print the check:

1. The Write Checks window with Morgan Knapp's check should be displayed.

2. Click [Print] . (If you are not connected to a printer, click on the down-arrow next to Print and select Print Preview.)

3. The Print Forms: Disbursement Checks window appears. Click [Select Form] . Then select OCR AP Laser Preprinted to highlight it.

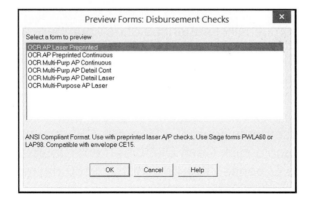

> **Comment**
>
> Step 3 instructs you to select OCR AP Laser Preprinted as the form to print. If this form does *not* print, select another one. The form you select is tied to the kind of printer you are using. Depending on your printer, you may need to make a different selection.

4. Click [OK]. Type **3030** in the First check number field.

5. The Print Forms: Disbursements Checks window appears. The Use this form field shows OCR AP Laser Preprinted; the First check number shows 3030. (*Hint:* The check number, 3030, was entered in step 4.)

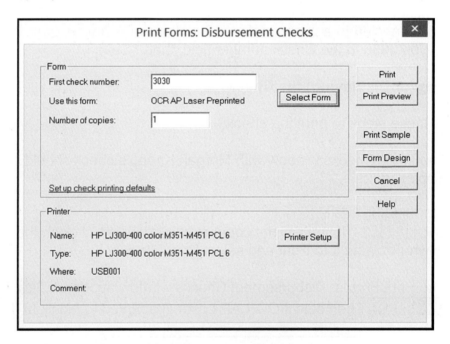

6. Sage 50 automatically sequences check numbers after the first one is entered. Click [Print] (or [Print Preview]). The check starts to print. Printing also posts the check to the Cash Disbursements Journal. If you are **not** printing, read the How to Fix box on the next page. (*Hint:* You can make sure the check posted by going to the Cash Disbursements Journal – Reports & Forms > Accounts Payable > double-click Cash Disbursements Journal. Check # 3030, Maintenance Expense, is shown for the $160 payment to Morgan Knapp.)

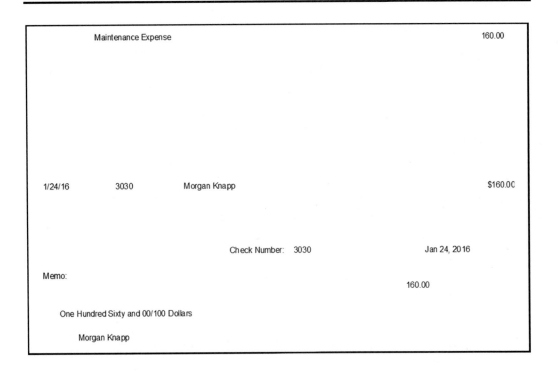

```
              Maintenance Expense                                                  160.00




    1/24/16          3030            Morgan Knapp                                  $160.0C


                                   Check Number:   3030                   Jan 24, 2016

    Memo:
                                                                      160.00


         One Hundred Sixty and 00/100 Dollars

             Morgan Knapp
```

Comment

If your check does not show the same amount, go back to the Write Checks window

and click 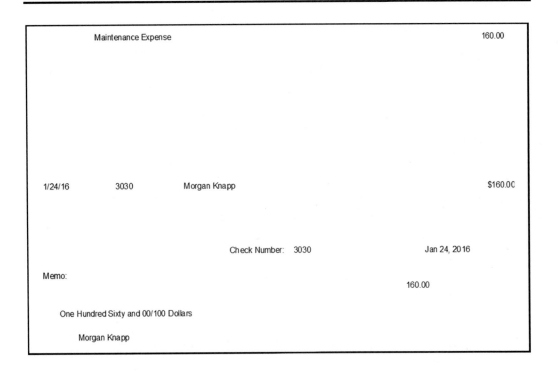. Double-click Check No. 3030, 1/24/2016; the Write Checks window appears. Make the necessary corrections. When you reprint Check No. 3030, Duplicate will be shown on the printout.

After you print a check, the Write Checks window is ready for another payment. Remember, the check form that you select is tied to the kind of printer you are using. If necessary, select a different form to print.

How to fix? If you are <u>not</u> connected to a printer, close the print preview window. Type **3030** in the Check num<u>b</u>er field. Then, click <<u>S</u>ave> on the Write Checks window.

Record the additional payments shown below. Since you are *not* going to print Check Nos. 3031-3035, type the appropriate check number in the Check num*ber* field on the Write Checks window.

Date	*Transaction Description*
1/24/16	Wendy's Service Merchandise issued Check No. 3031 in the amount of $45.00 to the U.S. Post Office (*Hint: Since you are not going to print checks, type* **3031** *in the Check num*ber *field. Click* Save *after each entry.*)
1/24/16	Issued Check No. 3032 in the amount of $107.65 to Main Office Supplies for letterhead paper, envelopes, and note pads. (Debit Account No. 75500, Supplies Expense.)
1/24/16	Issued Check No. 3033 in the amount of $72.14 to LRI Phone Co.
1/25/16	Issued Check No. 3034 to Alex Ziegler for $500.
1/25/16	Issued Check No. 3035 to Wendy Lincoln for $500.

8. Click List to see if you have issued Check Nos. 3030 through 3035.

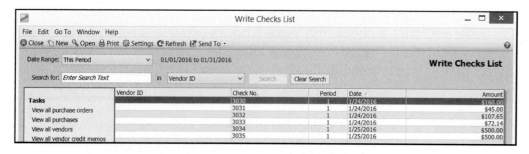

9. If you have any transactions to edit, highlight the line. Double-click. When the Write Checks window appears, make the necessary corrections. Remember to click Save for any revised transactions. If no corrections are needed, close the Write Checks List window.

10. Close the Write Checks window and the Write Checks List window.

PURCHASE RETURNS: CREDITS & RETURNS

Sometimes it is necessary to return merchandise that has been purchased from a vendor. When entering a purchase return, you need to record it as a vendor credit memo.

The following transaction is for merchandise returned to a vendor:

Date   *Transaction Description*

1/25/16   Returned one roll of vinyl flooring to Len Lacey Products, Invoice 90 and paid the invoice on the same day.

Follow these steps to enter a purchase return:

1. From the Vendors & Purchases Navigation Center, click . New Vendor Credit Memo. The Vendor Credit Memos window appears.

2. In the Vendor ID field, select Len Lacey Products.

3. Type **25** in the Credit <u>d</u>ate field.

4. Type **VCM90** in the Credit No field. For the credit number you are using the abbreviation VCM for Vendor Credit Memo, then the invoice number.

5. The Apply to In<u>v</u>oice No. tab is selected. Click on the down-arrow to select 90.

Observe that the Item, Quantity, Description, GL Account, and Unit Price fields are completed.

6. Type **1** in the Returned field > Press <Enter>. After you type 1 in the Returned field, the Amount field shows 54.00. Also, notice that the Credit Applied to Invoice shows 54.00. This agrees with the Credit Total.

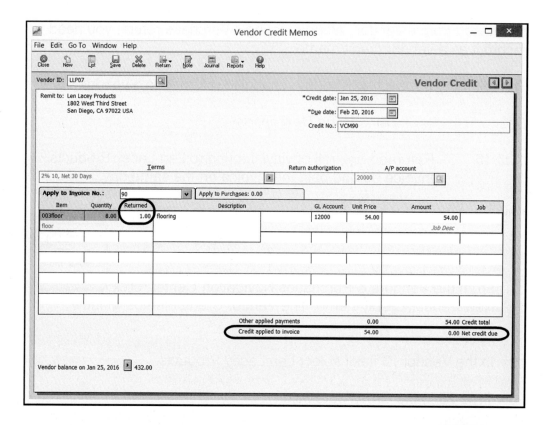

7. To see how the vendor credit memo is journalized, click Journal. Notice that Account No. 12000, Merchandise Inventory, is credited for $54.00 and Account No. 20000, Accounts Payable, is debited for $54.00.

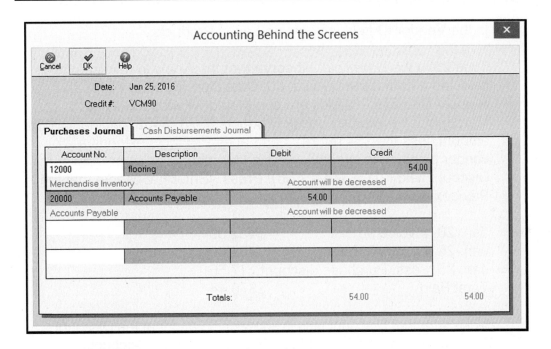

8. Click [OK] to close the Accounting Behind the Screens window.

9. Click [Save] to post, then [Close] the Vendor Credit Memos window.

Paying a Vendor, Minus a Return of Merchandise

How does the return of merchandise affect the payment to the vendor? Follow these steps to pay Invoice No. 90 less the return.

1. From the Vendors & Purchases Navigation Center, select [Pay Bills] > Pay Bill. The Payments window appears.

Date	Transaction Description
1/25/16	Wendy's Service Merchandise issued Check No. 3036 to Len Lacey Products in payment of Invoice No. 90 (less the return of merchandise). Print Check No. 3036.

2. In the Vendor ID field, select Len Lacey Products.

3. Type **25** in the Date field. Observe that the Apply to Invoices tab is selected and that the Invoice, 90; Date Due (Feb 20, 2016) and Amount Due 378.00 fields are completed. Wendy's Service Merchandise owes Len Lacey Products $378 ($432, original invoice amount, less the $54 return). Len Lacey Products extends a 2% vendor discount to Wendy's Service Merchandise. Type **7.56** in the Discount field (.02 x 378 = 7.56). Press <Enter>. Observe that the Pay box is checked. The payment was calculated as follows:

Jan. 20	Invoice 90	$432.00
Jan. 25	Less, VCM90	(54.00)
Jan. 25	Less, Purchase discount	(7.56)
Total Paid		$370.44

Make sure that Discount field is shows 7.56 and that the Discount Account field shows Account No. 59500, Purchase Discounts.

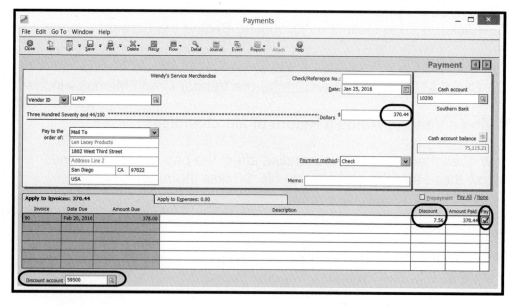

> ➤ **Troubleshooting Tip:** What if your Cash Account Balance field does not show an amount? Close the Payments window without saving. Then, from the menu bar, go to Options > Global. A checkmark should be placed next to Recalculate cash balance automatically in Receipts, Payments, and Payroll Entry. If

necessary, click on the appropriate field, then 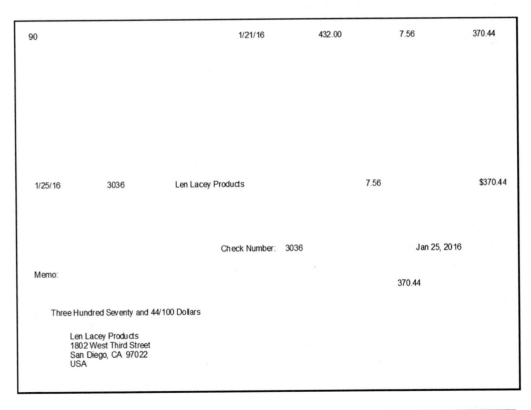 OK . Go back to step 1, on page 445.

4. Click [🖨 Print ▾] (or select Print Preview).

5. The Print Forms: Disbursement Checks window displays. Type **3036** in the First check number field.

6. The Use this form field shows OCR AP Laser Preprinted. If this selection is *not* made, click [Select Form], then select OCR AP Laser Preprinted.

7. Click [Print]. Check No. 3036 starts to print. Make sure the check amount is $370.44. (*Hint:* If you do <u>not</u> have a printer, click <Cancel> on the Print Forms: Disbursements Checks window. On the Payments window, type **3036** in the Check/Reference No. field > click <Save>.

90		1/21/16	432.00	7.56	370.44
1/25/16	3036	Len Lacey Products		7.56	$370.44

Check Number: 3036   Jan 25, 2016

Memo: 370.44

Three Hundred Seventy and 44/100 Dollars

Len Lacey Products
1802 West Third Street
San Diego, CA 97022
USA

8. Close the Payments window.

9. Record the following purchase return and payment:

Date	Transaction Description
1/28/16	Returned two curtain rods (001hardware) to James Jarvis Hardware, Invoice No. 78JJ; VCM78JJ. Wendy's Service Merchandise paid $50 each for the two curtain rods; credit total, $100.00.
1/28/16	Issued Check No. 3037 to pay James Jarvis Hardware for Invoice No. 78JJ (minus returned merchandise). (*Hint: Type the check number in the Check/Reference No. field instead of printing it. The discount is 8.00*)

▶ PAYING SPECIFIC VENDOR INVOICES

Once you have entered a vendor invoice in the Purchases/Receive Inventory window, you can apply payments to specific invoices. You enter the vendor invoice using the Purchases/Receive Inventory window; then when you post, the purchase journal is updated. To pay for the merchandise purchased, you select the specific invoice from the vendor's transaction list. When you print a check, you are also posting to the cash disbursements journal. The journal entry below shows a specific vendor payment.

Account Name	Debit	Credit
Accounts Payable/Ronnie Becker Fabrics	$120.00	
Purchase Discounts		$2.40
Southern Bank		$117.60

You should take advantage of both the Purchases/Receive Inventory and Payments features. Because amounts are disbursed and discounts are tracked automatically, your job is made easier. This also provides a detailed and complete audit trail. An audit trail is the path from the source document to the accounts. (Refer to pages 178-186 for more information about Sage 50's internal controls and audit trail.)

The diagram below shows how Purchases/Receive Inventory works together with Payments.

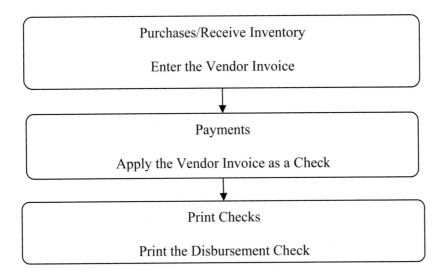

Purchases/Receive Inventory

Enter the Vendor Invoice

Payments

Apply the Vendor Invoice as a Check

Print Checks

Print the Disbursement Check

Date	Transaction Description
1/28/16	Issued Check No. 3038 to Ronnie Becker Fabrics in payment of Invoice No. 210.

Follow these steps to pay vendor invoice 210:

1. From the Payments window, select Ronnie Becker Fabrics as the vendor.

2. If necessary, type **3038** in the Check Number field.

3. Type **28** in the Date field.

4. The Apply to Invoices tab should already be selected. For Invoice No. 210, click on the Pay box.

5. Click 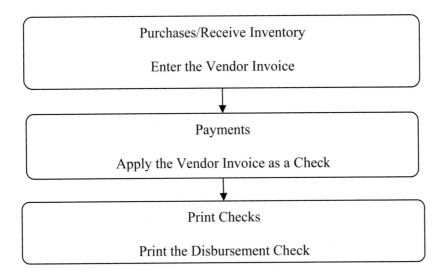 to post.

Editing Payments

If you have already paid a vendor, you can edit payments. Follow these steps to see what vendors have been paid.

1. Display the Payments window.

2. Click 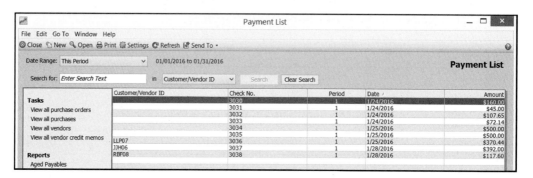. The Payment List window appears. Compare your Payment List window to the one shown below.

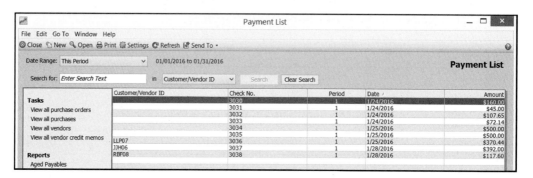

3. If you need to edit a payment, double-click on the appropriate one. Or, if no corrections are needed, close the Payment List window.

4. Make any necessary changes, then post.

5. When you are finished close all windows.

PRINTING THE PURCHASE JOURNAL AND CASH DISBURSEMENTS JOURNAL

Observe that the Vendors & Purchases Navigation Center shows the following sections.

- Vendors & Purchases Tasks: The flowchart that shows the Sage 50's accounts payable system.

- Vendors: Each vendor is shown. You can link to individual vendors or View Detailed List.

- Recently Used Vendor Reports: You can link to view or print vendor reports from this section or View All Vendor & Purchases Reports.

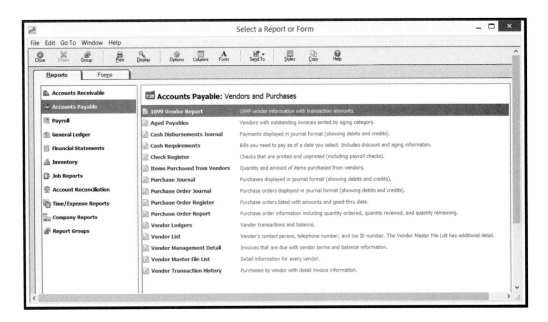

- Aged Payables: From this section, graphs or tables may be viewed.

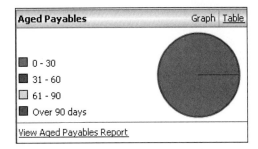

- Sage Advisor: Three links are shows — <u>Where do I get started</u>?, <u>What type of purchase information can I enter</u>?, and How <u>can I keep track of my purchases</u>? Link to one of them *or* click <u>Expand</u> to go to the Sage Advisor Getting Started window to watch videos

  ▶. When through, close the Getting Started window.

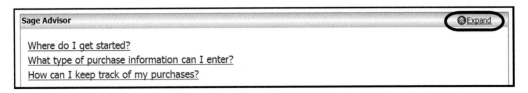

1. From the Recently Used Vendor Reports area, click <u>View</u> next to Purchase Journal.

Wendy's Service Merchandise
Purchase Journal
For the Period From Jan 1, 2016 to Jan 31, 2016
Filter Criteria includes: 1) Includes Drop Shipments. Report order is by Date. Report is printed in Detail Format.

Date	Account ID Account Description	Invoice/CM #	Line Description	Debit Amount	Credit Amount
1/3/16	12000 Merchandise Inventory 20000 Accounts Payable	56JJ	restoration hardware James Jarvis Hardware	300.00	300.00
1/21/16	12000 Merchandise Inventory 20000 Accounts Payable	210	wall coverings Ronnie Becker Fabrics	120.00	120.00
1/21/16	12000 Merchandise Inventory 20000 Accounts Payable	78JJ	restoration hardware James Jarvis Hardware	500.00	500.00
1/21/16	12000 Merchandise Inventory 20000 Accounts Payable	90	flooring Len Lacey Products	432.00	432.00
1/25/16	12000 Merchandise Inventory 20000 Accounts Payable	VCM90	flooring Len Lacey Products	54.00	54.00
1/28/16	12000 Merchandise Inventory 20000 Accounts Payable	VCM78JJ	restoration hardware James Jarvis Hardware	100.00	100.00
				1,506.00	1,506.00

2. Click <u>View</u> next to the Cash Disbursements Journal.

Wendy's Service Merchandise
Cash Disbursements Journal
For the Period From Jan 1, 2016 to Jan 31, 2016
Filter Criteria includes: Report order is by Date. Report is printed in Detail Format.

Date	Check #	Account ID	Line Description	Debit Amount	Credit Amount
1/24/16	3030	70000	Maintenance Expense	160.00	
		10200	Morgan Knapp		160.00
1/24/16	3031	73500	Postage Expense	45.00	
		10200	U.S. Post Office		45.00
1/24/16	3032	75500	Supplies Expense	107.65	
		10200	Main Office Supplies		107.65
1/24/16	3033	76000	Telephone Expense	72.14	
		10200	LRI Phone Co.		72.14
1/25/16	3034	39007	Alex Ziegler, Drawing	500.00	
		10200	Alex Ziegler		500.00
1/25/16	3035	39009	Wendy Lincoln, Drawing	500.00	
		10200	Wendy Lincoln		500.00
1/25/16	3036	59500	Discounts Taken		7.56
		20000	Invoice: 90	378.00	
		10200	Len Lacey Products		370.44
1/28/16	3037	59500	Discounts Taken		8.00
		20000	Invoice: 78JJ	400.00	
		10200	James Jarvis Hardware		392.00
1/28/16	3038	59500	Discounts Taken		2.40
		20000	Invoice: 210	120.00	
		10200	Ronnie Becker Fabrics		117.60
	Total			**2,282.79**	**2,282.79**

Comment

Observe that the Line Description on the Cash Disbursements Journal shows the account name (for example, Account No. 70000, Maintenance Expense) for the debit amount. The person to whom the check was written (Morgan Knapp) is shown for the amount credited. Your Line Descriptions may differ.

VENDOR LEDGERS

Follow these steps to print a Vendor Ledger for Wendy's Service Merchandise.

1. From the Recently Used Vendor Reports area, link to <u>View All Vendor & Purchases Reports</u>. The Select a Report or Form window appears.

2. Double-click Vendor Ledgers then make the selections to print.

Wendy's Service Merchandise
Vendor Ledgers
For the Period From Jan 1, 2016 to Jan 31, 2016

Filter Criteria includes: Report order is by ID.

Vendor ID Vendor	Date	Trans No	Type	Paid	Debit Amt	Credit Amt	Balance
JJH06	1/3/16	56JJ	PJ			300.00	300.00
James Jarvis Hardware	1/21/16	78JJ	PJ	*		500.00	800.00
	1/28/16	VCM78JJ	PJ	*	100.00		700.00
	1/28/16	3037	CDJ		8.00	8.00	700.00
	1/28/16	3037	CDJ		400.00		300.00
LLP07	1/21/16	90	PJ	*		432.00	432.00
Len Lacey Products	1/25/16	VCM90	PJ	*	54.00		378.00
	1/25/16	3036	CDJ		7.56	7.56	378.00
	1/25/16	3036	CDJ		378.00		0.00
RBF08	1/21/16	210	PJ	*		120.00	120.00
Ronnie Becker Fabrics	1/28/16	3038	CDJ		2.40	2.40	120.00
	1/28/16	3038	CDJ		120.00		0.00
Report Total					**1,069.96**	**1,369.96**	**300.00**

3. Close the Vendor Ledgers.

PRINTING THE GENERAL LEDGER TRIAL BALANCE

1. In the Reports list, highlight General Ledger > double-click General Ledger Trial Balance.

2. Make the selections to print. Compare your printout with the one shown on the next page.

	Wendy's Service Merchandise		
	General Ledger Trial Balance		
	As of Jan 31, 2016		

Filter Criteria includes: Report order is by ID. Report is printed in Detail Format.

Account ID	Account Description	Debit Amt	Credit Amt
10200	Southern Bank	74,235.17	
10400	Tucson Savings & Loan	22,000.00	
12000	Merchandise Inventory	28,938.00	
13000	Supplies	1,750.00	
14000	Prepaid Insurance	2,400.00	
15000	Furniture and Fixtures	5,000.00	
15100	Computers & Equipment	7,500.00	
15500	Building	100,000.00	
20000	Accounts Payable		300.00
27000	Long-Term Notes Payable		20,500.00
27400	Mortgage Payable		75,000.00
39006	Alex Ziegler, Capital		73,695.00
39007	Alex Ziegler, Drawing	500.00	
39008	Wendy Lincoln, Capital		73,695.00
39009	Wendy Lincoln, Drawing	500.00	
59500	Purchase Discounts		17.96
70000	Maintenance Expense	160.00	
73500	Postage Expense	45.00	
75500	Supplies Expense	107.65	
76000	Telephone Expense	72.14	
	Total:	**243,207.96**	**243,207.96**

3. Close all windows.

BACKING UP CHAPTER 12 DATA

Back up to this point in your data. The suggested file name is **Chapter 12**.

EXPORT REPORTS TO EXCEL

Follow these steps to export the following Sage 50 reports to Excel: Chart of Accounts, Purchase Journal, Cash Disbursements Journal, Vendors Ledgers, General Ledger Trial Balance.

1. From the menu bar, select Reports & Forms > General Ledger > double-click Chart of Accounts. The Chart of Accounts appears.

   Expand the Account Description column. (Click [⟷] to widen the column.)

2. Click 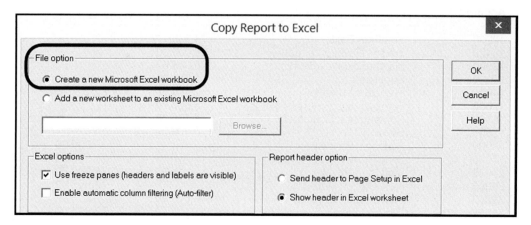 On the Copy Report to Excel window, accept the default for Create a new Microsoft Excel workbook. In the Report header option field, Show header in Excel worksheet is selected.

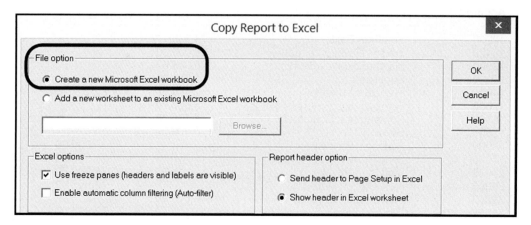

3. Click OK. The chart of accounts exports to Excel.

4. Save. Use the file name **Chapter 12_CofA_PJ_CDJ_VL_GLTB. xlsx**. (Abbreviations are Chart of Accounts, Purchase Journal, Cash Disbursements Journal, Vendor Ledgers, and General Ledger Trial Balance.)

5. Go back to Sage 50's Select a Report or Form window. In the Reports list, select Accounts Payable. Double-click Purchase Journal.

6. Click Excel. On the Copy Report to Excel window, select Add a new worksheet to an existing Microsoft Excel workbook.

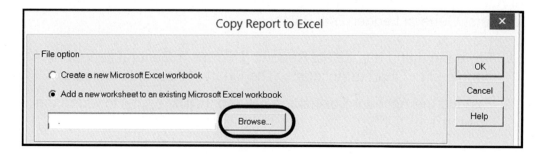

7. Click [Browse...] to go to the appropriate file. (*Hint:* File name is Chapter 12_CofA_PJ_CDJ_VL_GLTB.xlsx.) Click [Open]. You are returned to the Copy Report to Excel window. Observe that the Browse field shows the location of the file selected. Click [OK].

8. Observe that two sheets are shown at the bottom of the Excel file: Chart of Accounts and Purchase Journal. Save the file.

9. Repeat steps 5, 6, 7, and 8 to export the Cash Disbursements Journal, Vendor Ledgers, and General Ledger Trial Balance to the Excel File. There should be five sheets: Chart of Accounts, Purchase Journal, Cash Disbursements Journal, Vendor Ledgers, and General Ledger Trial Balance. When you are through, the Excel file has five sheets.

10. Save. Exit Excel.

    NOTE: If your instructor would like you to save the Chart of Accounts, Purchase Journal, Cash Disbursements Journal, Vendor Ledgers, and General Ledger Trial Balance as PDF files, do that. Depending on your instructor's preference, additional reports could be turned in. The suggested file name is **Chapter 12_Chart of Accounts.pdf**, etc.

ONLINE LEARNING CENTER

Complete end-of-chapter activities at www.mhhe.com/yacht2016 > Student Edition > Chapter 12.

1. Quizzes: Multiple Choice and True False questions. Interactive online tests that are graded and can be emailed to your instructor.

2. More Resources:

    a. QA Templates: Answer 10 true/make true questions and three Analysis Questions.

    b. Videos: Watch the Purchases and Payments videos.

    c. Narrated PowerPoints: Listen to the narrated PowerPoints.

d. Going to the Net Exercises: Watch Sage YouTube videos.

e. Assessment Rubric: Complete the rubric to review Sage 50's journals, navigation centers, modules, task windows, and reports.

The OLC also includes links to the Appendixes:

- Appendix A: Troubleshooting
- Appendix B: Accounting Information Systems
- Appendix C: Review of Accounting Principles
- Appendix D: Glossary (words that are boldfaced and italicized in chapter)

Exercise 12-1: Follow the instructions below to complete Exercise 12-1.

1. Start Sage 50. From the menu bar, select File > New Company. (One company should be open.) Set up a retail business using *your last name*; for example, *Your Last Name Sales and Service.* For the address, use 1834 East Peachtree Blvd., Norcross, GA 30092; Telephone, 404-555-4311; Fax, 404-555-4412; Business Type, Sole Proprietorship. For the Tax ID information, use the information below.

   Federal Employer ID: 99-1245334

   State Employer ID: 17-1588765

   State Unemployment ID: 174412-8

   Leave the Web Site and E-mail address fields blank.

2. At the New Company – Setup; Chart of Accounts window > select Copy settings from an existing Sage 50 Accounting company.

3. Highlight Wendy's Service Merchandise (*or,* your name Service Merchandise), then click [Next >].

4. Observe that the information on the Copy Company Information window includes a selection for Accounting Periods. Since this company is using the same accounting period (January 1 - 31, 2016) as Wendy's Service Merchandise, leave that box checked. For

purposes of Exercise 12-1 accept all the defaults on the Copy Company Information window by clicking on [Next >].

5. Read the information about the Accounting Method. Accept the default for accrual accounting by clicking on [Next >].

6. Accept the default for Real Time posting by clicking on [Next >].

7. At the Create a New Company – Finish window, click [Finish]. If the screen prompts You can use this company in the student version of Sage 50 for the next 14 months and then it will expire, click [OK].

8. Close the Setup Guide. (*Hint:* Click on the box next to Don't show this screen at startup to place a checkmark in it.) The Sage Advisor Getting Started window includes videos and PDF documents. You may want to watch the videos and read the PDF documents. When through, close the Sage Advisor Getting Started window.

9. Make sure the Period shows Period 1 - 01/01/16-01/31/16 [Period 1 - 01/01/16-01/31/16].

General Ledger

1. Delete the following accounts:

   3900A Owner's Draw
   40400 Sales-Floor

   Change the following accounts:

10200	Southern Bank	**First Interstate**
10400	Tucson Savings & Loan	**City Savings & Loan**
39009	Owner's Contribution	**Student Name, Capital** (Equity, doesn't close)
40200	Sales-Wall	**Sales-Tools**
50500	Cost of Sales-Wall	**Cost of Sales-Tools**
57000	Cost of Sales-Floor	**Cost of Sales**

Add the following account:

23755	**SUTA2 Payable**	Other Current Liabilities
39010	**Student Name, Drawing**	Equity-gets closed
72545	**SUTA2 Expense**	Expenses

2. Back up. The suggested file name is **Exercise 12-1 Chart of Accounts**.

3. To record chart of accounts beginning balances, use the Balance Sheet on the next page. You purchased the retail business in December 2015. Remember to select the period From 12/1/15 through 12/31/15. Record beginning balances as of December 31, 2015.

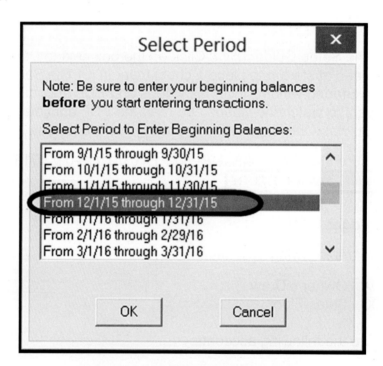

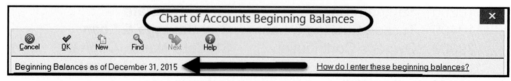

Student Name Sales and Service Balance Sheet January 1, 2016		
ASSETS		
Current Assets		
10200 - First Interstate	$65,500.00	
10400 - City Savings & Loan	13,300.00	
12000 - Merchandise Inventory	14,750.00	
13000 - Supplies	1,000.00	
14000 - Prepaid Insurance	2,400.00	
Total Current Assets		$96,950.00
Property and Equipment		
15000 - Furniture and Fixtures	$3,500.00	
15100 - Computers & Equipment	5,500.00	
15500 - Building	85,000.00	
Total Property and Equipment		$94,000.00
Total Assets		$190,950.00
LIABILITIES AND CAPITAL		
Long Term Liabilities		
27000 - Long-Term Notes Payable	10,000.00	
27400 - Mortgage Payable	60,000.00	
Total Long-Term Liabilities		$70,000.00
Capital		
39009 - Student Name, Capital		120,950.00
Total Liabilities and Capital		$190,950.00

4. Print the chart of accounts.

5. Print the December 31, 2015 balance sheet.

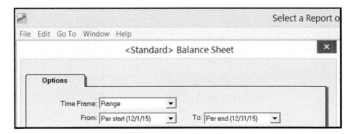

6.   Back up. The suggested file name is **Exercise 12-1 Starting Balance Sheet**.

Accounts Payable

Follow the instructions below to set up vendor information.

1.   From the Vendors & Purchases Navigation Center, click Vendors >
     Set up Vendor Defaults. Make sure the following defaults are set. If
     not, set them up.

Standard Terms:	Due in number of days
Net due in:	30 days
Discount in:	10 days
Discount %:	2.00
Credit Limit:	10,000.00

GL Link Accounts:

Expense Account:	12000 Merchandise Inventory
Discount GL Account:	59500 Purchase Discounts

2.   Click Vendors > New Vendor. Set up the following vendors:

a.	Vendor ID:	**CPT12**
	Name:	**Curt Perkins Tools**
	Contact:	**Curt Perkins**
	Mailing Address:	**2301 Thunderbird Avenue**
	City, ST, Zip	**Phoenix, AZ 85120**
	Country:	**USA**
	Vendor Type:	**tools**
	1099 Type:	select Independent Contractor
	Expense Account:	12000 Merchandise Inventory
	Telephone 1:	**602-555-3945**
	Fax:	**602-555-3950**
	E-mail:	**info@curtperkins.com**

Web Site: **www.curtperkins.com**

Purchase Info:

Tax ID Number: **44-2255277**

b. Vendor ID: **SJH14**
    Name: **Sally Jackson Hardware**
    Contact: **Sally Jackson**
    Mailing Address: **123 Citrus Avenue**
    City, ST, Zip   **Los Angeles, CA 90036**
    Country: **USA**
    Vendor Type: **hardware**
    1099 Type: select Independent Contractor
    Expense Account: 12000 Merchandise Inventory
    Telephone 1:   **310-555-1133**
    Fax: **310-555-3315**
    E-mail: **info@jacksonhardware.net**
    Web Site: **www.jacksonhardware.net**

Purchase Info:

Tax ID Number: **98-3129833**

Inventory

Follow these steps to set up inventory defaults:

1. From the Inventory & Services Navigation Center, click ,
   Set Up Inventory Defaults.

2. On the <u>G</u>eneral tab, the Default Item Class field shows Stock item. If
   not, select Stock item.

3. Select the G<u>L</u> Accts/Costing tab. If necessary, set up Average as the
   inventory costing method (Stock item, Master Stock item, Assembly).

4. If necessary, select Account No. 45500, Shipping Charges. This GL
   Link is for Freight Charges in Sales/Invoicing.

5. Click [Inventory Items] > New Inventory Item. Set up the following inventory stock items:

a.
Item ID:	**002tools**
Description:	**tools**
Item Class:	Stock item
Description for Sales:	**tools**
Price Level 1:	**85**
Last Unit Cost:	**30**
Cost Method:	Average
GL Sales Acct:	**40200 Sales-Tools**
GL Inventory Acct:	**12000 Merchandise Inventory**
GL Cost of Sales Acct:	**50500 Cost of Sales-Tools**
Item Tax Type:	1 Regular Taxable
Item Type:	**tools**
Stocking U/M:	**each**
Minimum Stock:	**10**
Reorder Quantity:	**4**
Preferred Vendor ID:	**CPT12, Curt Perkins Tools**

b.
Item ID:	**003hardware**
Description:	**hardware**
Item Class:	Stock item
Description for Sales:	**copper hardware**
Price Level 1:	**150**
Last Unit Cost:	**50**
Cost Method:	Average
GL Sales Acct:	**40000 Sales-Hardware**
GL Inventory Acct:	**12000 Merchandise Inventory**
Cost of Sales Acct:	**50000 Cost of Sales-Hardware**
Item Tax Type:	1 Regular Taxable
Item Type:	**hardware**
Stocking U/M:	**each**
Minimum Stock:	**10**
Reorder Quantity:	**4**
Preferred Vendor ID:	**SJH14, Sally Jackson Hardware**

Click on <u>B</u>eginning Balances. Record the beginning balances shown below.

Item ID	Description	Quantity	Unit Cost	Total Cost
002tools	tools	175	30	5,250.00
003hardware	hardware	190	50	9,500.00

6. Click .

7. Save the Chart of Accounts and December 31 2015 Balance Sheet as PDF files. The file names are **Exercise 12-1_Chart of Accounts**, **Exercise 12-1_Dec 31 2015 Balance Sheet**.

8. Back up. The suggested file name is **Exercise 12-1**.

Exercise 12-2: Follow the instructions below to complete Exercise 12-2. Exercise 12-1 *must* be completed before starting Exercise 12-2.

1. If necessary, restore the Exercise 12-1.ptb file. (*Hint:* You can restore from your back up file even if <u>no</u> company exists. From the startup window, select File > Restore. Select the location of your backup file. On the Restore Wizard's Select Company window, select *Create a new company using the restored data* which restores your backup data and sets up the company. For more information, refer to Troubleshooting, pages 279-280.)

2. Journalize and post the following transactions and print each check.

   1/4/16   Invoice No. 480CP was received from Curt Perkins Tools for the purchase of 10 tool kits for a unit cost of $30.

   1/5/16   Invoice No. SJH52 was received from Sally Jackson Hardware for the purchase of 8 hardware sets at a unit cost of $50.

   1/6/16   Returned two tool kits to Curt Perkins Tools, Invoice No. 480CP. Paid $30 for each tool kit; VCM480CP.

1/11/16	Issued First Interstate Check No. 2020 to pay Sally Jackson Hardware for Invoice No. SJH52. (*Hint:* Type the check number, 2020, in the Check/Reference No. field.)
1/11/16	Issued Check No. 2021 to pay Curt Perkins Tools for merchandise purchased on January 3, less the January 6 return, Invoice No. 480CP. (*Hint: Remember to calculate, then type the correct discount amount in the Discount field.*)
1/14/16	Issued Check No. 2022 to Nikki Bell for $125 for cleaning and maintenance.
1/15/16	Issued Check No. 2023 to the U.S. Post Office for $45.
1/15/16	Issued Check No. 2024 to Office Staples for $145.72 for cell phone. (Debit Account No. 71000, Office Expense.)
1/15/16	Issued Check No. 2025 to TeleCom for $46.65 to pay the telephone bill.
1/25/16	Issued Check No. 2026 to the owner of the business for $400.

3. Print the Purchase Journal. (*Hint:* If you are not connected to a printer, you can select Adobe PDF or a Microsoft XPS Document Writer in the Print Properties field.)

    GO GREEN & SAVE: Instead of printing, select Display or Print Preview, and save as an Adobe PDF file or Microsoft XPS file. In other words, you do <u>not</u> need to print hard copy. Check with your instructor for his or her preference. Instead of printing, email PDFs or Microsoft XPS files.

4. Print the Cash Disbursements Journal.

5. Print the Vendor Ledgers.

6. Print the General Ledger Trial Balance.

    Check Your Figures:

10200, First Interstate	$64,110.43
12000, Merchandise Inventory	15,390.00
20000, Accounts Payable	0.00
59500, Purchase Discounts	12.80

7. Back up. The suggested file name is **Exercise 12-2**.

8. Export the following reports to Excel – Chart of Accounts, Purchase Journal, Cash Disbursements Journal, Vendor Ledgers, and General Ledger Trial balance. The suggested file name is **Exercise 12-2_ CofA _PJ_CDJ_VL_GLTB.xlsx**.

9. Save these files as PDFs: Purchase Journal, Cash Disbursements Journal, Vendor Ledgers, and General Ledger Trial Balance. The suggested file name is **Exercise 12-2_Purchase Journal.pdf**, etc.

CHAPTER 12 INDEX

Chapter

13 Customers & Sales

LEARNING OBJECTIVES

1. Restore data from Chapter 12. (This backup was made on page 455.)
2. Set up customer default information.
3. Set up sales tax information.
4. Set up customer maintenance information.
5. Record credit sales, cash sales, and sales returns.
6. Record customer receipts, partial payments, and edit invoices.
7. Use the Financial Manager to view financial ratios and key Income Statement and Balance Sheet account balances.
8. Make four backups, save two Excel files, and save three PDF files.[1]

In Chapter 12, you learned how to use Sage 50's Purchases/Receive Inventory and Payments features. Now that you have purchased merchandise from vendors, you are ready to sell that merchandise. To do that, you use Sage 50's Customers & Sales Navigation Center.

In Chapter 3, Customers, when you entered a sales invoice for Bellwether Garden Supply, the unit price, description, account number, and sales taxes were automatically calculated for you. (See pages 107-117.)

Before using the Sales/Invoicing window, you need to set up customer defaults, sales tax information, and customer maintenance information. After you set up these defaults, Sage will use this information when you record a sale.

Chapter 13 explains how Sage's accounts receivable system works. *Accounts receivable* are what customers owe your business. Credit transactions from customers are called *accounts receivable transactions*.

---

[1]For the size of files backed up and saved, refer to the chart on pages 400-401.

Customer receipts work similarly to paying vendor invoices. When a customer pays an existing *invoice* there are two steps:

1. Enter the customer's ID code so that a list of existing invoices for the customer displays.

2. Select the invoice that applies to the customer's check, then select the Pay box.

This diagram illustrates Sage 50's accounts receivable system.

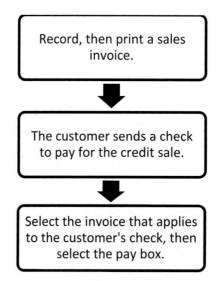

On the Customers & Sales Navigation Center, Sage 50 illustrates the accounts receivable system. In Chapter 13, you work with customers, sales invoices, credits and returns, and receipts from customers.

The Customers & Sales Navigation Center shows the flow of customer-related tasks and takes you where you need to go to perform those tasks. In Sage 50, this represents the accounts receivable module or accounts receivable system.

The Customers & Sales workflow diagram is shown on the next page.

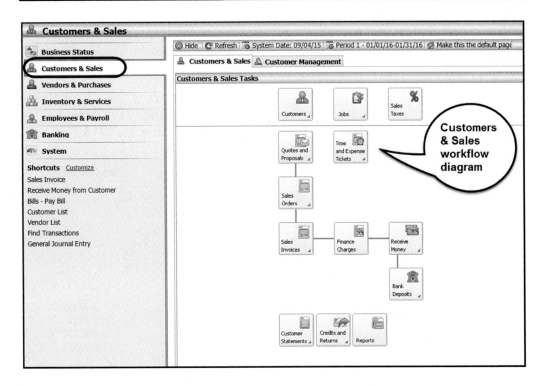

GETTING STARTED

1. Start Sage 50. Open Wendy's Service Merchandise, or if you used a unique name, select it. This company was set up in Chapter 12 on pages 404-409. (*Hint:* If another company opens, click File > Open Previous Company > select Wendy's [your name] Service Merchandise. Open one company.)

2. If necessary, restore data from the Chapter 12.ptb file. This file was backed up on page 455.

> **Read Me: Do I need to restore?**
>
>   If you are working on your own PC or laptop, you may be able to skip restore. Refer to the disk icon ▣ on the next page to make sure you are starting with the work completed in Chapter 12. *If you are working in the computer lab or classroom, start [Your First Name] Service Merchandise, then restore the Chapter 12.ptb file from your USB drive.*

To make sure you are starting in the appropriate place in the data (Chapter 12.ptb backup) display the General Ledger Trial Balance.

Wendy's Service Merchandise
General Ledger Trial Balance
As of Jan 31, 2016

Filter Criteria includes: Report order is by ID. Report is printed in Detail Format.

Account ID	Account Description	Debit Amt	Credit Amt
10200	Southern Bank	74,235.17	
10400	Tucson Savings & Loan	22,000.00	
12000	Merchandise Inventory	28,938.00	
13000	Supplies	1,750.00	
14000	Prepaid Insurance	2,400.00	
15000	Furniture and Fixtures	5,000.00	
15100	Computers & Equipment	7,500.00	
15500	Building	100,000.00	
20000	Accounts Payable		300.00
27000	Long-Term Notes Payable		20,500.00
27400	Mortgage Payable		75,000.00
39006	Alex Ziegler, Capital		73,695.00
39007	Alex Ziegler, Drawing	500.00	
39008	Wendy Lincoln, Capital		73,695.00
39009	Wendy Lincoln, Drawing	500.00	
59500	Purchase Discounts		17.96
70000	Maintenance Expense	160.00	
73500	Postage Expense	45.00	
75500	Supplies Expense	107.65	
76000	Telephone Expense	72.14	
	Total:	**243,207.96**	**243,207.96**

This is the same trial balance shown in Chapter 12 on page 455.

Setting Up Customer Defaults

In Chapter 12, you entered General Ledger, Accounts Payable, and Inventory Item defaults. The directions that follow show how to enter customer defaults.

1. From the Navigation Bar, select [Customers & Sales] >
   [Customers], Set Up Customer Defaults. The Customer Defaults window appears.

2. If necessary, click on the Discount Percent field. Type **0** (zero) in the Discount Percent field, then press **<Enter>**. Wendy's Service Merchandise does *not* offer a discount to its credit customers.

3. If necessary, type **2500** in the Credit Limit field, press **<Enter>**.

4. Accept the default for GL Sales Account 40000, Sales-Hardware by pressing **<Enter>**. (When you set up individual customers, you will select a GL Sales Account for that customer.)

5. Accept the default for Discount GL Account 49000, Sales Discounts by pressing **<Enter>**.

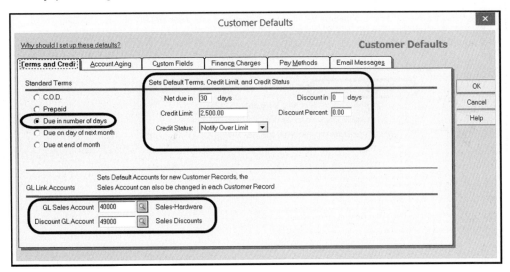

Observe that the default for Standard Terms is Due in number of days.

6. Click [OK].

Setting Up Sales Tax Defaults

You can enter sales tax default information for these areas:

➤ Sales Tax Authorities: codes for governments or other tax authorities and their tax rates. These are used to assemble the sales tax codes.
➤ Sales Tax Codes: the overall rate applied to taxable items on invoices to customers. This is composed of rates entered as Sales Tax Authorities.

Follow these steps to set up sales tax defaults.

1. From the Customers & Sales Navigation Center, click 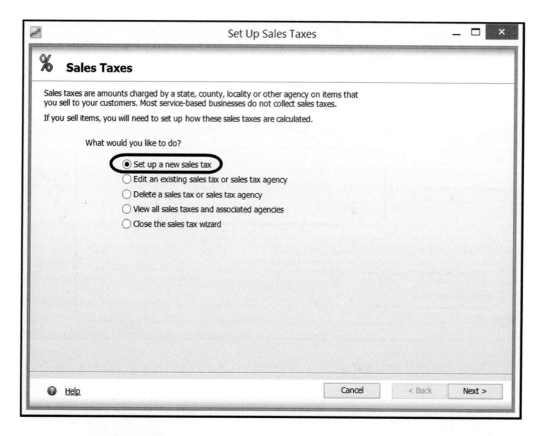. The Sales Taxes window appears. Set up a new sales tax is the default.

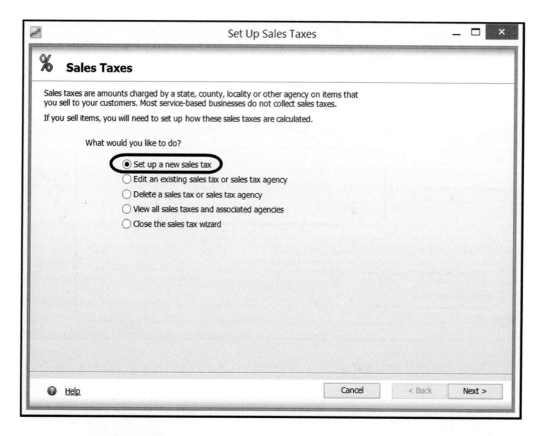

2. Click Next > The Set Up New Sales Tax window appears.

3. Type **8.00**% in the What is the total rate that you will charge? Press **<Enter>.** Accept the default for 1 in the How many individual rates make up this total rate? field.

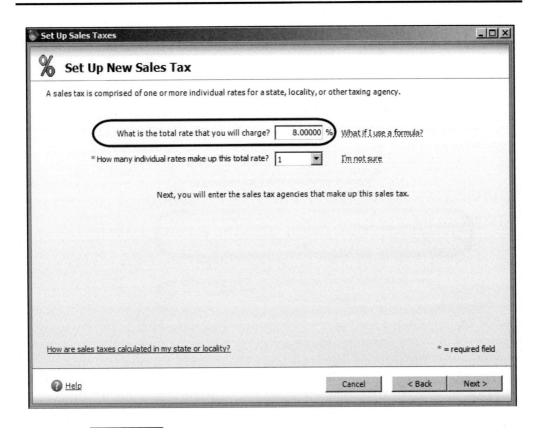

4. Click [Next >]. The Add Sales Tax Agency window appears.

5. Type **AZ** in the Sales tax agency ID field. Press **<Enter>**.

6. Type **Arizona Dept. of Revenue** in the Sales tax agency name field.

7. Accept the default by single rate in the How are sales taxes calculated for this agency? field.

8. Type **8.00**% in the Rate field. Press **<Enter>**.

9. Select Account No. 23100, Sales Tax Payable in the Select an account to track sales taxes field. Press **<Enter>**.

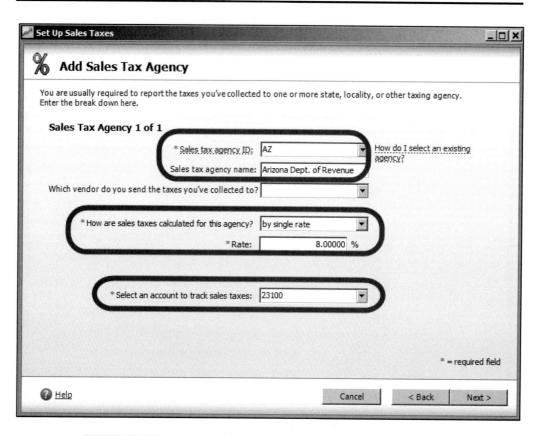

10. Click [Next >]. The Sales Tax Entered window appears.

11. Type **AZ** in the Sales tax ID field. Press **<Enter>**.

12. Type **Arizona sales tax** in the Sales tax name field. Compare your Sales Tax Entered window to the one shown on the next page.

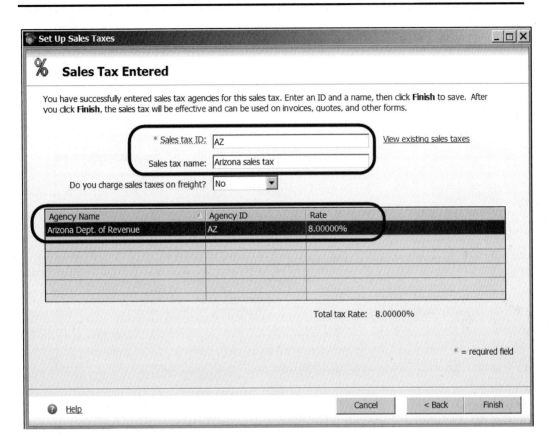

13. Click [Finish]. The Sales Taxes window appears. To make sure you have set up sales taxes for Wendy's Service Merchandise select View all sales taxes and associated agencies

. Click [Next >].

14. The View All Sales Taxes window appears and shows the sales tax that was set up on pages 474-477. The 8.00% sales tax rate for Arizona is shown. Compare your View All Sales Taxes window with the one shown on the next page.

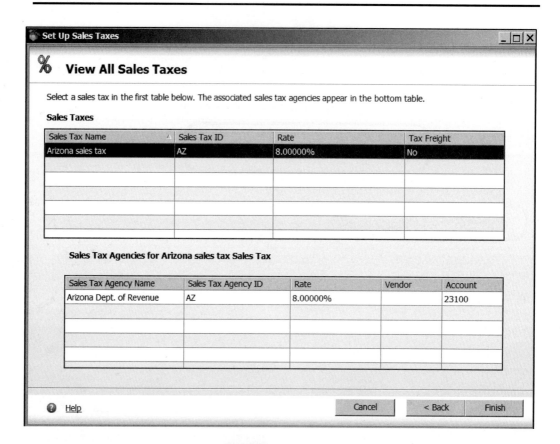

15. Click [Finish]. Click [×] on the title bar to close the Set Up Sales Taxes window.

Setting Up Customer Maintenance Information

To enter default information about your customers, follow these steps:

1. Select [Customers] > New Customer. The Maintain Customers/Prospects window appears.

2. Complete the following fields.

Customer ID:	**ap001** (Use lowercase letters and zeroes)
Name:	**Arlene Petty**
Billing address:	**1500 E. Cedar Avenue**
City, ST, Zip:	**Tucson, AZ 85713**

Country:	**USA**
Sales tax:	Select AZ (for Arizona sales tax)
Customer type:	**PIM**[2]
Telephone 1:	**520-555-8111**
Fax:	**520-555-9303**
E-mail:	**ap@tucson.com**
Web site:	**www.tucson.com/arlene**

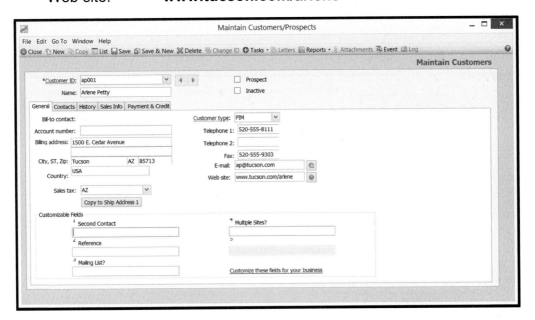

3. Click on the Sales Info tab.

4. In the GL Sales Acct field, if necessary, select Account No. 40000, Sales-Hardware.

---

[2]PIM is an abbreviation of Pima County. Customer Type groups similar customers together. In this case, customers in Tucson (PIM) are grouped together.

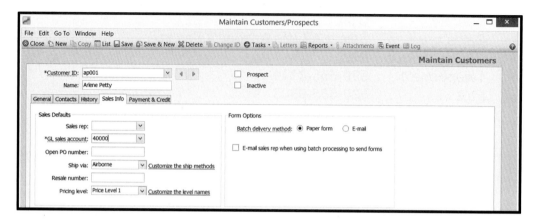

5. Click **Save & New**.

6. Click on the General tab. Add in the following customers.

Customer ID:	**bb002**
Name:	**Bonni Berman**
Billing address:	**115 North Seneca Street**
City, ST, Zip:	**Tucson, AZ 85715**
Country:	**USA**
Sales tax:	**AZ**
Customer type:	**PIM**
Telephone 1:	**520-555-1613**
Fax:	**520-555-2733**
E-mail:	**bonni@mail.com**
Web site:	**www.mail.com/berman**

In the Sales Info tab, select the GL Sales Acct 40200, Sales-Wall for Bonni Berman.

Customer ID:	**dc003**
Name:	**Denise Crosby**
Billing address:	**3088 Davis Road**
City, ST, Zip:	**Ft. Lauderdale, FL 33309**
Country:	**USA**
Sales tax:	Skip this field--see footnote.[3]
Customer type:	**FL**

---

[3]Since this customer is out of state, there is no Sales Tax.

Telephone 1:   **954-555-3292**
Fax: **954-555-9234**
E-mail: **denise@mail.net**
Web site: **www.mail.net/deniseC**

In the Sales Info tab, select the GL Sales Acct 40400, Sales-Floor for Denise Crosby.

Customer ID: **jp004**
Name: **Jessica Prince**
Billing address: **9001 Second Street**
City, ST, Zip: **Tucson, AZ 85704**
Country: **USA**
Sales tax: **AZ**
Customer type: **PIM**
Telephone 1:   **520-555-3203**
Fax: **520-555-0307**
E-mail: **prince@tucsonmail.com**
Web site: **www.tucsonmail.com/jessica**

In the Sales Info tab, select the GL Sales Acct 40000, Sales-Hardware for Jessica Prince.

Customer ID: **pm005**
Name: **Peter Malin**
Billing address: **7009 Western Avenue**
City, ST, Zip: **Tucson, AZ 85717**
Country: **USA**
Sales tax: **AZ**
Customer type: **PIM**
Telephone 1:   **520-555-0513**
Fax: **520-555-9515**
E-mail: **peter@mymail.com**
Web site: **www.mymail.com/peter**

In the Sales Info tab, select the GL Sales Acct 40200, Sales-Wall for Peter Malin. Close the Maintain Customers/Prospects window.

BACKING UP YOUR DATA

Back up. This backup saves your data to this point, including Chapter 12 and Chapter 13's work with Wendy's [your first name] Service Merchandise. The suggested file name is **Chapter 13 Begin**.

RECORDING SALES

Two types of sales are entered in Sage 50:

> ➢ Credit sales or invoiced sales—sales where you enter an invoice.
> ➢ Cash sales—sales where you do not enter an invoice.

All the information about a sale is recorded on the Sales/Invoicing window. Then, Sage takes the necessary information from the window and automatically journalizes the transaction in the *sales journal*. Only sales on account are recorded in the sales journal. You can also print sales invoices.

Cash sales are entered on the Receive Money window. Then, Sage takes that information and journalizes the transaction in the *cash receipts journal*.

On the Sales/Invoicing window, enter invoices for the customers stored in Sage's customer file. You entered five credit customers for Wendy's Service Merchandise. (Click [C Refresh] on the Customers & Sales Navigation Center to see the customer list.)

Customers			View Detailed List
Customer ID ⁄	Customer Name	Telephone 1	Balance
ap001	Arlene Petty	520-555-8111	$0.00
bb002	Bonni Berman	520-555-1613	$0.00
dc003	Denise Crosby	954-555-3292	$0.00
jp004	Jessica Prince	520-555-3203	$0.00
pm005	Peter Malin	520-555-0513	$0.00

All journal entries made to the Sales Journal (Sales/Invoicing window) are posted both to the General Ledger and to the Customer Ledger or *Accounts Receivable Ledger*. You can apply transactions to inventory items and jobs.

Entering sales works hand in hand with entering receipts. Once an invoice is posted it is simple to show that a customer has paid. Just display the appropriate invoice and click on the Pay box. Sage takes care of all the correct account distributions for you.

▶ Entering Invoices for Credit Sales (Remember, the icon means there is a video at www.mhhe.com/yacht2016.

In the steps that follow, you record the following transaction:

Date	Transaction Description
1/7/16	Sold two doorknobs on account to Arlene Petty; $324 ($300 plus $24, sales tax). (*Hint: Doorknobs are classified as hardware.*)

1. From the Customers & Sales Navigation Center, select > New Sales Invoice. The Sales/Invoicing window appears.

2. Your cursor is in the Customer ID field. Click 🔍 and select **Arlene Petty**. Sage supplies the customer default information: billing address, payment terms, GL account default, A/R Account default, and the sales tax code. (*Hint: If the GL Account field and A/R Account field do* not *display Account Nos. 40000 and 11000, refer* step 1, page xix *The Hide General Ledger Accounts boxes should be unchecked.*)

3. Type **7** in the Invoice date field and press **<Enter>**. Since the invoice is printed later, skip the Invoice # field. When the invoice is printed, the invoices are numbered automatically. (*Hint: If you do* not *have a printer, type* **101** *in the Invoice # field.*)

4. Click on the Quantity field, type **2** and press **<Enter>**.

5. In the Item field, click 🔍. Select **001hardware** for hardware.

6. In the Description field, type **Two doorknobs** and press **<Enter>**.

Notice that the GL Account,[4] Unit Price, Amount field, A/R Account, and Sales Tax Code are automatically completed.

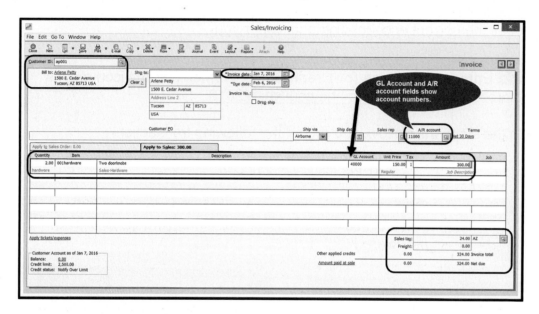

Printing Sales Invoices

When you print the sales invoice, it also posts the transaction to the Sales Journal. To print this sales invoice, follow these steps:

1. Click [Print]. (If you do not have a printer, click on the down-arrow next to Print > select Print Preview.)

2. The Print Forms: Invoices window appears. Click [Select Form].

3. The Print Forms: Invoices/Pkg. Slips window appears. If necessary, select Invoice.

---

[4]If the G/L Account field and A/R Account fields are *not* displayed on your Sales/Invoicing window, click on Options, Global. Make sure the boxes in the Hide General Ledger Accounts section are unchecked.

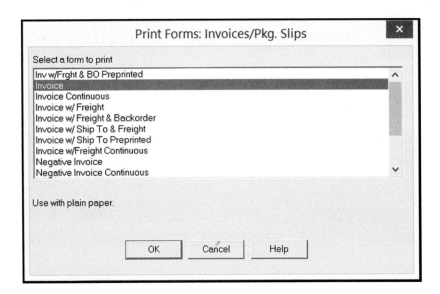

4. Click OK.

5. The Print Forms [or Preview Forms]: Invoices window appears. The First invoice number field shows 101. Subsequent invoices are numbered consecutively. The Use this form field shows Invoice.

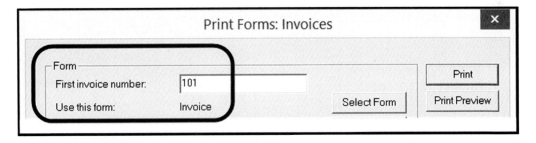

6. Click Print [or Print Preview]. The invoice starts to print. (*Hint:* When you print the invoice, it also posts to the sales journal.) If you are not connected to a printer, you post (save) the invoice *after* displaying it. Since you are not printing, an invoice number is not automatically generated. If needed, type the invoice number in the Invoice # field. Refer to the paragraph below the displayed invoice on the next page.

Wendy's Service Merchandise
1341 Farrington Road
Tucson, AZ 85750
USA

Voice: 520-555-3900
Fax: 520-555-3902

INVOICE

Invoice Number: 101
Invoice Date: Jan 7, 2016
Page: 1

Bill To:	Ship to:
Arlene Petty 1500 E. Cedar Avenue Tucson, AZ 85713 USA	Arlene Petty 1500 E. Cedar Avenue Tucson, AZ 85713 USA

Customer ID	Customer PO	Payment Terms
ap001		Net 30 Days

Sales Rep ID	Shipping Method	Ship Date	Due Date
	Airborne		2/6/16

Quantity	Item	Description	Unit Price	Amount
2.00	001hardware	Two doorknobs	150.00	300.00

Subtotal		300.00
Sales Tax		24.00
Total Invoice Amount		324.00
Payment/Credit Applied		
TOTAL		**324.00**

Check/Credit Memo No:

If you are not connected to a printer, close the Print Preview window. On the Sales/Invoicing window, type **101** in the Invoice No. field, select <u>S</u>ave to post.

How to fix?
The form you select is tied to the kind of printer you are using. If your invoice does not print, you should select a different form to print. Refer to step 2 on page 484 to change the form for printing invoices.

---

7. The Sales/Invoicing window is ready for the next sales invoice. (*Hint:* When you printed the invoice, the transaction was posted to the sales journal, accounts receivable account in the general ledger, and customer account in the customer ledger. Once the transaction is posted, cost of sales is also calculated. If you displayed the invoice, saving also posts.)

8. Record the following credit sales in the Sales/Invoicing window:

Date	Transaction Description
1/7/16	Sold four rolls of vinyl flooring on account to Denise Crosby. Print Invoice No. 102. (*Hint: Vinyl flooring is classified as floor. Ms. Crosby's sales invoice shows no tax because this sale is made to an out-of-state customer.*)

Wendy's Service Merchandise
1341 Farrington Road
Tucson, AZ 85750
USA

INVOICE

Invoice Number: 102
Invoice Date: Jan 7, 2016
Page: 1

Voice: 520-555-3900
Fax: 520-555-3902

Bill To:
Denise Crosby
3088 Davis Road
Ft. Lauderdale, FL 33309
USA

Ship to:
Denise Crosby
3088 Davis Road
Ft. Lauderdale, FL 33309
USA

Customer ID	Customer PO	Payment Terms	
dc003		Net 30 Days	
Sales Rep ID	**Shipping Method**	**Ship Date**	**Due Date**
	Airborne		2/6/16

Quantity	Item	Description	Unit Price	Amount
4.00	003floor	Four rolls of vinyl flooring	160.00	640.00

Subtotal		640.00
Sales Tax		
Total Invoice Amount		640.00
Payment/Credit Applied		
TOTAL		**640.00**

Check/Credit Memo No:

Date	*Transaction Description*
1/7/16	Sold four pairs of curtains on account to Peter Malin. Print Invoice No.103. (*Hint: Curtains are classified as wall.*)

Wendy's Service Merchandise
1341 Farrington Road
Tucson, AZ 85750
USA

Voice: 520-555-3900
Fax: 520-555-3902

INVOICE

Invoice Number:	103
Invoice Date:	Jan 7, 2016
Page:	1

Bill To:

Peter Malin
7009 Western Avenue
Tucson, AZ 85717
USA

Ship to:

Peter Malin
7009 Western Avenue
Tucson, AZ 85717
USA

Customer ID	Customer PO	Payment Terms	
pm005		Net 30 Days	
Sales Rep ID	**Shipping Method**	**Ship Date**	**Due Date**
	Airborne		2/6/16

Quantity	Item	Description	Unit Price	Amount
4.00	002wall	Four pairs of curtains	100.00	400.00

Subtotal		400.00
Sales Tax		32.00
Total Invoice Amount		432.00
Payment/Credit Applied		
TOTAL		**432.00**

Check/Credit Memo No:

Date

Transaction Description

1/7/16   Sold three curtain rods on account to Jessica Prince. Print
Invoice No. 104. (*Hint: Curtain rods are classified as
hardware.*)

Wendy's Service Merchandise
1341 Farrington Road
Tucson, AZ 85750
USA

INVOICE

Invoice Number: 104
Invoice Date: Jan 7, 2016
Page: 1

Voice: 520-555-3900
Fax: 520-555-3902

Bill To:	Ship to:
Jessica Prince 9001 Second Street Tucson, AZ 85704 USA	Jessica Prince 9001 Second Street Tucson, AZ 85704 USA

Customer ID	Customer PO	Payment Terms	
jp004		Net 30 Days	
Sales Rep ID	**Shipping Method**	**Ship Date**	**Due Date**
	Airborne		2/6/16

Quantity	Item	Description	Unit Price	Amount
3.00	001 hardware	Three curtain rods	150.00	450.00

Subtotal		450.00
Sales Tax		36.00
Total Invoice Amount		486.00
Payment/Credit Applied		
TOTAL		**486.00**

Check/Credit Memo No:

Entering a Service Invoice

Wendy's Service Merchandise sells and repairs household items. When repairs are done, a **service invoice** is used. A service invoice is an alternative to the standard invoice. It is used when you want to create an invoice without inventory items.

Follow these steps to enter a service invoice:

Date   *Transaction Description*

1/10/16   Repaired curtains for Bonni Berman, $49.89, plus
                 sales tax of $3.99, for a total of $53.88.

1. From the Sales/Invoicing window, click [Layout]. Then select
    <Predefined> Service.

    The Sales/Invoicing window changes to include only the information
    necessary for a service invoice. This means that you no longer can
    select inventory items. When you complete the service transaction,

    click [Layout] again. Then, you are ready to enter an inventory sale on
    the Sales/Invoicing window.

2. In the Customer ID field, select Bonni Berman.

3. Type **10** in the Invoice date field, then press **<Enter>**.

4. Click on the Description field. Type **Repair** and press **<Enter>**.

5. In the GL Account field, select Account No. 40600, Service Fees.

6. Type **49.89** in the Amount field. Compare your Sales/Invoicing
    window to the one shown on the next page.

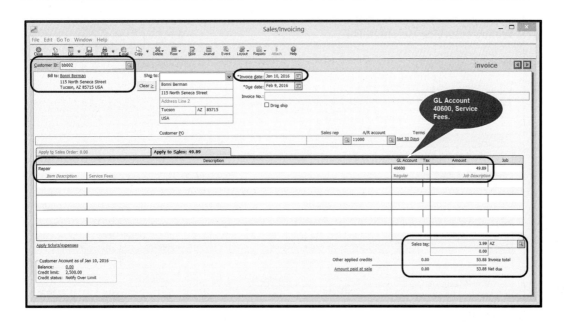

7. Print Invoice No. 105 and compare it to the one shown on the next page.

Wendy's Service Merchandise
1341 Farrington Road
Tucson, AZ 85750
USA

INVOICE

Invoice Number: 105
Invoice Date: Jan 10, 2016
Page: 1

Voice: 520-555-3900
Fax: 520-555-3902

Bill To:	Ship to:
Bonni Berman 115 North Seneca Street Tucson, AZ 85715 USA	Bonni Berman 115 North Seneca Street Tucson, AZ 85715 USA

Customer ID	Customer PO	Payment Terms	
bb002		Net 30 Days	
Sales Rep ID	**Shipping Method**	**Ship Date**	**Due Date**
	Airborne		2/9/16

Quantity	Item	Description	Unit Price	Amount
		Repair		49.89

			Subtotal	49.89
			Sales Tax	3.99
			Total Invoice Amount	53.88
Check/Credit Memo No:			Payment/Credit Applied	
			TOTAL	**53.88**

If you are not connected to a printer, close the Print Preview window. On the Sales/Invoicing window, type **105** in the Invoice No. field, then click <<u>S</u>ave> to post.

8. Click  > then <Predefined> Product. Click .

Sales Returns: Credits & Returns

A sales return, or credit memo, is used when merchandise is returned by a customer. Credit memos for sales returns are entered similarly to vendor credit memos.

Before you can apply a credit, you must post the invoice. Invoice Nos. 101–105 were posted to the sales journal when you printed (or saved) the sales invoices (see pages 486-492). This work must be completed *before* you can apply a sales return. When a credit memo is entered, select the customer's ID code and the appropriate invoice number. Then, the return will be applied to that invoice and the customer's account balance will be adjusted.

In the steps that follow, you record the following transaction:

Date	Transaction Description
1/14/16	Peter Malin returned one pair of curtains that he purchased on January 6, Invoice No. 103. He also paid the balance of that invoice.

1. From the Customers & Sales Navigation Center, select New Credit Memo.

2. In the Customer ID field, select Peter Malin.

3. In the Credit date field, type **14** and press **<Enter>**.

4. Type **CM103** in the Credit No. field. (CM is an abbreviation for Credit Memo> use the sales invoice number to identify the credit memo.) Press **<Enter>**.

5. The Apply to Invoice No. tab is selected. Click on the down-arrow and select 103.

6. Type **1** in the Returned field. Press **<Enter>**

7. Type **Returned one pair of curtains** in the Description field.

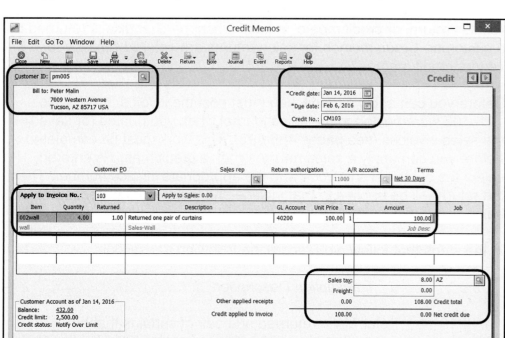

8. Click [Save] to post, then click [Close].

Apply a sales return: Follow these steps.

1. From the Customers & Sales Navigation Center, select [Receive Money] > Receive Money From Customer. At the Select a Cash Account window, accept the default for Southern Bank by clicking [OK].

2. On the Receive Money window, type **1/14/16** in the Deposit ticket ID field. Press **<Enter>** two times.

3. In the Customer ID field, select Peter Malin.

4. In the Check/Reference No. field, type **Invoice 103** then press **<Enter>** key two times.

5. In the <u>D</u>ate field, type **14**, then press the **<Enter>** key two times.

6. Observe that the Payment method field displays Check, and that the Cash Account field displays Account No. 10200, Southern Bank. In the Apply to <u>I</u>nvoices list, click on the Pay box. The Receipt amount shown is 324.00 ($432 original invoice - $108, return).

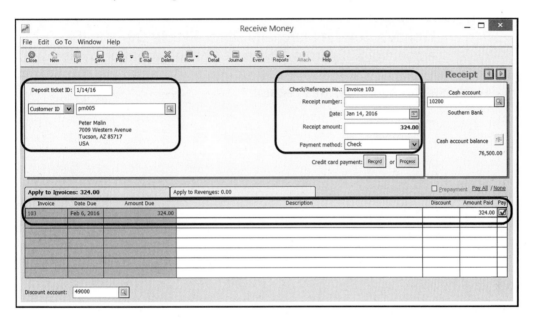

7. Click  to post, then click [Close].

RECORDING RECEIPTS AND CASH SALES

The Receive Money window is used for recording checks, cash, and credit card sales that are received and deposited in the checking account. The information from the Receive Money window is automatically journalized in the Cash Receipts Journal. If the receipt is from a credit customer, then the receipt is posted to the customer's subsidiary ledger as well.

There are two categories for receipts that result from sales:

➢ Receipts for which an invoice was entered in the Sales/Invoicing window.

> Direct sales receipts for which no invoice was entered in the Sales/Invoicing window.

▶ **Entering a Receipt**

| *Date* | *Transaction Description* |

1/21/16   Wendy's Service Merchandise received a check in the amount of $324 from Arlene Petty in payment of Invoice 101.

Follow these steps to enter this receipt:

1. Select [Receive Money] > Receive Money From Customer. The Receive Money window appears.

2. Type **1/21/16** in the Deposit ticket ID field.

3. In the Customer ID field, select Arlene Petty.

4. In the Check/Reference No. field, type **Invoice 101**. (This is the Invoice that is being paid.) Press the **<Enter>** key two times.

5. Type **21** in the Date field.

6. Verify that Account No. 10200, Southern Bank, is displayed in the Cash Account field. The Apply to Invoices tab is selected. Click on the Pay box for Invoice 101. Compare your Receive Money window to the one shown on the next page.

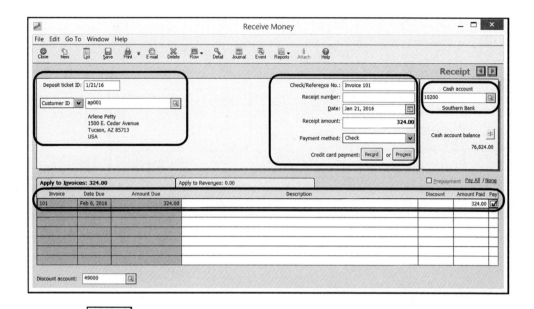

7. Click [Save] to post this receipt. The Receive Money window is ready for another transaction.

In the preceding steps, each customer paid the invoice in full. What if a customer made a partial payment on an invoice?

Date	Transaction Description
1/23/16	Jessica Prince paid $105 on account, Invoice No. 104.

Follow these steps for partial payment:

1. The Receive Money window should be displayed. Type **1/23/16** in the Deposit ticket ID field.

2. Select Jessica Prince as the customer.

3. Type **Invoice 104** in the Check/Reference No. field. Press the **<Enter>** key two times.

4. Type **23** in the Date field. If necessary, in the Payment method field, select Check.

5. Jessica Prince's Invoice number, Date Due, and Amount Due display in the Apply to Invoices table. Click on the Amount Paid field. Type **105** in the Amount Paid field and press **<Enter>**. A check mark is automatically placed in the Pay box.

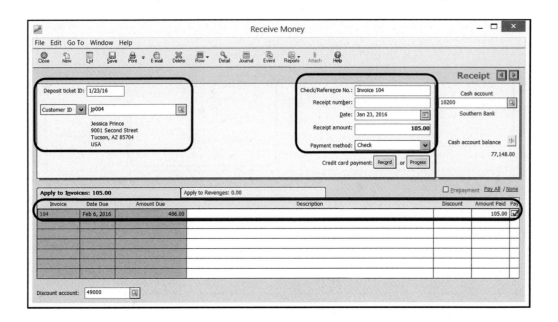

6. Click [Save] to post.

Enter the following receipts:

Date   *Transaction Description*

1/28/16   Received a check in the amount of $53.88 from Bonni Berman in full payment of Invoice No. 105.

1/28/16   Received a check in the amount of $640 from Denise Crosby in full payment of Invoice No. 102.

Cash Sales

Follow these steps to record a cash sale.

Date   *Transaction Description*

1/30/16   Sold two pairs of curtains for cash to Bertha Rabago, $200.

1. On the Receive Money window, type **1/30/16** in the Deposit ticket ID field.

2. Click on the Name field, then type **Bertha Rabago**. You do not enter address information for a cash sale.

3. Since this is a cash sale, type **Cash** in the Check/Reference No. field. Press **<Enter>** two times.

4. Type **30** as the date.

5. If necessary, in the Payment method field, select Check.

6. Verify that account 10200, Southern Bank, is displayed in the Cash Account field.

7. Make sure that the Apply to Revenues tab is selected.

   Sage assumes you are going to apply the receipt to revenue unless you select a customer with open invoices.

   You can also apply a portion of the receipt to both invoices and revenue. You do this by selecting each heading, then entering the distribution information for that portion of the receipt. A running subtotal is kept to show how much of the receipt has been applied.

8. Type **2** in the Quantity field.

9. Select 002wall as the inventory item.

10. Type **Two pairs of curtains** as the Description and press the **<Enter>** key.

11. Observe that the GL Account field, shows Account No. 40200, Sales-Wall (this is the default account). (*Hint:* Make sure the correct sales account is selected.)

12. In the Sales tax field, select AZ. Observe that 16.00 is automatically calculated in the Sales tax field.

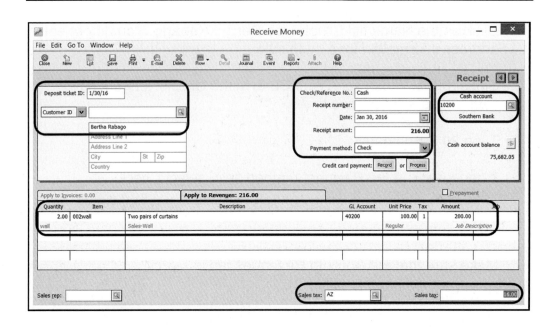

13. Click , then close the Receive Money window.

Finance Charges

Sage 50 includes a feature in the Tasks menu for computing finance or interest charges. This option computes and applies finance charges for customers and/or prints a report listing all finance charges.

You use this feature by selecting the Finance Charge option. You may want to try this out on your own. Use the Tasks menu and select Finance Charge to see how this feature works.

PRINTING CUSTOMER FORMS

Sage 50 provides forms for the following types of customer correspondence:

➢ Invoices.

➢ Statements.

➢ Mailing labels.

➢ Collection letters.

These reports can be accessed by selecting Reports & Forms from the menu bar, then Forms. Select a predefined form to print customer information or design your own form. In Part 4 of this book you will learn more about Custom Forms.

Printing Invoices

You can print a single invoice from the Sales/Invoicing window by selecting [Print]. This saves and prints the invoice.

A batch of invoices can be printed from the Reports & Forms menu by selecting Forms, then Invoices and Packing Slips. There are several types of predefined invoices available for printing customer information or you can design your own form.

Printing Statements

The information that is printed on customer statements is defined in the Statement/Invoices Defaults which are set up from the Maintain menu. You can set up collection letters and also select from these print options.

➤ Whether to print your company name, address, phone, and fax on the statement.

➤ Whether to print zero and credit balance statements.

➤ The minimum balance necessary to print a statement.

➤ The number of grace days before printing a statement.

➤ Whether to print statements for accounts with no activity.

You can print or display statements. Or, if you want to display customer information before printing, display or print the customer ledger.

Statements can be printed from the Reports & Forms menu by selecting Forms, then Invoices and Packing Slips. There are several types of predefined statements available for printing customer account balances. Select the form that best suits your needs. As mentioned before, you can also design your own statement.

When the statements stop printing, a message box displays, asking if the statements printed okay and if you want to update the customer file. Look at your printed statements carefully before you answer Yes to this question. When you answer Yes, Sage records the statement date in the customer record. This is used as the balance brought forward date the next time you print a statement. This way the ending balance on one statement is the same as the beginning balance on the next statement.

You should enter, print, and post all invoices prior to printing statements. In this way the Balance Forward amounts are correct from month to month.

Printing Mailing Labels

Labels can be printed by selecting the Reports & Forms menu, Accounts Receivable, Forms, then Customer Labels and Letters. Select one of the Customer Labels, then print. There are several predefined labels available for printing. You can elect to use these forms or design your own. When printing labels you can do the following.

➢ Select a range of customers.

➢ Enter all or part of a zip code to limit the mailing labels to customers in a certain area.

➢ Print labels for customers, prospects, or both.

➢ Enter a Status for customers so that you print labels for all, active, or inactive customers.

➢ Enter a Type Code for customers so that only customers of a specific Type Code will print.

Preparing Collection Letters

What if credit customers are slow to pay their bills? Collection letters can play an important role in generating revenue from customers who are slow to pay off their balances. Sometimes just a friendly reminder is all that is needed.

The table below shows how important it is to get paid on time because the longer a bill remains unpaid, the less chance there is of collecting.

Number of Days Overdue	Percent Uncollectible
1 to 30 days	2%
31 to 60 days	10%
61 to 90 days	20%
91 to 180 days	30%
181 to 365 days	50%
over 365 days	90%

Collection letters are an effective way to remind customers to pay their unpaid balances. Most customers will pay after they receive a friendly reminder of a past-due account. It is worthwhile to send these letters because past-due amounts can be a burden on a company's cash flow.

Depending on how late the payment is, collection letters vary in tone and urgency. For example, a friendly reminder may be all that's needed for someone who is 30 days past due, but a different letter may be needed for someone who is more than 90 days past due. Remember that while it is important to collect past-due amounts, you would also like to keep the customer.

Sage 50's letters are grouped by lateness of payment and severity of tone. The less than 30 days overdue letter is soft while the 61-90 days overdue letter is much firmer. You may edit all of these letters to suit your needs.

To print a collection letter you use the analysis menu. Follow these steps to do that:

1. From the menu bar, select Analysis > Collection Manager.

2. Type **1/31/16** in the As of Date field. Press **<Enter>**. The Collection Aging bar graph appears.

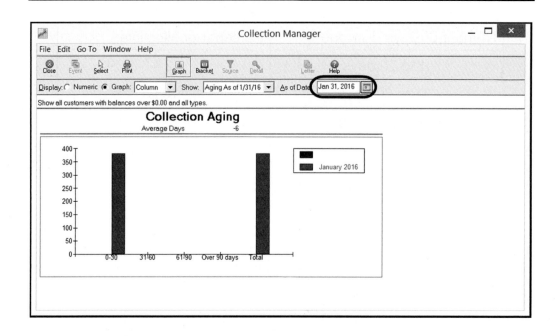

3. Click 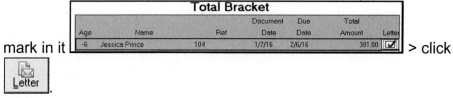 Bracket . The Total Bracket table lists an invoice for Jessica Prince.

4. Click on the Letter box on the Total Bracket table to place a check

	Total Bracket					
Age	Name	Ref	Document Date	Due Date	Total Amount	Letter
-6	Jessica Prince	104	1/7/16	2/6/16	381.00	☑

mark in it ... > click

Letter .

5. The Print Forms: Collection Letters window appears. Click

Select Form . You may want to try one of these selections and see what Sage 50's collection letters look like. The sample letters are sorted as follows.

   ➤ Overdue < 30 Days - Soft
   ➤ Overdue >90 Days
   ➤ Overdue >90 Days – Coll Agency
   ➤ Overdue 31-60 Days - Medium
   ➤ Overdue 61-90 Days - Firm

6. Select a form to print, then click   OK   .

7. Click [Print]. A collection letter prints. Read the letter that you printed. The collection letter that prints is an example. When the window prompts, Did the collection letters print properly?, click [Yes]. Since Ms. Prince does *not* have an overdue bill, no amount shows in the letter's Amount Overdue field.

8. Close the Collection Manager.

FINANCIAL MANAGER

The *Financial Manager* provides a brief, overall financial picture of how your business is performing. By default, the first window you see is a numeric table of summary data consisting of various business ratios. Both the Business Summary and Key Balances can be displayed.

1. From the menu bar, select Analysis > Financial Manager.

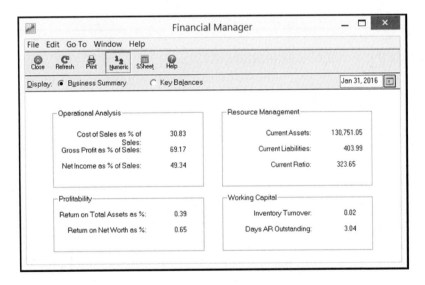

The radio button next to Business Summary is the default. The information is separated into four areas: Operational Analysis, Resource Management, Profitability, and Working Capital. Ratios are shown within each area.

2. Select the Key Balances radio button. Within Key Balances, Specific asset and liability balances are shown. The Operations column shows key balances from the income statement. Current and Year

to Date amounts are shown but since Wendy's Service Merchandise data is only for one year, those columns are the same. The cash balance is the total of Southern Bank and Tucson Savings & Loan: 75,898.05 + 22,000.00 = 97,898.05.

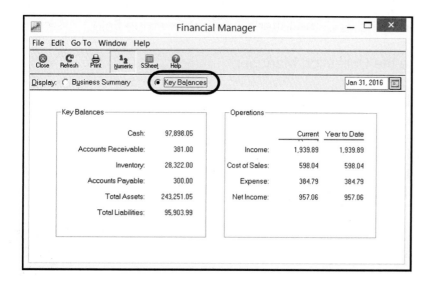

3. Close the Financial Manager.

PRINTING THE SALES JOURNAL

The Sales/Invoicing window is the Sales Journal. Credit sales are recorded in the Sales/Invoicing window. Follow these steps to print the Sales Journal:

1. From the Recently Used Customer Reports area on the Customers & Sales Navigation Center, link to <u>Print</u> or <u>View</u> the Sales Journal.

2. If you linked to <u>Print</u>, If the Modify Report – Sales Journal window appears. Click OK Make the selections to print. Compare your sales journal report to the one shown on the next page.

			Wendy's Service Merchandise		
			Sales Journal		
			For the Period From Jan 1, 2016 to Jan 31, 2016		
Filter Criteria includes: Report order is by Invoice/CM Date. Report is printed in Detail Format.					
Date	**Account ID**	**Invoice/CM #**	**Line Description**	**Debit Amnt**	**Credit Amnt**
1/7/16	23100	101	AZ: Arizona Dept. of Revenue		24.00
	40000		Two doorknobs		300.00
	50000		Cost of sales	100.00	
	12000		Cost of sales		100.00
	11000		Arlene Petty	324.00	
1/7/16	40400	102	Four rolls of vinyl flooring		640.00
	57000		Cost of sales	216.00	
	12000		Cost of sales		216.00
	11000		Denise Crosby	640.00	
1/7/16	23100	103	AZ: Arizona Dept. of Revenue		32.00
	40200		Four pairs of curtains		400.00
	50500		Cost of sales	120.00	
	12000		Cost of sales		120.00
	11000		Peter Malin	432.00	
1/7/16	23100	104	AZ: Arizona Dept. of Revenue		36.00
	40000		Three curtain rods		450.00
	50000		Cost of sales	150.00	
	12000		Cost of sales		150.00
	11000		Jessica Prince	486.00	
1/10/16	23100	105	AZ: Arizona Dept. of Revenue		3.99
	40600		Repair		49.89
	11000		Bonni Berman	53.88	
1/14/16	23100	CM103	AZ: Arizona Dept. of Revenue	8.00	
	40200		Returned one pair of curtains	100.00	
	50500		Cost of sales		30.00
	12000		Cost of sales	30.00	
	11000		Peter Malin		108.00
		Total		2,659.88	2,659.88

PRINTING THE CASH RECEIPTS JOURNAL

The Receive Money window is the Cash Receipts Journal. Payments from customers and cash sales are recorded in the Receive Money window. Follow these steps to print the Cash Receipts Journal.

1. From the Recently Used Customer Reports area on the Customers & Sales Navigation Center, link to Print or View the Cash Receipts Journal. If the Cash Receipts Journal is not listed, link to View All Customer & Sales Reports. (Or, from the menu bar select Reports, then Accounts Receivable, then highlight Cash Receipts Journal.)

				Wendy's Service Merchandise

Wendy's Service Merchandise
Cash Receipts Journal
For the Period From Jan 1, 2016 to Jan 31, 2016

Filter Criteria includes: Report order is by Check Date. Report is printed in Detail Format.

Date	Account ID	Transaction Ref	Line Description	Debit Am	Credit A
1/14/16	11000	Invoice 103	Invoice: 103		324.00
	10200		Peter Malin	324.00	
1/21/16	11000	Invoice 101	Invoice: 101		324.00
	10200		Arlene Petty	324.00	
1/23/16	11000	Invoice 104	Invoice: 104		105.00
	10200		Jessica Prince	105.00	
1/28/16	11000	Invoice 105	Invoice: 105		53.88
	10200		Bonni Berman	53.88	
1/28/16	11000	Invoice 102	Invoice: 102		640.00
	10200		Denise Crosby	640.00	
1/30/16	23100	Cash	AZ: Arizona Dept. of Revenue		16.00
	40200		Two pairs of curtains		200.00
	50500		Cost of sales	60.00	
	12000		Cost of sales		60.00
	10200		Bertha Rabago	216.00	
				1,722.88	1,722.88

2. If you linked to <u>Print</u>, The Modify Report - Cash Receipts Journal window displays. Click [OK] Make the selections to print.

PRINTING THE CUSTOMER LEDGERS

Follow these steps to print the Customer Ledgers for Wendy's Service Merchandise:

1. From the Recently Used Customer Reports area on the Customers & Sales Navigation Center, link to <u>View All Customer & Sales Reports</u>. The Select a Report or Form window appears.

2. In the Accounts Receivable: Customers and Sales list, select Customer Ledgers. Then, make the selections to display or print.

Wendy's Service Merchandise
Customer Ledgers
For the Period From Jan 1, 2016 to Jan 31, 2016

Filter Criteria includes: Report order is by ID. Report is printed in Detail Format.

Customer ID Customer	Date	Trans No	Type	Debit Amt	Credit Amt	Balance
ap001 Arlene Petty	1/7/16 1/21/16	101 Invoice 101	SJ CRJ	324.00	324.00	324.00 0.00
bb002 Bonni Berman	1/10/16 1/28/16	105 Invoice 105	SJ CRJ	53.88	53.88	53.88 0.00
dc003 Denise Crosby	1/7/16 1/28/16	102 Invoice 102	SJ CRJ	640.00	640.00	640.00 0.00
jp004 Jessica Prince	1/7/16 1/23/16	104 Invoice 104	SJ CRJ	486.00	105.00	486.00 381.00
pm005 Peter Malin	1/7/16 1/14/16 1/14/16	103 CM103 Invoice 103	SJ SJ CRJ	432.00	108.00 324.00	432.00 324.00 0.00
Report Total				**1,935.88**	**1,554.88**	**381.00**

PRINTING THE GENERAL LEDGER TRIAL BALANCE

1. In the Reports list, highlight General Ledger. Then, in the General Ledger: Account Information list highlight General Ledger Trial Balance.

2. Make the selections to display or print. Compare your general ledger trial balance to the one shown on the next page.

	Wendy's Service Merchandise		
	General Ledger Trial Balance		
	As of Jan 31, 2016		

Filter Criteria includes: Report order is by ID. Report is printed in Detail Format.

Account ID	Account Description	Debit Amt	Credit Amt
10200	Southern Bank	75,898.05	
10400	Tucson Savings & Loan	22,000.00	
11000	Accounts Receivable	381.00	
12000	Merchandise Inventory	28,322.00	
13000	Supplies	1,750.00	
14000	Prepaid Insurance	2,400.00	
15000	Furniture and Fixtures	5,000.00	
15100	Computers & Equipment	7,500.00	
15500	Building	100,000.00	
20000	Accounts Payable		300.00
23100	Sales Tax Payable		103.99
27000	Long-Term Notes Payable		20,500.00
27400	Mortgage Payable		75,000.00
39006	Alex Ziegler, Capital		73,695.00
39007	Alex Ziegler, Drawing	500.00	
39008	Wendy Lincoln, Capital		73,695.00
39009	Wendy Lincoln, Drawing	500.00	
40000	Sales-Hardware		750.00
40200	Sales-Wall		500.00
40400	Sales-Floor		640.00
40600	Service Fees		49.89
50000	Cost of Sales-Hardware	250.00	
50500	Cost of Sales-Wall	150.00	
57000	Cost of Sales-Floor	216.00	
59500	Purchase Discounts		17.96
70000	Maintenance Expense	160.00	
73500	Postage Expense	45.00	
75500	Supplies Expense	107.65	
76000	Telephone Expense	72.14	
	Total:	245,251.84	245,251.84

EDITING RECEIPTS

Is your Customer Ledger correct? Jessica Prince's account is used to show how to edit the Customer Ledger. Follow these steps to see how the editing feature works:

1. From the Customers & Sales Navigation Center, select **Receive Money** > View and Edit Money Received.

2. The Receipt List appears. Click on Invoice 104, $105.00 to highlight it.

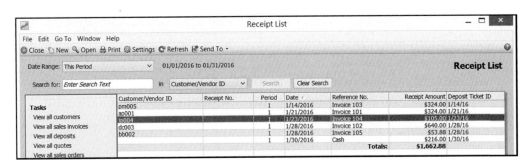

3. Click [🔍 Open]. The original Receive Money window with Jessica Prince's partial payment appears. Make any necessary corrections, then <Save>.

4. Close the Receive Money window and Receipt List window.

BACKING UP CHAPTER 13 DATA

Back up. (*Hint:* Close all windows before backing up.) This backup saves your data to this point, including Chapter 12 and Chapter 13's work with Wendy's [your first name] Service Merchandise. The suggested file name is **Chapter 13**.

EXPORT REPORTS TO EXCEL

1. Export the following Sage 50 reports to Excel:

   - Sales Journal
   - Cash Receipts Journal
   - Customer Ledgers
   - General Ledger Trial Balance.

2. Use the file name **Chapter 13_ SJ_ CRJ_ CL_GLTB.xlsx**.

   NOTE: If your instructor would like you to save the Sales Journal, Cash Receipts Journal, Customer Ledgers, and General Ledger Trial Balance as PDF files, do that. The suggested file name is **Chapter 13_Sales Journal.pdf**, etc.

ONLINE LEARNING CENTER

Complete end-of-chapter activities at <u>www.mhhe.com/yacht2016</u> >
<u>Student Edition</u>, then Chapter 13.

1. Quizzes: Multiple Choice and True False questions. Interactive
   online tests that are graded and can be emailed to your instructor.

2. More Resources:

   a. QA Templates: Answer 10 multiple-choice questions and one
      Analysis Question.
   b. Videos: Watch the Sales Invoice and Customer Payments videos.
   c. Narrated PowerPoints: Listen to the narrated PowerPoints.
   d. Going to the Net Exercises: Read information about accounts
      receivable on the Business Owner's Toolkit website.
   e. Assessment Rubric: Complete the rubric to review Sage 50's
      journals, navigation centers, modules, task windows, and reports.

The OLC also includes links to the Appendixes:

- Appendix A: Troubleshooting
- Appendix B: Accounting Information Systems
- Appendix C: Review of Accounting Principles
- Appendix D: Glossary (words that are boldfaced and italicized in
  chapter)

Exercise 13-1: You must complete Exercises 12-1 and 12-2 before
starting Exercise 13-1.

1. Start Sage 50. Open the company that you set up in Exercise 12-1
   on pages 458-459, Your last name Sales and Service.

2. If necessary, restore your data from Exercise 12-2. (*Hint:* This backup
   was made on page 467.) To make sure you are starting in the right
   place, display Exercise 12-2's general ledger trial balance (step 6,
   page 466).

   FYI: You can restore from your back up file even if <u>no</u> company exists. From the startup
   window, select File > Restore > select the location of your backup file. On the Restore
   Wizard's Select Company window, choose *Create a new company using the restored data*
   which restores your backup data and sets up the company. For more information, refer to
   Troubleshooting, pages 279-280.

3. If necessary, enter the following customer defaults:

   a. Standard Terms: Due in number of days

   b. Net due in: 30 days
       Discount in: 0 days
       Discount %:   0.00
       Credit Limit: 2,500.00
       GL Sales Account: 40000 Sales Hardware
       Discount GL Account: 49000 Sales Discounts

4. Set up GA sales taxes. The sales tax rate is 8.00%. (*Hint:* Refer to pages 473-478. Use Georgia Dept. of Revenue and Georgia sales tax.)

5. Enter the following customers:

   a. Customer ID: **ac001**
       Name: **Aaron Costa**
       Billing address: **4318 Eastern Blvd.**
       City, ST, Zip: **Norcross, GA 30092**
       Country: **USA**
       Sales Tax: **GA**
       Customer type: **GWI** (for Gwinnett County)
       Telephone 1:   **770-555-2621**
       Fax: **770-555-2694**
       E-mail: **info@aaroncosta.com**
       Web site: **www.aaroncosta.com**

       In the Sales Info tab, select the GL Sales Acct 40200, Sales-Tools for Aaron Costa.

   b. Customer ID: **bb002**
       Name: **Bryan Burris**
       Billing address: **45062 Camelback Road**
       City, ST, Zip: **Atlanta, GA 30343**
       Country: **USA**
       Sales tax: **GA**
       Customer type: **FUL** (for Fulton County)
       Telephone 1:   **404-555-0920**
       Fax: **404-555-0922**
       E-mail: **info@bryanburris.net**

Web site: **www.bryanburris.net**

In the Sales Info tab, select the GL Sales Acct 40000, Sales-Hardware for Bryan Burris.

c. Customer ID: **rn003**
Name: **Rose Norris**
Billing address: **3220 College Lane**
City, ST, Zip: **Atlanta, GA 30303**
Country: **USA**
Sales tax: **GA**
Customer type: **FUL**
Telephone 1: **404-555-2418**
Fax: **404-555-4262**
E-mail: **info@rosenorris.com**
Web site: **www.rosenorris.com**

In the Sales Info tab, select the GL Sales Acct 40000, Sales-Hardware for Rose Norris.

6. Make a backup of your work. (Use **Exercise 13-1** as the file name.)

Exercise 13-2: Exercise 13-1 must be completed before Exercise 13-2.

1. Start Sage 50. Open your last name Sales and Service company.

2. If necessary, restore the Exercise 13-1.ptb file.

3. Record the following transactions:

1/7/16   Sold five tool kits on account to Aaron Costa, Customer ac001. Type **101** in the Invoice No. field. Subsequent invoices will be numbered automatically.

1/7/16   Sold three hardware sets on account to Bryan Burris, Customer bb002.

1/7/16   Sold six hardware sets on account to Rose Norris, Customer rn003.

1/10/16   Aaron Costa returned one of the tool kits that he purchased on January 7, Invoice No. 101, CM101. Mr. Costa also paid the balance of Invoice 101. (*Hint: This transaction requires two entries*. If necessary, select Account No. 10200, First Interstate as the cash account.)

1/14/16   Received a check in full payment of Invoice No. 102 from Bryan Burris.

1/17/16   Sold two hardware sets *and* two tool kits for cash to Laura McFadden. (*Hint:* Remember to enter two quantities and two items. Make sure GA sales tax is being charged.)

1/18/16   Sold three tool kits for cash to Randy Hunt.

4. Print the Sales Journal, Cash Receipts Journal, Customer Ledgers, and General Ledger Trial Balance.

Check Your Figures:

10200, First Interstate:	$65,746.63
11000, Accounts Receivable	972.00
12000, Merchandise Inventory	14,570.00
23100, Sales Tax Payable	193.20
40000, Sales-Hardware	1,650.00
40200, Sales-Tools	765.00

5. Print the Financial Manager's Business Summary and Key Balances.

6. Backup. Use **Exercise 13-2** as the file name.

7. Export the following reports to Excel: Sales Journal, Cash Receipts Journal, Customer Ledgers, General Ledger Trial Balance. Use the file name **Exercise 13-2_SJ_CRJ_CL_GLTB.xlsx**.

8. Save these files as PDFs: Sales Journal.pdf, Cash Receipts Journal.pdf, Customer Ledgers.pdf, and General Ledger Trial Balance.pdf. The suggested file name is Exercise 13-2_Sales Journal.pdf, etc.

CHAPTER 13 INDEX

Chapter

14 Inventory & Services

LEARNING OBJECTIVES

1. Restore data from Chapter 13. (This backup was made on page 510.)
2. Enter inventory maintenance and default information.
3. Enter inventory item information, including Sales account, Merchandise Inventory account, and Cost of Sales account.
4. Enter item codes when recording purchases and sales.
5. Enter inventory adjustments.
6. Compare Chapter 14's Financial Manager's Business Summary and Key Balances to Chapter 13's Financial Manager.
7. Make three backups, save two Excel files, and save five PDF files.

Merchandise inventory includes all goods owned by the business and held for sale. The account used for merchandise inventory is Account No. 12000, Merchandise Inventory.

Sage 50's inventory system tracks inventory items at both the purchasing and sales level. When you set up an inventory item, you establish the General Ledger accounts that are updated by purchases and sales. Sage 50 keeps track of cost of goods sold, stock levels, sales prices, and vendors.

Sage uses a perpetual inventory system. In a perpetual inventory system a *merchandising business* continuously updates inventory each time an item is purchased or sold.

Inventory calculations include FIFO, LIFO, and average cost methods. The *FIFO* (first in, first out) method assumes that the items in the beginning inventory are sold first. The *LIFO* (last in, first out) method assumes that the goods received last are sold first. The average cost method (also known as weighted average method) is the default for inventory items sold. The formula used is: Average Cost x Quantity Sold = Cost of Sales.

Sage tracks the inventory items that you buy and sell. After you post, the cost and quantity of each inventory item is updated automatically. Generally, all of your inventory should use the same costing method.

Tracking inventory is a three-step process:

➢ Enter item information, including Sales account, Merchandise Inventory account, and Cost of Sales account.

➢ Use item codes when entering purchases and sales. Sage automatically calculates and tracks average cost, which is the default, using this to calculate and enter the Cost of Sales. You can change the cost method to LIFO (last in, first out) or FIFO (first in, first out). This chapter explains these inventory cost methods in detail.

➢ If necessary, enter inventory adjustments.

Sage does the rest automatically: adjusts inventory levels each time you post a purchase or sale of an inventory item, tracks the cost of each item, and makes a Cost of Goods Sold journal entry at the end of the accounting period.

COST METHODS

There are three types of inventory cost methods: average cost, LIFO, and FIFO. Once you select the costing method for an inventory item, you cannot change it if transactions have been posted. Therefore, if you want to change the cost method for an item with posted transactions, you must enter the item again.

Average Cost

When you set up inventory items for Wendy's Service Merchandise, you selected the Average cost method. In Chapter 12, Wendy's Service Merchandise purchased four pairs of curtains from Ronnie Becker Fabrics for $30 each (Invoice 210, page 437). What happens when these curtains are sold?

The journal entries would look like this:

Purchased four pairs of curtains from Ronnie Becker Fabrics at $30 each (Invoice 210, page 437). The account distribution is shown on the next page.

Account ID	Account Description, Purchase Invoice 210	Debit	Credit
12000	Merchandise Inventory	120.00	
20000/RBF08	Accounts Payable/Ronnie Becker Fabrics		120.00

Sold four pairs of curtains to Peter Malin for $100 each (Invoice 103, page 488).

Account ID	Account Description, Sales Invoice 103	Debit	Credit
50500	Cost of Sales-Wall	120.00	
11000/pm005	Accounts Receivable/Peter Malin	432.00	
12000	Merchandise Inventory		120.00
40200	Sales-Wall		400.00
23100	Sales Tax Payable		32.00

You can see from these journal entries that the Merchandise Inventory account is updated with each purchase and sale. After these transactions, the balance in Merchandise Inventory looks like this:

Merchandise Inventory, Account No. 12000

Purchased inventory	120.00	Sold Inventory	120.00
Balance	0.00		

LIFO (Last In, First Out)

The LIFO (last in, first out) method of inventory pricing assumes that the last goods received are sold first. LIFO assumes that cost is based on replacement and that the last price paid for merchandise is more accurate.

Accountants recommend that you select LIFO when you desire to charge the most recent inventory costs against revenue. LIFO yields the lowest amount of net income in periods of rising costs because the cost of the most recently acquired inventory more closely approximates the replacement cost.

FIFO (First In, First Out)

The FIFO (first in, first out) method of inventory pricing assumes that the items in the beginning inventory are sold first. FIFO costs your sales and values your inventory as if the items you sell are the ones that you have had in stock for the longest time.

Accountants recommend that you select FIFO when you desire to charge costs against revenue in the order in which costs occur. FIFO yields a higher amount of profit during periods of rising costs. This happens because merchandise was acquired prior to the increase in cost.

TYPES OF INVENTORY ITEMS

There are nine types of inventory items:

➢ Stock item: This is the default in the Item Class list. It is the traditional inventory item where the program tracks descriptions, unit prices, stock quantities, and cost of sales. For stock items, you should complete the entire window. Once an item has been designated as a stock item, the type cannot be changed.

➢ Master Stock Item: Sage uses this item class as a special item that does not represent inventory stocked but contains information (item attributes) shared with a number of substock items.

➢ Non-stock item: Sage tracks the description and a unit price for sales. You can also track default accounts. You might use this type for service items such as hours where the unit price is set.

➢ Description only: Sage keeps track of the description of an Inventory Item. This saves time when entering purchases and sales because you don't have to retype the description. You might use this type for service items where the price fluctuates.

➢ Service: This is for services you can apply to your salary and wages account.

➢ Labor: This is for labor you can apply to your salary and wages account. You cannot purchase labor items but you can sell them.

➢ Assembly: You can specify items as assembly items and create a bill of materials for a unit made up of component stock or subassembly items.

➢ Activity item: To indicate how time is spent when performing services for a customer, for a job, or for internal administrative work. Activity items are used with the Time & Billing feature.

➢ Charge item: Expenses recorded by an employee or vendor when company resources are used for a customer or job.

GETTING STARTED

In the preceding chapters, you set up inventory items. The instructions that follow show how to add inventory items to Wendy's Service Merchandise.

1. Start Sage 50. Open Wendy's [your first name] Service Merchandise.

2. If necessary, restore data from the Chapter 13.ptb file. This backup was made on page 511.

💾 To make sure you are starting in the appropriate place in the data (Chapter 13.ptb backup) display the General Ledger Trial Balance.

Wendy's Service Merchandise
General Ledger Trial Balance
As of Jan 31, 2016

Filter Criteria includes: Report order is by ID. Report is printed in Detail Format.

Account ID	Account Description	Debit Amt	Credit Amt
10200	Southern Bank	75,898.05	
10400	Tucson Savings & Loan	22,000.00	
11000	Accounts Receivable	381.00	
12000	Merchandise Inventory	28,322.00	
13000	Supplies	1,750.00	
14000	Prepaid Insurance	2,400.00	
15000	Furniture and Fixtures	5,000.00	
15100	Computers & Equipment	7,500.00	
15500	Building	100,000.00	
20000	Accounts Payable		300.00
23100	Sales Tax Payable		103.99
27000	Long-Term Notes Payable		20,500.00
27400	Mortgage Payable		75,000.00
39006	Alex Ziegler, Capital		73,695.00
39007	Alex Ziegler, Drawing	500.00	
39008	Wendy Lincoln, Capital		73,695.00
39009	Wendy Lincoln, Drawing	500.00	
40000	Sales-Hardware		750.00
40200	Sales-Wall		500.00
40400	Sales-Floor		640.00
40600	Service Fees		49.89
50000	Cost of Sales-Hardware	250.00	
50500	Cost of Sales-Wall	150.00	
57000	Cost of Sales-Floor	216.00	
59500	Purchase Discounts		17.96
70000	Maintenance Expense	160.00	
73500	Postage Expense	45.00	
75500	Supplies Expense	107.65	
76000	Telephone Expense	72.14	
	Total:	245,251.84	245,251.84

INVENTORY DEFAULTS

1. From the Navigation Bar, select 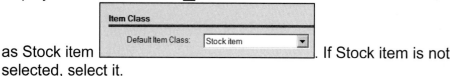 > Set Up Inventory Defaults. The Inventory Item Defaults window displays. Observe that the General tab shows the Default Item Class as Stock item [Item Class / Default Item Class: Stock item]. If Stock item is not selected, select it.

2. Click on the GL Accts/Costing tab. The default for inventory costing is the Average method. Since this is what Wendy's Service Merchandise uses, there is no need to make any changes to this window. These inventory defaults were set up in Chapter 12, pages 424-426.

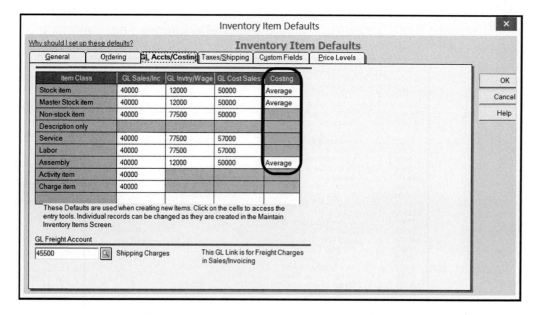

3. Click on the Taxes/Shipping tab.

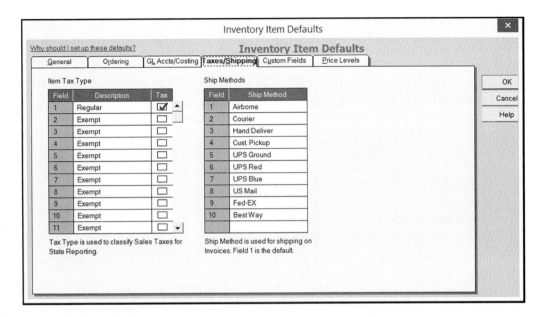

The Regular tax type is selected with a check mark. This is correct because there is an 8% sales tax in Arizona. The Ship Methods that appear on this tab are also shown on the Sales/Invoicing and Purchases/Receive Inventory windows. You can also use these ship methods to set up defaults for customers and vendors.

3. Click [OK] to close this window. (Remember: If you click [Cancel], you close the window without saving any changes.)

ENTERING INVENTORY ITEM MAINTENANCE INFORMATION

Inventory items are set up on the Maintain Inventory Items window. You can establish general ledger accounts, vendors, tax exemptions, sales prices and reorder quantities. The information on the Maintain Inventory Items window displays three active tabs: General, Custom Fields, and History; two tabs are inactive—Bill of Materials, and Item Attributes. Select an active tab to view its fields.

Follow the steps on the next page to enter inventory maintenance information.

1. From the Inventory & Services Navigation Center, select
   > New Inventory Item. The Maintain Inventory Items window
   appears.

2. Complete the following information:

Item ID:	**004lights**
Description:	**lighting**
Item Class:	Stock Item
Description(for Sales):	**light fixtures**
Price Level 1:	**175**
Last Unit Cost:	**64**
Cost Method:	Average
GL Sales Acct:	Add Account No. **40500 Sales-Lights** (Account Type, Income)
GL Inventory Acct:	12000 Merchandise Inventory
GL Cost of Sales Acct:	Add Account No. **57050 Cost of Sales-Lights** (Account Type, Cost of Sales)
Item Tax Type:	1
Item Type:	**lights**
Stocking U/M:	**each**
Minimum Stock:	**8**
Reorder Quantity:	**4**
Preferred Vendor ID:	

   You need to add a new vendor. Click in the Preferred Vendor ID

   field > then . The Maintain Vendors window displays.

Vendor ID:	**TSS09**
Name:	**Tom's Sales and Service**
Mailing Address:	**8300 Tumbleweed Street**
City, ST, Zip:	**Tucson, AZ 85724**
Country:	**USA**
Vendor Type:	**lights**
1099 Type:	**Independent Contractor**
Expense Account:	12000 Merchandise Inventory
Telephone 1:	**520-555-1322**

Fax:	**520-555-1544**
E-Mail:	**info@tomsaleserv.com**
Web Address:	**www.tomsaleserv.com**

Purchase Info:

Tax ID Number: **52-4344313**

a. Click ⊞ Save , then close the Maintain Vendors window. You are returned to the Maintain Inventory Items window. In the Preferred Vendor ID field, select Tom's Sales and Service as the vendor. Click ⊞ Save

b. Click on the Beginning Balances arrow (lower right corner of the Maintain Inventory Items window.) The Inventory Beginning Balances window displays. Select lighting. Complete the following:

Quantity:	125
Unit Cost:	64.00
Total Cost:	8,000.00 (completed automatically)

3. Observe that the Total Beginning Balances field shows 27,740.00. This amount agrees with the Merchandise Inventory balance on page 416 (Chapter 12's January 1, 2016 balance sheet).

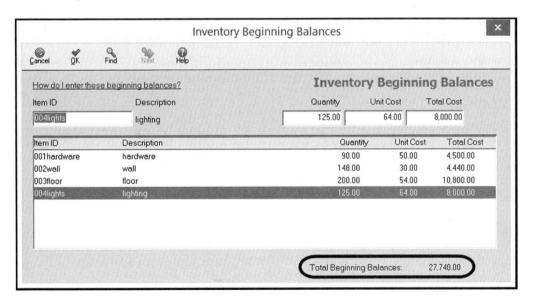

4. Click [OK] to close the Inventory Beginning Balances window.

5. Make sure, TSS09, Tom's Sales and Service, is shown in the Preferred Vendor ID field.

6. Save, then close the Maintain Inventory Items window.

BACKING UP YOUR DATA

Back up. This backup saves your data to this point, including work completed in Chapters 12, 13, and up to this point in Chapter 14 with Wendy's [your first name] Service Merchandise. The suggested file name is **Chapter 14 Begin**.

INVENTORY ADJUSTMENTS

Follow these steps to record a purchase and inventory adjustment.

Date	Transaction Description
1/14/16	Tom's Sales and Service sent Invoice No. 112 for the purchase of eight light fixtures for a unit cost of $64 each, and a total of $512.

1. From the Vendors & Purchases Navigation Center, select [Enter Bills] > New Bill. The Purchases/Receive Inventory window appears. Record the January 14, 2016 transaction. Compare your Purchases/Receive Inventory window with the one shown on the next page.

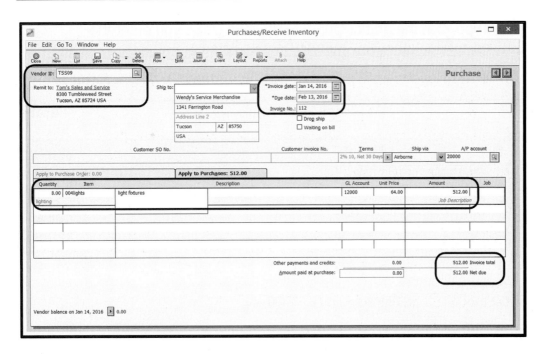

2. Save to post, then close.

Record the following transaction.

Date	Transaction Description
Date	*Transaction Description*

1/16/16   Two light fixtures were damaged when they were dropped on the floor by the owner, Alex Ziegler.

Follow the steps below to make an inventory adjustment.

1. From the Inventory & Services Navigation Center, select ____. The Inventory Adjustments window appears.

2. In the Item ID field, select lighting.

3. In the Reference field, type **AZ** (Alex Ziegler's initials).

4. Type **16** in the Date field.

5. Type **-2** in the Adjust Quantity By field. (After you enter the adjustment, the New quantity is calculated.)

6. In the Reason to Adjust field, type **Two damaged light fixtures**.

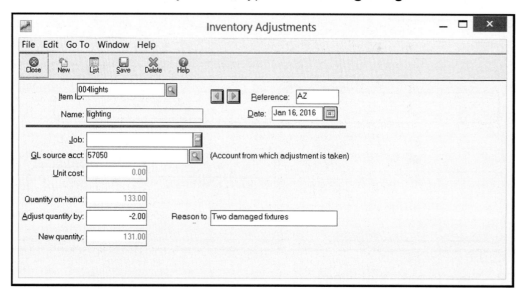

7. Click [Save] to post, then close the Inventory Adjustments window.

ADDITIONAL TRANSACTIONS

Record the following transactions for Wendy's Service Merchandise.

Date	Transaction Description

1/18/16   Sold two doorknobs on account to Arlene Petty. Type **106** in the Invoice No. field. Subsequent invoices will be numbered automatically. (*Hint: Select hardware as the inventory item for doorknobs. Make sure the Sales Tax field shows 24.00, or 8% of the sales amount for AZ sales taxes.*)

1/18/16   Sold two rolls of vinyl flooring on account to Denise Crosby, Invoice No. 107. There is no sales tax because merchandise is being shipped out of state.

1/18/16   Sold two pairs of curtains on account to Peter Malin, Invoice No. 108. (*Hint: Select wall as the inventory item for curtains. Remember to check Sales Tax field for 16.00 AZ sales taxes.*)

1/21/16   Wendy's Service Merchandise completed repair work for Bonni Berman at a cost of $75, plus 6.00 sales taxes, Invoice No. 109. (*Hint: Remember to credit Account No. 40600, Service Fees.*)

1/23/16   Cash sales in the amount of $1,404 ($1,300 plus $104, AZ sales taxes) were deposited at Southern Bank: 10 pairs of curtains, $1,000; 2 doorknobs, $300. (*Hint: Remember to select AZ in the Sales Tax field.*)

1/25/16   Received a check in the amount of $324 from Arlene Petty in full payment of Invoice 106.

1/25/16   Received a check in the amount of $216 from Peter Malin in full payment of Invoice No. 108.

1/29/16   Issued Check No. 3039 to CME Mortgage Co. in the amount of $685.80. Type **685.80** in the Dollars field. To distribute this amount between the principal amount of $587.95 and Interest Expense of $97.85, click Split .

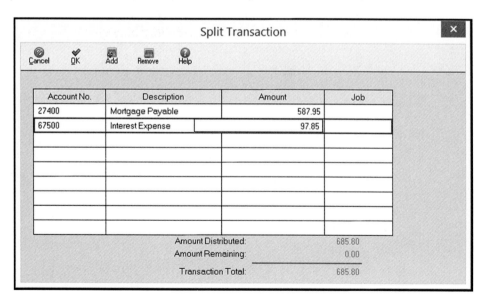

Click [✔ OK] to accept the split transaction. These steps assume you are using the Write Checks window. (*Hint: On the Write Checks window, type **3039** in the Check number field.*)

1/29/16	Issued Check No. 3040 in the amount of $500 to Alex Ziegler.
1/29/16	Issued Check No. 3041 in the amount of $500 to Wendy Lincoln.
1/30/16	Cash sales in the amount of $2,376 ($2,200 plus $176, AZ sales taxes) were deposited at Southern Bank: 8 doorknobs, $1,200; 10 pairs of curtains, $1,000. (*Remember to select AZ sales taxes.*)

PRINTING REPORTS

1. Print the Sales Journal. Compare your Sales Journal with the one shown on the next page.

Wendy's Service Merchandise
Sales Journal
For the Period From Jan 1, 2016 to Jan 31, 2016
Filter Criteria includes: Report order is by Invoice/CM Date. Report is printed in Detail Format.

Date	Account ID	Invoice/CM #	Line Description	Debit Amnt	Credit Amnt
1/7/16	23100	101	AZ: Arizona Dept. of Revenue		24.00
	40000		Two doorknobs		300.00
	50000		Cost of sales	100.00	
	12000		Cost of sales		100.00
	11000		Arlene Petty	324.00	
1/7/16	40400	102	Four rolls of vinyl flooring		640.00
	57000		Cost of sales	216.00	
	12000		Cost of sales		216.00
	11000		Denise Crosby	640.00	
1/7/16	23100	103	AZ: Arizona Dept. of Revenue		32.00
	40200		Four pairs of curtains		400.00
	50500		Cost of sales	120.00	
	12000		Cost of sales		120.00
	11000		Peter Malin	432.00	
1/7/16	23100	104	AZ: Arizona Dept. of Revenue		36.00
	40000		Three curtain rods		450.00
	50000		Cost of sales	150.00	
	12000		Cost of sales		150.00
	11000		Jessica Prince	486.00	
1/10/16	23100	105	AZ: Arizona Dept. of Revenue		3.99
	40600		Repair		49.89
	11000		Bonni Berman	53.88	
1/14/16	23100	CM103	AZ: Arizona Dept. of Revenue	8.00	
	40200		Returned one pair of curtains	100.00	
	50500		Cost of sales		30.00
	12000		Cost of sales	30.00	
	11000		Peter Malin		108.00
1/18/16	23100	106	AZ: Arizona Dept. of Revenue		24.00
	40000		Two doorknobs		300.00
	50000		Cost of sales	100.00	
	12000		Cost of sales		100.00
	11000		Arlene Petty	324.00	
1/18/16	40400	107	Two rolls of vinyl flooring		320.00
	57000		Cost of sales	108.00	
	12000		Cost of sales		108.00
	11000		Denise Crosby	320.00	
1/18/16	23100	108	AZ: Arizona Dept. of Revenue		16.00
	40200		Two pairs of curtains		200.00
	50500		Cost of sales	60.00	
	12000		Cost of sales		60.00
	11000		Peter Malin	216.00	
1/21/16	23100	109	AZ: Arizona Dept. of Revenue		6.00
	40600		Repair		75.00
	11000		Bonni Berman	81.00	
		Total		**3,868.88**	**3,868.88**

If any of your transactions do *not* agree with the Sales Journal, you can drill-down ( ) to the original entry, make any needed corrections, then save and reprint.

2. Print the Cash Receipts Journal.

			Wendy's Service Merchandise		
			Cash Receipts Journal		
			For the Period From Jan 1, 2016 to Jan 31, 2016		
Filter Criteria includes: Report order is by Check Date. Report is printed in Detail Format.					
Date	**Account ID**	**Transaction Ref**	**Line Description**	**Debit Amnt**	**Credit Amnt**
1/14/16	11000	Invoice 103	Invoice: 103		324.00
	10200		Peter Malin	324.00	
1/21/16	11000	Invoice 101	Invoice: 101		324.00
	10200		Arlene Petty	324.00	
1/23/16	11000	Invoice 104	Invoice: 104		105.00
	10200		Jessica Prince	105.00	
1/23/16	23100	Cash sales	AZ: Arizona Dept. of Revenue		104.00
	40200		Ten pairs of curtains		1,000.00
	50500		Cost of sales	300.00	
	12000		Cost of sales		300.00
	40000		Two doorknobs		300.00
	50000		Cost of sales	100.00	
	12000		Cost of sales		100.00
	10200		Cash	1,404.00	
1/25/16	11000	Invoice 106	Invoice: 106		324.00
	10200		Arlene Petty	324.00	
1/25/16	11000	Invoice 108	Invoice: 108		216.00
	10200		Peter Malin	216.00	
1/28/16	11000	Invoice 105	Invoice: 105		53.88
	10200		Bonni Berman	53.88	
1/28/16	11000	Invoice 102	Invoice: 102		640.00
	10200		Denise Crosby	640.00	
1/30/16	23100	Cash	AZ: Arizona Dept. of Revenue		16.00
	40200		Two pairs of curtains		200.00
	50500		Cost of sales	60.00	
	12000		Cost of sales		60.00
	10200		Bertha Rabago	216.00	
1/30/16	23100	Cash	AZ: Arizona Dept. of Revenue		176.00
	40000		Eight doorknobs		1,200.00
	50000		Cost of sales	400.00	
	12000		Cost of sales		400.00
	40200		Ten pairs of curtains		1,000.00
	50500		Cost of sales	300.00	
	12000		Cost of sales		300.00
	10200		Cash sales	2,376.00	
				7,142.88	7,142.88

3. Print the Customer Ledgers.

Wendy's Service Merchandise
Customer Ledgers
For the Period From Jan 1, 2016 to Jan 31, 2016

Filter Criteria includes: Report order is by ID. Report is printed in Detail Format.

Customer ID Customer	Date	Trans No	Type	Debit Amt	Credit Amt	Balance
ap001 Arlene Petty	1/7/16 1/18/16 1/21/16 1/25/16	101 106 Invoice 101 Invoice 106	SJ SJ CRJ CRJ	324.00 324.00	 324.00 324.00	324.00 648.00 324.00 0.00
bb002 Bonni Berman	1/10/16 1/21/16 1/28/16	105 109 Invoice 105	SJ SJ CRJ	53.88 81.00	 53.88	53.88 134.88 81.00
dc003 Denise Crosby	1/7/16 1/18/16 1/28/16	102 107 Invoice 102	SJ SJ CRJ	640.00 320.00	 640.00	640.00 960.00 320.00
jp004 Jessica Prince	1/7/16 1/23/16	104 Invoice 104	SJ CRJ	486.00	 105.00	486.00 381.00
pm005 Peter Malin	1/7/16 1/14/16 1/14/16 1/18/16 1/25/16	103 CM103 Invoice 103 108 Invoice 108	SJ SJ CRJ SJ CRJ	432.00 216.00	 108.00 324.00 216.00	432.00 324.00 0.00 216.00 0.00
Report Total				**2,876.88**	**2,094.88**	**782.00**

4. Print the Purchase Journal and compare it to the one shown on the next page.

Wendy's Service Merchandise
Purchase Journal
For the Period From Jan 1, 2016 to Jan 31, 2016
Filter Criteria includes: 1) Includes Drop Shipments. Report order is by Date. Report is printed in Detail Format.

Date	Account ID Account Description	Invoice/CM #	Line Description	Debit Amount	Credit Amount
1/3/16	12000 Merchandise Inventory	56JJ	restoration hardware	300.00	
	20000 Accounts Payable		James Jarvis Hardware		300.00
1/14/16	12000 Merchandise Inventory	112	light fixtures	512.00	
	20000 Accounts Payable		Tom's Sales and Service		512.00
1/21/16	12000 Merchandise Inventory	210	wall coverings	120.00	
	20000 Accounts Payable		Ronnie Becker Fabrics		120.00
1/21/16	12000 Merchandise Inventory	78JJ	restoration hardware	500.00	
	20000 Accounts Payable		James Jarvis Hardware		500.00
1/21/16	12000 Merchandise Inventory	90	flooring	432.00	
	20000 Accounts Payable		Len Lacey Products		432.00
1/25/16	12000 Merchandise Inventory	VCM90	flooring		54.00
	20000 Accounts Payable		Len Lacey Products	54.00	
1/28/16	12000 Merchandise Inventory	VCM78JJ	restoration hardware		100.00
	20000 Accounts Payable		James Jarvis Hardware	100.00	
				2,018.00	2,018.00

5. Print the Cash Disbursements Journal and compare it to the one shown on the next page.

			Wendy's Service Merchandise **Cash Disbursements Journal** **For the Period From Jan 1, 2016 to Jan 31, 2016**		
Filter Criteria includes: Report order is by Date. Report is printed in Detail Format.					
Date	**Check #**	**Account ID**	**Line Description**	**Debit Amount**	**Credit Amount**
1/24/16	3030	70000 10200	Maintenance Expense Morgan Knapp	160.00	 160.00
1/24/16	3031	73500 10200	Postage Expense U.S. Post Office	45.00	 45.00
1/24/16	3032	75500 10200	Supplies Expense Main Office Supplies	107.65	 107.65
1/24/16	3033	76000 10200	Telephone Expense LRI Phone Co.	72.14	 72.14
1/25/16	3034	39007 10200	Alex Ziegler, Drawing Alex Ziegler	500.00	 500.00
1/25/16	3035	39009 10200	Wendy Lincoln, Drawing Wendy Lincoln	500.00	 500.00
1/25/16	3036	59500 20000 10200	Discounts Taken Invoice: 90 Len Lacey Products	 378.00	7.56 370.44
1/28/16	3037	59500 20000 10200	Discounts Taken Invoice: 78JJ James Jarvis Hardware	 400.00	8.00 392.00
1/28/16	3038	59500 20000 10200	Discounts Taken Invoice: 210 Ronnie Becker Fabrics	 120.00	2.40 117.60
1/29/16	3039	27400 67500 10200	Mortgage Payable Interest Expense CME Mortgage Co.	587.95 97.85	 685.80
1/29/16	3040	39007 10200	Alex Ziegler, Drawing Alex Ziegler	500.00	 500.00
1/29/16	3041	39009 10200	Wendy Lincoln, Drawing Wendy Lincoln	500.00	 500.00
	Total			**3,968.59**	**3,968.59**

6. Print the Vendor Ledgers.

Wendy's Service Merchandise
Vendor Ledgers
For the Period From Jan 1, 2016 to Jan 31, 2016

Filter Criteria includes: Report order is by ID.

Vendor ID Vendor	Date	Trans No	Type	Paid	Debit Amt	Credit Amt	Balance
JJH06	1/3/16	56JJ	PJ			300.00	300.00
James Jarvis Hardware	1/21/16	78JJ	PJ	*		500.00	800.00
	1/28/16	VCM78JJ	PJ	*	100.00		700.00
	1/28/16	3037	CDJ		8.00	8.00	700.00
	1/28/16	3037	CDJ		400.00		300.00
LLP07	1/21/16	90	PJ	*		432.00	432.00
Len Lacey Products	1/25/16	VCM90	PJ	*	54.00		378.00
	1/25/16	3036	CDJ		7.56	7.56	378.00
	1/25/16	3036	CDJ		378.00		0.00
RBF08	1/21/16	210	PJ	*		120.00	120.00
Ronnie Becker Fabrics	1/28/16	3038	CDJ		2.40	2.40	120.00
	1/28/16	3038	CDJ		120.00		0.00
TSS09	1/14/16	112	PJ			512.00	512.00
Tom's Sales and Servic							
Report Total					**1,069.96**	**1,881.96**	**812.00**

7. Follow these steps to print the Cost of Goods Sold Journal and the Inventory Adjustment Journal:

   a. From the Reports area of the Select a Report or Form window, select Inventory.

   b. Highlight Cost of Goods Sold Journal, then make the selections to print. Compare your printout to the one shown on the next page.

Wendy's Service Merchandise
Cost of Goods Sold Journal
For the Period From Jan 1, 2016 to Jan 31, 2016

Filter Criteria includes: Report order is by Date. Report is printed in Detail Format and with shortened descriptions.

Date	GL Acct I	Reference	Qty	Line Description	Debit Amount	Credit Amount
1/7/16	12000	101	2.00	Two doorknobs		100.00
	50000		2.00	Two doorknobs	100.00	
1/7/16	12000	102	4.00	Four rolls of vinyl flooring		216.00
	57000		4.00	Four rolls of vinyl flooring	216.00	
1/7/16	12000	103	4.00	Four pairs of curtains		120.00
	50500		4.00	Four pairs of curtains	120.00	
1/7/16	12000	104	3.00	Three curtain rods		150.00
	50000		3.00	Three curtain rods	150.00	
1/14/16	12000	CM103	-1.00	Returned one pair of curtains	30.00	
	50500		-1.00	Returned one pair of curtains		30.00
1/18/16	12000	106	2.00	Two doorknobs		100.00
	50000		2.00	Two doorknobs	100.00	
1/18/16	12000	107	2.00	Two rolls of vinyl flooring		108.00
	57000		2.00	Two rolls of vinyl flooring	108.00	
1/18/16	12000	108	2.00	Two pairs of curtains		60.00
	50500		2.00	Two pairs of curtains	60.00	
1/23/16	12000	Cash	10.00	Ten pairs of curtains		300.00
	50500		10.00	Ten pairs of curtains	300.00	
	12000		2.00	Two doorknobs		100.00
	50000		2.00	Two doorknobs	100.00	
1/30/16	12000	Cash	2.00	Two pairs of curtains		60.00
	50500		2.00	Two pairs of curtains	60.00	
	12000		8.00	Eight doorknobs		400.00
	50000		8.00	Eight doorknobs	400.00	
	12000		10.00	Ten pairs of curtains		300.00
	50500		10.00	Ten pairs of curtains	300.00	
		Total			**2,044.00**	**2,044.00**

c. Highlight the Inventory Adjustment Journal, then make the selections to print.

Wendy's Service Merchandise
Inventory Adjustment Journal
For the Period From Jan 1, 2016 to Jan 31, 2016

Filter Criteria includes: Report order is by Date. Report is printed in Detail Format and with shortened descriptions.

Date	GL Acct ID	Reference	Qty	Line Description	Debit Amount	Credit Amount
1/16/16	12000	AZ	-2.00	lighting		128.00
	57050		-2.00	Two damaged fixtur	128.00	
		Total			**128.00**	**128.00**

8. Print the Inventory Profitability Report.

Wendy's Service Merchandise
Inventory Profitability Report
For the Period From Jan 1, 2016 to Jan 31, 2016

Filter Criteria includes: 1) Stock/Assembly. Report order is by ID. Report is printed with shortened descriptions.

Item ID Item Description	Units Sold	Sales($)	Cost($)	Gross Profit($)	Gross Profi	% of Total
001hardware hardware	17.00	2,550.00	850.00	1,700.00	66.67	40.23
002wall wall	27.00	2,700.00	810.00	1,890.00	70.00	44.72
003floor floor	6.00	960.00	324.00	636.00	66.25	15.05
004lights lighting						
	50.00	6,210.00	1,984.00	4,226.00		100.00

9. Print the General Ledger Trial Balance.

Wendy's Service Merchandise
General Ledger Trial Balance
As of Jan 31, 2016

Filter Criteria includes: Report order is by ID. Report is printed in Detail Format.

Account ID	Account Description	Debit Amt	Credit Amt
10200	Southern Bank	78,532.25	
10400	Tucson Savings & Loan	22,000.00	
11000	Accounts Receivable	782.00	
12000	Merchandise Inventory	27,338.00	
13000	Supplies	1,750.00	
14000	Prepaid Insurance	2,400.00	
15000	Furniture and Fixtures	5,000.00	
15100	Computers & Equipment	7,500.00	
15500	Building	100,000.00	
20000	Accounts Payable		812.00
23100	Sales Tax Payable		429.99
27000	Long-Term Notes Payable		20,500.00
27400	Mortgage Payable		74,412.05
39006	Alex Ziegler, Capital		73,695.00
39007	Alex Ziegler, Drawing	1,000.00	
39008	Wendy Lincoln, Capital		73,695.00
39009	Wendy Lincoln, Drawing	1,000.00	
40000	Sales-Hardware		2,550.00
40200	Sales-Wall		2,700.00
40400	Sales-Floor		960.00
40600	Service Fees		124.89
50000	Cost of Sales-Hardware	850.00	
50500	Cost of Sales-Wall	810.00	
57000	Cost of Sales-Floor	324.00	
57050	Cost of Sales-Lights	128.00	
59500	Purchase Discounts		17.96
67500	Interest Expense	97.85	
70000	Maintenance Expense	160.00	
73500	Postage Expense	45.00	
75500	Supplies Expense	107.65	
76000	Telephone Expense	72.14	
	Total:	249,896.89	249,896.89

FINANCIAL MANAGER

1. Display the Financial Manager's Business Summary. Compare it to the one shown on page 505 in Chapter 13.

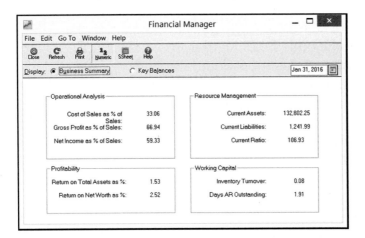

2. Display the Key Balances. Compare it to the one shown on page 506 in Chapter 13.

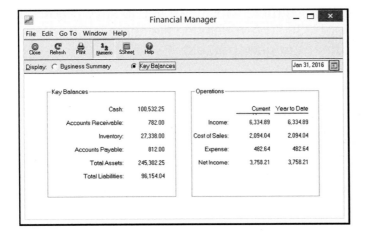

BACKING UP CHAPTER 14 DATA

If your reports agree with the ones shown, make a backup of Chapter 14 data. If your printouts do not agree with the ones shown, make the necessary corrections.

Back up. The suggested file name **Chapter 14**.

EXPORT REPORTS TO EXCEL

1. Export the following Sage 50 reports to Excel:

   - Customer Ledgers
   - Vendor Ledgers
   - Cost of Goods Sold Journal
   - Inventory Adjustment Journal
   - Inventory Profitability Report
   - General Ledger Trial Balance

   Check with your instructor to see if he or she also wants you to include the following journals in this Excel file: Purchase Journal, Cash Disbursements Journal, Sales Journal, and Cash Receipts Journal.

2. If needed, refer to pages 329-331 for detailed steps to add multiple sheets to one Excel file. Use the file name **Chapter 14_ CL_ VL_CGSJ_IAJ_IPR_GLTB.xlsx**.

   NOTE: If your instructor would like you to save reports as PDF files, refer to page 331. The suggested file name is **Chapter 14_Customer Ledgers.pdf**, etc.

ONLINE LEARNING CENTER

Complete end-of-chapter activities at www.mhhe.com/yacht2016 > Student Edition > Chapter 14.

1. Quizzes: Multiple Choice and True False questions. Interactive online tests that are graded and can be emailed to your instructor.

2. More Resources:

   a. QA Templates: Answer 10 short-answer questions and one Analysis Question.

   b. Narrated PowerPoints: Listen to the narrated PowerPoints.

   c. Going to the Net Exercises: Access the BizMov Business Guides.

d. Assessment Rubric: Complete the rubric to review Sage 50's journals, navigation centers, modules, task windows, and reports.

The OLC also includes links to the Appendixes:

- Appendix A: Troubleshooting
- Appendix B: Accounting Information Systems
- Appendix C: Review of Accounting Principles
- Appendix D: Glossary (words that are boldfaced and italicized in chapter)

Exercise 14-1: You must complete Exercises 12-1, 12-2, 13-1, and 13-2 before starting Exercise 14-1.

1. Start Sage. Open the company that you set up in Exercise 12-1, Your last name Sales and Service.

2. If necessary, restore the data that you backed up in Exercise 13-2. (This backup was made on page 515.) To make sure you are starting in the right place, display Exercise 13-2's general ledger trial balance (step 4, page 515).

3. Make the following inventory purchase.

   1/28/16   Curt Perkins Tools sent Invoice No. 732CP for the purchase of 8 tool kits for a unit cost of $30.

4. Make the following inventory adjustment:

   1/30/16   Two tool kits purchased from Curt Perkins Tools on 1/27/16 were accidentally damaged by the owner. (*Hint:* Use your initials.)

Complete the following additional transactions:

   1/30/16   Received check in the amount of $972 from Rose Norris in payment of Invoice No. 103.

   1/31/16   Cash Sales in the amount of $4,752, ($4,400 plus $352, GA sales taxes) were deposited at First Interstate: 20 tool kits, $1,700; 18 hardware sets, $2,700.

5. Make a backup of Exercise 14-1. (Use **Exercise 14-1** as the file name.)

Exercise 14-2: Follow the instructions below to complete Exercise 14-2.

1. Print the Cash Receipts Journal.

2. Print the Purchase Journal.

3. Print the Cost of Goods Sold Journal.

4. Print the Inventory Adjustment Journal.

5. Print the Inventory Profitability Report.

6. Print the General Ledger Trial Balance.

   Check Your Figures:

10200, First Interstate	$71,470.63
11000, Accounts Receivable	0.00
12000, Merchandise Inventory	13,250.00
23100, Sales Tax Payable	545.20
50000, Cost of Sales-Hardware	1,450.00
50500, Cost of Sales-Tools	930.00
59500, Purchase Discounts	12.80

7. Export the following reports to Excel.

   a. Cash Receipts Journal
   b. Purchase Journal
   c. Cost of Goods Sold Journal
   d. Inventory Adjustment Journal
   e. Inventory Profitability Report
   f. General Ledger Trial Balance

8. Save the Excel file as **Exercise 14-2_CRJ_PJ_ CGSJ_ IAJ_ IPR_ GLTB.xlsx**.

9. Save these reports as PDFs: Cash Receipts Journal, Cost of Goods Sold Journal, Inventory Adjustment Journal, Purchase Journal, Inventory Profitability Report, and General Ledger Trial Balance. The suggested file name is **Exercise 14-2_Cash Receipts Journal.pdf**, etc.

10. There is no need to backup Exercise 14-2. The Exercise 14-1.ptb file has the data needed to print Exercise 14-2's reports.

CHAPTER 14 INDEX

Chapter

15

Employees, Payroll, and Account Reconciliation

LEARNING OBJECTIVES

1. Restore data from Chapter 14. (This backup was made on page 539.)
2. Complete the Payroll Setup Wizard.
3. Enter employee and employer default information.
4. Journalize and post Payroll Journal entries.
5. Print paychecks.
6. Reconcile the Southern Bank account and the Payroll Checking Account.
7. Compare the vendor ledgers, customer ledgers, and inventory valuation report to the general ledger's controlling accounts.
8 Print the financial statements.
9. Make four backups, save two Excel files, and save nine PDF files.

Employers withhold local, state, and federal taxes from their employees' paychecks. The amount withheld for federal taxes is determined from tax tables published by the Internal Revenue Service (IRS). Circular E, Employer's Tax Guide, is available from the IRS. It shows the applicable tax tables and forms that are necessary for filing employee payroll information. Sage includes payroll tax tables built into the software. In this chapter you learn how to access and use the payroll tax tables.

The amount withheld also depends on the employee's earnings and the number of *exemptions* or *withholding allowances* claimed by the employee. The number of withholding allowances usually includes one for the employee, one for the employee's spouse, and one for each dependent.

Also deducted from employees' paychecks are *FICA taxes* or social security taxes. This deduction from wages provides qualified workers who retire at age 62 or older with monthly payments from the federal government. The retiree also receives medical benefits called *Medicare* after reaching age 65. In addition to these retirement benefits, social

---

security also provides payments to the surviving family of a qualified deceased worker.

By January 31 of each year employers are required to issue *W-2 Forms* to employees and to the Internal Revenue Service. The W-2 Form is an annual report of the employee's wages subject to FICA and federal income tax and shows the amounts that were withheld.

Using the years 2015 and 2016 as an example, Social Security is funded by a 12.4% tax on wages up to $118,500. Half is paid by employers and half is paid by employees.

The employee's W-2 Form shows the Federal Income Tax, State Income Tax, Social Security, and Medicare withheld. In 2015 and 2016, yearly income up to $118,500 is subject to the social security portion of the FICA tax. FICA is two taxes—the Social Security portion and the Medicare portion. For additional information, refer to this website https://www.imercer.com/content/social_security_figures.aspx.

This table compares 2015 and 2016 FICA tax rates and maximum social security earnings for tax contributions. For purposes of comparison, in 2014 the social security portion of the FICA tax was based on income up to $117,000. The amount subject to social security tax is the same for 2015 and 2016, $118,500.

Social Security	2015	2016
FICA tax rate:		
• Social Security for employees	6.2%	6.2%
• Social Security for employers	6.2%	6.2%
• Medicare for employees	1.45%	1.45%
• Medicare for employers	1.45%	1.45%
Maximum Social Security earnings for tax contributions	$118,500	$118,500
Medicare taxable earnings	No limit	No limit

Sage 50's payroll tax calculations are for example purposes only. After annual federal legislation, payroll products can be purchased from Sage at http://www.sage.com/us/need/human-resources-and-payroll.

Employees may also voluntarily deduct other amounts from wages. These voluntary deductions include: charitable contributions, medical insurance premiums, U.S. savings bonds, or union dues.

It is the purpose of this chapter to show you how to use Sage 50 to enter payroll default information, add employees, make journal entries for payroll, and print the various payroll reports. Once you set up the default information and employee information, Sage automates the payroll process. *The automatic withholding calculations are for example purposes only. They do not reflect accurate amounts.*

You establish the following default information for processing payroll:

1. The cash account that is credited when disbursing paychecks. Wendy's Service Merchandise credits Account No. 10300, Payroll Checking Account.

2. The accounts that comprise the employee's fields.

3. The accounts that comprise the employer's fields.

4. The payroll fields that go on the W-2 form.

5. The employee-paid taxes.

6. The employer-paid taxes.

At the Maintain Employees level, you enter the following types of information:

1. The employee name, address, telephone number, and information from the Employee's Withholding Allowance Certificate, Form W-4.

2. Information about employee pay: hourly, salaried, and amount.

3. The tax filing status of the employee for federal, state, and local purposes, including withholding allowances.

When the payroll tables included with the student version or educational version software are used, the payroll tax withholdings are calculated automatically. Once payroll defaults are set up, all you need to do is select the employee you want to pay, date the paycheck and pay period, and post the paycheck. For a yearly fee, Sage 50's payroll tax service offers the appropriate payroll tax withholdings.

The diagram below shows the steps for setting up and using Sage's payroll system.

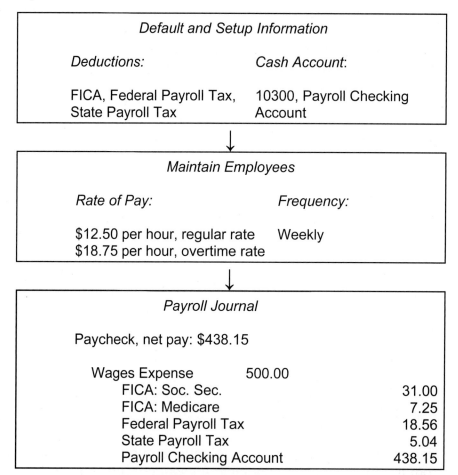

Default and Setup Information

Deductions:	*Cash Account:*
FICA, Federal Payroll Tax, State Payroll Tax	10300, Payroll Checking Account

↓

Maintain Employees

Rate of Pay:	*Frequency:*
$12.50 per hour, regular rate $18.75 per hour, overtime rate	Weekly

↓

Payroll Journal

Paycheck, net pay: $438.15

Wages Expense	500.00	
FICA: Soc. Sec.		31.00
FICA: Medicare		7.25
Federal Payroll Tax		18.56
State Payroll Tax		5.04
Payroll Checking Account		438.15

Sage 50's payroll tax calculations are for example purposes only. The automatic Social Security tax is calculated as $500.00 X .062 = $31.00. Medicare is calculated as $500 X .0145 = $7.25. The State and Federal Payroll taxes are calculated by Sage 50 and are examples of that employee withholding tax. The net pay amount, $438.15, is that same as Laurie Gallardo's paycheck, page 568.

GETTING STARTED

Follow these steps to start:

1. Start Sage 50. Open Wendy's [your first name] Service Merchandise. (*Hint:* If a different company opens, select File > Open Previous Company. Open one company.)

2. If necessary, restore the Chapter 14.ptb file. This backup was made on page 539.

To make sure you are starting in the appropriate place in the data (Chapter 14.ptb backup) display the General Ledger Trial Balance. The trial balance is also shown in Chapter 14 on page 538.

	Wendy's Service Merchandise **General Ledger Trial Balance** **As of Jan 31, 2016**		
Filter Criteria includes: Report order is by ID. Report is printed in Detail Format.			
Account ID	**Account Description**	**Debit Amt**	**Credit Amt**
10200	Southern Bank	78,532.25	
10400	Tucson Savings & Loan	22,000.00	
11000	Accounts Receivable	782.00	
12000	Merchandise Inventory	27,338.00	
13000	Supplies	1,750.00	
14000	Prepaid Insurance	2,400.00	
15000	Furniture and Fixtures	5,000.00	
15100	Computers & Equipment	7,500.00	
15500	Building	100,000.00	
20000	Accounts Payable		812.00
23100	Sales Tax Payable		429.99
27000	Long-Term Notes Payable		20,500.00
27400	Mortgage Payable		74,412.05
39006	Alex Ziegler, Capital		73,695.00
39007	Alex Ziegler, Drawing	1,000.00	
39008	Wendy Lincoln, Capital		73,695.00
39009	Wendy Lincoln, Drawing	1,000.00	
40000	Sales-Hardware		2,550.00
40200	Sales-Wall		2,700.00
40400	Sales-Floor		960.00
40600	Service Fees		124.89
50000	Cost of Sales-Hardware	850.00	
50500	Cost of Sales-Wall	810.00	
57000	Cost of Sales-Floor	324.00	
57050	Cost of Sales-Lights	128.00	
59500	Purchase Discounts		17.96
67500	Interest Expense	97.85	
70000	Maintenance Expense	160.00	
73500	Postage Expense	45.00	
75500	Supplies Expense	107.65	
76000	Telephone Expense	72.14	
	Total:	**249,896.89**	**249,896.89**

Establishing the Payroll Account

In order to establish the payroll checking account, transfer funds from Southern Bank (Account No. 10200) to the Payroll Checking Account (Account No. 10300). Journalize and post the following General Journal transaction:

Date   *Transaction Description*

01/4/16   Wendy's Service Merchandise transferred $6,500 from Account No. 10200, Southern Bank, to Account No. 10300, Payroll Checking Account.

After posting this general journal entry, display the general journal. (*Hint: Reports & Forms > General Ledger > General Journal > Display.*)

		Wendy's Service Merchandise				
		General Journal				
		For the Period From Jan 1, 2016 to Jan 31, 2016				
Filter Criteria includes: Report order is by Date. Report is printed with Accounts having Zero Amounts and with shortened descriptions and in Detail Format.						
Date	**Account ID**	**Reference**	**Trans Description**		**Debit Amt**	**Credit Amt**
1/4/16	10300	Transfer	Payroll Checking Account		6,500.00	
	10200		Southern Bank			6,500.00
		Total			**6,500.00**	**6,500.00**

Close all windows.

PAYROLL SETUP WIZARD

The Payroll Setup wizard walks you through setting up most payroll defaults and standard payroll fields. As you answer the prompts, Sage 50 creates most of the common payroll fields used in calculating deductions and taxes.

The Sage 50 Payroll Setup Wizard establishes the following:

- State and locality defaults.
- State unemployment percentage.
- Common federal and state payroll fields for employee-paid and company-paid taxes.
- General ledger account defaults for payroll fields.
- Optional payroll fields for tips, meals, 401K contributions, etc.

1. From the Navigation Bar, select **Employees & Payroll**, Payroll Setup >
Payroll Setup Wizard. Read the information on the Payroll Setup
Wizard window. Observe that the left pane shows Home, Payroll
Options, Company Information, Benefits, Taxes, Setup Complete.
(*Hint:* You may want to watch the Sage Advisor employees and
payroll videos ⊙ and read the PDF documents.)

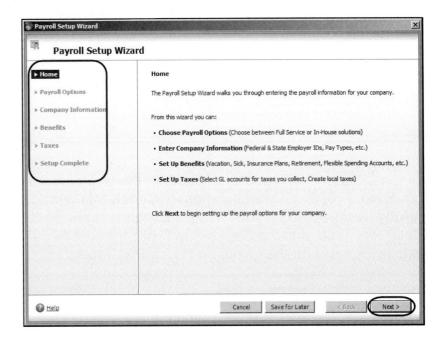

2. Click [Next >]. Payroll Options is selected. Read the information
in the Other Payroll Options, Direct Deposit, and E-filing areas.

3. Click [Next >]. Company Information is selected. The Federal
Employer ID, State Employer ID, State (AZ), and State
Unemployment ID are automatically completed. These fields agree
with the company information entered on page 405 in Chapter 12.

4. Type **3.4** in the State Unemployment Rate field. No is selected for
Do you want to record employee meals and tips. Compare your
Company Information window to the one shown on the next page.

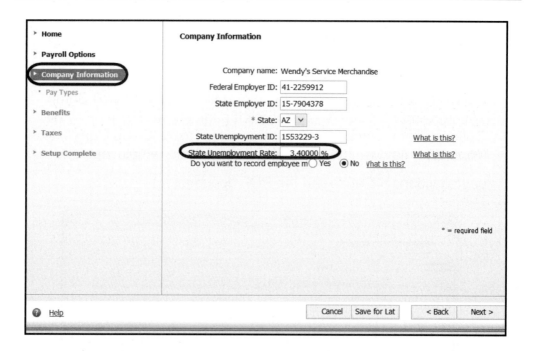

5. Click [Next >]. Pay Types is selected. In the Overtime field, select Account No. 77600 - Overtime Expense. **Check this window carefully**. Account No. 77500 - Wages Expense is shown for the Regular Pay Type, and the Salary Pay Type. Account No. 77600 - Overtime Expense for the Overtime Hourly Pay Type.

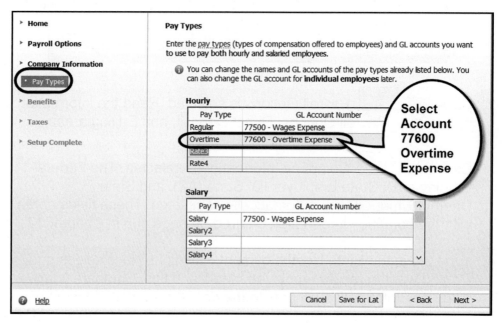

6. Click [Next >]. The Benefits window appears. Do not make any selections. Click [Next >] to continue.

7. The Payroll Taxes window appears. Observe that the Tax liability acct no. (23400) and Tax Expense acct no. (72000) is selected. To accept these defaults, click [Next >].

8. The Setup Complete window appears, click [Finish]. After completing employee defaults in the next section, you return to the Payroll Setup Wizard to assign employee and company-paid tax fields.

ENTERING EMPLOYEE AND EMPLOYER DEFAULT INFORMATION

Follow these steps to enter employee and employer default information:

1. From the Employees & Payroll Navigation Center, click [Employees ▲] > Set Up Employee Defaults. The Employee Defaults window displays. In the Employee Defaults window, you enter account numbers that serve as the basis for payroll withholdings.

   There are five tabs:

   ➢ <u>G</u>eneral
   ➢ Employe<u>e</u> Fields
   ➢ Compan<u>y</u> Fields
   ➢ <u>R</u>eview Ratings
   ➢ Employment <u>S</u>tatus

2. Select the Employe<u>e</u> Fields tab.

3. The Fed_Income line shows the default G/L Account as 23400 (Federal Payroll Taxes Payable) for FIT. Account No. 23400, Federal Payroll Taxes Payable, is the correct account for the Fed Income line.

4. Click on the G/L Account field for Soc_Sec and select Account No. 24000, Soc. Sec. Employee Taxes Payable.

5. Click on the G/L Account field for MEDICARE and select Account No. 24200, Medicare Employee Taxes Payable.

6. Click on the G/L Account field for St_Income and select Account No. 23600, State Payroll Taxes Payable.

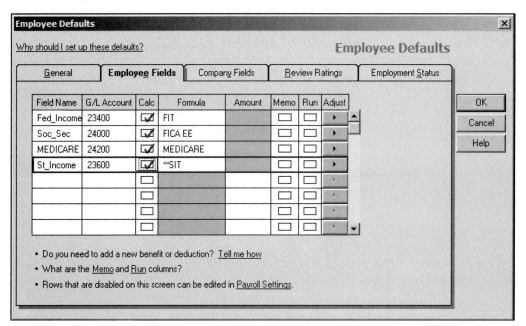

7. Click on the Company Fields tab. Change the following account numbers:

	Liability Column	Expense Column
Soc_Sec_C	24100, Soc. Sec. Employer Taxes Payable	72510, Soc. Sec. Expense
Medicare_C	24400, Medicare Employer Taxes Payable	72520, Medicare Expense
Fed_Unemp_C	23500, FUTA Tax Payable	72530, FUTA Expense
State_Unemp_C	23700, SUTA Payable	72540, SUTA Expense

Compare your Employee Defaults/Company Fields window, to the one shown on the next page. Make sure the Liability and Expense accounts are correctly selected.

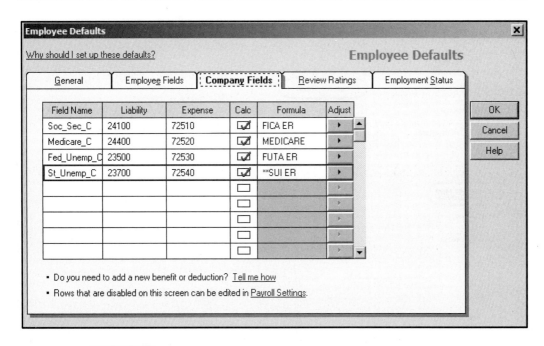

8. Click [OK] to save your changes and return to the menu bar.

COMPLETING PAYROLL SETUP

After completing the initial payroll setup and entering employee defaults, the next step is to use the Payroll Setup Wizard to assign tax fields. Follow these steps to do that.

1. From the Employees & Payroll Navigation Center, click [Payroll Setup] > Payroll Setup Wizard. On the left pane select Taxes > Assign Tax Fields.

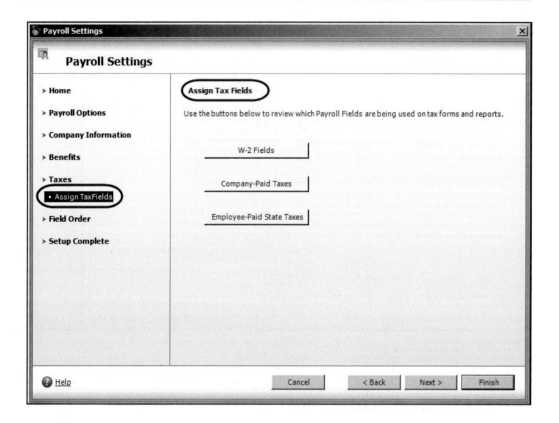

2. The Assign Tax Fields Taxes window appears. There are three buttons: W-2 Fields, Company-Paid Taxes, and Employee-Paid State Taxes. Click $\boxed{\text{W-2 Fields}}$. The Assign Tax Fields for W-2s window appears. These selections appear. (If not, select them.)

Federal income tax withheld:	Fed_Income
Social Security tax withheld:	Soc_Sec
Medicare tax withheld:	MEDICARE
State income tax:	St_Income

    Compare your Assign Tax Fields for W-2s window to the one shown on the next page.

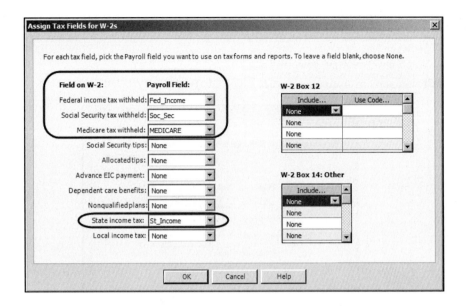

3. Click OK. You are returned to the Assign Tax Fields window.

4. Click Company-Paid Taxes. The Assign Company-Paid Tax Fields window appears. These selections appear. (If not, select them.)

Federal Unemployment (FUTA):   Fed_Unemp_C
State Unemployment (SUTA):   St_Unemp_C

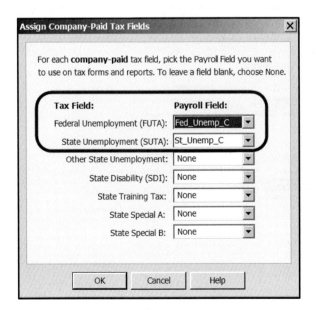

5. Click [OK]. You are returned to the Assign Tax Fields window.

6. Click [Employee-Paid State Taxes]. Do not make any changes.

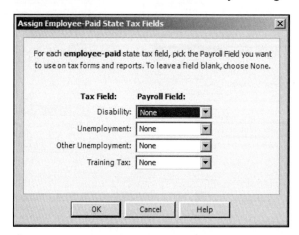

7. Click [OK]. You are returned to the Assign Tax Fields window. Click [Next >].

8. The Field Order window appears. Do not make any changes. Click [Next >].

9. The Setup Complete window appears. Read the information.

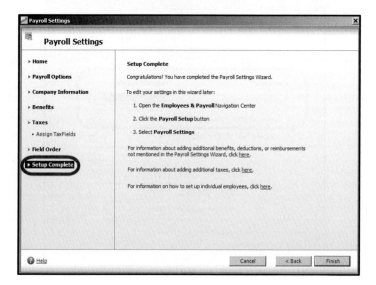

10. Click [Finish].

ENTERING EMPLOYEE MAINTENANCE INFORMATION

The Maintain Employees/Sales Reps window includes information about your employees or sales representatives. The information is displayed as seven tabs: General, Additional Info, Pay Info, Withholding Info, Vacation/Sick Time, Employee Fields, and Company Fields.
Follow these steps to set up employee maintenance information.

1. Select [Employees ▲] > New Employee. The Maintain Employees & Sales Reps window appears.

2. Complete the following fields.

Employee ID:	**A001** (use zeroes)
Name:	**Tim Anderson**
Accept the default for Employee	
Address:	**17 Sycamore Lane**
City, ST, Zip:	**Tucson, AZ 85718**
E-mail	**tim@mail.com**
Home phone:	**520-555-3482**
Social Security No	**040-00-0280**
Type:	**FULL**

3. Click on the Withholding Info tab. Complete the following fields.

Filing Status:	Single for Federal, State, and Local
Allowances:	**1** for Federal, State, and Local
State Addl Withholding:	**11.68** (Type **11.68** in the State, Additional Withholding field.)

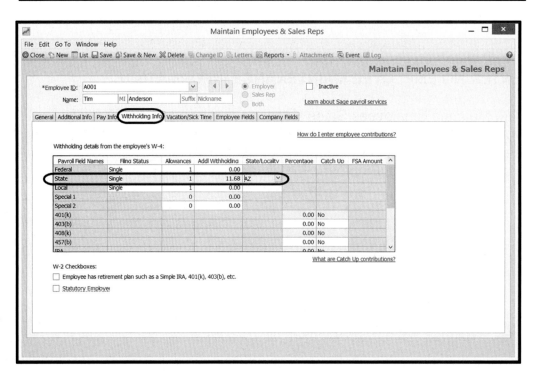

4. Click on the Pay Info tab.

5. Type **12.50** in the Hourly Pay Rate column. Press the **<Enter>** key two times.

6. Type **18.75** in the Hourly Pay Rate column for Overtime. Press the **<Enter>** key. Make sure that the Pay Method field displays Hourly - Hours per Pay Period, the Pay Frequency field displays Weekly, and the Hours Per Pay Period field shows 40.00. Compare your Maintain Employees & Sales Reps/Pay Info window to the one shown on the next page.

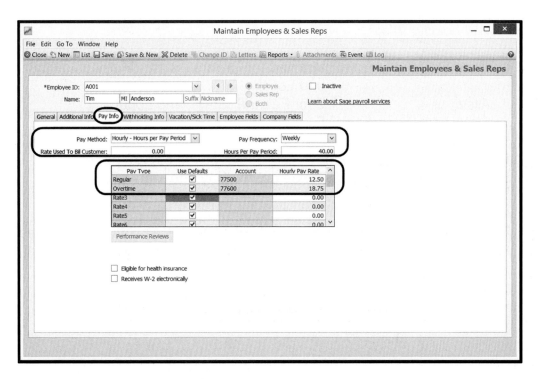

7. Select the Employee Fields tab. Notice that the accounts selected for Fed_Income, Soc_Sec, MEDICARE, and St_Income match the accounts shown on page 554, Employee Defaults/Employee Fields window.

8. Click on the Company Fields tab. These are the employer payroll tax liabilities. Notice that the accounts match the Employee Defaults/Company Fields window shown on page 555.

9. Click Save & New.

10. Click on the General tab. Enter another employee.

Employee ID:	**G001**
Name:	**Laurie Gallardo**
Accept the default for Employee.	
Address:	**33 West Second Street**
City, ST, Zip:	**Tucson, AZ 85716**
E-mail:	**laurie@mail.com**
Home phone:	**520-555-0722**
Social Security No:	**001-00-0083**
Type:	**FULL**

Withholding Info:

Filing Status:	**Married** for Federal, State (Married/Jointly), and Local
Allow:	**2** for Federal, State, and Local
State Addl Withholding:	**5.04**

11. Ms. Gallardo is paid hourly. Her regular pay is $12.50 per hour and her overtime pay is $18.75. Select the Pay Info tab and record this information.

12. Save the employee information. Then, close the Maintain Employees & Sales Reps window. (If necessary, close the Sage Advisor Getting Started window.)

13. On the Employees & Payroll Navigation Center, click [Refresh]. The Employee list appears.

Employees				View Detailed List
Employee ID ∕	Last Name	First Name	Home Phone	Pay Method
A001	Anderson	Tim	520-555-3482	Hourly - Hours per Pay Period
G001	Gallardo	Laurie	520-555-0722	Hourly - Hours per Pay Period

BACKING UP YOUR DATA

When you backup, you are saving work completed for Wendy's [your first name] Service Merchandise in Chapters 12, 13, 14, and to this point in Chapter 15. The suggested file name is **Chapter 15 Begin**.

PAYROLL ENTRY

Once the defaults for payroll are set up, you have very little work to do. In Chapter 4, Employees, Bellwether Garden Supply already had the default information set up. Since the payroll tax tables were included for the sample company, all you needed to do for payroll was:

➢ Enter or select the Employee ID.

➢ Specify the pay period (period-ending date).

➢ Verify the information the window displays (name and address of employee, amount of hours, and employee/employer fields.)

> Print or post the paycheck.

In Chapter 15, you use the payroll tax tables included with the software. These tables are for example purposes only and are not meant for exact computation of payroll withholding amounts.

In Sage 50, the Payroll Entry window is also the *payroll journal*. All entries saved in the Payroll Entry window are posted to the payroll journal, the General Ledger, and to the Employee file.

Payroll entry is a simple process after completing the Payroll Setup Wizard and employee and company (employer) default and maintenance information. When employee and company defaults are selected, you are setting up the payroll liability and expense accounts for payroll entry. The employee maintenance information includes the employee's name; address; social security number; Federal, State, and Local withholding allowances; and pay levels.

All entries made to the Payroll Journal are posted both to the General Ledger and to the Employee file. Once an Employee ID is selected, the rest of the employee information is completed automatically. Enough information is entered in the Maintain Employees record, Default Information, and the payroll tax tables included with the software to determine what the paycheck amount should be. If the information is correct, you print or post the paycheck and proceed to the next employee.

The check amount (or net pay) is automatically credited to Account No. 10300, Payroll Checking Account. The withholding amounts are calculated based on the Payroll Fields which were defined in the Default Information that you previously entered. The rate and frequency of pay were set up in the Employee/Sales Rep record. For Wendy's Service Merchandise, employees are paid weekly.

1. From the Employees & Payroll Navigation Center, click >

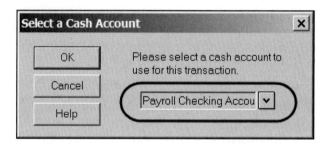

   Enter Payroll For One Employee .

2. The Select a Cash Account window displays. Select the Payroll Checking Account.

3. Click ___OK___ . The Payroll Entry window appears.

4. In the Employee ID field, select Tim Anderson.

5. Leave the Check Number field blank. Type or select **8** as the Date.

6. Make sure that Account No. 10300, Payroll Checking Account, is displayed in the Cash Account field.

7. In the Pay Period End field, type **8** and press **<Enter>**.

8. Accept the default for Weeks in Pay Period which is 1 week.

9. In the Hours Worked table go to the Overtime Hours field. Type **2** and press **<Enter>**.

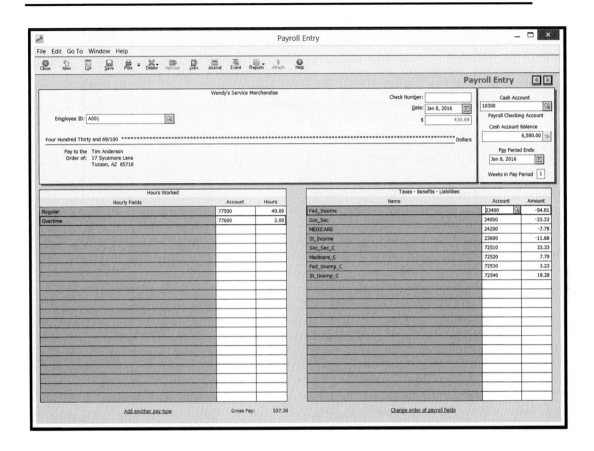

Comment

Observe that the Taxes- Benefits - Liabilities table on the Payroll Entry window includes withholding amounts. These amounts are for example purposes only and do not reflect accurate payroll taxes. For an explanation of Sage 50's payroll calculations, refer to the chart on page 546.

A separate service provided by Sage 50 at an additional cost includes payroll tax tables. More information about Sage 50's Payroll Tax Service is included on their website at http://na.sage.com/us/need/human-resources-and-payroll.

---

10. Click [Print]. (*Or,* click on the down-arrow and select Print Preview.)

11. The Print Forms: Payroll Checks window appears. Click [Select Form]. Select OCR Multi-Purpose PR Laser.

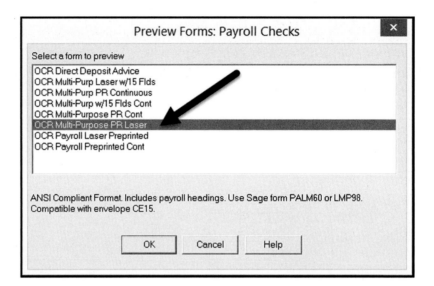

Comment: The form you select is tied to the kind of printer you are using. You may need to make a different selection depending on your printer.

12. Click [OK].

13. The Print Forms: Payroll Checks window appears. Make sure that the form you chose is shown in the Use this form field.

14. Type **101** as the First check number.

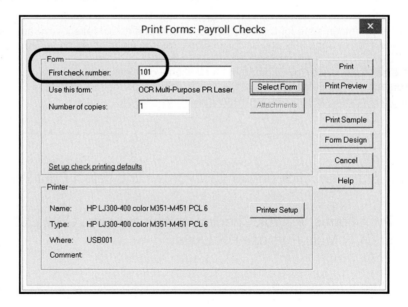

15. Click [Print] (or [Print Preview]). Your check starts to print. (*Or,* Close the Print Preview window. Then, type **101** in the Check Number field. Click <Save> to post. When you <Save>, the check posts to the Payroll Journal. Printing also posts.)

	This Check	Year to Date				
Tim Anderson				Employee ID: A001		
				Social Sec # xxx-xx-0280		
Gross	537.50	537.50		Hours	Rate	Total
Fed Income	-54.01	-54.01	Regular	40.00	12.50	500.00
Soc Sec	-33.33	-33.33	Overtime	2.00	18.75	37.50
MEDICARE	-7.79	-7.79				
St Income	-11.68	-11.68				

Net Check: $430.69   Total   42.00   537.50

Pay Period Beginning: Jan 2, 2016   Check Date: 1/8/16
Pay Period Ending: Jan 8, 2016   Weeks in Pay Period: 1

Check Number: 101   Jan 8, 2016

430.69

Four Hundred Thirty and 69/100 Dollars

Tim Anderson
17 Sycamore Lane
Tucson, AZ 85718

16. Make the selections to pay Ms. Gallardo on January 8, 2016. She worked 40 regular hours. Compare your Payroll Entry window with the one shown on the next page.

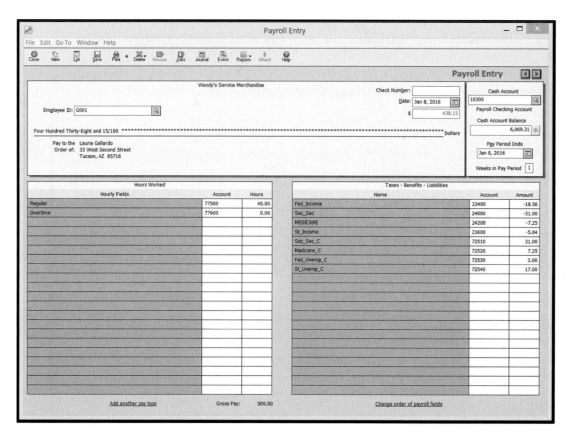

17. Print (or display) Check No. 102. Compare your check with the one shown on the next page.

```
    Laurie Gallardo                                          Employee ID: G001
                                                             Social Sec # xxx-xx-0083
                          This Check        Year to Date
    Gross                  500.00            500.00          Hours        Rate        Total
    Fed Income             -18.56            -18.56  Regular  40.00        12.50       500.00
    Soc Sec               -31.00            -31.00
    MEDICARE               -7.25             -7.25
    St Income              -5.04             -5.04




    Net Check:             $438.15            Total          40.00                     500.00
         Pay Period Beginning: Jan 2, 2016                        Check Date: 1/8/16
         Pay Period Ending: Jan 8, 2016                       Weeks in Pay Period: 1




                              Check Number:  102                      Jan 8, 2016



                                                                        438.15



    Four Hundred Thirty-Eight and 15/100 Dollars


         Laurie Gallardo
         33 West Second Street
         Tucson, AZ  85716
```

18. Make the following payroll entries for Tim Anderson and Laurie Gallardo.

Date	Name	Hours Worked	Overtime	Check No.
1/15/16	T. Anderson	40	2	103
	L. Gallardo	40		104
1/22/16	T. Anderson	40	2	105
	L. Gallardo	40		106
1/29/16	T. Anderson	40	2	107
	L. Gallardo	40		108

After recording the paycheck information, **type the check number**, then click [Save] to post. You do *not* need to print the paychecks.

19. Close the Payroll Entry window.

PRINTING THE PAYROLL JOURNAL

From the Recently Used Employee Reports area of the Employees & Payroll Navigation Center, link to Print or View the Payroll Journal. The Payroll Journal is shown in the next two pages.

Wendy's Service Merchandise
Payroll Journal
For the Period From Jan 1, 2016 to Jan 31, 2016
Filter Criteria includes: Report order is by Check Date. Report is printed in Detail Format.

Date Employee	GL Acct ID	Reference	Debit Amt	Credit Amt
1/8/16	77500	101	500.00	
Tim Anderson	77600		37.50	
	23400			54.01
	24000			33.33
	24200			7.79
	23600			11.68
	24100			33.33
	24400			7.79
	23500			3.23
	23700			18.28
	72510		33.33	
	72520		7.79	
	72530		3.23	
	72540		18.28	
	10300			430.69
1/8/16	77500	102	500.00	
Laurie Gallardo	23400			18.56
	24000			31.00
	24200			7.25
	23600			5.04
	24100			31.00
	24400			7.25
	23500			3.00
	23700			17.00
	72510		31.00	
	72520		7.25	
	72530		3.00	
	72540		17.00	
	10300			438.15
1/15/16	77500	103	500.00	
Tim Anderson	77600		37.50	
	23400			54.01
	24000			33.33
	24200			7.79
	23600			11.68
	24100			33.33
	24400			7.79
	23500			3.23
	23700			18.28
	72510		33.33	
	72520		7.79	
	72530		3.23	
	72540		18.28	
	10300			430.69
1/15/16	77500	104	500.00	
Laurie Gallardo	23400			18.56
	24000			31.00
	24200			7.25
	23600			5.04
	24100			31.00
	24400			7.25
	23500			3.00
	23700			17.00
	72510		31.00	
	72520		7.25	
	72530		3.00	
	72540		17.00	
	10300			438.15
1/22/16	77500	105	500.00	
Tim Anderson	77600		37.50	
	23400			54.01
	24000			33.33

Page: 2

Wendy's Service Merchandise
Payroll Journal
For the Period From Jan 1, 2016 to Jan 31, 2016

Filter Criteria includes: Report order is by Check Date. Report is printed in Detail Format.

Date Employee	GL Acct ID	Reference	Debit Amt	Credit Amt
	24200			7.79
	23600			11.68
	24100			33.33
	24400			7.79
	23500			3.23
	23700			18.28
	72510		33.33	
	72520		7.79	
	72530		3.23	
	72540		18.28	
	10300			430.69
1/22/16 Laurie Gallardo	77500	106	500.00	
	23400			18.56
	24000			31.00
	24200			7.25
	23600			5.04
	24100			31.00
	24400			7.25
	23500			3.00
	23700			17.00
	72510		31.00	
	72520		7.25	
	72530		3.00	
	72540		17.00	
	10300			438.15
1/29/16 Tim Anderson	77500	107	500.00	
	77600		37.50	
	23400			54.01
	24000			33.33
	24200			7.79
	23600			11.68
	24100			33.33
	24400			7.79
	23500			3.23
	23700			18.28
	72510		33.33	
	72520		7.79	
	72530		3.23	
	72540		18.28	
	10300			430.69
1/29/16 Laurie Gallardo	77500	108	500.00	
	23400			18.56
	24000			31.00
	24200			7.25
	23600			5.04
	24100			31.00
	24400			7.25
	23500			3.00
	23700			17.00
	72510		31.00	
	72520		7.25	
	72530		3.00	
	72540		17.00	
	10300			438.15
			4,633.52	4,633.52

ACCOUNT RECONCILIATION

In Chapters 12-15, you worked with Sage 50's accounts payable, accounts receivable, inventory, and payroll systems. The general ledger is integrated with the other parts of the program. For example, when a vendor is paid, that entry is recorded in *both* the general ledger, Southern Bank *and* Accounts Payable accounts, and the individual vendor's account. In other words, the subsidiary ledger (vendor ledger) works together with the general ledger.

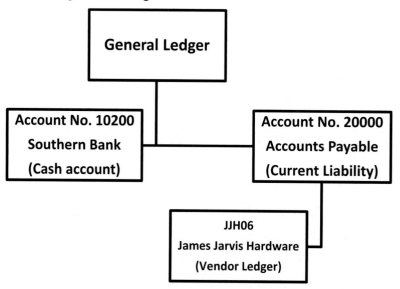

To see how this works, you are going to reconcile two bank statements.

- The January 31, 2016 bank statement from Southern Bank, page 573.

- The January 31, 2016 bank statement from the Payroll Checking Account, page 574.

Then, you are going to check the accounts receivable, accounts payable, and merchandise inventory account balances against the general ledger. This shows you that Sage 50's subsidiary ledgers (customer ledgers, vendor ledgers, and inventory valuation) are in agreement with the associated general ledger accounts.

Southern Bank Statement

You may want to review the steps for Account Reconciliation in Chapter 10, pages 317-319, steps 1-6.

Statement of Account Southern Bank January 1 to January 31, 2016		Account No. 21383-21-01		Wendy's Service Merchandise 1341 Farrington Road Tucson, AZ 85750	
REGULAR CHECKING					
Previous Balance	12/31/15	76,500.00			
8 Deposits(+)		3,390.88			
11 Checks (-)		9,450.63			
Service Charges (-)	1/31/16	18.00			
Ending Balance	1/31/16	**70,422.25**			
DEPOSITS					
1/17/16	324.00	1/25/16	1,404.00	1/28/16	53.88
1/23/16	324.00	1/26/16	324.00	1/31/16	640.00
1/25/16	105.00	1/27/16	216.00		
CHECKS (Asterisk * indicates break in check number sequence)					
	1/4/16	Transfer	6,500.00		
	1/26/16	3030	160.00		
	1/26/16	3031	45.00		
	1/26/16	3032	107.65		
	1/27/16	3033	72.14		
	1/27/16	3034	500.00		
	1/27/16	3035	500.00		
	1/28/16	3036	370.44		
	1/30/16	3037	392.00		
	1/30/16	3038	117.60		
	1/30/16	3039	685.80		

NOTE: Deposits that are recorded on the same day may be added together on the Account Reconciliation window.

$$1,404.00 + 105.00 = \$1,509.00$$
$$324.00 + 216.00 \quad\quad 540.00$$
$$53.88 + 640.00 = \quad 693.88$$

Payroll Checking Account Bank Statement

Statement of Account Payroll Checking Account January 1 to January 31, 2016		Account No. 961-782239	Wendy's Service Merchandise 1341 Farrington Road Tucson, AZ 85750	
		REGULAR CHECKING		
Previous Balance	12/31/15	0.00		
1 Deposits(+)		6,500.00		
6 Checks (-)		2,606.52		
Service Charges (-)	1/31/16	15.00		
Ending Balance	1/31/16	**3,878.48**		
		DEPOSITS		
	1/4/16	6,500.00		
		CHECKS (Asterisk * indicates break in check number sequence)		
	1/11/16	101	430.69	
	1/11/16	102	438.15	
	1/18/16	103	430.69	
	1/18/16	104	438.15	
	1/25/16	105	430.69	
	1/25/16	106	438.15	

Printing Reports: Account Reconciliation, Accounts Receivable, Accounts Payable, and Inventory

1. Print the Southern Bank account reconciliation report.

Wendy's Service Merchandise
Account Reconciliation
As of Jan 31, 2016
10200 - Southern Bank
Bank Statement Date: January 31, 2016

Filter Criteria includes: Report is printed in Detail Format.

Beginning GL Balance				76,500.00
Add: Cash Receipts				5,982.88
Less: Cash Disbursements				(3,950.63)
Add (Less) Other				(6,518.00)
Ending GL Balance				72,014.25
Ending Bank Balance				70,422.25
Add back deposits in transit				
	Jan 30, 2016	1/30/16	2,592.00	
Total deposits in transit				2,592.00
(Less) outstanding checks				
	Jan 29, 2016	3040	(500.00)	
	Jan 29, 2016	3041	(500.00)	
Total outstanding checks				(1,000.00)
Add (Less) Other				
Total other				
Unreconciled difference				0.00
Ending GL Balance				72,014.25

2. Print the Payroll Checking Account reconciliation report. (*Hint:* On the Account Reconciliation Select a Report or Form window, click

    ⚙ Options . In the Select a filter field, select Account No. 10300, Payroll Checking Account.)

Wendy's Service Merchandise
Account Reconciliation
As of Jan 31, 2016
10300 - Payroll Checking Account
Bank Statement Date: January 31, 2016

Filter Criteria includes: Report is printed in Detail Format.

Beginning GL Balance				
Add: Cash Receipts				
Less: Cash Disbursements				(3,475.36)
Add (Less) Other				6,485.00
Ending GL Balance				3,009.64
Ending Bank Balance				3,878.48
Add back deposits in transit				
Total deposits in transit				
(Less) outstanding checks				
	Jan 29, 2016	107	(430.69)	
	Jan 29, 2016	108	(438.15)	
Total outstanding checks				(868.84)
Add (Less) Other				
Total other				
Unreconciled difference				0.00
Ending GL Balance				3,009.64

3. Print the General Ledger accounts 10200 and 10300. (*Hint:* On the General Ledger Select a Report or Form window, select General

    Ledger > [Options]. On the Modify Report - General Ledger window > select the filter GL Account ID > One or more > check the boxes next to 10200 and 10300. Click <OK>.

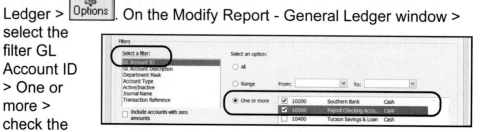

Wendy's Service Merchandise
General Ledger
For the Period From Jan 1, 2016 to Jan 31, 2016
Filter Criteria includes: 1) IDs: Multiple IDs. Report order is by ID. Report is printed with shortened descriptions and in Detail Format.

Account ID Account Descri	Date	Reference	Jrnl	Trans Description	Debit Amt	Credit A	Balance
10200	1/1/16			Beginning Balance			76,500.00
Southern Bank	1/4/16	Transfer	GENJ	Southern Bank		6,500.00	
	1/14/16	Invoice 103	CRJ	Peter Malin	324.00		
	1/21/16	Invoice 101	CRJ	Arlene Petty	324.00		
	1/23/16	Invoice 104	CRJ	Jessica Prince	105.00		
	1/23/16	Cash	CRJ	Cash sales	1,404.00		
	1/24/16	3030	CDJ	Morgan Knapp		160.00	
	1/24/16	3031	CDJ	U.S. Post Office		45.00	
	1/24/16	3032	CDJ	Main Office Supplies		107.65	
	1/24/16	3033	CDJ	LRI Phone Co.		72.14	
	1/25/16	3034	CDJ	Alex Ziegler		500.00	
	1/25/16	3035	CDJ	Wendy Lincoln		500.00	
	1/25/16	3036	CDJ	Len Lacey Products		370.44	
	1/25/16	Invoice 106	CRJ	Arlene Petty	324.00		
	1/25/16	Invoice 108	CRJ	Peter Malin	216.00		
	1/28/16	3037	CDJ	James Jarvis Hardware		392.00	
	1/28/16	3038	CDJ	Ronnie Becker Fabrics		117.60	
	1/28/16	Invoice 105	CRJ	Bonni Berman	53.88		
	1/28/16	Invoice 102	CRJ	Denise Crosby	640.00		
	1/29/16	3039	CDJ	CME Mortgage Co.		685.80	
	1/29/16	3040	CDJ	Alex Ziegler		500.00	
	1/29/16	3041	CDJ	Wendy Lincoln		500.00	
	1/30/16	Cash	CRJ	Bertha Rabago	216.00		
	1/30/16	Cash	CRJ	Cash sales	2,376.00		
	1/31/16	01/31/16	GENJ	Service Charge		18.00	
				Current Period Change	5,982.88	10,468.6	-4,485.75
	1/31/16			**Ending Balance**			72,014.25
10300	1/1/16			Beginning Balance			
Payroll Checking	1/4/16	Transfer	GENJ	Payroll Checking Account	6,500.00		
	1/8/16	101	PRJ	Tim Anderson		430.69	
	1/8/16	102	PRJ	Laurie Gallardo		438.15	
	1/15/16	103	PRJ	Tim Anderson		430.69	
	1/15/16	104	PRJ	Laurie Gallardo		438.15	
	1/22/16	105	PRJ	Tim Anderson		430.69	
	1/22/16	106	PRJ	Laurie Gallardo		438.15	
	1/29/16	107	PRJ	Tim Anderson		430.69	
	1/29/16	108	PRJ	Laurie Gallardo		438.15	
	1/31/16	01/31/16	GENJ	Service Charge		15.00	
				Current Period Change	6,500.00	3,490.36	3,009.64
	1/31/16			**Ending Balance**			3,009.64

Observe that Account No. 10200, Southern Bank; and Account No. 10300, Payroll Checking Account agree with the Ending GL Balances shown on the account reconciliation reports on pages 575 and 576: $71,014.25 and $3,009.64, respectively.

4. Print the general ledger account balance for Account No. 11000, Accounts Receivable.

Wendy's Service Merchandise
General Ledger
For the Period From Jan 1, 2016 to Jan 31, 2016
Filter Criteria includes: 1) IDs: 11000. Report order is by ID. Report is printed with shortened descriptions and in Detail Format.

Account ID Account Description	Date	Reference	Jrnl	Trans Description	Debit Amt	Credit Amt	Balance
11000	1/1/16			Beginning Balance			
Accounts Receivable	1/7/16	101	SJ	Arlene Petty	324.00		
	1/7/16	102	SJ	Denise Crosby	640.00		
	1/7/16	103	SJ	Peter Malin	432.00		
	1/7/16	104	SJ	Jessica Prince	486.00		
	1/10/16	105	SJ	Bonni Berman	53.88		
	1/14/16	CM103	SJ	Peter Malin		108.00	
	1/14/16	Invoice 103	CRJ	Peter Malin - Invoice: 103		324.00	
	1/18/16	106	SJ	Arlene Petty	324.00		
	1/18/16	107	SJ	Denise Crosby	320.00		
	1/18/16	108	SJ	Peter Malin	216.00		
	1/21/16	Invoice 101	CRJ	Arlene Petty - Invoice: 101		324.00	
	1/21/16	109	SJ	Bonni Berman	81.00		
	1/23/16	Invoice 104	CRJ	Jessica Prince - Invoice: 10		105.00	
	1/25/16	Invoice 106	CRJ	Arlene Petty - Invoice: 106		324.00	
	1/25/16	Invoice 108	CRJ	Peter Malin - Invoice: 108		216.00	
	1/28/16	Invoice 105	CRJ	Bonni Berman - Invoice: 10		53.88	
	1/28/16	Invoice 102	CRJ	Denise Crosby - Invoice: 10		640.00	
				Current Period Change	2,876.88	2,094.88	782.00
	1/31/16			Ending Balance			782.00

5. Compare the general ledger's accounts receivable balance to the customer ledgers balance.

Wendy's Service Merchandise
Customer Ledgers
For the Period From Jan 1, 2016 to Jan 31, 2016
Filter Criteria includes: Report order is by ID. Report is printed in Detail Format.

Customer ID Customer	Date	Trans No	Typ	Debit Amt	Credit Amt	Balance
ap001	1/7/16	101	SJ	324.00		324.00
Arlene Petty	1/18/16	106	SJ	324.00		648.00
	1/21/16	Invoice 101	CRJ		324.00	324.00
	1/25/16	Invoice 106	CRJ		324.00	0.00
bb002	1/10/16	105	SJ	53.88		53.88
Bonni Berman	1/21/16	109	SJ	81.00		134.88
	1/28/16	Invoice 105	CRJ		53.88	81.00
dc003	1/7/16	102	SJ	640.00		640.00
Denise Crosby	1/18/16	107	SJ	320.00		960.00
	1/28/16	Invoice 102	CRJ		640.00	320.00
jp004	1/7/16	104	SJ	486.00		486.00
Jessica Prince	1/23/16	Invoice 104	CRJ		105.00	381.00
pm005	1/7/16	103	SJ	432.00		432.00
Peter Malin	1/14/16	CM103	SJ		108.00	324.00
	1/14/16	Invoice 103	CRJ		324.00	0.00
	1/18/16	108	SJ	216.00		216.00
	1/25/16	Invoice 108	CRJ		216.00	0.00
Report Total				**2,876.88**	**2,094.88**	**782.00**

6. Print the general ledger account balance for Account No. 20000, Account Payable. (A minus sign in front of a general ledger balance means it is a credit balance.)

Wendy's Service Merchandise
General Ledger
For the Period From Jan 1, 2016 to Jan 31, 2016

Filter Criteria includes: 1) IDs: 20000. Report order is by ID. Report is printed with shortened descriptions and in Detail Format.

Account ID Account Descript	Date	Reference	Jrnl	Trans Description	Debit Amt	Credit Am	Balance
20000	1/1/16			Beginning Balance			
Accounts Payable	1/3/16	56JJ	PJ	James Jarvis Hardware		300.00	
	1/14/16	112	PJ	Tom's Sales and Service		512.00	
	1/21/16	90	PJ	Len Lacey Products		432.00	
	1/21/16	210	PJ	Ronnie Becker Fabrics		120.00	
	1/21/16	78JJ	PJ	James Jarvis Hardware		500.00	
	1/25/16	VCM90	PJ	Len Lacey Products	54.00		
	1/25/16	3036	CD	Len Lacey Products - Invoice: 90	378.00		
	1/28/16	VCM78JJ	PJ	James Jarvis Hardware	100.00		
	1/28/16	3037	CD	James Jarvis Hardware - Invoice: 78	400.00		
	1/28/16	3038	CD	Ronnie Becker Fabrics - Invoice: 210	120.00		
				Current Period Change	1,052.00	1,864.00	-812.00
	1/31/16			**Ending Balance**			-812.00

7. Compare the general ledger's accounts payable balance to the vendor ledgers balance.

Wendy's Service Merchandise
Vendor Ledgers
For the Period From Jan 1, 2016 to Jan 31, 2016

Filter Criteria includes: Report order is by ID.

Vendor ID Vendor	Date	Trans No	Type	Paid	Debit Amt	Credit Amt	Balance
JJH06	1/3/16	56JJ	PJ			300.00	300.00
James Jarvis Hardware	1/21/16	78JJ	PJ	*		500.00	800.00
	1/28/16	VCM78JJ	PJ	*	100.00		700.00
	1/28/16	3037	CDJ		8.00	8.00	700.00
	1/28/16	3037	CDJ		400.00		300.00
LLP07	1/21/16	90	PJ	*		432.00	432.00
Len Lacey Products	1/25/16	VCM90	PJ	*	54.00		378.00
	1/25/16	3036	CDJ			7.56	378.00
	1/25/16	3036	CDJ		378.00		0.00
RBF08	1/21/16	210	PJ	*		120.00	120.00
Ronnie Becker Fabrics	1/28/16	3038	CDJ		2.40	2.40	120.00
	1/28/16	3038	CDJ		120.00		0.00
TSS09	1/14/16	112	PJ			512.00	512.00
Tom's Sales and Service							
Report Total					1,069.96	1,881.96	812.00

8. Print the general ledger account balance for Account No. 12000, Merchandise Inventory.

Wendy's Service Merchandise
General Ledger
For the Period From Jan 1, 2016 to Jan 31, 2016
Filter Criteria includes: 1) IDs: 12000. Report order is by ID. Report is printed with shortened descriptions and in Detail Format.

Account ID Account Description	Date	Reference	Jrnl	Trans Description	Debit Amt	Credit A	Balance
12000	1/1/16			Beginning Balance			27,740.00
Merchandise Inventory	1/3/16	56JJ	PJ	James Jarvis Hardware - Item: 0	300.00		
	1/7/16	101	COGS	Arlene Petty - Item: 001hardwar		100.00	
	1/7/16	102	COGS	Denise Crosby - Item: 003floor -		216.00	
	1/7/16	103	COGS	Peter Malin - Item: 002wall - Fou		120.00	
	1/7/16	104	COGS	Jessica Prince - Item: 001hardw		150.00	
	1/14/16	CM103	COGS	Peter Malin - Item: 002wall - Ret	30.00		
	1/14/16	112	PJ	Tom's Sales and Service - Item:	512.00		
	1/16/16	AZ	INAJ	lighting		128.00	
	1/18/16	106	COGS	Arlene Petty - Item: 001hardwar		100.00	
	1/18/16	107	COGS	Denise Crosby - Item: 003floor -		108.00	
	1/18/16	108	COGS	Peter Malin - Item: 002wall - Tw		60.00	
	1/21/16	90	PJ	Len Lacey Products - Item: 003fl	432.00		
	1/21/16	210	PJ	Ronnie Becker Fabrics - Item: 0	120.00		
	1/21/16	78JJ	PJ	James Jarvis Hardware - Item: 0	500.00		
	1/23/16	Cash	COGS	Cash sales - Item: 001hardware		100.00	
	1/23/16	Cash	COGS	Cash sales - Item: 002wall - Ten		300.00	
	1/25/16	VCM90	PJ	Len Lacey Products - Item: 003fl		54.00	
	1/28/16	VCM78JJ	PJ	James Jarvis Hardware - Item: 0		100.00	
	1/30/16	Cash	COGS	Bertha Rabago - Item: 002wall -		60.00	
	1/30/16	Cash	COGS	Cash sales - Item: 001hardware		400.00	
	1/30/16	Cash	COGS	Cash sales - Item: 002wall - Ten		300.00	
				Current Period Change	1,894.00	2,296.00	-402.00
	1/31/16			**Ending Balance**			**27,338.00**

9. Compare the general ledger's merchandise inventory account balance to the Inventory Valuation Report's item value. (*Hint:* From the Reports list, select Inventory > Inventory Valuation Report. If your reports do not agree, refer to How to Fix?, page 583.)

Wendy's Service Merchandise
Inventory Valuation Report
As of Jan 31, 2016
Filter Criteria includes: 1) Stock/Assembly. Report order is by ID. Report is printed with shortened descriptions.

Item ID Item Class	Item Descriptio	Stocking U/M	Cost Met	Qty on Hand	Item Value	Avg Cost	% of Inv Value
001hardware Stock item	hardware	each	Average	87.00	4,350.00	50.00	15.91
002wall Stock item	wall	each	Average	125.00	3,750.00	30.00	13.72
003floor Stock item	floor	each	Average	201.00	10,854.00	54.00	39.70
004lights Stock item	lighting	each	Average	131.00	8,384.00	64.00	30.67
					27,338.00		**100.00**

PRINTING THE GENERAL LEDGER TRIAL BALANCE

Wendy's Service Merchandise
General Ledger Trial Balance
As of Jan 31, 2016

Filter Criteria includes: Report order is by ID. Report is printed in Detail Format.

Account ID	Account Description	Debit Amt	Credit Amt
10200	Southern Bank	72,014.25	
10300	Payroll Checking Account	3,009.64	
10400	Tucson Savings & Loan	22,000.00	
11000	Accounts Receivable	782.00	
12000	Merchandise Inventory	27,338.00	
13000	Supplies	1,750.00	
14000	Prepaid Insurance	2,400.00	
15000	Furniture and Fixtures	5,000.00	
15100	Computers & Equipment	7,500.00	
15500	Building	100,000.00	
20000	Accounts Payable		812.00
23100	Sales Tax Payable		429.99
23400	Federal Payroll Taxes Payable		290.28
23500	FUTA Tax Payable		24.92
23600	State Payroll Taxes Payable		66.88
23700	SUTA Payable		141.12
24000	Soc. Sec. Employee Taxes Payab		257.32
24100	Soc. Sec. Employer Taxes Payab		257.32
24200	Medicare Employee Taxes Payabl		60.16
24400	Medicare Employer Taxes Payabl		60.16
27000	Long-Term Notes Payable		20,500.00
27400	Mortgage Payable		74,412.05
39006	Alex Ziegler, Capital		73,695.00
39007	Alex Ziegler, Drawing	1,000.00	
39008	Wendy Lincoln, Capital		73,695.00
39009	Wendy Lincoln, Drawing	1,000.00	
40000	Sales-Hardware		2,550.00
40200	Sales-Wall		2,700.00
40400	Sales-Floor		960.00
40600	Service Fees		124.89
50000	Cost of Sales-Hardware	850.00	
50500	Cost of Sales-Wall	810.00	
57000	Cost of Sales-Floor	324.00	
57050	Cost of Sales-Lights	128.00	
59500	Purchase Discounts		17.96
62000	Bank Charges	33.00	
67500	Interest Expense	97.85	
70000	Maintenance Expense	160.00	
72510	Soc. Sec. Expense	257.32	
72520	Medicare Expense	60.16	
72530	FUTA Expense	24.92	
72540	SUTA Expense	141.12	
73500	Postage Expense	45.00	
75500	Supplies Expense	107.65	
76000	Telephone Expense	72.14	
77500	Wages Expense	4,000.00	
77600	Overtime Expense	150.00	
	Total:	251,055.05	251,055.05

PRINTING THE FINANCIAL STATEMENTS

1. Print the <Standard> Balance Sheet.

Wendy's Service Merchandise
Balance Sheet
January 31, 2016

ASSETS

Current Assets		
Southern Bank	$ 72,014.25	
Payroll Checking Account	3,009.64	
Tucson Savings & Loan	22,000.00	
Accounts Receivable	782.00	
Merchandise Inventory	27,338.00	
Supplies	1,750.00	
Prepaid Insurance	2,400.00	
Total Current Assets		129,293.89
Property and Equipment		
Furniture and Fixtures	5,000.00	
Computers & Equipment	7,500.00	
Building	100,000.00	
Total Property and Equipment		112,500.00
Other Assets		
Total Other Assets		0.00
Total Assets	$	241,793.89

LIABILITIES AND CAPITAL

Current Liabilities		
Accounts Payable	$ 812.00	
Sales Tax Payable	429.99	
Federal Payroll Taxes Payable	290.28	
FUTA Tax Payable	24.92	
State Payroll Taxes Payable	66.88	
SUTA Payable	141.12	
Soc. Sec. Employee Taxes Payab	257.32	
Soc. Sec. Employer Taxes Payab	257.32	
Medicare Employee Taxes Payabl	60.16	
Medicare Employer Taxes Payabl	60.16	
Total Current Liabilities		2,400.15

Continued

Long-Term Liabilities		
Long-Term Notes Payable	20,500.00	
Mortgage Payable	74,412.05	
Total Long-Term Liabilities		94,912.05
Total Liabilities		97,312.20
Capital		
Alex Ziegler, Capital	73,695.00	
Alex Ziegler, Drawing	(1,000.00)	
Wendy Lincoln, Capital	73,695.00	
Wendy Lincoln, Drawing	(1,000.00)	
Net Income	(908.31)	
Total Capital		144,481.69
Total Liabilities & Capital	$	241,793.89

Unaudited - For Management Purposes Only

2. Print the <Standard> Income Stmnt. Compare your Income Statement with the one shown on the next page.

How to Fix?

What if the general ledger Account No. 12000, Merchandise Inventory, does not agree with the Item Value balance on the Inventory Valuation report? If they are different, make sure that you selected inventory items on both the Sales/Invoicing window (Sales Journal) and Purchases/Receive Inventory window (Purchase Journal).

Wendy's Service Merchandise
Income Statement
For the One Month Ending January 31, 2016

		Current Month				Year to Date	
Revenues							
Sales-Hardware	$	2,550.00	40.25	$		2,550.00	40.25
Sales-Wall		2,700.00	42.62			2,700.00	42.62
Sales-Floor		960.00	15.15			960.00	15.15
Service Fees		124.89	1.97			124.89	1.97
Total Revenues		6,334.89	100.00			6,334.89	100.00
Cost of Sales							
Cost of Sales-Hardware		850.00	13.42			850.00	13.42
Cost of Sales-Wall		810.00	12.79			810.00	12.79
Cost of Sales-Floor		324.00	5.11			324.00	5.11
Cost of Sales-Lights		128.00	2.02			128.00	2.02
Purchase Discounts		(17.96)	(0.28)			(17.96)	(0.28)
Total Cost of Sales		2,094.04	33.06			2,094.04	33.06
Gross Profit		4,240.85	66.94			4,240.85	66.94
Expenses							
Bank Charges		33.00	0.52			33.00	0.52
Interest Expense		97.85	1.54			97.85	1.54
Maintenance Expense		160.00	2.53			160.00	2.53
Soc. Sec. Expense		257.32	4.06			257.32	4.06
Medicare Expense		60.16	0.95			60.16	0.95
FUTA Expense		24.92	0.39			24.92	0.39
SUTA Expense		141.12	2.23			141.12	2.23
Postage Expense		45.00	0.71			45.00	0.71
Supplies Expense		107.65	1.70			107.65	1.70
Telephone Expense		72.14	1.14			72.14	1.14
Wages Expense		4,000.00	63.14			4,000.00	63.14
Overtime Expense		150.00	2.37			150.00	2.37
Total Expenses		5,149.16	81.28			5,149.16	81.28
Net Income	$	(908.31)	(14.34)	$		(908.31)	(14.34)

3. Print the <Standard> Cash Flow. Compare your Statement of Cash Flow to the one shown on the next page.

Wendy's Service Merchandise
Statement of Cash Flow
For the one Month Ended January 31, 2016

		Current Month		Year to Date
Cash Flows from operating activities				
Net Income	$	(908.31)	$	(908.31)
Adjustments to reconcile net				
income to net cash provided				
by operating activities				
Accounts Receivable		(782.00)		(782.00)
Merchandise Inventory		402.00		402.00
Accounts Payable		812.00		812.00
Sales Tax Payable		429.99		429.99
Federal Payroll Taxes Payable		290.28		290.28
FUTA Tax Payable		24.92		24.92
State Payroll Taxes Payable		66.88		66.88
SUTA Payable		141.12		141.12
Soc. Sec. Employee Taxes Payab		257.32		257.32
Soc. Sec. Employer Taxes Payab		257.32		257.32
Medicare Employee Taxes Payabl		60.16		60.16
Medicare Employer Taxes Payabl		60.16		60.16
Total Adjustments		2,020.15		2,020.15
Net Cash provided by Operations		1,111.84		1,111.84
Cash Flows from investing activities				
Used For				
Net cash used in investing		0.00		0.00
Cash Flows from financing activities				
Proceeds From				
Used For				
Mortgage Payable		(587.95)		(587.95)
Alex Ziegler, Drawing		(1,000.00)		(1,000.00)
Wendy Lincoln, Drawing		(1,000.00)		(1,000.00)
Net cash used in financing		(2,587.95)		(2,587.95)
Net increase <decrease> in cash	$	(1,476.11)	$	(1,476.11)
Summary				
Cash Balance at End of Period	$	97,023.89	$	97,023.89
Cash Balance at Beg of Period		(98,500.00)		(98,500.00)
Net Increase <Decrease> in Cash	$	(1,476.11)	$	(1,476.11)

Unaudited - For Internal Use Only.

BACKING UP CHAPTER 15 DATA

If your reports agree with the ones shown, make a backup. If your printouts do not agree with the ones shown, make the necessary corrections.

Back up. The suggested file name **Chapter 15.ptb**.

EXPORT REPORTS TO EXCEL

1. Export the following reports to Excel:

    - Payroll Journal
    - General Ledger Trial Balance
    - Balance Sheet
    - Income Statement
    - Statement of Cash Flow

2. Save. Use the file name **Chapter 15_PayJ_GLTB_BS_IS_SCF.xlsx**.

    NOTE: If your instructor would like you to save reports as PDF files, do that. The suggested file name is **Chapter 15_Payroll Journal.pdf**, etc. Your instructor may require additional reports.

ONLINE LEARNING CENTER

Complete end-of-chapter activities at www.mhhe.com/yacht2016 > select Student Edition, then Chapter 15.

1. Quizzes: Multiple Choice and True False questions. Interactive online tests that are graded and can be emailed to your instructor.

2. More Resources:

    a. QA Templates: Answer 10 multiple-choice questions and one Analysis Question.

    b. Narrated PowerPoints: Listen to the narrated PowerPoints.

    c. Going to the Net Exercises: Access the Employer Reporting website.

d. Assessment Rubric: Complete the rubric to review Sage 50's journals, navigation centers, modules, task windows, and reports.

The OLC also includes links to the Appendixes:

- Appendix A: Troubleshooting
- Appendix B: Accounting Information Systems
- Appendix C: Review of Accounting Principles
- Appendix D: Glossary (words that are boldfaced and italicized in chapter)

Exercise 15-1: Follow the instructions below to complete Exercise 15-1. Exercises 12-1, 12-2, 13-1, 13-2, 14-1, and 14-2 must be completed before starting Exercise 15-1.

1. Start Sage. Open the company that you set up in Exercise 12-1, Your last name Sales and Service.

2. If necessary, restore the Exercise 14-1.ptb file which was backed up on page 542. To make sure you are starting with the correct data, display Exercise 14-2's General Ledger Trial balance (step 6, page 542).

3. Journalize and post the following General Journal entry:

   01/4/16   Transfer $5,450 from Account No. 10200, First Interstate, to Account No. 10300, Payroll Checking Account.

4. Print the January 3, 2016 General Journal.

5. For setting up payroll, refer to the Payroll Setup Wizard, pages 550-553. Use the following information:

   State: GA
   State Unemployment   Rate: **3.4%**
   Georgia Administrative   Assessment Tax Rate: **.08%**

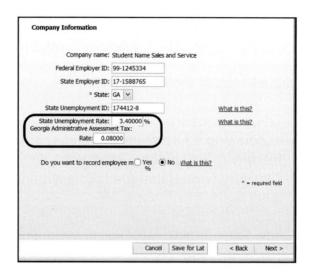

Overtime Expense: Account No. 77600, Overtime Expense

6. For entering employee and employer defaults, refer to pages 553-555. Use the Employee Fields shown below.

Field Name	GL Account
Fed_Income	23400, Federal Payroll Taxes Payable
Soc_Sec	24000, Soc. Sec. Employee Taxes Payable
MEDICARE	Account No. 24200, Medicare Employee Taxes Payable
St_Income	Account No. 23600, State Payroll Taxes Payable

Verify your Employee Fields window with the one shown on page 554.

7. Use the following Company Fields.

Field Name	Liability column	Expense column
Soc_Sec_C	24100, Soc. Sec. Employer Taxes Payable	72510, Soc. Sec. Expense

Medicare_C	24400 Medicare Employer Taxes Payable	72520, Medicare Expense
Fed_Unemp_C	23500, FUTA Tax Payable	72530, FUTA Expense
St_Unemp_C	23700, SUTA Payable	72540, SUTA Expense
St2_Unemp_C	23755, SUTA2 Payable	72545, SUTA2 Expense

Verify your Company Fields window with the one shown on page 555. St2_Unemp_C is specific to Georgia payroll tax.

8. Refer to pages 555-559 to complete the payroll setup wizard. The Assign Company-Paid Taxes window shows ST2_Unemp_C for Other State Unemployment which is specific to GA payroll taxes.

   (*Hint:* Other State Unemployment is not shown on page 557 for the company in Arizona. For Georgia, this field is completed)

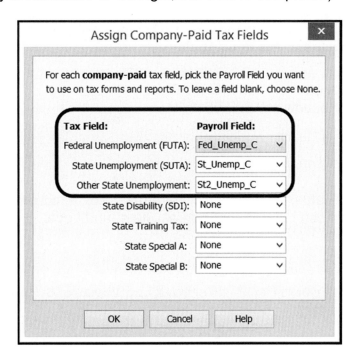

9. Add the following employees.

    Employee ID: C50
    Name: Rick Cooke
    Accept the default for Employee
    Address: 5300 Atlantic Avenue
    City, ST, Zip: Norcross, GA 30092
    E-mail: cooke@email.com
    Home phone: 404-555-3203
    Social Security #: 001-00-4000
    Type: FULL

    Withholding Info:

    Filing Status: Single for Federal, State, and Local
    Allowances: 1 for Federal, State, and Local

    Pay Info: Hourly - Hours per Pay Period, $12.50/hour; $18.75/hour,
    overtime; paid weekly

    Employee ID: M60
    Name: Madison Malloy
    Accept the default for Employee
    Address: 14821 East Oakwood Street
    City, ST, Zip: Norcross, GA 30092
    E-mail: malloy@email.com
    Home phone: 770-555-2934
    Social Security #: 002-00-1241
    Type: FULL

    Withholding Info:

    Filing Status: Single for Federal, State, and Local
    Allowances: 1 for Federal, State, and Local

    Pay Info:

    Hourly - Hours Per Pay Period, $12.50/hour; $18.75/hour, overtime;
    paid weekly

10. Print an employee list. (*Hint:* Reports & Forms > Payroll > Employee
    List.)

11. Save the General Journal as a PDF file.

12. Back up. (Use **Exercise 15-1** as the file name.)

13. Exit or continue.

Exercise 15-2: Follow the instructions below to complete Exercise 15-2.

1. Start Sage. Open your company.

2. If necessary, restore data from Exercise 15-1.

3. On January 8, 2016, issue payroll check 6050 to Rick Cooke. Mr. Cooke worked 40 regular hours. Issue paychecks from the Payroll Checking Account. Type **6050** in the Check Number field. To post, save after each payroll transaction.

4. On January 8, 2016, issue payroll check 6051 to Madison Malloy. Ms. Malloy worked 40 regular hours.

5. Make the following payroll entries for Rick Cooke and Madison Malloy.

Date	Name	Hours Worked	Overtime	Check No.
1/15/16	R. Cooke	40		6052
	M. Malloy	40		6053
1/22/16	R. Cooke	40		6054
	M. Malloy	40		6055
1/29/16	R. Cooke	40		6056
	M. Malloy	40		6057

After recording the paycheck information, type the check number, then post. You do *not* need to print paychecks 6050–6057.

6. Print the Payroll Journal.

7. Complete account reconciliation for Account No. 10200, First Interstate.

Statement of Account				Student Name Sales and Service		
First Interstate January 1 to January 31, 2016		Account No. 920-3933-12		10200 Pine Street Norcross, GA 30092		
REGULAR CHECKING						
Previous Balance		12/31/15	$65,500.00			
6 Deposits(+)			7,360.20			
8 Checks (-)			6,839.57			
Service Charges (-)		1/31/16	12.00			
Ending Balance		1/31/16	**66,008.63**			
DEPOSITS						
1/15/16	367.20	1/25/16	275.40			
1/22/16	486.00	1/30/16	972.00			
1/23/16	507.60	1/30/16	4,752.00			
CHECKS (Asterisk * indicates break in check number sequence)						
		1/5/16	Transfer	5,450.00		
		1/15/16	2020	392.00		
		1/25/16	2021	235.20		
		1/25/16	2022	125.00		
		1/27/16	2023	45.00		
		1/27/16	2024	145.72		
		1/27/16	2025	46.65		
		1/30/16	2026	400.00		

8. Complete account reconciliation for Account No. 10300, Payroll Checking Account. The bank statement is shown on the next page.

Statement of Account Payroll Checking Account January 1 to January 31, 2016		Account No. 99-114401	Student Name Sales and Service 1834 East Peachtree Blvd. Norcross, GA 30092	
REGULAR CHECKING				
Previous Balance	12/31/15	0.00		
1 Deposits(+)		5,450.00		
8 Checks (-)		3,142.24		
Service Charges (-)	1/31/16	15.00		
Ending Balance	1/31/16	**2,292.76**		
DEPOSITS				
	1/4/16	5,450.00		
CHECKS (Asterisk * indicates break in check number sequence)				
	1/11/16	6050	392.78	
	1/11/16	6051	392.78	
	1/14/16	6052	392.78	
	1/14/16	6053	392.78	
	1/21/16	6054	392.78	
	1/21/16	6055	392.78	
	1/28/16	6056	392.78	
	1/28/16	6057	392.78	

9. Print the account reconciliation reports for First Interstate and the Payroll Checking Account.

10. Print the Customer Ledgers; Vendor Ledgers; and Inventory Valuation Report.

11. Print the General Ledger Trial Balance.

12. Print the following financial statements: Balance Sheet, Income Statement, and Statement of Cash Flow.

Check Your Figures:

Total Assets:	$192,251.39
Gross Profit	4,447.80
Net Increase in Cash	2,801.39

13. Make a backup. (Use **Exercise 15-2** as the file name.)

14. Export the following files to Excel:

    - Employee List
    - Customer Ledgers
    - Vendor Ledgers
    - Inventory Valuation Report
    - Payroll Journal

    - General Ledger Trial Balance
    - Balance Sheet
    - Income Statement
    - Statement of Cash Flow.

15. Use the file name **Exercise 15-2_EL_CL_VL_IVR_PayJ_GLTB_
    BS_IS_SCF.xlsx.**

16. Save these reports as PDF files: Employee List, Customer Ledgers,
    Vendor Ledgers, Inventory Valuation Report, Payroll Journal,
    General Ledger Trial Balance, Balance Sheet, Income Statement,
    and Statement of Cash Flow.

CHAPTER 15 INDEX

In Project 2, you complete the Computer Accounting Cycle for Highland Sports, a merchandising business. Highland Sports sells mountain bicycles, road bicycles, and children's bicycles. It is organized as a corporation. You purchased Highland Sports in December 2015.

It is the purpose of Project 2 to review what you have learned in Chapters 12 through 15, Part 3 of Sage 50 for Merchandising Businesses. Accounts payable, accounts receivable, payroll, and inventory transactions are included in this project. Account reconciliation is also completed.

Vendors offer Highland Sports a purchase discount of 2% 15, Net 30 days. Highland Sports is located in OR where there is no sales tax.

At the end of Project 2, a checklist is shown listing the reports that you should have. The step-by-step instructions also remind you to print reports and back up.

Follow these steps to complete Project 2, Highland Sports:

Step 1: Start Sage 50.

Step 2: If a company opens, from the menu bar, select File > New Company > [No] for keeping another company open > click [Next >]. (Or, from the startup window, select Create a new Company.)

Step 3: Complete the following company information:

Company Name: Highland Sports (use your last name, then the company name; for example Smith Highland Sports)
Address Line 1: 98 Highland Road, Store 15

City, State, Zip:	Eugene, OR 97401
Country:	USA
Telephone:	541-555-3555
Fax:	541-555-3557
Business Type:	Corporation
Federal Employer ID:	98-4814362
State Employer ID:	21-7139842
State Unemployment ID:	214132-9
Web Site:	www.highlandsports.com
E-mail:	mail@highlandsports.com

Step   4:   Accept the default for Use a sample business type that closely matches your company.

Step   5:   Scroll down the list. In the **Detailed types** list, select Retail Company. (*Hint:* Account numbers have 5 digits.)

Step   6:   Accept the default for Accrual accounting.

Step   7:   Accept the default for Real Time posting.

Step   8:   Accept the default for 12 monthly accounting periods.

Step   9:   The Choose the first period of your fiscal year window appears. If necessary, select 2016 as the year.

Step 10:   At the You are ready to create your company window, click [Finish]. When the Sage 50 Setup Guide window appears, click on the box next to Don't show this screen at startup to place a checkmark in it. Close the Setup Guide window. Watch the Getting Started videos and read the PDF documents. Close the Sage Advisor Getting Started window.

Step 11:   Change the accounting period to 01-Jan 01, 2016 to Jan 31, 2016—[Period 1 - 01/01/16-01/31/16].

General Ledger

1. Delete the accounts shown below and on the next page.

    10000   Petty Cash
    10100   Cash on Hand

10300	Payroll Checking Account
11500	Allowance for Doubtful Account
14200	Notes Receivable-Current
15400	Leasehold Improvements
15500	Building
15600	Building Improvements
16900	Land
17400	Accum. Depreciation - Leasehold
17500	Accum. Depreciation - Building
17600	Accum. Depreciation - Bldg Imp
19000	Deposits
19200	Note Receivable-Noncurrent
19900	Other Noncurrent Assets
23000	Accrued Expenses
24200	Current Portion Long-Term Debt
60500	Amortization Expense
63000	Charitable Contributions Exp
63500	Commissions and Fees Exp
65000	Employee Benefit Programs Exp
66000	Gifts Expense
68000	Laundry and Cleaning Exp
89000	Other Expense

Change these account names:

10200	Regular Checking Account to US Bank
10400	Savings Account to NW Savings & Loan
12000	Product Inventory to Inventory-Mountain Bikes
14000	Prepaid Expenses to Prepaid Insurance
23300	Deductions Payable to Medicare Employee Taxes Payabl
24000	Other Taxes Payable to Soc. Sec. Employee Taxes Payab
24100	Employee Benefits Payable to Soc. Sec. Employer Taxes Payab
24800	Other Current Liabilities to Short-Term Notes Payable
27000	Notes Payable-Noncurrent to Long-Term Notes Payable
40000	Sales-Merchandise to Sales-Mountain Bikes
50000	Cost of Goods Sold to Cost of Sales-Mountain Bikes
72500	Penalties and Fines Exp to FUTA Expense
73000	Other Taxes to SUTA Expense
74000	Rent or Lease Expense to Rent-Mall Space

Add the accounts shown below and on the next page:

12020	Inventory-Road Bikes	Inventory
12030	Inventory-Children's Bikes	Inventory
23350	Medicare Employer Taxes Payabl	Other Current Liabilities

40020	Sales-Road Bikes	Income
40030	Sales-Children's Bikes	Income
50020	Cost of Sales-Road Bikes	Cost of Sales
50030	Cost of Sales-Children's Bikes	Cost of Sales
73200	Soc. Sec. Expense	Expenses
73300	Medicare Expense	Expenses
73350	Local Payroll Taxes Expense	Expenses

2. Back up. Use **Highland Sports Chart of Accounts** as the file name.

3. Record chart of accounts beginning balances as of December 31, 2015.

Highland Sports, Balance Sheet January 1, 2016		
ASSETS		
Current Assets		
US Bank	$ 86,400.00	
NW Savings & Loan	15,000.00	
Inventory-Mountain Bikes	6,000.00	
Inventory-Road Bikes	8,250.00	
Inventory-Children's Bikes	4,050.00	
Prepaid Insurance	2,400.00	
Total Current Assets		$122,100.00
Property and Equipment: Furniture and Fixtures	6,000.00	
Total Property and Equipment and Other Assets		6,000.00
Total Assets		$128,100.00
LIABILITIES AND STOCKHOLDERS' EQUITY		
Short-Term Notes Payable	4,000.00	
Long-Term Notes Payable	5,500.00	
Total Liabilities		$9,500.00
Stockholder's Equity: Common Stock		118,600.00
Total Liabilities and Stockholders' Equity		$128,100.00

4. Print the December 31, 2015 balance sheet. Save the Project 2 Dec 31, 2015 Balance Sheet as a PDF file.

5. Back up. Use **Highland Sports Starting Balance Sheet** as the file name.

Accounts Payable

Follow the instructions below to set up vendor information for Highland Sports.

1. Set up the following vendor defaults.

Standard <u>T</u>erms:	Due in number of days
Net due in:	30 days
Discount in:	15 days
Discount %	2.00
Credit Limit:	15,000.00

GL Link Accounts:

Expense Account:	12000 Inventory-Mountain Bikes
Discount GL Account:	59500 Purchase Discounts

2. Set up the following vendors.

Vendor ID:	ABC111
Name:	ABC Mountain Bikes
Contact:	Amanda Glass
Mailing Address:	7700 Century Blvd.
City, ST, Zip:	Los Angeles, CA 90082
Vendor Type:	mountain
1099 Type:	Independent Contractor
Expense Account:	12000, Inventory-Mountain Bikes
Telephone 1:	323-555-8919
Fax:	323-555-7648
E-Mail	info@abcmountainbikes.net
Web Site:	www.abcmountainbikes.net

Purchase Info:

Tax ID Number:	41-8354824

Vendor ID:	ERB112
Name:	Escalante Road Bikes
Contact:	Daniel Escalante
Mailing Address:	4822 West Third Street
City, ST, Zip:	El Paso, TX 76314
Vendor Type:	road
1099 Type:	Independent Contractor
Expense Account:	12020, Inventory-Road Bikes
Telephone 1:	915-555-0633
Fax:	915-555-0789
E-mail:	escalante@roadbikes.com
Web Site:	www.roadbikes.com

Purchase Info:

Tax ID Number:	89-9943442

Vendor ID:	TTW113
Name:	Tiny Tots Wheels
Contact:	Mike McDonald
Mailing Address:	1842 San Francisco Street
City, ST, Zip:	Flagstaff, AZ 86003
Vendor Type:	children
1099 Type:	Independent Contractor
Expense Account:	12030, Inventory-Children's Bikes
Telephone 1:	928-555-5831
Fax:	928-555-3249
E-mail:	info@tinytotswheels.biz
Web Site:	www.tinytotswheels.biz

Purchase Defaults:

Tax ID Number:	78-9441402

Accounts Receivable

Follow these steps to set up customer information for Highland Sports.

1. Set up the following customer defaults.

Standard Terms:	Due in number of days
Net due in:	30 days
Discount in:	0 days

Discount %:	0.00
Credit Limit:	5,000.00
GL Sales Account:	40000 Sales-Mountain Bikes
Discount GL Account:	49000 Sales Discounts

2. Set up the following customers.

Customer ID:	DB001
Name:	Denise Barson
Billing address:	48900 Clark Street
City, ST, Zip:	Eugene, OR 97404
Customer type:	LANE (for Lane County)
Telephone 1:	541-555-9233
Fax:	541-555-3934
E-mail	barson@eugene.com
Web site:	www.eugene.com/barson

Sales Info:

GL sales acct:	40000, Sales-Mountain Bikes

Customer ID:	RL002
Name:	Richard Lindner
Billing address:	1434 Princeton Drive
City, ST, Zip:	Eugene, OR 97402
Customer type:	LANE
Telephone 1:	541-555-4893
Fax:	541-555-0622
E-mail:	richard@eugene.com
Web site:	www.eugene.com/lindner

Sales Info:

GL sales acct:	40020, Sales-Road Bikes

Customer ID:	SW003
Name:	Sharon Wilson
Billing address:	13 Lake Street
City, ST, Zip:	Eugene, OR 97404
Customer type:	LANE
Telephone 1:	541-555-4852
Fax:	541-555-0550

E-mail:	wilson@eugene.com
Web site:	www.eugene.com/sharon
Sales Info:	
GL sales acct:	40030, Sales-Children's Bikes

Payroll

1. Use the following information for the Payroll Setup Wizard:

State: OR
State Unemployment Rate: 3.4%
Do you have any localities for which you collect taxes in the state of OR? **Yes**

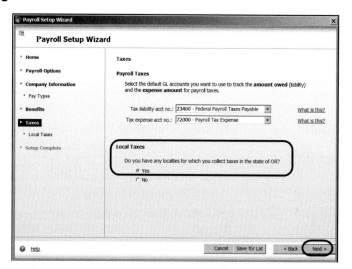

Locality: **Tri-Met**

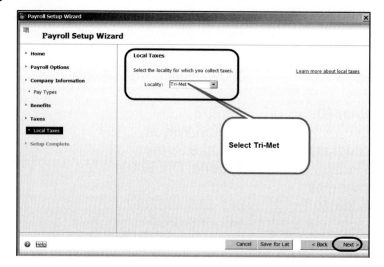

2. For entering employee and employer default information, refer to pages 553-555. Use the Employee Fields shown below.

Field Name	GL Account
Fed_Income	23400, Federal Payroll Taxes Payable
Soc_Sec	24000, Soc. Sec. Employee Taxes Payable
MEDICARE	23300, Medicare Employee Taxes Payable
St_Income	23600, State Payroll Taxes Payable

3. Use the Company Fields shown below.

Field	Liability column	Expense column
Soc_Sec_C	24100, Soc. Sec. Employer Taxes Payable	73200, Soc. Sec. Expense
Medicare_C	23350 Medicare Employer Taxes Payable	73300, Medicare Expense
Fed_Unemp_C	23500, FUTA Tax Payable	72500, FUTA Expense
Loc_IncomeC	23800, Local Payroll Taxes Payable	73350, Local Payroll Taxes Expense
St_Unemp_C	23700, SUTA Payable	73000, SUTA Expense

4. Refer to pages 555-559 to complete the Payroll Setup Wizard's Taxes and Assign Tax Fields.

   a. Compare your Assign Tax Fields for W-2s to page 557.

   b. Compare your Assign Company-Paid Tax Fields to page 557. The State Special A field shows Loc_IncomeC.

   c. Compare Employee-Paid State Taxes to page 558.

5. Add the following employees.

| **Employee ID:** | ML |
| Name: | Mark Lucas |

Accept the default for Employee

Address:	490 School Street
City, ST, Zip:	Eugene, OR 97401
E-mail:	mark@mail.net
Home phone:	541-555-9145
Social Security #:	003-00-0004
Type:	FULL

Withholding Info:

Filing Status:	Married for Federal and State
	Local (Married/Jointly)
Allow:	2 for Federal, State and Local

Pay Info: Salary, $500 per week. (*Hint:* Remember to select Salary as the Pay Method. Weekly is the default.)

| **Employee ID:** | JW |
| Name: | Jane Welch |

Accept the default for Employee

Address:	1300 State Street, Apt. 1D
City, ST, Zip:	Eugene, OR 97402
E-mail:	jane@mail.net
Home phone:	541-555-7997
Social Security #:	050-00-0003
Type:	FULL

Withholding Info:

Filing Status:	Married for Federal and State
	Local (Married/Jointly)
Allow:	2 for Federal, State and Local

Pay Info: Salary, $500 per week.

6. Close.

Inventory

1. Set up the following inventory defaults. On the <u>G</u>eneral Tab select Stock item as the Default Item Class.

2. Click on the G<u>L</u> Accts/Costing tab. For Stock item, Master Stock item, and Assembly, select LIFO as the inventory costing method

3. Set up the following Inventory items.

Item ID:	mbikes
Description:	mountain bikes
Item Class:	Stock item
Description for Sales:	mountain bikes
Price Level 1:	300.00
Last Unit Cost:	150.00
Cost Method:	LIFO
GL Sales Acct:	40000 Sales-Mountain Bikes
GL Inventory Acct:	12000, Merchandise Inventory-Mountain Bikes
GL Cost of Sales Acct:	50000, Cost of Sales-Mountain Bikes
Item Tax Type:	1
Item Type:	mountain
Stocking U/M:	each
Minimum Stock:	10
Reorder Quantity:	5
Preferred Vendor ID:	ABC Mountain Bikes
Beginning Balances:	mountain bikes
Quantity:	40.00
Unit Cost:	150.00
Total Cost:	6,000.00

Item ID:	rbikes
Description:	road bikes
Item Class:	Stock item
Description for Sales:	road bikes
Price Level 1:	150.00
Last Unit Cost:	75.00
Cost Method:	LIFO

GL Sales Acct:	40020, Sales-Road Bikes
GL Inventory Acct:	12020, Inventory-Road Bikes
GL Cost of Sales Acct:	50020, Cost of Sales-Road Bikes
Item Tax Type:	1
Item Type:	road
Stocking U/M:	each
Minimum Stock:	10
Reorder Quantity:	5
Preferred Vendor ID:	Escalante Road Bikes

Beginning Balances: Road Bikes

Quantity:	110.00
Unit Cost:	75.00
Total Cost:	8,250.00

Item ID:	cbikes
Description:	children's bikes
Item Class:	Stock item
Description for Sales:	children's bikes
Price Level 1:	90.00
Last Unit Cost:	45.00
Cost Method:	LIFO
GL Sales Acct:	40030, Sales-Children's Bikes
GL Inventory Acct:	12030, Inventory-Children's Bikes
Cost of Sales Acct:	50030, Cost of Sales-Children's Bikes
Item Tax Type:	1
Item Type:	children
Stocking U/M:	each
Minimum Stock:	10
Reorder Quantity:	5
Preferred Vendor ID:	Tiny Tots Wheels

Beginning Balances: children's bikes

Quantity:	90.00
Unit Cost:	45.00
Total Cost:	4,050.00

4. Back up. Use **Highland Sports Begin** as the filename.

Journalize and post the following transactions:

Date	Description of Transaction

1/08/16   Issued pay checks 5001 and 5002 from US Bank for Jane Welch and Mark Lucas. Type the check number on the Payroll Entry window.

1/08/16   Invoice No. 74A was received from ABC Mountain Bikes for 10 mountain bikes at $150 each.

1/08/16   Invoice No. 801 was received from Tiny Tots Wheels for 15 children's bikes at $45 each.

1/08/16   Invoice No. ER555 was received from Escalante Road Bikes for 12 road bikes at $75 each.

1/10/16   Deposited cash sales of $2,670: 4 mountain bikes, $1,200; 5 road bikes, $750; 8 children's bikes, $720. Cash sales are deposited in the US Bank account. (*Hint: Make sure the correct Sales account is credited.*)

1/11/16   Deposited cash sales of $1,950: 5 children's bikes, $450; 4 road bikes, $600; and 3 mountain bikes, $900.

1/15/16   Issued pay checks 5003 and 5004 for Jane Welch and Mark Lucas. (*Hint: If necessary, complete the Check Number field.*)

1/15/16   Sold one mountain bike to Denise Barson on account, Sales Invoice 101. (*Hint: Type the invoice number in the Invoice No. field. If necessary, select Layout, <Predefined> Product as the Invoice type.*)

1/18/16   Deposited cash sales of $1,920: 3 children's bikes, $270; 2 mountain bikes, $600; 7 road bikes, $1,050.

1/18/16   Issued Check No. 5005 to ABC Mountain Bikes in payment of purchase Invoice No. 74A. Complete the Check/Reference No. field. Issue checks from the US Bank account. (Make sure that the Discount Account field shows 59500 for Purchase Discounts.)

1/18/16   Issued Check No. 5006 to Escalante Road Bikes in payment of purchase Invoice No. ER555.

1/19/16   Issued Check No. 5007 to Tiny Tots Wheels in payment of purchase Invoice No. 801.

1/22/16   Issued pay checks 5008 and 5009 for Jane Welch and Mark Lucas.

1/22/16   Issued Check No. 5010 to Gibson Rentals for $1,350 in payment of mall space rent for Highland Sports. (*Hint: Remember to complete the Check/Reference No. field.*)

1/26/16   Deposited cash sales of $3,810: 6 mountain bikes, $1,800; 8 road bikes, $1,200; 9 children's bikes, $810.

1/26/16   Sold one children's bike to Sharon Wilson on account, Sales Invoice 102. (*Hint: Type the invoice number in the Invoice No. field.*)

1/26/16   Invoice No. 88A was received from ABC Mountain Bikes for three mountain bikes at $150 each.

1/26/16   Invoice No. 962 was received from Tiny Tots Wheels for five children's bikes at $45 each.

1/27/16   Invoice No. ER702 was received from Escalante Road Bikes for five road bikes at $75 each.

1/27/16   Deposited cash sales of $3,240: 6 mountain bikes, $1,800; 6 road bikes, $900; 6 children's bikes, $540.

1/29/16   Issued pay checks 5011 and 5012 for Jane Welch and Mark Lucas.

1/29/16   Issued Check No. 5013 to Jamie Ross for $245 in payment of Short-Term Notes Payable.

1/29/16   Issued Check No. 5014 to US Bank for $175.80 in payment of Long-Term Notes Payable.

1/30/16   Issued Check No. 5015 to City Utilities for $226.65 in payment of utilities.

5. Backup. Use **Highland Sports January** as the file name.

6. Complete account reconciliation for the US Bank account. The January 31, 2016 bank statement is shown below.

Statement of Account US Bank January 1 to January 31, 2016		Account No. 340-5621-214	Highland Sports 98 Highland Road, Store 15 Eugene, OR 97401	
REGULAR CHECKING				
Previous Balance	12/31/15	$86,400.00		
5 Deposits(+)		13,590.00		
12 Checks (-)		7,299.44		
Service Charges (-)	1/31/16	15.00		
Ending Balance	1/31/16	**92,675.56**		
DEPOSITS				
1/11/16	2,670.00	1/25/16	3,810.00	
1/12/16	1,950.00	1/28/16	3,240.00	
1/19/16	1,920.00			
CHECKS (Asterisk * indicates break in check number sequence)				
	1/8/16	5001	419.19	
	1/8/16	5002	419.19	
	1/15/16	5003	419.19	
	1/15/16	5004	419.19	
	1/22/16	5005	1,470.00	
	1/22/16	5006	882.00	
	1/22/16	5007	661.50	
	1/22/16	5008	419.19	
	1/22/16	5009	419.19	
	1/26/16	5010*	1,350.00	
	1/31/16	5013	245.00	
	1/31/16	5014	175.80	

Print the following reports:

1. Print the General Ledger Trial Balance.

2. Print the Account Reconciliation report for the US Bank.

3. Print the Inventory Valuation Report.

4. Print the financial statements: Balance Sheet, Income Statement, and Statement of Cash Flow.

5. Print the Customer Ledgers and Vendor Ledgers.

6. Back up. Use **Highland Sports Financial Statements** as the file name.

7. Export the following reports to Excel: Chart of Accounts, Customer Ledgers, Vendor Ledgers, General Ledger Trial Balance, Account Reconciliation, Balance Sheet, Income Statement, Statement of Cash Flow. Use the file name **Highland Sports_CofA_CL_VL_GLTB_ AcctRec_BS_IS_SCF.xlsx**.

8. Save the following reports as PDF files: Chart of Accounts, Customer Ledgers, Vendors Ledger, General Ledger Trial Balance, Account Reconciliation, Balance Sheet, Income Statement, and Statement of Cash Flow. (Your instructor may require more reports saved as PDF files.)

		CHECKLIST OF PRINTOUTS, Highland Sports
	1	General Ledger Trial Balance
	2	Account Reconciliation – US Bank
	3	Inventory Valuation Report
	4	Balance Sheet
	5	Income Statement
	6	Statement of Cash Flow
	7	Customer Ledgers
	8	Vendor Ledgers
		OPTIONAL PRINTOUTS
	9	Chart of Accounts
	10	December 31, 2015 Balance Sheet
	11	General Ledger
	12	Customer List
	13	Vendor List
	14	Purchase Journal
	15	Cash Disbursements Journal
	16	Sales Journal
	17	Cash Receipts Journal
	19	Payroll Journal
	19	Cost of Goods Sold Journal

Student Name_____**Date**_____

CHECK YOUR PROGRESS: PROJECT 2, Highland Sports

1. What are the total debit and credit balances on your
    General Ledger Trial Balance?   _____

2. What are the total assets on January 31?   _____

3. What is the balance in the US Bank account
    on January 31?   _____

4. How much are total revenues as of January 31?   _____

5. How much net income (net loss) is reported on
    January 31?   _____

6. What is the balance in the Inventory-Mountain Bikes
    account on January 31?   _____

7. What is the balance in the Inventory-Road Bikes
    account on January 31?   _____

8. What is the balance in the Inventory-Children's Bikes
    account on January 31?   _____

9. What is the balance in the Short-Term Notes Payable
    account on January 31?   _____

10. What is the balance in the Common Stock account
    on January 31?   _____

11. What are the total expenses reported on January 31?   _____

12. Were any Accounts Payable incurred during the
    month of January? (Circle your answer.)   YES   NO

Project 2A

Student-Designed Merchandising Business

In Chapters 12, 13, 14, 15 and Project 2, you learned how to complete the Computer Accounting Cycle for merchandising businesses. Project 2A gives you an opportunity to design a merchandising business of your own.

You select the type of merchandising business you want, edit your business's Chart of Accounts, create an opening Balance Sheet and transactions, and complete Sage 50's computer accounting cycle. Project 2A also gives you an opportunity to review the software features learned so far.

You should think about the kind of business you want to create. In Chapters 12, 13, 14 and 15 you worked with Wendy's Service Merchandise, a partnership form of business; and Your Last Name Sales and Service, a sole proprietorship. In Project 2, you worked with Highland Sports, a corporate form of business. You could design a similar business. Other merchandising businesses include: jewelry store, automobile dealer, convenience store, florist, furniture dealer, etc.

Before you begin, you should design your business. You need the following:

1. Company information that includes business name, address, telephone number, and form of business.
2. One of Sage 50's sample companies.
3. A Chart of Accounts: 80 accounts minimum, 110 accounts maximum.
4. A Balance Sheet for your business.
5. One month's transactions for your business. These transactions must include accounts receivable, accounts payable, inventory, and payroll. You should have a minimum of 25 transactions; a maximum of 35 transactions. Your transactions should result in a net income.
6. A bank statement.
7. Complete another month of transactions that result in a net loss.

After you have created your business, you should follow the steps of Sage 50's computer accounting cycle to complete Project 2A.

After completing the Student-Designed Merchandising Business, you should have the following printouts.

		CHECKLIST OF PRINTOUTS
		Student-Designed Merchandising Business
	1	General Ledger Trial Balance
	2	Account Reconciliation Report
	3	Inventory Valuation Report
	4	Balance Sheet
	5	Income Statement
	6	Statement of Cash Flow
	7	Customer Ledgers
	8	Vendor Ledgers
		OPTIONAL PRINTOUTS
	9	Chart of Accounts
	10	General Ledger
	11	Customer List
	12	Vendor List
	13	Purchase Journal
	14	Cash Disbursements Journal
	15	Sales Journal
	16	Cash Receipts Journal
	17	Payroll Journal
	18	Cost of Goods Sold Journal

Part 4

Advanced Sage 50 2016 Applications

Part 4 includes three chapters and three projects.

Chapter 16, Customizing Forms, shows how to change the preprinted forms included with the software.

Chapter 17, Import/Export, shows how to use Sage 50 2016 with a word processing program.

Chapter 18, Microsoft Word and Templates, shows you how to copy Sage 50 reports to Microsoft Word, use Sage 50's write letters feature, and create templates.

Projects 3 and 4 complete your study of *Computer Accounting with Sage 50 2016, 19th Edition*. All features of the software are included for review in these projects.

Project 4A gives you an opportunity to add another month's worth of transactions to any of the projects that you have completed.

The chart on the next page shows the size of the files saved and Sage 50 backups made in Part 4--Chapters 16, 17, 18, Project 3 and Project 4. You may back up or save to a USB flash drive, the hard drive, or network. *To complete work in Chapters 16-18, the Exercise 6-2.ptb file is restored.*

Chapter	Sage 50 Backup (.ptb) Excel (.xlsx) and Adobe (.pdf)	Kilobytes	Page No.
16	Exercise 16-2.ptb	3,661 KB	641
	Exercise 16-2_Copy of Income Stmnt.pdf	8 KB	641
	Exercise 16-2_Copy of Income Stmnt.xlsx	16 KB	641
17	customer.csv	34 KB	648-649
	customer.txt	34 KB	651
	Exercise 17-1_Chart of Accounts.pdf	35 KB	659
	Exercise 17-1.Chart of Accounts.xlsx	16 KB	659
	Exercise 17-2.ptb	936 KB	659
18	Bellwether Garden Supply.docx	12 KB	663
	Customer Letters.docx	3,102 KB	665
	Bellwether Sales Special.doc	579 KB	669
	Exercise 18-1.docx	3,102 KB	672
	Exercise 18-2.docx	3,102 KB	672
Project 3	Springfield Computer Club Chart of Accounts.ptb	933 KB	680
	Springfield Computer Club Starting Balance Sheet.ptb	934 KB	681
	Springfield Computer Club January.ptb	979 KB	682
	Springfield Computer Club_CofA_ CDJ_CRJ_ GLTB_ BS_ IS_ SCF_SRE. xlsx	37 KB	682
	Project 3_Chart of Accounts.pdf	17 KB	683
	Project 3_General Ledger Trial Balance.pdf	6 KB	683
	Project 3_Balance Sheet.pdf	10 KB	683
	Project 3_Income Statement.pdf	11 KB	683
	Project 3_Statement of Cash Flow.pdf	10 KB	683
	Project 3_Statement of Retained Earnings.pdf	8 KB	683
Project 4	CW Mftg Chart of Accounts.ptb	933 KB	687
	CW Mftg Starting Balance Sheet.ptb	935 KB	688
	CW Mftg Begin.ptb	1,027 KB	698
	CW Mftg January.ptb	1,116 KB	703
	CW Mftg_CofA_GLTB_BS_IS_SCF_ SRE.xlsx	34 KB	703
	Project 4_Chart of Accounts.pdf	26 KB	703
	Project 4_General Ledger Trial Balance.pdf	7 KB	703
	Project 4_Balance Sheet.pdf	6 KB	703
	Project 4_Income Statement.pdf	5 KB	703
	Project 4_Statement of Cash Flow.pdf	5 KB	703
	Project 4_Statement of Retained Earnings.pdf	3 KB	703

The size of your backup files may differ from the amounts shown on the table.

Chapter 16 Customizing Forms

LEARNING OBJECTIVES

1. Define Sage 50 forms.
2. Customize a form (invoice).
3. Print a practice form.
4. Use design tools.
5. Use the Financial Statement Wizard.
6. Make one backup and save one PDF file.

You have used many different kinds of forms: invoices, statements, checks, etc. There may be times when you want to create your own form or customize one of the formats that come with Sage 50. You can customize forms with the Forms Designer.[1]

PRINTING FORMS

There are three types of documents that can be accessed from the Reports & Forms menu:

- Reports
- Financial Statements
- Forms

The rules for each type of document are different for printing and designing. This chapter will explain the rules for designing forms.

WHAT IS A FORM?

A form in Sage 50 is a document that you exchange with customers, vendors, or employees. The forms that come with Sage 50 include checks, tax forms, invoices, statements, mailing labels, quotes, and collection letters.

---

[1]You need a mouse to use the forms designer.

Usually, these documents are printed on preprinted forms, but you can also design a form and print on blank paper. When you are ready to print or design a form, you select Reports & Forms, then select Forms. Select the appropriate form from the Forms Types list. The illustration below shows the Checks selection. From the Forms list, additional selections can be made.

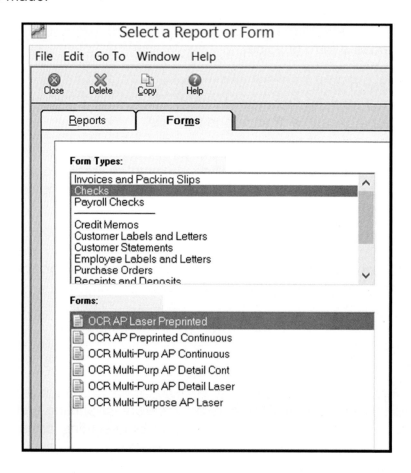

The Select a Report or Form window lists all the reports and forms currently set up in Sage 50. Reports include financial statements, aging reports, etc. Forms are usually tied to a transaction, such as an invoice or check. Letters are also listed on the Forms tab.

The following table lists the forms that can be printed or edited:

Accounts Receivable	Accounts Payable	Payroll
Collection letters	1099 Forms	Payroll checks
Credit memos	Disbursement checks	Employee mailing labels
Customer labels	Purchase orders	
Customer quotes	Vendor mailing labels	
Customer statements		
Invoices/packing slips		
Receipts		
Sales orders		

Preprinted paper forms require special attention because the forms must be aligned in the printer correctly and the printer must be configured to accommodate the form. That is why forms cannot be displayed on your screen prior to printing. You can print practice forms to test alignment and printer configuration, or you can view the layout of the form.

GETTING STARTED

In this chapter, you are going to use Bellwether Garden Supply (the sample company that you used in Chapters 1 through 7).

1. Start Sage 50.

2. Open the sample company, Bellwether Garden Supply. (The instructions in this chapter assume that you are using data from the Exercise 6-2.ptb backup made on page 202. No new data was added in Chapter 7.) If necessary, restore the Exercise 6-2.ptb file.

Comment

You can use beginning Bellwether Garden Supply data or any subsequent Bellwether backup. To install Bellwether's starting data, restore the bgs.ptb backup file. Steps for restoring the bgs.ptb backup are on pages 29-33.

■ To verify Exercise 6-2 data, display the balance sheet. A partial balance sheet is shown below. Chapter 7's balance sheet is shown on pages 213-214. (If you restored the bgs.ptb backup file, your balance sheet will differ.)

Bellwether Garden Supply - Student Name
Balance Sheet
March 31, 2016

ASSETS

Current Assets		
Petty Cash	$ 327.55	
Cash on Hand	1,850.45	
Regular Checking Account	9,046.52	
Payroll Checking Account	8,836.40	
Savings Account	7,500.00	
Money Market Fund	4,500.00	
Accounts Receivable	176,026.47	
Other Receivables	7,681.84	
Allowance for Doubtful Account	(5,000.00)	
Inventory	12,386.46	
Prepaid Expenses	14,221.30	
Employee Advances	3,000.65	
Notes Receivable-Current	11,000.00	
Other Current Assets	120.00	
Total Current Assets		251,497.64
Property and Equipment		
Furniture and Fixtures	62,769.25	
Equipment	38,738.33	
Vehicles	86,273.40	
Other Depreciable Property	6,200.96	
Buildings	185,500.00	
Building Improvements	26,500.00	
Accum. Depreciation-Furniture	(54,680.57)	
Accum. Depreciation-Equipment	(33,138.11)	
Accum. Depreciation-Vehicles	(51,585.26)	
Accum. Depreciation-Other	(3,788.84)	
Accum. Depreciation-Buildings	(34,483.97)	
Accum. Depreciation-Bldg Imp	(4,926.28)	
Total Property and Equipment		223,378.91
Other Assets		
Deposits	15,000.00	
Organization Costs	4,995.10	
Accum Amortiz - Organiz Costs	(2,000.00)	
Notes Receivable- Noncurrent	5,004.90	
Other Noncurrent Assets	3,333.00	
Total Other Assets		26,333.00
Total Assets		$ 501,209.55

CUSTOMIZING A FORM

1. From the Navigation Bar, select [👤 **Customers & Sales**] > in the Recently Used Customer Reports area, link to <u>View All Customer & Sales Reports</u>. The Select a Report or Form window displays.

2. Select the For<u>m</u>s tab. In the Form Types list, Invoices and Packing Slips is highlighted.

3. In the Forms list > select Invoice. Observe that the Description field shows Use with plain paper.

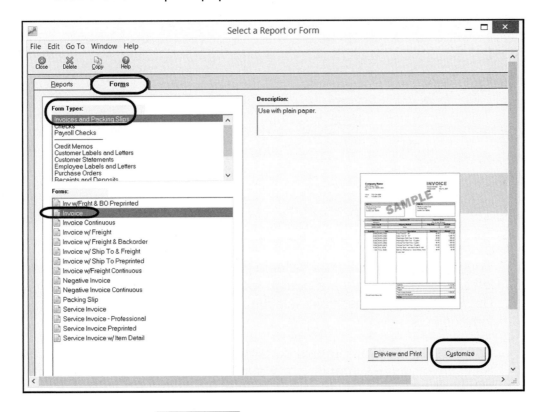

4. After selecting [Cu̲stomize], the window for designing an invoice form appears. A partial Invoice window is shown on the next page. This window allows you to create new customized forms or edit existing forms to match your business's needs.

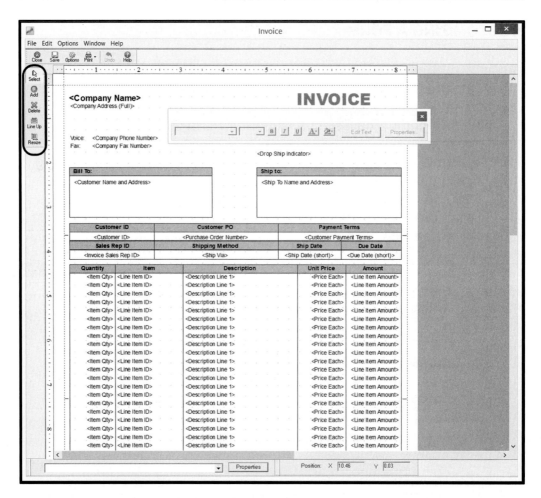

You have several options available for customizing the form. On the left side of the window are design tools: Select, Add, Delete, Line Up, Resize. These assist in selecting and adding various types of form objects.

You can also design forms in certain task windows (for example, Sales/Invoicing, Payments, and Payroll Entry) by selecting the Print button, then Form Design on the Print dialog.

5. To select an object for customizing, use the Select tool [Select]. With your mouse pointer, you can drag and drop objects to move them

    around. Click Select Then move your mouse cursor to the inside of the form (inside the red outline). Click on the <Company Name> field to select it (field selection is indicated by a box).

6. With the <Company Name> field selected (blue box is around it), right-click.

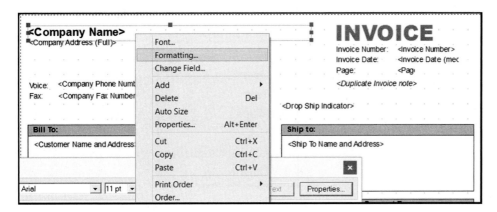

7. Left-click Formatting. The Data field Options window appears. In the Text alignment field, select Center.

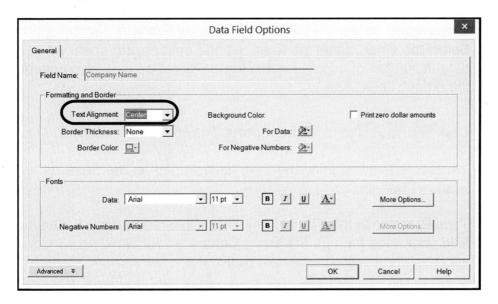

8. Click ▢ OK ▢. Observe that the <Company Name> field moves to the center. Right-click on the <Company Address (Full)> field and center it. You may want to Right-click on various fields and make changes such as font size, alignment, etc. You can delete a field or two as well.

9. Click 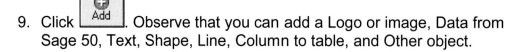. Observe that you can add a Logo or image, Data from Sage 50, Text, Shape, Line, Column to table, and Other object.

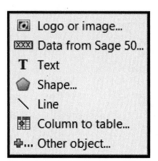

10. On the icon bar of the Forms Designer, click Options. The Forms Design Options window appears.

    If necessary, select the Display tab to select various display options. Select the Grid/Copies tab to adjust grid options and specify a default number of copies for this form. (*Hint:* You may also accept the default selections.)

11. Click OK to close the Forms Design Options window.

12. When finished designing the form, select Save. The Save As window appears.

13. Type **Practice** in the Form Name field. Observe that the Filename field shows the path for this form. Compare your Save As window with the one shown on the next page.

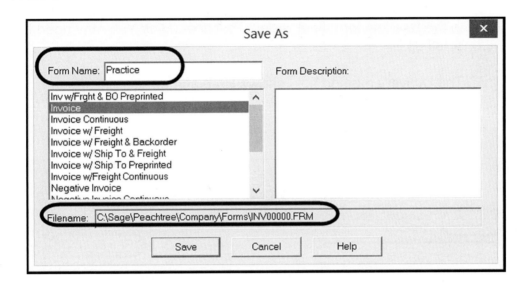

14. Click [Save] > [Close]. Observe that Practice is shown on the Forms list with a wrench next to it. A wrench indicates a Custom Sage 50 form. Select Practice.

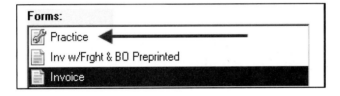

15. Click [Preview and Print]

PRINTING CUSTOMIZED FORMS

The Preview and Print Invoices and Packing Slips window should be displayed. Follow these steps to see the redesigned Invoice.

1. Make the following selections on the Preview and Print Invoices and Packing Slips window

   a. Type or select **3/15/2016** in the through field. Mar 15, 2016 should be displayed in the through field.

   b. The Number the first invoice field shows 103.

c. In the Use this form field, select Practice. (*Hint:* You may need to scroll up.)

d. The Delivery method field shows Print and e-mail.

e. Click [⟳ Refresh List].

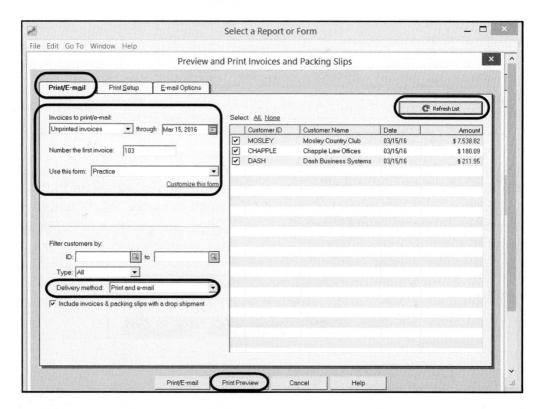

2. After selecting [Print Preview], Invoice Number 103 appears. Notice in the illustration on the next page that Bellwether Garden Supply and its address information is centered. Your Invoice may differ depending on which fields you changed. Invoice Number 103 is shown on the next page.

Bellwether Garden Supply - Student Name
1505 Pavilion Place
Norcross, GA 30093-3203
USA

INVOICE

Invoice Number: 103
Invoice Date: Mar 15, 2016
Page: 1

Voice: 770-724-4000
Fax: 770-555-1234

Bill To:	Ship to:
Mosley Country Club 1 Howell Walk Duluth, GA 30096	Mosley Country Club 1 Howell Walk Duluth, GA 30096

Customer ID	Customer PO	Payment Terms	
MOSLEY		2% 10, Net 30 Days	
Sales Rep ID	**Shipping Method**	**Ship Date**	**Due Date**
SPRICHARD	None		4/14/16

Quantity	Item	Description	Unit Price	Amount
20.00	NURS-21900	Ficus Tree 22" - 26"	55.95	1,119.00
25.00	NURS-22000	Ginko Tree 14" - 16"	49.95	1,248.75
10.00	NURS-23000	Washington Palm Tree - 5 Gallon	49.00	490.00
20.00	NURS-23010	Washington Palm Tree - 10 gallon	119.00	2,380.00
10.00	NURS-24000	Chinese Fan Palm Tree - 5 gallon	49.95	499.50
10.00	NURS-24010	Chinese Fan Palm Tree - 10 gallon	122.00	1,220.00
15.00	SOIL-34160	GA Pine Straw - wire tied 4 cubic ft. bale	6.99	104.85
1.00	TOOL-35300	Bell-Gro Wheelbarrow - Green Metal; Holds 6 cubic feet	49.99	49.99

	Subtotal	7,112.09
	Sales Tax	426.73
	Total Invoice Amount	7,538.82
Check/Credit Memo No:	Payment/Credit Applied	
	TOTAL	**7,538.82**

3. Click [Next] to see Invoice Numbers 104 and 105. Click [Print].
    (*Hint:* If you do not have a printer, in the Print window's Name box,
    select Adobe PDF. Save the file.) When the Did the Invoices print
    and e-mail properly window appears, click [Yes].

4. Close the Select a Report or Form window.

EDITING A FORM DESIGN

1. From the menu bar, select Reports & Forms > Forms > Invoices and Packing Slips.

2. In the Forms list, select Practice.

3. Click [C̲ustomize]. Select the fields you want to change.

4. On the Practice window's icon bar, click [Options]. Select the Display tab to select various display options. Select the Grid/Copies tab to adjust grid options and specify a default number of copies for this form.

5. When through, click [OK].

6. Save the form. Use the same filename, Practice.

DESIGN TOOLS

The forms designer includes design tools: Select, Add, Delete, Line Up, Resize. These terms are defined as follows:

Object Toolbar

[Select] Select: Select this to use the Selection tools to highlight or select one or more form objects.

[Add] Add: Select Add to add an object to the form. You can add an image or logo, data field, text field, column field, shape, line or other object using this tool.

Delete: Select Delete to delete the object or objects that you have selected on the form.

Line Up: Select Line Up to align the objects that you have selected on the form. You can Line Up-Left, Right, Top, Bottom.

Resize: Select Resize to resize the objects that you have selected on the form. You can resize the width and height.

Click **Close** to return to the Select a Report or Form window. Close to return to the menu bar.

Formatting Toolbar

Use the formatting toolbar to change the format of the selected object on your form. Use this toolbar to change the font, color, and background color of the selected object. If you have selected a text object, you can click the Edit Text button to change the text. Clicking the Properties button will open the corresponding property window, where you can modify the object's properties. The Fonts section of the Data Field Options window is shown below.

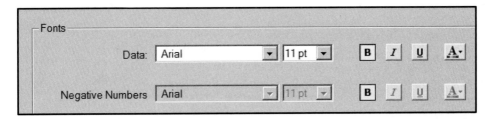

You may want to experiment with the Practice form to see some of these design features.

FINANCIAL STATEMENT DESIGN TOOLS

When you design a financial statement, use the financial statement Design Tools window. It has three major areas: the toolbar at the top of the window, the design toolbar at the side of the window where you select the type of fields you want to place on the designer, and the design area where you actually create the financial statement.

When you create a financial statement, you work with five areas: 1) the header; 2) lines of text; 3) columns; 4) totals; 5) footer. Follow these steps to see the designing tools that are available on the Statement of Cash Flow.

1. From the Reports & Forms menu, select Financial Statements > <Standard> Cash Flow.

2. Click ☐Design☐. The <Standard> Cash Flow window includes the design tools necessary for customization. Compare yours with the one shown below.

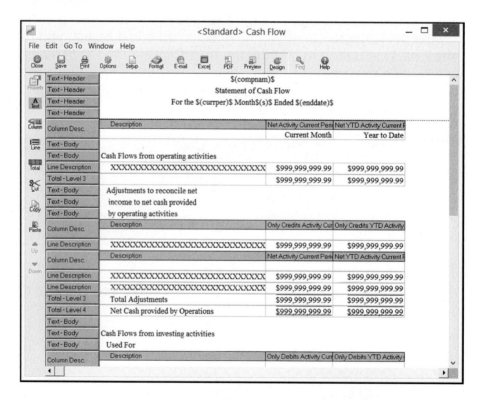

On the left side of the design window, observe that each row has a button next to it that defines the row; for example, Text – header, Column Desc., Text – Body, etc. The icon bar at the top of the window contains the following buttons: Close, Save, Print, Options, Setup, Format, E-mail, Excel, PDF, Preview, Design, and Help.

The information that follows is for explanation purposes only. You may want to experiment with some of the design tools to make changes to Sage 50's <Standard> Cash Flow.

When designing a new form or modifying an existing one, you need to save the form to record your changes. If you change one of the standard forms (those that came with Sage 50), you must rename the form before saving your changes. You cannot save changes to the standard forms using the original form name. This allows you to keep the standard form in case you make a design error and need to start over.

A custom form appears on the report list with a different icon than a <Standard> form. Predefined or standard forms and reports are included with the software.

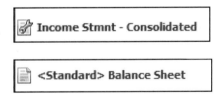

The financial statement design tools are shown below.

Use the Property tool to work with the properties window for the selected row type. For example, if you select a text row, the text window opens.

Use the Text tool to insert text that you will not change from statement to statement (for example, section headings).

Use the Column tool to define columns, enter a title for each column, select the alignment of each column title (left, right, or center) and select the style, size and color of the text.

Once the columns are defined, use the Line tool to define what data to put in each row of a column. Line objects are placed below column objects.

Use the Total tool to tell the program how to calculate totals and subtotals.

Use the Cut tool to remove the selected row and copy it to the Windows Clipboard.

Use the Copy tool to copy the selected row to the Windows Clipboard.

Use the Paste tool to insert the current row from the Windows Clipboard.

Use the Up tool to move the selected row up one position in the list of rows.

Use the Down tool to move a selected row down one position in the list of rows.

You can select multiple rows in the window and then apply the cut, copy, and paste functions to all of them. To select multiple rows, hold down the Ctrl key, and then with the cursor select the buttons that define the rows you want. When through looking at the <Standard> Cash Flow Design window, close it.

FINANCIAL STATEMENT WIZARD

The Financial Statement Wizard walks you through the process of designing financial statements. Follow these steps to use the Financial Statement Wizard.

1. If necessary start Sage 50. Open Bellwether Garden Supply.

2. From the Reports & Forms menu, select Financial Statements.

3. Link to <u>Financial Statement Wizard</u> (upper right side of window).

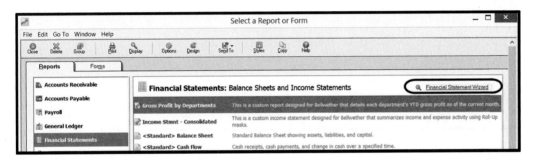

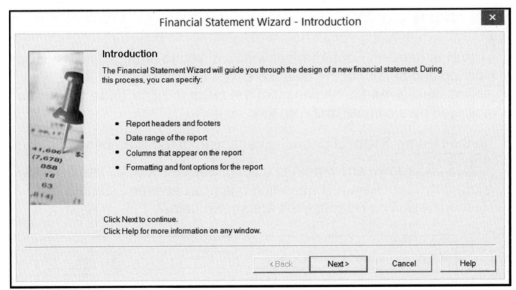

4. After reading the information on the Introduction window, click <u>Next ></u>.

5. Make sure <Standard> Balance Sheet appears in the Financial Statement Template field. If necessary, select it.

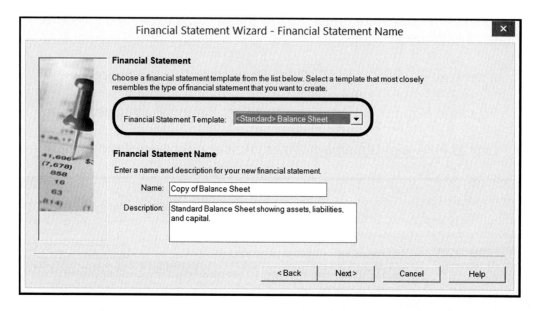

6. After reading the information on the Financial Statement window, click **Next >** . The Headers and Footers window appears.

7. The Headers and Footers window allows you to change information at the top and bottom of the balance sheet. For purposes of this exercise, click on the beginning of the Header 1 line. Type **your name** followed by a comma and a space.

8. In the Header 3 line, click on the beginning of the line, then click **Insert** ▼ (down arrow next to Insert). Select Today's Date from the drop-down list. Type a comma and a space between $(Date)$ and $(enddate)$. The Header lines are shown below.

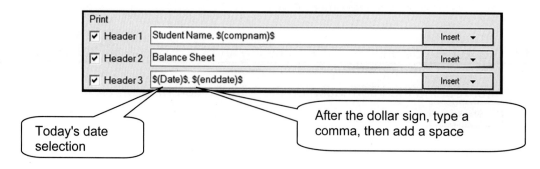

Today's date selection

After the dollar sign, type a comma, then add a space

Compare your Headers and Footers window with the one shown.

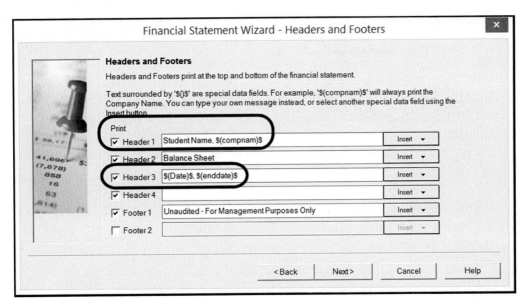

9. Click [Next >]. The Date Range and Account Masking window appears. Read the information in the Dates and General Ledger Account Masking sections. Accept the defaults on this window, by clicking on [Next >].

10. Accept the defaults on the Column Properties window by clicking on [Next >].

11. Accept the defaults on the Column Options window by clicking on [Next >].

12. Unless you want to change fonts, accept the defaults on the Fonts window by clicking on [Next >].

13. Accept the defaults on the Formatting and Default Printer window by clicking on [Next >].

14. The Congratulations window appears. To display your new financial statement, click [Finish]. The Copy of Balance Sheet window appears, click [OK].

Compare your balance sheet to the partial one shown below. Observe that the header shows your name on line one; today's date is shown on line 3 before March 31, 2016 (your current date will differ). This balance sheet is from the Exercise 6-2.ptb backup file. In Chapter 7 on pages 213-214, you printed Bellwether Garden Supply's balance sheet.

If you added your name to Bellwether Garden Supply in Chapter 1 on page 43, your name appears at the beginning of header line 1 and at the end of the line.

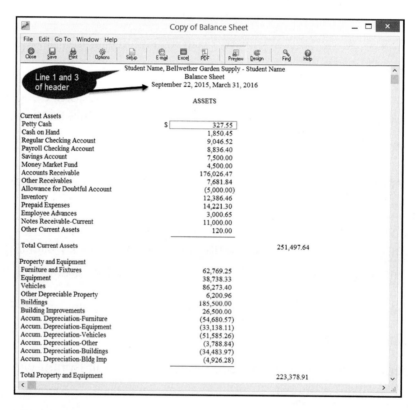

15. Close the Copy of Balance Sheet window. Observe a wrench is shown next to Copy of Balance Sheet, which indicates a custom form.

16. Close the Select a Report or Form window. Exit Sage 50 or continue.

ONLINE LEARNING CENTER

Complete end-of-chapter activities at www.mhhe.com/yacht2016 >
Student Edition > Chapter 16.

1. Quizzes: Multiple Choice and True False questions. Interactive
    online tests that are graded and can be emailed to your instructor.

2. More Resources:

    a. QA Templates: Answer 10 multiple-choice questions and two
        Analysis Questions.

    b. Narrated PowerPoints: Listen to the narrated PowerPoints.

    c. Going to the Net Exercises: On the Our News website, select
        two articles to read.

    d. Assessment Rubric: Complete the rubric to review Sage 50's
        journals, navigation centers, modules, task windows, and
        reports.

The OLC also includes links to the Appendixes:

- Appendix A: Troubleshooting
- Appendix B: Accounting Information Systems
- Appendix C: Review of Accounting Principles
- Appendix D: Glossary (words that are boldfaced and italicized in
  chapter)

Exercise 16-1: Use the forms designer to customize a Service Invoice.

1. From the Customers & Sales Navigation Center, link to View All Customer and Sales Reports.

2. From the Forms list, select Service Invoice > Customize.

3. Change Company Name's font size to 16.

4. Change the font size of the Company Address to Arial 12.

5. Change the font size of the Customer Name and Address to Arial 12.

6. Save the Service Invoice as Exercise 16-1.

7. On the Preview and Print Invoices and Packing Slips window, select Printed invoices. Type **103** in the Numbered fields. Filter the customers by MOSLEY. Remember to refresh the list.

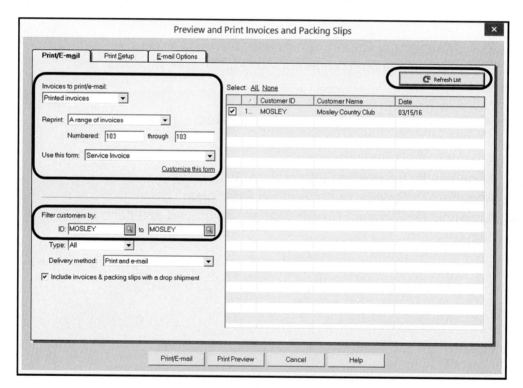

8. Preview and print the service invoice number 103 for Mosley.

Exercise 16-2: Use the Financial Statement Wizard.

1. Use the Financial Statement Wizard to add your name and today's date to <Standard> Income Statement.

2. Print the income statement. (*Hint:* Uncheck Show Zero Amounts.) If you added your name to Bellwether Garden Supply in Chapter 1, page 43, your name appears at the beginning of header line 1 and at the end of the line.

3. Backup. The suggested file name is **Exercise 16-2.ptb**.

4. Save the Copy of the Income Statement as a PDF file and export to Excel. The suggested file name is **Exercise 16-2_Copy of Income Stmnt**. Check with your instructor to see if he or she would also like an Excel file.

CHAPTER 16 INDEX

Chapter

17 Import/Export

LEARNING OBJECTIVES

1. Export information from Sage 50 to a word processing program.
2. Select the customer list from Bellwether Garden Supply to export.
3. Import Bellwether Garden Supply's chart of accounts into a new company.
4. Save two files: a comma separated value file (.csv) and a text file (.txt).
5. Make one backup, save one Excel file, and save one PDF file.

Importing translates data from other programs into a format that Sage 50 can use. The diagram below shows how importing works. Data can be imported into Sage 50.

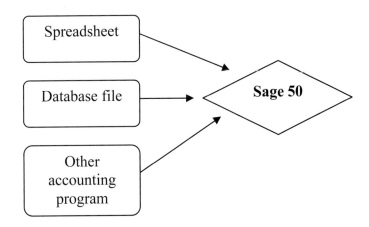

Exporting copies Sage 50 data into a format that other programs can read and use. The diagram on the next page illustrates exporting. Data is exported from Sage 50.

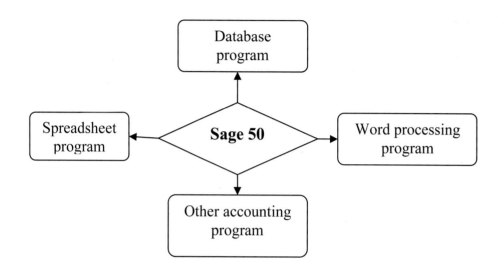

The chart below shows how Sage 50 organizes data.

Customer	**Files**	Journal

Records	General Journal	Purchase Journal	Cash Disbursements Journal	Sales Journal	Cash Receipts Journal

Fields	Invoice Number	Account Number	Debit Amount	Credit Amount

➤ **Files** are a group of related records; for example, customer files and journal files.

➤ **Records** are a group of fields that contain information on one subject; for example, the general journal, purchase journal, cash disbursements journal, sales journal, or cash receipts journal.

➤ **Fields** are an individual piece of data; for example, invoice numbers, account numbers, debit amount, credit amount.

Files

When you import or export files, you use templates to format the data.

The templates included in Sage 50 are:

- ➤ Accounts Receivable: Customer List, Sales Journal, and Cash Receipts Journal

- ➤ Accounts Payable: Vendor List, Purchase Journal, and Cash Disbursements Journal

- ➤ Payroll: Employee List

- ➤ General Ledger: Chart of Accounts and General Journal

- ➤ Inventory: Inventory Item List

- ➤ Job Reports: Jobs List

Records

When you select a file to export, you can define which information you want. For instance, when you select the Customer List, you can select which customers you want to export.

Fields

When export is used, you export individual fields of information. You can see what fields are exported by selecting the Format tab. You may uncheck fields to exclude them from being exported or move fields around to change their order.

When you export, the information is exported in a ***comma separated values*** (CSV) format. This means that the fields for each record are written in one line, with commas between them. You see how this looks when you export one of Sage 50's customer lists into Microsoft Word. Comma separated value files (CSV extensions) are commonly used for transferring data between applications in a text-based format.

The file created during the export process is an ***ASCII*** file, which contains only text characters. Each record is on a separate line. ASCII is an acronym for American Standard Code for Information Interchange. It is one of the standard formats used for representing characters on a computer. Most word processing, spreadsheet, and database programs can read ASCII files.

GETTING STARTED: EXPORTING

1. Start Sage 50.

2. Open Bellwether Garden Supply. (In this chapter data is used from the Exercise 6-2.ptb backup file made on page 202.)

3. If necessary, restore the Exercise 6-2.ptb file. (*Hint:* Any Bellwether Garden Supply file can be used to complete work in Chapter 17.)

4. From the menu bar, select File > Select Import/Export. The Select Import/Export window appears. *Or*, from the System Navigation page, click Import/Export Data .

5. In the Accounts Receivable list, highlight Customer List.

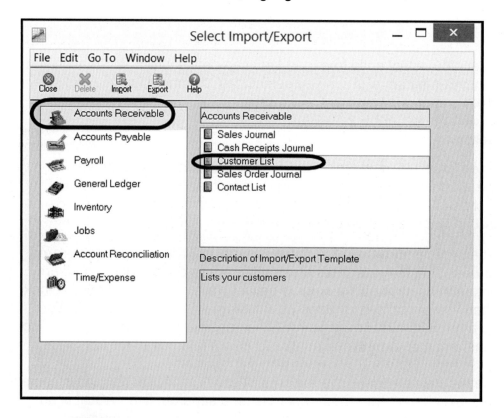

6. Click Export . The Customer List window appears.

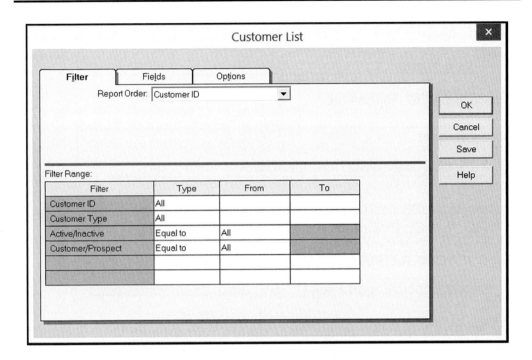

7. Click on the Fields tab, then click 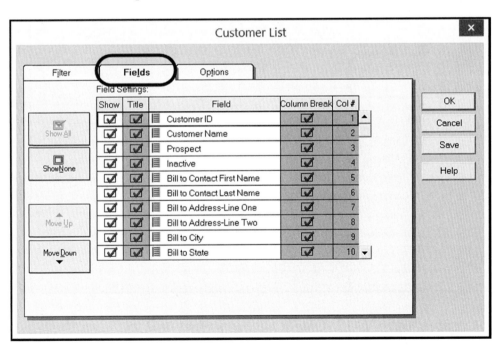.

> **Comment**
>
> Show All places a check mark in all the fields.

8.   Click on the Options tab.

> **Comment**
>
> The radio button next to Ask, Then Overwrite is the default.

9.   Insert a USB flash drive. Click on the arrow ▶ below Import/Export File. The Open window appears. The File name field shows

     CUSTOMER.CSV `File name: CUSTOMER.CSV`. The field to the right

     shows Import/Export Files (*.CSV) `Import/Export Files (*.CSV)  ▼`.

10. Select the appropriate location for your USB. The author's is

     F – `▷ USB DISK (F:)`. (Your USB location may differ.) Click

     `Open`.

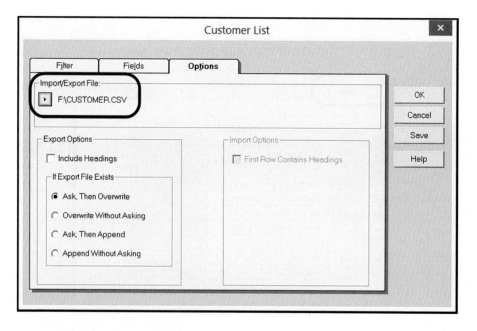

Observe that F:\CUSTOMER.CSV is shown next to the arrow ▶ under Import/Export File. (Substitute your USB location for F.)

---

11. Click Save . The Save As window appears. Type **Customers** in the Template Name field.

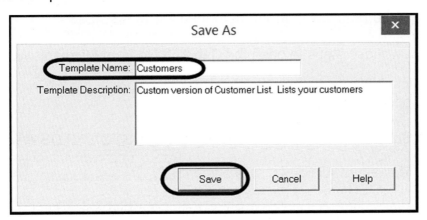

12. After clicking Save , you are returned to the Customers Options window. Make sure X:\CUSTOMER.CSV is shown as the Import/Export File name. (Substitute your USB location for X.)

13. Click OK . The Select Import/Export window shows Customers with a red arrow. Select it. The Description field describes the custom version.

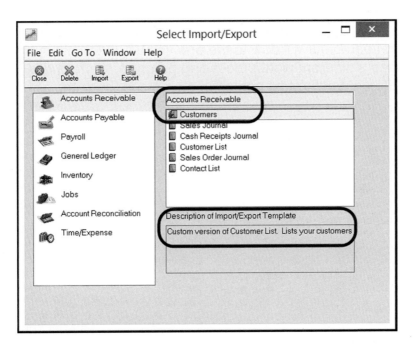

14. Close the Select Import/Export window.

15. Start your word processing program. You can use Microsoft Word, or any word processing program that supports ASCII.

16. Follow these steps to open the Sage 50 file from Microsoft Word.

   a. Start Word or other word processing program. Click ⬛ (the open file icon).

   b. Select the appropriate location of the CUSTOMER.CSV file. Make sure All Files (*.*) is shown `All Files (*.*) ▼`.

   c. Highlight the CUSTOMER.CSV file. The File name field is completed `File name: CUSTOMER.CSV ▼  All Files (*.*) ▼`.

   d. Click `Open`. (*Hint:* If a Convert File window appears, select Plain Text, then <OK>.)

   The data on your window was exported in a comma separated format. The fields for each record are written in one line, with commas between them. To use this information, you would need to edit its contents, then save it.

   Compare your window to the one shown on the next page. If you used a different word processing program, your window will look different but the text portion of the data is the same.

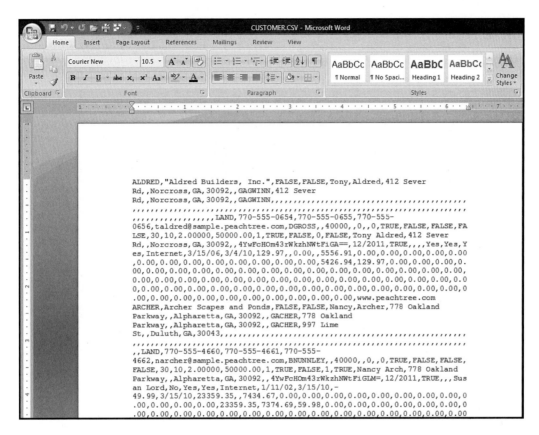

e. To keep the original ASCII file, use Word's Save <u>A</u>s command and rename the file **CUSTOMER.txt**. When you save, the file converts to a text document file from its original ASCII format. If a File Conversion – CUSTOMER.txt window appears, click

    OK

f. Exit the word processing program.

TEXT AND COMMA SEPARATED VALUES FILES

To look at the files you just created, do this:

1. Open File Explorer.

2. Go to the location of the CSV file.

3. Observe that the CUSTOMER.CSV file is an Excel file saved as Comma Separated Values. The CUSTOMER.txt file is a Text document.

| CUSTOMER.CSV | Microsoft Office Excel Comma Separated Values File | 34 KB |
| CUSTOMER.txt | Text Document | 34 KB |

4. Double-click CUSTOMER.CSV to see the Excel file created from Bellwether Garden Supply's customer list. Close the window.

5. Double-click CUSTOMER.txt to see the text file.

6. Exit the Notepad window and File Explorer. If the CUSTOMER.txt file is open in Microsoft Word, close it. Close MS Word.

IMPORTING

Importing data from another accounting, database, or spreadsheet program into Sage 50 works similarly to exporting. Any information that is entered in Sage 50 during setup and maintenance can be imported.

In Sage 50, the Maintain windows allow you to perform tasks associated with lists, such as the Customer List, Employee List, Chart of Accounts, etc. The Tasks windows allow you to perform tasks that consist of journalizing various kinds of transactions. When you import data, it is important to know that Sage 50 permits the importing of new transactions, for example, the information entered within the Tasks windows. Once transactions are imported they cannot be edited.

In the example that follows, you are going to copy Bellwether Garden Supply's chart of accounts to another company. To start this process, you export the chart of accounts list first, then import the chart into a newly set up company.

Import a Chart of Accounts

To import the chart of accounts from Bellwether Garden Supply to another company, do the following.

1. If necessary start Sage 50 and open Bellwether Garden Supply. From the File menu > Select Import/Export > General Ledger. The Chart of Accounts Lists is the default.

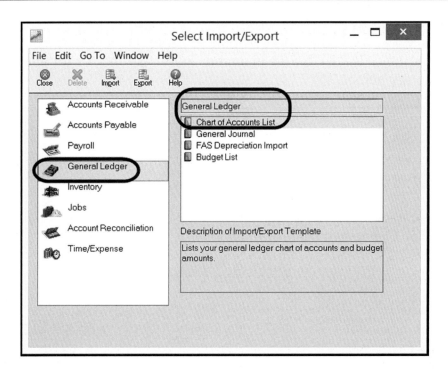

2. Click [Export]. The Chart of Accounts List window appears. Select the Options tab. Observe the default location for the CHART.CSV file. The file will be imported from the default location. The default location is C:\Users\[computer name]\ Documents\ CHART.CSV.

3. Click [Save]. In the Template Name field, type **Chart**.

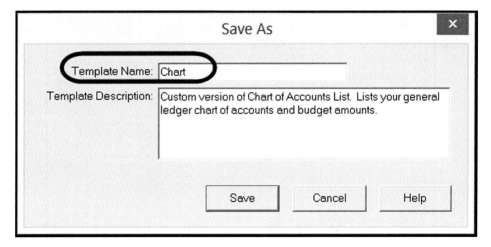

4. Click [Save]. The Chart window appears. Observe the location where the CHART.CSV file is stored. Substitute the X's for your computer name.

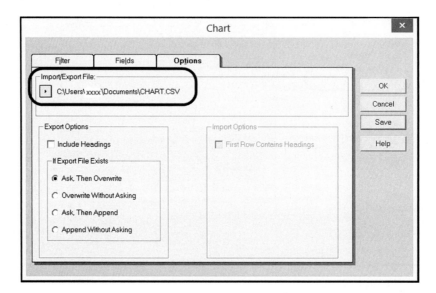

5. Click [OK]. The Select/Import Export window shows the custom version of the Chart.

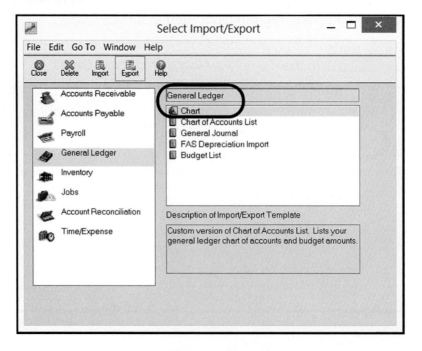

6. Close the Select Import/Export window.

7. Set up a new company. From the menu bar, select File > New Company. When the window prompts, do you want to keep Bellwether Garden Supply open, select ⬚ No ⬚ . The Create a New Company window appears. Click ⬚ Next > ⬚

   a. Use your first name Company; for example, Carol Company.

   b. Accept the default for Corporation. Click ⬚ Next > ⬚ .

   c. On the Select a method to create your company, select Build your own chart of accounts.

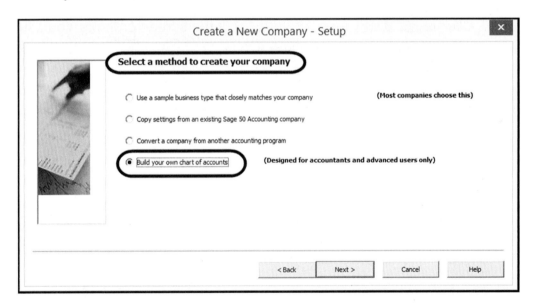

   d. Click ⬚ Next > ⬚ until the Choose the first period of your fiscal year window appears. Select January 2016.

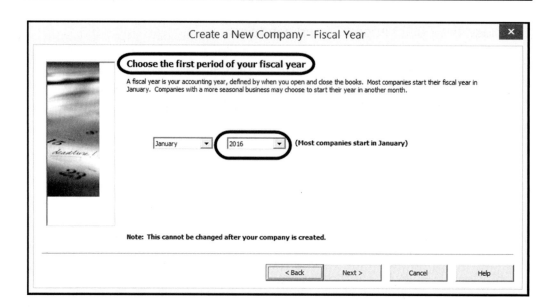

e. Click [Next >], then [Finish]. If the screen prompts You can use this company in the student version of Sage 50 for the next 14 months and then it will expire, click [OK].

8. If necessary, close the Setup Guide and the Sage Advisor Getting Started. The title bar shows Your Name Company - Sage 50 Accounting. From the File menu, click Select Import/Export. Select General Ledger > Chart of Accounts List > [Import].

9. On the Chart of Accounts List window, select Options. Observe that the file name location is the same as the illustration at the top of page 654. (Substitute the x's for your computer name.)

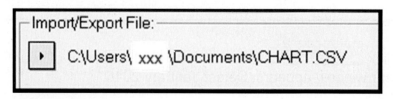

10. Click [OK]. When the screen prompts You should make a backup before attempting to import. Would you like to continue?, click [Yes]. Close the Select Import/Export window.

11. Display your Chart of Accounts (Reports & Forms > General Ledger > Chart of Accounts). Your company shows the same chart of accounts as Bellwether Garden Supply. A partial chart of accounts is shown below. The month on your chart of accounts will differ from the one shown. The month defaults to the period when the company was set up.

Carol Company
Chart of Accounts
As of Sep 30, 2016

Filter Criteria includes: Report order is by ID. Report is printed with Accounts having Zero Amounts and in Detail Format.

Account ID	Account Description	Active?	Account Type
10000	Petty Cash	Yes	Cash
10100	Cash on Hand	Yes	Cash
10200	Regular Checking Account	Yes	Cash
10300	Payroll Checking Account	Yes	Cash
10400	Savings Account	Yes	Cash
10500	Money Market Fund	Yes	Cash
11000	Accounts Receivable	Yes	Accounts Receivable
11100	Contracts Receivable	Yes	Accounts Receivable
11400	Other Receivables	Yes	Accounts Receivable
11500	Allowance for Doubtful Account	Yes	Accounts Receivable
12000	Inventory	Yes	Inventory
14000	Prepaid Expenses	Yes	Other Current Assets
14100	Employee Advances	Yes	Other Current Assets
14200	Notes Receivable-Current	Yes	Other Current Assets
14700	Other Current Assets	Yes	Other Current Assets
15000	Furniture and Fixtures	Yes	Fixed Assets
15100	Equipment	Yes	Fixed Assets
15200	Vehicles	Yes	Fixed Assets
15300	Other Depreciable Property	Yes	Fixed Assets
15400	Leasehold Improvements	Yes	Fixed Assets
15500	Buildings	Yes	Fixed Assets
15600	Building Improvements	Yes	Fixed Assets
16900	Land	Yes	Fixed Assets
17000	Accum. Depreciation-Furniture	Yes	Accumulated Depreciation
17100	Accum. Depreciation-Equipment	Yes	Accumulated Depreciation
17200	Accum. Depreciation-Vehicles	Yes	Accumulated Depreciation
17300	Accum. Depreciation-Other	Yes	Accumulated Depreciation
17400	Accum. Depreciation-Leasehold	Yes	Accumulated Depreciation
17500	Accum. Depreciation-Buildings	Yes	Accumulated Depreciation
17600	Accum. Depreciation-Bldg Imp	Yes	Accumulated Depreciation
19000	Deposits	Yes	Other Assets

In this chapter, you exported and imported data. To learn more about these features, use Sage 50's Help feature. Exit Sage 50, or continue.

ONLINE LEARNING CENTER

Complete end-of-chapter activities at www.mhhe.com/yacht2016 >
Student Edition > Chapter 17.

1. Quizzes: Multiple Choice and True False questions. Interactive
   online tests that are graded and can be emailed to your instructor.

2. More Resources:

   a. QA Templates: Answer 10 multiple-choice questions and one
      Analysis Question.

   b. Narrated PowerPoints: Listen to the narrated PowerPoints.

   c. Going to the Net Exercises: Access the Sage Knowledgebase.

   d. Assessment Rubric: Complete the rubric to review Sage 50's
      journals, navigation centers, modules, task windows, and
      reports.

The OLC also includes links to the Appendixes:

- Appendix A: Troubleshooting
- Appendix B: Accounting Information Systems
- Appendix C: Review of Accounting Principles
- Appendix D: Glossary (words that are boldfaced and italicized in
  chapter)

Exercise 17-1: Follow the instructions below to complete Exercise 17-1.

1. Print your company's Chart of Accounts.

2. Save the Chart of Accounts as a PDF file, and export it to Excel. Use the file name **Exercise 17-1_Chart of Accounts**.

Exercise 17-2: Follow the instructions below to complete Exercise 17-2.

1. Backup. The suggested file name is **Exercise 17-2.ptb**.

2. Exit Sage 50.

CHAPTER 17 INDEX

LEARNING OBJECTIVES

1. Copy Sage 50 report data to Microsoft Word.
2. Use the write letters feature.
3. Edit and save letter templates.
4. Save Word files.
5. Extract the PAWMail.zip folder.
6. Save five Word files.

Sage 50's write letters feature allows you to send information to a large number of people quickly. For example, you can send personally addressed letters to all the company's customers. The Tasks menu and the Select a Report or Forms window include a selection for write letters. Use Sage 50's write letters feature to create mailings or e-mail messages from existing or custom letter templates using customer, vendor, and employee information. A *template* is a document pattern or part of a document that is stored so that it can be used again.

You can create mailings such as newsletters, announcements, collection letters, individual letters, e-mail messages, and other types of mailings. Sage 50 integrates with Microsoft Word's mail merge feature, using Word to edit and create custom templates, then generates mailings using selected Sage 50 information.

GETTING STARTED

1. Start Sage 50. Open Bellwether Garden Supply. (*Hint:* If another company opens, select File > Open Previous Company > Bellwether Garden Supply – Student Name. Open one company.

2. If necessary, restore the Exercise 6-2 file. This backup was made on page 202.

> **Comment**
>
> If you no longer have your Exercise 6-2 back up file, use starting data for Bellwether Garden Supply. Refer to pages 29-33, Using Sage 50's Restore Wizard, to restore Bellwether's starting data.

COPYING SAGE 50 REPORT DATA TO MICROSOFT WORD

A displayed report or financial statement can be copied to the Windows clipboard. Then you can paste that data into other applications, such as Microsoft Word or another word processing program. The steps that follow show you how to copy and paste a report using Microsoft Word.

1. If necessary start Sage. Open the sample company, Bellwether Garden Supply.

2. From Bellwether's menu bar, select Reports & Forms > Financial Statements > <Standard> Retained Earnings > [Display]. The Statement of Retained Earnings displays.

3. Click [Options]. Uncheck Print Page Numbers and Show Zero Amounts > [OK].

4. From the menu bar, select Edit > Copy.

5. Start Microsoft Word or other word processing program. Click Paste. Or, right-click on the document, left-click <u>P</u>aste. Bellwether's statement of retained earnings appears. You need to format the statement in order for it to look like the one shown on the next page. (These account balances reflect data from the Exercise 6-2.ptb backup file. If you restored a different backup file, your account balances will differ.)

Bellwether Garden Supply - Student Name
Statement of Retained Earnings
For the Three Months Ending March 31, 2016

Beginning Retained Earnings	$	189,037.60
Adjustments To Date		0.00
Net Income		25,579.22
Subtotal		214,616.82
Ending Retained Earnings	$	214,616.82

For Management Purposes Only

The copied file was formatted with Microsoft Word.

6. Save As. In the Save in field, select the appropriate drive. Accept the file name Bellwether Garden Supply.docx. Observe that the File as type field shows Word Document (*.docx). (Some templates add the extension .doc.)

7. Click [Save].

8. Exit Word.

9. Close all Sage 50 windows.

CREATE A MAILING TO CUSTOMERS

Follow these steps to use one of Sage 50's Write Letters templates.

1. From the Tasks menu, select Write Letters > Customer Letters.

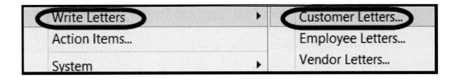

2. The Select a Report or Form window appears. Observe that the Form Types list shows Customer Labels and Letters highlighted. Select Bellwether Sales Special. The Description field shows 2nd Qtr Sales Promotion letter.

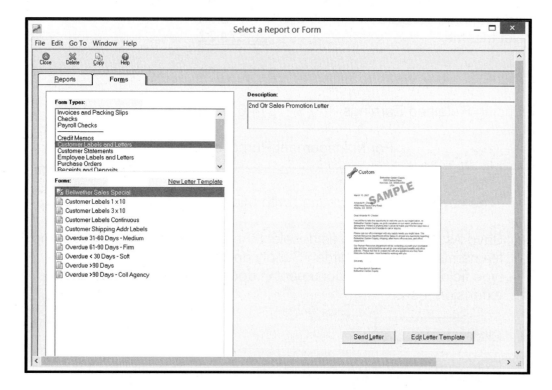

3. Click [Send Letter]. The Write Letters - Bellwether Sales Special window appears. Observe there are two tabs: Select Recipients and E-mail Options. Select Recipients is the default.

4. Click [Word]. Wait a few moments for the first customer letter to appear. Observe that the taskbar shows Page 1 of 34 – PAGE 1 OF 34. This means there are 34 customer letters. The Aldred Builders, Inc. letter is shown on your screen and on the next page. Read the letter.

GARDEN SUPPLY
1505 Pavilion Place
Norcross, GA 30093-3203
770-724-4000

*BUY ONE ITEM GET THE 2nd ITEM 50% OFF
PROMOTION!!!*

Aldred Builders, Inc.
412 Sever Rd
Norcross, GA 30092

Dear Tony Aldred:

As one of our loyal customers, we would like to *thank you* by extending you a
special offer. Buy any item in our catalog at the regular price and receive any
2nd item (at an equal or lesser value) for *50%* off.

This offer is also good for purchases made online!! Check us out on the web at
www.sage50accounting.com.

Again, thank you for your continued business.

Regards,

Derrick P. Gross
Sales Representative

Go to pages 2, 3, etc. Observe that each customer receives an
individually addressed letter.

5. Save the letter. The suggested filename is **Customer Letters**. If the
    screen prompts, You are about to save your document to one of the
    new file formats, click [OK].

6. Close the document.

7. If necessary, go to the taskbar. Select the Sage icon and Select and
    Report or Form.

EDIT LETTER TEMPLATES

Follow these steps to create a letter template from the promotion letter shown on page 665.

1. From the Select a Report window, make sure Bellwether Sales Special is selected. (If necessary, select Tasks > Write Letters > Customers Letters.)

2. Click ⬛ Edit Letter Template . The Edit Letter Template – Bellwether Sales Special window appears. Observe that the Letter Template Description shows 2nd Qtr Sales Promotion Letter. Compare your Edit Letter Template window with the one shown below.

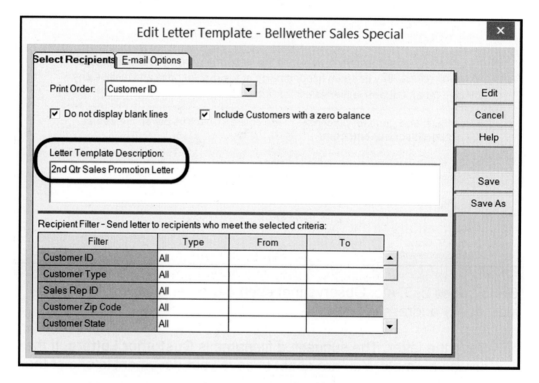

3. Review the information on the Edit Template window. Click ⬛ Edit . The letter appears with fields identified.

You can use this letter as a template or model to create a similar letter. Observe that the information in the letter is the same as the customer letter shown on page 665, *except* for the customizable information—<<Company_Address_Line_1>>, etc.

4. To add a date to the letter, click on a line or two above

    <<Customer_Name>>. Select Date & Time [Date & Time] from Word's Insert selections. Select the appropriate format and the date is inserted.

5. Select Save As. If you are using Microsoft Word 2013, your screen shows a CUSTOMER Current folder. If you open that folder, a list of letter templates appears. (*Hint:* If you do <u>not</u> see the list of customer letter templates, you may need to extract the PAWMail.zip folder. Unzipping or extracting the PAWMail.zip folder is shown on pages 669-670.)

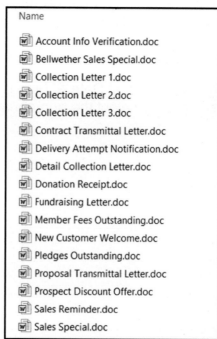

6. To save to a USB location, select it. Accept the default file name Bellwether Sales Special.doc. (*Hint:* Sage 50's letter templates default to .doc files.) Insert your USB flash drive. Select the appropriate drive letter. Click Save .

PAWMail.Zip FOLDER

The letter templates are included on drive C within the Sage folder. Follow these instructions to see all the letters.

1. Open Windows Explorer.

2. Go to C:\Sage\Peachtree\Company\Letters.

3. Copy the PAWMail.zip folder to the desktop.

4. Extract the files. (Right-click on the PAWMail.Zip folder. Left-click Extract All. Click Extract .) Open the templates from these folders: Customer; Employee; Vendor.

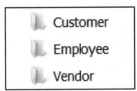

a. The Customer folder includes these documents.

Name	Type
Account Info Verification.doc	Microsoft Word 97 - 2003 Document
Collection Letter 1.doc	Microsoft Word 97 - 2003 Document
Collection Letter 2.doc	Microsoft Word 97 - 2003 Document
Collection Letter 3.doc	Microsoft Word 97 - 2003 Document
Contract Transmittal Letter.doc	Microsoft Word 97 - 2003 Document
Delivery Attempt Notification.doc	Microsoft Word 97 - 2003 Document
Detail Collection Letter.doc	Microsoft Word 97 - 2003 Document
Donation Receipt.doc	Microsoft Word 97 - 2003 Document
Fundraising Letter.doc	Microsoft Word 97 - 2003 Document
Member Fees Outstanding.doc	Microsoft Word 97 - 2003 Document
New Customer Welcome.doc	Microsoft Word 97 - 2003 Document
Pledges Outstanding.doc	Microsoft Word 97 - 2003 Document
Proposal Transmittal Letter.doc	Microsoft Word 97 - 2003 Document
Prospect Discount Offer.doc	Microsoft Word 97 - 2003 Document
Sales Reminder.doc	Microsoft Word 97 - 2003 Document
Sales Special.doc	Microsoft Word 97 - 2003 Document

b. The Employee folder includes the Employee Welcome.doc file.

c. The Vendor folder includes two documents: Disputed Charge.doc and Request Credit Increase.doc.

5. Observe that the letters end in a .doc extension which means that the Sage 50 templates were saved as Word 97-2003 files. Open the Vendor folder. Double-click the Request Credit Increase.doc.

«Company_Name»
«Company_Full_Address»

«Todays_Date_Long»

«Vendor_Name»
«Vendor_Full_Address»

Re: Request for increase in credit limit

Dear «Vendor_Contact»:

«Company_Name» has enjoyed doing business with your company for the past twelve months. We are very happy with your product, and are looking forward to a continued business relationship. After reviewing the past year's records, I would like you to consider increasing our credit limit. An increase of available credit in the amount of $500.00 should suffice.

Thank you for your consideration in this matter. If you have any questions, please feel free to contact me at my direct extension.

Sincerely,

Office Manager
«Company_Name»

6. Close the Request for increase in credit limit letter.

7. To see the Customer Templates, go to your desktop and open the Customers folder.

8. Double-click Contract Transmittal Letter.

«Company_Name»
«Company_Full_Address»

«Todays_Date_Long»

«Customer_Contact»
«Customer_Name»
«Customer_Full_Address»

Dear «Customer_Contact»:

Enclosed are two copies of the contract. If it meets with your approval, please sign both copies and return one in the enclosed, preaddressed envelope.

Please do not hesitate to contact me should you have any questions or concerns.

We at «Company_Name» are pleased to come to this agreement and look forward to working with you.

Sincerely,

«Customer_Sales_Rep_Name»
«Company_Name»
«Company_Telephone_Number»
«Company_Full_Address»

---

9. Look at some of the other templates.

10. Exit Word without saving documents.

11. If necessary, maximize Sage 50. Close all windows.

12. Exit Sage 50.

ONLINE LEARNING CENTER

Complete end-of-chapter activities at www.mhhe.com/yacht2016 > Student Edition > Chapter 18.

1. Quizzes: Multiple Choice and True False questions. Interactive online tests that are graded and can be emailed to your instructor.

2. More Resources:

   a. QA Templates: Answer 10 short-answer questions and two
       Analysis Questions.

   b. Narrated PowerPoints: Listen to the narrated PowerPoints.

   c. Going to the Net Exercises: Access the Sage 50 Accounting –
       Small Business Accounting Software website. Link to these add-
       on services: payroll services, credit cards, and mobile sales.

   d. Assessment Rubric: Complete the rubric to review Sage 50's
       journals, navigation centers, modules, task windows, and
       reports.

The OLC also includes links to the Appendixes:

- Appendix A: Troubleshooting
- Appendix B: Accounting Information Systems
- Appendix C: Review of Accounting Principles
- Appendix D: Glossary (words that are boldfaced and italicized in
  chapter)

Exercise 18-1: Follow the instructions below to complete Exercise 18-1.

1. Print the sales promotion letter to Chapple Law Offices. Use March 15,
   2016 as the date. (*Hint:* Use the Bellwether Special letter template.
   Send a letter to Chapple Law Office.)

2. Save the file as Exercise 18-1.

Exercise 18-2: Follow the instructions below to complete Exercise 18-2.

1. Print a sales promotion letter to Cummings Construction. (Use the
   current date.)

2. Save the file as Exercise 18-2.

CHAPTER 18 INDEX

Project

3 Springfield Computer Club

In Project 3, you complete the computer accounting cycle for the Springfield Computer Club which is located in Springfield, Illinois. The computer club is a nonprofit business organized as a corporation.

Because the Springfield Computer Club is a nonprofit business, observe that there are some differences in its Chart of Accounts and some of its transactions. For example, revenues are derived from membership fees and seminars. Club members also contribute computers to local schools. When you work with this project, you see how these transactions are handled.

The club sponsors a trip to the International Consumer Electronics Show (ICES), a trade show in Las Vegas, Nevada. The trip involves expenses for bus rental, motel rooms, meals, and entrance fees to the trade show. Since so many club members attend ICES, a special rate is offered to them.

In this project, you complete the accounting cycle for the month of January 2016. Springfield Computer Club's Balance Sheet, transaction register, and bank statement are provided as source documents.

At the end of this project there is a Checklist that shows the printed reports you should have. The step-by-step instructions also remind you when to print. Your instructor may ask you to turn in these printouts for grading purposes. Remember to make backups at periodic intervals.

Follow these steps to complete Project 3, Springfield Computer Club:

Step 1: Start Sage 50.

Step 2: Make the selections to create a new company.

Step   3:   The company information for Springfield Computer Club is:

Company Name:	Springfield Computer Club
Address Line 1:	1102 South Third Street
City, State, Zip:	Springfield, IL 62705
Country:	USA
Phone:	217-555-2980
Fax:	217-555-2235
Business Type:	Corporation
Federal Employer ID:	41-7855344
State Employer ID:	45-3148921
State Unemployment ID:	458010-8
Web Site:	www.springfieldcomputerclub.com
E-mail:	info@springfieldcomputerclub.com

Step   4:   Accept the default to Use a sample business that closely matches your company.

Step   5:   Select Non-Profit Organizations. (*Hint:* Scroll down the Detailed types list. Chart of Account numbers have five digits.)

Step   6:   Accept the default for Accrual accounting.

Step   7:   Accept the default for Real Time posting.

Step   8:   Accept the default for Choose an accounting period structure, 12 monthly accounting periods per year.

Step   9:   The Choose the first period of your fiscal year window appears. If necessary, select January 2016.

Step   10:   At the You are ready to create your company window, click
Finish . If the screen prompts You can use this company in the student version of Sage 50 for the next 14 months and
then it will expire, click OK . If necessary, close the
Setup Guide and Sage Advisor Getting Started windows.

Step 11:   Change the accounting period to Period 1 – 01/01/16 to
01/31/16 - Period 1 - 01/01/16-01/31/16 .

Step 12:   Delete, add, and change the following General Ledger
accounts in the Chart of Accounts:

Delete these accounts:

Acct. #   Account Name

10000   Petty Cash
10100   Cash on Hand
10300   Payroll Checking Account
10500   Special Account
10600   Cash-Restricted Fund
10700   Investments
11400   Other Receivables
11500   Allowance for Doubtful Account
12100   Inventory-Kitchen
12150   Inventory-Golf & Tennis
12200   Inventory-Snack Stand
14100   Employee Advances
14700   Other Current Assets
15200   Automobiles
15300   Other Depreciable Property
15400   Leasehold Improvements
15500   Building
15600   Building Improvements
16900   Land
17200   Accum. Depreciation-Automobi
17300   Accum. Depreciation-Other
17400   Accum. Depreciation-Leasehol
17500   Accum. Depreciation-Building
17600   Accum. Depreciation-Bldg Imp
19000   Deposits
19150   Accum. Amortiz. - Org. Costs
19200   Note Receivable-Noncurrent
19900   Other Noncurrent Assets
23000   Accrued Expenses
23100   Sales Tax Payable

23300	Deductions Payable
23400	Federal Payroll Taxes Payable
23500	FUTA Tax Payable
23600	State Payroll Taxes Payable
23700	SUTA Payable
23800	Local Payroll Taxes Payable
24000	Other Taxes Payable
24100	Employee Benefits Payable
24200	Current Portion Long-Term Debt
24800	Other Current Liabilities
24900	Suspense-Clearing Account
27000	Notes Payable-Noncurrent
27100	Deferred Revenue
27400	Other Long-Term Liabilities
40200	Sales-Kitchen/Dining Room
40400	Sales-Golf/Tennis
40600	Sales-Snack Stand
40800	Sales-Other
41000	Contributions-Unrestricted
41200	Grants
41400	Program Service Revenue
41800	Investment Income
42000	Realized gain in Investment
42200	Miscellaneous Income
42400	Contributions-Restricted
42600	Investment Income-Restricted
43000	Other Income
48000	Fee Refunds
58000	Cost of Sales-Other
59000	Purchase Returns and Allowance
60000	Default Purchase Expense
60100	Grant and Allocation Exp.
61500	Bad Debt Expense
65000	Employee Benefit Programs Exp
65500	Other Employee Benefits
72000	Payroll Tax Expense
76500	Compensation of Officers
77000	Salaries Expense
89000	Other Expense

Change these accounts:

Acct. #	Account Name	New Account Name
10200	Regular Checking Account	National Bank
12000	Inventory-Bar	Inventory-Computers/Schools
14000	Prepaid Expenses	Prepaid Rent
15100	Equipment	Computer Equipment
17000	Accum. Depreciation-Furnitur	Accum. Depreciation-Furn&Fix
17100	Accum. Depreciation-Eq.	Accum. Depreciation-Comp Equip
20000	Accounts Payable	Credit Card Payable
40000	Sales-Bar	Fees-Seminars/Classes
66000	Supplies Expense	Office Supplies Expense
67500	Occupancy Expense	Rent Expense
70000	Travel Expense	Bus Rental-ICES
72500	Depreciation Expense	Depr. Exp.-Furniture & Fixture

Add these accounts:

Acct. #	Account Name	Account Type
39002	Membership Contributions	Equity-doesn't close
60000	Advertising Expense	Expenses
60400	Bank Service Charge	Expenses
70010	Meals-ICES	Expenses
70020	Motel-ICES	Expenses
70030	Fees-ICES	Expenses
72520	Depr. Exp.-Comp Equip	Expenses

How to Fix? How do I show my name on printouts?

Follow these steps to add your name to the company name.

1. From the menu bar, select Maintain > Company Information. The Maintain Company Information window appears.
2. Type your first and last name after Springfield Computer Club. The Company Name field shows: Springfield Computer Club—Your first and last name.
3. Click OK.

Step 13: Back up. The suggested file name is **Springfield Computer Club Chart of Accounts.ptb**.

Step 14: Use the Springfield Computer Club Balance Sheet to record the chart of accounts beginning balances.

Springfield Computer Club Balance Sheet January 1, 2016		
ASSETS		
Current Assets		
National Bank	$21,250.00	
Inventory-Computers/Schools	500.00	
Inventory-Office	1,500.00	
Total Current Assets		$23,250.00
Property and Equipment		
Furniture and Fixtures	1,500.00	
Computer Equipment	3,000.00	
Total Property and Equipment		4,500.00
Total Assets		$27,750.00
LIABILITIES		
Credit Card Payable	250.00	
Total Liabilities		250.00
CAPITAL		
Retained Earnings		27,500.00
Total Liabilities and Capital		$27,750.00

Step 15:   Back up your data. The suggested file name is **Springfield Computer Club Starting Balance Sheet.ptb**. To check that your beginning balances are entered correctly, display the December 31, 2015 balance sheet.

Step 16:   The transaction register provides you with the information necessary for Springfield Computer Club's Cash Receipts Journal and Cash Disbursements Journal entries for January. The Springfield Computer Club issues checks and makes deposits to National Bank.

Springfield Computer Club Transaction Register					
Ck. No.	**Date**	**Description of Transaction**	**Payment**	**Deposit**	**Balance**
	12/31/15				21,250.00
	1/4/16	Deposit (membership dues)[1]		2,850.00	24,100.00
8001	1/11/16	Payment - Credit Card	250.00		23,850.00
8002	1/11/16	Kevin Advertising	205.00		23,645.00
8003	1/11/16	Sepulveda Office Supplies	155.65		23,489.35
8004	1/18/16	Meals-ICES	800.00		22,689.35
8005	1/18/16	Bus Rental-ICES	600.00		22,089.35
8006	1/18/16	Entrance Fees-ICES	725.00		21,364.35
8007	1/18/16	Motel Rooms-ICES	835.27		20,529.08
8008	1/26/16	Springfield Telephone	41.76		20,487.32
8009	1/26/16	Shipping Charges	45.00		20,442.32
	1/29/16	Deposit (seminar fees)		800.00	21,242.32

Step 17:   *Additional journal entry*: On January 31, a club member donated a computer system and printer to the club. The value of the computer and printer is $250. (Debit, Inventory - Computers/Schools; Credit, Membership Contributions. Use the General Journal for this entry)

---

[1]For each deposit shown on the transaction register, type the date of the transaction in the Deposit ticket ID field. For each check, use Banking > Write Checks.

Step 18: Springfield Computer Club's bank statement is shown below. Complete the Account Reconciliation for the National Bank.

Statement of Account National Bank Jan. 1 to Jan. 31, 2016		Account No. 931-49786	Springfield Computer Club 5902 Sixth Street Springfield, IL 62705	
REGULAR CHECKING				
Previous Balance	12/31/15	$ 21,250.00		
2 Deposits(+)		3,650.00		
7 Checks (-)		2,887.68		
Service Charges (-)		12.00		
Ending Balance	1/31/16	**$ 22,000.32**		
DEPOSITS				
	1/5/16	2,850.00	1/29/16	800.00
CHECKS (Asterisk * indicates break in check number sequence)				
	1/14/16	8001	250.00	
	1/14/16	8002	205.00	
	1/18/16	8003	155.65	
	1/26/16	8004	800.00	
	1/28/16	8005*	600.00	
	1/29/16	8007	835.27	
	1/29/16	8008	41.76	

Step 19: Make a backup. The suggested file name is **Springfield Computer Club January.ptb**.

Step 20: Export these reports to Excel: Chart of Accounts, Cash Receipts Journal, Cash Disbursements Journal, General Ledger Trial Balance, Balance Sheet, Income Statement, Statement of Cash Flow, Statement of Retained Earnings. Use the file name **Springfield Computer Club_CofA_CRJ_CDJ_ GLTB_ BS_ IS_ SCF_SRE.xlsx**.

Step 21: Save the following reports as PDF files: Chart of Accounts, General Ledger Trial Balance, Balance Sheet, Income Statement, Statement of Cash Flow, and Statement of Retained Earnings. The suggested file name is **Project 3_Chart of Accounts.pdf**, etc. Your instructor may require additional PDF files.

Your instructor may want to collect this project. A Checklist of Printouts is shown below.

Checklist of Printouts, Project 3: Springfield Computer Club		
1		Chart of Accounts
2		December 31, 2015 Starting Balance Sheet
3		Account Reconciliation
4		Account Register – National Bank
5		Cash Disbursements Journal
6		Cash Receipts Journal
7		General Journal
8		General Ledger Trial Balance
9		General Ledger
10		Balance Sheet
11		Income Statement
12		Statement of Cash Flow
13		Statement of Retained Earnings

Student Name_____**Date**_____

CHECK YOUR PROGRESS: PROJECT 3
SPRINGFIELD COMPUTER CLUB

1. What are the total debit and credit balances on your general ledger trial balance?   _____

2. What is the total amount of checks outstanding?   _____

3. How much are the total expenses on January 31?   _____

4. How much are the total revenues on January 31?   _____

5. How much is the net income (net loss) on January 31?   _____

6. What is the account balance in the Membership Contributions account on January 31?   _____

7. What are the total assets on January 31?   _____

8. What is the ending retained earnings on January 31, 2016?   _____

9. What is the balance in the Credit Card Payable account on January 31?   _____

10. What is the balance in the Office Supplies Expense account on January 31?   _____

11. Is there an Increase or Decrease in cash for the month of January?   _____

12. Was any Credit Card Payable incurred during the month of January? (Circle your answer)   YES   NO

Project 4 — CW Manufacturing, Inc.

In Project 4, you complete the computer accounting cycle for CW Manufacturing, Inc. This company manufactures backpacks, sleeping bags, and tents.

CW Manufacturing, Inc. offers its customers a sales discount of 2% 15, Net 30 days. Vendors offer CW Manufacturing, Inc. a purchase discount of 1% 15, Net 30 days.

Follow these steps to complete Project 4, CW Manufacturing, Inc.

Step 1:   Start Sage 50.

Step 2:   Make the selections to create a new company.

Step 3:   Type the following company information for CW Manufacturing, Inc.:

Company Name:	CW Manufacturing, Inc. (*use your initials, then Manufacturing, Inc.*)
Address Line 1:	2100 Broad Street
City, State, Zip:	Philadelphia, PA 19122
Country:	USA
Phone:	215-555-3444
Fax:	215-555-3446
Business Type:	Corporation
Federal Employer ID:	82-8505202
State Employer ID:	34-5848232
State Unemployment ID:	340307-3
Web Site:	www.cwmftg.net
E-mail:	info@cwmftg.net

Step 4:   Accept the default for Use a sample business type that closely matches your company.

Step   5:   Scroll down the list. In the **Detailed types** list, select Manufacturing Company. (*Hint:* The Chart of Accounts has five-digit account numbers.)

Step   6:   Accept the default for Accrual accounting.

Step   7:   Accept the default for Real Time posting.

Step   8:   Accept the default for 12 monthly accounting periods.

Step   9:   The Choose the first period of your fiscal year window appears. If necessary, select January 2016 as the month and year.

Step 10:   At the You are ready to create your company window, click Finish. If the screen prompts You can use this company in the student version of Sage 50 for the next 14 months and then it will expire, click OK.

Step 11:   When the Sage 50 Setup Guide window appears, click on the box next to Don't show this screen at startup to place a checkmark in it. Close the Setup Guide and Sage Advisor Getting Started windows.

Step 12:   Change the accounting period to 01-Jan 01,2016 to Jan 31,2016—Period 1 - 01/01/16-01/31/16.

General Ledger

1.   Delete the following accounts:

   10100   Cash on Hand
   10400   Savings Account
   10500   Special Account
   10600   Investments-Money Market
   15400   Leasehold Improvements
   16900   Land
   17300   Accum. Depreciation-Other
   17400   Accum. Depreciation-Leasehol
   24800   Other Current Liabilities

2. Change these account names:

10200   Regular Checking Account to Penn Bank
10300   Payroll Checking Account to Hancock Savings & Loan
14000   Prepaid Expenses to Prepaid Insurance
15100   Equipment to Computers & Equipment
15200   Automobiles to Trucks/Autos
17100   Accum. Depreciation - Equipment to Accum. Depreciation - Comp&Eq
17200   Accum. Depreciation - Automobil to Accum. Depreciation - Trks/Aut
23300   Deductions Payable to Medicare Employee Taxes Payabl
24000   Other Taxes Payable to Soc. Sec. Employee Taxes Payab
24100   Employee Benefits Payable to Soc. Sec. Employer Taxes Payab
27000   Notes Payable-Noncurrent to Mortgage Payable
40000   Sales #1 to Sales-Backpacks
40200   Sales #2 to Sales-Sleeping Bags
40400   Sales #3 to Sales-Tents
72500   Penalties and Fines Exp to Employer FUTA Expense
73000   Other Taxes to Employer SUTA Expense

3. Add these accounts:

Acct. ID	Acct. Description	Account Type
12010	Inventory-Backpacks	Inventory
12020	Inventory-Sleeping Bags	Inventory
12030	Inventory-Tents	Inventory
22000	Credit Card Payable	Other Current Liabilities
23350	Medicare Employer Taxes Payabl	Other Current Liabilities
23650	Employee SUI Taxes Payable	Other Current Liabilities
51050	Overtime Costs	Cost of Sales
73200	Employer Soc. Sec. Taxes Expen	Expenses
73300	Employer Medicare Expense	Expenses

4. Back up. The suggested file name is **CW Mftg Chart of Accounts.ptb**.

5. You purchased CW Manufacturing, Inc. in December 2015. Use the Balance Sheet below to record the chart of account beginning balances.

CW Manufacturing, Inc. Balance Sheet January 1, 2016		
ASSETS		
Current Assets		
Penn Bank	$80,650.00	
Hancock Savings & Loan	31,300.00	
Investments-Cert. of Deposit	14,500.00	
Inventory-Backpacks	1,612.50	
Inventory-Sleeping Bags	1,760.00	
Inventory-Tents	2,679.60	
Prepaid Insurance	3,600.00	
Total Current Assets		$136,102.10
Property and Equipment		
Furniture and Fixtures	2,500.00	
Computers & Equipment	6,000.00	
Trucks/Autos	25,000.00	
Building	105,000.00	
Total Property and Equipment		138,500.00
Total Assets		$274,602.10
LIABILITIES AND STOCKHOLDER'S EQUITY		
Credit Card Payable	15,900.00	
Mortgage Payable	97,500.00	
Total Liabilities		$113,400.00
Stockholder's Equity: Common Stock		161,202.10
Total Liabilities and Stockholder's Equity		$274,602.10

6. Backup. The suggested filename is **CW Mftg Starting Balance Sheet.ptb**. To check beginning balances, display the December 31, 2015 balance sheet

Accounts Payable

1. Set up the following vendor defaults.

Standard Terms:	Due in number of days
Net due in:	30 days
Discount in:	15 days
Discount %:	1.00
Credit Limit:	20,000.00

GL Link Accounts:

Expense Account:	12010 Inventory-Backpacks
Discount GL Account:	59500 Purchase Discounts

2. Set up the following vendors:

Vendor ID:	dd22
Name:	Dana Dash Fabrics
Contact:	Dana Dash
Mailing Address:	315 Oak Drive
City, ST, Zip:	Hartford, CT 06108
Vendor Type:	slpg bgs
1099 Type:	Independent Contractor
Expense Account:	12020 Inventory-Sleeping Bags
Telephone 1:	860-555-2211
Fax:	860-555-2322
E-mail:	dana@ddfabrics.com
Web Site:	www.ddfabrics.com

Purchase Info:

Tax ID Number:	13-4338452

Vendor ID:	ep33
Name:	Evans Products
Contact:	Donna Evans
Mailing Address:	4201 Erie Blvd.
City, ST, Zip:	Cleveland, OH 44192
Vendor Type:	tents
1099 Type:	Independent Contractor

Expense Account:	12030 Inventory-Tents
Telephone 1:	216-555-2113
Fax:	216-555-2144
E-mail:	donna@evansproducts.com
Web Site:	www.evansproducts.com

Purchase Info:

Tax ID Number:	39-1880248

Vendor ID:	rk44
Name:	RK Supplies
Contact:	Rita Kalmar
Mailing Address:	92311 Jefferson Circle
City, ST, Zip:	Trenton, NJ 07092
Vendor Type:	backpack
1099 Type:	Independent Contractor
Expense Accounting:	12010 Inventory-Backpacks
Telephone 1:	609-555-9822
Fax:	609-555-8230
E-mail:	info@rksupplies.net
Web Site:	www.rksupplies.net

Purchase Info:

Tax ID Number:	32-4284141

Accounts Receivable

1. Set up the following customer default settings:

Standard Terms:	Due in number of days
Net due in:	30 days
Discount in:	15 days
Discount Percent:	2.00
Credit Limit:	$15,000.00
GL Sales Account:	40000 Sales-Backpacks
Discount GL Account:	49000 Sales Discounts

2. Enter the following customer records:

Customer ID: 001BOS
Name: Burton's Outdoor Suppliers
Billing address: 5201 Dogwood Street
City, ST, Zip: Gainesville, FL 32652
Customer Type: FL (for Florida)
Telephone 1:   352-555-9200
Fax: 352-555-9208
E-mail: info@burtonoutdoor.biz
Web Site: www.burtonoutdoor.biz

Contacts:

Contact name: Victor Burton

Sales Info:

G/L Sales Acct: 40000, Sales-Backpacks
Resale Number: 7231350-2

Customer ID: 002SCS
Name: Sally's Camping Store
Billing address: 3901 Chestnut Street
City, ST, Zip: Philadelphia, PA 19131
Customer type: PA (for Pennsylvania)
Telephone 1:   215-555-3388
Fax: 215-555-3390
E-mail: sally@campingstore.biz
Web Site   www.campingstore.biz

Contacts:

Contact name: Sally Carlton

Sales Info:

G/L Sales Acct: 40200, Sales-Sleeping Bags
Resale Number: 9393192-1

Customer ID: 003WST
Name: West's Store
Billing address: 8900 Clark Street
City, ST, Zip: Cincinnati, OH 45227
Customer type: OH (for Ohio)
Telephone 1:   513-555-2001
Fax: 513-555-3118
E-mail: janet@weststore.com
Web Site: www.weststore.com

Contacts:

Contact name: Janet West

Sales Info:

G/L Sales Acct: 40400, Sales-Tents
Resale Number: 3936801-4

Payroll

1. Use the following information for the Payroll Setup Wizard.

   State: PA
   State Unemployment Rate: **3.4**
   Hourly Pay Types: Regular, Select 51000 - Direct Labor Costs
                     Overtime, Select 51050 - Overtime Costs
   Salary Pay Type: Select 77000 - Salaries Expense

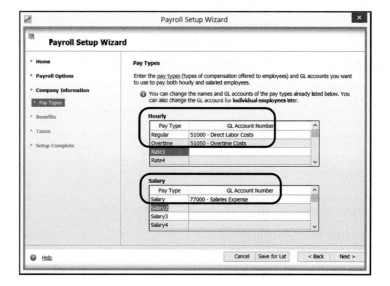

Do you have any localities for which you collect taxes in the state of PA? **Yes**

Locality: **Phila**
Tax rate: **1.0**

Local Taxes

Enter the name of the locality for which you collect taxes.

Locality: Phila

Tax rate: 1.00000 %

2. Set up these employee defaults. Use the Employee Fields information shown below.

Field Name	G/L Account
Fed_Income	Account No. 23400, Federal Payroll Taxes Payable
Soc_Sec	Account No. 24000, Soc. Sec. Employee Taxes Payable
MEDICARE	Account No. 23300, Medicare Employee Taxes Payable
St_Income	Account No. 23600, State Payroll Taxes Payable
Loc_Income	Account No. 23800, Local Payroll Taxes Payable
St_Unemp	Account No. 23650, Employee SUI Taxes Payable

3. Use the Company Fields shown below.

Field Name	Liability column	Expense column
Soc_Sec_C	24100, Soc. Sec. Employer Taxes Payable	73200, Employer Soc. Sec. Taxes Expense
Medicare_C	23350 Medicare Employer Taxes Payable	73300, Employer Medicare Expense
Fed_Unemp_C	23500, FUTA Tax Payable	72500, Employer FUTA Expense
St_Unemp_C	23700, SUTA Payable	73000, Employer SUTA Expense

4. Complete the Payroll Setup Wizard's Taxes and Assign Tax Fields.

5. Add the following employees.

Employee ID: EK40
Name: Ellie Kern
Accept the default for Employee
Address: 5220 Brockton Street
City, ST, Zip: Upper Darby, PA 19112
E-mail: ellie@mail.net
Home phone: 215-555-0368
Social Security #:   000-01-0002
Type: FULL

Pay Info:

Salary, $1,500. Ms. Kern is paid monthly.

Withholding Info:

Filing Status: Single for Federal, State, and Local
Allow: 1 for Federal, State and Local

Employee ID: JS50
Name: Jackie Sanchez
Accept the default for Employee
Address: 131 Girard Avenue
City, ST, Zip: Philadelphia, PA 19191
E-mail: jackie@mail.net
Home phone: 215-555-2843
Social Security #:   001-00-0402
Type: FULL

Pay Info: Hourly, $13.00 per hour; Overtime, $19.50. Ms. Sanchez is paid weekly.

Withholding Info:

Filing Status: Married for Federal, State, and Local
Allow: 2 for Federal, State and Local

Employee ID: LS60
Name: Len Simpkins
Accept the default for Employee
Address: 81 Montgomery Avenue
City, ST, Zip: Philadelphia, PA 19122
E-mail: len@mail.net
Home phone: 215-555-1208
Social Security #:   003-00-0003
Type: FULL

Pay Info: Hourly, $13.00 per hour; Overtime, $19.50. Mr. Simpkins is paid weekly.

Withholding Info:

Filing Status: Married for Federal, State, and Local
Allow: 2 for Federal, State and Local

Employee ID: OW70
Name: Owen Williams
Accept the default for Employee
Address: 321 West Oxford, Apt. 1E
City, ST, Zip: Philadelphia, PA 19131

E-mail:	owen@mail.net
Home phone	215-555-7218
Social Security #:	000-00-2000
Type:	FULL

Pay Info: Hourly, $13.00 per hour; Overtime, $19.50. Mr. Williams is paid weekly.

Withholding Info:

Filing Status:	Married for Federal, State, and Local
Allow:	2 for Federal, State and Local

Inventory

1. Set up inventory defaults. On the <u>G</u>eneral Tab, select Stock item as the Default Item Class.

2. Make sure that FIFO is the default inventory costing method.

3. Set up the following inventory items:

Item ID:	backpacks
Description:	backpacks
Item Class:	Stock item
Description for Sales:	backpacks
Price Level 1:	150.00
Last Unit Cost:	37.50
Cost Method:	FIFO
GL Sales Acct:	40000 Sales-Backpacks
GL Inventory Acct:	12010, Inventory-Backpacks
GL Cost of Sales Acct:	50500, Raw Material Purchases
Item Tax Type:	2 Exempt
Item Type:	backpack
Stocking U/M:	each
Minimum Stock:	10
Reorder Quantity:	5
Preferred Vendor ID:	rk44, RK Supplies
Beginning Balances:	backpacks
Quantity:	43.00
Unit Cost:	37.50
Total Cost:	1,612.50

Item ID: sleeping bags
Description: sleeping bags
Item Class: Stock item
Description for Sales: sleeping bags
Price Level 1:   105.00
Last Unit Cost: 27.50
Cost Method: FIFO
GL Sales Acct: 40200, Sales-Sleeping Bags
GL Inventory Acct: 12020, Inventory-Sleeping Bags
GL Cost of Sales Acct: 50500, Raw Material Purchases
Item Tax Type: 2 Exempt
Item Type: slpg bgs
Stocking U/M: each
Minimum Stock: 10
Reorder Quantity: 5
Preferred Vendor ID: dd22, Dana Dash Fabrics

Beginning Balances: sleeping bags

Quantity: 64.00
Last Unit Cost   27.50
Total Cost: 1,760.00

Item ID: tents
Description: tents
Item Class: Stock item
Description for Sales: tents
Price Level 1:   175.00
Last Unit Cost: 47.85
Cost Method: FIFO
GL Sales Acct: 40400, Sales-Tents
GL Inventory Acct: 12030, Inventory-Tents
GL Cost of Sales Acct: 50500, Raw Material Purchases
Item Tax Type: 2 Exempt
Item Type: tents
Stocking U/M: each
Minimum Stock: 10
Reorder Quantity: 5
Preferred Vendor ID: ep33, Evans Products

Beginning Balances: tents

Quantity: 56.00
Unit Cost: 47.85
Total Cost: 2,679.60

Jobs

1. Set up the following job records:

Job ID:	13-221
Description:	backpacks
For Customer:	001BOS
Start Date:	1/2/16
Projected End Date:	12/31/16
Job Type:	backpack

Job ID:	14-331
Description:	sleeping bags
For Customer:	002SCS
Start Date:	1/2/16
Projected End Date:	12/31/16
Job Type:	slpg bgs

Job ID:	15-441
Description:	tents
For Customer:	003WST
Start Date:	1/2/16
Projected End Date:	12/31/16
Job Type:	tents

2. Back up. Use **CW Mftg Begin.ptb** as the filename.

3. Exit or continue.

Journalize and post the following transactions:

Date   Description of Transaction

1/5/16   Invoice No. 315 was received from Dana Dash Fabrics for 15 sleeping bags @ $27.50 each for a total of $412.50. Post invoice 315.

1/5/16   Invoice No. 45 was received from RK Supplies for 20 backpacks @ $37.50 each for a total of $750.00. Post invoice 45.

1/5/16   Invoice No. 800 was received from Evans Products for 16 tents @ $47.85 each for a total of $765.60. Post invoice 800.

1/8/16   Pay the factory employees for 40 hours of direct labor. Select Account No. 10300, Hancock Savings & Loan, as the Cash Account. In the Check Number field, type **101** for Ms. Sanchez's paycheck. The check numbers for Mr. Simpkins and Mr. Williams are automatically completed. (Do *not* print the payroll checks.) Remember, click [Jobs] to complete the following:

Check No.	Employee	Job	Hours
101	Jackie Sanchez	15-441	40
102	Len Simpkins	14-331	40
103	Owen Williams	13-221	40

Click [Save] *after each payroll entry.*

1/12/16   Sold 20 backpacks on account to Burton's Outdoor Suppliers for a total of $3,000.00, Job 13-221. In the Invoice No. field, type **101**.[1] Post sales invoice 101.

1/12/16   Sold 12 sleeping bags on account to Sally's Camping Store for a total of $1,260.00, Job 14-331. Post sales invoice 102.

1/12/16   Sold 20 tents on account to West's Store for a total of $3,500.00, Job 15-441. Post sales invoice 103.

1/15/16   Pay the factory employees for 40 hours of direct labor. (Refer to the information on the next page.) *Remember to post each payroll entry.*

---

[1]Since you are not printing sales invoices, it is necessary to complete this field.

Check No.	Employee	Job	Hours
104	Jackie Sanchez	15-441	40
105	Len Simpkins	14-331	40
106	Owen Williams	13-221	40

1/15/16   Issued Check No. 1001 to RK Supplies in payment of purchase Invoice No. 45. Select Account No. 10200, Penn Bank as the cash account. In the Check/Reference field, type **1001**. Do *not* print vendor checks. In the Discount Account field, make sure that Account No. 59500, Purchase Discounts is shown. Post Check No. 1001 in the amount of $742.50.

1/15/16   Issued Check No. 1002 to Dana Dash Fabrics in payment of purchase Invoice No. 315. Post Check No. 1002 in the amount of $408.37.

1/15/16   Issued Check No. 1003 to Evans Products in payment of purchase Invoice No. 800. Post Check No. 1003 in the amount of $757.94.

1/19/16   Invoice No. 328 was received from Dana Dash Fabrics for 15 sleeping bags @ $27.50 each for a total of $412.50. Post invoice 328.

1/19/16   Invoice No. 900 was received from Evans Products for 20 tents @ $47.85 each for a total of $957.00. Post invoice 900.

1/22/16   Pay the factory employees for 40 hours of direct labor. *Remember to click on* <u>S</u>ave *after each payroll check is recorded*.

Check No.	Employee	Job	Hours
107	Jackie Sanchez	15-441	40
108	Len Simpkins	14-331	40
109	Owen Williams	13-221	40

1/22/16   Received payment from Burton's Outdoor Suppliers for sales invoice 101. Select Account No. 10200, Penn Bank, as the cash account. Use the date of the transaction in the Deposit ticket ID field. In the Check/Reference field, type **Inv. 101**. Post this receipt in the amount of $2,940.

1/22/16   Received payment from Sally's Camping Store for sales invoice 102. In the Check/Reference field, type **Inv. 102**. Post this receipt in the amount of $1,234.80.

1/22/16   Received payment from West's Store for sales invoice 103. In the Check/Reference field, type **Inv. 103**. Post this receipt in the amount of $3,430.

1/22/16   Sold 25 sleeping bags on account to Sally's Camping Store for a total of $2,625.00, Job 14-331. In the Invoice No. field, type **104**. Post sales invoice 104.

1/22/16   Sold 21 tents on account to West's Store for a total of $3,675.00, Job 15-441. Post sales invoice 105.

1/29/16   Pay the factory employees for 40 hours of direct labor. *Remember to click on* Save *after each payroll check is recorded.*

Check No.	Employee	Job	Hours
110	Jackie Sanchez	15-441	40
111	Len Simpkins	14-331	40
112	Owen Williams	13-221	40

1/29/16   Pay the salaried employee, Ellie Kern. In the Salary Amounts table, make sure that account 77000, Salaries Expense, is shown in the Account column. If not, select that account. Post Check No. 113.

1/29/16   Issued Check No. 1004 to Penn Bank for $709.23 in payment of Mortgage Payable; split the mortgage payment between principal in the amount of $584.06, and interest in the amount of $125.17. In the Check number field, type **1004**. (Use the Write Checks task and the split feature. Make sure that account 10200, Penn Bank, is selected as the Cash Account.) Post Check No. 1004.

1/29/16	Issued Check No. 1005 to Hancock Savings & Loan for $800 in payment of Credit Card Payable. Post Check No. 1005.
1/29/16	Issued Check No. 1006 to the Hill Power Company for $204.75 in payment of utilities. (Debit Utilities Expense, Account No. 78000.) Post Check No. 1006.
1/29/16	Issued Check No. 1007 to Eastern Telephone for $189.10 in payment of telephone bill. Post Check No. 1007.
1/30/16	Received payment from West's Store for sales invoice 105. In the Reference field, type **Inv. 105**. Post this receipt in the amount of $3,601.50.

Account Reconciliation

1. Complete the bank reconciliation for Penn Bank and Hancock Savings & Loan. The January 31, 2016, bank statements are shown below and on the next page.

Bank Statement: Penn Bank

Statement of Account Penn Bank January 1 to January 31, 2016 Account #54672			CW Manufacturing, Inc. 2100 Broad Street Philadelphia, PA 19122	
REGULAR CHECKING				
Previous Balance	12/31/15	$80,650.00		
2 Deposits(+)		11,206.30		
3 Checks (-)		1,908.81		
Service Charges (-)	1/31/16	22.00		
Ending Balance	1/31/16	**$89,925.49**		
DEPOSITS				
	1/26/16	7,604.80		
	1/31/16	3,601.50		
CHECKS (Asterisk * indicates break in check number sequence)				
	1/28/16	1001	742.50	
	1/30/16	1002	408.37	
	1/30/16	1003	757.94	

Bank Statement: Hancock Savings & Loan

Statement of Account Hancock Savings & Loan January 1 to January 31, 2016 Account #32310-38002			CW Manufacturing, Inc. 2100 Broad Street Philadelphia, PA 19122	
PAYROLL CHECKING				
Previous Balance	12/31/15	31,300.00		
Deposits(+)				
9 Checks (-)		3,943.26		
Service Charges (-)	1/31/16	20.00		
Ending Balance	1/31/16	**27,336.74**		
DEPOSITS				
CHECKS (Asterisk * indicates break in check number sequence)				
	1/08/16	101	438.14	
	1/08/16	102	438.14	
	1/08/16	103	438.14	
	1/15/16	104	438.14	
	1/15/16	105	438.14	
	1/15/16	106	438.14	
	1/22/16	107	438.14	
	1/22/16	108	438.14	
	1/22/16	109	438.14	

2. Back up. Use **CW Mftg January.ptb** as the file name.

3. Export the following reports to Excel: Chart of Accounts, General Ledger Trial Balance, Balance Sheet, Income Statement, Statement of Cash Flow, and Statement of Retained Earnings. Use the file name **CW Mftg_CofA_GLTB_ BS_IS_SCF_SRE.xlsx**

4. Save the following reports as PDF files: Chart of Accounts, General Ledger Trial Balance, Balance, Sheet, Income Statement, Statement of Cash Flow, Statement of Retained Earnings. The suggested file

name is **Project 4_Chart of Accounts.pdf**, etc. Your instructor may require additional reports.

		CHECKLIST OF PRINTOUTS, CW MANUFACTURING, INC.
	1	Account Reconciliation Report: Penn Bank
	2	Account Reconciliation Report: Hancock Savings & Loan
	3	Account Register: Penn Bank
	4	Account Register: Hancock Savings & Loan
	5	General Ledger Trial Balance
	6	General Ledger
	7	Balance Sheet
	8	Income Statement
	9	Statement of Cash Flow
	10	Statement of Retained Earnings
	11	Customer Ledgers
	12	Vendor Ledgers
	13	Job Ledger
	14	Job Profitability Report
	15	Inventory Profitability Report
	16	Payroll Register
		Optional printouts, CW Manufacturing, Inc.
	17	Chart of Accounts
	18	December 31 2015 Balance Sheet
	19	Customer List
	20	Vendor List
	21	Payroll Journal
	22	Purchase Journal
	23	Cash Disbursements Journal
	24	Sales Journal
	25	Cash Receipts Journal
	26	Cost of Goods Sold Journal
	27	General Journal

Student Name_____**Date**_____

CHECK YOUR PROGRESS: PROJECT 4
CW MANUFACTURING, INC.

1. What are the total debit and credit balances on your General Ledger Trial Balance? _____

2. What are the total assets on January 31? _____

3. What is the balance in the Penn Bank account on January 31? _____

4. What is the balance in the Hancock Savings & Loan account on January 31? _____

5. What is Sally's Camping Store account balance on January 31? _____

6. What are the direct labor costs on January 31? _____

7. How many backpacks were sold during the month of January? _____

8. How many sleeping bags were sold during the month of January? _____

9. How many tents were sold during the month of January? _____

10. What is the ending retained earnings amount on on January 31? _____

11. What are the total expenses reported on January 31? _____

12. Was any Accounts Payable incurred during the month of January? (Circle your answer)   YES   NO

Project

4A   Student-Designed Project

You have completed four projects: Shelly Martin, Accounting; Highland Sports; Springfield Computer Club; and CW Manufacturing, Inc. In each project you completed the Computer Accounting Cycle for one month.

It is the purpose of Project 4A, to have you write the next month's transactions for one of the four projects. You pick the project and complete the accounting cycle: Project 1, Shelly Martin, Accounting, a service business; Project 2, Highland Sports, a merchandising business; Project 3, Springfield Computer Club, a nonprofit business; or Project 4, CW Manufacturing, Inc., a manufacturing business. At the end of your month's transactions, you are required to complete adjusting entries.

Good luck! It is your turn to create the transactions for another month and complete the Computer Accounting Cycle. Remember to back up periodically.

Appendix A — Troubleshooting

Refer to the Online Learning Center for the most recent troubleshooting information. Appendix C, Review of Accounting Principles; and Appendix D, Glossary is on the OLC at www.mhhe.com/yacht2016 > Troubleshooting Tips.

The last page of each chapter is an index. Refer to the chapter index for specific troubleshooting, how to fix, comments, and Read Me boxes.

Appendix A, Troubleshooting, includes the following.

1. Troubleshooting Installation, page 709

   a. System Requirements Warning, pages 709-710
   b. Sage 50 Installer: IPV4 vs. IPV6, page 710
   c. Remove PCWxxx.ini Files, pages 710

2. PDF Files, pages 710-711
3. Using Excel 2007, 2010, or 2013, page 711
4. Go Green and Save, *or* No Printer, page 711
5. Opening the Sample Companies, pages 711-712
6. Problem Backing Up to USB Drive, page 712
7. Restoring Starting Data for the Sample Companies, pages 712-713
8. Restoring Sage 50 2013 and 2015 backup files (.ptb extensions), pages 713
9. Payroll Entry, page 713-714
10. Serial Number in Use, page 714
11. Deleting Sage 50, page 714-715

TROUBLESHOOTING INSTALLATION

System Requirements Warning

If a System Requirements window warns RAM is not large enough or processing speed is too slow, you may continue installation but Sage 50 2016 may run slower.

The minimum requirements for Sage 50 2016 installation is 1 GB of RAM for single user, 2GB of RAM for multiple users, and 2.4 GHz of processor speed. Refer to pages iv-v for System Requirements.

Sage 50 Installer: IPV4 vs. IPV6

During installation, if a window prompts "Your computer is currently using a default network protocol, IPV6, which may cause Sage 50 to run slowly. Would you like to change to a default protocol, IPV4, which will make Sage 50 run faster? Click <Yes>.

The database engine that Sage 50 uses internally is not compatible with IPV6. It requires the use of IPV4. In some configurations, it can cause Sage 50 to run very slowly. Very few network installations actually use IPV6, so it is generally safe to make the switch to IPV4.

Remove PCWxxx.ini Files

If you are having difficulty installing Sage 50 2016, do a search to check if a PCWXXX.ini file resides on your hard drive. Search and then delete these files:

1. PCW160.ini (Peachtree 2009)
2. PCW170.ini (Peachtree 2010)
3. PCW180.ini (Peachtree 2011)

Once the PCWXXX.ini file is deleted, reinstall Sage 50.

PDF FILES

To convert Sage 50 reports to PDF files, you need Adobe Reader software, an Adobe Corporation product. This software lets you view, navigate, and print the contents of a file. Free Adobe Reader software is available at https://get.adobe.com/reader/.

If you are having difficulty using Sage 50's PDF feature, do the following:

1. Update to the latest version of Adobe Reader https://get.adobe.com/reader/.
2. Exit Sage 50. Insert the Sage 50 DVD and select Repair.

USING EXCEL 2007, 2010, OR 2013

Exporting two or more Sage 50 reports to Excel is shown on pages 85-87. If a window prompts that additional reports cannot be exported to the same file, save the Excel report, then Exit. Go to the Sage 50 report you want to export, then add a new worksheet to an existing workbook. When saving multiple Sage reports to an Excel file, you may need to exit Excel between exporting each report to an existing workbook.

GO GREEN AND SAVE, *OR* NO PRINTER

Reminders to Go Green and Save are included within chapters of the textbook. *Or,* if your computer is not connected to a printer, you have these choices:

1. In the Print Properties field, save the file as either an Adobe PDF file or a Microsoft XPS Document Writer file. If needed, you can attach the file to your instructor.

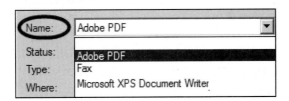

2. In the Check number field or Invoice number field, type the appropriate number. Since printing a check or invoice numbers the entry and posts it to the ledger, typing the number in the appropriate field before posting will also include the number on the journal and ledger.

OPENING THE SAMPLE COMPANIES

When selecting one of the sample companies – Bellwether Garden Supply or Stone Arbor Landscaping – the Explore a Sample Company Window does <u>not</u> show the <OK>, <Close>, or <Help> buttons.

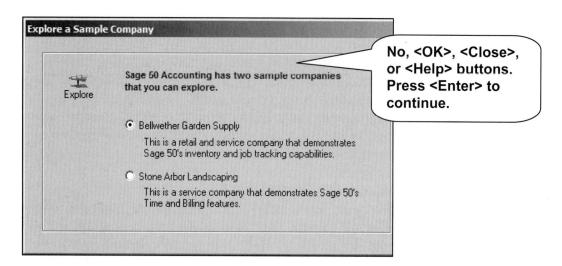

Screen resolution affects how Sage 50's windows look. The recommended screen resolution is 1024X768 with small fonts. Page v includes this recommended system requirement:

- At least high color (16-bit) SVGA video; supports 1024x768 resolution with small fonts required.

Higher screen resolution may be used. Higher resolution will not affect how the software functions, but the user interface might look different. For example, if you do not have an <OK> button, press <Enter> to start Bellwether Garden Supply or Stone Arbor Landscaping.

PROBLEM BACKING UP TO USB DRIVE

Instead of backing up to the USB drive, backup to your desktop. Then, copy the backup from your desktop to the USB drive.

RESTORING STARTING DATA FOR THE SAMPLE COMPANIES: BELLWETHER GARDEN SUPPLY AND STONE ARBOR LANDSCAPING

To start the sample companies from the beginning (before any data was added), restore these files:

1. In Chapter 1, on pages 23-25, you backed up Bellwether Garden Supply. This back up was made *before* any data was added. Restore the bgs.ptb file. Refer to Using Sage 50's Restore Wizard on

pages 29-33 for detailed steps. Once the bgs.ptb file is restored you have starting (beginning) data for Bellwether Garden Supply.

2. In Chapter 8, on page 243, you backed up Stone Arbor Landscaping. Restore the Chapter 8.ptb file.

RESTORING SAGE 50 2013 OR 2015 BACKUP FILES (.PTB EXTENSION)

To restore files from earlier versions of Sage 50, use the Educational version software. The student version *cannot* be used to restore .ptb backup files from earlier Sage 50 versions. The Educational version is free to schools, does not have a time limit, is multiuser ready, and has a different serial than the student version.

If your school is a member of the Sage Education Partner Program (http://www.sage.com/us/about-us/education), the new version of Sage 50 is automatically sent to schools. When installing the Educational version, use the serial number emailed by SageEducation@sage.com, 800-256-8807. The website for downloading free classroom software is http://www.sage.com/us/about-us/education-instructor.

PAYROLL ENTRY

If you are trying to use the payroll tax tables and a window prompts to register your product, you may not have not installed the software with the appropriate serial number. [Peachtree is used as an example; your window shows Sage 50.]

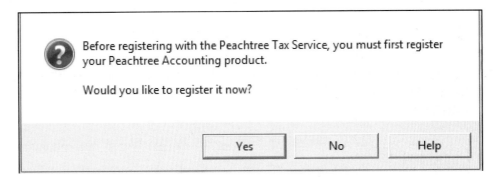

Before registering with the Peachtree Tax Service, you must first register your Peachtree Accounting product.

Would you like to register it now?

| Yes | No | Help |

If you select the Payroll Entry window and a window appears asking you to register payroll, click on the Do not display this message again box. Then click <OK>.

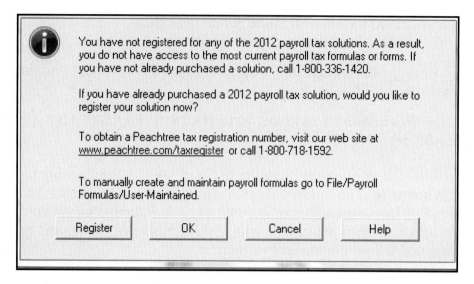

Sage 50 educational and student versions include *example* tax tables for 50 states (File; Payroll Formulas, Sage-Maintained, select the Formula ID field. Example payroll formulas are included for the 50 states.)

You may need to delete the software and reinstall.

SERIAL NUMBER IN USE; YOU CANNOT USE SAGE 50 BECAUSE IT HAS REACHED ITS MAXIMUM NUMBER OF USERS

If you are receiving Serial Number in use, Another Sage 50 user is using the same serial number, or Sage 50 has reached its maximum number of users, do the following.

1. If necessary, exit Sage 50.

2. Go to Task Manager by pressing the CTRL+ALT+DEL keys and on the Processes tab look for W3DBSMGR.EXE, click to highlight and choose End Task. The W3DBSMGR.EXE file is the Pervasive database which sometimes takes time to end. You may have exited Sage 50 and then tried to start it *before* Pervasive stopped running.

3. Restart Sage 50.

DELETING SAGE 50

Follow these steps to delete Sage 50 Accounting 2016. (Use similar steps to delete Sage 50 2015 or earlier version.)
1.   Insert the Sage 50 CD. Select Run autorun.exe. *Or,* go to Control Panel > Programs and Features > Uninstall Sage 50 Accounting 2016 (*or* other year). The InstallWizard window appears briefly.

2.   When the Maintenance Options window appears, select Remove > click <Next>.

3.   The Confirm Uninstall prompts This will remove Sage 50 Accounting 2016 (all versions), click <OK>. Be patient. Removing Sage 50 Accounting will take a while.

4.   When the Maintenance Complete window appears, click <Finish>. .

5.   If necessary, remove the CD. Close Control Panel.
After removal, you may want to delete these two folders:

1.   C:\Sage

2.   C:\Program Files (x86)\Sage

Before removing the folders, backup data that you want to keep. Once the Sage folder is deleted, all company data files are removed. (In Windows Vista, the Sage folder is within C:\Program Files.)

These steps are also shown on pages xxiii.

Appendix B

Accounting Information Systems

In *Computer Accounting with Sage 50 2016, 19e,* you learn about the relationship between Sage 50 and fundamental accounting principles and procedures. Throughout the textbook, you are shown how the initial decisions for setting up a company, setting defaults, processing transactions, and generating reports relates to what is learned in other accounting courses.

Another feature of the textbook explains how Sage 50's user interface organizes and processes data. Sage 50 is an example of an accounting information system. The following section defines *accounting information systems (AIS)* and their key components.

ACCOUNTING INFORMATION SYSTEMS

An accounting information system is the method of recordkeeping a business uses to maintain its financial information. This includes purchases, sales, and other financial processes of the business. The purpose of AIS is to accumulate data and provide decision makers (investors, creditors, and managers) with information.

Key characteristics of an accounting information system include providing timely accurate financial information to management and external users (creditors, investors, regulatory authorities, and taxation authorities). AIS software uses various modules to record data and produce reports. Users can easily produce financial statements or obtain information to manage the day-to-day activities of a business. This was previously a paper-based process but most businesses now use accounting software. In an electronic financial accounting system, the steps in the accounting cycle are built on the system itself.

Accounting information systems not only record the financial transactions of a business but also combine the study and practice of accounting within the design, implementation, and monitoring of records. Such systems use information technology resources together with traditional accounting controls and methods to provide users the financial information necessary to manage their organizations. The key components of an accounting information system are:

Input. The input devices commonly associated with AIS include: standard personal computers or workstations, scanning devices for standardized data entry, electronic communication devices for electronic data interchange (EDI) and e-commerce. In addition, many financial systems come Web-enabled to allow devices to connect to the Internet

Process. Basic processing is achieved through computer systems ranging from individual personal computers to large-scale enterprise servers. The underlying model is the double-entry accounting system initially introduced in Italy in the fifteenth century.

Output. Output devices used include computer displays, printers, and electronic communication devices for electronic data exchange and e-commerce. The output content may encompass almost any type of financial reports from budgets and tax reports to multinational financial statements.

ACCOUNTS PAYABLE SYSTEM: SAGE 50 AND QUICKBOOKS

Sage 50 and QuickBooks are two popular small business accounting software applications. To exemplify an accounting information system, let's look at how these two software applications process accounts payable.

Both software applications contain modules that reflect business processes. Typical business processes include sales, cash receipts, purchases, cash payments, and human resource functions such as payroll.

Sage 50

Sage 50 includes a Navigation Bar and Navigation Centers which take you to various business process areas or system modules. Another way to go to Sage 50's modules is to make selections from the menu bar. In order to show Sage 50's accounts payable system, the Vendors & Purchases Navigation Center is shown on the next page.

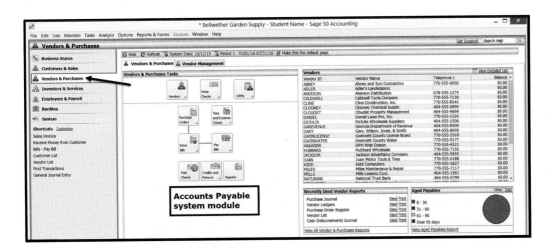

When Vendors & Purchases is selected, the Vendors & Purchases Navigation Center appears. A task diagram shows the flow of data through the accounts payable system. Other areas on the Vendors & Purchases Navigation Center include the Vendors list, Recently Used Vendor Reports, Aged Payables, and Sage 50 solutions. This is all in Sage 50's accounts payable system or accounts payable module.

Another way to use the accounts payable system is to make selections from the menu bar. The Maintain menu is where defaults are set up. The Maintain menu includes a Vendors selection and a selection for Default Information, Vendors.

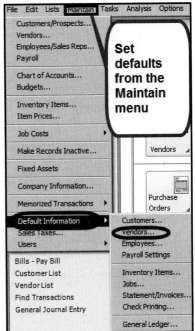

The menu bar's Tasks menu is also organized by module. For example, the accounts payable selections are in one area. The Tasks menu A/P area is shown on the next page.

The Reports & Forms menu includes an Accounts Payable selection. When the Select a Report or Form window appears, Accounts Payable: Vendors and Purchases selections are available. There are two tabs: Reports and Forms. The Forms tab allows you to select the appropriate accounts payable form. Notice that the Reports list includes each Sage 50 module: Accounts Receivable, Accounts Payable, Payroll, General Ledger, Inventory, etc.

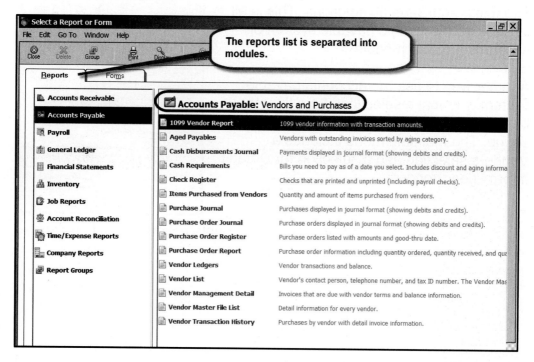

In addition, various system controls exist to ensure the accuracy and reliability of the data recorded. For example, preformatted screens facilitate the accuracy and completeness of data entry. Fields are restricted to either text or numeric data or a specific number of characters. Values are automatically calculated. The system prompts or requests the user to enter specific data and processing will not continue until the appropriate data is entered. Drop down lists or look-up tables allow the user to access master tables.

Master tables are used to set and maintain constant data, i.e. defaults. When a user enters a specific identification code such as a vendor number, the system accesses the master table and automatically completes information about the vendor within the transaction window. From these examples, you can see how Sage 50's accounts payable system is organized. Now let's look at QuickBooks and you will see many similarities as well as differences between the two accounting information systems.

QuickBooks Desktop

The QuickBooks desktop home page shows an Icon Bar (similar to Sage 50's Navigation Bar) on the left side of the screen, and Centers or areas on the right side of the screen. For example, Vendors, Customers, Employees, Company, Banking Centers. If you compare this to Sage 50's Navigation Bar you see a similar organization—QuickBooks's Icon Bar and Centers vs. Sage 50's Navigation Bar and Navigation Centers. QuickBooks's home page is shown below.

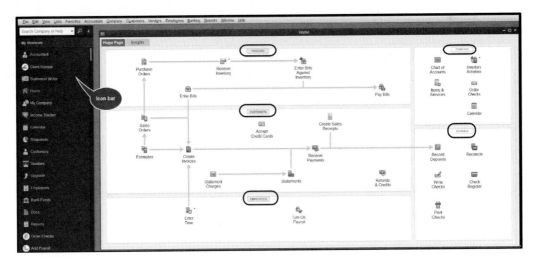

The QuickBooks Home page provides a big picture of how essential business tasks fit together. Tasks are organized

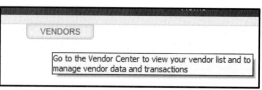

into groups (Customers, Vendors, Employees, Company, and Banking) with workflow arrows to help you learn how tasks relate to each other, and help decide what to do next. When the Vendors button is selected, the Vendor Center appears. If the Customers button or Employees button is selected, their Centers appear.

Another way to access the accounts payable module is to make selections from QuickBooks's Icon Bar. For example, from the Icon Bar, you can go to the Vendor Center by selecting Vendors–

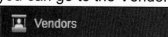

The Icon Bar also includes a 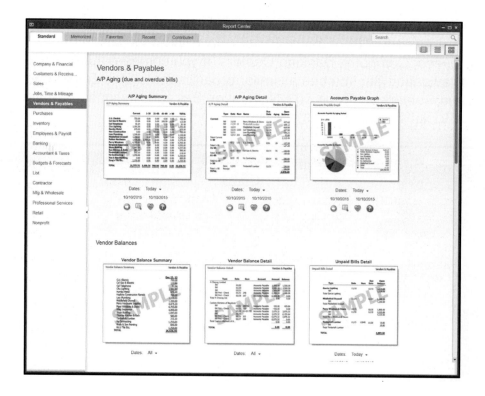 selection. From the Reports selection, the Vendors & Payables choice is listed, along with other report types. The Reports; Vendors & Payables selection is shown below.

Both the Icon Bar and the menu bar include Report selections organized by module. For example, if you select Reports from the menu bar, these Vendors & Payables selections appear.

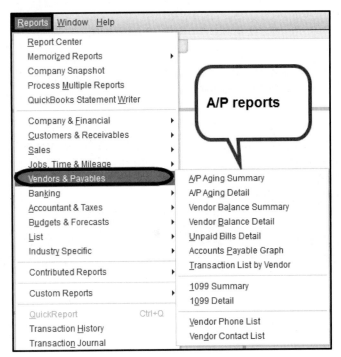

The table below and on the next page summarizes some of the similarities and differences between Sage 50 and QB Desktop (local computer installation) and QB Online (web delivered).

Features	Sage 50	QuickBooks Desktop	QuickBooks Online
Modules Customers (A/R) Vendors (A/P) Employees Banking Inventory	**Navigation Bar** Transaction windows include debit/credit fields LIFO/FIFO, and average inventory User-maintained payroll *or* third-party	**Icon Bar & Centers** Transaction window dr./cr. defaults cannot be changed Average inventory Intuit payroll add-on or third-party	**Navigation Bar** for menu of items *Same features as QB Desktop* Familiar icons: 🔍 Search ➕ Create 🔄 Recent Transactions

Features	Sage 50	QuickBooks Desktop	QuickBooks Online
Periods/Year End	Select period/fiscal year for accounting; year-end closing process	One period or list for all entries; select new year	*Same as QB Desktop*
Journals	**GL:** General Journal **A/P:** Purchase Journal and Cash Payments Journal **A/R:** Sales Journal and Cash Receipts Journal **Inventory:** Cost of Goods Sold Journal; Inventory Adjustments Journal **Payroll:** Payroll Journal	Transaction Journal	*Same as QB Desktop*
General Ledger **Subsidiary Ledgers** **Financial Statements**	YES	YES	*Same as QB Desktop*
Export and Save Reports	Excel and Adobe PDF	Excel and Adobe PDF	Excel and Adobe PDF
Backup/Restore/ Open Company	One file extension - .PTB - for backups/restore/open company	Backup extensions include .QBB, .QBM, .QBA. Open company, .QBW extension	Save or back up on Intuit web server. Start browser, sign into account.

Sage 50 and QuickBooks are examples of accounting information systems that are used for small business accounting. Even though the user interface looks different, the processing of accounting data and the reports generated are similar.

QuickBooks Online

The differences between desktop, or software that is installed locally on the hard drive, and Online accounting software are disappearing. QuickBooks desktop files can be converted to QB Online.

As more companies require cloud deployment so that all devices are working in sync (iPad, iPhone, Android, Macs or PCs), Intuit's customer base for QB Online grows. QB Online requires an Internet connection, not a specific Windows or Mac operating system. This means that Macs, PCs, tablets, and Smartphones can be used.

The QuickBooks Online home page is shown below. Using the Icon bar, you navigate the systems modules: vendors, customers, employees, transactions, reports, taxes and apps.

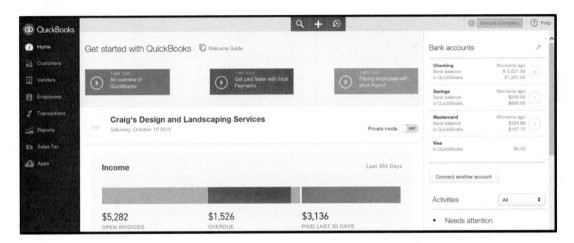

QuickBooks Online is an example of *cloud computing* or *Software as a Service*. SaaS is a way of delivering applications over the Internet as a service paid for with monthly or yearly subscriptions. Instead of installing software locally on the computer's hard drive, you access software via the Internet.

Sage One is the online version of Sage (formerly Peachtree) software.

Accounting Software

Accounting information systems use software applications like Sage 50, QuickBooks, and Microsoft Dynamics to process and manage business transactions.

The major difference between accounting software includes the depth of processing, enhanced features and functions, and the size of the database. As the database gets larger, the depth of processing increases and more features and functions are available. As companies grow in size, their accounting software needs change.

The diagram compares QuickBooks Online and Desktop, Sage 50 and Microsoft Dynamics. Because of its larger database, observe that Sage 50 can be used by both small and medium-sized business.

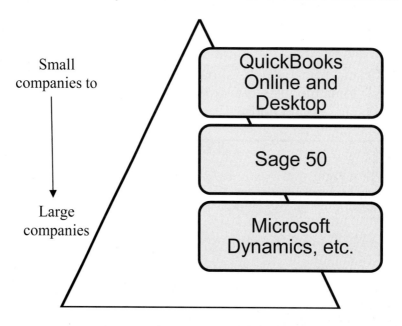

Sage 50 and QuickBooks are used by small companies. As the company grows to mid-size, Sage 50 and Microsoft Dynamics can be used. Large companies use Microsoft Dynamics, Oracle and SAP.

Company size	No. of Employees
Small business	1-50 employees
Medium-sized business	50-500 employees
Large business	500+ employees

You can see that accounting software addresses small, medium and large businesses. The high-end accounting software applications are generally referred to as **enterprise resource planning (ERP)** systems. ERP systems are designed to integrate all of the major functions of a business to promote efficient operations. ERP systems are company-wide software applications which manage and coordinate all the resources, information, and functions of a business from shared data sources.

Index